Profiles of

People in Power:

the World's Government Leaders

Profiles of
People in Power:
the World's Government Leaders

Roger East, Carina O'Reilly and Richard J. Thomas

SECOND EDITION

Routledge
Taylor & Francis Group

LONDON AND NEW YORK

First Edition 2003
Second Edition 2006

Published by Routledge
Haines House, 21 John Street, London WC1N 2BP, United Kingdom
(A member of the Taylor & Francis Group)

© **Cambridge International Reference on Current Affairs (CIRCA) Ltd 2005**
Compiled and typeset by Cambridge International Reference on Current Affairs
(CIRCA) Ltd, Cambridge, United Kingdom

ISBN 1-85743-346-7

The publishers make no representation, express or implied with regard to the accuracy
of the information contained in this book and cannot accept any legal responsibility
for any errors or omissions that may take place.

Printed and bound in Great Britain by MPG Books, Bodmin, Cornwall

FOREWORD

PROFILES OF PEOPLE IN POWER, first published in 2003, is here presented in a fully updated second edition. Its primary purpose is to provide, in a single volume, a comprehensive set of succinct biographical portraits of the heads of state and government of every sovereign country in the world as of September 2005. Where appropriate, the leaders of ruling parties, presidents-elect and outgoing presidents are also included.

A number of additional features have been included to enhance the value of this book as a work of reference.

The biographical profiles—arranged by country—are preceded by a concise description of the constitutional structure of the country's leadership, executive branch and legislature. These descriptions are drawn from *People in Power*, a bimonthly publication compiled by Cambridge International Reference on Current Affairs (CIRCA) Ltd, which provides accurate, comprehensive and up-to-date listings of government membership around the world.

Each country entry also contains a table listing the names of all those who have held the office of head of state, head of government or ruling party leader since 1 January 2000, with their dates of taking (and, where relevant, leaving) office.

The book is fully indexed by personal names and by dates of taking power. A further index lists countries by type of political regime, and an appendix provides address and contact data.

Roger East
Cambridge, September 2005

ACKNOWLEDGEMENTS

The authors gratefully acknowledge the assistance received with the compilation of this book from many of the governments concerned, and the co-operation of international organizations in providing us with photographs. We are also greatly indebted to Rosemary Payne, and to the staff of Cambridge International Reference on Current Affairs (CIRCA) Ltd, in particular Catherine Jagger, for their painstaking work in collecting and revising data. Special thanks are also due to Catherine Jagger for copy editing and project management.

We have made extensive use of material from the bimonthly *People in Power*, published by CIRCA Ltd. The *Europa World Year Book* and the *International Who's Who* have both been used extensively for the cross-checking of detailed factual information.

CONTENTS

Contents

Contents

Contents

xii

Contents

PHOTOGRAPHS

OF

WORLD LEADERS

United Nations (UN) World Summit

New York, USA, 2005

Asia–Pacific Economic Co-operation (APEC) Summit

Busan, South Korea, 2005

European Union (EU) Council

Brussels, Belgium, 2005

G8–Africa Summit

Gleneagles, Scotland, UK, 2005

United Nations World Summit (New York, USA, 2005)

(Front row) 1: Moisiu, Albania. 2: Mwanawasa, Zambia. 3: Mkapa, Tanzania. 4: Gnassingbé, Togo. 5: Crvenkovski, Macedonia. 6: Blair, UK. 7: Putin, Russia. 8: Bush, USA. 9: Persson, Sweden. 10: Annan, UN. 11: Bongo, Gabon. 12: Arroyo, Philippines. 13: Hu, China. 14: Villepin, France. 15: Gusmão, East Timor. 16: Museveni, Uganda. 17: Mugabe, Zimbabwe. 18: Bouteflika, Algeria. 19: Kérékou, Benin.

(Second row) 1: Rep., Iraq. 2: Guelleh, Djibouti. 3: Mesić, Croatia. 4: Azali, Comoros. 5: Bozizé, Central African Republic. 6: Biya, Cameroon. 7: Purvanov, Bulgaria. 8: da Silva, Brazil. 9: Jović, Bosnia and Herzegovina. 10–12: Representatives, UN. 13: Mogae, Botswana. 14: Bolkiah, Brunei. 15: Nkurunziza, Burundi. 16: Pires, Cape Verde. 17: Lagos, Chile. 18: Sassou-Nguesso, Rep. Congo. 19: Papadopoulos, Cyprus. 20: Obiang Nguema, Equatorial Guinea.

(Third row) 1: Gayoom, Maldives. 2: Adamkus, Lithuania. 3: Lahoud, Lebanon. 4: Bakiyev, Kyrgyzstan. 5: Kibaki, Kenya. 6: Talabani, Iraq. 7: Yudhoyono, Indonesia. 8: Maduro, Honduras. 9: Saakashvili, Georgia. 10: Halonen, Finland. 11: Rüütel, Estonia. 12: Jammeh, Gambia. 13: Kufuor, Ghana. 14: Sólyom, Hungary. 15: Ahmadinejad, Iran. 16: Abdullah II, Jordan. 17: Vike-Freiberga, Latvia. 18: Bryant, Liberia. 19: Ravalomanana, Madagascar. 20: Toumani Touré, Mali.

(Fourth row) 1: Morganti, San Marino. 2: Basescu, Romania. 3: Roh, South Korea. 4: Sampaio, Portugal. 5: Musharraf, Pakistan. 6: Obasanjo, Nigeria. 7: Pohamba, Namibia. 8: Enkhbayar, Mongolia. 9: Fox, Mexico. 10: Note, Marshall Islands. 11: Albert II, Monaco. 12: Guebuza, Mozambique. 13: Scotty, Nauru. 14: Remengesau, Palau. 15: Toledo, Peru. 16: Hamad, Qatar. 17: Voronin, Moldova. 18: Kagame, Rwanda. 19: Gasperoni, San Marino. 20: Wade, Senegal.

(Fifth row) 1: Arthur, Barbados. 2: Howard, Australia. 3: Spencer, Antigua and Barbuda. 4: Toafa, Tuvalu. 5: Alkatiri, East Timor. 6: Rakhmanov, Tajikistan. 7: Mswati III, Swaziland. 8: Kumaratunga, Sri Lanka. 9: Mbeki, South Africa. 10: Gašparovič, Slovakia. 11: Kabbah, Sierra Leone. 12: Drnovšek, Slovenia. 13: Juan Carlos I, Spain. 14: Venetiaan, Suriname. 15: Schmid, Switzerland. 16: Thaksin, Thailand. 17: Erdoğan, Turkey. 18: Pintat Santolària, Andorra. 19: Markarian, Armenia. 20: Zia, Bangladesh. 21: Verhofstadt, Belgium.

(Sixth row) 1: Badawi, Malaysia. 2: Bounnhang, Laos. 3: Patterson, Jamaica. 4: Sharon, Israel. 5: Ásgrímsson, Iceland. 6: Gomes, Guinea-Bissau. 7: Paroubek, Czech Republic. 8: Musa, Belize. 9: Martin, Canada. 10: Rasmussen, Denmark. 11: Karamanlis, Greece. 12: Diallo, Guinea. 13: Latortue, Haiti. 14: Ahern, Ireland. 15: Berlusconi, Italy. 16: Sabah, Kuwait. 17: Mosisili, Lesotho. 18: Gonzi, Malta.

(Seventh row) 1-5: Various representatives. 6: Rodríguez Zapatero, Spain. 7: Hama, Niger. 8: Jettou, Morocco. 9: Ramgoolam, Mauritius. 10: Balkenende, Netherlands. 11: Douglas, St Kitts and Nevis. 12: Kemakeza, Solomon Islands. 13-17: Various representatives.

(Eighth row) Various representatives.

(Back row) Various representatives.

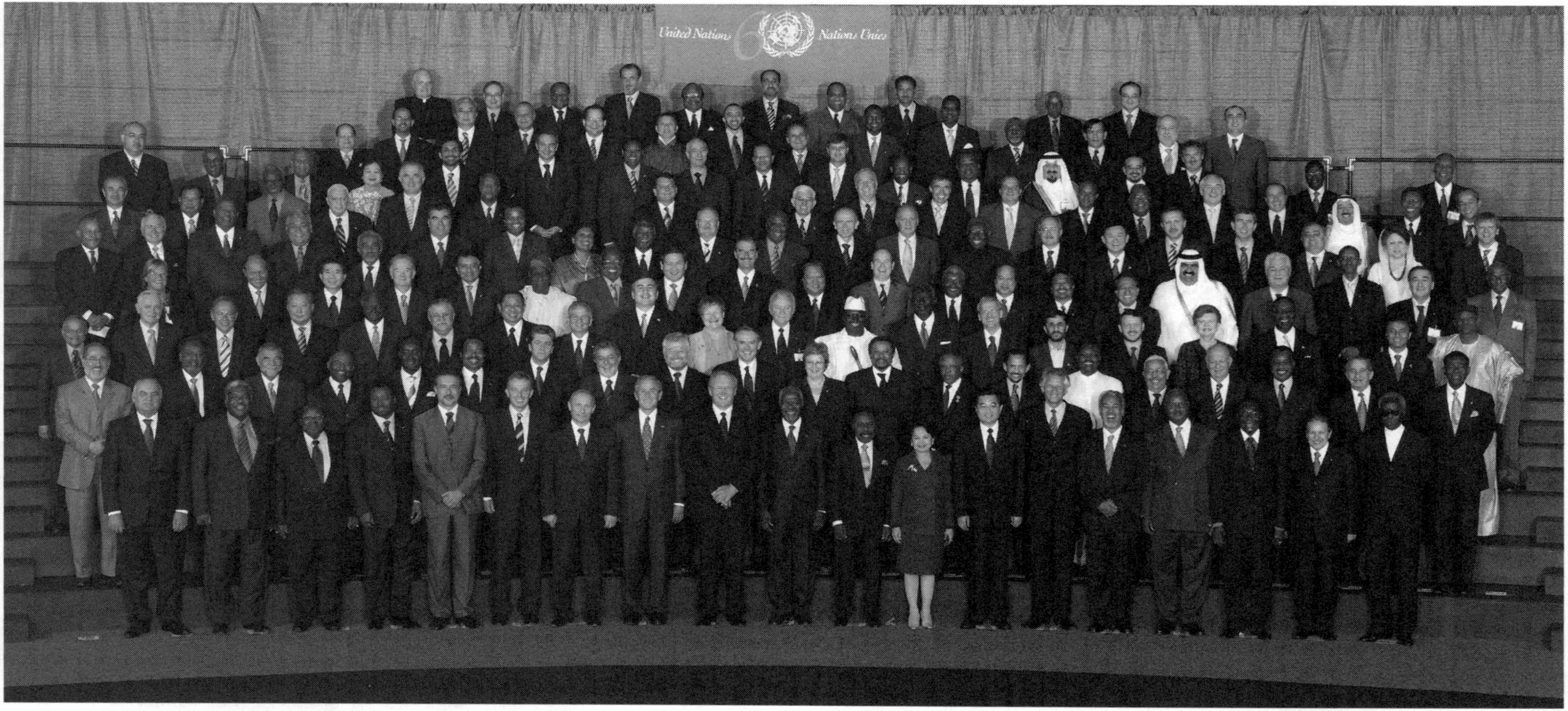
United Nations
Nations Unies

Asia–Pacific Economic Co-operation Summit (Busan, South Korea, 2005)

© APEC Secretariat, Singapore

(Front row) 1: Howard, Australia. 2: Bolkiah, Brunei. 3: Arroyo, Philippines. 4: Hu, China. 5: Luong, Viet Nam. 6: Roh, South Korea. 7: Lagos, Chile. 8: Badawi, Malaysia. 9: Koizumi, Japan. 10: Yudhoyono, Indonesia. 11: Rep., Hong Kong.

(Back row) 1: Fox, Mexico. 2: Clark, New Zealand. 3: Somare, Papua New Guinea. 4: Toledo, Peru. 5: Martin, Canada. 6: Bush, USA. 7: Thaksin, Thailand. 8: Rep., Taiwan. 9: Lee, Singapore. 10: Putin, Russia.

European Union Council (Brussels, Belgium, 2005)

Justus Lipsius © European Community, 2005. A/V Library of European Commission

(Front row) 1: Solana, EC. 2: Sócrates, Portugal. 3: Schüssel, Austria. 4: Barroso, EC. 5: Basescu, Romania. 6: Papadopoulos, Cyprus. 7: Halonen, Finland. 8: Juncker, Luxembourg. 9: Chirac, France. 10: Adamkus, Latvia. 11: Borrell Fontelles, European Parliament. 12: Blair, UK. 13: Schröder, Germany. 14: Janša, Slovenia.

(Second row) 1: Paroubek, Czech Republic. 2: Persson, Sweden. 3: Rodríguez Zapatero, Spain. 4: Verhofstadt, Belgium. 5: Gyurcsány, Hungary. 6: Belka, Poland. 7: Rasmussen, Denmark. 8: Ahern, Ireland. 9: Brazauskas, Lithuania. 10: Karamanlis, Greece. 11: Berlusconi, Italy. 12: Kalvitis, Latvia. 13: Balkenende, Netherlands. 14: Dzurinda, Slovakia. 15: Gonzi, Malta.

(Third row) 1-6: Various representatives. 7: Saxecoburggotski, Bulgaria. 8: Vanhanen, Finland. 9: Ansip, Estonia. 10-15: Various representatives.

(Back row) Various representatives.

G8–Africa Summit (Gleneagles, Scotland, 2005)

(Front row) 1: Obasanjo, Nigeria. 2: Bush, USA. 3: Chirac, France. 4: Blair, UK. 5: Putin, Russia. 6: Schröder, Germany. 7: Mbeki, South Africa.

(Second row) 1: Annan, UN. 2: Martin, Canada. 3: Koizumi, Japan. 4: Berlusconi, Italy. 5: Barroso, European Commission. 6: Kufuor, Ghana.

(Third row) 1: Wolfowitz, World Bank. 2: Wade, Senegal. 3: Meles, Ethiopia. 4: Mkapa, Tanzania. 5: Konaré, African Union. 6: Bouteflika, Algeria. 7: Rodrigo de Rato, IMF.

AFGHANISTAN

Full name: The Islamic State of Afghanistan.

Leadership structure: The head of state is a president, directly elected by universal adult suffrage. The president's term of office is five years. The president is also head of government and appoints the cabinet.

President:	Burhanuddin Rabbani	28 June 1992—22 Dec. 2001
	(ousted by *taliban* regime on 27 Sept. 1996)	
	Hamid **KARZAI**	Since 19 June 2002
	(chairman of interim government from 22 Dec. 2001)	
Leader of the Taliban:	Mohammad Omar	3 April 1996—13 Nov. 2001

Chairman of the Interim Council (under the Taliban):

	Mohammad Rabbani	27 Sept. 1996—16 April 2001
	Mawlawi Abdul Kabir	16 April 2001—13 Nov. 2001

Legislature: After the abolition in 1992 of the bicameral National Assembly (Meli Shura), no new legislature was established under the *taliban* regime. A Loya Jirga (traditional tribal council) convened on 13 December 2003 comprised 500 delegates, 450 of them elected by the 15,000 voters registered as electors at the last Loya Jirga in 2002, and 50 appointed by the president.

Under the 2004 Constitution the legislature (Jirga) will be bicameral; elections are scheduled for September 2005. The lower chamber, the House of the People (Wolesi Jirga), will have 249 members directly elected for a five-year term. The upper house, the House of Elders (Meshrano Jirga) will have 102 members: one-third elected by provincial councils for three-year terms, one-third elected by district councils for four-year terms and one-third appointed by the president for five-year terms.

Profile of the President:

Hamid **KARZAI**

Hamid Karzai, who was educated mainly in Pakistan and India and has strong family links in the USA, is leader (khan) of the Popolzai tribe of ethnic Pashtuns—the largest single ethnic group in Afghanistan. Having grown disillusioned with the post-Soviet-occupation government of Burhanuddin Rabbani, Karzai initially lent his support to the Islamic taliban *movement before turning against them in the late 1990s. He was initially chosen to head the post-*taliban *government by a conference of Afghan notables held in Germany in December 2001. Confirmed in this transitional role the following June, he went on to win the direct presidential elections held in October 2004, and was sworn in on 7 December for a five-year term.*

Hamid Karzai was born into the Popolzai tribe on 24 December 1957 in the southern Afghan city of Kandahar, the Popolzai stronghold. His father, Abdul Ahad Karzai, was khan of the Popolzai (from which almost all of Afghanistan's kings were drawn from the 18th century onward), and served as a prominent member of the government before the fall of King Zahir Shah (also a member of the Popolzai clan) in 1973. The Karzai family fled the Soviet invasion of Afghanistan and moved to Quetta, Pakistan, in 1983. Most of Hamid's seven brothers and his sister emigrated to the USA where they now head the successful Helmand franchise of Afghan restaurants. However, Hamid remained in the south Asian region and attended college in India.

During the struggle of the various *mujahideen* factions in the 1980s against Soviet domination, Karzai acted as an adviser and diplomat for the resistance forces. However, throughout this time he maintained a low profile, and is even said to have run a small hotel in Peshawar, Pakistan. His connection with the *mujahideen* movements brought him to prominence in 1992 when newly appointed President Rabbani chose him as deputy foreign minister. He was the most prominent Pashtun member of this regime.

The *mujahideen* government quickly fell into internal disputes which were reflected in violent struggle throughout the country. Various warlords held de facto dominion over their own territories and Karzai grew disaffected with the inability of the government to maintain control. He left the government in 1994 having been approached by the new *taliban* (Islamic student) movement which was drawn mostly from the Pashtuns. He gave his full support to the movement, supplying them with arms and advice. The *taliban* seized Kabul in 1996 and effectively controlled the majority of the country. In return for his backing the *taliban* nominated Karzai to be their representative to the UN—although the UN's refusal to recognize the regime made this nomination ineffective.

Within a year, Karzai had grown concerned at the extent to which the regime had fallen under what he saw as the dominant influence of 'foreign' Islamic fundamentalists, principally Arabs such as Osama bin Laden, and the Pakistani secret service. In 1998 he began to foment an anti-*taliban* opposition based in Quetta, along with his father, and looked unsuccessfully to the West for assistance. In 1999 Abdul Ahad Karzai was shot dead by unknown assailants on his way home from mosque. Hamid Karzai immediately blamed the *taliban* regime, and anti-*taliban* sentiment gathered pace among the horrified Popolzai and other Pashtuns. Hamid was appointed khan of the clan ahead of his older, but

US-based, brothers. In defiance of the *taliban* and the Pakistani authorities he arranged a 300-vehicle convoy to take his father's body from Quetta to be buried in their ancestral home of Kandahar. The *taliban* are thought to have allowed the funeral for fear of creating further division within their own Pashtun stronghold.

Karzai continued to press for Western assistance from his base in Pakistan. He was not rewarded until international attention was focused on his home country following the 11 September 2001 attacks in the USA, committed by followers of Afghan-based Osama bin Laden. Karzai slipped back into Afghanistan in October 2001 as the US bombing campaign got under way, and this time received overt logistical and even military support from the USA in his attempts to build on anti-*taliban* sentiment among the Pashtuns. In a celebrated event he escaped a heavy-handed assassination attempt by the *taliban* with the assistance of US warplanes.

Karzai was named as a prime candidate to lead the post-*taliban* government during talks held in Bonn, Germany, despite the fact that he himself remained in Afghanistan. His dominant position among the Pashtuns, and his close relationship with ex-king Zahir Shah, increased Karzai's standing and he was chosen to be interim leader on 5 December 2001. One day later he was at the centre of negotiations which saw the handover of the last *taliban* stronghold, Kandahar.

The interim government was installed in Kabul on 22 December and was formalized by a Loya Jirga (traditional tribal council) in June 2002 as a permanent administration, with Karzai as president, and supported by an international UN peacekeeping force. Karzai's government immediately sought to reverse the social prohibitions of the *taliban*, notably those against women, and set about planning to encourage private investment and market reforms in the war-ravaged country. In his efforts to strengthen central authority, he remained heavily dependent on international backing, with Northern Alliance commanders reluctant to relinquish their hard-won power, and the battle against the *taliban* far from over, especially in the south and east. Violent attacks continued even in Kabul, many of them attributed to *taliban* supporters, and Karzai himself has been the subject of several assassination attempts.

Gradual progress towards a fully elected government structure saw the approval of a new draft constitution in January 2004, and Karzai's own position strengthened by a convincing victory in presidential elections held on 9 October 2004. He won 55.4% of the vote, well ahead of his nearest rival, Yunus Qanuni, with 16.3%, and a UN investigation concluded that 'shortcomings' during the ballot had not changed the outcome significantly. He had been effectively unable to campaign in many areas, however, holding only one rally outside the capital (amid massive security precautions in the town of Ghazni).

Sworn in for his new five-year term on 7 December, Karzai named a new government on 23 December, pending the holding of legislative elections. His government's grip on the security situation in much of the country remained so tenuous, however, that legislative elections planned for May 2005 had to be postponed until later in the year.

Hamid Karzai married Zinat, a doctor, late in life and they have no children. He speaks six languages, including English.

ALBANIA

Full name: The Republic of Albania.

Leadership structure: The head of state is a president indirectly elected by the People's Assembly. The president's term of office is five years, with a maximum of two successive terms. The head of government is the prime minister, who is appointed by the president. Under the terms of the 1998 Constitution, the prime minister's appointment must be approved by the People's Assembly. The Council of Ministers is elected by the Assembly.

President:	Rexhep Mejdani	24 July 1997—24 July 2002
	Gen. (retd) Alfred **MOISIU**	Since 24 July 2002
Prime Minister:	Ilir Meta (acting from 29 Jan. 2002)	29 Oct. 1999—22 Feb. 2002
	Pandeli Majko	22 Feb. 2002—31 July 2002
	Fatos **NANO** (acting from 2 Sept. 2005)	Since 31 July 2002

Legislature: The legislature is unicameral. The sole chamber, the People's Assembly (Kuvendi Popullor), has 140 members under the 1998 Constitution, directly elected for a maximum of four years.

Profile of the President:

Gen. (retd) Alfred **MOISIU**

Alfred Moisiu is an independent politician who has served in both communist and postcommunist governments. The founding president of the Albanian Atlantic Association, he has been at the forefront of the country's attempts to integrate with the West. Indeed his personal motto reads, "West, Peace, Justice and Development". He was appointed president in June 2002 as a compromise candidate designed to end years of political infighting within the ruling Albanian Socialist Party (Partia Socialiste e Shqipërisë—PSSh). He took office in July.

Alfred Moisiu, a widower with four children, was born on 1 December 1929 in Shkodër, northern Albania. He joined the communist-led Albanian partisans in 1943 in their two-year struggle to liberate the country from Nazi forces, and afterwards went to St Petersburg (then Leningrad in the Soviet Union) to attend the Soviet military engineering school, from which he graduated in 1948. He went on to study at the Academy of Military Engineering in Moscow where he was awarded the Golden Medal. A legacy of his Soviet education is a fluency in Russian.

Returning to Albania in 1948, Moisiu began his military career at the Joint Officers' School in Tirana and worked as an instructor at the city's Military Academy. He eventually attained the rank of general. When he returned from Moscow in 1958 he began to diversify his military career with assignments at the engineering directorate of the ministry of defence until he was made a full director of engineering and fortification at the ministry in 1971. He served as deputy defence minister for a year from 1981 before leaving government service.

As Albania underwent its transition to democracy, Moisiu was appointed defence minister in the technical government from October 1991 until April 1992. After his term in office he acted as adviser to his successor at the ministry before becoming deputy minister once again in 1994. In the same year he founded the Albanian Atlantic Association which aims to promote Albania's ultimate membership of the North Atlantic Treaty Organization (NATO). He left the defence ministry in 1997.

His election five years later as president of Albania came as the supposed climax of a drawn-out battle within the PSSh between the then prime minister Pandeli Majko and his predecessor Ilir Meta on the one hand, and the long-time PSSh leader and next prime minister, Fatos Nano, on the other. Moisiu's candidacy arose after the country's ambassador to the European Union (EU), Artur Kuko, had declined to stand. Moisiu was inaugurated on 24 July 2002.

Profile of the Prime Minister:

Fatos **NANO**

Fatos Nano is leader of the ruling Albanian Socialist Party (Partia Socialiste e Shqipërisë—PSSh). Originally a lecturer in economics under the communist-era regime, he first became prime minister for a short period in 1991. Between then and 2002 he was imprisoned for three years for corruption, and returned as premier in 1997–98. Immediately prior to his reappointment in July 2002 he led internal party opposition to the incumbent government.

Fatos Thanas Nano was born on 16 September 1952 in Tirana. He married his second wife, Xhoana, in 2001, having divorced his first wife, Rexhina, with whom he had had two children.

He studied political economy at Tirana University and graduated in 1975. After a period working in the management of the state steelworks in Elbasan, southeast of Tirana, he went on to pursue a career as economic researcher and lecturer at the faculty of economy and at the Institute of Marxist-Leninist Studies in Tirana.

In the late 1980s he was one of the first individuals publicly to criticize the policies of the ruling Party of Labour of Albania (Partia e Punës e Shqipërisë—PPSh).

With the collapse of the communist regime in December 1990, Nano became secretary-general of the Council of Ministers, and by the following January had become deputy prime minister for economic reforms. In March 1991 he assumed the leadership of the provisional government formed in advance of the first multiparty elections held on 31 March. His election as chairman of the PSSh followed his appointment as prime minister for a second term in May 1991. Nano committed his government to the introduction of a free-market economy. However, a wave of anti-communist strikes obliged his government to resign within a month, although Nano continued to sit as a deputy in the People's Assembly.

On 30 July 1993 Nano was arrested and stripped of his parliamentary immunity from prosecution to face charges of embezzlement. In April 1994 he was convicted of mishandling US$8 million of aid from the Italian government, of dereliction of duty and of falsifying state documents. His detention and the arrest of several other ministers prompted protests against alleged gross violations of legal procedure. Sentenced to serve 12 years in prison, he was nevertheless re-elected to the PSSh leadership and continued to be regarded as the main political opponent of the then president, Sali Berisha.

The 1997 rebellion in the south of the country, precipitated by economic collapse, resulted in the release of many prison detainees. Nano, one of those released in this way, was formally pardoned by Berisha on 17 March. The PSSh went on to win a general election held in two rounds in June–July 1997; PSSh Secretary-General Rexhep Mejdani replaced Berisha as president, and immediately called on Nano to form a government. On 25 July Nano took office at the head of a coalition government but was forced to step down in October 1998 amid a return of popular protest against economic reforms.

Having been re-elected leader of the PSSh, Nano led a campaign within the party against the next PSSh prime minister, Ilir Meta, accusing him and his government of corruption. The struggle reached a head in January 2002 when Meta resigned. The resulting deadlock over who should succeed as head of government prompted international financial agencies to withhold payments from Albania. Nano's supporters within the party were finally included in the next government, headed by Pandeli Majko, which lasted from February until the party voted in July to merge the position of party leader with prime minister, guaranteeing Nano's return to power.

Tensions resurfaced the following year between Nano and Meta, who had been appointed as foreign minister. Meta resigned, accusing Nano of trying to take control of his ministry. In October 2003 Meta's faction in the PSSh threatened to withhold all support for Nano over his authoritarian manner. By February 2004, the embattled prime minister was also facing massive opposition demonstrations led by Berisha, demanding his resignation for failing to improve living standards and implement much-needed reforms. Meta's block broke away from the PSSh and formed a new party in September.

A further political stir was caused in November by allegations, denied by Nano, that he had been involved with smuggling weapons to Kosovo in 1997; the People's Assembly voted against launching a parliamentary inquiry due to the lack of evidence.

With legislative elections set for 3 July 2005, Nano's Socialists and Berisha's Democrats were neck-and-neck in the polls. The vote was keenly observed by the international community as a "crucial test" of democracy in the country. Results announced finally on 2 September gave victory narrowly to Berisha. Nano remained in office, however, in an interim capacity pending the formation of a new government.

ALGERIA

Full name: The People's Democratic Republic of Algeria.

Leadership structure: The head of state is a president, directly elected by universal adult suffrage. The president's term of office is five years. The president appoints a prime minister, who has the formal status of head of government and who appoints the Council of Ministers. The president, not the prime minister, presides at meetings of the Council.

President:	Abdelaziz **BOUTEFLIKA**	Since 27 April 1999
Prime Minister:	Ahmed Benbitour	23 Dec. 1999—27 Aug. 2000
	Ali Benflis	27 Aug. 2000—5 May 2003
	Ahmed **OUYAHIA**	Since 5 May 2003

Legislature: The legislature, the Parliament (Barlaman), is bicameral. The lower chamber, the National People's Assembly (Majlis al-Chaabi al-Watani), has 389 members (eight of them representing Algerians abroad), directly elected for a five-year term. The upper chamber, the National Council (Majlis al-Oumma), has 144 members; one-third of the members are appointed by the president, the other two-thirds indirectly elected for six-year terms, half of the seats being elected every three years.

Profile of the President:

Abdelaziz **BOUTEFLIKA**

Abdelaziz Bouteflika was a long-serving member of the National Liberation Front (Front de Libération Nationale—FLN) and foreign minister for much of the 1960s and 1970s, but then spent some seven years in exile as the tide turned against those closely associated with the government of the late President Houari Boumedienne. 'Rehabilitated' in 1988, he kept a relatively low profile until emerging as the regime's preferred consensus candidate for the April 1999 presidential election, leading the National Democratic Rally (Rassemblement National Démocratique—RND). Bouteflika is well connected in Algeria's upper social strata, and has a strong support base among the urban elite and the military.

Abdelaziz Bouteflika was born on 2 March 1937 in Oujda, on the Algeria–Morocco border, where he was also educated. In 1956 he joined Algeria's

National Liberation Army, the military wing of the FLN, and was promoted to the rank of major, although he did not take part in any fighting. By the early 1960s he was working in the headquarters of military commanders of the southern regions and his administrative career was greatly boosted when he joined a secret Algerian delegation to France in 1961.

Following national independence in 1962, Bouteflika was appointed by President Ahmed Ben Bella as minister of youth, sport and tourism. He went on to become foreign minister from 1963 to 1979 under Ben Bella and his military successor, Col. Boumedienne. In this capacity Bouteflika was a key figure, overseeing the international recognition of the country's territorial borders and forging strong ties with the rest of the Arab world notably at the conference of Khartoum in 1967 and during the Arab–Israeli war in 1973. In 1971 he helped to ride out the embargo imposed by France following the nationalization of Algeria's hydrocarbon reserves, and from 1974 to 1975 he was president of the UN General Assembly. On the global stage, Bouteflika has also been a strong supporter of decolonization.

The death of Boumedienne in 1978 was followed by a power struggle and a backlash against the 'Boumediennists'. Bouteflika, charged with corruption, went into exile in 1980, and, although the case against him was later dropped, he did not return permanently to Algeria until January 1987. His rehabilitation into national politics followed the signing of the 'motion of the 18' in protest at the violence unleashed by the government against reformist protestors in October 1988. At a party congress the following year he was appointed to the central committee of the FLN.

During the violence of the 1990s Bouteflika kept a low profile. Bloodshed followed the nullification of election results in 1992 which would have led to an Islamic government. Bouteflika rejected an offer to sit on the High Council of State which was formulated as an interim presidency. In 1994 he even refused the presidency itself, but in the somewhat more promising circumstances of December 1998 he did announce his candidacy for the April 1999 presidential elections. Dubbed the 'candidate of consensus', he realized this unfortunate title when all six of his opponents stepped down from the competition at the last minute, accusing him of large-scale electoral fraud. Unopposed, Bouteflika easily swept the board at the polls with nearly 80% of the vote. He was backed in the National People's Assembly by a majority coalition which includes his own authoritarian RND, the FLN and two moderate Islamic parties.

The long-running civil conflict was high on the national agenda and Bouteflika was quick to act towards its resolution. A referendum showed massive public support for his 'civil reconciliation' programme which included an amnesty for Islamic militants until January 2000, which was followed by the release of 5,000 political prisoners. By the deadline of the amnesty, 1,500 militants had handed themselves over including the major paramilitary organization, the Islamic Salvation Army, which voluntarily decommissioned its arms in July 1999.

Although this decommissioning received the backing of the main Islamist movement, the Islamic Salvation Front, Bouteflika maintained the political ban on the latter. Two other insurrectionary forces ignored the amnesty, but despite the continuing violence Bouteflika remained keen to talk of peace. Meanwhile he made several firebrand speeches against outside interference in Algerian affairs aimed both at other Arab nations and the West, which he accused in February 2000 of "rubbing Africa off the map" through its economic imperialism. The former colonial power, France, had renewed diplomatic ties in 1999, having broken off relations in 1992.

The FLN pulled out of the government in October 2003, following a rift in April between Prime Minister Ali Benflis and the president over Bouteflika's candidature for the 2004 presidential poll. The election campaign saw demonstrations by the FLN against Bouteflika's 'authoritarian' rule and by Berbers disappointed by the breakdown of talks over the status of their Tamazight language. Bouteflika was re-elected on 8 April 2004, winning 83% of votes cast, comfortably ahead of Benflis, who took 8% and immediately accused Bouteflika of massive fraud. International observers indicated, however, that the poll was one of Algeria's fairest since the introduction of multiparty politics in 1989.

Plans were announced in 2005 for a fresh referendum on Bouteflika's 'national reconciliation' plan, which would allow for a second period of amnesty, releasing prisoners in return for Islamic militants laying down their arms. However, international human rights organizations feared that the amnesty would allow crimes by both sides in the war to go unpunished.

Profile of the Prime Minister:

Ahmed **OUYAHIA**

Ahmed Ouyahia was appointed as prime minister of Algeria on 5 May 2003. A career diplomat, he had previously held the post under President Liamine Zeroual from December 1995 to December 1998, when he was noted for his hard and ruthless policies. He joined a new pro-Zeroual party, the National Democratic Rally (Rassemblement National Démocratique—RND), when it was formed in April 1997. Now a powerful figure in the RND, he has the backing of both President Abdelaziz Bouteflika and the armed forces. There are rumours that he is the favoured successor for the regime.

A Berber from the Kabylie region, Ahmed Ouyahia was born on 2 July 1952 in Bouadnane in Tizi Ouzou district. Educated locally and in the capital, he worked in government administration after graduating from the University of Algiers, in the president's office and from 1979 in the ministry of foreign affairs. He is married and has two children.

Between 1984 and 1989 he was posted to Algeria's UN mission in New York. As ambassador to Mali in the early 1990s, he was credited with having played a key role in arranging a peace accord between the government of Mali and Tuareg rebels in April 1992. He joined the Algerian cabinet in September 1993 as secretary of state for co-operation and Maghreb affairs, and in March 1994 became a presidential adviser and director of the president's office.

His appointment as prime minister on 31 December 1995—the first civilian Berber-speaker to hold the post, and at 43 Algeria's youngest ever prime minister—was seen as part of an attempt to win support for President Zeroual's regime from younger Algerians. Critics were worried, however, about his lack of political experience and he was at that time not affiliated to any party. His first cabinet included members of the Hamas party (the largest legal Islamic party, later renamed the Movement for a Peaceful Society (Mouvement de la Société pour la Paix—MSP)) and the Algerian Renewal Party, two pro-government parties which had not boycotted the presidential elections.

Ouyahia joined the pro-Zeroual RND, formed in April 1997 in the run-up to legislative elections held on 5 June under a revised parliamentary structure. The RND secured 156 of the 380 seats in the National Assembly, thereby giving his government a relatively secure base in the legislature, although all the opposition parties made accusations of fraud and vote rigging, and the supposed return to civilian rule did nothing to reduce the intensity of the conflict between the army and militant Islamists. In the wake of the elections, Ouyahia was reappointed; his new cabinet, announced on 25 June, comprised members of the RND, members of the former ruling National Liberation Front (Front de Libération Nationale—FLN), which held 62 Assembly seats, and three members of the MSP (which had won only 69 seats in the elections, about 100 less than it had been expecting).

By December 1998, however, with the economy struggling and no end in sight to the Islamist insurgency, Ouyahia resigned, taking responsibility for the country's woes—critics described him as Algeria's most unpopular prime minister ever. The presidential election in April 1999 saw victory for Abdelaziz Bouteflika of the RND, who had the backing of the FLN, MSP and the Islamic Renewal Movement, and promised national reconciliation. Ouyahia returned to a senior post in the cabinet in December 1999 as minister of state for justice, which he retained under Prime Minister Ali Benflis from August 2000. He also chaired the committee that drew up government policy. A key ally of Bouteflika, in June 2002 he was made minister of state and personal representative of the president.

Ouyahia was reappointed as prime minister on 5 May 2003, following the dismissal of Benflis, who had refused to approve the early endorsement by his FLN of Bouteflika's candidature in the forthcoming 2004 presidential poll. Ouyahia appointed a mostly unchanged cabinet, though in September the FLN ministers resigned and the following month the party pulled out of the coalition. Following Bouteflika's successful re-election, Ouyahia was confirmed in post on 26 April, heading a reshuffled cabinet.

ANDORRA

Full name: The Principality of Andorra.

Leadership structure: Under the 1993 Constitution, the titular heads of state are the president of France and the bishop of Urgel (in Spain), whose powers relate solely to relations with France and Spain. The head of government is the president of the Executive Council, which is appointed by the General Council. There is a permanent delegation for Andorran affairs in Andorra headed respectively by the prefect of the Pyrénées-Orientales department in France and a vicar-general from the Urgel diocese.

Co-prince (Bishop of Urgel):

Joan Martí Alanis	31 Jan. 1971—12 May 2003
Joan Enric **VIVES** i Sicília	Since 12 May 2003

Co-prince (President of France):

Jacques Chirac	Since 17 May 1995

President of the Executive Council:

Marc Forné Molné	7 Dec. 1994—27 May 2005
Albert **PINTAT** Santolària	Since 27 May 2005

Legislature: The legislature is unicameral. The sole chamber, the General Council of the Valleys (Consell General del Valles), has 28 members, directly elected for a maximum four-year term.

Profile of the Co-prince (Bishop of Urgel):

Joan Enric **VIVES** i Sicília

Joan Enric Vives i Sicília, from Barcelona, became a co-prince of Andorra on his appointment as bishop of Urgel in May 2003. His role is almost entirely ceremonial.

Joan Enric Vives i Sicília was born in Barcelona on 24 July 1949, the son of Francesc Vives i Pons and Cornèlia Sicília Ibáñez, who were small traders. Following his education at the Pere Vila school and the Jaume Balmes High School, Vives entered the Barcelona Seminary in 1965. He was ordained as a priest in September 1974. He taught at the faculty of theology in Barcelona until

1976, and also worked as a teacher of the Catalan language. Vives was appointed auxiliary bishop of Barcelona and titular bishop of Nona in 1993. He became coadjutor bishop of Urgel in 2001 and succeeded the bishop of Urgel on 12 May 2003, thus becoming a co-prince of Andorra in accordance with the constitution of the principality.

Profile of the Co-prince (President of France):

Jacques **CHIRAC**—*see France.*

Profile of the President of the Executive Council:

Albert **PINTAT** Santolària

Albert Pintat Santolària had a long career in ministerial and diplomatic service prior to his appointment as president of the Executive Council in May 2005. He is a member of the Liberal Party of Andorra (Partit Liberal d'Andorra—PLA).

Albert Pintat Santolària was born on 23 June 1943 and graduated in economic sciences from the Catholic University of Freiburg (Switzerland). He served as personal secretary to the then head of government Josep Pintat from 1984 to 1985 before becoming minister of foreign trade. He was elected to the General Council in 1986 and remained there until 1991 when he became the Andorran ambassador to the Benelux countries and in 1995 ambassador to the European Union.

Pintat returned to Andorra in 1997 to become foreign minister, a post he held until 2001. He then served as ambassador to Switzerland and later to the UK. Following the victory of the PLA in elections in 2005 Pintat was named as president of the Executive Council on 27 May. He is married to Carmen Pintat Rossell, with three children.

ANGOLA

Full name: The Republic of Angola.

Leadership structure: The head of state is a president, directly elected by universal adult suffrage. The president's term of office is five years, but elections have not been held since 1992. The president is head of government and appoints the prime minister, a post reintroduced in December 2002. The president also appoints and presides over the Council of Ministers.

President:	José Eduardo **DOS SANTOS** (acting from 10 Sept. 1979)	Since 21 Sept. 1979
Prime Minister:	Fernando **DA PIEDADE**	Since 5 Dec. 2002

Legislature: The 223-member unicameral National Assembly (Assembléia Nacional) is directly elected for a four-year term, but elections have not been held since 1992. The Assembly extended its own mandate for the second time on 17 October 2000. On 24 August 2004 the government announced a timetable for voter enrolment leading to elections in September 2006.

Profile of the President:

José Eduardo **DOS SANTOS**

José Eduardo dos Santos was involved from his youth in the struggle to end Portuguese colonial rule, as a member of the Marxist-Leninist guerrilla Popular Movement for the Liberation of Angola (Movimento Popular de Libertação de Angola—MPLA). He succeeded to the presidency four years after independence, but his regime remained dogged until 2002 by a protracted civil war against Jonas Savimbi's National Union for the Total Independence of Angola (União Nacional para a Independência Total de Angola—UNITA).

Born in Luanda on 28 August 1942, the son of a bricklayer, José Eduardo dos Santos joined the MPLA in 1961 while still a student in Luanda, and set up a youth organization within it. In November of that year he fled north across the Congolese border, initially to Léopoldville (now Kinshasa) to escape the Portuguese colonial authorities. Enlisting in the MPLA guerrilla army the following year, he soon became the organization's chief representative in Brazzaville.

In 1963 he went to study in the Soviet Union at the Baku Petroleum and Gas Institute, receiving degrees in petroleum engineering and in radar communications. After completing his studies in 1969 he did a one-year military communications course before returning to Angola in 1970 to resume his role in the anti-colonial struggle. He was head of the MPLA's principal communications centre on the northern front, where he became in 1974 a member of the readjustment commission and also head of finances. In September 1974 he was elected to the MPLA central committee.

In June 1975 he was named as the MPLA's foreign affairs secretary, and after the proclamation of independence on 11 November he was appointed minister of external relations, later transferring to become minister of planning. He also held the office of first deputy premier until it was abolished in 1978, and was put in charge of national reconstruction on the party central committee.

After President Agostinho Neto's death in 1979, dos Santos moved up to take over the MPLA leadership, which carried with it the roles of state president and commander-in-chief of the armed forces, to which he was sworn in on 21 September 1979. The dos Santos succession marked a setback for hard-line pro-Soviet elements within the embattled party leadership, and the ascendancy of those who favoured a sustained attempt to negotiate an end to the civil war with UNITA. For most of the next decade this proved unattainable, however, with the Reagan administration in the USA and the South African apartheid government (itself also embroiled in Namibia) both increasingly committed to backing and arming UNITA. The MPLA regime for its part remained militarily reliant on the Cuban forces which had helped avert its defeat in the months after independence.

Prospects for peace apparently improved with two sets of agreements in which dos Santos played a major part—those signed in New York in 1988 to end South African and Cuban involvement, and the 1991 Bicesse Accords with UNITA which provided for a peace process, a UN presence and a transition to multiparty democracy. Elections held in September 1992 were dominated by the presidential contest between dos Santos (who won 49.6% of the vote in the first round) and Savimbi (who won 40%). UNITA responded by launching an intensified civil war, however, which prevented the holding of a second-round runoff.

Dos Santos was generally credited with supporting the peace process, and with having overseen the reorientation of the MPLA away from its Marxist-Leninist ideological foundation in the wake of the collapse of communism in Eastern Europe and the Soviet Union. At successive party congresses in December 1990 and May 1992, reforms were adopted and he was re-elected as party chairman. A more hard-line element in the party, however, backed the election of Lopo do Nascimento as secretary-general in 1993, and reflected concern that the party's forces had weakened themselves dangerously vis-à-vis UNITA by observing the terms of the peace process, which remained mired in continuing conflict until the death of Savimbi in February 2002. The president, his family and his immediate circle of advisers were accused by critics of lacking answers to the country's pressing problems, and of corruption and preoccupation with their own business interests, while dos Santos himself suffered serious illness, believed to be prostate cancer.

Since the abortive 1992 polls, no elections have been held. Dos Santos postponed polls promised for 2001 to late 2002, but announced that he would not stand for re-election. However, a peace accord in 2002 began a four-year period of transition, and legislative polls are scheduled for 2006, though delays are likely. Dos Santos was re-elected as MPLA leader in December 2003 and is widely expected to stand as the party's candidate in the next presidential poll. He is married to businesswoman Ana Paula dos Santos and they have two children.

Profile of the Prime Minister:

Fernando **DA PIEDADE**

Fernando 'Nandó' da Piedade is a very close ally of President José Eduardo dos Santos. A former active participant in the liberation struggle, he is a member of the politburo of the Popular Movement for the Liberation of Angola (Movimento Popular de Libertação de Angola—MPLA), and was interior minister before being chosen to fill the resurrected post of prime minister in December 2002 as part of the country's peace process.

Fernando da Piedade Dias dos Santos was born on 5 March 1952 in Luanda, then the administrative capital of the Portuguese overseas province of Angola. Drafted into the colonial army, he was briefly imprisoned for his pro-independence views. In June 1974 he deserted and joined the MPLA in Cabinda, in its struggle against the Portuguese. He eventually reached the rank of major. Angola became an independent country in November 1975 amid a civil war between the MPLA and the US-backed National Union for the Total Independence of Angola (União Nacional para a Independência Total de Angola—UNITA).

In the early 1970s da Piedade occupied posts in the now defunct People's Army for the Liberation of Angola and the national police force. He entered direct government service as deputy interior minister in 1984 and studied law at the newly opened Agostinho Neto University. President dos Santos appointed him deputy minister of state security in 1986 and chose him to head the commission for reorganization of the ministry of state security later that year. Under da Piedade's guidance the commission purged the ministry of several senior members, jailing them for corruption. The commission was disbanded in 1988.

Da Piedade was elected to the MPLA's politburo in 1998 and in February 1999 he was made full interior minister in a cabinet reshuffle which saw President dos Santos take over the functions of prime minister. In the meantime the attempts of the early 1990s to end the civil war had given way to renewed violence. As part of the government's effort to find a resolution of the apparent impasse, da

Angola: *Fernando da Piedade*

Piedade was made co-ordinator of the peace process and national reconciliation. In 2002 the death of UNITA leader Jonas Savimbi opened up the way for peace and a lasting ceasefire was signed in April. By December the country was beginning to restructure itself after 27 years of war. UNITA members were inducted into government and President dos Santos appointed da Piedade to the resurrected post of prime minister.

ANTIGUA AND BARBUDA

Full name: Antigua and Barbuda.

Leadership structure: The head of state is the British sovereign, styled 'Queen of Antigua and Barbuda and of Her other Realms and Territories, Head of the Commonwealth', represented by a governor-general who is appointed on the advice of the prime minister of Antigua and Barbuda. The head of government, the prime minister, is the leader of the majority in the House of Representatives and is appointed by the governor-general. The governor-general also appoints, on the prime minister's advice, the cabinet, which is responsible to Parliament.

Queen:	Elizabeth II	Since 6 Feb. 1952
Governor-General:	Sir James B. **CARLISLE**	Since 10 June 1993
Prime Minister:	Lester Bird	9 March 1994—24 March 2004
	Baldwin **SPENCER**	Since 24 March 2004

Legislature: The legislature, the Parliament, is bicameral. The lower chamber, the House of Representatives, has 17 members, directly elected for up to five years. The upper chamber, the Senate, has 17 members, appointed by the governor-general on the advice of the prime minister and the leader of the opposition, for the life of the Parliament.

Profile of the Governor-General:

Sir James B. **CARLISLE**

Sir James Carlisle has been governor-general of Antigua and Barbuda since 1993. He represents the monarch, Queen Elizabeth II, as titular head of state. His appointment came after a long career in dentistry.

James Beethoven Carlisle was born on 5 August 1937 and has been married three times. He most recently married Nalda Amelia Meade in 1984 and he has a total of five children. He attended Bolans Public School, Antigua, between 1946 and 1954, and afterwards worked as a primary school teacher. In 1960 he went to the UK, joining the Royal Air Force while also pursuing courses at North West London Polytechnic and (in 1963–64) at Singapore University. Returning to the UK he did an 'A-level' course at Northampton College of Technology and then attended the University of Dundee in 1967–72, qualifying as a dentist.

From 1972 to 1992 he worked in general practice in Scotland, Wales, England and Antigua, and was also a part-time school dental officer in Scotland and Antigua. Between 1981 and 1983 he was a volunteer dentist at the Baptist Dental Clinic, and from 1983 to 1986 was manager of the fluoride programme with the Catholic Dental Centre. In 1990–91 he studied laser dentistry at Orlando, Florida. In 1993 he instituted a free dental care programme for children and the elderly. He was also chairman of the National Parks Authority (1986–90) and chairman of the Tabitha Senior Citizen's Home (1987–90). He took up his appointment as governor-general in June 1993 and was created a Knight Grand Cross of the Most Distinguished Order of St Michael and St George in November of that year.

Profile of the Prime Minister:

Baldwin **SPENCER**

Baldwin Spencer and his United Progressive Party (UPP) won a landslide victory in general elections on 23 March 2004, ending the political dynasty of the Bird family which had ruled Antigua and Barbuda since 1960. A lifelong labour activist, Spencer was born in Antigua's poor working-class neighbourhood of Green Bay. He spent most of his political life campaigning against the Birds, and when he eventually won elections in 2004 he pledged to invest in supporting the poor through education and unemployment benefits.

Winston Denfield Baldwin Spencer was born on 8 October 1948, and is married to office clerk Jackie Baldwin, with whom he has a son and a daughter. Born in Green Bay to a single mother, his early years were spent in poverty. His personal history, like that of Antigua and Barbuda itself, is entwined with the history of the Bird dynasty. A youth leader of the Antigua Trades and Labour Union formed by Vere Bird Sr in the 1950s, Spencer was sent by the organization on a scholarship to the UK to study labour relations at Ruskin College, Oxford. (He also holds qualifications from the Coady International Institute in Canada and Oslo University in Norway.) By the time he returned, the movement was in disarray. Bird had fired three senior labour leaders because their popularity threatened the cult of personality he was gradually constructing.

Spencer joined the breakaway Progressive Labour Movement (PLM), which had split from the Antigua Trades and Labour Union in 1968. The new party defeated Bird's Antigua Labour Party (ALP) in general elections in 1971, but five years later the ALP wrested back power. It was to hold on to that power for 28 years, with the office of prime minister passing to Vere's son Lester in 1994. The ALP lavished gifts on voters and rewarded party members with sought-after government jobs; the PLM could hope to match neither its strength nor its extravagance. Spencer joined the United National Democratic Party and later became head of the UPP opposition alliance, but could only watch as voters ignored blatant corruption to keep the Birds and the ALP in power.

Of the scandals that finally brought down the Birds, the most important involved the national health insurance fund, to which every working Antiguan contributes. Allegations flew that senior members of the government and their friends and families had been handed vast sums from the fund for cosmetic surgery in the USA. Two years ahead of the 2004 general election, the Privy Council ordered Lester Bird to relinquish his absolute control over broadcasting outlets and allow opposition voices to be heard, and momentum began to build behind Spencer's challenge to the Bird family's domination of island politics. Finally, in the early morning of 24 March 2004, Bird conceded defeat in the previous day's general election, and Antigua and Barbuda woke up to a celebration that had been nearly three decades in the making.

ARGENTINA

Full name: The Republic of Argentina.

Leadership structure: The head of state is a president, directly elected by universal adult suffrage. The president's term of office is four years, renewable once only. The head of government is the president. The cabinet is appointed by the president.

President:	Fernando de la Rúa	10 Dec. 1999—21 Dec. 2001
	Ramón Puerta (acting)	21 Dec. 2001—23 Dec. 2001
	Adolfo Rodríguez Saá (interim)	23 Dec. 2001—31 Dec. 2001
	Eduardo Camaño (acting)	31 Dec. 2001—2 Jan. 2002
	Eduardo Alberto Duhalde	2 Jan. 2002—25 May 2003
	Néstor **KIRCHNER**	Since 25 May 2003
Cabinet Chief:	Rodolfo Terragno	10 Dec. 1999—5 Oct. 2000
	Chrystian Colombo	5 Oct. 2000—21 Dec. 2001
	Humberto Schiavoni	21 Dec. 2001—23 Dec. 2001
	Luis Lusquiños (acting)	23 Dec. 2001—31 Dec. 2001
	Antonio Cafiero	31 Dec. 2001—3 Jan. 2002
	Jorge Capitanich	3 Jan. 2002—3 May 2002
	Alfredo Atanasof	3 May 2002—25 May 2003
	Alberto **FERNÁNDEZ**	Since 25 May 2003

Legislature: The legislature, the National Congress (Congreso de la Nación), is bicameral. The lower chamber, the Chamber of Deputies (Cámara de Diputados), has 257 members, directly elected for four-year terms (with half of the seats renewed every two years). The upper chamber, the Senate (Senado), has 72 members, who until December 2001 were indirectly elected. The terms of all sitting senators ended in December 2001. The whole Senate was directly elected for the first time in October 2001, with one-third renewable every two years.

Profile of the President:

Néstor **KIRCHNER**

Néstor Kirchner, a Peronist with leftist leanings, became Argentinian president by default on 25 May 2003 following the withdrawal of his controversial opponent (and fellow Peronist) Carlos Menem from the second round of elections. Kirchner assumed the presidency at the tail end of the worst economic crisis in Argentinian history, with middle-class savings wiped out, the near collapse of the banking system, and many people slipping below the poverty line. Described by his opponents as 'decaffeinated' and 'grey', Kirchner described himself to the electorate as a serious and efficient administrator, and immediately won respect for purging the higher echelons of the justice system and security services. Having been elected president with just 22% of the vote in the first-round ballot, opinion polls a year later gave him an approval rating of 80%.

Néstor Carlos Kirchner Ostoic is of mixed Swiss/Croatian descent and was born on 25 February 1950 in Río Gallegos, in the Patagonian province of Santa Cruz. A vehement opponent of the military junta that ousted Juan Perón, Kirchner was throughout the 1970s active in the Young Peronists and the Justicialist National Movement (Movimiento Nacionalista Justicialista, forerunner of the Justicialist Party, Partido Justicialista—PJ). He was imprisoned twice during the 1976–83 military dictatorship, and several of his friends were among the thousands who 'disappeared'. During the 1970s Kirchner studied law at La Plata National University, graduating in 1976. He returned to Río Gallegos to practise law with his wife, Cristina Fernández, also a lawyer and member of the PJ and now a popular and influential senator.

Following the restoration of democracy in 1983, Kirchner became a public officer in the provincial government. The following year, he was briefly president of the Río Gallegos social welfare fund, but was forced out by the governor because of a dispute over financial policy. The affair made him a local celebrity; in 1987 he won the mayoral race for Río Gallegos, and in 1991 he became governor of the province of Santa Cruz. In 1995, having introduced constitutional reforms to allow himself another gubernatorial term, Kirchner was easily re-elected with 66.5% of the votes.

Over the next three years he was beginning to distance himself from the charismatic and controversial President Carlos Menem, leader of the PJ; the president's decision to stand again in 1999 had prompted fury on the part of the party's rank and file, and Kirchner had aligned himself with the camp of Menem's chief opponent within the PJ, the governor of the Buenos Aires province (and later president) Eduardo Duhalde.

Defeat in the 1999 elections at national level, and the loss of the presidency to Fernando de la Rúa, came as a shock to the PJ. Kirchner lost ground in Santa Cruz too, but managed to be re-elected to a third term as governor there. The financial crisis that hit Argentina in 2001, however, destroyed de la Rúa. Three stopgap presidents followed in quick succession as the Argentinian people openly displayed their contempt for the political classes, with Duhalde taking the reins in January 2002.

Both factions of the PJ fielded candidates in the 2003 presidential poll. Menem, attempting a comeback and standing for the Front for Liberty, won the first round with just 24%—only 2% more than Kirchner, candidate of the Front for Victory. Recognizing that he was too unpopular in the country as a whole to win, Menem withdrew from the race, leaving Kirchner to take the presidency by default.

Expectations were low, but Kirchner acted decisively on several fronts. Shortly after coming into office, he suspended the laws of immunity for former military leaders and hinted that he would be happy to see them extradited. He then sacked 50 senior officers linked with the corruption of earlier regimes. Most prominently, Kirchner refused—and refuses—to bend his policies to the demands of the International Monetary Fund and economic orthodoxy, and is emerging as one of the biggest thorns in the US side in the Latin American region—a significant departure from the pro-US policies of Menem. Some, indeed, are beginning to compare him to the founder of his party, Juan Perón, a populist who nationalized foreign-owned industries while railing against US imperialism as Argentina's president half a century ago.

Profile of the Cabinet Chief:

Alberto **FERNÁNDEZ**

Alberto Fernández is a career lawyer and academic who specialized in insurance and later cofounded an anti-corruption think tank. A close ally of Néstor Kirchner in the Justicialist Party (Partido Justicialista—PJ), he was appointed as his cabinet chief on 25 May 2003 when Kirchner won the presidency.

Alberto Angel Fernández was born in the city of Buenos Aires on 2 April 1959 and is married with one son. At the age of 24 he graduated from the faculty of law of the University of Buenos Aires as a solicitor. In 1989, when he was just 30 years of age, he was appointed as national superintendent of insurance. Until then he had worked as an adviser to the municipal council of Buenos Aires and the national Chamber of Deputies, and also the subdirector-general of legal affairs in the ministry of the economy.

On the international stage, between 1989 and 1999, Fernández was president of the Association of Superintendents of Insurance of Latin America, and also negotiator for Argentina in the Uruguay round of GATT trade talks. In business, he was responsible for the development of the insurance arms of the Buenos Aires Provincial Bank; later, as president of Gerenciar SA, he developed and set in motion an expansion of its insurance business and in 1997 he was made executive vice president of the group. In recognition of his work, he received the

Securities Prize for 'manager of the year' in 1997 and the Millennium Prize as 'manager of the century' in 2000.

In 1997 he cofounded a think tank known as los Servicios de Transparencia, focusing on the impact of corruption on private and public organizations, and in 1999 he was installed as programme director for transparency in public and private organizations at the University of Buenos Aires. He is also a professor of penal law and gives classes in law and in criminology. Fernández is the author of a number of publications and journals.

When Néstor Kirchner won the presidency of Argentina on 25 May 2003, he immediately chose Fernández to head his cabinet.

ARMENIA

Full name: The Republic of Armenia.

Leadership structure: The head of state is a president, directly elected by universal adult suffrage. The president's term of office is five years, renewable once only. The president appoints the prime minister, and the other members of the cabinet as proposed by the prime minister. The prime minister is head of government, and directs and co-ordinates its work.

President:	Robert **KOCHARIAN** (acting from 3 Feb. 1998)	Since 9 April 1998
Prime Minister:	Aram Sarkissian	3 Nov. 1999—2 May 2000
	Robert Kocharian (acting)	2 May 2000—12 May 2000
	Andranik **MARKARIAN**	Since 12 May 2000

Legislature: The legislature is unicameral. The sole chamber, the National Assembly (Azgayin Joghov), has 131 members, directly elected for a four-year term.

Profile of the President:

Robert **KOCHARIAN**

Robert Kocharian was once a member of the Soviet-era communist party. In the last years of the Soviet Union he became prominent in the pro-independence movement in the Armenian-dominated enclave of Nagorno-Karabakh (inside Azerbaijan), of which he is a native. His term as the enclave's first 'president' (1994–97) was followed by a one-year spell as prime minister of Armenia. He was elected president of Armenia after the incumbent's surprise resignation in early 1998, and was re-elected in 2003.

Robert Sedrakovich Kocharian, who is married with three children, was born on 31 August 1954 in Stepanakert (now known as Xankändi), Nagorno-Karabakh, and joined the Soviet army in 1972 for three years. He then studied electronics and technology at the Polytechnic Institute in Yerevan, the Armenian capital, graduating in 1982. The previous year he had begun a job as an engineer and electrotechnician at the Karabakh silk production factory in Stepanakert. In 1987 he became secretary on the committee of the factory's communist party. The following year he began campaigning for the formation of a unified Republic of Armenia, to include Nagorno-Karabakh. He founded Unification (Miatsum), an ostensibly non-political movement which became the leading faction in the Karabakh movement.

In 1989, the year in which he left the communist party, Kocharian became a deputy in the Armenian Supreme Council. Towards the end of the year the council declared an Armenian republic which included Nagorno-Karabakh, although the Soviet government declared this move unconstitutional. On 2 September 1991 Nagorno-Karabakh declared itself a republic, then the Communist Party of Armenia dissolved itself and on 23 September Armenia voted for independence from the Soviet Union. At this time Kocharian was elected a deputy to the Supreme Council of Nagorno-Karabakh. From August 1992, when a state of emergency was declared, he became chairman of the defence committee which effectively governed the region. In December 1994 he was elected the first president of the Republic of Nagorno-Karabakh by the Supreme Council, his position being confirmed in a direct election in the enclave in November 1996.

Kocharian was appointed prime minister of Armenia on 19 March 1997 by Armenian president Levon Ter-Petrossian, who hoped to use this nationalistic gesture to relieve popular discontent at the high unemployment and rising poverty brought about by recent economic reforms. Kocharian expressed hopes that his appointment might speed up the resolution of the status of his war-ravaged home territory. In Azerbaijan, however, it was regarded as an insult and as evidence of de facto Armenian annexation of the Nagorno-Karabakh enclave.

The two men's close relationship soon soured, with Kocharian critical of any attempts to dilute the enclave's claims. Ter-Petrossian unexpectedly resigned in February 1998 amid disagreements with the government over a proposal from the Organization for Security and Co-operation in Europe (OSCE) to end the dispute. Kocharian was successfully elected in his place and was inaugurated on 9 April.

His first term as president was fraught with conflict between himself and the government. He clashed in particular with Aram Sarkissian, who was prime minister for six months after the incumbent, his brother Vazgen Sarkissian, was killed in a shoot-out in the parliament in October 1999. Sources of friction included the enclave, alleged corruption, and Kocharian's authoritarian approach.

There have been several unsuccessful attempts to have Kocharian impeached, including one for his refusal to allow the military prosecutor-general to testify in the 1999 parliament massacre. Consequently, his rule is frequently protested by large demonstrations in Yerevan, where over 10,000 people rallied in September 2001 against his declared intention to run for a second term in 2003. He won the election in the second round with 67% of the vote, but OSCE observers reported irregularities in the poll, and popular protests demanding Kocharian's resignation for rigging the vote carried on into 2004. A referendum held on 25 May 2003 proposed constitutional amendments to reduce the power of the presidency. However, it failed to achieve a large enough majority amid cries from the opposition that the reforms did not go far enough; they demand, in particular, that the prime minister should be responsible to the National Assembly rather than the president. Constitutional reform was a condition of Armenia's accession to the Council of Europe in 2001, so redrafting of the amendments continued into 2005.

There remains no end in sight for the Nagorno-Karabakh dispute, though at Kocharian's first meeting with the new leader of Azerbaijan Ilham Aliyev in December 2003, both presidents committed to renewing talks.

Profile of the Prime Minister:

Andranik **MARKARIAN**

A computer specialist and career politician who was briefly detained for seditious nationalism under Soviet rule, Andranik Markarian is seen as a close ally of President Robert Kocharian. Markarian heads the large Unity (Miasnutiun) parliamentary bloc and was appointed prime minister in May 2000.

Andranik Markarian was born in the early 1950s in what was then the Soviet Socialist Republic of Armenia. From an early age he became involved with nationalist activists. In the early 1970s he joined the banned National Unity Party and was arrested by the Soviet authorities in 1974. After two years in a penitential gulag he returned to Armenia. His prisoner-of-conscience past is renowned in Armenia where he insists it does not equate with modern-day anti-Russian sentiment.

Following the assassination of Prime Minister Vazgen Sarkissian in a shoot-out in the parliament building in October 1999, his brother Aram took on the position only to be dismissed in May 2000 after months of political wrangling with President Kocharian. The president filled the vacuum with Markarian, who had become the new head of the Republican Party of Armenia (Hayastani Hanrapetakan Kusaktsutiun—HHK) which was the leading member of the powerful Unity parliamentary bloc.

Upon his appointment Markarian faced hostility from large factions of the Unity bloc and promptly relieved himself of dissident ministers mostly from the Yerkrapah Union of Veterans of the Karabakh War. Despite resistance from the National Assembly Markarian pledged to continue the policies of his immediate predecessors and to rule a government of accord. A major part of his new policy revolved around an ending of conflict between the government and Kocharian.

Pro-presidential parties dominated the National Assembly after the May 2003 elections and Markarian remained in post heading a coalition of the HHK, the Law-Based State party and the Armenian Revolutionary Federation—Dashnaktsutyun.

AUSTRALIA

Full name: The Commonwealth of Australia.

Leadership structure: A Constitutional Convention voted by an overwhelming majority, on 14 February 1998, to hold a referendum on whether Australia should become a republic. The referendum, held on 6 November 1999, rejected the suggested format, involving replacement of the monarchy by a president selected by Parliament. The head of state thus remains the British sovereign, styled 'Queen of Australia and Her other Realms and Territories, Head of the Commonwealth', and represented by a governor-general who is appointed on the advice of the Australian prime minister. The head of government is the prime minister, who is appointed by the governor-general and responsible to Parliament. The cabinet is selected by the prime minister and appointed by the governor-general. Members of the cabinet must be members of the federal Parliament.

Queen:	Elizabeth II	Since 6 Feb. 1952
Governor-General:	Sir William Deane	16 Feb. 1996—29 June 2001
	Peter Hollingworth	29 June 2001—28 May 2003
	Sir Guy Green (acting)	15 May 2003—11 Aug. 2003
	Michael **JEFFERY**	Since 11 Aug. 2003
Prime Minister:	John **HOWARD**	Since 11 March 1996

Legislature: The legislature, the Parliament, is bicameral. The lower chamber, the House of Representatives, has 150 members, directly elected for a maximum of three years. The upper chamber, the Senate, has 76 members (12 members for each of the six states, directly elected for a maximum of six years, and two each for the Northern Territory and the Australian Capital Territory, directly elected for three years). Half of the Senate is normally elected at the same time as the House of Representatives.

Profile of the Governor-General:

Michael **JEFFERY**

Michael Jeffery became governor-general of Australia on 11 August 2003. A career soldier, he served in Malaya, Borneo, Viet Nam, and Papua New Guinea. He left the army to become governor of Western Australia in 1993, and on leaving that post founded a public policy think tank. Although he is a social conservative, Jeffery's role in the largely ceremonial office of the presidency restricts his freedom to speak out on controversial issues.

Philip Michael Jeffery was born on 12 December 1937 in the remote town of Wiluna in Western Australia and was educated at state schools in Perth before attending the Royal Military School in Duntroon, Canberra. He graduated in 1958 and was posted to Malaya with the Royal Australian Regiment before being seconded to the British Special Air Service (SAS) for a tour of duty in Borneo.

From 1966 until 1969 he served in Papua New Guinea with 1st Battalion, the Pacific Islands Regiment, during which time he married Marlena Kerr; they have three sons and a daughter. Jeffery then served a tour of duty in Viet Nam, during which time he was awarded the Military Cross and the South Vietnamese Cross of Gallantry. In 1972, he was promoted to lieutenant-colonel following a stint at the British Army Staff College in Camberley, and took command of the 2nd Battalion, the Pacific Islands Regiment, in Papua New Guinea. After three years he assumed command of the SAS Regiment in Perth and was later promoted to colonel as the first director of the army's special action forces.

In 1981 he was promoted to brigadier and headed the national counterterrorist co-ordination authority. He remained in this post until 1983 when he assumed command of the 1st Mechanized and Airborne Brigade in Sydney. Jeffery attended the Royal College of Defence Studies in London in 1985, and was promoted again to major-general, taking command of the army's 1st Division the following year. In 1990 he was appointed deputy chief of the general staff and in 1991 he became assistant chief of the general staff for materiel.

In November 1993 Jeffery became governor of Western Australia, a position he held for seven years. On leaving the post, he founded the public policy think tank Future Directions International and chaired the corporation until 2003. He was sworn in as Australian governor-general on 11 August 2003, following the resignation of Peter Hollingworth. Jeffery is known to be a conservative on moral issues and has spoken out critically on single parenthood and homosexuality.

Profile of the Prime Minister:

John **HOWARD**

John Howard is a former lawyer and a member of Parliament since 1974. He was leader of the Liberal Party of Australia from 1985 to 1989, and the party turned to him once again in early 1995, by which time he had moved from his former 'radical conservative' stance to redefine himself as a 'tolerant conservative'. He became prime minister the following March, after leading a Liberal–National coalition to a general election victory, defeating the Australian Labor Party (ALP) which had been in government for the previous 13 years.

John Winston Howard was born in Earlwood, New South Wales, on 26 July 1939, and was educated locally at Canterbury Boys' High School. He graduated in 1961 from Sydney University with a degree in law, and was admitted as a solicitor of the New South Wales Supreme Court the following year, becoming a partner in a Sydney law firm (1968–74). He married Alison Janette Parker in 1971 and they have two sons and one daughter.

From 1972 to 1974 Howard was the vice president of the New South Wales Liberal Party, and in May 1974 he was elected to the federal Parliament as a Liberal MP for Bennelong, a suburb of Sydney. For a brief period in 1975 he served as a member of the opposition shadow ministry, speaking on consumer affairs.

When Gough Whitlam's ALP government was ousted in late 1975, and Liberal leader Malcolm Fraser was invited to form a government in his place, Howard became a government minister for the first time, serving as minister for business and consumer affairs, then briefly as minister of state for special trade negotiations in 1977. He was treasurer in Fraser's government from November 1977 to March 1983. After the electoral defeat for the Liberal–National coalition in 1983, Howard was chosen to be deputy leader of the Liberal Party (and of the opposition), with Andrew Peacock as the new party leader. A rivalry between these two saw the party leadership change hands a number of times during a long period in opposition. Howard became leader in September 1985, adopting a right-wing stance against a range of ALP policies, including increased Asian immigration. In May 1989 he was ousted as party leader by Peacock. Howard held several shadow cabinet posts, especially in the field of industrial relations and employment. He also chaired the manpower and labour market reform group, and made an unsuccessful bid for the party leadership again after the general election in 1993.

Having redefined himself as a 'tolerant conservative', Howard made his political comeback in January 1995, and was re-elected leader of the Liberal Party unanimously on 30 January when Alexander Downer stood down after only eight months in the post. As leader of the opposition, Howard confirmed his party's retreat from proposals to raise indirect taxes. He refrained from making a clear commitment, however, on the issue of the proposed move from a monarchy to a republican system which was a key part of the ALP government's pre-election position. Howard led the Liberal Party in its strong showing in the general election of 2 March 1996, enabling him to claim the post of prime minister as head of a Liberal–National coalition government sworn in on 11 March.

The Howard government was re-elected in early elections held in October 1998 but over the course of his first two terms as prime minister Howard's popularity declined, despite progress on the management of the economy. He was criticized for weak handling of a challenge from the far right, while he risked a major rural–urban split on the race issue by advocating legislation to make it more difficult for Aborigines to claim native title rights over lands leased from the state by white farmers. His referendum on whether Australia should become a republic produced a 'no' vote on the basis that the alternatives offered, such as an indirectly elected president, were unacceptable. By 2001 it was generally expected that the Liberal–National coalition would be resoundingly ousted in the next election, and the ALP surged to victory in local elections, taking all but one state by February.

However, public opinion took a sudden and dramatic swing to the right towards the end of that year based on two issues: international terrorism and immigration. The attempt by 450 Afghan refugees to enter Australia illegally aboard the *Tampa* in August 2001, and the 11 September attacks in the USA, galvanized support for Howard's hard-line stance on these issues. The Liberal–National coalition was consequently re-elected in November 2001 for a third term.

In the ensuing year the government's popularity at the national level was damaged by discomfort over the conditions in detention camps for asylum seekers and a fierce row over government claims that some asylum seekers aboard a vessel known as SIEV 4 had deliberately thrown their children overboard in order for them to be rescued by the Australian coastguard. This row lingered on until 2004. At the local level, the ALP completed its clean sweep of state legislatures in March 2002.

The October 2002 Islamist terrorist bombing in Bali, where Australian tourists were the most numerous of the victims, saw Howard reiterate his hard line on international terrorism which struck a chord with many voters. He capitalized on his image as the guardian of Australian national security by sending Australian troops to support the US-led invasion of Iraq in March 2003. Though he was subject to considerable criticism for the decision, especially when no weapons of mass destruction—the justification for the invasion—had been found, his popularity among much of the electorate remained undimmed. Opposition leader Mark Latham pledged to withdraw all Australian troops from Iraq, but the expected backlash against Howard's Liberal–National coalition did not occur. The Liberal–National coalition had expanded homeownership, and coupled with accusations that a Labour government would lead to higher interest rates, Howard's strategy of portraying Latham as undermining US–Australian relations in the end proved effective. In the 2004 elections the Liberal–National coalition won an increased majority in Congress and a majority in the Senate; Howard thus became the first prime minister in decades to have control of both houses.

The rapid and effective government response to the Asian tsunami in December 2004 won plaudits at home and abroad, including from the opposition ALP, though a decision in February 2005 to send 450 more troops to Iraq was not greeted with the same enthusiasm. Discontent with government policies on asylum led to a minor backbench revolt in May 2005, but the planned introduction of new terror legislation in late 2005 reinforced Howard's identification with a firm stance on these issues.

AUSTRIA

Full name: The Republic of Austria.

Leadership structure: The head of state is a federal president, directly elected by universal adult suffrage. The president's term of office is six years, renewable once only. The head of government is the federal chancellor, who is appointed by the president. The federal government is appointed by the president at the chancellor's recommendation.

Federal President:	Thomas Klestil	8 July 1992—6 July 2004
	Andreas Khol (acting)	6 July 2004—8 July 2004
	Heinz **FISCHER**	Since 8 July 2004
Federal Chancellor:	Viktor Klima	28 Jan. 1997—4 Feb. 2000
	Wolfgang **SCHÜSSEL**	Since 4 Feb. 2000

Legislature: The legislature, the Parliament (Parlament), is bicameral. The lower chamber, the National Council (Nationalrat), has 183 members, directly elected for a four-year term. The upper chamber, the Federal Council (Bundesrat), has 62 members elected for various terms by the provincial assemblies. Powers relating to some formal acts of state are vested in the two chambers meeting together as the Federal Assembly (Bundesversammlung).

Profile of the Federal President:

Heinz **FISCHER**

Heinz Fischer became Austria's first socialist president for 18 years on 8 July 2004 after beating Foreign Minister Benita Ferrero-Waldner of the Austrian People's Party (Österreichische Volkspartei—ÖVP) in a close-fought election. His victory was a blow to Chancellor Wolfgang Schüssel, the leader of the ÖVP. Fischer is known as a professional politician who prefers to avoid controversy and conflict; he has said, however, that he wants to use his largely ceremonial position to act as a counterweight to the right-wing administration.

Born in Graz, Styria, on 9 October 1938, Heinz Fischer received a classical education before studying law at the University of Vienna from 1956 and earning his doctorate in 1961. He continued in academia as well as following a political career and was appointed associate professor of political science at the University

33

of Innsbruck in 1978, becoming full professor in 1994. Fischer has been married to his wife Margit since 1968 and has two children. He co-edited the Austrian *Zeitschrift für Politikwissenschaft* (Journal of Political Science) and the quarterly *Journal für Rechtspolitik* (Journal of Law Policy), and is the author of several books in the fields of law and political science.

Fischer began his own political career with the Social Democratic Party of Austria (Sozialdemokratische Partei Österreichs—SPÖ) in the 1960s. From 1971 to 2004 he served as a member of the National Council, interrupted only when he served as federal minister of science and research from 1983 to 1987. In November 1990 Fischer was elected speaker of the National Council, to which he was re-elected three times, holding the office for 12 consecutive years until December 2002, when he was elected deputy speaker.

He was elected president of Austria on 25 April 2004, beating Benita Ferrero-Waldner, foreign minister in the ruling conservative coalition headed by the ÖVP. Fischer's predecessor as president, Thomas Klestil, died of a heart attack two days before he was due to hand over the post in July 2004.

Profile of the Federal Chancellor:

Wolfgang **SCHÜSSEL**

Wolfgang Schüssel is a career politician with a background in law, and has led the right-of-centre Austrian People's Party (Österreichische Volkspartei—ÖVP) since 1995. He held various ministerial posts, and was vice chancellor in a socialist-led coalition government from 1995 onward, before becoming federal chancellor on 4 February 2000. He has retained office since then at the head of a controversial coalition between the ÖVP and the far right.

Wolfgang Schüssel was born on 7 June 1945 in Vienna. He attended the renowned Schottengymnasium grammar school until graduation in 1963, and went on to obtain a doctorate in law from the University of Vienna. He is married to Krista, with two children.

Schüssel became secretary of the parliamentary group of the ÖVP in 1968 and in 1975 he moved to the party's Austrian Business Federation where he served as secretary-general until 1991. He entered Parliament at the 1979 elections and headed the ÖVP's parliamentary economic group from 1987.

In April 1989 Schüssel was appointed as minister of economic affairs in a coalition led by the Social Democratic Party of Austria (Sozialdemokratische Partei Österreichs—SPÖ). Over the course of the early 1990s, however, the ÖVP suffered from falling popular support, mostly due to the rise of the far-right Freedom Party of Austria (Freiheitliche Partei Österreichs—FPÖ). The October 1994 federal elections saw ÖVP support fall to an all-time low of only 27.7% of the vote. This poor showing brought a change of leadership in 1995, in which

Schüssel became party chairman, and therefore federal vice chancellor in the continuing SPÖ-led coalition government. Later that same year the ÖVP scored a slight recovery in a snap election.

Schüssel added the foreign affairs portfolio to his responsibilities from 1996, but the coalition was brought to the point of collapse in 1999, when the far-right FPÖ made further gains in parliamentary elections, achieving parity of seats with the ÖVP, both behind the SPÖ. With the SPÖ unwilling to countenance a coalition with the far right, the then chancellor Viktor Klima stepped down, making way for Schüssel to form a controversial government which included six FPÖ cabinet members on 4 February 2000.

The resulting ostracization of Austria by other EU member states proved relatively short-lived, but Schüssel's government was nevertheless beset by repeated disputes about—and among—its far-right contingent. The FPÖ's popularity began to plummet, and the resignation of its charismatic but controversial leader Jörg Haider did nothing to improve its standing. The coalition reached breaking point in September 2002, over Schüssel's plans to postpone tax cuts in order to cover the damage caused by that year's severe flooding. The FPÖ walked out of government in protest, and fresh elections were called for 24 November.

The ÖVP's impressive 42% of the vote in this poll made it the largest party, and ensured that Schüssel would remain in office as chancellor if he could put together another coalition. After prolonged and unsuccessful negotiations with the SPÖ and the Greens, in late February 2003 he re-formed the previous alliance with the FPÖ, even though the latter's support in the elections had fallen dramatically to just 10% of the vote. In April 2005 the junior coalition partner's ministers transferred their party affiliation from the FPÖ to a new Alliance for the Future of Austria (Bündnis Zukunft Österreich—BZÖ), formed by Haider.

AZERBAIJAN

Full name: The Republic of Azerbaijan.

Leadership structure: The head of state is a president, who is directly elected by universal adult suffrage. Under the 1995 Constitution the president's term of office is five years, nonrenewable. Executive power is held by the president. The highest executive body is the cabinet of ministers appointed by the president. The prime minister, appointed by the president, is head of government. There is, in addition, a National Security Council, set up under presidential authority by a decree of 10 April 1997.

President:	Heydar Aliyev (acting from 24 June 1993)	10 Oct. 1993—31 Oct. 2003
	Ilham **ALIYEV**	Since 31 Oct. 2003
Prime Minister:	Artur Rasizade (acting from 20 July 1996)	26 Nov. 1996—4 Aug. 2003
	Ilham Aliyev	4 Aug. 2003—4 Nov. 2003
	Artur **RASIZADE** (acting from 6 Aug. 2003)	Since 4 Nov. 2003

Legislature: The legislature is unicameral. The sole chamber, the National Assembly (Milli Majlis), has 125 members, directly elected for a five-year term.

Profile of the President:

Ilham **ALIYEV**

Ilham Aliyev is the son of Heydar Aliyev, the long-time president of Azerbaijan. He inherited his post from his father following disputed elections just before the latter's death in December 2003; Heydar had been ill and had been considering his succession for some time. Ilham had once wanted to become a Soviet diplomat, but the collapse of the Soviet Union led him to become a roving businessman and minor oil magnate. He is a sports fan with a reputation as a 'playboy' and remains president of the National Olympic Committee.

Ilham Heydar oglu Aliyev was born on 24 December 1961 in the Azeri capital, Baku. His father, Heydar Aliyev, later to be president, had at that time just become head of the Azeri KGB. Ilham Aliyev was educated in Baku until 1977 when he entered the Moscow State University of International Relations (MSUIR), graduating in 1982, the year his father joined the Soviet politburo. Ilham received his doctorate in history in 1985. He remained at MSUIR as a lecturer until 1990; reportedly his first ambition was to become a Soviet diplomat, but the Soviet Union collapsed before he got the chance. He is married with one son and two daughters.

From 1991 until 1994 Aliyev ran a number of private industrial and commercial enterprises, spreading his time between Moscow and Istanbul. It was during this period that he gained a reputation as a roulette-loving playboy. His father was elected president of Azerbaijan in 1993, and by 1994 Ilham had become vice president of the State Oil Company of the Azerbaijani Republic (SOCAR) and was actively promoting his father's oil strategy. The following year he was elected to parliament for the first time.

In 1997, he became the president of the National Olympic Committee of Azerbaijan. In 1999 he was elected deputy and in 2001 first deputy of the ruling New Azerbaijan Party (Yeni Azerbaijan Partiyasi—YAP). From 2001 until 2003 he served as the head of the Azeri parliamentary delegation to the Parliamentary Assembly of the Council of Europe (PACE). He was appointed prime minister on 4 August 2003; his father had collapsed in the spring of the same year and was openly considering his succession. In early October Heydar withdrew his own candidacy from the forthcoming presidential elections to allow Ilham to take his place. The polls on 15 October were marred by voter intimidation, media bias and violence; Ilham Aliyev won 80% of the vote and was sworn in on 31 October.

Though some Western observers, particularly those with an interest in Azerbaijan's oil industry, have made much of Aliyev as an urbane pro-Western modernizer, others consider this account preposterous and claim he has inherited his father's corrupt police state intact.

Profile of the Prime Minister:

Artur **RASIZADE**

Artur Rasizade is an engineer by training who worked in machine construction for the oil industry before becoming involved in the state planning committee. For the last five years of the communist era (1986–91) and the first year of independence he was a deputy prime minister at republican level. He is a member of the New Azerbaijan Party (Yeni Azerbaijan Partiyasi—YAP), a party of former communists founded in September 1992 by the country's dominant political figure and long-term president, Heydar Aliyev.

Artur Tahir oglu Rasizade was born on 26 February 1935 in Gyandja. He trained as an engineer at the Azerbaijan Institute of Industry and joined the Azerbaijan Institute of Oil Machine Construction when he was 22. He worked there for 21 years, rising to the post of director in 1973. From 1973 to 1977 he was also chief engineer of Trust Soyuzneftemash. In 1978 he left the engineering sector to become deputy head of the Azerbaijan state planning committee for three years. Then he joined the central committee of the Communist Party of Azerbaijan as a head of section from 1981 until 1986, before his appointment as first deputy prime minister. He retained this position until 1992, the year after the independence of Azerbaijan.

When the former communists were defeated in presidential elections in 1992 by the Azerbaijan Popular Front (Azerbaijan Khalq Cabhasi—AKC), Rasizade had to resign and became an adviser to the Foundation of Economic Reforms. Meanwhile Aliyev broke away from the AKC, which had declared a new age limit for presidential candidates which would have disqualified him from contesting elections. He formed the YAP, which Rasizade subsequently joined, and was elected president in 1993.

In February 1996 Rasizade became Aliyev's assistant, before being appointed first deputy prime minister again in May. After the resignation of the prime minister on 19 July, following accusations from Aliyev of bad management of the economy, Rasizade became acting prime minister. He was confirmed in this position on 26 November 1996, and remained in office following the November 2000 legislative elections.

In August 2003, as part of the manoeuvring around the succession to the ailing veteran president, the National Assembly approved the appointment of Aliyev's son Ilham as prime minister, but two days later he took leave to contest the October presidential elections and Rasizade took control again in an acting capacity. Ilham Aliyev reappointed Rasizade prime minister on 4 November 2003, after his inauguration as president.

BAHAMAS

Full name: The Commonwealth of the Bahamas.

Leadership structure: The head of state is the British sovereign, styled 'Queen of the Commonwealth of the Bahamas and of Her other Realms and Territories, Head of the Commonwealth', and represented by a governor-general who is appointed on the advice of the Bahamian prime minister. The head of government is the prime minister, appointed by the governor-general. The cabinet is appointed by the governor-general on the advice of the prime minister.

Queen:	Elizabeth II	Since 6 Feb. 1952
Governor-General:	Sir Orville Turnquest	3 Jan. 1995—13 Nov. 2001
	Dame Ivy **DUMONT** (acting from 13 Nov. 2001)	Since 1 Jan. 2002
Prime Minister:	Hubert Ingraham	21 Aug. 1992—3 May 2002
	Perry **CHRISTIE**	Since 3 May 2002
	Cynthia Pratt (acting)	4 May 2005—21 June 2005

Legislature: The legislature, the Parliament, is bicameral. The lower chamber, the House of Assembly, has 40 members, directly elected for a maximum five-year term. The upper chamber, the Senate, has 16 members, nominated immediately after the election of the House of Assembly for the same term.

Profile of the Governor-General:

Dame Ivy **DUMONT**

Dame Ivy Dumont is a member of the right-of-centre Free National Movement (FNM). Trained as a teacher, she had served in the cabinet of FNM prime minister Hubert Ingraham before being appointed acting governor-general in November 2001. On 1 January 2002 she was made the country's first ever female full governor-general, acting as the nominal representative of the head of state, Queen Elizabeth II.

Ivy Leona Dumont, née Turnquest, was born on 2 October 1930 at Roses on Long Island in the central Bahamas, which was then a British Crown Colony. On leaving school in 1948 she began a career in education, graduating from the teacher training college in 1951 and receiving the Bahamas Teacher's Certificate in 1954. For the next 21 years she worked as a teacher, gaining a teaching degree in 1970 and ultimately becoming a head teacher. She married Police Inspector Reginald Dumont. They have a son and a daughter.

In 1975, two years after the Bahamas became independent, Ivy Dumont entered political service as a deputy permanent secretary in the ministry of works and utilities where she stayed until 1978. In this time she gained a master's degree (1977) and a doctorate (1978) in public administration. Between 1978 and 1992 she worked in the human resources department of the Roy West Trust Corporation, a private financial firm.

Following legislative elections held in mid-1992 Dumont was appointed to the Senate to represent the FNM, of which she was also to serve as secretary-general. Prime Minister Hubert Ingraham brought her into the cabinet, one of its three women members, and she headed the ministry of health and environment for three years. She moved across to the education and training ministry in January 1995. She remained in charge at the ministry when it was transformed into the ministry of education in March 1997 after the FNM was re-elected. She retired from front-line politics in January 2000, retaining her seat in the Senate.

In November 2001 the then governor-general, Sir Orville Turnquest (no relation), stepped down so that his son, FNM leader Tommy Turnquest, could lead the party into the 2002 general elections (which it went on to lose resoundingly). Senator Dumont was drafted in as an interim replacement on 13 November, and was confirmed in the role on 1 January 2002.

Profile of the Prime Minister:

Perry **CHRISTIE**

Perry Christie is leader of the left-leaning Progressive Liberal Party (PLP). A career politician, he became in 1974 the youngest Bahamian appointed to the Senate. He has represented the Centreville constituency in the House of Assembly continuously since 1977, the same year he entered the cabinet. He led the PLP to a sweeping victory in elections in May 2002.

Perry Gladstone Christie was born on 21 August 1943 in Nassau, the capital of the Bahamas, which was then a British Crown Colony. After graduating in law in 1969 from Birmingham University in the UK, he was appointed to the Senate in 1974, one year after the Bahamas gained independence. Three years later he was elected to the House of Assembly and was drafted into the cabinet as minister of health and national insurance. He was assigned to the tourism ministry in 1982.

Having fallen out with the government and the party in 1984, Christie was dismissed from the cabinet. He left the PLP and successfully stood as an independent in the 1987 legislative elections, once again representing Centreville. Following a rapprochement he rejoined the party in March 1990 and was brought back into government, this time as minister of agriculture, trade and industry. Two years later the PLP suffered its first electoral defeat since independence.

In opposition, Christie became joint deputy leader of the PLP in 1993 and rose to full leader in 1997 after a further defeat for the PLP in the face of a resurgent Free National Movement. Rallying the party in opposition to Prime Minister Hubert Ingraham's privatization policies, Christie led the PLP to victory in May 2002 taking a clear majority of 28 seats in the 40-seat Assembly.

Christie suffered a mild stroke in early May 2005, and Deputy Prime Minister Cynthia Pratt took over his duties while he convalesced. He returned to work on 21 June, initially on a part-time basis.

Christie was a keen athlete in his youth and represented the Bahamas in the triple jump at the 1960 West Indies Federation Games, and in the 1963 Central American and Caribbean Games where he won the bronze medal. He is married to Bernadette Christie, née Hanna, who is an accountant and attorney. They have two sons and a daughter.

BAHRAIN

Full name: The Kingdom of Bahrain.

Leadership structure: The head of state is a hereditary monarch. As part of the movement towards a constitutional monarchy, Sheikh Hamad proclaimed himself king on 14 February 2002 and the country's official name became the Kingdom of Bahrain. The king appoints the cabinet. The prime minister is formally the head of government.

King: Sheikh **HAMAD** bin Isa al-Khalifa Since 6 March 1999
(amir until 14 Feb. 2002)

Prime Minister: Sheikh **KHALIFA** bin Sulman al-Khalifa Since 19 Jan. 1970
(president of the State Council until 16 Aug. 1971)

Legislature: Under the 2002 Constitution the National Assembly is bicameral. The lower house, the Chamber of Deputies (Majlis al-Nuwab), has 40 directly elected members. The upper house, the Consultative Council (Majlis al-Shura), is a consultative body appointed by the king, and has 40 members. Both houses have a four-year mandate, although the king is able to extend the term of each house for a maximum of two years. All adult Bahrainis, including women, are eligible to vote for the members of the lower house. In preparation for the first election of the National Assembly, the process of legalizing political parties was started in September 2001 and the 1975 law suspending elections was repealed by the king in February 2002.

Profile of the King:

Sheikh **HAMAD** bin Isa al-Khalifa

Sheikh Hamad bin Isa al-Khalifa has been head of state of Bahrain since the death of his father Sheikh Isa in March 1999. Following a Western military education Sheikh Hamad has had a long association with Bahrain's armed forces. His reign has been characterized by a degree of leniency towards opponents and by the initiation of moves towards a constitutional monarchy. As amir he was absolute ruler, advised by a cabinet. Sheikh Hamad proclaimed himself king in February 2002.

Hamad bin Isa al-Khalifa was born in Riffa on 28 January 1950. After completing his primary education in Bahrain in 1964 he was proclaimed as crown prince and received a British public school education at the Leys School in Cambridge.

Returning briefly to Bahrain in 1967, he then went back to England to be trained as an officer at the Mons Officer Cadet School in Aldershot. After graduating he played a central role in the creation of the Bahrain Defence Force (BDF) and has been its commander-in-chief ever since. From 1972 to 1973 Sheikh Hamad was at the US Army Command and Staff College at Fort Leavenworth, Kansas. He also received the US military honour certificate for his work with the BDF since 1968.

Sheikh Hamad's main interests are sports, especially horse riding, and aviation. In 1975 he was appointed president of the supreme council of youth and sports and in 1977 he established the amiri stables which were welcomed into the World Arabian Horses Organization the following year. He also founded the al-Areen Wildlife Parks Reserve in 1976 and cites falconry as a favourite pastime. As a keen aviator Sheikh Hamad pushed for the establishment of the Bahrain Amiri Air Force and created the Defence Air Wing in 1978. After learning to fly helicopters in the same year he was admitted to the Helicopters Club of the UK in 1979. Another interest is historical research. He founded the Historical Documents Centre at his court in 1978, and from the centre's collection he published *al-Watheqa* magazine as a source of historical documents and photographs. He also founded the Bahrain Centre for Studies and Research in 1981.

As a member of Bahrain's ruling dynasty and its heir apparent, Sheikh Hamad took an active role in politics from early on. Head of the defence directorate and a member of the State Council (precursor to the cabinet) in 1970, he became minister of defence in the cabinet of the newly independent amirate in 1971. His father made him a member of the al-Khalifa Family Council in 1974.

Since becoming head of state on his father's death in March 1999, Sheikh Hamad has maintained continuity by retaining a substantially unchanged cabinet, which includes his uncle as prime minister, while also developing his own liberal image, notably with the holding of legislative elections in October 2002 and the appointment of the first female cabinet minister in 2004. Measures of clemency towards opponents began early in his reign with the release of 320 prisoners in June 1999 including Bahrain's top Shi'a Muslim opposition leader, Sheikh Abdel Amir al-Jamri. In 2004 he sacked the interior minister after police had tried to suppress a Shi'a demonstration against the US-led invasion of Iraq; the royal decree stated that the right to express anger against occupation and oppression "was a legitimate right of the citizens".

Alongside domestic advances, he has tried to improve Bahrain's relations with the outside world. As well as establishing a human rights commission in October 1999 Sheikh Hamad established diplomatic relations with the Vatican City, reiterating his government's tolerance of the country's Christian minority. He also brokered a thawing of tensions between the amirate and neighbouring Qatar, exchanging ambassadors and setting up channels to discuss their long-running border dispute, which was finally resolved by the International Court of Justice in 2001.

Sheikh Hamad married his cousin Sheikha Sabeeka bint Ibrahim al-Khalifa on 9 October 1968. He has seven sons (the eldest of whom, the heir apparent Sheikh Salman bin Hamad al-Khalifa, was born in 1969) and four daughters.

Profile of the Prime Minister:

Sheikh **KHALIFA** bin Sulman al-Khalifa

Sheikh Khalifa was appointed head of government of Bahrain on 19 January 1970, the year before Bahrain gained its independence from the UK. Sheikh Khalifa is the brother of the late amir, Sheikh Isa, and uncle of the current ruler Sheikh Hamad, and heads a cabinet dominated by members of the ruling al-Khalifa dynasty.

Khalifa bin Sulman al-Khalifa was born on 28 November 1935 in Bahrain, the second son of the then heir apparent, Sheikh Sulman. Married with two sons and a daughter, he was educated, like his elder brother Sheikh Isa, at the royal court, but then continued his studies in London, UK. In 1957 he became chairman of the country's education council, and in 1961, the year of his father's death, he was appointed director of finance and president of the electricity board. Between 1966 and 1970 he was also president of the Council of Administration.

On 19 January 1970 the Council of Administration was replaced by a 12-member State Council in moves to make the country appear less of an autocracy. Sheikh Khalifa became its president, a position equivalent to that of prime minister, and other council members were also given ministerial portfolios.

The following year Bahrain gained its independence. This had little immediate effect on the structure of the ruling body apart from redesignating the State Council as the cabinet and Sheikh Khalifa as prime minister. Under a new constitution introduced in 1973, a partially elected National Assembly was formed. In August 1975, however, the assembly was abolished because it was considered to obstruct the governing of the country, and only the cabinet, led by Sheikh Khalifa, was retained, putting power firmly back in the hands of the royal family.

Sheikh Khalifa, who retained the premiership when his nephew succeeded his brother as amir in 1999, is also chairman of many other official bodies including the board of directors of the Bahrain Monetary Agency and the councils for civil aviation, the civil service, defence, petroleum, projects and water resources.

BANGLADESH

Full name: The People's Republic of Bangladesh.

Leadership structure: The head of state is a president, elected by Parliament. The president's term of office is five years. The head of government is the prime minister, who is the dominant political figure but is nominally appointed by the president, as is the cabinet (on the advice of the prime minister).

President:	Shahabuddin Ahmed	9 Oct. 1996—14 Nov. 2001
	A. Q. M. Badruddoza Chowdhury	14 Nov. 2001—21 June 2002
	Jamiruddin Sircar (acting)	21 June 2002—6 Sept. 2002
	Iajuddin **AHMED**	Since 6 Sept. 2002
Prime Minister:	Sheikh Hasina Wajed	23 June 1996—15 July 2001
	Latifur Rahman (chief adviser)	15 July 2001—10 Oct. 2001
	Khaleda **ZIA**	Since 10 Oct. 2001

Legislature: The legislature is unicameral. The sole chamber, the Parliament (Jatiya Sangsad), has 345 members, directly elected for a five-year term. Under a constitutional amendment passed by Parliament in 2004, 45 seats are reserved for women.

Profile of the President:

Iajuddin **AHMED**

Iajuddin Ahmed is the first non-politician to be appointed president of Bangladesh. A senior authority in soil sciences, he has been connected with Dhaka University since 1950. He advised the transitional government in 1991 and headed the University Grants Commission in the late 1990s. He was appointed as the country's 17th president on 6 September 2002.

Iajuddin Ahmed was born in the village of Nayagaon, near Munshiganj, on 1 February 1931. He is married to Anwara Begum, a professor of zoology, and they have three children. He graduated in earth sciences from Dhaka University in 1952 and went on to receive a master's degree from the same university in 1954. He then travelled to the USA where he obtained a master's degree (1958) and then a doctorate (1962) from Wisconsin University. His work on soil salinity and rice yields has created a process to better conserve soil nutrients in rice fields.

Returning to what was by then East Pakistan, Ahmed joined the staff of Dhaka University and began a 40-year career at the institution. He began as an assistant professor of soil sciences in 1963, became an associate professor the next year and a full professor in 1973. Administratively he was provost (head) of the university's Salimullah Muslim Hall between 1975 and 1983, and dean of the biological sciences faculty in 1989–90 and 1990–91. He also sat on various councils and committees in the university administration.

In 1991 Ahmed was called to advise the caretaker government of Acting President Shahabuddin Ahmed. A government structure with power centred on the prime minister was then introduced in place of the previous presidential system. Under Prime Minister Begum Khaleda Zia, Iajuddin Ahmed was made chairman of the University Grants Commission. He remained in this position until 1999. In June 2002 the incumbent president, A. Q. M. Badruddoza Chowdhury, elected shortly after the return to power of Prime Minister Zia the previous year, left office amid a dispute with her government, and Ahmed was nominated to fill the position. He came out of retirement to become president in September.

Profile of the Prime Minister:

Khaleda **ZIA**

Begum Khaleda Zia was inaugurated for her third official term as prime minister of Bangladesh on 10 October 2001. Originally a retiring housewife, she came to prominence as the political heir of her assassinated husband, military leader and president Gen. Ziaur Rahman. Hounded by the military regime in the 1980s, she led the right-wing Bangladesh Nationalist Party (BNP) to power in 1991, becoming the country's first female head of government. She led the BNP back to victory in 2001. In her first term as premier she pushed hard for the reform of the education system, and particularly for women's rights. She currently heads a coalition government which includes hard-line Islamic parties.

Khaleda Zia, née Majumder, was born on 15 August 1945 in Dinajpur district in what was then northern Bengal in British-controlled India. She married Capt. Ziaur Rahman in 1960 and was educated at Surendranath College in Dinajpur. She concentrated on bringing up her two sons while her husband rose through the Pakistani army to reach the rank of general, and led calls for the secession of East Pakistan in 1971. Bangladesh was born later that year after a brief civil war. In 1975 Gen. Zia seized power in a military coup and proclaimed himself president of Bangladesh in 1977. Even during this period Khaleda Zia kept a very low public profile. However, this was all changed when her husband was murdered in May 1981 during an abortive coup attempt.

Vice President Justice Abdus Sattar, who took over as head of state and chairman of the BNP (which Gen. Zia had founded in 1979), was overthrown by Gen. Ershad in 1982. In opposition he appointed Khaleda Zia as vice chair of the BNP. She inherited the leadership of the party on Sattar's retirement in February 1984 and was confirmed in the post by the party in August. As chair, she worked to unify political opposition to the authoritarian Ershad regime, forming a seven-party coalition alongside a similar grouping formed by the BNP's main rival, the Awami League (AL). During the nine years of military rule, Khaleda Zia was arrested on seven separate occasions. Deriding an apparent return to democracy in 1986, the BNP boycotted elections and remained in opposition along with the AL.

By 1990 popular discontent against Ershad and support for the opposition political parties had grown sufficiently to convince the president to step down and organize fresh elections. Khaleda Zia led the BNP to a convincing victory in February 1991 and was appointed the country's first female prime minister. Her BNP government revised the presidential system in favour of a 'parliamentary' system with a more powerful prime minister as head of government (implemented from 19 September 1991). In her first term, Khaleda Zia worked to ensure equality and improvement in education and attempted to achieve autarky in food production while ensuring provision for the needy. However, her courting of the Islamic right and her support for strict free-market economics provoked mass discontent. Riots and popular demonstrations convinced her to organize early elections in 1996.

The polls were boycotted by the AL, ensuring a BNP victory, and Khaleda Zia was inaugurated for her second term in February. However, the agitation continued and she called new elections for June. The BNP was narrowly defeated by the AL and became the largest opposition party in the country's recent history. In opposition Khaleda Zia led an increasingly outspoken voice of dissent against the government. In 1999 she formed a four-party opposition alliance and led a prolonged boycott of Parliament. In return Prime Minister Sheikh Hasina Wajed had charges of corruption levelled at her, and she was forced to appear in court to defend herself in September 2000. The BNP led a series of increasingly aggressive strikes as the country headed into elections in 2001 but failed to bring about a premature collapse of the AL government.

Elections on 1 October 2001 were preceded by high levels of violent unrest and yielded a sweeping victory for the BNP and its coalition allies. The BNP secured 66% of the seats in Parliament leaving the AL with just 20%. Khaleda Zia was inaugurated as prime minister nine days later. Within months of taking power, she had in turn filed corruption charges against Sheikh Hasina, while demonstrations by the AL followed a familiar pattern, descending into violence in January 2002. A year-long boycott of Parliament by the AL, whose deputies claimed that they had not been permitted to criticize the government, ended in June 2004, but demonstrations and strikes continued.

Bangladesh: *Khaleda Zia*

Khaleda Zia's government is continuing to work for women's rights; in 2004 a constitutional amendment expanded the 300-seat Parliament to include 45 seats reserved for women, and controversial plans were announced to amend *shari'a* (Islamic law) to allow women to initiate divorce proceedings—which could cause fractions with the BNP's Islamic coalition partners.

BARBADOS

Full name: Barbados.

Leadership structure: The head of state is the British sovereign, styled 'Queen of Barbados and of Her other Realms and Territories, Head of the Commonwealth', and represented by a governor-general who is appointed on the advice of the Barbadian prime minister. The head of government is the prime minister, who is responsible to Parliament and appointed by the governor-general. The cabinet is appointed by the governor-general on the advice of the prime minister.

Queen:	Elizabeth II	Since 6 Feb. 1952
Governor-General:	Sir Clifford **HUSBANDS**	Since 1 June 1996
Prime Minister:	Owen **ARTHUR**	Since 7 Sept. 1994

Legislature: The legislature, the Parliament, is bicameral. The lower chamber, the House of Assembly, has 30 members, directly elected for a five-year term. The upper chamber, the Senate, has 21 members, appointed to office for a five-year term by the governor-general, 12 of them on the advice of the prime minister, two on the advice of the leader of the opposition and seven representing religious, economic and social interests.

Profile of the Governor-General:

Sir Clifford **HUSBANDS**

Sir Clifford Husbands has been governor-general of Barbados since June 1996. He represents the monarch, Queen Elizabeth II, as titular head of state. A British-trained barrister, he was a Supreme Court judge before his appointment as governor-general.

Clifford Straughn Husbands was born on 5 August 1926 at Morgan Lewis Plantation in St Andrew parish. He was educated locally at Harrison College, before travelling to the UK to begin his legal training. He was called to the Bar in 1952, and later that year was admitted to practise in Barbados, working in private practice from 1952 to 1954. For the next six years, he practised in Barbados, Grenada, Antigua, Montserrat and elsewhere, before returning to Barbados in 1960 to work in the attorney general's chambers.

49

In 1967 Sir Clifford was appointed director of public prosecutions, a year later becoming a Queen's Counsel. In 1976 he was appointed a judge of the Supreme Court in Barbados, and he has held the position of justice of appeal since 1991; he has acted as chief justice of Barbados on a number of occasions. He also acted as governor-general for a brief period in 1990, before his formal appointment as governor-general on 1 June 1996.

Sir Clifford has been chairman of the community legal services commission and the penal reform committee, and also a member of the judicial and legal services commission. He received the Gold Crown of Merit in 1986, and was made a Companion of Honour of Barbados in 1989. Sir Clifford was created a Knight of St Andrew in 1995 in recognition of his outstanding legal and judicial service to Barbados, and upon becoming governor-general in 1996 was made a Knight Grand Cross of the Most Distinguished Order of St Michael and St George. He is married to Lady Ruby Husbands, and they have one son and two daughters.

Profile of the Prime Minister:

Owen ARTHUR

Leader of the moderate social-democratic Barbados Labour Party (BLP), Owen Arthur is an economist by training and has been a member of Parliament since the early 1980s. When taking office at the age of 44 in 1994, he was the country's fifth prime minister since independence.

Owen Seymour Arthur was born in Barbados on 17 October 1949, and educated at All Saints' Boys' School and Parry School on a government scholarship. He graduated in economics and history from the University of the West Indies in 1971, gaining a master's degree in economics in 1974. He is married to Beverley, née Batchelor.

He worked at the national planning agency in Jamaica in 1974–79, becoming chief economic planner, then taking up a post as director of economics at the Jamaica Bauxite Institute for three years (1979–81). In 1981 he was appointed as chief project analyst in the ministry of finance and planning, assisting in the preparation of Barbados's 1983–88 development plan, and taking part in negotiations with the International Monetary Fund (IMF). Other positions held by Arthur include membership of the board of directors of the Central Bank of Barbados, and of the Barbados Industrial Development Corporation. He has also served as a member of the board of directors of Jamaica's scientific research council.

Becoming a member of the Senate in 1983, Arthur became chairman of the BLP in the same year. In 1984 he was elected to the House of Assembly as a BLP candidate, the party being then in government. He was parliamentary secretary at the ministry of finance and planning from 1985 until 1986, when the BLP lost the election and began a period of eight years in opposition. During this period Arthur held a part-time lectureship in management at the University of the West Indies, and worked as a consultant with the Caribbean Community (Caricom) in 1992.

Arthur was elected leader of the BLP, and thus leader of the parliamentary opposition, in July 1993. The September 1994 general election, called early following a revolt within the Democratic Labour Party, resulted in the BLP winning 19 of the House of Assembly's 28 seats, and Arthur became prime minister. The relative success of Arthur's government saw the party go on to win a landslide 26 seats, and a further five-year term in the January 1999 elections. The May 2003 elections saw the BLP re-elected for a third term, albeit with a slightly reduced majority of 23 seats in the expanded 30-seat House.

In addition to the premiership Arthur holds the portfolios of defence and security, finance and economic affairs, civil service and information. Committed to equal opportunity, he allocated ministerial portfolios in his first cabinet to all three of his party's women MPs and now has five female ministers. As prime minister, his priorities are the growth of the economy and international competitiveness. Having campaigned in the 2003 election with a pledge to cut ties with the British monarchy within his next term, in January 2005 he announced plans for Barbados to become a republic with an elected ceremonial president by the end of the year. Following a voluble public reaction, he agreed to hold a referendum on the issue.

BELARUS

Full name: The Republic of Belarus.

Leadership structure: The head of state is a president, directly elected by universal adult suffrage. A president could only serve two five-year terms under the 1994 Constitution, but a referendum held with the 2004 legislative elections approved amendments removing the limit to presidential terms. The president appoints the chair of the Council of Ministers (prime minister). The Council of Ministers exercises executive power; it is accountable to the president, and responsible to the National Assembly and its chair is the head of government.

President:	Aleksandr **LUKASHENKA**	Since 20 July 1994
Prime Minister:	Sergei Ling (acting from 18 Nov. 1996)	19 Feb. 1997—18 Feb. 2000
	Vladimir Yermoshin (acting from 18 Feb. 2000)	14 March 2000—1 Oct. 2001
	Gennady Novitsky (acting from 1 Oct. 2001)	10 Oct. 2001—10 July 2003
	Sergei **SIDORSKY** (acting from 10 July 2003)	Since 19 Dec. 2003

Legislature: The legislature, the National Assembly (Natsionalnoye Sobranie), is bicameral. The lower chamber, the House of Representatives (Palata Predstaviteley), has 110 members, directly elected for a maximum of four years. The upper chamber, the Council of the Republic (Soviet Respubliki), has 56 members elected by regional soviets, and eight members appointed by the president, all for four-year terms.

Profile of the President:

Aleksandr **LUKASHENKA**

Aleksandr Lukashenka was manager of a collective farm in the Soviet and immediate post-Soviet era. He continues to favour a considerable degree of state regulation of the economy. At the international level he has made close relations with Russia the centrepiece of his presidency, but has become increasingly isolated within Europe as the head of a regime which lacks convincing democratic credentials.

Aleksandr Grigorjevich Lukashenka was born on 30 August 1954 in the village of Kopys in northeastern Belarus. He graduated from the history faculty of the Mogilev Pedagogical Institute in 1975. He also has a degree in agricultural and industrial economics from the Belarussian Agricultural Academy (1985). He is married to Galina Rodionovna, and they have two sons.

During his military service in 1975 and 1977, he worked as a political propagandist with the Soviet border troops in Brest and then in 1977–78 in Komsomol, the communist youth league. From 1980 to 1982 he rejoined the army as a deputy company commander but then moved to various positions within the command economy. He rose to the post of deputy chairman of the collective farm in Shklov and then deputy manager of a construction materials factory in the same town. In 1987 he became head of the Harazdiec farm in the Mogilev region, a post he held until 1994.

In July 1990 Lukashenka was elected as a deputy to the Supreme Soviet of the Belarussian Soviet Socialist Republic and founded a Communists for Democracy deputies' group. At the time of the short-lived coup against Soviet President Mikhail Gorbachev in August 1991 he supported the 'national emergency committee' which briefly seized power in the Kremlin. In December of the same year he was the only deputy in the Belarus Supreme Soviet to vote against the formation of the Commonwealth of Independent States (CIS).

Lukashenka subsequently built up his popularity as chairman of the Supreme Soviet's Commission for the Struggle against Corruption, a post to which he was appointed in April 1993. The commission's allegations played a key role in ousting the reformist Stanislau Shushkevich as chairman of the Supreme Soviet in January the following year. A new constitution providing for a presidential form of government opened the way for direct presidential elections held in two rounds in June and July 1994. In an unexpected result, Lukashenka was elected president for a five-year term, polling 44.8% of the vote in the first round and 80.1% in the second.

During his period in office Lukashenka has promoted close political relations with Russia. Working with the then Russian president Boris Yeltsin, Lukashenka oversaw the drafting of a full union treaty in December 1999, setting 2005 as the deadline for full integration of Belarus and Russia. However, the election of President Vladimir Putin in Russia in 2000 put a brake on the pace of unification and strained relations, weakening Lukashenka's position. A draft agreement on the adoption of the Russian rouble as the common currency in the proposed Russia–Belarus union was signed in June 2003, but Lukashenka stalled the process later that year as relations deteriorated.

Domestically Lukashenka has come increasingly into conflict with parliament, the judiciary, the media and the wider public, as he has strengthened his hold on power. In August 1996 he announced that a nationwide referendum would be held on proposals to change the 1994 Constitution in order to strengthen his presidential position still further. In this referendum, on 24 November, the results were recorded as a turnout of 84% and a 70.4% 'yes' vote for establishing a bicameral parliament and extending Lukashenka's term of office to the year 2001. The opposition denounced the vote as a 'farce' designed to legitimize a dictatorship and strongly denounced the later extension of Lukashenka's term to 2002.

Nevertheless, Lukashenka was re-elected in 'early' presidential elections on 9 September 2001, with 75% of the vote. The opposition candidate Vladimir Goncharik was backed by the international community in claiming large-scale fraud and intimidation during the election. In 2002 the European Union (EU) responded to Lukashenka's authoritarian regime by banning him and his government from travelling to the Union's member states. He replied by allegedly threatening to help illegal immigrants across the border into Poland in protest at the EU's refusal to compensate Belarus for maintaining its border security.

In February 2003 the EU censured Lukashenka's government for the parlous state of the economy and its authoritarian attitude towards domestic critics. Meanwhile, Lukashenka condemned his own cabinet, and promised to protect the Belarussian people from their corruption. He dismissed Prime Minister Gennady Novitsky on 10 July accusing him and his "ineffective" government of having "failed to keep presidential orders ... [or to] pay agrarian workers and ... [of having] falsified and misrepresented information".

A crackdown on dissenting media outlets in August 2004 preceded a referendum held alongside parliamentary elections in October that proposed removing the constitutional limit of two presidential terms in office. Lukashenka, who had been quick to capitalize on neighbouring Russia's recent spate of terrorist attacks, claiming to be the sole guarantor of his country's security, easily won support for the change, with 80% of the vote, in what the opposition decried as a move that gave Lukashenka the presidency for life. US and EU election observers said that the poll fell "significantly" short of being free and fair; the USA imposed sanctions and the EU reinstated and broadened its visa ban.

In 2005 US secretary of state Condoleezza Rice labelled Belarus as Europe's 'last true dictatorship' and one of the world's six 'outposts of tyranny'. Many in the West openly hoped for a 'colour' revolution mirroring those that recently ousted repressive leaders in Georgia, Ukraine and Kyrgyzstan. Lukashenka has warned that any such attempt would be doomed to failure.

Profile of the Prime Minister:

Sergei **SIDORSKY**

Sergei Sidorsky was appointed acting prime minister of Belarus on 10 July 2003, and confirmed on 19 December. He trained as an electrical engineer in Soviet-

era Belarus before entering the government in 1998. Like his predecessor, Gennady Novitsky, Sidorsky is very much in the shadow of the more constitutionally powerful president. Indeed, it could be argued that he was appointed precisely because he poses little threat to President Aleksandr Lukashenka: Sidorsky is unpopular with the Russian leadership due to his previous role as a tough negotiator over oil and gas transhipments and would be unlikely to gain any backing from that vital quarter should he have any ambitions for the presidency.

Sergei Sidorsky was born on 13 March 1954 in the town of Gomel. In 1976 he graduated from the Belarussian Institute of Railroad Engineers (faculty of electrical engineering), and began his working life as an electrician. He speaks three languages—Belarussian, Russian and German—and has more than 40 scientific articles to his name. Sidorsky is married with two daughters.

Sidorsky's career began in the Gomel Radio Equipment Plant, where he worked his way up from foreman to director over a 25-year span. By 1992, he had moved to become the general manager of the Gomel Scientific Production Association (RATON). In 1998 Sidorsky became a serious regional political player, as the first deputy chairman of the Gomel Regional Administration, but it was not until 2001 that he was appointed deputy prime minister of Belarus.

In July 2003 Lukashenka dismissed Prime Minister Gennady Novitsky and three senior members of the cabinet, accusing them of massaging statistics relating to an outstanding debt owed to the agricultural sector for cattle and milk deliveries to the state. Observers initially questioned the appointment of Sidorsky as replacement; as one of the leaders of negotiations with giant neighbour Russia on oil and gas supplies, he was hardly a favourite of Moscow, the major power broker in Belarus.

However, Lukashenka had determined to hold a referendum to extend his own rule, for which he needed Russian backing. Were he to step down instead, then traditionally the serving prime minister—Sidorsky—would stand for president in his place. By appointing Sidorsky as prime minister, he weighted Russian elite opinion in favour of a referendum—which passed in 2004—allowing the extension of his own rule by re-election. Sidorsky has continued as the main negotiator with Russia on the price of supplies of oil and gas.

BELGIUM

Full name: The Kingdom of Belgium.

Leadership structure: The head of state is a hereditary constitutional monarch. The head of government is the prime minister, who is appointed by the monarch, and is responsible to the Chamber of Representatives. The cabinet is appointed by the monarch on the prime minister's advice.

King:	**ALBERT II**	Since 9 Aug. 1993
Prime Minister:	Guy **VERHOFSTADT**	Since 12 July 1999

Legislature: The legislature, the Federal Chambers (Chambres Législatives Fédérales/Federale Wetgevende Kamers), is bicameral. The lower chamber, the Chamber of Representatives (Chambre des Représentants/Kamer van Volksvertegenwoordigers), has 150 members, directly elected by proportional representation for a four-year term. The upper chamber, the Senate (Sénat/ Senaat), has 71 members, also with a four-year term; 40 senators are elected, and the rest co-opted by the elected members. Regional parliaments have since 1995 been directly elected and elect regional governments.

Profile of the King:

ALBERT II

Albert II took the constitutional oath at the age of 59 and ascended the throne as the sixth king of the Belgians on 9 August 1993 after the death of his brother, Baudouin I. Keenly interested in sport, he plays no direct political role as head of state, but is regarded as a key unifying figure in a country with three distinct linguistic and cultural heritages: that of French-speaking Wallonia, Dutch-speaking Flanders and the small German-speaking minority.

Albert was born in Brussels on 6 June 1934, the son of Léopold III and Queen Astrid. He married Donna Paola Ruffo di Calabria in 1959. They have two sons and a daughter.

As prince of Liège (his title before his accession to the throne) he held several posts relating to his academic studies in harbour management and transport policy, as a vice admiral of the navy, and as honorary president (from 1962) of the Belgian office of foreign trade. In this capacity Albert has presided over almost 90 economic missions abroad, seeking to win foreign investment for

Belgium. Between 1954 and 1992 he also served as president of the Caisse Générale d'Epargne et de Retraite. He was president of the Belgian Red Cross from 1958 until 1993, and set up the Prince Albert Fund for the Training of Foreign Trade Experts in 1984. This fund was designed to award grants to young Belgian graduates or executives to undergo training in the branches of Belgian companies located outside western Europe.

In the political sphere, Albert fulfilled a variety of roles, especially after 1967 when he began to carry out projects in the fields of town planning, housing, environmental protection and management. In 1969 he was appointed president of the conference of European ministers responsible for the preservation of cultural heritage. He represented Belgium at the 1972 UN environmental conference in Stockholm, Sweden, and has presided over the Belgian committee for the European 'year of the renaissance of the city'.

Profile of the Prime Minister:

Guy **VERHOFSTADT**

Guy Verhofstadt was appointed prime minister of Belgium after the resignation of Jean-Luc Dehaene in June 1999. The first liberal premier in 61 years, he headed a multiparty coalition consisting of his own Flemish Liberals and Democrats (Vlaamse Liberalen en Demokraten—VLD), the Walloon liberals and the socialist and ecologist parties. Returned to office after the May 2003 elections, his new coalition consisted just of the liberals and socialists. A career politician who put much energy into pressing for party reforms, Verhofstadt had become leader of the Flemish liberal Party for Freedom and Progress (Partij voor Vrijheid en Vooruitgang—PVV) in 1981, and masterminded their metamorphosis into the VLD in 1992.

Guy Verhofstadt was born in Dendermonde, near Ghent, on 11 April 1953. His father, Marcel, was a magistrate and adviser to the leader of the PVV's Ghent branch, Willy de Clercq. At school Guy was noted as a difficult pupil and admits to having done only enough to get by. From 1971 he studied law at the University of Ghent and took an active role in the Flemish Liberal Student Union, and upon graduation in 1975 he immediately threw himself into liberal politics, becoming a town councillor. Two years later he found a mentor in the old family friend de Clercq, who was by now the PVV chairman, and became his political secretary. The position stood him in good stead to re-energize the PVV youth movement (Jongeren) which he chaired from 1979 to 1981—the year of his marriage to Dominique Verkinderen, with whom he has one son and one daughter. He made a name for himself in party politics as a reformist by producing a radical manifesto advocating a thorough overhaul in the party's structure.

In 1981 the PVV became the right flank to the ruling centre-left coalition. De Clercq was drawn into the cabinet which left the way free for Verhofstadt to become the country's youngest party leader as chairman of the PVV. Verhofstadt became a member of parliament in 1985 and was subsequently appointed as deputy prime minister and minister for the budget. He maintained these positions until 1988 when the ruling Christian People's Party (Christelijke Volkspartij—CVP) reaffirmed their alliance with the socialists, and the liberals were elbowed out of the governing coalition. After re-election as party chairman in 1989 Verhofstadt sat in the Chamber of Representatives as the leader of the opposition, giving him the opportunity to flesh out the reformist politics he had long been conceiving. In November 1992 these policies were put into practice when the PVV transformed into the VLD; the move was, in essence, an exercise in political inclusivism. Verhofstadt put everything behind renewed success in the 1995 elections on the back of his reforms and was bitterly disappointed by the electoral defeat of that year. In response he took a short sabbatical from active politics in Tuscany, Italy.

In 1996 Verhofstadt staged a comeback acting as a reporter on the Rwanda Committee, which had been organized to investigate the 1994 genocide of Tutsis, and by 1997 he had been re-elected as chairman of the VLD in time for the run-up to the 1999 elections. The VLD campaigned on promises to lower taxes and increase morality in policy-making, and following the food contamination scandal that shocked the country two weeks before polling, it became the biggest single party in the 150-seat Chamber of Representatives with 23 seats ahead of the CVP's 22. When the then prime minister Jean-Luc Dehaene resigned over the scandal, Verhofstadt was asked to form a government by King Albert II on 23 June 1999 and took office in July, thereupon resigning the chairmanship of the VLD. His multiparty coalition included the two socialist parties and the two ecologist parties. As prime minister, Verhofstadt introduced a conference aimed at revamping governing bodies, a wave of privatizations and a promise to guarantee social security. He also paid his debt to his ecologist coalition partners by proposing a gradual phasing out of nuclear power by 2025, despite its major role in the country's current energy mix. However, the issue of increased night flights over Brussels by international courier company DHL caused a rift in early 2003.

The VLD tied with the French socialists in early elections held in May 2003, both on 25 seats, with the French liberals on 24 and the Flemish socialists on 23. Both ecologist parties lost support in the poll, and Verhofstadt's new coalition was formed in July from just the two main blocs. The controversial DHL night flights issue re-emerged the following year and threatened to bring down Verhofstadt's government as he negotiated with regional governments to enable the firm to expand its major hub in Belgium. A deal could not be achieved, causing the prospective loss of 1,700 jobs.

A staunch supporter of a federalist Europe, Verhofstadt backed the Franco-German opposition to the US-led invasion of Iraq in 2003, and joined leaders of those countries and Luxembourg in a mini-summit to draw up plans for a

European Security and Defence Union. In June 2004 he was the French and German choice to succeed Romano Prodi as president of the European Union's Commission, but he was opposed by the UK, Poland and Italy, and withdrew his candidacy after the Union summit had failed to reach an agreement; the Portuguese prime minister José Manuel Durão Barroso went on to win the nomination.

BELIZE

Full name: Belize.

Leadership structure: The head of state is the British sovereign, styled 'Queen of Belize and of Her other Realms and Territories, Head of the Commonwealth', and represented by a governor-general who is appointed on the advice of the Belizean prime minister. The head of government is the prime minister, who is responsible to parliament, and appointed by the governor-general. The governor-general appoints the rest of the cabinet on the prime minister's advice.

Queen:	Elizabeth II	Since 6 Feb. 1952
Governor-General:	Sir Colville **YOUNG**	Since 17 Nov. 1993
Prime Minister:	Said **MUSA**	Since 28 Aug. 1998

Legislature: The legislature, the National Assembly, is bicameral. The lower chamber, the House of Representatives, has 29 members, directly elected for a five-year term. The upper chamber, the Senate, has 13 members appointed by the governor-general, six of them on the advice of the prime minister, three on the advice of the leader of the opposition, three representing various sectors of society, and the Senate president.

Profile of the Governor-General:

Sir Colville **YOUNG**

Sir Colville Young's background is in linguistics and education, and his career moved from teaching to university lecturing. In 1986 he became president of the University College of Belize, a post he held for four years. He was appointed as governor-general in November 1993.

Colville Norbert Young was born in Belize City on 20 November 1932, and was educated at St Michael's College (1946–50) before going on to obtain a first-class teacher's certificate in 1955. He studied for a degree in English at the University of London and then at the University College of the West Indies, graduating in 1961. He gained a doctorate in linguistics from York University in 1973, his thesis being based on a study of the creolized English spoken in Belize.

Young is married to Norma, née Trapp, and has three sons and one daughter. He followed a career in education, and was principal of St Michael's College in

1974–76. Having spent a decade as lecturer in English and general studies at the Belize Technical College, he became president of the new University College of Belize in 1986. He held this office for four years, and was one of its lecturers until 1993. He presented papers at the 1980 and 1990 conferences of the Society for Caribbean Linguistics, and received a citation from the prime minister in 1988 for his contribution to Belizean culture.

Young was appointed governor-general in November 1993, after the prime minister had requested his predecessor's resignation. He has also been a trustee of the Belize Urban Development Corporation. Young has written a number of books, including *Creole Proverbs of Belize* (1980), *Caribbean Corner Calling* (1988), *Language and Education in Belize* (1989) and *From One Caribbean Corner* (poems) (1983). He was a founding member of First Belizean Steel Band and of the Beltek Steel Orchestra, and has composed music including *Missa Caribeña*, the first Belizean setting of the mass.

Profile of the Prime Minister:

Said **MUSA**

Said Musa was a successful lawyer before going into politics. He has been a member of the House of Representatives for the People's United Party (PUP) since 1979 and party leader since 1996. As foreign minister he secured a celebrated recognition of Belize's territorial integrity from Guatemala in 1991, only to see Guatemala's claim reopened in 2000 while he was prime minister (having led the PUP to electoral triumph in August 1998). In March 2003 the PUP secured a historic re-election.

Said Wilbert Musa was born in the border town of San Ignacio on 19 March 1944. A boy from humble origins who improved his prospects through education, he moved on from secondary school in Belize City to study law at the University of Manchester, England, graduating in 1966. He was called to the Bar at Gray's Inn in London and briefly stayed in England (where he married his wife Joan; they have four children). He returned to Belize in 1967 where he served as a circuit magistrate and then a Crown Counsel in the office of the director of public prosecutions the following year. In 1970 he left public service and set up as an independent partner in law with his associate, Lawrence Balderamos.

In the course of the early 1970s Musa was active in nongovernmental politics, joining the United Black Association for Development and running the People's Action Committee and the Society for the Promotion of Education and Research, both of which he had helped to found in 1969. He also cofounded the *Journal of Belizean Affairs* in 1972, but his nonparty political activity ended when he joined the PUP in 1974.

Despite losing the election in the Fort George constituency of Belize City in 1974, Musa was nominated to the Senate, where he sat until 1979, at the request of the PUP prime minister, George Price. He eventually won the Fort George seat in a sensational victory against the opposition United Democratic Party leader Dean Lindo in 1979 and has represented it in government ever since. Between 1979 and 1984 Musa was attorney general and minister of education, sports and culture. As a member of the cabinet Musa was involved with independence negotiations with the UK in 1981, and the drafting of the new constitution. Following independence he represented his country at the Caribbean Community (Caricom), the Commonwealth of Latin American Nations and the UN. In the first postindependence elections in 1984 the PUP suffered a crushing defeat, relegating Musa to the opposition benches in the House of Representatives.

In 1989 the PUP clawed back into power and Musa rejoined the cabinet, this time as foreign minister. The year 1991 was one of particular achievement for Musa when he oversaw Belize's admission to the Organization of American States (OAS) and, most significantly, secured territorial recognition of Belize's borders from Guatemala. Following another electoral defeat for the party in 1993, Musa went on to take first the deputy leadership of the PUP in 1994 and then full leadership in 1996.

He led a reinvigorated party to a stunning victory in the elections of August 1998 winning almost 60% of the vote and giving them an overpowering 26 seats in the 29-seat House of Representatives. As prime minister, Musa faced an international crisis in 2000 when Guatemala renewed its territorial claim to half of Belize, severing once again the diplomatic ties established in 1991.

Musa won a historic re-election on 5 March 2003—the first time since independence that the ruling party had been given a second term—with a slightly reduced majority for his PUP of 22 seats in the 29-seat House of Representatives.

BENIN

Full name: The Republic of Benin.

Leadership structure: The head of state is a president, directly elected by universal adult suffrage. The president's term of office is five years, renewable once only. The president is head of government as well as head of state. The president appoints and presides over the Council of Ministers.

President: Gen. Mathieu **KÉRÉKOU**   Since 24 March 1996

Legislature: The legislature is unicameral. The sole chamber, the National Assembly (Assemblée Nationale), has 83 members, directly elected for a maximum of four years.

Profile of the President:

Gen. Mathieu **KÉRÉKOU**

Gen. Mathieu (Ahmed) Kérékou, a French-trained army officer who ruled Benin from 1972 to 1991, then had the distinction of being the first former dictator in mainland Africa to hand over power after returning his country to multiparty democracy. Five years later, in March 1996, he won back power by the ballot box, and is currently serving a second (and, according to the current constitution, final) five-year term.

Born on 2 September 1933 in Natitingou, in the north of what was then Dahomey, Mathieu (Ahmed) Kérékou was educated initially in Mali and Senegal. He then enrolled at the Saint-Raphaël military school in France, and served in the French army until 1961 when he was appointed second lieutenant in the army of newly independent Dahomey. He was an aide-de-camp to President Hubert Coutoucou Maga between 1961 and 1963. In 1967, when his cousin Maj. Maurice Kouandété led a military coup, Kérékou became chairman of the Military Revolutionary Council. He returned to French military schools from 1968 to 1970, when he became commander of the Ouidah paratroop unit and deputy chief of staff.

In October 1972, following five years of coups and political crises, Maj. Kérékou led a military coup which ousted the then president Justin Ahomadegbé. On coming to power he declared the country a Marxist-Leninist state and appointed a military revolutionary government of army officers who were all under the age of 40, assuming for himself the positions of president, head of government and minister of national defence. He executed some of his political opponents, imprisoned others, dismissed senior army officers and has been accused of human rights abuses. In 1975 he changed the country's name from Dahomey to Benin. Four years later, when his power base was sufficiently strong for him to be confident of retaining the presidency, he staged elections, nominally returning the country to civilian rule.

During nearly two decades in power he nationalized private business and expanded government control but by the late 1980s began to be accused of destroying the economy, while public pressure grew for him to introduce reforms reversing these policies. In 1989, facing further mass protests and pressure from the French government, he dropped single-party Marxism for multiparty politics. A national conference in February 1990 appointed former finance minister Nicéphore Soglo as interim prime minister and Kérékou reluctantly agreed to hold free elections. In the ensuing March 1991 presidential election he won only 32.2% of the vote. Conceding victory to Soglo, Kérékou stepped down in what was the first example in mainland Africa of a former dictator relinquishing power following a democratic election. Kérékou was given immunity from prosecution, made a public apology for the mistakes and abuses of his term, and was allowed to remain active in politics.

In the next presidential election, in March 1996, Kérékou was returned to power. Although he polled only one-third of the total vote and trailed Soglo in the first round, he picked up support from the eliminated candidates and won 52.5% of the vote in the second round. Soglo, whose popularity had suffered both from his perceived autocratic attitudes and his economic austerity policies, contested the result before the Constitutional Court, but conceded defeat when the court on 24 March formally declared Kérékou the winner.

His first term in office as an elected president was a relative success, despite a dip in the country's economic growth prompted by drought in 1998. In February 2001 Kérékou announced that he would stand for re-election. He led with 47% in the first poll, and was left to face a token candidate after his main opponents boycotted the second round. They claimed widespread fraud but Kérékou countered by claiming that democracy was "alive and kicking" in Benin. The alliance of pro-Kérékou parties, the Presidential Tendency (Mouvance Présidentielle—MP), won an overall majority in the legislative elections held in March 2003.

The constitution bars Kérékou from standing in the 2006 election—both because it allows a maximum of two terms and because it states candidates must be under 70 years of age. While Kérékou has not announced any desire to stand for a third term, there may well be an attempt to amend the constitution; accusations that the president has been bribing legislators began appearing in 2005 in the local press.

Kérékou has two sons by his first marriage to Béatrice Lakoussan, a former member of the National Assembly, and two sons by his current wife Marguerite.

BHUTAN

Full name: The Kingdom of Bhutan.

Leadership structure: The head of state is a hereditary monarch, who until 1998 was also automatically the head of government. On 6 July 1998, however, the king dissolved his cabinet (Lhengyal Shungtshog) for the first time in 26 years, instituting a system whereby it is headed by an annually rotating chairman. The king's role is now reserved to matters of sovereignty and national security.

Druk Gyalpo (Dragon King):   **JIGME** Singye Wangchuk   Since 24 July 1972

Chairman of the Cabinet:	Sangay Ngedup	9 July 1999—31 July 2000
	Yeshey Zimba	31 July 2000—8 Aug. 2001
	Khandu Wangchuk	8 Aug. 2001—14 Aug. 2002
	Kinzang Dorji	14 Aug. 2002—30 Aug. 2003
	Jigme Thinley	30 Aug. 2003—18 Aug. 2004
	Yeshey **ZIMBA**	Since 18 Aug. 2004

Legislature: The legislature is unicameral. The sole chamber, the National Assembly (Tshogdu), has 154 members, of whom 105 are directly elected by universal adult suffrage for three-year terms. There are 12 seats reserved for representatives of religious bodies and 37 nominated by the government.

Profile of the Druk Gyalpo (Dragon King):

JIGME Singye Wangchuk

King Jigme acceded to the throne of Bhutan in 1972 at the age of 16 on the death of his father, Jigme Dorji Wangchuk. As king he has followed the cautious modernizing approach of his father, although he remains firmly rooted in Bhutan's traditional heritage, which he has sought to protect against being overwhelmed by outside cultural influences.

Jigme Singye Wangchuk was born in Dechenchholing Palace, Thimphu, on 11 November 1955. He was initially educated by private tutors, and later at St Joseph's School in Darjeeling, India. He studied in England from 1965 to 1969, returning to Bhutan in 1970 to complete his education at the Wangchuk Academy in Paro. He was named crown prince in March 1972, after which he began participating in cabinet meetings, and was appointed chairman of the planning commission. Installed formally as crown prince on 5 May 1972, he acceded to the throne as *druk gyalpo* (dragon king) only just over two months later, on 24 July, on the sudden death of his father. His coronation took place in June 1974.

As king of Bhutan he chaired the cabinet until the political reforms of 1998, and is commander-in-chief of the armed forces. He has also retained the chairmanship of the planning commission and regularly tours the country, attempting to combine the ideals of technological development with principles of continuity in a traditional society. He has, however, taken a strong stance against the growth of political opposition, especially from those of Nepalese descent in the banned left-wing Bhutan People's Party. In 1988 he imposed a code of conduct, and his attempt to forge a new national identity has alienated the ethnic Nepalese of the south, inspiring a fierce minority rights campaign. Partly to counter the threat of cross-border dissident activity, he has worked to promote diplomatic links with India and with China.

A regular participant in summit meetings of the Non-Aligned Movement and the South Asian Association for Regional Co-operation (SAARC), King Jigme has been instrumental in the very gradual opening up of Bhutan to economic development and to strictly limited tourism.

King Jigme married four sisters, Ashi Dorji Wangmo Wangchuk, Ashi Tshering Pem Wangchuk, Ashi Tshering Yangdon Wangchuk and Ashi Sangay Choden Wangchuk, in a private ceremony in 1979. A public ceremony was held in 1988. He has five sons and five daughters, and his eldest son Jigme Khesar Namgyal Wangchuk was installed formally as crown prince in October 2004.

Profile of the Chairman of the Cabinet:

Yeshey **ZIMBA**

Yeshey Zimba became chairman of the Council of Ministers of Bhutan on 18 August 2004, having previously served from 2000 to 2001: in Bhutan each minister takes turns holding the chairmanship for one year. He was elected finance minister by the National Assembly in 1998, after political reforms in which King Jigme Singye Wangchuk relinquished his right to single-handedly appoint the cabinet. Zimba played a key role in negotiating Bhutan's entry into the World Trade Organization, a process that will lower trade barriers and may open up the insular mountain kingdom—which did not allow television until 1999—to the outside world.

Yeshey Zimba was born in Omladama village in Punakha, in northwest Bhutan. After completing high school in Darjeeling, India, in 1969, he graduated from St Joseph's College, also in Darjeeling, with a degree in economics in 1973 and went on to complete a master's degree at the University of Wisconsin in the USA. Zimba first joined the ministry of development in 1976.

Zimba became the deputy secretary of the ministry of finance in 1979 and served as managing director of the royal monetary authority when it was set up in 1982. He was transferred as the director of the ministry of trade and industry and then became joint secretary in the planning commission.

In 1991 he was appointed as the joint secretary in the finance ministry and became the finance secretary in 1994. Four years later he was elected as the finance minister by the members of the National Assembly. After being appointed minister of trade and industry, Zimba took over as chairman of the Bhutan Power Corporation.

Since the 1998 reforms, the chairmanship of the cabinet has rotated annually between the ministers. Zimba was chairman from 2000 until 2001, and again from August 2004. In his second term he faced continued challenges over the treatment of the Nepalese minority, youth unemployment, national debt, and the introduction of the country's first constitution.

BOLIVIA

Full name: The Republic of Bolivia.

Leadership structure: The head of state is a president, directly elected by universal adult suffrage, but chosen by Congress if no candidate gains a majority of the vote. The presidential term is five years. The incumbent may not seek re-election. The head of government is the president, who appoints the cabinet.

President:	Gen. Hugo Bánzer Suárez	6 Aug. 1997—7 Aug. 2001
	Jorge Quiroga Ramírez	7 Aug. 2001—6 Aug. 2002
	Gonzalo Sánchez de Lozada	6 Aug. 2002—17 Oct. 2003
	Carlos Mesa	17 Oct. 2003—9 June 2005
	Eduardo **RODRÍGUEZ** Veltzé	Since 9 June 2005

Legislature: The legislature, the National Congress (Congreso Nacional), is bicameral. The lower chamber, the Chamber of Deputies (Cámara de Diputados), has 130 members, directly elected for a five-year term. The upper chamber, the Chamber of Senators (Cámara de Senadores), has 27 members, also directly elected for a five-year term.

Profile of the President:

Eduardo **RODRÍGUEZ** Veltzé

Eduardo Rodríguez Veltzé was head of the Supreme Court when President Carlos Mesa resigned in June 2005 amid a political crisis over control of the country's natural resources. The two politicians next in line for the presidency both declined the post, and Rodriguez was sworn in on 9 June.

Eduardo Rodríguez Veltzé was born on 2 March 1956 in Cochabamba in central Bolivia. He graduated in law from the Universidad Mayor de San Simón in Cochabamba in 1981, and obtained a master's degree in public administration from the Kennedy School of Government, Harvard University, in the USA in 1988. Rodríguez worked as head of department and professor of law at the Catholic University of Bolivia and taught at several other universities. He is the author of several articles and papers. In March 1999 he became a member of the Supreme Court, and later became president of the court.

Popular unrest in Bolivia over the export of the country's natural resources led President Carlos Mesa to resign in June 2005. The presidency was offered to the two men next in the line of succession, Hormando Vaca Díez and Mario Cossío, head of the Chamber of Senators and the Chamber of Deputies respectively, but both men refused. Rodríguez, as head of the judiciary, accepted the post and was inaugurated on 9 June 2005. In his acceptance speech he said that he felt his mandate was concerned with the renovation of the whole political system—a grim task as the two sides in the dispute over energy reserves appeared irreconcilable. Rodríguez scheduled early elections for 4 December.

BOSNIA AND HERZEGOVINA

Full name: Bosnia and Herzegovina.

Leadership structure: The head of state is a collective presidency, with one member representing each ethnic group (Bosniac, Serb and Croat), all directly elected for a four-year term. The chair of the presidency rotates every eight months among its three members. Both the (Bosniac-Croat) Federation and the Republika Srpska (RS) also have their own presidents. The (Bosniac-Croat) Federation president and vice president are elected by the Bosniac and Croat members of the House of Peoples for a four-year term. A second vice president is also elected to represent the Serb population. The Republika Srpska has a directly elected president, also with a four-year term.

The executive consists of a central Council of Ministers and separate executives for the two entities. Appointments to the executives must be in consultation with, and can be vetoed by, the UN's international high representative. From December 2002 the post of prime minister became fixed, with a four-year term, rather than rotating every eight months.

Chairman of the Presidency:

Ante Jelavić (Croat)	15 June 1999—14 Feb. 2000
Alija Izetbegović (Bosniac)	14 Feb. 2000—14 Oct. 2000
Zivko Radišić (Serb)	14 Oct. 2000—14 June 2001
Jozo Križanović (Croat)	14 June 2001—14 Feb. 2002
Beriz Belkić (Bosniac)	14 Feb. 2002—28 Oct. 2002
Mirko Sarović (Serb)	28 Oct. 2002—2 April 2003
vacant	2 April 2003—10 April 2003
Borislav Paravać (Serb)	10 April 2003—27 June 2003
Dragan Covíć (Croat)	27 June 2003—28 Feb. 2004
Sulejman Tihić (Bosniac)	28 Feb. 2004—28 Oct. 2004
Borislav Paravać (Serb)	28 Oct. 2004—28 June 2005
Ivo Miro **JOVIĆ** (Croat)	Since 28 June 2005

Prime Minister:	Haris Silajdžić & Svetozar Mihajlović	4 Feb. 1999—6 June 2000
	Spasoje Tusevljak	6 June 2000—18 Oct. 2000
	Martin Raguz (acting)	18 Oct. 2000—11 Nov. 2000
	vacant	11 Nov. 2000—22 Feb. 2001
	Bozidar Matić	22 Feb. 2001—18 July 2001
	Zlatko Lagumdžija	18 July 2001—15 March 2002
	Dragan Mikerević	15 March 2002—23 Dec. 2002
	Adnan **TERZIĆ**	Since 23 Dec. 2002

International High Representative:

	Wolfgang Petritsch	18 Aug. 1999—27 May 2002
	Paddy **ASHDOWN**	Since 27 May 2002

Legislature: The legislature of Bosnia and Herzegovina, the Parliamentary Assembly (Parlamentarna Skupština), is bicameral. The House of Representatives (Predstavnički Dom/Zastupnički Dom) has 42 members who are directly elected to the two constituent chambers, the Chamber of Deputies of the (Bosniac-Croat) Federation, with 28 members, and the Chamber of Deputies of the Republika Srpska, with 14 members. The House of Peoples (Dom Naroda) has 15 members, ten of them appointed from the Federation and five from the Republika Srpska. Both houses have four-year terms.

The Federation also has a bicameral Assembly (Skupština), including a House of Representatives (Predstavnički Dom/Zastupnički Dom) with 140 directly elected members, and a 74-member House of Peoples (Dom Naroda), comprising 30 Bosniacs, 30 Croats and 14 members elected indirectly by the cantonal assemblies. The Republika Srpska has a People's Assembly (Narodna Skupština) with 83 directly elected members. All of these bodies have four-year terms.

Profile of the Chairman of the Presidency:

Ivo Miro **JOVIĆ**

Ivo Miro Jović, a former headmaster and deputy education minister, was elected as the Croat member of the tripartite presidency of Bosnia and Herzegovina on 9 May 2005, and assumed the chair of the presidency for an eight-month term on 28 June.

Ivo Miro Jović was born on 15 July 1950 in the town of Trebižat, Capljina, in the south of Bosnia and Herzegovina. He graduated in philosophy from the

University of Sarajevo and undertook a postgraduate degree in economics at the University of Rijeka in Croatia. Jović worked as a teacher in the towns of Ilijaš and Kiseljak before becoming director of an adult education centre and headmaster of a secondary school in the latter town. Jović is married to Lucija with three children.

In 1997 Jović was appointed deputy minister of education, science, culture and sport for the Central Bosnia canton before becoming the deputy minister of education, science, culture and sport for the entire Federation in 1999, remaining in this post until 2001. The following year he was elected to the House of Representatives as a member of the Croatian Democratic Union of Bosnia and Herzegovina (Hrvatska Demokratska Zajednica Bosne i Hercegovine— HDZBiH), where he served until elected as the Croat representative of the presidency of Bosnia and Herzegovina on 9 May 2005. The international high representative had demanded the resignation of his predecessor Dragan Čović following charges of corruption and abuse of office. Jović became chairman of the presidency on 28 June, a position he will hold until the next rotation in February 2006.

Profile of the Prime Minister:

Adnan **TERZIĆ**

Adnan Terzić is member of the Bosniac-nationalist Party of Democratic Action (Stranka Demokratske Akcije—SDA). Based in the central Bosnian town of Travnik, he has been an integral part of the Bosniac-nationalist movement since the 1992–95 civil war. However, on his appointment as federal prime minister on 23 December 2002 he promised to oversee a multi-ethnic and liberal government.

Adnan Terzić was born on 5 April 1960 into the Muslim Bosniac community in Bosnia and Herzegovina, which was then a constituent republic of socialist Yugoslavia. Trained as a geodetic engineer, he was a prominent advocate of the Bosniac-nationalist movement from the early 1990s. He is married with one child.

While serving as mayor of the town of Travnik in 1996, Terzić officially denied that ethnic Croat families in the region had been banished following the Dayton Peace Accord. In the new cantonal structure adopted after the war, Terzić soon rose to prominence and was elected governor of the Central Bosnia canton for 1997–98, and again for 2000–01. During his governorships he oversaw the return of refugees and the implementation of redevelopment plans.

The SDA took on a more liberal stance at its congress in October 2001 and Terzić was elected to its vice presidency as part of these changes. He was key in leading the party to electoral success in the 2002 general elections which saw gains for the three traditional nationalist parties. Under new constitutional arrangements he was confirmed by a majority in parliament on 23 December as the country's first prime minister to have a fixed four-year term. In January he announced a five-party coalition comprising nationalist parties from each of the three ethnicities—the Bosniac-dominated SDA, the Croatian Democratic Union of Bosnia and Herzegovina and the Serb Democratic Party—plus two more moderate parties.

Terzić submitted his resignation and that of his government on 5 November 2004, over a controversial measure approved by parliament to set value-added tax (VAT) at 17% on all products except basic foodstuffs. The draft of the bill was very different from that which Terzić and international financial institutions had supported. However, representatives of the five ruling parties agreed to refuse the resignation and to support Terzić's reform programme.

Profile of the International High Representative:

Lord **ASHDOWN** ('Paddy' Ashdown)

'Paddy' Ashdown is a liberal democrat from the UK. During the wars of the Yugoslav succession he was a very vocal advocate of international military intervention. He was nominated to be the UN's high representative in Bosnia and Herzegovina in early 2002. Ashdown's position is constitutionally the most powerful in the country.

Jeremy John Durham Ashdown (known as 'Paddy') was born on 27 February 1941 in Delhi, India. His family returned to Northern Ireland, in the UK, in 1945. Ashdown enlisted with the Royal Marines while still studying at Bedford School in east England, and joined the military full-time in 1959. He married Jane Courtenay in 1961; they have two children.

A commander in the elite Special Boat Service from 1965, Ashdown saw active service in Borneo, the Persian Gulf and Belfast. He left the army in 1972 and took up a position at the UK's mission to the UN in Geneva, Switzerland. Many have since speculated that this post acted as cover for an assignment as a member of MI6, the UK foreign secret service. In 1976 Ashdown settled in England working with local industries. Having joined the then Liberal Party in 1975 he unsuccessfully stood for election in 1979. After two years as a local youth worker (1982–83), Ashdown was elected to the House of Commons, the lower house of the UK parliament, in 1983.

When the Liberals merged with the Social Democratic Party in 1988, Ashdown was elected leader of the resultant Liberal Democratic Party (LDP). In this position he pressed the government to take direct military action to try and halt the bloodshed in the disintegrating Yugoslavia and later in Kosovo. In August 1999 he stepped down as LDP leader and announced that he would retire from parliament at the next election. He was knighted in 2000 and was made Baron Ashdown of Norton-sub-Hamdon in 2001 when he left the House of Commons.

As a life peer he is now a member of the House of Lords, the upper house of the UK parliament.

Ashdown was nominated to be international high representative in Bosnia in February 2002 to replace Wolfgang Petritsch, who stepped down in May. In his new role Ashdown has been notably proactive. In June 2002 he dismissed the federal finance minister, citing corruption, and in December that year he restructured the federal government to increase its power and create a prime ministerial post that no longer rotated every eight months.

The following year he dissolved the RS defence council and struck out much of the nationalist language from the RS constitution, claiming that it had gone too far in promoting the idea of a separate Bosnian Serb state, rather than an entity within Bosnia and Herzegovina. In June 2004 he sacked 60 Bosnian Serb officials including the parliamentary speaker and interior minister over the government's failure to arrest war crimes suspect Radovan Karadžić. He told a press conference that a small band of corrupt politicians had been protecting Karadžić and other war criminals and preventing Bosnia from making progress towards joining the North Atlantic Treaty Organization (NATO) and the European Union. He said that it was necessary to remove "the cancer of obstructionism and corruption" in the Bosnian Serb political structure. Nine more officials were sacked in December.

Meanwhile, he demanded that the members of Bosnia's joint presidency should take responsibility for the large-scale embezzlement and waste of public funds that had been revealed in six institutions, including the presidency. When the Croat member Dragan Cović was charged with corruption in 2005, Ashdown dismissed him.

BOTSWANA

Full name: The Republic of Botswana.

Leadership structure: The head of state is a president, who is elected by parliament. A limit of two terms, to apply from 1999, was confirmed by referendum on 4 October 1997. The president's term of office is five years. The head of government is the president. The vice president and the cabinet are appointed by the president.

***President*:**	Festus **MOGAE**	Since 1 April 1998

Legislature: The legislature is unicameral. The sole chamber, the National Assembly, has 57 members, directly elected for a five-year term. There are also a variable number, currently four, nominated by the president from both the majority party and the opposition, and elected by the parliament itself. A 15-member House of Chiefs (Ntlo ya Dikgosi) acts as an advisory body on tribal matters and on alterations to the constitution.

Profile of the President:

Festus **MOGAE**

Festus Mogae took over as president of Botswana in 1998. He was elected to a full five-year term by the National Assembly the following year and was re-elected in 2004. An Oxford-educated economist with an illustrious previous career within the national bank and the International Monetary Fund (IMF), he leads the Botswana Democratic Party (BDP), which has maintained a parliamentary majority since the country's first general election in 1965.

Festus Gontebanye Mogae was born on 21 August 1939 in Serowe in eastern Botswana. After receiving his initial education in Botswana, he travelled to the UK to study economics, first at the North West London Polytechnic, and then at the universities of Oxford and Sussex. He returned to newly independent Botswana in 1968 to become a planning officer at the ministry of development planning. He married Barbara Gemma Modise that year and they have three daughters.

In 1971 Mogae was appointed as senior planner at the ministry and was attached to the Botswanan branch of the IMF as an alternate governor. He also worked with the African Development Bank and the International Bank for Reconstruction and Development. In 1972 he was made director of economic affairs at the ministry and was permanent secretary from 1975. During the early 1970s he was also on the board of various companies, including De Beers Botswana diamond mining company among others. In 1976 he moved to a permanent position with the IMF first as an alternate executive director. From 1978 he moved to Washington D.C. to work as a full executive director with responsibility for anglophone Africa.

Mogae returned to Botswana in 1980 to take up the governorship of the national bank and begin his high-level political career. In 1982 he was appointed as permanent secretary to President Ketumile Masire, a position he held for seven years in all. After Masire began his third term in 1989 he appointed Mogae to head the same ministry of finance and development planning where he had begun his career. As a trusted member of Masire's government, Mogae was appointed as vice president in 1992. He contested, and won, a seat in the National Assembly representing the Palapye constituency in 1994.

In November 1997 President Masire announced his desire to retire at the end of March the following year. Mogae, as his deputy, took over the remainder of the presidential term from 1 April 1998. On taking office he made no changes to his predecessor's cabinet apart from the introduction of Lt.-Gen. Ian Seretse Khama, the son of Botswana's first president, as minister of presidential affairs and ultimately his vice president. The move began a rift between the executive and the ranks of the ruling BDP as the then party chairman, Ponatshego Kedikilwe, had been groomed for the position.

In legislative elections held in October 1999 Mogae's BDP managed to reverse a recent downward trend in its popularity and increase its number of seats in the National Assembly, which duly re-elected Mogae as president. Mogae provoked outrage from the opposition and public alike in December when he agreed to grant Khama a one-year sabbatical. The leave of absence was cut short in August 2000 when Mogae recalled his deputy and, despite removing his ministerial position, installed him as his ministerial co-ordinator—effectively the head of government. Mogae explained that he had brought Khama back to give momentum to the eighth national development plan, current mid-term reviews of which had shown that it was lagging behind schedule. The move prompted criticism from his own cabinet who had little personal affection for the abrasive Khama who rides on the inherited popularity of his father.

The rift within the BDP deepened in 2003 as Khama, with Mogae's backing, ousted Kedikilwe as party chairman. The BDP retained its majority in an enlarged National Assembly at the 2004 elections, thereby re-electing Mogae for his second (and final) term. Then the tension rose, as the Assembly voted on Mogae's choice to retain Khama as vice president—and therefore very likely to be Mogae's eventual successor—a choice not supported by Kedikilwe's faction in the BDP. Mogae managed to split the dissenters with the lure of unfilled cabinet posts and the threat of dissolving the Assembly.

Mogae has campaigned hard to raise awareness of AIDS in a country where HIV has reached epidemic levels, affecting 38% of the population—the highest rate in the world in 2003. He takes every opportunity to openly discuss the disease and to stress the dangers of unsafe sex. In 2002 Botswana became the first African country to provide free anti-retroviral drugs nationwide.

BRAZIL

Full name: The Federative Republic of Brazil.

Leadership structure: The head of state is a president, directly elected by universal adult suffrage. The term of office is four years. A president is permitted to stand for re-election once only. The head of government is the president. The cabinet is appointed by the president.

President:	Fernando Henrique Cardoso	1 Jan. 1995—1 Jan. 2003
	Luiz 'Lula' **DA SILVA**	Since 1 Jan. 2003

Legislature: The legislature, the National Congress (Congresso Nacional) is bicameral. The lower chamber, the Chamber of Deputies (Câmara dos Deputados), has 513 members, directly elected for a four-year term. The upper chamber, the Federal Senate (Senado Federal), has 81 members, elected for eight-year terms, one-third and two-thirds alternately every four years.

Profile of the President:

Luiz 'Lula' **DA SILVA**

Luiz da Silva, popularly known simply as 'Lula', was a metalworker-turned-trade unionist who cofounded the socialist Workers' Party (Partido dos Trabalhadores—PT) and came to symbolize left-wing opposition to the military-backed regimes of the 1970s and 1980s. Having failed in successive challenges for the presidency in 1989, 1994 and 1998, he toned down his socialist rhetoric in order to win elections in October 2002, and embraced liberal economics, while still maintaining that globalization should be tempered by truly fair trade. He took office on 1 January 2003.

Luiz Inácio da Silva, whose nickname 'Lula' translates as 'squid', was born in October 1945; official records and his mother differ on the exact date. His impoverished family lived near Garanhuns, in the northeastern state of Pernambuco, but his father left to seek a way out of poverty in the southern state of São Paulo. The rest of the family—mother and six siblings—followed in 1952, moving to São Paulo city itself in 1956. Lula soon lost his 'northern' accent, sparing him the discrimination often suffered by northern Brazilians in mainstream society.

Lula was put to work as a street vendor as soon as he arrived in the south, peddling newspapers and shining shoes. At the age of 14 he became a metalworker, a full-time job which brought his schooling to an end, although he did a night-school course on metalworking until 1963. He lost a finger while working as a lathe operator. He married Maria de Lourdes in 1966 but was widowed three years later when Maria, and their child, died in childbirth. In 1974 he remarried, to Marisa Letícia Rocco, with whom he has three children; Lula also has two other children.

In 1966 Lula began working at Villares Industries and threw himself into trade union activism in the face of a recently installed autocratic military regime. In 1969 he was elected as an executive member of the São Bernando do Campo and Diadema Metalworkers' Union. By 1975 he had become its president. During his presidency he led two major industrial strikes against the Vauxhall motor company. His activities were gravely noted by the regime and he was briefly imprisoned.

Party politics was liberalized in 1979 and on 10 February 1980 Lula became one of the founder members of the PT. Its support for the radical movement of the landless, and industrial action, played a key role in toppling the military-backed government in 1985. During that period Lula helped create the Workers' Central Union in 1983 and led the 'Direct Elections Now' campaign in 1984 in an ultimately successful bid to press for direct presidential elections. In 1986 he was elected to the National Constituent Assembly with 650,000 votes—the largest personal mandate in the election. In 1987 he stepped down as PT president and put his popularity to the test as a presidential candidate for the 1989 poll.

Lula was beaten into second place by Fernando Collor de Mello, but formed a 'parallel government' in 1990 and successfully campaigned to have Collor de Mello impeached in 1992. He stood for the presidency two more times but was defeated on both occasions by the conservative Fernando Henrique Cardoso.

As the economy in neighbouring Argentina collapsed and began to impact on Brazil, Lula stepped up once more in 2002. This time he distanced himself from the landless movement and watered down his socialist rhetoric, replacing a promise to default on Brazil's international debts with a pledge to maintain the liberal economic policies of his predecessor. He also smartened his image and courted big business by sharing his candidacy with running mate José Alencar, a textile magnate and a champion of capitalism from the small Liberal Party.

Lula's popularity in pre-election polling alarmed international investors, who went so far as to devalue the country's credit rating and warn of bleak times ahead. Nonetheless he secured victory in the second round of voting on 27 October 2002, against José Serra, the candidate favoured by the incumbent President Cardoso, who was constitutionally barred from standing again himself. Lula's mandate rests on an unprecedented popular base as he received 61% of the vote, a record 52.7 million ballots in his favour. He was inaugurated for a four-year term on 1 January 2003.

Just over a month into his presidency, Lula faced the first major backlash from a bloc of PT members in parliament over his pledge to continue the market economy policy of his predecessors.

A racial equality programme launched by Lula on 20 November aimed to redress historic inequalities faced by the country's black population—the largest outside Africa—and pledged to grant land rights to the descendants of runaway slaves.

The landless movement for its part restarted its invasions of fallow and unproductive land, complaining that the new government had not tackled the issue. A major wave of protest and illegal property invasions took place across Brazil in early April 2004 as peasants and unemployed city dwellers demanded that Lula make good on his promises of sweeping land reform. On the other hand he impressed foreign investors and the International Monetary Fund by his determination to keep a tight rein on the economy. In December 2004 he was saved from political humiliation when pro-government members of the Brazilian Democratic Movement Party, including two government ministers and 19 of the party's 22 senators, announced that they would ignore their party's decision to withdraw from Lula's governing coalition.

Opposition continued to grow in 2005, however, with a strong campaign to impeach Lula, focusing on a cash-for-votes scheme in Congress over which he was eventually compelled to make an apology on nationwide television, claiming that he had known nothing about the alleged corruption himself.

BRUNEI

Full name: The Sultanate of Brunei (Negara Brunei Darussalam).

Leadership structure: The head of state is the sultan. As head of government, the sultan presides over and is advised by a Council of Cabinet Ministers, a Religious Council and a Privy Council. The cabinet is appointed by the sultan.

Sultan:	Sir Hassanal **BOLKIAH**	Since 5 Oct. 1967
	(also prime minister from 1 Jan. 1984)	

Legislature: The 21-member appointed Legislative Council was reconvened on 25 September 2004 for the first time in 20 years. It approved amendments to the constitution which would increase the size of the Council to 45 members, one-third of whom would be directly elected.

Profile of the Sultan:

Sir Hassanal **BOLKIAH**

Sir Hassanal Bolkiah, who trained at the UK's Sandhurst military academy and succeeded to the throne at the age of 21 following his father's abdication, is frequently cited as one of the richest people in the world, thanks to his tiny country's oil wealth. He has placed increasing emphasis in recent years on Brunei's Islamic identity, putting behind him his earlier image as something of a 'jet-setter' and playboy.

Hassanal Bolkiah was born on 15 July 1946 in Brunei Town (now known as Bandar Seri Begawan), and was educated privately in Brunei and in Kuala Lumpur, Malaysia. In 1961 he was installed as the crown prince and heir apparent. From 1963 he attended the Royal Military Academy, Sandhurst, as an officer cadet and gained his captain's commission in 1967, before succeeding to the throne on 5 October. He was crowned as the 29th sultan and *yang di-pertuan* (ruler) on 1 August 1968. He married his first cousin, Queen Saleha, in 1965, and his second wife, Mariam Bell, a former flight attendant in 1981—they were divorced in 2003. He has ten children: four sons and six daughters.

In 1978 the sultan led a diplomatic mission to London to discuss with the British government a change of status for Brunei. A Treaty of Friendship and Co-operation was drawn up, whereby the British government relinquished its responsibilities for the conduct of Brunei's foreign affairs and its defence. The treaty confirmed that Brunei would, at the end of 1983, "assume its full international responsibilities as a sovereign and independent state". On the day Brunei formally became fully independent, 1 January 1984, the sultan appointed himself prime minister. He also took on the portfolios of finance and home affairs, swapping these in 1986 for the defence portfolio, and regaining the finance portfolio in 1997. A major reshuffle in 2003—the most significant since independence—saw the appointment of the sultan's son Crown Prince Al-Muhtadee Billah as senior minister in the prime minister's office.

The sultan's status as the richest man in the world has slipped in recent years and in 2000 he was knocked from the top spot even in Asia. Indeed money scandals tarnished his family's reputation when in that year he launched a lawsuit against his younger brother, Prince Jefri, who had been finance minister from 1986 until 1997, for the alleged embezzlement of more than US$35,000 million. The suit was dropped and Jefri's assets frozen and returned to the state.

While not showing any inclination towards introducing democracy in Brunei, the sultan reopened the country's parliament in September 2004. In a speech to the Legislative Council's 21 appointed members, he described the move as a "cautious" reform to "enhance co-operation" with the people. An appointed Council had not met since Brunei became independent; a previous semi-elected legislature had been disbanded by the sultan's father in 1962 after voters supported a party that backed the abolition of the monarchy. The new parliament voted to amend the constitution to enlarge itself to 45 members and allow one-third of them to be elected in future, though parties remain banned.

BULGARIA

Full name: The Republic of Bulgaria.

Leadership structure: The head of state is a president, directly elected by universal adult suffrage. The president's term of office is five years. The head of government is the prime minister, who is responsible to the National Assembly. The cabinet is appointed by the prime minister.

President:	Petar Stoyanov	22 Jan. 1997—22 Jan. 2002
	Georgi **PURVANOV**	Since 22 Jan. 2002
Prime Minister:	Ivan Kostov	21 May 1997—24 July 2001
	Simeon Saxecoburggotski	24 July 2001—16 Aug. 2005
	Sergey **STANISHEV**	Since 16 Aug. 2005

Legislature: The legislature is unicameral. The sole chamber, the National Assembly (Narodno Sobranie), has 240 members, directly elected for a four-year term.

Profile of the President:

Georgi **PURVANOV**

Georgi Purvanov is a former chairman of the reformed-communist Bulgarian Socialist Party (BSP). A communist-era historian and a member of the old Bulgarian Communist Party (BCP), he became a key leader of the reformist wing of the renamed BSP in the 1990s. Following the party's defeat in the 2001 elections, Purvanov was an unexpected victor in presidential elections in November 2001. He took office in January 2002 and saw his party return to government in mid-2005.

Georgi Sedefchov Purvanov was born in Sirishtnik in western Bulgaria on 28 June 1957. He served two years in the army from 1975 before studying history at Sofia University. After graduating in 1981 he joined the BCP and worked as a researcher in the party's Institute of History, specializing in the emergence of the modern Bulgarian state at the turn of the 20th century. He is married to the academic Zorka Purvanova and they have two sons.

In 1991 Purvanov was elected to the recently renamed BSP's Supreme Council and championed the realignment of the party towards a more centrist approach in the newly democratic Bulgaria. The BSP was returned to power in elections in 1994, but faced increasing political and economic problems. Although his faction within the party gained the ascendancy, and he was elected party chairman in December 1996, Purvanov realized how untenable the government's position had become, and he and the new prime minister, Nikolai Dobrev, refused a further mandate in February 1997, instead leading the BSP into opposition.

From here Purvanov worked to transform the party in line with other social-democratic parties elsewhere in Europe. Although he led its opposition to the bombing in Yugoslavia by the North Atlantic Treaty Organization (NATO) in 1999, the following year he pledged its support for Bulgaria's campaigns to join both NATO and the European Union (EU).

Purvanov was one of five candidates to stand against incumbent president Petar Stoyanov in presidential elections in November 2001. The personal prestige of Stoyanov, who also had the full backing of the hugely popular and newly elected prime minister, Simeon Saxecoburggotski, made Purvanov's electoral victory all the more surprising. He stood down from the leadership of the BSP and was inaugurated as president on 22 January 2002. His commitment to pursue his predecessor's policies of promoting Bulgaria's ties to the West was shared by his party when it returned to government following the June 2005 elections.

Profile of the Prime Minister:

Sergey **STANISHEV**

Sergey Stanishev was appointed prime minister on 16 August 2005. He leads the Bulgarian Socialist Party (BSP), which won the most seats in the June 2005 election and eventually formed a coalition with the former ruling party of ex-king Simeon II (Saxecoburggotski) and the ethnic Turkish party.

Sergey Dmitriev Stanishev was born on 5 May 1966 in Kherson in Ukraine. He was educated at Moscow State University, from which he graduated in history in 1989, and took his doctorate in 1994, after which he worked as a freelance journalist for a year. In 1995 Stanishev worked at the BSP's foreign affairs department as a staff member and was head of foreign policy and international relations from 1996 to 2001, though he spent some time at the Moscow School of Political Studies in 1998 and was a visiting fellow at the London School of Economics from 1999 until 2000. Stanishev speaks fluent English and Russian and has some knowledge of French and Polish; he is in a long-time partnership with journalist Elena Yoncheva.

Stanishev was elected as a member of the Supreme Council of the BSP in 2000, and as a member of the National Assembly for the city of Ruse in June 2001, despite his party's defeat in that general election. In December that year at the BSP congress, he was elected to succeed president-elect Georgi Purvanov as chair of the party. He was re-elected to the National Assembly on 25 June 2005; the BSP won the parliamentary elections but failed to muster an outright majority. It took nearly two months of negotiations before the BSP came to a coalition agreement with the National Movement Simeon II and the largely ethnic Turkish Movement for Rights and Freedoms. Stanishev was elected prime minister by the National Assembly on 16 August 2005 and was sworn in the following day. His priorities include meeting the reform criteria for European Union accession.

BURKINA FASO

Full name: Burkina Faso.

Leadership structure: The head of state is a president, directly elected by universal adult suffrage. A parliamentary vote on 11 April 2000 fixed the presidential term at five years, with a maximum of two terms. Executive authority is vested jointly in the president, who is responsible to parliament, and in the Council of Ministers, which is headed by the prime minister (appointed by the president) and which is also responsible to parliament.

President:	Capt. Blaise **COMPAORÉ** (seized power on 15 Oct. 1987)	Since 31 Oct. 1987
Prime Minister:	Kadré Désiré Ouédraogo	6 Feb. 1996—7 Nov. 2000
	Paramanga Ernest **YONLI**	Since 7 Nov. 2000

Legislature: The legislature is unicameral. The National Assembly (Assemblée Nationale), has 111 members, directly elected for a five-year term.

Profile of the President:

Capt. Blaise **COMPAORÉ**

Capt. Blaise Compaoré has been president since the 1987 military coup which overthrew his former fellow parachute officer Thomas Sankara. Compaoré's military regime gave way to a multiparty system in 1991; that December he was elected under controversial circumstances, and re-elected in 1998. Constitutional changes in 2000 established that this should be his final term in office, expiring in 2005, but the ruling party nevertheless nominated him for a third term.

Born on 3 February 1951 in Ouagadougou, Blaise Compaoré joined the army and was sent as a parachute trainee to the Yaoundé military school in Cameroon, where he first met fellow trainee Sankara. He graduated as an officer in 1978, going on to become a commander at the National Commando Training Centre in the town of Po in southern Burkina. When Sankara took power in a 1983 coup, establishing an avowedly Marxist-Leninist government, he appointed Compaoré as minister of state to the presidency and as a member of the National Revolutionary Council. Compaoré subsequently became minister of justice, holding this post from 1984 to 1987. In 1985 he married Chantal Terrasson from Côte d'Ivoire; they have one daughter.

In October 1987, following disagreements with Sankara, Compaoré mounted his own coup. Together with up to 100 others, Sankara was killed in fighting in the capital during the struggle. Compaoré declared himself chairman of the Popular Front (Front Populaire—FP) and head of state, and formed a new government on 31 October. Over the succeeding years he followed policies of 'rectification' which, although nominally socialist, in fact featured economic reforms including the privatization of state-run industry. In 1989 he founded the Organization for Popular Democracy–Labour Movement (Organisation pour la Démocratie Populaire–Mouvement du Travail—ODP–MT).

In June 1991 Compaoré retired from the army under public pressure and announced multiparty elections. On 1 December he was elected president in a direct election in which he was the sole candidate. Opposition parties boycotted the contest (in which there was a turnout of only 28%) after the breakdown of tripartite talks, complaining of the lack of any prospect of a national conference. Violent protests followed, and a leading opposition figure was killed in a bomb explosion.

Condemning this violence as the work of the enemies of democracy, Compaoré postponed legislative elections due in January 1992 and announced that a national reconciliation forum would be convened forthwith to consider democracy, human rights and development. When the legislative elections did take place, in May 1992, opposition parties claimed that massive fraud had occurred. Compaoré's ODP–MT won three-quarters of the seats, and repeated this success five years later, having in the meantime absorbed several opposition groupings and restyled itself as the Congress for Democracy and Progress (Congrès pour la Démocratie et le Progrès—CDP).

Although Compaoré's personal hold on power appears to remain strong, his CDP government has suffered from continuing accusations of human rights abuses. The death of journalist Norbert Zongo in 1998 caused particular discontent. A variety of opposition parties chose to compete in the 2002 legislative elections, having boycotted previous polls, and the CDP was reduced to a narrow overall majority. A coup plot was foiled in September 2003, and four months later the defence minister was dismissed in connection with it.

Despite the constitutional amendments passed in 2000 that limit a president to two terms, in June 2005 the CDP nominated Compaoré as its candidate for the forthcoming presidential elections, victory in which would give him a third term.

Profile of the Prime Minister:

Paramanga Ernest **YONLI**

Paramanga Ernest Yonli is an economist by training, with a university education completed in France, and a background in agricultural development, on which he has written extensively. Fluent in English as well as French, he worked in Burkina as a researcher on regional food-related issues before entering government in 1996.

Paramanga Ernest Yonli was born on 15 March 1956 at Tansarga, Tapoa province. He moved to the capital for his secondary education in 1969, and in 1976 he entered the University of Ouagadougou to study economics, graduating in 1979. Two years later he gained a master's degree in economics, specializing in planning and development, from the University of Benin (Togo). In 1981 he moved to France for further study at the Sorbonne in Paris, gaining a diploma in international economy and development in 1984, and a doctorate from the University of Paris in agricultural development in 1985. He is married with four children.

An association with the Netherlands, marked by the award of a doctorate from the University of Ouagadougou/University of Groningen (Netherlands) in 1987, led to his involvement in the latter part of the 1980s with agricultural development studies and projects in Burkina Faso undertaken with Dutch co-operation and financing. Between December 1988 and October 1990 his work was based at the Dutch embassy in Ouagadougou. In 1990 the focus of his work moved to the Centre d'Etudes, de Documentation, de Recherches Economiques et Sociales (CEDRES) at the University of Ouagadougou and the University's faculty of economics and management, where he stayed until 1994. During this time he was a member of a Dutch–Burkinabé–Ghanaian research group on regional food security and sustainable development and gained a bursary from the Dutch Foundation for the Advancement of Tropical Research (WOTRO).

Yonli was appointed to the government in February 1996 by President Blaise Compaoré, serving firstly as director of the prime minister's office, and subsequently as minister of public office and institutional development, before becoming prime minister in November 2000. He was reappointed on 6 June 2002, after that year's legislative elections.

BURUNDI

Full name: The Republic of Burundi.

Leadership structure: The first post-transition president was elected by the members of the National Assembly and Senate in August 2005. In future the president will be directly elected. The president's term of office is five years, renewable once only. Two vice presidents are appointed by the president with the approval of the National Assembly and the Senate. The first vice president must be from a different ethnic group and political party from the president. The head of government is the president, who appoints and presides over the Council of Ministers. The 2004 Constitution specifies the proportion of Hutu and Tutsi members of the cabinet, and also the number of women it should include.

President:	Maj. Pierre Buyoya (head of military junta from 25 July 1996)	11 June 1998—30 April 2003
	Domitien Ndayizeye	30 April 2003—26 Aug. 2005
	Pierre **NKURUNZIZA**	Since 26 Aug. 2005

Legislature: The 2004 Constitution provides for a bicameral Parliament (Parlement). The lower chamber, the National Assembly (Assemblée Nationale), elected for the first time on 4 July 2004, has 100 directly elected members. Up to 21 members (currently 15) can be co-opted to achieve a split of 60% Hutu and 40% Tutsi members, and at least 30% women; three members of the Twa ethnic group are also co-opted. The upper chamber, the Senate (Sénat), elected for the first time in July 2005 to replace the co-opted Transitional Senate (Sénat de Transition) in office since February 2002, has 49 members, comprising 34 elected members (one Hutu and one Tutsi from each province); three co-opted Twa; all former presidents (currently four); and eight women co-opted to bring the total number of women senators to 30% of the total. All members of both houses serve a five-year term.

Profile of the President:

Pierre **NKURUNZIZA**

Pierre Nkurunziza was a PE teacher and lecturer until the murder of President Melchior Ndadaye in 1993 plunged the country into ethnic bloodletting. Following an attack on his university campus, Nkurunziza joined the Hutu rebel National Council for the Defence of Democracy—Forces for the Defence of

Democracy (Conseil National pour la Défense de la Démocratie—Forces pour la Défense de la Démocratie—CNDD–FDD), rising through the ranks to become the movement's leader in 2001. He signed a peace deal with the government in 2003, opening the way for him to enter the transitional government, and following poll victories in 2005 for the CNDD–FDD he was elected president by Parliament. He was sworn in on 26 August.

Pierre Nkurunziza was born on 18 December 1963 in the capital Bujumbura. His father, Eustache Ngabisha, a Roman Catholic, was elected as a member of the National Assembly in 1965 while his Anglican mother was a nurse; his father was assassinated during the Hutu massacres of 1972. Nkurunziza was schooled first in the province of Ngozi before going to secondary school in Kitenga.

He was admitted in 1987 to the University of Burundi's faculty of physical education (PE) and sports, despite having applied to the faculty of economic sciences and the High Military Institute; admissions to various faculties were at that time determined on an ethnic basis and Hutus such as Nkurunziza were not admitted to the High Military Institute. He graduated with a degree in physical education and sports in 1991 and taught PE at the Vugizo and Muramvya secondary schools, before returning to the University of Burundi as an assistant lecturer. Nkurunziza, a born-again Christian, is married with three sons.

In 1993 Burundi's first ethnic Hutu leader, Melchior Ndadaye, was assassinated. Nkurunziza lost two of his brothers in the ethnic violence that immediately followed. By 1995 he had been forced to join the CNDD–FDD as a soldier, narrowly escaping after Tutsi soldiers and some of his own students had attacked Hutus on the university campus. Nkurunziza was appointed deputy secretary-general of the CNDD–FDD in 1998, and was seriously injured in fighting in 1999, forcing him to hide out in the bush with no medical care for four months.

In 2001 he was elected as leader of the CNDD–FDD at the movement's first congress. After considerable negotiations, he signed a ceasefire accord with the transitional government in November 2003, and became minister of good governance. Following a series of electoral victories in 2005 on the part of the CNDD–FDD, Nkurunziza was nominated as the party's presidential candidate and was elected unopposed by Parliament on 19 August. He took office on 26 August. Nkurunziza's main task will be that of reassuring the minority Tutsis that a government led by ethnic Hutus can ensure their physical security.

CAMBODIA

Full name: Kingdom of Cambodia.

Leadership structure: The head of state under the 1993 Constitution is the king, who is elected by a nine-member Throne Council appointed by Parliament. The head of government is the prime minister, responsible to the Parliament but appointed by the king. The Royal Government of Cambodia is appointed by the prime minister.

King:	Norodom Sihanouk (head of state from 20 Nov. 1991)	24 Sept. 1993—6 Oct. 2004
	Samdech Chea Sim (acting)	10 April 2004—13 July 2004
	Nhek Bun Chhay (acting)	13 July 2004—22 July 2004
	Samdech Chea Sim (acting)	22 July 2004—20 Oct. 2004
	Norodom **SIHAMONI**	Since 14 Oct. 2004
Prime Minister:	**HUN SEN** (head of government from 14 Jan. 1985)	Since 26 Nov. 1998

Legislature: The legislature, the Parliament, is bicameral. The lower chamber, the National Assembly (Radhsphea Ney Preah Recheanachakr Kampuchea), has 123 members, directly elected for a five-year term. A 61-member Senate was approved by the National Assembly on 4 March 1999, and held its first session on 25 March. Its membership was determined in proportion to the results of the 1998 legislative elections, with senators serving a five-year term. The mandate of the current Senate was extended to January 2006, when the senators will be indirectly elected for a six-year term by the members of the National Assembly and the commune councils.

Profile of the King:

Norodom **SIHAMONI**

Norodom Sihamoni was nominated as king of Cambodia on 14 October 2004 following the abdication of his father Sihanouk. A professional dancer, Sihamoni spent much of his life living outside Cambodia, most recently for two decades in Paris. Observers have warned that the political inexperience of the new king should not persuade politicians to mistake him for a soft touch.

Norodom Sihamoni was born on 14 May 1953, the eldest son of King Norodom Sihanouk and his sixth wife Monique. He was schooled initially at the Norodom School and at the Descartes High School in the capital Phnom Penh, before being sent to what was then Czechoslovakia at the age of nine for the remainder of his schooling. He is unmarried with no children.

In 1967 he entered the National Conservatory of Prague. He remained in Czechoslovakia during the 1970 Cambodian coup d'etat by Lon Nol and graduated in 1975 from the Academy of Musical Art, having written a thesis on the conception and administration of artistic schools in Cambodia. He went from Czechoslovakia to North Korea, where he studied cinematography, returning to Cambodia two years after the Khmer Rouge assumed power. Sihamoni was put under house arrest with the rest of the royal family, several members of whom died in the chaos and violence of the Khmer Rouge's four-year rule, before being liberated by the 1979 Vietnamese invasion. He moved to Paris in 1981 to teach ballet.

Since 1984 Sihamoni has been president of the Khmer Dance Association based in Paris and the artistic director of the 'Deva' ballet troupe. He is also the director-general and artistic director of the Khmer cinematographic society Khemara Pictures, an interest he shares with his father. He visited Cambodia regularly during this period and in 1992 was appointed as permanent representative to the UN, and in 1993 as Cambodian delegate to the UN Educational, Scientific and Cultural Organization (UNESCO) based in his beloved Paris, where he won plaudits for his commitment and his hard work, while remaining distant from Cambodian domestic politics.

Sihamoni was selected to be the next king on 14 October 2004 by a nine-member Throne Council, one week after the surprise resignation of his father. He returned to Cambodia six days later and was crowned on 29 October. Sihamoni's status as an outsider may have contributed to his selection; the relationship between his father and Cambodian prime minister Hun Sen was notoriously frosty. However, observers say Sihamoni's pliancy should not be mistaken for weakness, and Hun Sen should not take the new king's acquiescence for granted.

Profile of the Prime Minister:

HUN SEN

Hun Sen is vice chairman of the socialist Cambodian People's Party (CPP). A one-time Khmer Rouge guerrilla who fell out with that movement's 1975–79 regime, he returned from exile as part of the Vietnamese-backed government when the Khmers Rouges were driven out, and then led one side of the coalition government formed after the UN-sponsored May 1993 elections. Ousting his co-premier in 1997, he was effectively re-elected in 1998 and 2003, and heads a surprisingly durable coalition with the royalists.

Hun Sen was born in Kampong Cham province on 5 August 1952, although his official birth date is given as 4 April 1951. He studied in Phnom Penh before joining the Khmer Rouge guerrillas in 1970, eventually rising to commandant, and losing an eye in 1975 in the successful Khmer Rouge attack on Phnom Penh which ended their long insurgency. That year Hun Sen married Bun Sam Heang, now known as Bun Rany, and they have three sons and three daughters.

In 1977, alienated from the genocidal new regime, and facing the threat of a purge, Hun Sen fled to Viet Nam, becoming leader of an anti-Pol Pot group there and founding in 1978 the Kampuchean National United Front for National Salvation (KNUFNS). This formed a nucleus for the government installed in Phnom Penh after the Vietnamese-backed military operation which drove the Khmer Rouge regime from the capital in 1979.

Hun Sen was foreign minister between 1979 and 1985 in this government, which renamed the country the People's Republic of Kampuchea (PRK), but was denied wide international recognition, the West backing instead an exile coalition government including both Prince Sihanouk's royalists and the Khmers Rouges. Heavily involved in the fighting, mainly against Khmer Rouge forces, Hun Sen became in addition deputy prime minister in 1981 and prime minister, despite his youth, in January 1985. He was thus a signatory of the October 1991 Paris accords which allowed for the return of Sihanouk and the holding of elections. That same month the PRK's ruling party, the Kampuchean People's Revolutionary Party (KPRP), renounced Marxism-Leninism and adopted the new CPP name. Hun Sen, a moderate in party terms, became deputy party leader with hard-liner Chea Sim as president.

The elections held in May 1993 under UN supervision (but boycotted by the Khmers Rouges) resulted in a victory for the royalist National United Front for an Independent, Neutral, Peaceful and Co-operative Cambodia (Front Uni National pour un Cambodge Indépendant, Neutre, Pacifique et Co-opératif—Funcinpec). Hun Sen's government, however, refused to relinquish power, and the compromise coalition formula, with two co-premiers—Hun Sen and Prince Ranarridh—was eventually agreed in June. Under the new constitution, adopted in September, Ranarridh became 'first' prime minister and Hun Sen 'second' prime minister. In the ensuing years (until the events of July 1997) the government, still dogged by a Khmer Rouge insurgency in the northwest, moved gradually to introduce free-market economic reforms. However there were growing signs of authoritarianism and a Hun Sen personality cult, fostered in the face of tensions within the coalition (and factional differences within both of its constituent halves). Assessments of Hun Sen stressed his hard work, tactical astuteness and continual drive to extend his power base, while also noting the fear he inspired in opponents and his displays of anger when crossed.

In July 1997 Hun Sen ousted Ranariddh. Despite some attempts to explain this as a preemptive strike against a royalist deal with remaining elements of the Khmers Rouges, Hun Sen's move was generally portrayed as a cynical consolidation of his power, encouraged also by personal animosities. Despite the misgivings of the international community, elections held in July 1998 were described as 'free and fair' by the UN joint inspection team. Hun Sen, having initially refused to stand in the election, emerged as the power broker in coalition negotiations which were increasingly dogged by violence. Four months later a coalition was finally agreed between the CPP and the royalist Funcinpec, with Hun Sen as sole prime minister and Ranarridh as speaker of the National Assembly.

During this term Hun Sen oversaw a relatively liberal government. He stepped down as commander-in-chief of the armed forces in January 1999 and the government promoted its environmental policies. Discussions continued with the UN on setting up trials of the former members of the Khmers Rouges, legislation for which was approved by the National Assembly in 2004.

In the July 2003 elections the CPP increased its share of the seats in the National Assembly, but again fell short of the two-thirds' majority required to form a government. Protracted coalition discussions dragged on for almost a year, with a deal eventually being signed to re-form the coalition with Funcinpec on 30 June 2004. Hun Sen was reappointed prime minister by King Sihanouk on 13 July.

CAMEROON

Full name: The Republic of Cameroon.

Leadership structure: The head of state is a president, directly elected by universal adult suffrage. The president's term of office is seven years. The president appoints the ministers, including the prime minister, who is head of government.

President:	Paul **BIYA**	Since 6 Nov. 1982
Prime Minister:	Peter Mafany Musonge	19 Sept. 1996—8 Dec. 2004
	Ephraïm **INONI**	Since 8 Dec. 2004

Legislature: The unicameral legislature, the National Assembly (Assemblée Nationale), has 180 members, directly elected for a five-year term.

Profile of the President:

Paul **BIYA**

Trained in France in law and public administration, Paul Biya became president of Cameroon in 1982 on the resignation of Ahmadou Ahidjo, whom he had previously served under as prime minister. A Roman Catholic and a southerner, he oversaw a transition from single-party rule to multiparty politics in the early 1990s. He was elected for further presidential terms in 1992, 1997 and 2004.

Paul Biya was born on 13 February 1933 in Mvomeka'a, in the south of Cameroon. His first wife Jeanne née Atyam, with whom he had one son, died in 1992. He married his second wife Chantal in 1994, and they have one son and one daughter.

He was educated at local Catholic schools and at the Lycée Général Leclerc in Yaoundé, before going to France in 1956 to study for a degree in public law at the University of Paris. Graduating in 1960, he spent the subsequent two years at the Institut d'Etudes Politiques and the Institut des Hautes Etudes d'Outre-mer. He returned to Cameroon in 1962, going into the postindependence civil service as a *chargé de mission* in the department of foreign aid (1962–63). In 1963 he obtained a postgraduate diploma in public law. In 1964 he moved to the ministry of national education, youth and culture. Biya also served on a goodwill mission to Ghana and Nigeria.

In December 1967 he was appointed director of the civil cabinet of Cameroon. Early the next year he was also made general secretary to the president, and in 1970 he became a minister of state in the president's office. He was appointed prime minister in June 1975, but was regarded as still having a relatively low-profile advisory role until November 1982, when Ahidjo stepped aside for health reasons and handed over the presidency to Biya as his designated successor.

The appointment of Biya, a francophone Catholic from southern Cameroon, directly challenged the political hegemony of the northern Muslims. Several revolts seriously threatened his rule in 1983–84, the first of them blamed on Ahidjo himself, who fled the country and resigned his remaining post as head of the ruling party, the Cameroon National Union (Union Nationale Camerounaise—UNC). Biya consolidated his position, taking over the party leadership himself and having his role as president confirmed by an overwhelming majority in the January 1984 election. Promising some gradual steps towards greater democratization, he restyled the ruling party in 1985 as the Cameroon People's Democratic Movement (Rassemblement Démocratique du Peuple Camerounais—RDPC), and initiated some measures of social and economic liberalization.

Presidential elections in April 1988 were held on the basis that he was the sole candidate, producing the required near-unanimous endorsement, but pressure for political pluralism ultimately led to the drafting of a new constitution, which was formalized in November 1990 and opened the way for multiparty elections. When these took place in 1992 the RDPC won most seats, but not an overall majority, in the legislature. Biya himself only narrowly won the presidential poll in October, claiming almost 40% of the vote against almost 36% officially credited to John Fru Ndi of the Social Democratic Front (SDF).

Thereafter the SDF mounted a sustained campaign for an all-party national conference and an interim government to supervise fresh elections. Biya refused to cede authority from his own government in this way, but his re-election as president on 17 May 1997, when he was recorded as having won 92.5% of the vote, was marred by opposition claims of fraud, and a low turnout in the north and west of the country in response to boycott calls.

Nonetheless, Biya remained in power, despite vocal and often physical opposition from the SDF accusing Biya and his government of corruption and sanctioning extrajudicial killings, and in the face of growing calls for autonomy from the anglophone west. The opposition sought to unite against him in the run-up to the 2004 election, but its attempt to choose a single candidate collapsed in acrimony. Biya was re-elected in October with more than 70% of the vote, and the Supreme Court rejected a complaint by opposition parties that the vote was unfair, a decision concurring with the opinion of the majority of observers.

Profile of the Prime Minister:

Ephraïm **INONI**

Ephraïm Inoni, a long-time aide to President Paul Biya, was sworn in as prime minister of Cameroon on 8 December 2004. An anglophone like his predecessor, he has a background in finance and business. Since taking office, Inoni has moved to tackle Cameroon's appalling corruption.

Ephraïm Inoni was born on 16 August 1967 in Bakingili in Fako division, a member of the Bakweri ethnic group. Educated in the USA with a master's degree in business and finance, Inoni is an anglophone financier. He is married to Gladys née Ngone, an ethnic Bakossi, and they have five children.

Inoni is a long-time loyalist of President Paul Biya and has been part of the Cameroonian government since 1994. He is a member of the ruling Cameroon People's Democratic Movement (Rassemblement Démocratique du Peuple Camerounais—RDPC) and has represented Biya in talks with Nigeria over the oil-rich Bakassi peninsula. His appointment, to succeed fellow anglophone Peter Mafany Musonge, is a nod to the quarter of Cameroon's population who are English-speaking and who have long complained of marginalization by the francophone majority.

Inoni faced an uphill struggle dealing with Cameroon's moribund and corruption-ridden economy. His predecessor had instigated a number of reforms which boosted annual growth to around 5%, but the majority of the population failed to garner the benefits of this success. Failure to meet the terms of the Highly Indebted Poor Country (HIPC) initiative means that Cameroon missed out on the cancellation of billions of dollars in external debts, which still loom over any attempts to lift its people out of poverty.

Real power in Cameroon remains in the hands of President Biya, who has not hitherto been known for his enthusiasm in countering corruption; Transparency International found in 2004 that 51% of Cameroonians had paid a bribe in the past year—more than anywhere else in the world. However, Inoni began an anti-corruption drive with confidence, insisting that disciplinary sanctions be applied to some 500 civil servants who had been faking documents to earn allowances and in some cases entire salaries to which they were not entitled.

CANADA

Full name: Canada.

Leadership structure: The head of state is the British sovereign, styled 'of the United Kingdom, Canada and Her other Realms and Territories, Queen, Head of the Commonwealth, Defender of the Faith', and represented by a governor-general who is appointed on the advice of the Canadian prime minister. The head of government is the prime minister, who is appointed by the governor-general. The cabinet is appointed by the governor-general on the recommendation of the prime minister.

Queen:	Elizabeth II	Since 6 Feb. 1952
Governor-General:	Adrienne **CLARKSON**	Since 7 Oct. 1999
Prime Minister:	Jean Chrétien	4 Nov. 1993—12 Dec. 2003
	Paul **MARTIN**	Since 12 Dec. 2003

Legislature: The legislature, the Parliament, is bicameral. The lower chamber, the House of Commons, has 308 members, directly elected for a five-year term. The upper chamber, the Senate, has 105 members appointed by the governor-general on the recommendation of the prime minister. Senators retain their seats until age 75.

Profile of the Governor-General:

Adrienne **CLARKSON**

Adrienne Clarkson has a long history as one of Canada's leading television journalists, producing and presenting many shows for the Canadian Broadcasting Corporation (CBC) since 1965. Her appointment in October 1999 as governor-general broke with the recent trend of ex-politicians, and her Chinese birth makes her the first immigrant to hold the post.

Adrienne Clarkson (née Poy) was born to Chinese parents in Hong Kong on 10 February 1939. Her family fled the Japanese advance in the Second World War, arriving as refugees in Canada in 1942. She received a public school education in Ottawa and graduated with a master's degree in English literature from the University of Toronto. She studied as a postgraduate at the Sorbonne in Paris, France, and as a member of the Chinese-Canadian minority she is notable for her ability to speak both English and French fluently. From 1965 to 1982 she forged her career as a producer, writer and host of a number of successful CBC television programmes including *Take Thirty* and *Adrienne at Large*. She has also written a number of articles and three books. During this period she was married (from 1963 to 1975), to the political scientist Stephen Clarkson, and they had two daughters. She married her current husband, the writer John Ralston Saul, in 1999 after a 15-year romance.

From 1982 to 1987 Clarkson was the first agent-general for the state of Ontario in Paris. Her duties in this post were to promote Ontario's business and cultural interests to Europe, foreshadowing her role as governor-general. In 1987 she became the president of the Canadian publisher McClelland & Stewart until returning to broadcasting in 1988. For the next ten years she was executive producer, writer and host for the programmes *Adrienne Clarkson's Summer Festival* and *Adrienne Clarkson Presents*. As well as these achievements she also wrote and directed several films, receiving various television industry awards from Canada and the USA. From 1998 until her appointment as governor-general, Clarkson served as chair of the Board of Trustees of the Canadian Museum of Civilization in Hull, Québec, and as president of IMZ (an international association of cultural programmers based in Vienna, Austria) as well as continuing her work as a television presenter and producer.

In 1999 she was taken by surprise at her nomination to be governor-general in succession to the retiring Roméo LeBlanc. She became the second female holder of this office, the first non-white, and the first person not of political or military background. She announced her desire to spend more time in the governor-general's second official residence, La Citadelle in Québec City.

During her tenure, Clarkson has travelled extensively in Canada to meet the people, as well as making many official visits overseas. She has been praised for modernizing and raising the profile of the governor-generalship, but has also met with frequent complaints about her office's soaring spending levels and from monarchists about actions that have undermined the British monarch's position as Canada's head of state. Despite these mixed reactions, her term was extended for a year to late 2005 in order to provide stability at a time when a minority government was in power.

Profile of the Governor-General-designate:

Michaëlle **JEAN**

Michaëlle Jean is an award-winning journalist and filmmaker whose family fled Haiti when she was a child. Married to fellow documentary-maker Jean-Daniel Lafond, she was nominated as Canada's first black governor-general in August 2005 to take office on 27 September.

Michaëlle Jean was born in Port-au-Prince in Haiti on 6 September 1957. She and her family fled the country in 1968; her father, a philosopher, had been tortured under the Duvalier regime. The family settled in Québec, Canada, and Jean studied Italian and Hispanic languages and literature at the University of Montréal. After graduating she began studying for a master's degree while teaching Italian studies and working at a shelter for battered women. Jean then went to Italy to study at the University of Perugia, the University of Florence and the Catholic University of Milan. She is fluent in French, English, Italian, Spanish and Haitian Creole, and can read Portuguese. She is married to Jean-Daniel Lafond and they have one adopted daughter; Lafond has two other daughters from a previous marriage.

Jean joined Radio Canada in 1988 as a reporter and quickly became a host on a variety of programmes. She and Lafond collaborated on several films, including the award-winning *Haiti dans tous nos rêves* in 1995. Four years later she also began hosting English-language documentaries for Canadian Broadcasting Corporation (CBC) Newsworld. By 2001 Jean had become a weekend anchor on Radio Canada's major news broadcasts and in 2004 started her own television show called *Michaëlle*.

Prime Minister Paul Martin nominated Jean as governor-general in August 2005 to take office on 27 September. She would be Canada's first black governor-general and the second to be foreign-born (after incumbent Adrienne Clarkson).

Profile of the Prime Minister:

Paul **MARTIN**

Paul Martin succeeded Jean Chrétien as prime minister of Canada on 12 December 2003 and was re-elected with a minority government on 28 June 2004. The son of a prominent Liberal backbencher of the same name, Martin first entered Parliament in 1988. He stood against Jean Chrétien for leadership of the Liberal Party of Canada in 1990, losing the bid after a bitter race that resulted in lasting animosity between their respective supporters. Nonetheless, Chrétien appointed Martin as finance minister following the Liberal landslide of 1993. Martin won plaudits for slashing federal government spending to eliminate the budget deficit, but not from Chrétien, who fired him in 2002. Martin formally declared his intention to run for the leadership of the Liberal Party at the next party convention and shortly afterwards Chrétien announced that he would not seek a fourth term; Martin went on to win 92% of delegates' votes and, as leader of the largest party, automatically became prime minister. A scandal over sponsorship contracts when he was finance minister forced him to call an election for June 2004; he won a strong minority and another term in office.

Paul Martin was born in Windsor, Ontario, on 28 August 1938, the son of the distinguished parliamentarian of the same name, who died in 1992. Paul Martin

Sr, who served almost two dozen years in Liberal cabinets under four different prime ministers, was regarded as one of the architects of the postwar social policy that is considered an enduring part of the Liberal legacy. The younger Paul Martin studied philosophy and history at St Michael's College at the University of Toronto and graduated from the University of Toronto Law School. He was called to the Bar in Ontario in 1966. Before entering politics, he had a distinguished career in the private sector. Martin is married to Sheila née Cowan, with three sons.

Martin was first elected to the House of Commons in 1988 as the member of Parliament for the constituency of LaSalle-Emard in Montréal, Québec. In 1990 he ran for the leadership of the Liberal Party at that year's party convention, losing to Jean Chrétien. The incident marked the beginning of a venomous personal rivalry between the two men. The key to their animosity was Québec; both Québécois, Martin backed greater autonomy for the province, while mocking Chrétien as being out of touch and selling out to the English. Chrétien never forgave Martin for his taunts, but brought him into government as finance minister in 1993. Martin served in that role until June 2002, using the post to position himself for a future assault on the leadership and building a substantial war chest from corporate donations, until he was unceremoniously replaced in a surprise cabinet reshuffle that coincided with a wave of scandals breaking over the higher echelons of the Liberal Party.

Relegated to the backbenches, Martin took advantage of the opportunity to reconnect with his substantial support among the grass roots of the party and plan for an immediate leadership battle. Meanwhile Chrétien, in an attempt to ride out the scandals and unify the party, announced his intention to stay on until February 2004, effectively instigating an 18-month unofficial leadership campaign. In the event, the showdown came in November 2003, when Martin was finally chosen as prime-minister-in-waiting, and he took over from Chrétien in December. Almost immediately engulfed in controversy, however, Martin was forced to call an early general election in 2004 to consolidate his somewhat tenuous hold on power. Continuing scandals meant that Martin failed to win the landslide victory that his initial popularity might have garnered, but he nevertheless won enough votes to form a minority government, albeit one propped up by the Bloc Québécois and the New Democratic Party (NDP). However, the taint of scandal followed the party. Martin set up a public inquiry into allegations that the Liberal Party had funnelled millions of dollars in the late 1990s—at the time when Martin was finance minister—from a government programme set up to promote Canadian unity in Québec to a set of companies sympathetic to the party in payment for little or no work. In 2005 he became the first sitting prime minister to testify before such an inquiry since 1873.

With the Liberal Party's popularity plummeting, the opposition pledged to bring down the government, accusing it of having lost the moral right to govern. Martin apologized for the "unjustifiable mess", pledged to hold a general election in

January 2006 within 30 days of the inquiry reporting its findings in December, and struck a deal with the tiny NDP for support in a confidence vote in parliament. Thus when a budget vote in May was turned into a confidence motion, the survival of Martin's government hinged on the votes of two independent MPs. Martin won by a single vote, and went on to survive several more confidence votes the following month, despite the defection of one of his Liberal MPs over plans to legalize gay marriage.

CAPE VERDE

Full name: The Republic of Cape Verde.

Leadership structure: The head of state is a president, directly elected by universal adult suffrage. The president's term of office is five years. The head of government is the prime minister, who is responsible to the National Assembly. The Council of Ministers is appointed by the prime minister.

President: António Mascarenhas Monteiro   22 March 1991—22 March 2001

   Pedro **PIRES**   Since 22 March 2001

Prime Minister: Carlos Veiga   4 April 1991—5 Oct. 2000
   (acting from 28 Jan. 1991)

   António Gualberto do Rosário   5 Oct. 2000—1 Feb. 2001
   (acting from 29 July 2000)

   José Maria **NEVES**   Since 1 Feb. 2001

Legislature: The legislature is unicameral. The sole chamber, the National Assembly (Assembléia Nacional), has 72 members, directly elected for a five-year term.

Profile of the President:

Pedro **PIRES**

Pedro Pires is a veteran of the armed struggle against Portuguese colonialism in Africa, and was independent Cape Verde's first prime minister in 1975. He led the ruling left-wing African Party for the Independence of Cape Verde (Partido Africano da Independência de Cabo Verde—PAICV) into multipartyism, and ultimately defeat in 1991, but returned to the limelight in 2001, riding the wave of the party's electoral revival. Although long seen as on the political left, he now champions a more pragmatic, liberal approach. As president his influence is overshadowed by the constitutional power of the prime minister.

Pedro Verona Rodrigues Pires was born on 29 April 1934 on the island of Fogo (Fire Island) in what was then the Portuguese colony of Cape Verde and Portuguese Guinea (modern-day Guinea-Bissau). He was educated in the islands before heading for Lisbon, Portugal, in 1956 to attend the faculty of science at the city's university. On graduation he was drafted into the Portuguese Air Force where he met with other people from Portugal's scattered colonies. He was already dedicated to the liberation of his homeland, and deserted from the air force in June 1961 in order to join the burgeoning anti-colonial movement back in Africa.

After taking an indirect route through Spain and France, Pires arrived in Ghana in September 1961. There he met the pro-independence leader Amílcar Cabral and joined his African Party for the Independence of Guinea and Cape Verde (Partido Africano da Independência da Guiné e Cabo Verde—PAIGC). The independence struggle in lusophone Africa was interconnected and Pires travelled to Morocco to join the secretariat of the Conference of the Nationalist Organizations within the Portuguese Colonies. The movement took up arms in Guinea in 1963 and Pires was appointed to the central committee of the PAIGC in 1965, and to its Council of War in 1967.

As the PAIGC forces gained ground, Pires served from 1971 in the administration of the liberated areas in the south of what is now Guinea-Bissau and was appointed assistant state commissioner in the first government of that country in 1973. In the same year he was also elected president of the national committee of the PAIGC for Cape Verde and was at the centre of successful negotiations for the independence of the two connected African territories in 1974. Cape Verde and Guinea-Bissau separated and Pires returned to his country of origin to serve as director of party policy in the transitional government of Cape Verde, before being elected to the newly created National Popular Assembly in June. In the country's first postcolonial government he was appointed prime minister. In the same year he married Adélcia Maria da Luz Lima Barreto; they have two daughters.

During Pires's three consecutive prime ministerial terms (1975–91), Cape Verde was run as a left-wing single-party state. Following a coup in Guinea-Bissau and the abandonment of the idea of reunifying the two states, the Cape Verdian branch of the PAIGC separated to form the PAICV in 1981. Pires served as its deputy secretary-general, under the leadership of the then president Aristides Pereira.

As part of a trend towards multipartyism throughout Africa, the PAICV agreed in 1990 to free elections. Pires replaced Pereira as secretary-general, but in the first free polls in February 1991 the PAICV was resoundingly beaten by the Movement for Democracy. Pires stayed at the helm of the defeated party for another three years.

The PAICV was beaten again in 1996 but saw its popularity return in the late 1990s. Pires resumed leadership of the party from 1997 to 2000. In legislative elections in January 2001 it secured a safe majority and nominated Pires as its presidential candidate for the following month. Despite the party's renewed vigour, Pires won the race by only 17 votes. He took office on 22 March.

Profile of the Prime Minister:

José Maria **NEVES**

José Maria Neves, a Brazilian-trained administrator, became head of the African Party for the Independence of Cape Verde (Partido Africano da Independência de Cabo Verde—PAICV) in time to lead it back to power in the 2001 elections after a ten-year stint in opposition. He is seen as a champion of the younger, more technocratic generation of Cape Verdian politicians now taking over from the veterans of the anti-colonial struggle.

José Maria Pereira Neves was born on 28 March 1960 in Santa Catarina, on the island of São Tiago (Santiago). He was educated in public administration at the Getúlio Vargas Foundation in São Paulo, Brazil. He has worked specifically on organizational development and management of human resources and was director of the National Public Administration Training Centre from 1988 to 1989.

In 1989 Neves became leader of the PAICV's youth movement, Amílcar Cabral African Youth. His political career began in local government in Santa Catarina. Going on to win election to the National Assembly in 1996, he became its vice president and chairman of the specialized committee on public administration, local government and regional development. In March 2000 he was appointed mayor of Santa Catarina, and was elected to lead the PAICV in June. After the PAICV's return to power in the January 2001 legislative elections, he was appointed prime minister and minister of defence in February. He also held the finance portfolio from October 2003 to April 2004.

CENTRAL AFRICAN REPUBLIC

Full name: The Central African Republic.

Leadership structure: The head of state is a president, directly elected by universal adult suffrage. Under the 2004 Constitution the presidential term is five years, renewable once only. The head of government is the prime minister, who is appointed by the president and appoints the ministers.

President:	Ange-Félix Patassé	22 Oct. 1993—15 March 2003
	François **BOZIZÉ**	Since 15 March 2003
Prime Minister:	Anicet Georges Dologuélé	4 Jan. 1999—1 April 2001
	Martin Ziguélé	1 April 2001—15 March 2003
	vacant	15 March 2003—23 March 2003
	Abel Goumba	23 March 2003—11 Dec. 2003
	Célestin Gaoumbalet	12 Dec. 2003—13 June 2005
	Elie **DOTÉ**	Since 13 June 2005

Legislature: Under the 2004 Constitution the legislature is unicameral. The National Assembly (Assemblée Nationale) has 105 members, directly elected for a five-year term.

Profile of the President:

François **BOZIZÉ**

François Bozizé was elected president of the Central African Republic (CAR) on 8 May 2005 in the second round of voting, two years after he seized power from Ange-Félix Patassé in a military coup. A career army officer and one of the country's great political survivors, Bozizé had long been a supporter of Patassé, and had put down many attempted putsches against him. Bozizé finally broke from Patassé in 2001 after a failed coup in which he was implicated. He led a rebel group from exile in Chad before his successful coup in 2003. In power, however, Bozizé has so far shown himself to be genuine in his desire for democratic reform.

François Bozizé was born Bozouissé Yangouvonda on 14 October 1946 in Mouila, French Equatorial Africa, today Gabon. He joined the army on leaving school and in 1966, following the overthrow of the country's first president David Dacko by Jean-Bédel Bokassa, was admitted into a military officers' training school in Bouar in the CAR. He became a lieutenant in 1969, and gradually worked his way into the country's elite inner circles, making the rank of captain in 1975. He is married to Monique.

Bokassa declared the Republic to be a monarchy and himself to be its emperor in 1976, spending US$20 million on his own coronation the following year. In 1978 he appointed Bozizé as brigadier-general and aide-de-camp. Following riots in the capital Bangui and the murder of dozens of schoolchildren, David Dacko led a successful coup against Bokassa, backed by France, in September 1979. Showing what would prove to be characteristic tenacity, Bozizé not only remained in favour under Dacko's renewed presidency but was appointed defence minister.

Two years later Dacko himself was overthrown once again in a bloodless coup, this time led by Gen. André Kolingba. Bozizé was made minister of information and culture, but in 1982 became entangled in the failed coup attempt of Ange-Félix Patassé. Initially taking refuge in the French embassy, the two men then shared a long exile in Togo before Patassé moved to France and Bozizé travelled to Benin, where he was arrested in Cotonou in July 1989 and handed over to the CAR authorities. He was imprisoned and tortured before finally being amnestied by Kolingba in 1991. Under international pressure, Kolingba held elections in 1993, which were won by Patassé. Bozizé, who was also a candidate, achieved a miserable seventh place.

Bozizé for many years gave staunch support to Patassé. He was named armed forces chief of staff and crushed numerous revolts against the president. UN troops were sent into the country to bolster a French contingent and ultimately the government was shored up by Libyan troops. In 2001, in the aftermath of one of these failed coups, Bozizé was implicated in the plot; rather than wait to be arrested by Patassé's supporters, he fled to Chad with around 300 supporters. From there he made frequent raids across the border with the assent of Chadian president Idriss Deby. In 2002 Bozizé led his exiles in an unsuccessful coup attempt which triggered renewed civil war, and his forces soon controlled swathes of the north of the country.

Following the replacement of the Libyan contingent of the peacekeeping force in CAR with troops from Gabon, Bozizé considered the time ripe to press home his advantage, calculating that the Gabonese had neither the interest in CAR nor the fighting capacity of the Libyans. On 15 March 2003, when Patassé was out of the country, Bozizé launched his coup. Patassé immediately moved to return to the CAR but his plane was shot at on attempting to land at Bangui and he was forced to fly to Cameroon, eventually returning to exile in Togo. The next day Bozizé declared himself head of state and suspended the constitution, promising fresh elections.

After a new constitution was approved by referendum in December 2004, Bozizé rescinded his pledge not to stand and ran successfully in presidential elections in 2005, winning the second round in May with 64% of the vote. While opposition politicians cried fraud, international observers said that the results reflected the will of the people, and Bozizé was congratulated by UN Secretary-General Kofi Annan, who promised UN backing for the process of reconstruction.

Profile of the Prime Minister:

Elie **DOTÉ**

Elie Doté is relatively unknown in politics in the Central African Republic (CAR), having worked mainly for the African Development Bank (AfDB). President Bozizé appointed him as prime minister in June 2005.

Elie Doté was born in 1947 and studied rural economy to doctorate level before joining the agriculture and animal husbandry ministry of the CAR. He remained in this post from 1974 until 1980, when he joined the AfDB. A technocrat, he spent much of his life abroad, particularly in Abidjan, Côte d'Ivoire, where the AfDB was based until its relocation to Tunis in 2003. Doté was appointed as prime minister of the CAR on 13 June 2005. He is married with six children.

CHAD

Full name: The Republic of Chad.

Leadership structure: The head of state is a president, directly elected by universal adult suffrage. The president's term of office is five years, renewable only once under the 1996 Constitution, but renewable indefinitely under a 2005 amendment. The head of government is the prime minister, who is appointed by the president. The cabinet is appointed by the prime minister.

President:	Idriss **DEBY** (seized power on 4 Dec. 1990)	Since 4 March 1991
Prime Minister:	Nagoum Yamassoum	13 Dec. 1999—12 June 2002
	Haroun Kabadi	12 June 2002—24 June 2003
	Moussa Faki Mahamat	24 June 2003—3 Feb. 2005
	Pascal **YOADIMNADJI**	Since 3 Feb. 2005

Legislature: The legislature is unicameral. The National Assembly (Assemblée Nationale), has 155 members, directly elected for a four-year term.

Profile of the President:

Idriss **DEBY**

Idriss Deby has been in power in Chad since his 1990 coup, and was elected president for five-year terms in 1996 and 2001. A French-trained soldier, he was the leader of the forces which enabled his fellow Muslim, northerner Hissène Habré, to take power in 1982. He turned against Habré in 1989 and subsequently mounted a successful Libyan-backed invasion from bases in Sudan.

Deby was born in 1952 in Fada, Ennedi, in eastern Chad, into the Muslim Zaghawa tribe. He trained as a soldier, attending the Aeronautic Institute in Amaury de la Grange in France in 1976–78. He quickly rose to become chief of staff in 1982 of the Armed Forces of the North (Forces Armées du Nord—FAN), the supporters of Habré. In the ongoing civil war Deby led the FAN forces and captured the capital N'Djamena, declaring Habré head of state in June 1982. Habré then promoted him to colonel and appointed him commander-in-chief of the armed forces and his military adviser. In 1985 Deby returned to France, this time attending the higher military academy in Paris.

Deby tried unsuccessfully to oust Habré on 1 April 1989, subsequently escaping into Sudan, where he founded a Patriotic Salvation Movement (Mouvement Patriotique du Salut—MPS) and launched a number of attacks into Chad. In November 1990 he led a successful invasion backed by Libyan troops, putting Habré to flight and proclaiming himself head of state and chairman of the interim council of state in December. He was inaugurated as president in March 1991, as fighting continued against troops loyal to Habré and against other tribal groups.

Since taking power Deby has sought progressively to bring the many rival factions in Chad into a 'national reconciliation' process, as part of which he eventually conceded the introduction of a multiparty system. A new constitution was approved by referendum in March 1996, which is secular in form (ostensibly to avoid closing the door to reconciliation with southern-based Christian opponents), although Deby's regime has in practice introduced many elements of Islamic *shari'a* law. As permitted by Islamic law, Deby himself has four wives, and about 12 children.

Presidential elections on 2 June 1996 saw Deby head a field of 15 candidates in the first round, and in the runoff on 3 July he won 69% of the vote. He suffered something of a setback when his MPS failed to win an overall majority in legislative elections in early 1997. Deby again managed to bring in more former opposition groups to support his regime, which has been greatly bolstered by the prospect of exploiting the country's enormous recently discovered oil resources.

A harsh policy of shooting criminals on sight, and other human rights violations, brought criticism from abroad, with European countries becoming increasingly attentive to the Chadian situation. Deby's re-election for a further presidential term on 27 May 2001, when he was credited with 67% of the vote, prompted opposition candidates to protest over targeted state violence, ballot-rigging and fraud. The ensuing demonstrations were met with a firm crackdown and a spate of arrests, and the Deby government's hold on power was underlined when the MPS won two-thirds of the seats in the legislature in elections in April 2002. A referendum on 3 June 2005 removed the constitutional two-term limit on the presidency, thus allowing Deby to stand for re-election in 2006.

Profile of the Prime Minister:

Pascal **YOADIMNADJI**

Pascal Yoadimnadji was born in 1950, a member of the Gor ethnic group from the extreme south of Chad. A lawyer before he entered politics, Yoadimnadji served as the chair of the electoral commission, overseeing the 1996 presidential elections that confirmed Deby in office, and has headed the Constitutional Court. He was from July 2004 the minister of agriculture in the government of his predecessor, Moussa Faki. He was chosen to succeed Faki on 3 February 2005.

CHILE

Full name: The Republic of Chile.

Leadership structure: The head of state is a president, directly elected by universal adult suffrage. The president's term of office is six years, and is not renewable. The head of government is the president, who is responsible to the National Congress. The cabinet is appointed by the president.

| ***President***: | Eduardo Frei Ruiz-Tagle | 11 March 1994—11 March 2000 |
| | Ricardo **LAGOS** Escobar | Since 11 March 2000 |

Legislature: The legislature, the National Congress (Congreso Nacional), is bicameral. The lower chamber, the Chamber of Deputies (Cámara de Diputados), has 118 members, directly elected for a four-year term. The upper chamber, the Senate (Senado), has 38 members elected for an eight-year term (half of which are renewed every four years), and another nine appointed directly by the outgoing government and the Supreme Court. In addition, former presidents of the Republic who filled that position for six uninterrupted years are ex officio life senators. Eduardo Frei, president until March 2000, is the only current life senator under this provision, the former military dictator Gen. Augusto Pinochet having resigned his senatorial seat on 20 August 2002. Constitutional amendments which came into force in 2005 provide for the election of the entire Senate. The current non-elected members will retire on 10 March 2006.

Profile of the President:

Ricardo **LAGOS** Escobar

Ricardo Lagos is an eminent academic, who has written five texts on Chilean politics and economics since 1969. He founded the Party for Democracy (Partido por la Democracia—PPD) in 1987 as a vehicle for the outlawed Socialist Party (Partido Socialista—PS). He was elected president in 1999–2000 as the candidate of the Coalition of Parties for Democracy (Concertación de Partidos por la Democracia—CPD), which includes the PPD and the PS. He was inaugurated on 11 March.

Ricardo Lagos Escobar was born on 2 March 1938 in Santiago. He attended the law school of the University of Chile in Santiago from 1955 to 1960, and was president of the students' union there. He went to Duke University in North Carolina, USA, in 1961 to study for a doctorate in economics. On returning to

Chile Lagos was appointed a professor of the University of Chile, eventually becoming its secretary-general in 1969. While remaining a prominent academic in the field of social sciences throughout the 1970s, in 1971 he held his first political post when he was sent as ambassador to the UN. In the same year he married Luisa Durán de la Fuente. They have two children each from previous marriages, and one daughter born in 1975.

Following the military coup which overthrew and killed the socialist president Salvador Allende in 1973 and installed Gen. Augusto Pinochet as head of state, Lagos spent some years abroad as a visiting academic, first in Buenos Aires in Argentina, and then at the University of North Carolina in Chapel Hill, USA. In 1982 he sat on the executive committee of the PS, and was president between 1983 and 1984 of the Democratic Alliance, a coalition of opponents of the Pinochet dictatorship. In 1987, following the legalization of non-Marxist political parties, he founded the PPD and, as part of the CPD, he canvassed the nation in support of the 'no' campaign against Pinochet's confirmation for a new term as president.

The 'no' vote won in the plebiscite held in October 1988 and Pinochet was forced to hold elections in 1989. The Christian Democratic Party (Partido Demócrata Cristiano—PDC) candidate, Patricio Aylwin Azócar, became president and Lagos's PPD was included in the ruling CPD coalition. In the legislative elections the PPD became the third-largest party in Congress despite a residual anti-left bias in the electoral law. President Aylwin appointed Lagos as minister of education in 1990 where he worked until 1992 to improve equality of access and raise teaching standards.

Lagos ran for president in 1993 against the official CPD candidate, Eduardo Frei of the PDC, who went on to a convincing win. Under Frei, Lagos was given the portfolio of the public works ministry which he ran from 1994 to 1998, investing around US$2,000 million in various projects designed to reinvigorate Chile's deprived sectors.

In 1999 Lagos stood once again as the PPD's presidential candidate and received the endorsement of the CPD. A close-fought election in December led to a runoff against the conservative Independent Democratic Union candidate, Joaquín Lavín, on 16 January 2000. Victory for Lagos made him the country's first socialist president since Allende.

CHINA

Full name: The People's Republic of China.

Leadership structure: The head of state is a president, indirectly elected by the National People's Congress (NPC). The president's term of office is five years, renewable once only. The head of government is the premier, who is responsible to the NPC. The State Council is elected by the NPC on the nomination of the premier.

President:	Jiang Zemin	27 March 1993—15 March 2003
	HU Jintao	Since 15 March 2003
Premier:	Zhu Rongji	17 March 1998—16 March 2003
	WEN Jiabao	Since 16 March 2003

General Secretary of the Communist Party of China (CPC):

Jiang Zemin	24 June 1989—15 Nov. 2002
HU Jintao	Since 15 Nov. 2002

Legislature: The legislature is unicameral. The sole chamber, the NPC or National People's Congress (Quanguo Renmin Daibiao Dahui), has 2,979 members, indirectly elected for a five-year term.

Profile of the President:

HU Jintao

Hu Jintao joined the Communist Party of China (CPC) while still a student, and quickly worked through the ranks to become leader of its youth wing, the Communist Youth League (CYL), the youngest ever alternate member of its central committee and the youngest ever provincial governor. It was no surprise when he took over from Jiang Zemin as CPC general secretary in 2002 and also succeeded him as president of China in 2003. He is closely identified with China's economic reforms, but cautious about any equivalent political liberalization.

Hu Jintao was born in December 1942 in Jixi in the eastern province of Anhui. He moved to Taizhou, in neighbouring Jiangsu province, in about 1948 after the death of his mother, and was raised by his great aunt Liu Bingxia. Hu travelled to

Beijing in the 1960s to study hydraulic engineering at the respected Tsinghua University, where he joined the CPC, met his future wife Liu Yongqing (with whom he has two children), and continued to work as a researcher and political instructor after graduating.

The Cultural Revolution (1966–76) targeted the new political class and Hu was sent to rural Gansu province in 1968 to be 're-educated' as a farm labourer. He was rehabilitated later that year and rejoined party work as party secretary at the engineering bureau of the ministry of water resources and electrical power. In 1974 he became secretary of the Gansu provincial construction commission and developed ties with senior CPC member Song Ping. Song was to play a major part in abetting Hu's subsequent rapid climb up the party hierarchy.

In 1982 Hu became the youngest ever alternate member of the CPC central committee, at age 39, and joined the secretariat of the Gansu CYL. The following year he returned to Beijing to work at the headquarters of the generally reformist CYL and became head of its secretariat in 1984. He left the CYL and headed back out west to Guizhou province in 1985 as the youngest ever provincial party chief, and cultivated a reputation as a compassionate reformer. While there he was also made a full member of the CPC central committee in 1987.

Pushed further west, Hu was made the first nonmilitary party chief of Tibet in 1988. He dropped his tolerant attitude in his new position when, within a month of his arrival, separatist activists began organizing bigger and more violent demonstrations. In March 1989 over 40 Tibetans were killed by police during rioting and Hu organized the deployment of 100,000 troops to suppress the separatists. His ability to maintain order in Tibet thereafter, even during Beijing's Tiananmen Square demonstrations in June, earned him special notice within the central CPC machinery. He was the first provincial leader to express support for the government's actions. In 1990 he returned once more to Beijing, claiming altitude sickness, and began to build the most powerful support network in the party.

China's then paramount leader Deng Xiaoping nominated Hu in 1992 to organize the 14th CPC congress and Hu replaced Song as a member of the politburo's standing committee—the party's highest organ. Over the course of the 1990s he moved into a number of high-profile positions and worked closely with President Jiang Zemin on his largely reformist agenda. He was appointed vice president in March 1998 and vice chairman of the central military commission in September 1999. However, he made a point of not disclosing his own political leanings.

By 2002 he was being identified worldwide as China's president-in-waiting. It surprised no one when on 15 November, at the conclusion of the 16th CPC congress, Hu was appointed general secretary of the party and recognized as the leading figure in the politburo. Four months later, on 15 March 2003, he was appointed president of China as part of a new generation of leaders selected by the National People's Congress. Outgoing president Jiang Zemin retained the chairmanship of the central military commission for a further 18 months, but the handover was completed to Hu Jintao's benefit when he took on this post too on 8 March 2005. Meanwhile his pre-eminence in the foreign policy field was confirmed by his assumption in June 2003 of the chair of the party's Leading Group on Foreign Affairs.

A rare but important indication of Hu Jintao's cautious attitude to political change came in his speech on 15 September 2004 on the eve of the central committee's annual meeting. Hu warned that China would never "blindly" copy other countries' political systems, implicitly rejecting Western-style pluralism, but pledged to improve and strengthen checks and balances on single-party rule.

Profile of the Premier of the State Council:

WEN Jiabao

Wen Jiabao, a geologist by training, became premier of the State Council of China on 16 March 2003. A strong administrator and technocrat, Wen was renowned as vice premier for his ability to convert complex issues into simple policy recommendations. While in charge of the agriculture portfolio, Wen had become well known among rural cadres, who had been relatively neglected by the previous emphasis on the rapidly industrializing coastal regions. Along with President Hu Jintao, Wen has positioned himself as something of a champion of the rural poor and has begun to remove the tax burden from impecunious small farmers.

Wen Jiabao was born in the province of Tianjin in September 1942 and joined the Communist Party of China (CPC) at the age of 22, after graduating from the Beijing Institute of Geology with a degree in geological structure. He then went on to postgraduate study at the institute, eventually taking up his first technician's post in 1968 with the geomechanics survey team in Gansu province in north-central China. He also became the team's political instructor and head of the Gansu provincial geological bureau's political section. Wen is married to Zhang Peili, also a geologist. The couple have one son and one daughter.

By the end of his stay in Gansu, Wen had worked his way up to deputy director of the bureau, and in 1982 he transferred to Beijing, where he worked in the ministry of geology and mineral resources, soon becoming vice minister. In 1985 Wen was appointed deputy director of the general office of the CPC central committee, and the following year was promoted to be director of the general office, where he stayed until 1993. Between 1993 and 1997, Wen remained a member of the party secretariat and an alternate politburo member, but his exact responsibilities remained vague, and he was not promoted as a full politburo member until 1997.

In 1998 Wen was entrusted with the vice-premier post that the deeply unpopular Qiang Chunyun forfeited—some believe that Wen had been covering for Qiang for some time. Wen quickly took on an extremely broad range of responsibilities, including rural issues. He was also put in charge of disaster relief, and during the floods of late summer 1998 Wen attracted substantial favourable publicity as the leader of relief efforts. He was widely regarded as the most capable of the vice premiers, and the one with the best relations with subordinates and colleagues. During the 16th party congress in late 2002, he was appointed to the standing committee of the politburo, and as premier-designate.

On taking office as premier in March 2003, Wen immediately moved to reduce the number of ministerial commissions from 29 to 21—following the example of his predecessor, Zhu Rongji, who had cut the number from 50. He then moved to shift the focus of financial reform away from the stock market and towards the banking system to try to create a stable and secure financial system to facilitate long-term domestic investment. Both these moves shifted oversight away from the National People's Congress, allowing decisions to be taken quickly without the need for enabling legislation. Wen has also, along with President Hu Jintao, set himself up as a champion of the rural poor. He has made a point of visiting centres for the rehabilitation of drug addicts, and in 2003 he became the first Chinese official to publicly address the issue of AIDS.

COLOMBIA

Full name: The Republic of Colombia.

Leadership structure: The head of state is a president, directly elected by universal adult suffrage. The president's term of office is four years. Under the 1991 Constitution, the president was not permitted to stand for a second consecutive term, but a bill passed by the House of Representatives on 30 November 2004 would allow the present incumbent to stand for re-election in 2006 once it was approved by the Constitutional Court. The head of government is the president, who is responsible to parliament. The cabinet is appointed by the president.

President:	Andrés Pastrana Arango	7 Aug. 1998—7 Aug. 2002
	Álvaro **URIBE** Vélez	Since 7 Aug. 2002

Legislature: The legislature, the Congress (Congreso), is bicameral. The lower chamber, the House of Representatives (Cámara de Representantes), has 166 members, directly elected for a four-year term. The upper chamber, the Senate (Senado), has 102 members, directly elected for a four-year term, including two senators representing indigenous people in specific areas.

Profile of the President:

Álvaro **URIBE** Vélez

Álvaro Uribe Vélez is an independent but is associated with right-wing politics and accused by his detractors of intimate ties to right-wing paramilitaries and the infamous Medellín drugs cartel. A career politician in the region of his birth, Antioquia, Uribe served as both a senator for the region and as its governor before successfully being elected president of Colombia in 2002. He has pushed through a constitutional amendment to allow him to stand for a second term in 2006, in order to provide stability and consolidate progress against rebel groups.

Álvaro Uribe Vélez was born on 4 July 1952 in Medellín. His father is popularly believed to have been associated with the Medellín cartel and was the subject of unsuccessful extradition requests from the USA. Uribe is married to Lina Moreno and they have two sons. He graduated in law from the University of Antioquia and began work in the public works department of the Medellín city council in 1976.

The following year Uribe moved up to national government level as secretary-general of the labour ministry before being appointed director of civil aeronautics in the Colombian aviation agency in 1980. During his time at the agency he is accused of corruption, particularly of providing the Medellín cartel with private airstrips. Four years later he was appointed mayor of Medellín. His detractors accuse him of gaining influence through illegal channels, claiming that he received the post after his father made significant donations to the president of the day. Medellín was renowned worldwide at the time as the base for the powerful drugs cartel of the same name, which was then headed by Pablo Escobar. Uribe was publicly linked to Escobar several times, but was still sufficiently popular to be elected to the Senate in 1986.

During two consecutive terms in the upper chamber Uribe proved consistently popular with both the public and his colleagues, polling among the top five in opinion polls and even winning the Best Senator award in 1993. That same year he studied for a postgraduate course in management and conflict resolution at Harvard University, USA.

On leaving the Senate, Uribe was appointed governor of the Antioquia province in 1995 for a one-year, nonrenewable term. His tenure has been shrouded in controversy. On the one hand he is praised for slashing government spending in the province, and providing an increase in education and welfare payments. He is also credited with greatly improving the region's road network. On the other hand he was the patron of a number of right-wing paramilitary groups under his Rural Vigilance Committee scheme. The resultant Convivir groups were condemned by Amnesty International among others as government-sanctioned death squads. They were scrapped by the national government in 1997 at the end of Uribe's governorship. It is alleged that the Convivir gunmen simply shifted their allegiance to the United Self-Defence Forces of Colombia (Autodefensas Unidas de Colombia—AUC) which was responsible for an escalation in the country's civil conflict until its official disbandment in 2002. From 1998 to 1999 Uribe worked as an associate professor at Oxford University, UK, on a British Council fellowship.

Uribe returned to high-profile political life in his campaign for the 2002 presidential elections. In his bid to replace the right-of-centre incumbent Andrés Pastrana Arango, he pledged to abandon the previous peace negotiations with the powerful left-wing rebel groups, and to revitalize the government's campaign with massive injections of funds into the defence and police budgets. He won the election with an unprecedented first-round victory, claiming 53% of the vote. Many observers predicted that his rise signalled the end of the country's traditional two-party system.

Uribe's inauguration on 7 August 2002 was met, as promised by left-wing guerrillas, with a concerted bombing campaign in Bogotá. Thirteen people were killed and Uribe introduced a state of emergency. Under the decree greater powers were soon granted to the police force. As president Uribe is accused of maintaining his links with right-wing paramilitaries while abandoning previous connections to the narcotics industry in favour of a close relationship with the USA. He is a keen supporter of the US-backed Plan Colombia and has welcomed an intensification of the USA's military campaign against narcotics growers, whose crops often provide the rebels with their source of income. He has held negotiations with the right-wing AUC, but has launched strong military action against the National Liberation Army (Ejército de Liberación Nacional—ELN) and the Revolutionary Armed Forces of Colombia (Fuerzas Armadas Revolucionarias de Colombia—FARC). However, in 2004 he did offer talks with the ELN, if it called a ceasefire, in an attempt to split the rebel alliance. FARC issued an order for Uribe's assassination, though he has already survived more than ten attempts. 2005 saw the continuance of the military offensive against FARC and a new law on demobilization of the AUC, controversially allowing its leaders to escape trial for the group's atrocities.

The national plan during his term in office, entitled 'Toward a Community State', aims to extend nationwide the initiatives that he set up at state level during his governorship. It emphasizes public participation and decentralization of security, efficient use of government resources, private provision of social welfare, and encourages a system of government informers among the public to tackle the left-wing guerrillas. Despite Uribe's high approval ratings, a package of reforms needed to meet the fiscal targets of the International Monetary Fund (IMF) were rejected by referendum in October 2003. Several ministers subsequently resigned to give Uribe a 'free hand' in reorganizing the reforms.

In April 2004 Uribe launched a campaign for a constitutional amendment to allow him to run for a second term in 2006, contending that the country needed stability in leadership to follow through the advances made on security and the economy. It was finally passed by the House of Representatives in November 2004, but still needs to be approved by the Constitutional Court, whose ruling is expected in late 2005.

COMOROS

Full name: The Union of the Comoros.

Leadership structure: Under the 2002 Constitution the Union president is elected from each of the three islands in turn, for a four-year term. Each island also has its own regional president. The head of government of the Union is the president. Each island's president is also head of its government.

President:	Col. Assoumani Azali (seized power 30 April 1999)	6 May 1999—21 Jan. 2002
	Hamada Madi 'Boléro' (interim)	21 Jan. 2002—26 May 2002
	Col. Assoumani **AZALI**	Since 26 May 2002
Prime Minister:	Bianrifi Tarmidi	1 Dec. 1999—11 Dec. 2000
	Hamada Madi 'Boléro' (post then abolished)	11 Dec. 2000—15 April 2002

Legislature: Under the 2002 Constitution, the islands each have a local parliament, elected for the first time in March 2004. The Union has a legislative assembly, the Assembly of the Union (Assemblée de l'Union), with 33 members, five members appointed by each of the three local parliaments and 18 elected through direct universal suffrage for a five-year term.

Profile of the President:

Col. Assoumani **AZALI**

Assoumani Azali has a military background and, like many previous heads of state in the Comoros, assumed power in a coup, in 1999. He justified his action on the grounds that the government was not taking adequate measures to control the current unrest stemming from separatist demands by the island of Nzwani. Having framed a new constitution for the newly entitled Union of the Comoros, Azali was declared its president and sworn in on 26 May 2002, after a complex process of elections in each of the Union's main constituent islands.

Assoumani Azali was born in Mitsoudjé on the island of Njazidja (formerly Grande Comore) on 1 January 1959 into a Muslim family of nine children. He went to school in Moroni, becoming president of the student union. From 1979 to

120

1981 he attended the Royal Military Academy in Morocco, before joining the Comoran Armed Forces. Spells of training at French military schools enabled him to rise rapidly through the ranks and he held various detachments, at the ministry of the interior handling immigration and at the office of the president handling military affairs. He was appointed provisional chief of staff in 1989 and the following year became head of the reorganized Comoran Defence Force, holding this post until 1996 and leading the action to put down the 1992 coup attempt and partial army mutiny. In 1996 he became the first Comoran to attend the elite Collège Interarmées de Défense in Paris and on his return he became involved in the Comoran army training schools. During this time he was promoted to colonel. He is married to Anbar Azali.

Unrest broke out on Nzwani (formerly known as Anjouan) in 1997, and the prolonged crisis led Azali to mount a bloodless coup in April 1999 to overthrow President Tadjidine Ben Saïd Massoundi and the elected government. Under a new constitutional charter Azali was declared head of state and government and commander-in-chief of the armed forces, and he also assumed legislative authority. Initially he announced his intention to stay in power for only one year, pending new constitutional arrangements.

The basis for the constitutional changes was the Antananarivo agreement, a document drawn up at a conference held in Antananarivo (Madagascar) in April 1999 (before the coup), providing for greater autonomy for the islands of Nzwani and Mwali (formerly known as Mohéli) within a new Union of the Comoros. The unrest which provided the occasion for Azali's coup broke out when the Nzwani delegates refused to sign the accord, which continued to be obstructed by the separatists there, who went on to form a 'government of national unity' on the island, and held a referendum in January 2000 to demonstrate support for full Nzwani independence.

The problem appeared intractable with Azali backtracking on a pledge to return the country to civilian rule by April 2000. However, with the backing of the Organization of African Unity (the precursor to the African Union), an accord known as the Fomboni Declaration was signed in August 2000. It took a further 18 months before Azali finally agreed to step down as 'president' of the Comoros on 21 January 2002 in order to run for the new post of union president in March–April. A long process of elections, annulments and political manoeuvring was finally resolved on 26 May when Azali was inaugurated as the new Union president. Also elected in the first half of 2002 were the regional presidents of each of the three Comoran islands who quickly sought to assert their powers in the new structure.

Authorities on Nzwani provocatively lowered the Union flag on 10 January 2003 in protest over Azali's 'dictatorial' decree outlining the role of internal security forces in the country, issued even though a debate on the subject was still in progress. The following month Njazidja's cabinet chief and two ministers were arrested amid rumours of an alleged coup plot. Azali postponed legislative elections indefinitely, and international arbitrators arrived, led by South African president Thabo Mbeki. They secured a deal in December to hold the elections in April 2004. Azali's supporters won only one-third of the seats, while most of the rest were secured by parties representing the individual islands and demanding greater autonomy.

DEMOCRATIC REPUBLIC OF THE CONGO

Full name: The Democratic Republic of the Congo.

Leadership structure: The head of state is the president. The succession to office of the current incumbent, Maj.-Gen. Joseph Kabila, was approved unanimously by parliament on 24 January 2001, eight days after the assassination of his father Laurent Kabila. On 26 January Joseph Kabila was sworn into office as president. He was inaugurated for a further two-year term on 7 April 2003 under the terms of the Final Act to end the civil war, heading an interim government with four vice presidents from the major factions until democratic elections are held. The head of government is the president, who appoints the cabinet.

| *President*: | Laurent Kabila (seized power on 17 May 1997) | 29 May 1997—16 Jan. 2001 |
| | Joseph **KABILA** (interim from 17 Jan. 2001) | Since 26 Jan. 2001 |

Legislature: A Constituent and Legislative Assembly was inaugurated on 21 August 2000. It has 300 members appointed by the president.

Profile of the President:

Joseph **KABILA**

Joseph Kabila was trained as a military officer in Rwanda and China. When he succeeded his assassinated father in January 2001 he raised hopes of revitalizing the country's neglected peace process, but a resolution of the complex regional conflict centred on his Democratic Republic of the Congo (DRC) did not emerge until late 2002.

Joseph Kabila was born on 4 December 1971 in Hewa Bora, in the eastern province of South Kivu, to an ethnic Tutsi woman from Rwanda while his father was in exile in Tanzania as an opponent of the Mobutu regime. He is believed to be the eldest of ten children fathered by Laurent Kabila, almost all born to different mothers. Joseph received his early education in Tanzania and went on to study in neighbouring Uganda. He began his military training in Rwanda in around 1995. He is married to Sandrine, daughter of Denis Sassou-Nguesso, the president of the Republic of Congo; they have one daughter.

As his father began to press for an armed overthrow of the Mobutu regime in what had become known as Zaïre, Joseph Kabila entered the country for the first time in 1996 as a commander in his father's rebel army. Gaining support from almost all regional powers, the rebels and their allies swept across the country and entered Kinshasa in 1997. Laurent was installed as the new president of the renamed DRC and Joseph was sent to China to receive a further six months of military education. On his return his father promoted him to major-general and placed him at the head of the Congolese armed forces.

Initial hopes of a swift return to democracy were thwarted, however, and Laurent Kabila soon lost the support of his Rwandan and Ugandan allies. As army chief of staff, and with the experience gained in the 1996–97 conflict, Joseph Kabila was despatched to the eastern front line and led the campaign there until 2001. During this time Joseph Kabila, who has the reputation of being painfully shy, remained firmly out of the international limelight, which was entirely taken up by his charismatic father. While his supporters applauded his command as instrumental in holding back the rebel advance, his detractors suggest that any victories by government forces were won mostly with the use of foreign assistance, and that Joseph would not arrive in 'liberated' areas until after they had fallen to his troops.

On 16 January 2001 Laurent Kabila was shot by a bodyguard at his offices in Kinshasa. The authorities denied initial reports while Joseph was rushed back to the capital. On the following day he was overwhelmingly accepted as interim leader, and was appointed president straight after his father's funeral. Analysts at the time suggested that he was a wholly unsuitable choice as head of state, pointing to his less-than-glorious career on the front line, his lack of political experience and even his alleged Rwandan heritage. However, he worked quickly to repair the damage done by his increasingly authoritarian father and talked the talk of a leader committed to achieving peace. He met with his Rwandan counterpart within days and UN-brokered peace talks were under way by February. Political parties were unbanned and the Congo River was reopened to commercial traffic in August.

Nevertheless, despite promising to hold fresh elections as soon as all foreign troops had left Congolese soil, Kabila then let the impetus of his first few months slowly slip away. A long-awaited inter-Congolese dialogue between warring factions was suspended within days of opening. Over the course of 2002, however, pressure for an end to the conflict finally seemed to be having an effect. Kabila met with his Rwandan and Ugandan counterparts, and oversaw continuing negotiations with rebel factions. Tens of thousands of Rwandan, Ugandan and Zimbabwean troops began withdrawing in August. Meanwhile, Kabila secured aid and the cancellation of debt for his war-ravaged country.

A power-sharing peace deal initially touted in April was signed on 16 December 2002. A transitional constitution was agreed in March 2003, and the Final Act was signed on 2 April. Under the plan, Kabila was confirmed as president with four major factions represented by vice presidents for a transitional period. Rebel groups were allowed to form themselves into political parties, militias were to be disarmed or incorporated into a new national army, and elections were to be held in 2005.

The transitional parliament adopted a new constitution in May 2005, decentralizing power and limiting the authority of the presidency; a referendum is set for November. Elections scheduled for June were postponed, following delays in voter registration. Kabila has pledged that they will be held in 2005, but the deadline under the peace plan is mid-2006.

REPUBLIC OF THE CONGO

Full name: The Republic of the Congo.

Leadership structure: The head of state under the 2002 Constitution is a president, directly elected by universal adult suffrage for a term of seven years. The head of government under the 2002 Constitution is the president, who appoints the cabinet. The post of prime minister was reinstated in 2005, having not been filled since 1997.

President:	Denis **SASSOU-NGUESSO**	Since 25 Oct. 1997
	(in de facto control from 15 Oct. 1997)	
Prime Minister:	Isidore **MVOUBA**	Since 7 Jan. 2005
	(minister of state in charge of co-ordination	
	of government action from 18 Aug. 2002)	

Legislature: Under the 2002 Constitution, the legislature, the Parliament (Parlement), is bicameral. The lower chamber, the National Assembly (Assemblée Nationale), has 137 members, directly elected for a five-year term. The upper chamber, the Senate (Sénat), has 66 members, indirectly elected for a six-year term (one-third of members every two years).

Profile of the President:

Denis **SASSOU-NGUESSO**

Gen. Denis Sassou-Nguesso, who returned to power in 1997, had dominated the Congolese political scene prior to the country's first multiparty elections in 1992. He was a prominent member of the military committee which took over the running of the then Marxist regime in 1977, and was president from 1979 to 1992, under a single-party structure. Defeated in the 1992 elections, he took his party (and its militia) into opposition. His return to power was assisted by Angolan forces in a decisive military offensive which ended five months of effective civil war. He subsequently won presidential elections in 2002.

A member of the Mboshi ethnic group, Denis Sassou-Nguesso was born in 1943 in Oyo in the territory then known as the Middle Congo, which was part of French Equatorial Africa. He joined the army of the newly independent Republic of the Congo and as a young junior officer he supported the self-declared Marxist regime established after a military coup in 1968. He has been married twice and is the father of seven children; his eldest daughter is married to Gabonese president Omar Bongo and another is married to Joseph Kabila, president of the Democratic Republic of the Congo.

Regarded in the 1970s as strongly pro-Soviet, Sassou-Nguesso headed the political police from 1974, and in late 1975, when he had reached the rank of major, he was appointed to a nine-member ruling Council of State. The military leadership sought to tighten its grip on the ruling Congolese Labour Party (Parti Congolais du Travail—PCT) after the assassination of the president, Maj. Ngouabi, in March 1977. Ngouabi's successor, Gen. Yhombi-Opango, set up a military committee in which Sassou-Nguesso was first vice president 'responsible for co-ordinating PCT activities' as well as minister of defence.

Using his party role as a power base, Sassou-Nguesso was within two years able to challenge Yhombi-Opango for power, forcing him to resign when he criticized the PCT in February 1979. A newly formed PCT presidium thereupon appointed Sassou-Nguesso as interim president. He was confirmed in this post, as well as becoming party chairman, at a special PCT congress on 27 March.

Although the single-party structure ensured Sassou-Nguesso's unopposed re-election at five-year intervals (in July 1984 and 1989), economic difficulties led his regime to turn increasingly away from state socialism and towards free-market policies which could satisfy the criteria for attracting International Monetary Fund (IMF) support. In October 1990 an extraordinary party congress (at which Sassou-Nguesso was elected president of a new central committee) formally abandoned Marxism-Leninism and endorsed the creation of a multiparty political system.

A national conference was convened from February 1991, and by June of that year it had secured the role of interim head of government for the prime minister rather than the president. Legislative elections in June–July 1992 established the recently formed Pan-African Union for Social Democracy (Union Panafricaine pour la Démocratie Sociale—UPADS) as the leading party, and when presidential elections were held in August 1992, Sassou-Nguesso as the PCT candidate was knocked out in the first-round ballot, finishing third with under 17% of the vote. Conceding defeat with what he claimed to be "serenity", he thereupon called on his supporters to vote for the UPADS leader Pascal Lissouba, who won the runoff and was sworn in on 31 August.

In the five years of the Lissouba regime, however, Sassou-Nguesso maintained a high profile within a series of alliances that combined parliamentary opposition with extraparliamentary protest and militia activity. Talks on a possible all-party coalition, and the integration of rival militias into the national army, produced a short-lived agreement in late 1994 on ending hostilities, and a similarly unimplemented peace pact a year later. With the approach of presidential elections due in July 1997, Lissouba tried unsuccessfully to disarm the PCT militia, and large-scale fighting broke out in the capital, Brazzaville, in June of that year. Attempts at external mediation failed to resolve the conflict, and were rendered irrelevant when a successful offensive by Sassou-Nguesso's forces, backed by Angola, left him in full control by mid-October.

Sassou-Nguesso was inaugurated as president on 25 October 1997. The following month, when his takeover was still not widely accepted internationally, his position was boosted by his long meeting with French President Jacques Chirac (with whom he shares membership of a French Masonic order) at a francophone summit in Hanoi, Viet Nam. An executive National Transitional Council was created in January 1998, but fighting and violence continued throughout the year, culminating in an inconclusive battle for Brazzaville itself in December. Sassou-Nguesso pursued talks with rival militias but remained at loggerheads with their key leaders, Lissouba and his former prime minister Bernard Kolélas.

By late 1999 a peace deal had been forged and the process of rehabilitation had begun. The civil war was officially declared over in February 2000 and a new draft constitution was proffered by Sassou-Nguesso in November that year, under which the president would hold considerable executive power as head of government. The document was approved by 84% in a referendum on 20 January 2002, and Sassou-Nguesso went on to win 90% of the vote in presidential elections on 10 March, but only after the main opposition candidate, André Milongo, had pulled out of the poll and called for a boycott. Less than a month later the fragile peace was shattered with renewed fighting between government forces and so-called Ninja rebels in the turbulent southern Pool region. Thousands of people were displaced and fighting spilled over into the outskirts of Brazzaville once again. A peace deal was signed in March 2003, though sporadic attacks have continued. The disarmament process stalled in 2005 when the leader of the rebels demanded his group's inclusion in a national unity government.

Profile of the Prime Minister:

Isidore MVOUBA

A railway engineer, Isidore Mvouba is a member of the ruling Congolese Labour Party (Parti Congolais du Travail—PCT). A close ally of President Denis Sassou-Nguesso, he has directed two election campaigns and held cabinet posts since 1997. He was chosen for the new post of minister of state and co-ordinator of government action in August 2002, and appointed to the reinstated post of prime minister in January 2005.

Isidore Mvouba was born in 1954 in Kindamba in the Pool region in the south of the country. He trained as a railway engineer and worked from 1977 for the Congo Ocean Railway. He joined the PCT and rose to become a member of its politburo and head of the youth movement.

Having directed President Denis Sassou-Nguesso's unsuccessful election campaign in 1992, Mvouba rejected an offer from the successful candidate Pascal

Lissouba to become minister of trade. Following Sassou-Nguesso's takeover of power in late 1997, Mvouba was appointed cabinet director and permanent undersecretary at the presidency. In a reshuffle in January 1999 he became minister of transport, civil aviation and merchant navy.

Campaign director again for Sassou-Nguesso in the March 2002 presidential elections, Mvouba retained his existing ministerial responsibilities, but ceased to be head of the president's office, when he was nominated to fill the new role of minister of state and co-ordinator of government action in August 2002. In his new capacity it was Mvouba who formally presented the newly reshuffled ministerial team to parliament on 18 August. He was awarded the post of prime minister on 7 January 2005, after it had been vacant since Sassou-Nguesso's 1997 coup.

Mvouba's prominence is particularly significant in view of the problems of violent conflict in his native Pool region in 2002; a peace deal was signed with the so-called Ninja rebels in 2003, but disarmament was stalling in 2005 when the rebel leader demanded his group's inclusion in a national unity government.

COSTA RICA

Full name: The Republic of Costa Rica.

Leadership structure: The head of state is a president, directly elected by universal adult suffrage. The president's term of office is four years. The head of government is the president, who appoints the cabinet.

President: Miguel Ángel Rodríguez Echeverría   8 May 1998—8 May 2002

              Abel **PACHECO** de la Espriella   Since 8 May 2002

Legislature: The legislature is unicameral. The sole chamber, the Legislative Assembly (Asamblea Legislativa), has 57 members, directly elected for a four-year term.

Profile of the President:

Abel **PACHECO** de la Espriella

Abel Pacheco is a leading figure in the right-wing Social Christian Unity Party (Partido Unidad Social Cristiana—PUSC). Although trained as a psychiatrist he achieved fame in Costa Rica as a television commentator and writer. He was elected president in an unprecedented second-round vote held on 7 April 2002, and took office on 8 May.

Abel de Jesús Pacheco de la Espriella was born in the capital, San José, on 22 December 1933. His family moved to Mexico when he was still young and he graduated in medicine from the Independent National University there before studying psychiatry at Louisiana State University in the USA. He has been married twice, firstly to Mexican Elsa Muñoz, with whom he had three daughters and two sons, and secondly in 1974 to Leila Rodríguez, a former Miss Costa Rica, with whom he has one son.

In the 1960s Pacheco worked at the National Psychiatric Hospital in San José, becoming director. He later resigned claiming that the hospital provided insufficient care to its patients. From medicine Pacheco moved into television. His first notable documentary *National Legends and Traditions* won him a prize from the University of Latin America. Later he became a well-known face on Costa Rican television as a political and social commentator. Other career directions included ventures in commerce and, most notably, writing. He has had seven books of poetry and short stories published, and has received a National Prize for his works.

Pacheco's centre-right conservatism and popular renown enabled him to become leader of the PUSC in 1996, the same year he was elected to the Legislative Assembly, representing a constituency in San José. After recovering from a minor stroke in 2000, he was selected to represent the party in presidential elections in 2002, which, for the first time ever, required a second round to determine a clear result. In the runoff poll, marked by an unprecedentedly low turnout, Pacheco won with 58% of the vote against the candidate from the National Liberation Party, Rolando Araya. He took office on 8 May.

Despite his conservatism, Pacheco's campaign pledged not to privatize key state-owned industries. His anti-corruption platform soon became engulfed by successive corruption scandals involving his party, forcing the resignations of several ministers and leading to charges against his three immediate presidential predecessors, two of whom were PUSC members.

During his term in office, he has pursued several environmental programmes. Good relations with the USA saw Pacheco voice support for the 2003 invasion of Iraq, though the Constitutional Court in 2004 ruled that Costa Rica could not be listed in the "Coalition of the Willing" due to its constitutional neutrality.

On the international stage Pacheco has also been a leading voice for a Central American Free Trade Agreement. However, the details of the agreement came unstuck on the issue of Costa Rica's nationalized telecommunications services, with the USA insisting on full privatization. When Costa Rica decided to pull out of the agreement altogether, the USA relented and settled for a part-privatization, though even this has caused divisions within Pacheco's government and massive strikes, with his popularity suffering for breaking this key campaign pledge.

CÔTE D'IVOIRE

Full name: The Republic of Côte d'Ivoire.

Leadership structure: The head of state is a directly elected president serving a five-year term, renewable once only. Under the 2000 Constitution the head of government is the president, who appoints the prime minister, and also appoints the cabinet on the proposal of the prime minister.

President:	Gen. Robert Guéï	4 Jan. 2000—26 Oct. 2000
	(seized power on 25 Dec. 1999)	
	Laurent **GBAGBO**	Since 26 Oct. 2000
Prime Minister:	*vacant*	25 Dec. 1999—18 May 2000
	Seydou Elimane Diarra	18 May 2000—26 Oct. 2000
	Pascal Affi N'Guessan	26 Oct. 2000—10 Feb. 2003
	Seydou Elimane **DIARRA**	Since 10 Feb. 2003

Legislature: The legislature is unicameral. The National Assembly (Assemblée Nationale) has 225 members, directly elected for a five-year term.

Profile of the President:

Laurent **GBAGBO**

Laurent Gbagbo was prominent in opposition politics in the 1980s and 1990s before eventually being elected president in 2000. During the early part of his period in opposition he spent six years as a political refugee in France. He stood against the long-established President Félix Houphouët-Boigny in the presidential elections of October 1990, when his party, the Ivorian Popular Front (Front Populaire Ivoirien—FPI), challenged the official outcome awarding Houphouët-Boigny over 80% of the vote. His term in office has been marred by civil war; a peace plan in 2003 has set a path towards fresh elections.

Laurent Gbagbo was born on 31 May 1945 at Gagnoa, in the south of the country. He studied at the Petit Séminaire St-Dominique Savio in Gagnoa, before moving to the Lycée Classique in Abidjan from 1962, receiving his baccalauréat in 1965. He went to university in Abidjan, before moving to the Université de Lyon, France, to study classics and French. He returned to Côte d'Ivoire to study history in 1968, then went back to France to complete his studies at the Sorbonne with a master's degree in history in 1970. In the same year he became a teacher of geography and history at the Lycée Classique in Abidjan, and divorced his first wife, with whom he had two children, in order to marry Simone Ehivet, a Catholic divorcee with three children; they now have seven children altogether. Simone is an active figure in the FPI and leads the party in the National Assembly.

In March 1971 Gbagbo was arrested and sent to military camps in Akoué, Séguéla and Bouaké. On his release in January 1973 he was appointed to the education directorate, where he worked until 1977. He resumed his history studies in Paris in 1979, and the following year he was elected director of the Institut d'Histoire.

In 1982 Gbagbo created the FPI, before going into exile in France, where he was granted political asylum in 1985. He returned to Côte d'Ivoire for the FPI Constitutional Congress, at which he was elected the party's secretary-general. He stood in the presidential elections of October 1990 as the FPI candidate against incumbent President Houphouët-Boigny. When Houphouët-Boigny was awarded over 80% of the vote, the FPI challenged the result.

In November 1990 Gbagbo was elected deputy to the National Assembly for Ouragahio, and was the president of the FPI parliamentary group between 1990 and 1995. He was among over 100 people arrested in February 1992 in the wake of a violent anti-government protest in the capital. He was convicted under a new presidential decree making political leaders liable for any offences committed during demonstrations by their supporters, and was given a two-year prison sentence and a fine. In June 1995 he was again nominated FPI presidential candidate, but did not run as the FPI boycotted the election in protest over the electoral code in a vain attempt to get the elections postponed. In 1996 he became president of the FPI.

When President Henri Konan Bédié was overthrown in December 1999 in a coup led by Gen. Robert Guéï, it was anticipated that Alassane Ouattara would become president. Bédié had tried to ban Ouattara from standing as a presidential candidate on the grounds of the status of his Ivorian nationality. By October 2000, however, Gen. Guéï had ceased to support Ouattara, and the main contenders in the election were Guéï and Gbagbo. After the poll both claimed victory, but a popular outcry forced Guéï to concede defeat. Gbagbo had not only favoured the banning of Ouattara, but had adopted an anti-northerner (and thereby anti-Muslim) stance in his election campaign. Although Gbagbo reached an agreement with Ouattara once in power and stressed the importance of national unity, the treatment of Ouattara prompted a sense of racial and religious division between the north and south of the country. Legislative elections in December, preceded by widespread violence, were won by the FPI.

A culture of fear, and frequent racist attacks on 'foreigners' in Abidjan and other major cities, continued throughout 2001 and 2002. For his part, Gbagbo made overtures to Ouattara's Rally of the Republicans (Rassemblement des Républicains—RDR) while openly accusing Ouattara himself of attempting to destabilize the country. A 'reconciliation forum' intended to ease relations between Gbagbo, Ouattara and Guéï was abandoned in September 2001 as neither of the main guests accepted the president's invitation.

A breakthrough in August 2002, when the RDR joined the government, was followed by a major setback, as Guéï led an army mutiny in Abidjan in September. Although Guéï died in early fighting, Gbagbo's position as civilian president became effectively only that of a factional leader, as the rebellion quickly escalated into a full-scale civil war between the north and the south of the country. Gbagbo's forces soon found themselves in control of just the southern half of the country, with at least three separate 'patriotic' movements holding sway over the north and west, and UN and French peacekeepers attempting to stabilize the situation.

A peace plan was signed by the main factions in Paris in January 2003, allowing for a power-sharing government, disarmament and the devolving of more power to a new prime minister, in advance of early elections. A ceasefire came into effect on 4 May and the war was officially declared over on 4 July, but tensions remained high, sporadic clashes continued, and disputes were constantly simmering over Gbagbo's delays in implementing reforms, with the rebels and opposition Democratic Party of Côte d'Ivoire intermittently boycotting the unity government. As the peace process stalled in 2004, government forces bombed a rebel base, killing nine French peacekeepers, and France retaliated by obliterating the small Ivorian air force; anti-French riots swept the capital and foreigners were evacuated. The UN imposed an arms embargo and threatened sanctions.

South African president Thabo Mbeki brought all factions back to the negotiating table and measures were agreed to revive the faltering peace accord, including a constitutional change to allow citizens with just one Ivorian parent to stand for the presidency, clearing the way for a bid by Ouattara. Gbagbo insisted that a referendum would have to be held on this issue. A "final cessation of all hostilities" was signed on 6 April 2005, and under intense pressure, Gbagbo agreed to take "exceptional measures" for the forthcoming presidential election to suspend the rule requiring candidates to have two Ivorian parents. More talks were needed in June when the disarmament process ground to a halt within days of a ceremony to launch it. Gbagbo looks set to face Ouattara and Bédié among other candidates when the presidential poll is eventually held.

Profile of the Prime Minister:

Seydou Elimane **DIARRA**

Seydou Elimane Diarra was appointed prime minister of Côte d'Ivoire by President Laurent Gbagbo in January 2003 and sworn in on 10 February. A technocrat, he was generally seen as a consensus figure who could help bridge the gap between Gbagbo's supporters and northern rebels. A resurgence of violence, between the two sides and involving French peacekeepers, left Diarra with a far harder task.

Seydou Elimane Diarra was born on 23 November 1933 to a Muslim family in the north of Côte d'Ivoire. He won a scholarship to study agriculture at the Lycée Fénelon in La Rochelle, France, returning to Côte d'Ivoire shortly after independence in 1960 to run the state-controlled agriculture and insurance company. He was jailed, briefly, in the early 1960s for agitation—he had become involved in a scheme to set up workers' co-operatives—but was quickly rehabilitated and in 1965 took up the post of commercial director for CAISTAB, Côte d'Ivoire's governmental supervisory body for the country's staple industries of coffee and cocoa.

Diarra represented CAISTAB in London before progressing to more influential positions abroad; he served as the African representative to the International Coffee Organization before joining Côte d'Ivoire's diplomatic corps, in which guise he served as ambassador to Brazil, the European Union and finally to the UK, before returning to Côte d'Ivoire in 1985. There he set up his own business (Saco et Chocodi) as a cocoa exporter.

Following Gen. Robert Guéï's seizure of power in a military coup in 1999, Diarra headed an interim government until presidential elections in 2000, when Laurent Gbagbo came into power. Despite his service under Guéï's tenure, he was seen by the Gbagbo administration as a consensus figure and was appointed to head up a short-lived national reconciliation forum, set up under pressure from France, that attempted to prevent the simmering ethnic tensions in the country from descending into all-out civil war.

A new government was set up in August 2002, but fighting broke out in the north and west the following month and lasted until the following year. In early 2003 a provisional settlement was brokered in Paris involving the creation of a government of national unity. The aim of the Linas–Marcoussis Agreement was to create a transitional power-sharing regime under the guidance of a consensual but powerful prime minister. Diarra, with his background as a technocrat and his reputation as a conciliator, was chosen to head the new administration which took office in 2003. A comprehensive ceasefire was signed in May of that year, though supporters of President Gbagbo accused Diarra of being too soft on rebels who failed to disarm.

CROATIA

Full name: The Republic of Croatia.

Leadership structure: The head of state is a president, directly elected by universal adult suffrage for a five-year term. The head of government is the prime minister, who, under the 2000 constitutional amendments, is appointed by and responsible to the Croatian Assembly. The cabinet is appointed by the prime minister.

President:	Vlatko Pavletić	26 Nov. 1999—2 Feb. 2000
	(acting up to and following the death of President Franjo Tudjman on 10 Dec. 1999)	
	Zlatko Tomčić (acting)	2 Feb. 2000—18 Feb. 2000
	Stipe **MESIĆ**	Since 18 Feb. 2000
Prime Minister:	Zlatko Matesa	7 Nov. 1995—27 Jan. 2000
	Ivica Račan	27 Jan. 2000—23 Dec. 2003
	Ivo **SANADER**	Since 23 Dec. 2003

Legislature: The legislature, the Croatian Assembly (Hrvatski Sabor), is unicameral. The sole chamber, the House of Representatives (Zastupnički Dom), currently has 152 members, directly elected for a four-year term; 140 are elected in ten constituencies, eight elected by ethnic minorities, and a variable number (not more than 15, and only four in the 2003 elections) chosen to represent Croatians abroad.

Profile of the President:

Stipe **MESIĆ**

Stipe Mesić's election as president in February 2000 marked a major shift for Croatia following the death the previous December of the stridently nationalistic Franjo Tudjman. Mesić was especially popular among female and younger voters due to his relaxed style. A career politician, Mesić was the last chairman of the joint presidency of the Socialist Federal Republic of Yugoslavia before Croatian independence and civil war in 1991. In 1994 he split with Tudjman over the government's growing authoritarianism and its pursuit of Croat nationalist ambitions in war-torn neighbouring Bosnia.

Stjepan Mesić was born in the eastern town of Slavonska Orahovica on 24 December 1934. A prominent student activist, he graduated from the University of Zagreb with qualifications in law, and served in the early 1970s as a member of the Croatian republican parliament (within what was then Yugoslavia) before being sentenced to one year in jail for his involvement in the 'Croatian Spring', the 1971 uprising against Yugoslav central control from Belgrade. He is married to Milka née Dudunić and they have two daughters.

In 1989 Mesić joined Tudjman in the newly formed nationalist Croatian Democratic Union (Hrvatska Demokratska Zajednica—HDZ) and following success at the polls in 1990 was appointed as president of the Executive Council—effectively the republic's prime minister—with Tudjman as the republic's president. In an effort to sustain the Zagreb–Belgrade relationship, Mesić was appointed to the joint Yugoslavian presidency in May 1991, becoming its chairman on 1 July. As the federation disintegrated beneath him the position became increasingly untenable; Croatia officially pronounced itself independent on 8 October, and on 5 December he resigned as president, famously declaring: "Yugoslavia no longer exists."

The ensuing war abated in 1992 and Mesić was elected as speaker of the Croatian parliament. From this position he led the growing criticisms of the HDZ's authoritarianism and especially the rising cult of personality surrounding President Tudjman. From 1993 tensions spiralled, with the war in neighbouring Bosnia raising the possibility of a 'greater Croatia' carved out of Bosnian territory, and in 1994 Mesić was relieved from his post as speaker after he formed the Croatian Independent Democrats (Hrvatski Nezavisni Demokrati—HND). Despite a renewed pact with the Bosnian Muslim-Croat federation Mesić remained in defiance of the HDZ and fared poorly at the polls following the Croat military successes of 1995. Mesić subsequently abandoned the HND to join the Croatian People's Party (Hrvatska Narodna Stranka—HNS) in 1997 and was soon promoted to its vice presidency.

In the autumn of 1999 President Tudjman's health deteriorated rapidly. His death on 10 December gave rise to an urgent race to fill the vacancy. Mesić, who stood as the HNS candidate, was at first seen as an outsider, but quickly rose in opinion polls, contrasting himself to Tudjman's authoritarian approach. He swept the polls to take 56% of the vote in the second round on 7 February 2000. He took office on 18 February. Part of his manifesto had been to reduce the role of president to that of a 'guarantor of balance' in the republic, and on taking office he immediately entered into a dialogue with the Assembly to define the new presidential remit. In September 2003 he made the first visit by a Croatian president to Belgrade since Croatia's independence. He easily secured re-election in January 2005, almost winning outright in the first round.

Profile of the Prime Minister:

Ivo **SANADER**

Ivo Sanader was appointed prime minister of Croatia on 23 December 2003 after his Croatian Democratic Union (Hrvatska Demokratska Zajednica—HDZ) became the single largest party following parliamentary elections—an impressive comeback following a trouncing in 2000 after the death of long-time leader Franjo Tudjman. The multilingual, well-travelled Sanader that year inherited a party riven by internal feuds and mired in scandal. He has since toned down its nationalism and is committed to steering Croatia on a pro-Western path.

Ivo Sanader was born on 8 June 1953 in Split, Croatia, and attended the University of Innsbruck in Austria, where he attained a doctorate in comparative literature and Romance languages in 1982. Sanader is married to archaeologist Mirjana Sanader and they have two children.

Immediately following his return to Croatia in 1982, Sanader went to work for the marketing department of the Dalmacijaturist tourist agency. By 1988 he had become editor-in-chief of the Logos publishing house. At the time, he was also one of the editors of the magazine *Mogućnosti* (Possibilities). In 1991, Sanader took up a management position at the National Theatre in Split.

In August 1992, after being elected to the House of Representatives of the Croatian Assembly (then bicameral), Sanader became minister of science and technology, a position he held until January 1993.

Sanader was subsequently appointed deputy foreign minister. In this new post, he participated in the bilateral talks which led to the establishment of the Muslim-Croat Federation of Bosnia and Herzegovina. At the end of November 1995, following the Dayton Peace Accords, Sanader left the cabinet to become chief of staff to President Tudjman, who also appointed him secretary-general of the defence and national security council and a member of the presidential council. In January 1996, he became a member of the joint council for co-operation between Croatia and Bosnia. Later, Sanader was reappointed as deputy foreign minister.

In 2000, he was elected president of the HDZ following the death of Tudjman. Sanader vowed to modernize and strengthen his party, which had acquired a reputation as a far-right nationalist organization and had been battered by a succession of scandals and allegations of corruption. In 2003 the HDZ won parliamentary elections and Sanader was confirmed as prime minister by the legislature on 23 December. Sanader insists that his party is now a mainstream conservative party, and he has repeatedly stressed his commitment to democracy, the market economy and human rights, including co-operation with the International Criminal Tribunal for the former Yugoslavia. However, it was the issue of failing to surrender war crimes suspect Gen. Ante Gotovina, who is regarded as a war hero by Croatians, that caused the European Union to delay the start of accession talks in 2005.

CUBA

Full name: The Republic of Cuba.

Leadership structure: The head of state is a president, indirectly elected by the National Assembly. The president's term of office is five years. The head of government is the president. The Council of Ministers is appointed by the National Assembly.

President of the Council of State and Council of Ministers:

Fidel **CASTRO** Ruz	Since 2 Dec. 1976
(prime minister since 16 Feb. 1959,	
having taken power on 1 Jan. 1959)	

Legislature: The legislature is unicameral. The sole chamber, the National Assembly of the People's Power (Asamblea Nacional del Poder Popular— ANPP), has 609 members, directly elected for a five-year term. It elects the Council of State, which represents it between its sessions.

Profile of the President of the Council of State and Council of Ministers:

Fidel **CASTRO** Ruz

Targeted as an object of particular hatred by successive US administrations, Fidel Castro survives in power as a lone remnant from the gallery of internationally known communist figures of the Cold War era. The leader of the Cuban revolution in 1959, he has been in power longer than any other current nonhereditary ruler in the world, although despite his age he still presents himself as the fatigue-clad, bearded revolutionary. He still runs a one-party state, but the pope's visit in January 1998 marked the beginning of an improvement in his regime's international relations, and its partial emergence from the isolation it had suffered since the collapse of communism elsewhere.

Fidel Alejandro Castro Ruz was born on 13 August 1926 in Birán in the Oriente region of southeast Cuba. His father Ángel Castro, who had arrived as an immigrant farm labourer from Galicia, Spain, owned a 23,000-acre sugar plantation. One of seven children, Fidel Castro had a strict upbringing in a large Roman Catholic family, although he was later to be excommunicated. After attending the local primary school he went to Jesuit schools in Santiago and Havana, and graduated in law from the University of Havana in 1949. He practised as a lawyer in Havana, and planned to stand for parliament, until Gen. Batista seized power in 1952.

After first attempting unsuccessfully to use the law to oppose Batista, by bringing a suit against the dictator for contravening the constitution, Castro became involved in underground resistance. On 26 July 1953 he led an assault on the Moncada barracks in Oriente. Half of his force were killed and both Fidel Castro and his brother Raúl were captured and sentenced to 15 years in prison. Defending himself at the trial, Castro closed his defence with the much-quoted words, "History will absolve me." His marriage to Mirta Díaz-Bilart, with whom he had one son Fidelito, ended with her divorcing him while he was in prison.

Released under a general amnesty in May 1955, Castro fled to Mexico and then on to the USA. He returned to Cuba aboard the *Granma* on 2 December 1956 as leader of an 82-man group of Cuban exiles calling themselves the 26 July Revolutionary Movement. Batista's troops killed 70 of them soon after they landed, leaving the Castro brothers, Che Guevara and just nine others to form the nucleus of a guerrilla movement in the mountainous Sierra Maestra region. Gathering strength over the next two years, the guerrilla army marched on Havana and put Batista to flight on 1 January 1959. The USA recognized Castro's government on 7 January and on 16 February Castro declared himself prime minister.

It was the expropriation of US-owned firms which underlay the rapid deterioration in relations with the USA. Castro responded to Soviet overtures by concluding deals on trade, oil, food and credit, while the USA retaliated on the expropriation issue by imposing an economic embargo. Fearing a Marxist and pro-Soviet state 'in its back yard', the new Kennedy administration in the USA gave the go-ahead for a disastrous attempted invasion of Cuba by CIA-backed Cuban exiles, who were wiped out at the Bay of Pigs in April 1961. In 1962 Castro agreed to a Soviet nuclear weapons base being established on the island. Global nuclear war seemed imminent as the USA imposed a naval blockade to stop the missiles reaching their new base. Superpower negotiation between Presidents Kennedy and Khrushchev ended the crisis, with the Soviet ships turning back with their cargo of missiles, but from then on Castro's government was viewed with even more hostility by the USA and several attempts were made to assassinate Castro.

Castro had declared Cuba a communist single-party state in December 1961, the year in which he was awarded the Lenin Peace Prize. His regime pressed ahead with the nationalization of industry, setting up farm collectives and appropriating property from the wealthy or from foreigners. Thousands of opponents of his regime were imprisoned or executed and many of the middle and upper classes left Cuba, forming a substantial community of exiles in Miami.

In 1963 Castro became first secretary of the United Party of the Cuban Socialist Revolution, which became the Cuban Communist Party (Partido Comunista de

Cuba—PCC) in 1965. He did not formally join the party's politburo, however, until 1976. Cuba approved its first constitution in that year and, instead of prime minister, Castro officially became head of state and government as president of the Council of State and the Council of Ministers. Since then he has been re-elected to the presidency a number of times, most recently by the National Assembly in March 2003 when he began a new five-year term in office. He also retains the leadership of the PCC as its first secretary, and in 1992 became, in addition, chairman of the National Defence Council.

From the 1960s until the 1990s Castro governed Cuba on strict Marxist lines. Within Cuba he pointed with particular pride to achievements in the national education and health services. Keen to export the Cuban example, he was active in the Non-Aligned Movement and supported revolutions in Latin America, Ethiopia and Angola, with substantial commitments of military hardware, training and troops.

Through the 1990s Castro insisted on maintaining Cuba's Marxist identity, and came under criticism for the suppression of dissent (with a strong clampdown as late as 1999) as well as for his cautious approach on economic reform. The loss of the once substantial Soviet aid and the ending of preferential trade deals contributed to the problems of the economy, as did, above all, the maintenance of the US trade embargo. Concessions to free enterprise included the introduction of farmers' markets, and a foreign investment law in 1995. In March 1996, however, at a rare meeting of the PCC's central committee, Castro announced stronger measures to restrict private business ventures, emphasizing again his hard-line stance. (The previous December, during a visit to China, he had praised his hosts for holding out against capitalism, thereby reinforcing his own reputation for last-ditch resistance, if not for perceptive analysis of Chinese affairs.) The emergence of a dollarized tourist sector has nevertheless become a major factor in changing the nature of the economy. In late 2004 Castro banned the free circulation of US dollars in protest over the continuing US sanctions, causing economic chaos as people rushed to exchange the currency.

Relations with EU countries have also been rocky, with disputes over treatment of dissidents and the policy ties between the EU and the USA. Mexico and Peru have also been temporarily out of favour for backing a UN censure motion of Cuba's human rights record. However, elsewhere in Latin America and the Caribbean Castro has tried to extend his influence, in particular forging strong links with Venezuelan president Hugo Chávez, whose left-wing anti-American views find a natural ally in Castro. A summit in 2005 forged an alliance of Caribbean countries including Cuba that would benefit from subsidized oil from Venezuela.

On the issue of religious freedom, the unprecedented visit to Cuba by Pope John Paul II in January 1998 helped to encourage the regime's loosening of controls over the Roman Catholic Church, which was even given time for broadcasts on state television, and Christmas was reinstated as a national holiday. The pope's death in 2005 was marked by three days of national mourning and Castro joined hundreds of Cubans at a funeral mass.

Since July 1998 the matter of Castro's health has repeatedly hit the headlines. Officials strongly denied claims made by a Cuban surgeon and recent defector that she had been part of a team which had operated on him for a serious brain condition. His habit for making long-winded speeches in the blazing Cuban sun wearing no hat led to a public collapse in 2001, and in late 2002 an insect bite that he had scratched forced him to take bed rest for a number of days, causing him to miss his first National Assembly session in 25 years. A fall in 2004 resulted in a broken arm and knee. Castro's age and increasing infirmity have made the issue of the succession one of the main focuses of political life.

CYPRUS

Full name: The Republic of Cyprus.

Leadership structure: The head of state is a president, directly elected by universal adult suffrage. The president's term of office is five years. The head of government is the president, who appoints the Council of Ministers.

President:	Glafcos Clerides	28 Feb. 1993—28 Feb. 2003
	Tassos **PAPADOPOULOS**	Since 28 Feb. 2003

Legislature: The legislature is unicameral. The sole chamber, the House of Representatives (Vouli Antiprosopon), has 80 members (56 seats for Greek-Cypriots, 24 seats nominally reserved for Turkish-Cypriots), directly elected for a five-year term.

Profile of the President:

Tassos **PAPADOPOULOS**

Tassos Papadopoulos took office as president of Cyprus on 1 March 2003. A lawyer by training, Papadopoulos had first entered government after Cyprus's independence from British rule in 1960. He held a variety of cabinet posts under Cyprus's first president, Archbishop Makarios, and had long been involved in negotiations with the island's Turkish community, but was known—as was his Democratic Party—for his hard line on the peace process, so there was little surprise when Papadopoulos refused to back a UN plan to reunify the island in time for its accession to the European Union (EU). Greek Cypriots rejected the plan in a referendum in April 2004, and Papadopoulos guided his still-divided island into the EU in May.

Tassos Papadopoulos was born in Nicosia, Cyprus, on 7 January 1934. He studied law in London at Gray's Inn and returned to Cyprus to set up practice in the mid-1950s. Papadopoulos, like many other young men of his generation, became involved in the struggle for independence from British rule. He quickly became a senior figure in the political arm of the liberation movement, and was the youngest minister in the government following independence in August 1960. He is married to Photini Michaelides (the widow of interior minister Polycarpos Georgadjis, murdered in 1970) and they have two sons and two daughters.

In the early 1960s, as arguments over constitutional interpretation brought political deadlock and sectarian violence grew between Greek and Turkish

143

Cypriots, Papadopoulos served successively as minister of the interior, minister of finance, minister of labour and social insurance, minister of health and minister of agriculture and natural resources. The UN Peacekeeping Force in Cyprus (UNFICYP) was established in 1963 and the two warring communities segregated, but nonetheless the island was brought to the brink of war twice in a decade.

In February 1969, Papadopoulos joined with Glafcos Clerides, a moderate right-wing politician, to establish the Unified Party (Eniaion), and was elected as a deputy for Nicosia. In 1974 the great crisis of Cypriot history took place; President Makarios was deposed by the Greek military junta, Turkish forces invaded the north and the island was partitioned. Papadopoulos served as adviser to Clerides in his role as the first representative of the Greek Cypriot side in the intercommunal talks, until April 1976 when he broke openly with Clerides; that same year he was re-elected as an independent deputy. He subsequently took up Clerides's post of negotiator himself, serving until July 1978.

Spyros Kyprianou, who took over from Makarios as president and formed the Democratic Party (Dimokratikon Komma—DIKO), did not count Papadopoulos among his supporters. But when Papadopoulos failed in his efforts to form his own party, he turned to DIKO, and in the 1991 and 1996 parliamentary elections he was returned as a DIKO candidate. He served as a member of the National Council and chaired the House of Representatives committee on foreign and European affairs. He was also a member of the committees on legal affairs and financial and budgetary affairs. In the 2003 presidential election he stood as the DIKO candidate and defeated the two-term incumbent, Clerides.

Papadopoulos, who took a hard-line approach towards attempts at reunifying the island, led the successful 'no' campaign in the 2004 referendum on a UN-backed proposal on reunification, meaning that in effect just the Greek part of the island acceded to the EU in May 2004. However, Papadopoulos's intransigence on the issue could yet backfire; international aid has been promised to the Turkish north—which voted 'yes'—with the USA particularly keen to see the imbalance in trade links and wealth redressed.

TURKISH REPUBLIC OF NORTHERN CYPRUS

The internationally unrecognized Turkish Republic of Northern Cyprus (TRNC) adopted a constitution in May 1985 creating an executive presidency, directly elected by universal adult suffrage for a five-year term. The TRNC also has an Assembly (Cumhuriyet Meclisi), with 50 members directly elected for a five-year term.

TRNC 'President':	Rauf Denktaş	15 Nov. 1983—24 April 2005
	('president' of Turkish Federated State from 13 Feb. 1975)	
	Mehmet Ali **TALAT**	Since 24 April 2005
TRNC 'Prime Minister':	Derviş Eroglu	16 Aug. 1996—13 Jan. 2004
	Mehmet Ali Talat	13 Jan. 2004—23 April 2005
	vacant	23 April 2005—25 April 2005
	Ferdi Sabit **SOYER**	Since 25 April 2005

Profile of the TRNC 'President':

Mehmet Ali **TALAT**

Mehmet Ali Talat was inaugurated as president of the Turkish Republic of Northern Cyprus (TRNC) on 24 April 2005. Previously prime minister, he is credited with leading the successful 'yes' campaign in the TRNC in a referendum on a UN-sponsored plan to unify the island. After its rejection by Greek Cypriots, the international community promised an increase in aid to the TRNC.

Mehmet Ali Talat was born in Girne (Kyrenia) in northern Cyprus on 6 July 1952, to a farming family. He first became involved in politics while studying for a degree in electrical engineering at the Middle East Technical University (METU) in Ankara, Turkey, from where he graduated in 1977. On his return to Cyprus he joined the left-of-centre Republican Turkish Party (Cumhuriyetçi Türk Partisi—CTP) and supported himself by repairing refrigerators and air conditioners. He is married with a son and a daughter.

Talat became minister of education and culture in 1993 in the coalition government formed by the Democrat Party (Demokrat Partisi—DP) and the CTP following general elections, and continued in the same post in the second DP–CTP coalition government. Elected as leader of the CTP in January 1996, he first became an Assembly member in 1998 for the constituency of Lefkosa (Nicosia), and was re-elected in 2003.

Talat formed a CTP–DP government in January 2004 at the request of then-president Rauf Denktaş when Prime Minister Derviş Eroglu found himself unable to do so, and was credited with leading the successful campaign to persuade Turkish Cypriots to accept a UN-backed proposal to reunite the island, though the plan was scuppered when Greek Cypriots voted 'no'. Following the CTP–DP victory in parliamentary elections in February 2005, Talat served as prime minister until his election as president on 17 April 2005. He was inaugurated on 24 April and the following month stepped down as CTP leader.

Profile of the TRNC 'Prime Minister':

Ferdi Sabit **SOYER**

Ferdi Sabit Soyer was appointed prime minister in April 2005. A career politician, he leads the Republican Turkish Party (Cumhuriyetçi Türk Partisi— CTP).

Ferdi Sabit Soyer was born in Lefkosa (Nicosia) in 1952. He was educated in Cyprus before attending a Turkish university to study medicine, a degree he never completed. He returned to Cyprus to become active in politics and joined the CTP. He was elected to parliament for the first time in 1985, and in the mid-1990s was minister of agriculture, natural resources and energy in the coalition government formed by the CTP and the Democrat Party (Demokrat Partisi—DP).

Soyer was named prime minister on 25 April 2005 by new president Mehmet Ali Talat. He became chairman of the CTP in May, replacing Talat who gave up the post shortly after taking over the presidency. Soyer is married with two children.

CZECH REPUBLIC

Full name: The Czech Republic.

Leadership structure: The head of state is a president, indirectly elected by a joint session of both houses of Parliament. The president's term of office is five years, with a maximum of two consecutive terms. The head of government is the prime minister, who is responsible to the Chamber of Deputies. The Council of Ministers is appointed by the president after nomination by the prime minister.

President:	Václav Havel	2 Feb. 1993—2 Feb. 2003
	Vladimír Špidla (acting)	2 Feb. 2003—7 March 2003
	Václav **KLAUS**	Since 7 March 2003
Prime Minister:	Miloš Zeman	17 July 1998—12 July 2002
	Vladimír Špidla	12 July 2002—30 June 2004
	Stanislav Gross (acting from 30 June 2004)	26 July 2004—25 April 2005
	Jirí **PAROUBEK**	Since 25 April 2005

Legislature: The legislature, the Parliament (Parlament), is bicameral. The lower chamber, the Chamber of Deputies (Poslanecká Sněmovna), has 200 members, directly elected for a four-year term. The upper chamber, the Senate (Senát), has 81 directly elected members. All members of the Senate were first elected in November 1996; one-third of the seats come up for re-election every two years, and senators now serve six-year terms.

Profile of the President:

Václav **KLAUS**

Václav Klaus was elected to the largely ceremonial post of president by Parliament at the third attempt on 28 February 2003, a decade after leading, as prime minister, the peaceful division of Czechoslovakia and the foundation of an independent Czech Republic. Highly regarded by neoliberals as an economist, Klaus joined the Civic Forum (Občanská Fórum) during the 'velvet revolution' of 1989 and after its split cofounded the Civic Democratic Party (Občanská Demokratická Strana—ODS), remaining as its leader until 2002. In 2004 Klaus finished the task that his predecessor and erstwhile rival Václav Havel had begun, overseeing the Czech Republic's accession to the European Union (EU).

Václav Klaus was born in the Vinohrady district of Prague on 19 July 1941. He studied at the Prague School of Economics and eventually took advantage of the relative thaw in Czechoslovakian politics in the 1960s to study in Italy and the USA. As a research worker at the Institute of Economics of the Czech Academy of Sciences, he completed a doctorate in economics in 1968. In 1970, in the clampdown which followed the suppression of Czechoslovakia's 'Prague Spring' experiment in liberalized communism, he was forced to abandon his research career for political reasons and left to work for many years at the Czechoslovak State Bank. He returned to an academic post at the Forecasting Institute of the Czech Academy of Sciences in late 1987. Klaus is married to fellow economist Livia Klausová and has two sons. He has published over 20 books on general social, political and economics subjects and he holds a number of international awards and honorary doctorates from universities all over the world.

Václav Klaus started his political career following the fall of the Berlin Wall in Germany in December 1989. He became federal minister of finance, and in October 1991 was also appointed deputy prime minister. In late 1990, he became chairman of what was then the strongest political entity in the country—Civic Forum. After its demise in April 1991, he cofounded the ODS, and was its chairman from the outset until December 2002. He won the parliamentary elections with this party in 1992 and became prime minister of the Czech Republic within the federation. It was in this position that he took part in the peaceful division of Czechoslovakia and the foundation of an independent Czech Republic on 1 January 1993.

During this period he was careful to maintain his contacts with the world of economics. He continued his lectures and published occasionally and in 1991 he was appointed assistant professor of economics at Prague's Charles University. In 1995 he was appointed professor of finance at the Prague School of Economics.

In 1996, Klaus successfully defended his position as prime minister in the elections to the Chamber of Deputies, but he resigned after the breakup of the government coalition in November 1997. After the early elections of 1998, he became the chairman of the Chamber of Deputies for a four-year term of office. On 28 February 2003, Václav Klaus was elected president, and in 2004 he oversaw the accession of the Czech Republic into the EU.

Profile of the Prime Minister:

Jirí PAROUBEK

Jirí Paroubek is an economist who was appointed prime minister of the Czech Republic on 25 April 2005. A member of the Czech Social Democratic Party

(Česká strana sociálné demokratická—ČSSD), he is the country's third prime minister in a year.

Jirí Paroubek was born on 21 August 1952 in Olomouc, Moravia, in the east of what is now the Czech Republic. He first entered politics at the age of 18, joining the Czechoslovak Socialist Party. He studied at the University of Economics in Prague, graduating in 1976, whereupon he worked as an economist for various state companies, while simultaneously working his way up the party hierarchy. He attracted some attention from the secret police, but was left alone after 1982 as the authorities concluded that he had insufficient potential and contacts to merit closer surveillance.

In 1989, following the 'velvet revolution', Paroubek joined the ČSSD. Throughout the decade that followed, he worked as an economic consultant, specializing in small and medium-sized enterprises. He held various positions within the ČSSD, including his election in November 1998 as deputy mayor of Prague responsible for financial policy. He was regional development minister from mid-2004 under Prime Minister Stanislav Gross, whom he succeeded the following April after the latter was forced to resign after a financial scandal.

Paroubek's first cabinet was almost unchanged from that of his predecessor. In an awkward position, with opponents on every side, he warned the president over his habit of publicly disagreeing with government policy. With a tiny majority in Parliament, his administration seemed unlikely to be able to force through major reforms.

DENMARK

Full name: The Kingdom of Denmark.

Leadership structure: The head of state is a hereditary monarch. The head of government is the prime minister, who appoints a cabinet.

Queen:	**MARGRETHE II**	Since 15 Jan. 1972
Prime Minister:	Poul Nyrup Rasmussen	25 Jan. 1993—27 Nov. 2001
	Anders Fogh **RASMUSSEN**	Since 27 Nov. 2001

Legislature: The legislature is unicameral. The sole chamber, the Parliament (Folketing), has 179 members, directly elected for a four-year term.

Profile of the Queen:

MARGRETHE II

Queen Margrethe II succeeded to the Danish throne in January 1972 upon the death of her father Frederik IX. An amendment to the Danish constitution, adopted in 1953 through a referendum, permitted female descendants of the reigning monarch to ascend the throne as long as there were no male heirs. As is the rule with Scandinavian monarchs Queen Margrethe has no personal political power. Her titular roles include that of supreme commander of the Danish defence forces.

Margrethe II, popularly known as Daisy, was born on 16 April 1940 at Amalienborg. Given the names Margrethe Alexandrine Thorhildur Ingrid, she is the eldest daughter of King Frederik IX (1899–1972) and Queen Ingrid (1910–2000). Having completed her secondary education in Denmark at Zahles Skole, she took the philosophy examination at Copenhagen University in 1960, studied prehistoric archaeology at Cambridge University in 1960–61, and later specialized in political science at Århus (1961–62), the Sorbonne, Paris, (1963) and the London School of Economics (1965). In her youth she took part in several archaeological excavations in Greece, Sudan and Rome.

In April 1958 Margrethe first began attending the weekly meetings of the Council of State between the monarch and the cabinet. Since ascending the throne on 15 January 1972 she has taken an active interest in matters of state, meeting her ministers weekly and representing Denmark abroad.

Margrethe illustrated Tolkien's *The Lord of the Rings* in 1977 and as an artist she has also worked with handicrafts and textiles and designed seals, calendars and costumes for television and theatre productions. In 1981, with her French husband, she translated Simone de Beauvoir's *All Men Are Mortal*. She was awarded the Danish Language Society Prize in 1989 and is an honorary member of the Swedish Royal Academy of Science, History and Antiquities.

Margrethe married on 10 June 1967 the French diplomat Count Henri-Marie-Jean-André de Laborde de Monpezat, who took the courtesy title Prince Henrik of Denmark. They have two sons, Crown Prince Frederick and Prince Joachim.

Profile of the Prime Minister:

Anders Fogh **RASMUSSEN**

Anders Fogh Rasmussen was originally an outspoken right-winger within the Liberal Party (Venstre—V), but softened his style after taking over the party leadership in 1998. Remodelling himself along the lines of the so-called 'third way' associated with UK prime minister Tony Blair and German chancellor Gerhard Schröder, Rasmussen has earned the nickname 'Mr Perfect'. He combines his recently developed support for Denmark's welfare state with stricter rules on immigration, heading a minority coalition with the Conservative People's Party (re-formed after the 2005 elections) that depends on support in Parliament from the far-right Danish People's Party (Dansk Folkeparti—DF).

Anders Fogh Rasmussen was born on 29 January 1953 in Ginnerup, east Jutland. He grew up on the family farm and completed his secondary education in 1972 at the Viborg Cathedral School, where he had already begun his career in right-wing politics, founding and chairing the school branch of the Young Liberals. He went on to Århus University to study economics, graduating in 1978 with a master's degree. While at university he headed the Young Liberals Party from 1974 and joined the Danish Youth Council in 1976. In the year of his graduation he was successfully elected to Parliament as a member of Venstre, and married his wife Anne-Mette, with whom he has one son and two daughters.

Since 1978 Rasmussen has been re-elected to Parliament at every election. At first he combined his rapid political career with a professional line as an economics consultant, beginning at the Danish Federation of Crafts and Small Industries. His work also included positions with the Building Council's Mortgage Credit Fund, the insurance company Østifterne and the investment firm Andelsinvest. During these early years in Parliament he was a strident critic of the postwar welfare state, and wrote a number of vehement articles against it, including *From Social State to Minimal State* which prompted much discussion. In the meantime he was also sitting on parliamentary fiscal affairs and housing committees.

Following Venstre's electoral successes in the 1980s Rasmussen rose high and fast. From 1987 to 1992 he was minister of taxation in the Conservative-led coalition of Poul Schlüter, and from 1990 he combined that portfolio with the ministry of economic affairs. His meteoric career was threatened in 1992 when he was forced to step down from the cabinet after opposition claims that he had misled Parliament. With his own downfall came that of the coalition and Venstre was forced into opposition in 1993. For five years Rasmussen remained vocally prominent in Parliament as vice chairman of the economic and political affairs committee, while also resuming some consultancy work.

In 1998 Rasmussen was elected leader of Venstre ahead of legislative elections. The party's failure to oust the incumbent Social Democrat government that year was largely put down to the electorate's fear that under Rasmussen Venstre would dismantle the welfare state. The defeat prompted a rethink and the beginning of Rasmussen's remarkable transformation. In just three years he distanced himself from the right-wing rhetoric of his past, learning to embrace both welfare state and Denmark's membership of the European Union (EU). Seeking to dominate the middle ground of Danish politics, he mixed these newer philosophies with some mainstream conservatism, support for lower taxation and an even harsher approach to immigration. He struck a populist chord when he referred to unemployed immigrants, of whom there are few in Denmark, as "scroungers".

In the November 2001 elections a positive response among voters to Rasmussen's new image, combined with widespread disappointment with the pro-EU Social Democrats, gave Venstre the largest share of the vote, for the first time since the 1920s. However, the party still lacked an overall majority, with only 31% of the seats in Parliament. Rasmussen formed a minority coalition with the Conservatives, which left him dependent on the far-right DF for support in Parliament.

During his first term in office Rasmussen maintained high popularity ratings by fulfilling his pledges to cut taxes and slash the number of asylum seekers by nearly three-quarters. He even suggested that Denmark should reconsider adopting the euro currency—rejected in a referendum in 2000. Venstre retained its position as the largest party in Parliament at the February 2005 elections, and Rasmussen re-formed the minority coalition with the Conservatives, again relying on external DF support for a (comfortable) parliamentary majority.

DJIBOUTI

Full name: The Republic of Djibouti.

Leadership structure: The head of state is a president, directly elected for a six-year term, renewable once only. The president appoints the Council of Ministers, which is responsible to the president. The prime minister presides at meetings of the Council of Ministers and is formally head of government.

President:	Ismaïl Omar **GUELLEH**	Since 8 May 1999
Prime Minister:	Barkat Gourad Hamadou (acting since 6 Feb. 2001)	30 Sept. 1978—7 March 2001
	Dilleita Mohamed **DILLEITA**	Since 7 March 2001

Legislature: The legislature is unicameral. The sole chamber, the National Assembly (Assemblée Nationale), has 65 members, directly elected for a five-year term.

Profile of the President:

Ismaïl Omar **GUELLEH**

Ismaïl Omar Guelleh was handpicked as successor by his uncle, the aging president Hassan Gouled Aptidon, whom he served as chief of staff for 22 years. As he was seen as the regime's strongman, his election to the presidency in 1999, as the candidate of the ruling Popular Rally for Progress (Rassemblement Populaire pour le Progrès—RPP), was hotly contested by the rebel Front for the Restoration of Unity and Democracy (Front pour la Restauration de l'Unité et de la Démocratie—FRUD). Since becoming president, however, he has overseen the end of the civil war and encouraged the FRUD's participation in politics.

Ismaïl Omar Guelleh, widely known as 'IOG', was born into the ethnic Issa community on 27 November 1947 in the Ethiopian town of Dire Dawa. His parents sent him to a French religious school there for his primary studies, and then to secondary school in neighbouring Djibouti, which was under French colonial rule as French Somaliland. After leaving school he joined the French administration's police force in 1968 and was promoted to inspector in 1970. He is married to Kadra Mahamoud Haïd and has two sons and two daughters.

Despite his chosen profession within the colonial social structure, Guelleh became involved in the illegal Issa-dominated separatist movement, the African

Popular League for Independence (Ligue Populaire Africaine pour l'Indépendance—LPAI). When the authorities discovered Guelleh's connection with the LPAI in 1975 he was suspended from the police force. Over the next two years he participated in several LPAI missions overseas, seeking support in Libya and Mogadishu, and entering discussions with the French government over independence for Djibouti, which finally came in 1977. Guelleh played an active role in the foundation of the separatist newspaper *Populaire*, which was run by his colleague Ahmed Dini, and his own publication *Djibouti Aujourd'hui*.

The newly independent Djibouti was run from 1977 to 1999 by President Gouled, Guelleh's uncle, and Guelleh was throughout this period head of the president's office with special remit over national security. As a prominent member of the LPAI he was included in the 1979 transformation of the League into the RPP which then ran the country as a single-party state until 1992. In 1983 Guelleh was elected to the party's central committee and directed a cultural commission to Paris before becoming a member of its executive from 1987. After a referendum in 1992 the country adopted a multiparty constitution but in practice the RPP still utterly dominated national politics. Political tensions mingled with ethnic divisions to fuel the fierce civil war which had erupted in 1991. The breakaway FRUD, headed by Guelleh's old LPAI comrade Ahmed Dini, backed an Afar uprising and rejected a power-sharing deal offered by the government in 1993.

As Gouled's heir apparent, Guelleh was elevated to be the third vice president of the RPP in 1996 before being nominated as its presidential candidate when Gouled finally announced his resignation in February 1999. He faced as little apparent opposition at the polls as his uncle had, and swept into office with 74% of the vote in the April elections. The results were immediately questioned by the FRUD candidate Moussa Ahmed Idriss and the international community at large.

Guelleh's greatest achievement after becoming president was the conclusion in February 2000 of a peace agreement to end the country's bitter ethnic-fuelled conflict. Later that same year he expanded his role as peace broker to the Horn of Africa region, inviting political leaders from neighbouring Somalia to Djibouti to negotiate the restoration of centralized government to that troubled state. Guelleh has also exploited Djibouti's location at the end of the Red Sea—it hosts the largest overseas French military base and the only US military base in Africa, and it has become a key US ally in the 'war on terrorism'.

The RPP and FRUD campaigned jointly in the 2003 legislative elections, winning all the seats. Despite being the sole candidate for the April 2005 presidential poll after a rival candidate withdrew due to lack of funds, Guelleh campaigned vigorously, focusing on reducing the country's dependence on imported food, and improving women's rights and transparency in local government. He polled 100% of the votes on 8 April in a turnout of almost 80%, despite opposition calls for a boycott. He has pledged that this will be his final term, and that he will not attempt to overturn the constitutional two-term limit.

Profile of the Prime Minister:

Dilleita Mohamed **DILLEITA**

Dilleita Mohamed Dilleita is a member of the ruling Popular Rally for Progress (Rassemblement Populaire pour le Progrès—RPP). A career diplomat, he served as ambassador to Ethiopia before being appointed prime minister in March 2001.

Dilleita Mohamed Dilleita was born on 12 March 1958 in Tadjoura in what was then French Somaliland. He is married and has one child. He was sent to Cairo, Egypt, and later Reims, France, for his education before attending the Centre for Vocational Training in Médéa, Algeria. He graduated in 1981 and returned to Djibouti where he worked at the ministry of foreign affairs, subsequently becoming an adviser to the country's embassies, and going back to France in 1986 to study diplomacy at the French foreign ministry.

Continuing his diplomatic career, Dilleita returned to Djibouti to become chief of protocol. He had a further spell in France from 1992, as an adviser to the Djibouti embassy there, and in 1997 he was made full ambassador to Ethiopia. In this role he also represented the country at the Organization of African Unity (OAU, now the African Union—AU) and played a key part in brokering peace talks between Ethiopia and Eritrea at the end of their two-year border war.

In February 2001 the aging veteran prime minister, Barkat Gourad Hamadou, was allowed to retire. President Ismaïl Guelleh appointed Dilleita in his place in March. The RPP, in alliance with the former rebel Front for the Restoration of Unity and Democracy (Front pour la Restauration de l'Unité et de la Démocratie—FRUD) and two other parties, won all seats in parliament at the 2003 election, despite the opposition winning over one-third of the vote. Dilleita retained the premiership after the poll and again in a May 2005 reshuffle following that year's presidential elections.

DOMINICA

Full name: The Commonwealth of Dominica.

Leadership structure: The head of state is a president, elected by the legislature. The president's term of office is five years, renewable once only. The head of government is the prime minister, who is appointed by the president from among the members of the House of Assembly.

President:	Vernon Shaw	6 Oct. 1998—2 Oct. 2003
	Nicholas **LIVERPOOL**	Since 2 Oct. 2003
Prime Minister:	Edison James	14 June 1995—3 Feb. 2000
	Roosevelt 'Rosie' Douglas	3 Feb. 2000—1 Oct. 2000
	Pierre Charles (acting from 1 Oct. 2000)	3 Oct. 2000—6 Jan. 2004
	Osborne Rivierre (acting)	6 Jan. 2004—8 Jan. 2004
	Roosevelt **SKERRIT**	Since 8 Jan. 2004

Legislature: The legislature is unicameral. The sole chamber, the House of Assembly, has 21 directly elected members and nine appointed senators who sit for a five-year term.

Profile of the President:

Nicholas **LIVERPOOL**

Nicholas Liverpool took office as president of Dominica on 2 October 2003. A respected jurist and legal consultant, Liverpool had served as a Justice of Appeal in Belize, the Bahamas and the Eastern Caribbean Court of Appeal, and as Dominican ambassador to the USA. He was initially reported to have turned down the post for personal reasons.

Nicholas Joseph Orville Liverpool was born in 1934. He was called to the Bar at the Inner Temple in London in 1961, and graduated with a doctorate from Sheffield University, also in the UK, in 1965. Liverpool taught law at the University of the West Indies for several years, and is considered an authority on Caribbean law.

Having prepared a new criminal code for Belize in 1980, he served as justice of appeal for that country from 1990 to 1992. From 1993 to 1995 he was a judge at the Eastern Caribbean Court of Appeal. As well as serving as a judge on the appeal court of Grenada and the high courts of Antigua and Montserrat, Liverpool has also been Dominica's ambassador to the USA and a member of the Organization of American States (OAS) administrative tribunal. His nomination for president was approved by the House of Assembly on 19 September 2003, following his predecessor Vernon Shaw's decision not to serve a second term. He was sworn in on 2 October.

Profile of the Prime Minister:

Roosevelt **SKERRIT**

Roosevelt Skerrit was sworn in as prime minister of Dominica on 8 January 2004, after being chosen by the Dominica Labour Party (DLP) to replace Pierre Charles who died a few days earlier from heart failure. Skerrit, who was just 31 when he took office, studied English and psychology in the USA before returning to Dominica to become a teacher and a lecturer. He faces a considerable challenge in boosting the island's economy, which relies heavily on tourism and the declining banana industry.

Roosevelt Skerrit was born on 8 June 1972. He went to university in the USA, graduating with a degree in English and psychology from the University of Mississippi in 1997, and also attended New Mexico State University before returning home to Dominica to work as a teacher and a lecturer on the island. He entered politics in 1999 and was elected to the House of Assembly in 2000 as a member of the DLP, and was soon appointed minister of education, sports and youth affairs. He was sworn in as Dominica's youngest ever prime minister (and one of the youngest heads of government anywhere in the world) two days after the sudden death of the former premier, Pierre Charles, in January 2004.

Charles was the second prime minister to die in office during a single five-year electoral period; former head Roosevelt Douglas had perished in October 2000, only months after his party had won the 2000 general elections. Facing a faltering economy and a politically divided electorate in shock at the loss of their second leader in three years, Skerrit's first move was to declare a national day of prayer for peace, unity and togetherness, and to pledge to follow a course of inclusive leadership.

The new prime minister inherited the challenge of boosting Dominica's sluggish economy, which relies heavily on tourism and the export of bananas. In 2004 Skerrit's government cut diplomatic relations with Taiwan in favour of ties with mainland China. The prime minister said the latter had agreed to give more than US$100 million in aid, a sum equivalent to US$1,750 for each Dominican—more than a third of his government's normal revenue.

DOMINICAN REPUBLIC

Full name: The Dominican Republic.

Leadership structure: The head of state is a president, directly elected by universal adult suffrage. The president's term of office is four years. A president may serve at most two consecutive terms. The head of government is the president, who appoints and presides over the cabinet.

President:		
	Leonel Fernández Reyna	16 Aug. 1996—16 Aug. 2000
	Hipólito Mejía Domínguez	16 Aug. 2000—16 Aug. 2004
	Leonel **FERNÁNDEZ** Reyna	Since 16 Aug. 2004

Legislature: The legislature, the National Congress (Congreso Nacional), is bicameral. The lower chamber, the Chamber of Deputies (Cámara de Diputados), has 150 members, directly elected for a four-year term. The upper chamber, the Senate (Senado), has 30 members, also directly elected for a four-year term.

Profile of the President:

Leonel **FERNÁNDEZ** Reyna

Leonel Fernández Reyna has been president of the Dominican Republic since August 2004, having previously held the presidency from 1996 to 2000. He was the candidate of the Dominican Liberation Party (Partido de la Liberación Dominicana—PLD). A student activist in the 1970s and supporter of ex-president and PLD founder Juan Bosch, Fernández combined journalism with an academic career as a political scientist, and in 1994 stood unsuccessfully for vice president as Bosch's PLD running mate.

Born on 26 December 1953 in Santo Domingo, Leonel Fernández Reyna was taken as a child to live in New York, where he completed high school before returning to the Dominican Republic and enrolling in the Free University of Santo Domingo (UASD). As a student in the faculty of political science and law, living once again in the capital's working-class Villa Juana district, he was attracted to Bosch's radical ideas, taking an active part in student politics and protests against the right-wing regime of President Joaquín Balaguer. He was awarded his doctorate in 1978, his thesis subsequently becoming an influential book on media law. He held a succession of professorships at UASD over the next 15 years, in political science, law and media studies, while also attending courses in Mexico and other centres in the region. Having completed a journalism course at

Columbia University in New York in 1984, he wrote columns for several Santo Domingo newspapers and ran the international section of the PLD's *Vanguardia del Pueblo*.

A founder member of the PLD, Fernández was elected in 1983 to its central committee and joined the inner party leadership in 1990 when he was elected to its political committee. By this time Bosch and other PLD leaders were espousing rapid privatization and the promotion of private enterprise, in marked contrast to the PLD's original stance, and in a major schism in 1992 a number of dissident left-wingers resigned from the party. In 1994 the PLD picked Fernández as vice-presidential candidate in a final bid for the presidency by the veteran Bosch, who resigned his party post after finishing a poor third in the poll in May. The eventual outcome of the controversial 1994 elections was an interparty agreement on a short further term for the elderly Balaguer, the incumbent president and leader of the conservative Social Christian Reformist Party (Partido Reformista Social Cristiano—PRSC). The PLD backed a subsequent deal to extend this from 18 months to two years, leading up to fresh presidential elections in 1996.

In the first round in May 1996 Fernández finished second with 38.9%, behind the candidate of the Dominican Revolutionary Party (Partido Revolucionario Dominicano—PRD) but well ahead of the PRSC. He then announced a "national patriotic front" electoral alliance with outgoing president Balaguer's PRSC supporters, enabling him to overtake his PRD rival and win the 30 June runoff with 51.25% of the vote. Sworn in as president on 16 August, he faced the problem of governing without a majority in the Congress, where his PLD had won few seats at the 1994 election. During his first term as president the country experienced rapid economic growth, averaging 7.7% per annum, and unemployment fell, but accusations of corruption and cronyism snowballed, and his final year in office was marred by an embezzlement scandal.

The scandals caused the 2000 election to be won by the candidate of the PRD, but the economy plummeted taking the new government's popularity with it, and inflation soared to 43%. With Dominicans desperate for a return to the growth and stability of the Fernández era, he was re-elected in May 2004, winning 51% of the vote in the first round.

EAST TIMOR

Full name: The Democratic Republic of East Timor.

Leadership structure: The head of state is a president, directly elected by universal adult suffrage. The president's term of office is five years, renewable once only. The head of government is the prime minister, who is appointed by the president and nominates the Council of Ministers.

UN Administrator:	Sérgio Vieira de Mello	25 Oct. 1999—19 May 2002
President:	José Alexandre 'Xanana' **GUSMÃO**	Since 20 May 2002
Prime Minister:	Mari **ALKATIRI** (chief minister from 20 Sept. 2001)	Since 20 May 2002

Legislature: The Constituent Assembly (Assembléia Constituinte), with 88 members, was elected in August 2001 and inaugurated on 15 September. In December 2001 the Assembly began debating the details of a constitution for a fully independent state in preparation for presidential elections. The Assembly voted on 31 January 2002 to convert itself into a full National Parliament (Parlamento Nacional) without further elections. The parliament's term of office is five years.

Profile of the President:

'Xanana' **GUSMÃO**

Active in the resistance from the time of the Indonesian invasion in 1975, 'Xanana' Gusmão was leader of the Revolutionary Front for an Independent East Timor (Frente Revolucionária do Timor Leste Independente—Fretilin) from the early 1980s, and a founder member of the broader-based National Council of Maubere Resistance (Conselho Nacional da Resistência Maubere—CNRM). He was captured by the Indonesian authorities in 1992 and imprisoned until September 1999, his release following Indonesian acceptance of the need to prepare a transition to independence. As the principal surviving hero of the resistance, he became a popular choice for the new state's presidency once he had overcome his initial reluctance to take on the task.

José Alexandre Gusmão was born in Manatuto, East Timor, on the night of 20–21 June 1947. His father was a schoolmaster and part-time factory inspector. Gusmão attended a Jesuit seminary for his secondary education, and spent the subsequent years either unemployed or in construction and low-grade clerical jobs. He married Emilia Baptista in 1970 and they had a son and a daughter. In 1974 political tensions in East Timor escalated, as Portuguese sovereignty came increasingly to be questioned and internecine conflict threatened, causing Gusmão to contemplate emigration to Australia. He remained in the country, however, and joined Fretilin after the Democratic Union of Timor (União Democrática Timorense—UDT) tried to seize power from the Portuguese in August 1975, precipitating a civil war.

In 1975 Gusmão helped organize Fretilin, working at the Fretilin department of information and later gaining election to the Fretilin central committee. Gusmão also helped set up the Armed Forces for the National Liberation of East Timor (Forças Armadas de Libertação Nacional de Timor Leste—Falintil). On 28 November 1975 Fretilin declared East Timor independent, but on 7 December Indonesian troops invaded, crushing Fretilin and leaving Gusmão separated in far-eastern Timor. After this Gusmão was given responsibility for a handful of resistance fighters in the far-eastern part of East Timor and he set about rebuilding the movement there.

In 1986 Gusmão presided over the formation of the CNRM which drew on much broader support within East Timor than just Fretilin. By 1988 he was the commander of a pan-East Timorese underground army, uniting several underground resistance movements, including Fretilin, the UDT and the youth movement Renetil. During this period he continued to seek a peaceful resolution to the conflict, pushing for negotiations with the Indonesian government and a UN presence on the island. He also tried to promote international awareness of the political situation in East Timor.

Gusmão was captured in November 1992 in a western suburb of Dili. Between February and May 1993 an Indonesian court tried him for rebellion, possession of firearms and causing death to villagers. He was sentenced to life imprisonment, later reduced to 20 years. Gusmão continued to appeal to the international community from his prison cell, and to demand UN involvement in East Timor. He received a high-profile visit from the world's most famous ex-prisoner, South Africa's Nelson Mandela, in July 1997, and was appointed president of the National Council of Timorese Resistance (Conselho Nacional da Resistência Timorense—CNRT), successor to the CNRM, in April 1998. The accession of B. J. Habibie as Indonesian president in May 1998 raised hopes of a breakthrough, but in the event Gusmão's sentence was only reduced by four months.

January 1999 proved to be a key month in East Timor's history. Gusmão was permitted to serve the rest of his sentence under house arrest (although he was not moved until April) and the Indonesian government surprisingly gave its consent to a referendum on Timorese independence. Tragically, this news prompted a dramatic increase in violence on the island and Gusmão urged Falintil to resume its struggle. Nonetheless, on 30 August 1999, an overwhelming 79% of voters endorsed independence. The violence increased following the announcement of the 'yes' result as anti-independence militias ravaged the territory. Gusmão was released from house arrest on 7 September, but, fearing for his safety, travelled to exile in Australia.

Once relative peace had been restored by a UN force, Gusmão made a triumphant return to Dili in October 1999. Although clearly the most popular figure in the country, he startled observers by declaring in February 2000 that he would not seek the presidency on independence. He resigned as leader of Falintil in August 2000 in order to concentrate on the political path to independence, and was appointed head of the transitional National Council (advisory assembly) in October. Becoming increasingly disillusioned with the whole process, however, he stepped down in March 2001, with a parting shot at the UN administration. In the meantime he had divorced his wife and married former Australian secret agent Kirsty Sword in July 2000. They now have two sons.

By August 2001 he had succumbed to growing public pressure and announced that he would, after all, stand for the presidency. His popularity was such that the only other candidate stood merely in order to provide voters with a choice. He was elected with 83% of the vote on 14 April 2002. East Timor became independent a month later on 20 May, on which day Gusmão was inaugurated as its president.

Profile of the Prime Minister:

Mari **ALKATIRI**

Mari Alkatiri was one of the founders of the Revolutionary Front for an Independent East Timor (Frente Revolucionária do Timor Leste Independente— Fretilin) independence movement which now governs East Timor. Noted in the past for his international left-wing connections, he was effectively exiled in Mozambique from 1975 until 1999, when he was appointed economics minister in the first interim government, and then chief minister in the second. He went on to become prime minister upon independence in May 2002, making him the most prominent member of the country's small Muslim community, while his brother is Dili's leading Islamic cleric.

Mari bin Hamud Alkatiri was born on 26 November 1949 in Dili, in what was then the Portuguese colony of East Timor. He is one of ten children. His family had moved to the East Indies in the 19th century from the al-Khatiri sultanate in what is now Yemen. He travelled to the then Portuguese colony of Angola in the late 1960s where he graduated as a surveyor from the Angolan School of Geography. Alkatiri is married to Marina Ribeiro, with two sons and a daughter.

Returning to East Timor, Alkatiri found work as a chartered surveyor in the colonial administration's public works department. Almost immediately he became active in the community's independence struggle and was a cofounder of the Movement for the Liberation of East Timor in January 1970. This secretive group was allowed to come into the open in 1974 following political revolution and liberalization in Portugal. Thus the movement was transformed first into the Timorese Social Democratic Association and then merged with other groups to form Fretilin on 11 September 1974.

With Indonesia rapidly seeking to incorporate East Timor, the local government sought to garner international support for the country's self-declared independence. Alkatiri was appointed state minister of political affairs in November 1975 and was despatched to Africa along with other prominent politicians to canvass world leaders. He left East Timor three days before the Indonesian invasion and did not return for almost 24 years. He lived in exile in Mozambique and continued to promote the Timorese cause. He was among the statesmen who managed to secure the UN's condemnation for the invasion and was subsequently appointed as East Timor's foreign minister-in-exile in 1977. In the following decades he found work in Mozambique as an academic and has said that he intends eventually to return to academia.

Alkatiri finally went back to East Timor in 1999, just before the UN-sponsored referendum on independence. As the violence which followed the resounding 'yes' vote died down he was appointed economics minister in the first interim, UN-supervised government. His most important task in this role was to secure an agreement with neighbouring Australia over sharing the significant mineral resources hidden beneath the Timor Sea. Although the agreement was hailed as a future boon to the Timorese economy it has since been sharply criticized for overly favouring Australia. Alkatiri has defended his work, citing the need to maintain good relations with the fledgling country's more powerful neighbours. Following elections to the Constituent Assembly in August 2001, a second transitional government was formed in September with Alkatiri as chief minister.

On 20 May 2002 East Timor emerged as the world's youngest independent country and Alkatiri was elected prime minister at the head of the Fretilin government. His position, however, was precarious because of his notoriously stormy relationship with the immensely popular president, 'Xanana' Gusmão. Alkatiri refused to vote in the presidential election himself. One of the major divisions between the two leaders was their attitude regarding the need to prosecute the militiamen responsible for the 1999 violence, with Alkatiri fervently calling for justice, while Gusmão proposed a more forgiving approach to reconciliation. Alkatiri also came under pressure from the Timorese opposition for his apparently authoritarian style of government. He was accused of trying to create a one-party state after refusing to create a 'unity' government and instead relying on the absolute majority enjoyed by Fretilin in the parliament. Furthermore he is derided for being one of the large number of politicians who stayed away from East Timor following the invasion and is criticized for filling his cabinet with other former exiles.

ECUADOR

Full name: The Republic of Ecuador.

Leadership structure: The head of state is a president, who is directly elected by universal adult suffrage. The president's term of office is four years. The head of government is the president, who appoints the cabinet.

President:	Jamil Mahuad	10 Aug. 1998—21 Jan. 2000
Head of Military Junta:	Lucio Gutiérrez Borbúa	21 Jan. 2000—22 Jan. 2000
President:	Gustavo Noboa Bejarano	22 Jan. 2000—15 Jan. 2003
	Lucio Gutiérrez Borbúa	15 Jan. 2003—20 April 2005
	Alfredo **PALACIO** González	Since 20 April 2005

Legislature: The legislature is unicameral. The sole chamber, the National Congress (Congreso Nacional), currently has 121 members; 101 members elected on a provincial basis, and 20 members directly elected on a national basis, all for four-year terms. Under the 1998 Constitution, the number of deputies will be adjusted to allow for increasing population, with two elected for each province, plus one more for each 200,000 inhabitants of a province.

Profile of the President:

Alfredo **PALACIO** González

Alfredo Palacio González, a medical doctor whose career included several years working in the USA, was vice president of Ecuador from January 2003 until April 2005, when he was sworn in as president following the ousting by Congress of his predecessor Lucio Gutiérrez.

Luis Alfredo Palacio González was born on 22 January 1939 in the city of Guayaquil in southwest Ecuador. He was schooled there, in the Escuela Abdón Calderón and the Colegio San José La Salle, before studying medicine at the University of Guayaquil. He later interned at Case Western Reserve University in Cleveland, Ohio, USA, as well as Mount Sinai Hospital. From 1971 to 1972 he was a resident at the Veterans Administration in Missouri, USA, then worked for two years as a fellow of cardiology in Barnes-Jewish Hospital, Washington University, St Louis, Missouri.

Palacio spent most of his life outside politics, and despite serving as minister of public health between 1994 and 1996, still maintains that he is not a politician. He ran alongside Lucio Gutiérrez for vice president in the elections of 2002 (often wearing surgical scrubs on campaign stops), and was sworn in in this post on 15 January 2003, though he later became a critic of Gutiérrez for doing too little to alleviate poverty.

In late 2004 Gutiérrez sacked the Supreme Court for alleged bias, prompting the beginning of a wave of protests that culminated in the Ecuadorian Congress removing him from office on 20 April 2005. Palacio was sworn in immediately as the new president. He appointed a cabinet mainly from the Democratic Left (Izquierda Democrática—ID) party and has promised to reform the political system, as well as spend more on health and education.

EGYPT

Full name: The Arab Republic of Egypt.

Leadership structure: The head of state is a president, nominated by the People's Assembly and confirmed by popular referendum. The president's term of office is six years. On 10 May 2005 parliament agreed the final details of a change to the constitution under which the president is directly elected from a number of candidates; each candidate must have the backing of at least 65 members of parliament, and be the candidate of an established party. The changes were endorsed in a referendum on 25 May 2005, and the necessary bill approved by parliament on 16 June. The president appoints all the members of the Council of Ministers. The prime minister chairs meetings of the Council of Ministers and is head of government.

President:	Mohammed Hosni **MUBARAK** (acting from 6 Oct. 1981)	Since 14 Oct. 1981
Prime Minister:	Atif Mohammad Obeid	5 Oct. 1999—14 July 2004
	Ahmed **NAZIF**	Since 14 July 2004

Legislature: The legislature is unicameral. The sole chamber, the People's Assembly (Majlis al-Sha'ab), has 444 members directly elected by universal adult suffrage, and ten members appointed by the president, all for a five-year term. There is also a Consultative Council (Majlis al-Shoura), which has advisory powers. It has 264 members, 88 appointed by the president and 176 directly elected, for a six-year term.

Profile of the President:

Mohammed Hosni **MUBARAK**

Hosni Mubarak has been president of Egypt and its dominant political figure for two and a half decades. A former air force commander and hero of the 1973 war with Israel, Mubarak had become vice president, and was standing next to President Anwar al-Sadat at the military parade at which Sadat was assassinated by Islamic militants in 1981. Mubarak, while maintaining Sadat's controversial 1979 treaty with Israel, has based his policies on achieving a rapprochement with other Arab states, while clamping down on dissent.

Mohammed Hosni Mubarak was born on 4 May 1928 in Kafr al-Musailha, within the al-Menoufiyah governorate. From 1947 until 1949 he studied for a degree in military sciences at the Egyptian Military Academy. Specializing in aviation sciences, he then attended the Air Force Academy and went on to join the Egyptian air force in 1950. Between 1952 and 1959 he lectured at the Air Force Academy, while he also briefly attended the Frunze Military Academy in the Soviet Union.

In the 1950s and 1960s Mubarak was a successful air force pilot, seeing action in the Yemen civil war as a bomber squadron commander and in the 1967 Arab–Israeli war. Later in 1967 he took up a two-year post as director of the Aeronautical Academy. He was appointed successively air force chief of staff in 1969 and then commander in 1972 (a post he held until 1975). Acclaimed as a war hero after leading a successful air offensive against Israel in the 1973 war, he was promoted in that year to the rank of lieutenant-general. Mubarak is married to Suzanne Thabet, who is half-Egyptian and half-Welsh; they have two sons, Gamal and Alaa.

Mubarak's political rise under the Sadat regime was an exceptionally rapid one. Within three years of his first government appointment, as deputy minister for military affairs in 1972, he was made vice president by Sadat. Taking up this post in 1975, he was also given special responsibilities for state security. In 1978 he took charge of the organization of the newly formed National Democratic Party (NDP), acting as vice president of the party until 1981 and thereafter as its chairman.

A smooth transfer of power to Mubarak took place following Sadat's assassination on 6 October 1981. He was nominated as the NDP's presidential candidate that same day and endorsed by a nationwide referendum a week later with an approval rating recorded as 98.4%.

When he took office Mubarak was seen as a political moderate, who promised a degree of continuity with Sadat's policies. In the event, his presidency has been notable particularly for the gradual rebuilding of relations with the Arab states which had ostracized Sadat over his Camp David accords with Israel. He has maintained a degree of independence in Egypt's foreign policy, despite heavy reliance on US aid, and has been notably cool in dealings with Israel, which he has visited only once, in 1995. Even this was a condolence call rather than an official visit, on the occasion of the funeral of the Israeli prime minister Yitzhak Rabin, on whom many of the hopes for an Israeli–Palestinian peace agreement had rested. His credit with the US government was boosted by his leading role among Arab states in opposing the Iraqi invasion of Kuwait in 1990 and by his decision to commit Egyptian troops to join the US-led forces in the 1991 Gulf War.

Mubarak has been re-elected for successive six-year presidential terms, in 1987, 1993 and 1999, and is set to stand again in late 2005, despite having initially proclaimed that no president should serve more than two terms. In each case up to and including 1999 he was nominated as the sole candidate by the National Assembly and endorsed overwhelmingly by national referendum.

Mubarak has proved uncompromising in his attitude towards Muslim militant groups in Egypt, and there have been several attempts on his life, most notably on 26 June 1995 when he narrowly escaped assassination during a visit to Addis Ababa, Ethiopia. His clampdown on fundamentalist activity, while incurring criticism from human rights groups over reprisal killings, political trials and the use of torture, has not succeeded in doing more than containing a situation that remains tense and potentially explosive.

In foreign affairs, Mubarak has leaned closer to his Arab contemporaries. In June 2000 he ended the 21-year deadlock between Egypt and Iran by calling President Mohammad Khatami to congratulate him for Iran's entrance to the G15 group of developing countries. Conversely he has increasingly criticized Israel, accusing it in April 2002 of state-sponsored terrorism against the Palestinians.

Mounting demonstrations from 2004, however, demanded the introduction of free and direct elections for the presidency. Mubarak capitulated to the pressure and proposed multicandidate polls, which were approved by the People's Assembly in May 2005 and backed by referendum later that month. However, the new system has been criticized by the opposition on the grounds that the strict rules for becoming a candidate would prevent many from being able to stand. If re-elected (as widely expected) in late 2005, Mubarak has announced that he would then appoint a vice president, a move that could indicate his plans for succession—it is thought that his son Gamal is being groomed to take over, despite Mubarak's assurances that the presidency is not hereditary.

Profile of the Prime Minister:

Ahmed **NAZIF**

Ahmed Nazif is a skilled electronic and computer engineer who was appointed as Egyptian prime minister on 14 July 2004. Aged 52 when he took office, he is much younger than his predecessors and made his reputation while minister of communications and technology, when he instigated a programme for widening Internet access that has become a model for other countries. He has moved to liberalize Egypt's economy even as President Mubarak has begun the liberalization of its political system.

Ahmed Nazif was born on 8 July 1952 in Alexandria. He is married with two sons. After graduating with a degree and a master's degree in electrical engineering from Cairo University, Nazif travelled to Canada to study for a doctorate in computer engineering from McGill University in 1983. When he returned to Egypt he worked as a teacher in the faculty of engineering at Cairo University, where he obtained his professorship in 1993.

In 1989 he worked as an executive director in the Cabinet Information Centre, as well as implementing several other information technology (IT) projects across government. At the same time he became executive manager of IDSC, one of the leading IT organizations in the world. In 1999 Mubarak appointed Nazif as communications and technology minister under Prime Minister Atif Obeid. One of his major achievements was the implementation of the national communication and information plan, developed later into the Initiative of the Egyptian Information Society. The programme, involving the expansion of access to the Internet, is considered to be a model for developing nations.

On 14 July 2004, Nazif, the youngest member of the outgoing cabinet, was appointed prime minister. He told reporters that his priority would be to revive Egypt's sluggish economy and to find, if necessary, unconventional ways to improve Egypt's unemployment rate. Nazif has a reputation for being open and honest, and his name literally translates as 'clean'. Since his appointment, he has steadily been pursuing one of the biggest sell-offs in Egyptian history. Nearly 700 state-owned assets are to be privatized, floated on the stock market or otherwise offered to the private sector, despite concern among labour and industrial groups.

EL SALVADOR

Full name: The Republic of El Salvador.

Leadership structure: The head of state is a president, directly elected by universal adult suffrage. The president's term of office is five years. The head of government is the president, who appoints a Council of State.

President:	Francisco Flores	1 June 1999—1 June 2004
	Tony **SACA**	Since 1 June 2004

Legislature: The legislature is unicameral. The sole chamber, the Legislative Assembly (Asamblea Legislativa), has 84 members, directly elected for a three-year term.

Profile of the President:

Tony **SACA**

Tony Saca was the victorious candidate for the National Republican Alliance (Alianza Republicana Nacionalista—ARENA) in the presidential elections of 21 March 2004. He was sworn in on 1 June as successor to fellow ARENA member and outgoing president Francisco Flores. Saca, who is descended from Palestinian immigrants, was a prominent businessman and broadcast journalist before the election, known particularly for his radio sports reporting. He made his fortune selling radio advertising and now owns nine radio stations. Supported in his childhood by the remittances of brothers working illegally in the USA, Saca has embraced the free-market and pro-US policies of his predecessor.

Elías Antonio ('Tony') Saca González was born in Usulután on 9 March 1965, a descendent of Catholic Arab immigrants from the West Bank town of Bethlehem who had fled military service under the Ottoman Empire in 1913. He remained in Usulután until his father's cotton business went bankrupt and the family was forced to move to San Salvador, where they lived largely on remittances from elder sons who had made the perilous journey to work illegally in the USA. Saca was just 14 years old when he jumped through a door to dodge a street demonstration and found himself in a small radio station. He sold commercials by telephone to disguise his age, then did sports broadcasts before studying for a degree in journalism at the University of El Salvador. He subsequently worked as a sports journalist on radio and television for more than ten years. Saca is married to Ana Ligia Mixco Sol de Saca (who now holds the post of secretary of state for family affairs); they have three sons.

In 1987, in partnership with Alfonso Rivas, Saca established Radio América. A series of state radio stations followed this initiative until Saca ended the partnership and established Radio Astral—the first for the SAMIX Group, which is made up of nine radio stations in different states of El Salvador. By 1997 Saca had become something of a media mogul, and became a member of the Salvadoran Association of Radio Stations, where he served as president on two occasions between 1997 and 2001.

Aged just 39 when he stood in the 2004 presidential elections, Saca is young enough not to be indelibly associated with the bitter civil war that divided El Salvador in the 1980s. Coupled with his lack of political experience, this impression of 'clean hands' set him apart from other Salvadoran politicians, and stood in clear contrast to his presidential rival, Shafik Handal, candidate of the National Liberation Front Farabundo Martí (Frente Farabundo Martí para la Liberación Nacional—FMLN). Handal, oddly enough also descended from a Christian Arab family from Bethlehem, had been involved in sourcing arms for the FMLN in the 1980s from the Fatah organization in Beirut.

Saca defeated Handal by a margin of 58% to 36%, with 70% voter turnout. He was seen to be very much the preferred candidate of US president George W. Bush's administration, to the extent that some accused the USA of undermining the impartiality of the elections. Saca has since been greeted with warmth by US officials, and has succeeded in securing an extension of the temporary work permits enjoyed by about 250,000 illegal Salvadoran immigrants in the USA, who were granted this Temporary Protection Status after devastating earthquakes in 2001.

EQUATORIAL GUINEA

Full name: The Republic of Equatorial Guinea.

Leadership structure: The head of state is a president, directly elected by universal adult suffrage. The president's term of office is seven years. The president appoints the Council of Ministers. The prime minister is head of government.

President: Teodoro **OBIANG NGUEMA** Mbasogo   Since 12 Oct. 1982 (seized power on 3 Aug. 1979)

Prime Minister: Ángel Serafin Dougan   29 March 1996—4 March 2001

Cándido Muatetema Rivas   4 March 2001—14 June 2004

Miguel Abia **BITEO** Boricó   Since 14 June 2004

Legislature: The legislature is unicameral. The sole chamber, the House of Representatives of the People (Cámara de Representantes del Pueblo), has 100 members, directly elected for a five-year term.

Profile of the President:

Brig.-Gen. Teodoro **OBIANG NGUEMA** Mbasogo

Brig.-Gen. Teodoro Obiang Nguema, having deposed and executed his brutal and despotic uncle Francisco Macías Nguema in 1979, went on to create his own single-party structure, paying little more than lip service to the notion that Equatorial Guinea made a transition to multiparty democracy in the early 1990s. In the 1996 presidential elections he was the sole candidate, and in 2002 the opposition candidates withdrew after voting had started, alleging irregularities.

Teodoro Obiang Nguema Mbasogo was born on 5 June 1942 in Acó Acam near Mongomo, on the eastern border with Gabon. He is a member of that region's Esangui ethnic group, a small subgroup of the country's Fang majority. He went to school in Bata, the principal mainland port, and then received military training at the Zaragoza Military Academy in Spain from 1963 to 1965. In 1968 under his uncle's regime he was appointed deputy minister of defence and then military governor of the island of Fernando Póo (now known as Bioko). In the early 1970s he worked in government service, in the planning department and in the ministry of education. From 1975 he was defence minister and aide-de-camp to the president. The 11-year dictatorship of Macías was known for its brutality and

Obiang Nguema's own brother was among victims who were executed, in his case for complaining about unpaid wages.

On 3 August 1979 Obiang Nguema led a coup against Macías, ordered his execution and declared himself president. Despite the release of many political prisoners, Obiang Nguema continued to rule despotically as his uncle had done, surrounding himself in the same way with Esangui relatives. Since 1980 Obiang Nguema has also held the positions of minister of defence (until 2004) and supreme commander of the armed forces.

After a number of coup attempts in the years immediately following his takeover, a new constitution was adopted in 1982 which provided for a handover to civilian rule after a seven-year period during which Obiang Nguema was to rule as president.

In 1987 Obiang Nguema founded the Equatorial Guinea Democratic Party (Partido Democrático de Guinea Ecuatorial—PDGE) as the sole legal political party and, having meanwhile arrested his opponents, was the only candidate for the presidential elections held in June 1989.

External pressure, including the withholding of foreign aid and funds from the International Monetary Fund (IMF), eventually induced him to allow a nominal change to multipartyism, with six parties legalized in 1992. Most of the opposition leaders remained in exile, however; those who were allowed back returned only at real personal risk, and there was frequent violent disruption of opposition meetings. In 1993 the USA withdrew its diplomatic representation, citing the government's abuse of human rights. In November of that year the PDGE won all but 12 seats in legislative elections which were boycotted by the opposition following more arrests. The results were disputed by the US and Spanish governments and the latter withdrew aid to the country. The 1999 elections were equally unsatisfactory, with the official results giving the PDGE an even more overwhelming parliamentary majority.

The presidential elections held in February 1996 had similarly been denounced by opposition parties, who had been given only six weeks notice of the poll. Among the instances of election malpractice was the fact that the electoral list supplied by the UN was replaced by a government one, omitting many voters from the register in the areas where opposition groups commanded most support. The official results, which gave Obiang Nguema nearly 98% of the vote, showed many more votes cast than there were registered voters.

In June 1997 a coup attempt was foiled and a spate of arrests followed. Another clampdown in 2002 saw 68 opposition leaders jailed in connection with this same 1997 coup attempt. Obiang Nguema stood again as the PDGE presidential candidate in December 2002. The opposition candidates withdrew after voting had started, complaining of widespread vote rigging and intimidation. He went on to receive almost 100% of the vote. Afterwards, Obiang Nguema called for the creation of a government of unity, but deep differences with the opposition

Convergence for Social Democracy (Convergencia para la Democracia Social—CPDS) remained, especially over imprisoned opposition leaders. Later that year state radio proclaimed that Obiang Nguema was "like God in heaven" and had regular contact with the deity.

A coup plot to install the government-in-exile of Severo Moto Nsa was foiled in March 2004 when 15 suspected mercenaries were arrested in Equatorial Guinea and 64 more were arrested in Zimbabwe, en route to Malabo from South Africa. The multinational group of plotters included Sir Mark Thatcher, son of the former UK prime minister, and was allegedly backed by the intelligence services of various Western governments including the USA.

The PDGE and its close allies, known collectively as 'the democratic opposition', took 98 of 100 seats in the House of Representatives in the May 2004 elections. The CPDS denounced the elections as fraudulent and illegal, while international observers described the results as "not very credible".

With rumours spreading that Obiang Nguema is suffering from prostate cancer, the question of succession is rising. A likely candidate is Teodoro Nguema Obiang Mangue, his eldest son by his first wife Constancia Mangue Nsue. He is currently agriculture minister. Obiang Nguema has recognized four other sons, including Gabriel Nguema Lima, born to his other wife Celestina Lima.

Profile of the Prime Minister:

Miguel Abia **BITEO** Boricó

Miguel Abia Biteo Boricó was appointed prime minister on 14 June 2004. A close ally of President Teodoro Obiang Nguema, he is a former finance minister, but had been forced to resign that post in 2000 over a corruption scandal.

Miguel Abia Biteo Boricó was born in 1961, a member of the Bubi ethnic group, and one of the few Bubi to attain political power in Equatorial Guinea, which is dominated by the Fang ethnic group of President Obiang Nguema. Biteo studied in the former Soviet Union, where he gained a master's degree in mining engineering, specializing in the drilling of oil and gas.

After his return to Equatorial Guinea he began working for the government in the mines and hydrocarbons directorate, rising eventually to the position of director-general, one of the most powerful positions in the country's oil industry. He participated from the very start in oil negotiations with North American companies, and is said to know all the secrets of the country's opaque oil industry.

He served as finance minister from 1999 until 2000, when he was forced to resign over a corruption scandal. Biteo was accused of embezzling millions of francs, using public money to pay for his family's holidays, and of employing 'ghost' personnel in the ministry. He nonetheless remained a close ally of President Obiang Nguema. According to the exiled opposition, he spent the following years organizing the transfer of funds originating from the oil sector for the ruling elite. Obiang Nguema appointed him prime minister on 14 June 2004.

ERITREA

Full name: The State of Eritrea.

Leadership structure: The head of state is a president, elected by the National Assembly, of which he is chairman. Under the 1997 Constitution the president's term of office is five years, but elections have not been held since 1993. The head of government is the president, who appoints and presides over a State Council which includes provincial administrators.

President:	Issaias **AFEWERKI**	Since 24 May 1993
	(headed provisional government	
	before independence, from 29 May 1991)	

Legislature: The legislature is unicameral. Under the 1997 Constitution the 150-member National Assembly (Hagerawi Baito) is to be elected directly for a four-year term. In March 1994 it was decided that for the rest of the transitional period 75 Assembly members should be the members of the ruling central committee of the People's Front for Democracy and Justice (PFDJ) and 75 should be elected, but no mechanism was provided for such elections.

Profile of the President:

Issaias **AFEWERKI**

Issaias Afewerki is the first president of the State of Eritrea, elected one month after the April 1993 referendum which overwhelmingly endorsed secession from Ethiopia. He had come to prominence as a military leader in the three decades of struggle against Ethiopian occupation, helping to found the Eritrean People's Liberation Front (EPLF) under whose leadership the country was liberated when the Mengistu regime in Ethiopia was overthrown in 1991.

Born on 2 February 1946 in Asmara, Issaias Afewerki completed one year as an engineering student at the University of Addis Ababa before going underground in 1966 and joining the Eritrean Liberation Front (ELF), which had begun an armed liberation struggle in 1962. Afewerki is married to Saba Haile and they have three children.

Part of his military training was undertaken in China. From 1967 to 1970 he was regional and then general commander of the ELF, which merged with other groups in 1970 to form the EPLF. As a founding EPLF member he held various leading positions, becoming deputy secretary-general in 1977 and secretary-general in 1987. Part of his contribution to the liberation struggle was his success in obtaining support for the movement in the Islamic world.

The EPLF's military victories played a major role in the downfall of the Mengistu regime in Ethiopia in May 1991. Afewerki immediately set up a provisional government, and at a conference in London, UK, in August he secured recognition of his administration as the legitimate provisional government of Eritrea, while agreeing to hold a referendum on independence within two years. When this took place, in April 1993, there was a 99.8% vote recorded in favour of secession. In a process facilitated by the close links maintained between Afewerki and Ethiopia's prime minister Meles Zenawi, Ethiopia accepted Eritrea's secession on 3 May. A provisional assembly, composed of the EPLF's central committee and an equal number of elected members, confirmed Afewerki as president on 22 May, two days before independence was formally declared.

In February 1994 the EPLF changed its name to the People's Front for Democracy and Justice (PFDJ), since when Afewerki has been chairman of the National Assembly and of the PFDJ. He has made it his priority to develop and modernize the infrastructure of Eritrea and lead the country out of its many years of warfare and famine. A national constitution was adopted in May 1997, but multiparty elections, due to have been held within four years of independence, have yet to be arranged. Even a promise to schedule polls in December 2001, made just after the end of hostilities with Ethiopia in late 2000, did not come to pass. In the meantime Afewerki has clamped down on opposition, and a number of pro-democracy activists have been arrested.

ESTONIA

Full name: The Republic of Estonia.

Leadership structure: The head of state is a president, elected by the Parliament. However, if no candidate receives the votes of at least 68 of the 101 members of Parliament in up to three rounds of voting, an electoral assembly is convened, which includes 266 local government representatives in addition to the members of Parliament. In the voting by the electoral assembly a simple majority is sufficient to elect the new president. The president's term of office is five years. The head of government is the prime minister, who is appointed by the president and who nominates the Council of Ministers.

President:	Lennart Meri	6 Oct. 1992—8 Oct. 2001
	Arnold **RÜÜTEL**	Since 8 Oct. 2001
Prime Minister:	Mart Laar (acting until 28 Jan. 2002)	25 March 1999—8 Jan. 2002
	Siim Kallas	28 Jan. 2002—10 April 2003
	Juhan Parts (acting until 13 April 2005)	10 April 2003—21 March 2005
	Andrus **ANSIP**	Since 13 April 2005

Legislature: The legislature is unicameral. The sole chamber, the Parliament (Riigikogu), has 101 members, directly elected for a four-year term.

Profile of the President:

Arnold **RÜÜTEL**

Arnold Rüütel is a respected agronomist and is also active on environmental issues. A former senior member of the communist hierarchy, he was briefly (until 1992) Estonia's first postcommunist head of state. He was leader of the right-of-centre Estonian People's Union (Eestimaa Rahvaliit—ERL) until 2000, and was elected to the country's presidency the following year.

Arnold Rüütel was born on 10 May 1928 on the island of Saaremaa during Estonia's brief period of interwar independence. Still only a child when the country came under Soviet control in the Second World War, he graduated from an agricultural college in 1949 and began a long career in the Soviet agricultural sector as head of the agronomic department on Saaremaa. He moved to the Estonian Institute of Cattle Breeding in 1957 as head zootechnician. A year later he married Ingrid née Ruus; they have two daughters. By the time he left the institute in 1963 he had become its assistant director. For the next six years he directed work at the Tartu Model State Farm. He also studied at the Estonian Agricultural Academy, graduating in 1964. From 1969 he acted as rector of the academy.

From 1977 Rüütel began combining his scientific and administrative work with politics. In 1983 he was elected chairman of the Supreme Soviet of the Estonian Soviet Socialist Republic (SSR). In this capacity he played a vital role in the emergence of a separate Estonian state in the late 1980s and the drafting of the 1988 *Resolution on the Sovereignty of the Estonian SSR*. He was re-elected in 1990 as the country began separating itself from the Soviet Union. He was de facto head of state until 1992, when he failed to win presidential elections.

In the Parliament Rüütel headed the Estonian Rural People's Party (later to merge to form the ERL) from 1994 until 2000. He was elected vice speaker in 1995 and headed the regional Baltic Assembly. He continued to promote agricultural issues and established a number of agricultural and environmental bodies, including the Estonian Society for Nature Protection and the Estonian Green Cross. Parliament elected him president on 21 September 2001 and he took office on 8 October.

Profile of the Prime Minister:

Andrus **ANSIP**

Andrus Ansip was appointed prime minister on 31 March 2005, following the resignation of his predecessor Juhan Parts, and was sworn in on 13 April. A popular former mayor of Tartu, Ansip was a businessman before entering politics. He had stood—and won—in several elections to the Parliament, but had always given up his seat in order to remain in Tartu as mayor. However, when the leader of the conservative Reform Party (Reformierakond—RE), former Prime Minister Siim Kallas, became a European Union (EU) commissioner in 2004, Ansip took over as party leader, moved to the capital, Tallinn, and joined the cabinet.

Andrus Ansip was born on 1 October 1956 in Tartu, Estonia. After graduating in chemistry from Tartu University, Ansip became involved in banking and economics. He has served on the board of directors of the People's Bank of Tartu, as chairman of the board of Livonia Privatization IF, and as chief executive officer of Investment Fund Broker Ltd. He studied business management at York University in the UK in 1992. From 1994 to 1999, he was also chairman of the board of Radio Tartu. He is married with three children.

In 1998 Ansip was elected mayor of Tartu as the candidate of the conservative Reform Party, a position which he held until 2004. Ansip was a popular mayor, and consistently won high ratings in opinion polls. However, in 2004 Reform founder and former prime minister Siim Kallas became an EU commissioner and moved to Brussels. Ansip became the chair of the party, and entered the coalition government of Prime Minister Juhan Parts as minister of economic affairs and communications.

Parts announced his resignation on 21 March 2005, over a controversial anti-corruption plan, and Ansip was appointed prime minister ten days later. His administration, sworn in on 13 April, is the eighth since Estonia became independent in 1992. Ansip leads a 'rainbow' coalition government made up of his own conservative Reform Party, the left-leaning Centre Party and the rural-based Estonian People's Union. It has been dubbed the 'garlic coalition', as the deal was struck in the Balthasar restaurant in Tallinn which specializes in garlic-based dishes. Ansip has said that he will continue steering Estonia towards membership of the eurozone in 2007.

ETHIOPIA

Full name: The Federal Democratic Republic of Ethiopia.

Leadership structure: The head of state is a president, elected by a joint session of the House of People's Representatives and the House of the Federation. The president's term of office is six years, renewable once only. The head of government is the prime minister, who is appointed by the House of People's Representatives, and appoints the Council of Ministers.

President:	Negaso Gidada	22 Aug. 1995—8 Oct. 2001
	Lt. **GIRMA** Wolde Giorgis	Since 8 Oct. 2001
Prime Minister:	**MELES** Zenawi	Since 23 Aug. 1995
	(acting head of state from 28 May 1991;	
	transitional president from 21 July 1991)	

Legislature: The legislature, the Federal Parliamentary Assembly (Yememakirtoch Mekir Bet), is bicameral. The lower chamber, the House of People's Representatives (Yehizb Tewokayoch Mekir Bet), currently has 547 members (with a maximum of 550), directly elected for a five-year term. The upper chamber, the House of the Federation (Yefedereshn Mekir Bet), has 110 members representing the nations, nationalities and peoples of Ethiopia, elected for a five-year term by the government councils of the nine states which make up the federation.

Profile of the President:

Lt. **GIRMA** Wolde Giorgis

Girma Wolde Giorgis is an independent politician with a long but low-profile career in government service. Heading the country's aviation department in the 1950s, he went on to lead the Red Cross in the then Ethiopian province of Eritrea. He was chosen by the Federal Parliamentary Assembly to be president of Ethiopia in 2001.

Girma Wolde Giorgis was born in December 1924 in Addis Ababa, into the majority Oromo ethnic group. He is married and has three sons and two daughters; his family all live abroad. After studying at an Italian school in Addis Ababa in the late 1930s, he was enlisted in the UK-established Ethiopian Military Radio Communication in 1941 in the midst of the Second World War. Towards the end of that conflict he graduated from the Genet Military School as a lieutenant, in 1944, and transferred to the Ethiopian air force in 1946.

Girma travelled abroad between 1950 and 1952 to complete his education in air traffic management in the Netherlands, Sweden and Canada. When he returned he taught the subject in Ethiopia. In 1955 he was appointed director of the government's new civil aviation department and became a board member of Ethiopian Airlines in 1958.

Girma switched from aviation to more direct government service in 1959 when he became director-general of the ministry of trade, industry and planning. He was elected to parliament for the first time in 1960 and was appointed speaker. Between 1965 and 1974 he worked in commerce, both as manager of the Import and Export Enterprise (IMPEX) and as a representative for the business community at various nongovernmental organizations. Under the Dergue military regime which came to power in 1974, and its successors, Girma worked for the regional branch of the International Red Cross in what was then the Ethiopian northern province of Eritrea. Amid increasing civil conflict in the country, and especially in Eritrea, Girma returned to Addis Ababa in 1991 and established Lem Ethiopia, an environmental protection agency.

After a 35-year absence from parliament, Girma returned in 2000 when he was elected to the House of People's Representatives as an independent candidate. A year later he was selected by the government of Prime Minister Meles Zenawi as the presidential nominee. His appointment was seen as a tactical move by the government, as he was a largely unknown figure, and particularly as his ethnic Oromo background contrasted with the predominance of Tigrayans in Ethiopia's principal positions of power. He took over from the outgoing head of state, the increasingly combative President Negaso Gidada, on 8 October 2001. Just six days later Girma was taken to hospital in Saudi Arabia with a serious heart condition, raising doubts about his ability to fulfil his full six-year term. However, he returned a month later and resumed his duties. He has used his position to raise AIDS awareness in Ethiopia, to promote cultural diversity and to highlight internationally Ethiopia's struggle against poverty, recent conflict and recurrent famine.

Profile of the Prime Minister:

MELES Zenawi

Meles Zenawi has been prime minister of Ethiopia since August 1995, following a general election dominated by the Ethiopian People's Revolutionary Democratic Front (EPRDF). For the preceding four years he had headed an interim government formed after the overthrow of the Marxist military dictatorship of Mengistu. Meles had risen to prominence through the Tigray People's Liberation Front (TPLF), which, apart from its Eritrean counterpart, had been the most effective of the anti-Mengistu forces during the long armed struggle. Having accepted that the Eritreans should proceed to separate independence, the Tigrayans are a dominant element in the ruling EPRDF coalition.

Meles Zenawi was born on 9 May 1955 in Adwa, in Tigray in northern Ethiopia. He went to the prestigious Gen. Wingate High School in Addis Ababa and entered the University of Addis Ababa Medical School. In 1975, however, he left to help found a rebel Marxist-Leninist League of Tigray, a core element in the TPLF alliance ten years later. As TPLF secretary-general, Meles became a figure of real national significance when TPLF forces, encouraged by military successes by the Eritrean secessionist movement, turned the tide of their own war against Mengistu's troops and overran most of Tigray between 1988 and 1989. An alliance with other guerrilla groups in September 1989 brought into being the broader multi-ethnic EPRDF coalition of guerrilla movements, with Meles as its chairman. The Mengistu regime, having failed to reach a negotiated settlement, was swept away by military defeat in May 1991, and in July Meles was elected president of a transitional government of Ethiopia and chairman of the Council of Representatives.

Although the transition process was affected by disputes and violence, mainly between rival groups organized along ethnic lines, the EPRDF dominated both the Constituent Assembly elections in June 1994, and the general election held under the new federal constitution in May 1995—and marred by opposition boycotts and allegations of intimidation. Meles was elected unanimously as prime minister by the House of People's Representatives on 23 August 1995, the day after the formal establishment of the Federal Democratic Republic of Ethiopia.

Meles Zenawi's role in Ethiopia's transition to democracy and federalism won him the 'good governance award' of the Washington D.C.-based intergovernmental Global Coalition for Africa, although his administration has been criticized on human rights grounds for its harsh measures against those expressing opposition or discontent. In October 1996 Meles dismissed one of the deputy prime ministers, Tamirat Layne, accusing him of abuse of power, and this and other changes enabled him to consolidate his own position ahead of the May 2000 legislative elections, when the EPRDF retained an overwhelming majority of seats. He was re-elected by acclamation in parliament on 10 October to another five-year term as prime minister.

A growing opposition movement posed a much greater challenge in the 2005 elections. Beforehand Meles signed a nonviolence pact with the Coalition for Unity and Democracy (CUD) to try to ensure a peaceful poll; EU election observers praised Ethiopian efforts, saying that such an open debate had never been held in the country before. After polling on 15 May, Meles imposed a month-long ban on demonstrations, though the opposition still held rallies, claiming fraud. Investigations into the allegations, and subsequent reruns, dragged on for several months, preventing the official publication of final results. However, it soon became clear that the EPRDF had retained a majority, while opposition representation rose from 12 seats to around 160 in the 547-seat House of People's Representatives.

Meles is married to Azeb Mesfin, and they have three children. Azeb was rarely seen in public until 2003 when she became a founding member of Ethiopia's Coalition of Women against AIDS. Since then she has been active in raising AIDS awareness, publicly taking an HIV test on World AIDS Day in 2004. She has also campaigned for women's rights and an end to female genital mutilation.

FIJI

Full name: The Republic of the Fiji Islands.

Leadership structure: The head of state is a president, appointed by the Great Council of Chiefs. The president's term of office is five years. The head of government is the prime minister, who is appointed by the president and responsible to the Parliament. The cabinet is appointed by the prime minister.

President:	Ratu Sir Kamisese Mara (acting from 29 Nov. 1993)	18 Jan. 1994—29 May 2000

Head of Interim Military Government:

	Commodore Josaia Voreqe 'Frank' Bainimarama	29 May 2000—18 July 2000
President:	Ratu Josefa **ILOILO** (interim until 15 March 2001)	Since 18 July 2000

Prime Minister:	Mahendra Chaudhry	19 May 1999—27 May 2000
	vacant	27 May 2000—3 July 2000
	Laisenia Qarase (interim)	3 July 2000—14 March 2001
	Ratu Tevita Momoedonu	14 March 2001—16 March 2001
	Laisenia **QARASE** (interim to 10 Sept. 2001)	Since 16 March 2001

Legislature: The legislature, the Parliament, is bicameral. The lower chamber, the House of Representatives, has 71 members, directly elected for a five-year term. Under the 1997 Constitution, 25 of the 71 seats are open to all races, but elected in single-member constituencies; the other 46 seats are allocated for election by Fiji's various ethnic communities. The upper chamber, the Senate, has 32 members, appointed by the president for five-year terms, following recommendations from the political parties, in proportion to their seats in the House of Representatives, and from the Great Council of Chiefs.

Profile of the President:

Ratu Josefa **ILOILO**

A prominent western chief, Ratu Josefa Iloilo had been vice president before the May 2000 Fijian nationalist coup, but he had not held any other government position. The coup overthrew the ethnic Indian prime minister and brought about the resignation of the incumbent president. Iloilo's appointment as president by the Great Council of Chiefs in July 2000 was repeated eight months later, after a court decision that the 1997 Constitution scrapped by the coup leaders actually remained in force. Ill health prevented him from taking on the full powers of the presidency but he did nominate a pro-military government after the end of the crisis.

Josefa Iloilovatu Uluivuda was born on 29 December 1920 on Taveuni island. From 1939 to 1968 he worked as a schoolteacher on the islands. During these 30 years he helped to introduce the Boy Scout movement to the country, establishing scout troops on many islands. He is married to Salaseini Kavunono Uluivuda.

As Tui Vuda (high chief of Vuda, on the main westerly island of Viti Levu) Iloilo represents the interests of the western isles. In the late 1990s he was appointed as vice president by the then president Ratu Sir Kamisese Mara. Having established a reputation as a corruption-free administrator, Iloilo was nominated in 1999 as a candidate for chairman of the Great Council of Chiefs, but was defeated in the body's first secret ballot by the incumbent prime minister Ratu Sitiveni Rabuka.

In May 2000 Fijian supremacist and local businessman George Speight took Mahendra Chaudhry, the country's first ever ethnic Indian prime minister, and his cabinet hostage, and demanded the revocation of the 1997 Constitution. In the ensuing crisis martial law was imposed and President Mara stepped down at the rebels' insistence. Iloilo, whose daughter (now dead) had been married to Speight's brother, was Speight's second choice as an acceptable candidate for president and was offered the position by the Great Council of Chiefs.

From the outset it was clear that Speight had miscalculated in expecting Iloilo to be amenable to his own objectives. In his acceptance speech Iloilo called for a multiracial country, and he defied the nationalists by appointing the military-backed Laisenia Qarase as prime minister. Speight was arrested soon afterwards. However, Iloilo's ill health—giving rise to speculation that he might have Parkinson's disease—cast a shadow over his inauguration.

Less than a year after the coup the Constitutional Court threw the country into political chaos when it ruled on 1 March 2001 that the dissolution of the 1997 Constitution and the removal of the government in 2000 had both been illegal. Iloilo's position came directly into question until he was renominated by the Great Council of Chiefs a few days later. On 14 March Iloilo officially dismissed Chaudhry and appointed his own nephew Ratu Tevita Momoedonu as prime minister. Iloilo was re-inaugurated the following day, along with Momoedonu, and then accepted Momoedonu's resignation 24 hours later. Closing the loop, Iloilo reappointed Qarase as prime minister.

Rumours of Iloilo's ill health arose again in mid-2005, with news that he had been confined to a wheelchair for three weeks. However, he was well enough to open Parliament at the beginning of August.

Profile of the Prime Minister:

Laisenia **QARASE**

Laisenia Qarase was appointed as interim prime minister of Fiji by the military authorities on 3 July 2000, confirmed in the position by President Ratu Josefa Iloilo later in the month, and formed a new government after his party's success in elections just over a year later. His initial appointment followed a nationalist coup, led by Fijian supremacist George Speight, which disenfranchised the country's large ethnic Indian minority after overthrowing the government of Mahendra Chaudhry. Qarase has been a prominent champion of Fijian rights in the Indian-dominated economic sector and has resisted the inclusion in government of the main Indian-backed party.

Laisenia Qarase was born on 4 February 1941 into the Tota clan in Mavana on Vanua Balavu, in the Lau group of eastern islands. After attending local schools he travelled to the country's main island, Viti Levu, to enrol at Suva Boys' Grammar School. He left Fiji in 1959 and studied commerce and co-operative development at Auckland University in New Zealand. Now married to Leba Qarase with four sons and one daughter, he is described as a quiet and modest man.

From his first job with the Fijian Affairs Board until becoming prime minister, Qarase has worked for the advancement of the country's ethnic Fijian population. His career as a civil servant included posts at the ministries of finance, commerce and industry and public services before he was appointed as the first ethnic Fijian managing director of the Fiji Development Bank (FDB) in 1983. While at the bank he has admitted he felt angered by the dominance of ethnic Indians in the financial sector.

Following the pro-Fijian coups of 1987 the new government turned to Qarase for help in rebuilding the damaged economy. His suggested policies centred on promoting the economic involvement of native Fijians. He introduced a nine-point plan which extended government assistance to Fijians and oversaw the creation of Fijian Holdings. However the plan mostly resulted in bankruptcies and large debts and he was embroiled in scandal at Fijian Holdings over the acquisition of shares by members of his family. From 1994 he was chairman of Fiji Television and clashed with the government of Prime Minister Sitiveni Rabuka over its plans to introduce US investment into the company without consulting him. In 1998 he quit both the television company and the FDB to take up a new position at the Merchant Bank of Fiji.

In the new regime inaugurated by the multiracial 1997 Constitution, Qarase was nominated to the Senate in 1999 by the powerful Great Council of Chiefs as a candidate for the opposition Fijian Political Party. From the Senate he became a vocal critic of the government's policies towards the indigenous islanders. He also sat on the boards of several indigenous Fijian investment companies.

George Speight's two-month coup in 2000 drew great sympathy from conservative Fijians anxious to turn back the advance of multiracialism. Qarase was nominated by the military to head an interim government, and won the backing of the Great Council of Chiefs for his appointment. Although this disappointed Speight's own political ambitions, Qarase proved a stalwart supporter of Speight's pro-Fijian policies, saying openly that the people "were not ready" for an ethnic Indian prime minister. He initially rejected calls to convene new elections, while the initial international pressure to reinstate Chaudhry subsided to demands to restore the 1997 Constitution.

Although this demand was met by the Constitutional Court ruling of 1 March 2001, Qarase resolutely resisted court pressure to incorporate Chaudhry and his opposition Fiji Labour Party (FLP). The direct result of the ruling saw Qarase temporarily dismissed in mid-March, but he returned to office in a complex manoeuvre within just two days as President Ratu Josefa Iloilo officially dismissed Chaudhry, nominally appointed his own nephew at the head of a new FLP government, and then accepted its resignation so as to allow Qarase to take back the reins of power.

Fresh elections were called for May 2001 and Qarase led his new United Fiji Party (Soqosoqo Duavata ni Lewenivanua—SDL) to a narrow victory. In defiance of the 1997 Constitution, which grants parties with more than eight seats at least one cabinet ministry, Qarase went on to completely ignore the FLP (which had gained 27 seats) in his new, nationalist government. He was sworn in for his first legitimate full term in office on 11 September 2001. Despite rulings by the High Court, which in August 2002 issued revised election results that put the SDL on a level footing in the House of Representatives with the FLP, Qarase still repeatedly refused to accept that the FLP was entitled to cabinet representation. It wasn't until the Supreme Court had upheld these rulings in July 2003 and ruled that Qarase's government was illegal that he finally offered posts to the FLP, mainly in new, minor ministries. Chaudhry himself was not included in the nominees and the FLP rejected the offer, claiming entitlement to a greater proportion of cabinet seats. In March 2004 Qarase and Chaudhry agreed to work together to end the political stalemate, but the Supreme Court failed to resolve the dispute over the number of seats the FLP was entitled to, and the FLP in July rejected an enlarged offer.

A controversial bill was proposed in 2005 to allow conspirators in the 2000 coup to seek amnesty if their actions were deemed political rather than criminal. The FLP walked out of the House of Representatives, and the army threatened to overthrow the government if the amnesty went ahead. Qarase defended the plans saying that they were designed to remove lingering resentment caused by the coup.

FINLAND

Full name: The Republic of Finland.

Leadership structure: The head of state is a president, directly elected by universal adult suffrage. The president's term of office is six years. The head of government is the prime minister, who is elected by Parliament and appointed by the president. The Council of State is appointed by the president as proposed by the prime minister.

President:	Martti Ahtisaari	1 March 1994—1 March 2000
	Tarja **HALONEN**	Since 1 March 2000
Prime Minister:	Paavo Lipponen	13 April 1995—17 April 2003
	Anneli Jäätteenmäki (acting until 24 June 2003)	17 April 2003—18 June 2003
	Matti **VANHANEN**	Since 24 June 2003

Legislature: The legislature is unicameral. The sole chamber, the Parliament (Eduskunta), has 200 members, directly elected for a four-year term.

Profile of the President:

Tarja **HALONEN**

Tarja Halonen is Finland's first female head of state—a career politician, left-winger and feminist. She appealed to Finnish voters to redress the imbalance of the sexes in politics through her election, and—having raised her daughter Anna on her own—caused some surprise when she married her subsequent partner Pentti Arajärvi six months after her election to the presidency. The role of president is an active one in Finnish politics, especially in foreign affairs, the portfolio she held as a minister from 1995 until her election in 2000.

Tarja Kaarina Halonen was born in Helsinki on 24 December 1943. She studied law and foreign languages, and speaks several European languages fluently. As a law graduate, she worked for the firm Lainvalvonta from 1967 to 1968. Strengthening her trade union credentials, she worked as social affairs secretary and then general secretary of the National Union of Finnish Students between 1969 and 1970, and as a lawyer with the Central Organization of Finnish Trade Unions from 1970 until 1974. She became parliamentary secretary to Prime

Minister Kalevi Sorsa of Finland's Social Democratic Party (Suomen Sosiali-demokraattinen Puolue—SDP) in the years 1974 to 1975.

In the late 1970s and early 1980s Halonen expanded her political life by joining many nongovernmental organizations as well as beginning an unbroken career as a deputy in Parliament in 1979 until her election as president. Since 1975 she has been a member of the representative body of the co-operative retail company Elanto, and in 1977 she joined the Helsinki city council, on which she served until 1996. She also sat on the supervisory board during this time. On top of these roles she was a director of the International Solidarity Foundation and, reflecting her passion for the theatre, chaired the TNL Theatre Organization.

The late 1980s saw Halonen hold a number of government posts. She chaired the parliamentary social affairs committee from 1984 until her appointment as a minister at the ministry of social affairs and health in 1987. From 1989 she was also minister for Nordic co-operation, and in 1990 she took on the justice portfolio as well. She lost all three positions following the defeat of the SDP in the March 1991 legislative elections. Following four years in opposition the party's popularity returned to a postwar high in the March 1995 election and Halonen was appointed as minister of foreign affairs, where she remained until her election as president in 2000. She won a closely fought second-round victory on 6 February over the Finnish Centre Party candidate Esko Aho, gaining 51.6% to his 48.4%. In her electoral address she outlined her socialist principles of high government spending and heavy taxation while maintaining a realist approach to funding.

Profile of the Prime Minister:

Matti **VANHANEN**

Matti Vanhanen became prime minister of Finland on 24 June 2003, following the resignation of his predecessor Anneli Jäätteenmäki after just two months in office. Vanhanen, who served as defence minister in Jäätteenmäki's centre-left coalition, was seen as a safe pair of hands after the shock of Jäätteenmäki's departure. A former journalist, Vanhanen is considered a specialist in European affairs, particularly the European Union's Common Defence Policy.

Matti Vanhanen was born on 4 November 1955 in the southern town of Jyväskylä, the son of controversial Professor Emeritus Tatu Vanhanen. He studied political science at university before becoming a journalist on *Kehäsanomat*, eventually being appointed editor-in-chief. He is married to Merja Hannele née Lemmetti and they have two daughters.

Vanhanen chaired the youth league of the Centre Party (Suomen Keskusta—KESK) from 1980–83. From 1981 to 1984 he also served on the Espoo city council. Vanhanen entered Parliament for the first time in 1991, representing

Nurmijärvi for KESK. He served as defence minister in Anneli Jäätteenmäki's 2003 centre-left coalition that lasted just 63 days; Jäätteenmäki was then forced to resign. It was alleged that she had arranged for secret documents to be leaked that implied that the position of her predecessor, Paavo Lipponen, over the Iraq invasion had been equivocal at best; the charges were later dropped in court. Vanhanen became prime minister on 24 June, retaining the same coalition, but regarded the job as a temporary one until anointed as KESK chairman three months later.

Vanhanen is considered a specialist in European affairs, particularly the European Union's Common Defence Policy. He is a teetotaller who dislikes the taste of alcohol and who lists chopping wood among his hobbies.

FRANCE

Full name: The French Republic.

Leadership structure: The head of state is a president, directly elected by universal adult suffrage. The president's term of office was reduced from seven years to five years with effect from 2002, bringing it into line with the term of the National Assembly, under legislation passed by both chambers of Parliament in June 2000, and approved by a referendum on 24 September 2000, although the referendum attracted a turnout of only around 30%. The head of government is the prime minister, who is appointed by the president. The Council of Ministers is appointed by the prime minister.

President:	Jacques **CHIRAC**	Since 17 May 1995
Prime Minister:	Lionel Jospin	2 June 1997—6 May 2002
	Jean-Pierre Raffarin	6 May 2002—31 May 2005
	Dominique de **VILLEPIN**	Since 31 May 2005

Legislature: The legislature, the Parliament (Parlement), is bicameral. The lower chamber, the National Assembly (Assemblée Nationale), has 577 members, directly elected for a five-year term. The upper chamber, the Senate (Sénat), currently has 331 members, indirectly elected for a nine-year term. One-third of the membership is renewed every three years.

Profile of the President of the Republic:

Jacques **CHIRAC**

Chirac has become western Europe's elder statesman since the departure from office of former German chancellor Helmut Kohl. As president of France since 1995, Chirac has far-reaching political powers under the constitution framed by Charles de Gaulle in 1958, in particular with regard to external relations, holding referendums, issuing decrees and declaring a state of emergency. He has been a prominent Gaullist politician for 30 years. He is strongly identified with Paris, where he was mayor from 1977 to 1995, and was twice prime minister before winning the presidency. The workings of the French political system obliged him to share power in 1997 in a so-called 'cohabitation' with the socialists, until the 2002 elections delivered him a strong pro-presidential majority.

Jacques Chirac was born in the fifth *arrondissement* of Paris on 29 November 1932. His father François was a bank clerk and later a company director. Jacques Chirac attended two prestigious Parisian *lycées*, went on to the Institut d'Etudes Politiques in Paris, and attended Harvard University summer school in the USA in 1953. As a junior officer with the French army he was wounded in Algeria in the mid-1950s. In 1956 he married Bernadette Chodron de Courcel; they have two daughters.

Between 1957 and 1959 Chirac was a student at France's elite civil service training institution, the Ecole Nationale d'Administration. Upon graduation he began his political career as an auditor in the government's finance office. In 1962 he became *chargé de mission* within the government of Georges Pompidou, soon moving from the government secretariat to a three-year spell as adviser in Pompidou's private office. He became a junior minister in 1967, with responsibility first for employment and, from 1968 to 1971, for economy and finance. He was also public auditor at the Cour des Comptes from 1965, a member of the Corrèze municipal council from 1965 to 1967, was first elected National Assembly deputy for Corrèze in 1967, and chaired the Corrèze general council from 1970 to 1979.

Chirac gained ministerial experience in the early 1970s at the ministry of agriculture and rural development (1972–74) and briefly as minister of the interior. When Valéry Giscard d'Estaing won the presidency in May 1974, Chirac at first prospered, as a leading Gaullist in Giscard's centre-right alliance. In addition to the post of prime minister from May 1974, he took on the general secretaryship of the Gaullist party, the Union of Democrats for the Republic (Union des Démocrates pour la République—UDR) from December. The two men fell out, however, less over policy than because of friction between their dominant personalities. Chirac resigned from the government in August 1976, and in December established his dominance within the Gaullist movement, transforming the UDR into the Rally for the Republic (Rassemblement pour la République—RPR) with himself as its president. The following March he won election for the first time as mayor of Paris, using this power base to keep himself in the political forefront; he retained both the RPR leadership and the Paris mayoralty until he launched his successful bid for the presidency in the mid-1990s.

In the run-up to the 1981 presidential election, Chirac increasingly distanced the RPR leadership from the Giscard government, seeking to project himself rather than the president as the leader of the centre-right 'majority'. In the election, the first of his three bids for the presidency, he split the centre-right vote on the first round but finished a poor third behind the incumbent Giscard and the eventually successful François Mitterrand.

The honeymoon of the left in government soon gave way to acrimonious divisions and a reversal of direction on the economy, and in 1986 the centre-right came back strongly in the legislative elections. Chirac's RPR, its leadership rejuvenated by him in the years in opposition, performed so well that Mitterrand had little option but to make him prime minister. Thus began the first so-called 'cohabitation', a two-year test of some hitherto unexplored aspects of the division of powers under the Fifth Republic's constitution. The experiment was made to work, but Chirac's economic policies—based on a radical privatization programme—proved less successful with the electorate, and his party was divided on how to deal with the challenge of the National Front from the extreme right, a minority favouring some form of alliance.

Challenging Mitterrand for the presidency in April–May 1988, Chirac this time went through to the runoff, but finished second, with just under 46% of the vote. The general election the following month restored a centre-left majority, while also tilting the balance on the right away from Chirac towards Giscard.

Chirac favoured a 'yes' vote in the 1992 referendum on the Maastricht Treaty on European Union. Although his RPR was divided on this issue, it gained fresh momentum in the 1993 legislative elections, again becoming the largest party in a united centre-right grouping which won a landslide victory. Chirac, remaining aloof to prepare a third presidential bid, put forward fellow party member Edouard Balladur as prime minister for the second 'cohabitation' government, little expecting that his loyal colleague would emerge as a rival for the presidency in 1995. Balladur's candidacy was backed by the centre-right Union for French Democracy, Giscard having decided against standing himself. Chirac overtook Balladur by campaigning strongly with populist calls to tackle unemployment and 'social exclusion'. Second in the first ballot in April, with socialist Lionel Jospin unexpectedly leading the poll, Chirac picked up most of the Balladur votes in the second round on 7 May, ending with 52.6%, and was sworn in as president for a seven-year term on 17 May 1995.

Two years into his own first presidential term, Chirac found himself in another 'cohabitation', this time on the other side, when the pendulum in the legislative elections (called early by Chirac in the hope of a vote of confidence) swung back to the left. With Jospin as prime minister, the new socialist-led government in office between June 1997 and May 2002 was in the forefront of dealing with tensions over the state of the economy. To some extent this took the spotlight off Chirac, who had been criticized for neglecting his presidential campaign promises in pursuit of austerity policies to prepare for European monetary union.

It also turned out to be the socialists who paid a heavy price in electoral popularity at the 2002 elections. On this occasion, following constitutional changes to bring the president's term of office into line with that of the National Assembly, the presidential poll took place in April–May and the legislative elections followed in June. The shock result of the first round of the presidential election, where the far-right candidate Jean-Marie Le Pen came second—behind Chirac but ahead of Jospin—left pro-democracy voters no alternative but to rally around Chirac in the second round. The outcome of this was to deliver him a massive majority, where once he had been thought fatally compromised by mounting accusations of financial impropriety and political skulduggery. Moreover, it enabled his RPR to build a coalition known as the Union for a Presidential Majority (Union pour la Majorité Présidentielle—UMP) which swept to an overall majority in the ensuing legislative elections. Chirac survived an assassination attempt later that year.

In line with a marked unwillingness to accept any notion of US or UK leadership on contentious issues, Chirac caused controversy among European Union (EU) leaders in January 2003 when he invited Zimbabwean leader Robert Mugabe to attend a summit in France. He then emerged as a leading voice against the 2003 US-led invasion of Iraq, threatening to veto any UN Security Council resolution authorizing the use of force until weapons inspectors had been given more time. He was subject to predictable and vitriolic criticism in the USA and UK for his position, especially after he vowed in March to veto any resolution regardless of any changes that were made. Many of his critics accused France of having commercial ties with Saddam Hussein's Iraq, Chirac's stance thus being less one of principle than of protecting France's industrial interests.

In early 2004, UMP leader Alain Juppé, a close ally of Chirac, was convicted of corruption and banned from political office for ten years. The UMP, which had changed its name to the Union for a Popular Movement (Union pour un Mouvement Populaire), went on to lose badly in regional elections in March, not least due to the unpopularity of Chirac's public service reforms. In November the UMP membership elected Nicolas Sarkozy, once seen as Chirac's protégé, as party leader to replace Juppé. Relations between Chirac and Sarkozy were increasingly embittered, however, with Sarkozy making no secret of his own presidential ambitions.

Meanwhile, campaigning was getting under way ahead of the referendum on the proposed new EU constitution, due to be held in May 2005. The decision to hold a referendum had apparently been prompted by the announcement that the UK was to hold one as well. Chirac and the UMP threw their considerable weight behind the 'yes' campaign. The firm rejection of the treaty—with 69% of voters saying 'no'—was a massive blow to Chirac and his camp. Prime Minister Jean-Pierre Raffarin resigned two days later, to be replaced by another Chirac loyalist, Dominique de Villepin; the new constitution was shelved indefinitely. The ensuing EU summit was derailed both by the constitution debacle and a furious row with the UK over farm subsidies under the Common Agricultural Policy and the UK's EU rebate.

Chirac further embroiled himself in controversy in the run-up to the decision on the host city for the 2012 Olympic Games. Paris had been firm favourite for the Games, but a late renaissance by the London bid had shaken the Paris team. Still caught up in the farm subsidies row, Chirac told journalists that the only food worse than British food was Finnish, and that the UK's only contribution to European agriculture had been mad cow disease. Two Finnish delegates sat on the Olympic Committee; Chirac's comments were blamed by many for London's ensuing narrow victory over Paris.

Political gaffes of this kind, and the evident intent not only of Sarkozy but also Villepin in standing for the presidency in 2007, left Chirac looking increasingly a lame duck two-thirds of the way through his term of office. The taint of corruption dating back to his years as mayor of Paris weakened his position further, while his age and health also began to tell against him. In early September 2005 he was banned under medical advice from travelling by air to the UN General Assembly in New York, after being briefly hospitalized over a blood vessel problem that had blurred his vision.

Profile of the Prime Minister:

Dominique de VILLEPIN

Dominique de Villepin is an unelected former diplomat who won plaudits for his high-profile and articulate criticism of the 2003 US-led invasion of Iraq. Castigated, especially by the US press, for arrogance and vainglory, Villepin could afford to ignore such criticism; he is notably close to President Jacques Chirac and is regarded by some as the leader's latest protégé. He was appointed prime minister on 31 May 2005 when Chirac discarded his predecessor Jean-Pierre Raffarin in the wake of the disastrous French 'no' vote in the referendum on the European Union (EU) constitution.

Dominique Marie François René Galouzeau de Villepin was born on 14 November 1953 in Rabat in Morocco, the son of Yvonne Hétier and former senator Xavier de Villepin. He spent his childhood away from France, growing up in Venezuela and the USA, to which he ascribes his 'vision' of France and its role in the world. He studied initially at the Institut d'Etudes Politiques where he gained a degree in literature and law, before attending the Ecole Nationale d'Administration, the elite French civil service training institution, from which he graduated in 1980. Villepin is married with three children.

Villepin joined the Rally for the Republic (Rassemblement pour la République— RPR) party of Jacques Chirac, then mayor of Paris, in 1977. He joined the ministry of foreign affairs in 1980, the year he was first presented to Chirac, and worked in the African and Malagasy affairs section until 1984. That year he was sent to Washington D.C. where he served as first secretary of the French embassy to the USA, responsible for the Middle East. In 1987 he transferred to the press and information unit, before being relocated to India in 1989. He served as second councillor of the embassy in New Delhi for a year and was promoted to first councillor in 1990.

He returned to France in 1992 and was appointed assistant director of the African and Malagasy affairs section of the ministry of foreign affairs. By the following year he had been promoted again to principal private secretary to the minister, Alain Juppé, then regarded as Jacques Chirac's heir apparent.

Villepin was director of Chirac's successful presidential campaign in 1995 and as a reward was appointed as secretary-general of the presidency. However, he was widely blamed by many for recommending that the president call an early general election in 1997; a National Assembly that had been dominated by the right fell to the socialists. Villepin offered his resignation following the debacle; although this was turned down, hostility towards him from members of his own party still persists and is reportedly reciprocated.

After Chirac's re-election in presidential elections in May 2002, followed by the sweeping victory of the RPR in legislative polls the following month, Villepin was appointed minister of foreign affairs. It was from this position that he developed his criticisms of US policy over the invasion of Iraq, winning him few friends in the USA but impressing many in the wider world; he won unprecedented applause from diplomats after his speech to the UN Security Council in 2003 condemning the invasion.

In March 2004 he was appointed to the interior ministry where he cracked down on Islamic militancy, forced through a measure making it mandatory for Muslim clerics in France to study the language, laws and customs of the country, and tightened immigration and security measures. He was appointed prime minister on 31 May 2005 after his predecessor Jean-Pierre Raffarin resigned in the wake of the French rejection of the EU constitution.

This appointment was widely criticized both at home and abroad; Villepin was portrayed as an arrogant aristocrat, who had never held elected office, while his closeness to Chirac prompted accusations of cronyism. However, he vowed to work to heal the nation's divisions. Unlike his rival within the government, Nicolas Sarkozy, he did not come out in favour of a sharp dose of economic restructuring, perceiving that many voters, in saying 'no' to the EU constitution, were implicitly rejecting this liberal market prescription for the country's problems of global competitiveness. He has received favourable opinion poll ratings, and is increasingly cited as a presidential contender for the 2007 election.

GABON

Full name: The Gabonese Republic.

Leadership structure: The head of state is a president, directly elected by universal adult suffrage for a seven-year term. The 2003 constitutional amendment removed restrictions on the number of terms which a president may serve. The head of government is the prime minister, who is appointed by the president. The Council of Ministers is appointed by the prime minister.

President:	Omar **BONGO**	Since 2 Dec. 1967
	(acting from 28 Nov. 1967)	

Prime Minister: Jean-François **NTOUTOUME-EMANE** Since 24 Jan. 1999

Legislature: The Parliament (Parlement) is bicameral. The lower chamber, the National Assembly (Assemblée Nationale), has 120 members, directly elected for a five-year term. The upper chamber, the Senate (Sénat), has 91 members, elected for a six-year term by municipal and regional councillors.

Profile of the President:

Omar **BONGO**

Omar Bongo Ondimba, head of state in a single-party regime for 25 years, continued in office after winning the country's first multiparty presidential elections in December 1993. This term was extended by constitutional amendment from five to seven years, but he nevertheless went to the polls in December 1998 and secured a further term. In 2003 constitutional amendments were passed removing the presidential two-term limit, allowing him to stand for re-election again in 2005. The death of Togolese president Gen. Gnassingbé Eyadema in February of that year made Bongo Africa's longest-serving head of state. Before first becoming president he had held a number of posts in government service and had been a close adviser to his predecessor, President Léon M'Ba.

Albert-Bernard Bongo (he renamed himself Omar when he converted to Islam in 1973) was born on 30 December 1935 in Lewai, Franceville, in the southeast of Gabon. His town of birth is now called Bongoville. He gained a diploma in commerce from Brazzaville Technical College in the Congo. From 1958 he worked briefly in the civil service and was in the French air force for two years prior to independence. In 1960 he joined the ministry of foreign affairs.

Appointed as assistant director in the Gabonese cabinet in 1962, he was director of President M'Ba's private office by that October. In the succeeding years he held a variety of positions in government administration and became one of the president's closest advisers. In 1965 he entered the cabinet, as minister-delegate to the presidency. By November the following year he was vice president, and he became president in 1967 following the death of President M'Ba. In 1968 he founded the Gabonese Democratic Party (Parti Démocratique Gabonais—PDG), introducing a single-party system.

Bongo was elected to a new seven-year term in February 1973, confirmed in office in 1980, and re-elected to a further term in 1986. His government was generally regarded as pro-Western, maintaining close relations with France in particular. His role in international organizations included chairing the Organization of African Unity (OAU, now the African Union—AU) in 1977, and he was active as a mediator in regional disputes.

Bongo married his second wife Edith Lucie Sassou-Nguesso, the daughter of the president of the Republic of the Congo, in August 1990. They have one daughter and one son. Bongo also had eight children from his first marriage to Joséphine Kama, whom he divorced in 1986.

In 1990 Bongo announced proposals to establish a multiparty democratic system. Parliamentary elections took place in late 1990 and early 1991. When the presidential elections were held on 5 December 1993, Bongo topped the poll with 51.18% of the vote, and he was sworn in for his new term on 22 January 1994. Although international observers endorsed the conduct of the poll, dissatisfied opposition supporters formed a 'parallel administration'; protracted political disputes led eventually to constitutional amendments and the holding in 1996–97 of fresh elections to the National Assembly and Senate. In March 1997 a constitutional amendment was approved extending future presidential terms from five to seven years.

Bongo was re-elected with 67% of the vote on 6 December 1998, an easy victory over his nearest rival, Pierre Mamboundou, who received only 17%. Bongo was re-inaugurated in January 1999 despite opposition claims of fraud. In October 2000 Bongo secured lifetime immunity from prosecution. He has sought to conciliate the political opposition and invited the Rally for Gabon to join the government, which it did in January 2002.

Constitutional amendments in 2003 removed the two-term limit on the presidency, allowing Bongo to stand again in the December 2005 presidential election. Meanwhile, his eldest son Ali was appointed minister of defence in 1999, and many believe he is being groomed as Bongo's successor. Bongo's eldest daughter, Pascaline, a former foreign minister, is head of the presidential office, and her husband is minister of state for finance.

Profile of the Prime Minister:

Jean-François **NTOUTOUME-EMANE**

Jean-François Ntoutoume-Emane is a member of the ruling Gabonese Democratic Party (Parti Démocratique Gabonais—PDG). A career politician, he held a number of different portfolios simultaneously in the late 1990s before he was appointed prime minister in January 1999.

Jean-François Ntoutoume (he took on the suffix Emane later in life) was born on 6 November 1939. He has a doctorate in political science from the University of Jussieu, Paris. He joined the government for the first time in February 1996 as the minister of state for habitat, lands and urban planning and welfare, and in 1997 he was appointed minister of state, minister of land registry, town planning and housing and minister of state control, decentralization, territorial administration and regional integration. After his nomination as prime minister in January 1999, he retained the lands and urban planning portfolio.

President Omar Bongo found reason to berate Ntoutoume-Emane in August 2000 for his government's "comatose" performance. Despite this reproach, Ntoutoume-Emane oversaw the PDG's re-election in December 2001 and remained at the helm of the new government, which included the opposition Rally for Gabon, and promised to fight corruption and poverty and to improve living standards. Ntoutoume-Emane's wife Sophie has occasionally acted as a deputy to First Lady Edith Lucie Bongo at diplomatic occasions. They have seven children.

GAMBIA

Full name: The Republic of The Gambia.

Leadership structure: The head of state is a president, directly elected by universal adult suffrage. The president's term of office is five years, with no limit on re-election. The head of government is the president. The cabinet is appointed by the president.

President:	Col. (retd) Yahya **JAMMEH**	Since 26 July 1994
	(seized power on 22 July 1994)	

Legislature: The legislature is unicameral. The sole chamber, the National Assembly, has 53 members, 48 of them directly elected by universal adult suffrage, and five appointed by the president, for a five-year term.

Profile of the President:

Col. (retd) Yahya **JAMMEH**

Yahya Jammeh has held power in The Gambia since his bloodless coup in 1994, and was elected as president in a poll held under controversial circumstances in September 1996. His re-election in 2001 was similarly contentious. Before taking power he was a military police officer, trained in part in the USA.

Yahya Alphonse Jamus Jebulai Jammeh was born on 25 May 1965 in Kanilai village in Foni Kansala district, He later changed his name to Yahya Abdul-Aziz Jemus Junkung Jammeh. He was educated locally at the Kanilai and Bwiam primary schools and then at Gambia High School. Joining Gambia's national police force in 1984, he was promoted to sergeant two years later. Then, in 1989, he was commissioned as an officer and was put in charge of the presidential escort of the presidential guard. He joined the military police unit in 1991. Promoted to lieutenant in 1992, he became commander of the National Military Police that year and was made a captain in 1994. His military training has taken him abroad to the USA, where he attended the military police officers' basic course in Fort McClellan, Alabama.

In July 1994 he led a coup organized by a small group of five young army lieutenants aged between 25 and 30. The coup ousted the veteran President Dawda Jawara, who had headed a succession of democratically elected governments since independence in 1965, and suspended the constitution.

Jammeh headed a five-member Armed Forces Provisional Ruling Council, and assumed the title of 'president', although this was not recognized internationally.

Under pressure both from within the country and from abroad, Jammeh drew up a revised constitution providing for a return to civilian rule and multiparty politics, which was approved in a referendum in August 1996. However, within a week of the referendum Jammeh banned the three main opposition parties and announced that anyone who had held presidential or ministerial office in the 30 years preceding the 1994 coup would not be permitted to stand in the forthcoming presidential election. Foreign observers refused to attend the poll because of the circumstances under which it was being held. When it took place, on 26 September, Jammeh was elected president with 56% of the vote. The Alliance for Patriotic Reorientation and Construction (APRC), which Jammeh had formed in August to back his presidential candidacy, won 33 of the 45 elected seats in the new National Assembly the following January. In 1998 he married Zineb née Soumah, and they have one daughter.

Two separate coup attempts against Jammeh were foiled in January and July 2000 while public confidence in the police force plummeted and violent demonstrations over police brutality rocked the country later that year. Jammeh's political stance grew ever more conservative and in June 2001 he publicly admitted that he was seriously considering introducing Islamic *shari'a* law in The Gambia. In order to legitimize his position, however, he lifted his previous ban on political parties in July that year, prompting ex-president Jawara to promise a swift return, but he was not in time to prevent Jammeh's re-election, with 53% of the vote, in October.

Soon after his re-inauguration Jammeh faced stiff criticism from international human rights bodies. Amnesty International, in particular, felt that the supposed liberalism engendered before the election was hollow, as a number of Jammeh's opponents suddenly found themselves incarcerated. The APRC was ensured victory in legislative elections in January 2002 as an insufficient number of opposition candidates registered to compete against it—33 APRC politicians were entirely unopposed. Jammeh's consolidation of power seemed complete in June 2002, when he welcomed Jawara's eventual return from exile and promised him a future role as a respected 'elder statesman'.

GEORGIA

Full name: Georgia.

Leadership structure: The head of state is a president directly elected by universal adult suffrage. The president's term of office is five years, renewable once only. The head of government is the prime minister, who is appointed by the president. The Council of Ministers is nominated by the prime minister, and must be approved by the president.

President:	Eduard Shevardnadze (head of state from 10 March 1992)	26 Nov. 1995—23 Nov. 2003
	Nino Burjanadze (acting)	23 Nov. 2003—25 Jan. 2004
	Mikhail **SAAKASHVILI**	Since 25 Jan. 2004
State Minister:	Vazha Lortkipanidze (acting from 1 May 2000)	7 Aug. 1998—11 May 2000
	Giorgi Arsenishvili	11 May 2000—21 Dec. 2001
	Avtandil Jorbenadze	21 Dec. 2001—27 Nov. 2003
Prime Minister:	Zurab Zhvania (state minister from 27 Nov. 2003)	17 Feb. 2004—3 Feb. 2005
	Mikhail Saakashvili (acting)	3 Feb. 2005—17 Feb. 2005
	Zurab **NOGHAIDELI**	Since 17 Feb. 2005

Legislature: The legislature is unicameral, but is to become bicameral "following the creation of appropriate conditions". The sole existing chamber, the Parliament (Sakartvelos Parlamenti), has 230 members, 85 elected in single-member constituencies and the rest from party lists, for a four-year term.

Profile of the President:

Mikhail **SAAKASHVILI**

A multilingual, Western-educated human rights lawyer, Mikhail Saakashvili (known to most as Misha) rode a wave of popular discontent to a landslide electoral victory and was sworn in as president of Georgia on 25 January 2004. A long-time campaigner against corruption, he had first served in government as justice minister in 2000 under President Eduard Shevardnadze, but resigned in 2001 claiming that it would have been immoral to remain. Saakashvili formed an opposition party, the United National Movement (UNM), and led street protests in November 2003 over allegations of fraud in that month's parliamentary elections. As pressure built up on Shevardnadze to resign, Saakashvili stormed parliament on live national television as his supporters placed flowers in the gun barrels of the soldiers outside. The events were described by one journalist as "a coup masked as a street party". Saakashvili went on to be elected president in January 2004 with 96% of the vote.

Mikhail Saakashvili was born on 21 December 1967 in Tbilisi. He studied at Kiev University in Ukraine and the International Institute of Human Rights in Strasbourg, before moving to the USA. He attended Columbia University in New York, where he gained his master's degree in law in 1994, and the following year he gained a doctorate in juridical science from the George Washington National Law Center in Washington D.C. He spent one year as an intern working for the New York-based law firm Patterson, Belknap, Webb & Tyler; although he was then offered a lucrative job with the firm, he declined, choosing instead to return to Georgia to take up a political career. He is married to Dutch national Sandra Roelof who used to work at the Dutch consulate in Tbilisi; they have one son.

Saakashvili's friend Zurab Zhvania, whose Green Party had been one of a number of opposition groups striving for Georgia's independence, recruited Saakashvili in the mid-1990s to join the government of Eduard Shevardnadze. He stood in the December 1995 elections along with Zhvania, and both men won seats in parliament, standing for Shevardnadze's Citizens' Union of Georgia (CUG). Saakashvili soon made a name for himself as chairman of the parliamentary committee charged with creating a new electoral system, an independent judiciary and a non-political police force. He achieved a high degree of public recognition, with opinion surveys finding him to be the second most popular person in Georgia, behind Shevardnadze, and in 1997 was named 'man of the year' by a panel of journalists and human rights advocates.

On 12 October 2000, Shevardnadze appointed Saakashvili to the post of minister for justice. He immediately moved to reform the decrepit, corrupt and highly politicized Georgian criminal justice and prisons system, winning plaudits from human rights activists and the international community. However, in a cabinet meeting in August 2001, Saakashvili accused Economics Minister Vano Chkhartishvili, State Security Minister Vakhtang Kutateladze and Tbilisi police chief Soso Alavidze of profiting from corrupt business deals and displayed photos of their opulent houses in Tbilisi to support his claims. On 5 September 2001 Saakashvili resigned, saying, "I consider it immoral for me to remain as a member of Shevardnadze's government." He declared that corruption had penetrated to the very centre of the Georgian government and that Shevardnadze lacked the will to deal with it, warning that "current developments in Georgia will turn the country into a criminal enclave in one or two years".

In October 2001 Saakashvili founded the UNM, a left-of-centre political party akin to the social democrats in Europe with a touch of nationalism. In June 2002 he was elected as chairman of the Tbilisi assembly—in effect, the city's mayor—following an agreement between the UNM and the Georgian Labour Party. This gave him a powerful new platform from which to criticize the government. It made him enemies as well; even his great friend and ally Zurab Zhvania was reluctant to align closely with him at this time, and Zhvania was quoted as criticizing what he termed Saakashvili's "excessive radicalism". In the run-up to the November 2003 parliamentary elections, Zhvania's United Democrats (UD) forged an election alliance not with Saakashvili's UNM but with the eponymous political bloc formed by Zhvania's successor as Parliament speaker, Nino Burjanadze.

Georgia held parliamentary elections on 2 November 2003. When the election bloc cobbled together by Shevardnadze to replace the CUG set about manipulating the election returns, Zhvania, Burjanadze and Saakashvili joined forces to mobilize popular protest. Initially their objectives differed: Burjanadze and Zhvania (on record as saying "I hate all revolutions") wanted the election returns invalidated and new elections held, whereas Saakashvili demanded that the authorities acknowledge his bloc as the winner and urged Georgians to demonstrate against President Shevardnadze's government and engage in nonviolent civil disobedience against the authorities.

Massive political demonstrations (the so-called 'rose revolution') were held in Tbilisi, with over 100,000 people participating and listening to speeches by Saakashvili and other opposition figures. After an increasingly tense three weeks, Shevardnadze resigned as president on 23 November to be replaced on an interim basis by Burjanadze in her capacity as speaker of Parliament. On 4 January 2004 Saakashvili was elected with 96% of the vote to be president of Georgia and was sworn in three weeks later. Zhvania, hitherto state minister, was redesignated as prime minister in mid-February, and a week later the UNM and the UD finally amalgamated and the new political movement was named the National Movement—Democrats (NMD).

Saakashvili positioned himself and his country firmly facing west, and has announced his intention to see Georgia become a member of both the North Atlantic Treaty Organization (NATO) and the European Union (EU)—even going so far as to hoist an EU flag over the Georgian Parliament. He has reined in the ambitions of one-time Ajarian leader Aslan Abashidze, forcing him to resign and flee to Russia, and has offered sweeping powers of autonomy to the breakaway republics of South Ossetia and Abkhazia. Since the death of Prime Minister Zhvania in February 2005 in a freak carbon monoxide accident, Saakashvili has faced the task of holding his government and his country together without the counsel of his long-standing friend and adviser.

Profile of the Prime Minister:

Zurab **NOGHAIDELI**

Zurab Noghaideli was first elected to Parliament in 1992 after the overthrow of President Zviad Gamsakhurdia. Like most politicians in the current government, he initially served under Eduard Shevardnadze before the 'rose revolution' of 2003. A technocrat with a background in natural sciences, Noghaideli's appointment as premier in February 2005 following the death of Zurab Zhvania came as a surprise to some; Zhvania was regarded as one of Georgia's few statesmen, and many doubted that Noghaideli would be able to fill the gap.

Zurab Noghaideli was born on 22 October 1964 in the coastal town of Kobuleti in Ajaria, southwest Georgia. He was educated at the Moscow State University, where he graduated in physics in 1987, and worked at the Geography Institute of the Georgian Academy of Sciences until 1989, when he moved to the Geology Institute at the Estonian Academy of Sciences. He is married with one child.

In 1991 Noghaideli joined the Green Party of Zurab Zhvania. He was elected as a deputy to the Georgian Parliament for the first time in 1992, after the overthrow of President Gamsakhurdia, and he became chairman of the parliamentary committee on environmental protection and natural resources. Along with Zhvania and current president Mikhail Saakashvili, Noghaideli joined President Eduard Shevardnadze's Citizens' Union of Georgia (CUG). He was re-elected as a deputy in 1995, and in 1996 served as a member of the Ajarian Supreme Court. In 1999 Noghaideli chaired the parliamentary tax and income committee. He joined the government for the first time in May 2000 as minister of finance, but was dismissed without explanation two years later. He joined Zhvania's United Democrats (UD), an opposition party founded the same year.

Following the 'rose revolution' of November 2003 which ousted Shevardnadze, Noghaideli became economic adviser to acting president Nino Burjanadze. He was reappointed finance minister in February 2004 by Prime Minister Zhvania, in a government of the National Movement—Democrats (NMD), formed by a merger of the UD with President Saakashvili's United National Movement.

Zhvania died of carbon monoxide poisoning in February 2005, and Noghaideli was nominated to replace him on 11 February; he was confirmed by Parliament on 17 February. Many analysts and commentators found the choice of Noghaideli puzzling. He is known as a technocrat with little political experience, and lacks the charisma of his predecessor. Others, however, see his appointment as partly a nod to Zhvania's supporters, and partly a desire on the part of Saakashvili to balance his own spontaneous and rather disorganized temperament with a premier known for strictness and organization. He is not expected to fill Zhvania's shoes—it is generally agreed that there is no politician in Georgia that could.

GERMANY

Full name: The Federal Republic of Germany.

Leadership structure: The head of state is a president, elected by the Bundesversammlung—a specially constituted body comprising the members of the lower chamber of the federal legislature and an equal number of representatives elected by the state legislatures. The president's term of office is five years. The head of government is the federal chancellor, who is elected by the Federal Assembly on the proposal of the federal president. The federal government (Bundesregierung) is appointed by the president on the proposal of the federal chancellor.

Federal President:	Johannes Rau	1 July 1999—30 June 2004
	Horst **KÖHLER**	Since 1 July 2004
Federal Chancellor:	Gerhard **SCHRÖDER**	Since 27 Oct. 1998

Legislature: The legislature is bicameral. The lower chamber, the Federal Assembly (Bundestag), has 603 members, directly elected for a four-year term. The upper chamber, the Federal Council (Bundesrat), has 69 members appointed for variable terms by the 16 states (*Länder*), including city states with equivalent status.

Profile of the Federal President:

Horst **KÖHLER**

Horst Köhler succeeded Johannes Rau as German president on 1 July 2004. A highly regarded economist, Köhler held posts in academia, the private sector and in government, including acting as 'sherpa' to Chancellor Helmut Kohl in the preparation of G7 summits in the early 1990s, before becoming head of the International Monetary Fund (IMF) in 2000. Köhler has emphasized the importance of globalization but has also been at pains to stress his patriotism. His role is largely ceremonial but carries considerable moral authority.

Horst Köhler was born into an ethnic German family who had moved from Romania to Skierbieszów in Nazi-occupied Poland on 22 February 1943. The Köhlers moved into a vacant house whose Polish owners had been deported by Nazi troops as part of a project to 'Germanize' the area. The family fled to eastern Germany as the Russian Red Army advanced, and moved to West Germany in

1953 where they lived in refugee housing. Köhler was the only one of the eight children who went to university. He earned a doctorate in economics and political sciences from the University of Tübingen, where he was later a scientific research assistant from 1969 to 1976. Köhler is married with two children.

After completing his education, he held various positions in Germany's ministries of economics and finance between 1976 and 1989. From 1990 to 1993 he was deputy minister of finance, responsible for international financial and monetary relations. During this time, he led negotiations on behalf of the German government on the European Union (EU) agreement that became the Maastricht Treaty, was closely involved in the process of German unification, and held the position of deputy governor for Germany at the World Bank. He also acted as 'sherpa' to the federal chancellor during preparation for the G7 Economic Summits in Houston, London, Munich and Tokyo.

Köhler was president of the German Savings Bank Association from 1993 to 1998, when he was appointed president of the European Bank for Reconstruction and Development (EBRD). The bank, given the job of boosting economic regeneration in Eastern Europe, had made headlines for the wrong reasons: numerous investments had gone wrong, while spending on its plush headquarters had attracted vocal criticism. Köhler, however, quickly managed to get the EBRD out of the red and refocus its efforts on Eastern Europe.

In 2000 Köhler assumed office as managing director of the IMF, a post which traditionally only former finance ministers and Central Bank presidents had held. He was the second choice for the post, the first having been vetoed by the USA. He revamped the IMF management team and introduced measures to make the IMF more efficient and accountable, setting up an International Capital Markets department to ensure that the fund was more aware of market developments and possible dangers. He also oversaw an IMF review aimed at focusing conditions on IMF loans to core demands and goals—a popular step with the developing countries among the IMF's member nations.

In 2004 he was nominated by the opposition Christian Democrats, Christian Social Union and Free Democrats for the German presidency and resigned immediately from the IMF. He was elected by 604 votes to 589 and took office on 1 July.

Exactly one year later, on 1 July 2005, he faced a tricky situation when the Social Democrat federal chancellor Gerhard Schröder engineered his own defeat in a no-confidence vote in the Federal Assembly as a device to oblige the president to call early parliamentary elections. Technically Köhler could have refused to oblige, on the grounds that Schröder was manipulating the rules, but in practice he decided that there was no real alternative to fresh elections, which he duly called for 18 September. A challenge to his decision, brought in the Constitutional Court by two outraged Assembly members, was rejected by the court by seven to one.

Profile of the Federal Chancellor:

Gerhard **SCHRÖDER**

Gerhard Schröder is the moderate leader of the Social Democratic Party of Germany (Sozialdemokratische Partei Deutschlands—SPD), heading since October 1998 a government coalition with the environmentalist Greens. The election which brought him to power ended Helmut Kohl's 16 years as federal chancellor. Schröder, who had completed his transition from radical young socialist to proponent of the 'new centre' as head of the regional government in the northwest German state (Land) of Lower Saxony, was frequently cited with UK prime minister Tony Blair as representative of a new centrist politics in western Europe. Designer-suited, media savvy and business-friendly, he failed to deliver, however, on the key issue of successful economic stewardship. Although his energy and charisma carried him to re-election once, in September 2002, he was widely regarded as having run out of credibility and his chances of another term written off as the September 2005 polls approached.

Gerhard Fritz Kurt Schröder was born in Mossenberg near Detmold, North Rhine-Westphalia, on 7 April 1944. His father was killed a few days later as German troops withdrew from Romania. His mother Erika, a Protestant and staunch social democrat, did cleaning work to support him and his elder sister; she went on to have three more children by a second marriage.

Schröder was obliged to leave school at the age of 14 and work as an apprentice in a china shop. He went to night school to gain his school-leaving certificate, going on to study law at the University of Göttingen, and financing his studies by working on a building site. He joined the SPD in 1963, and has been a member of the public service union ÖTV since 1973.

Upon qualifying he set up a legal practice in Hanover in 1978 and in the same year was elected chairman of the Young Social Democrats (Jusos). He gained an early reputation as a radical firebrand, opposing the stationing of US nuclear weapons on West German soil, courting conservative criticism by appearing without a tie to deliver his maiden speech in the Federal Assembly (where he became a deputy on the SPD list in the October 1980 elections) and, in his law practice, defending former terrorists. A widely circulated—though possibly apocryphal—story told to illustrate Schröder's personal ambition describes him rattling the gates of the chancellor's residence in Bonn after a drinking spree, shortly after Helmut Kohl became federal chancellor in 1982, and shouting, "I want in there!"

Although still a Federal Assembly deputy until 1986, it was in regional politics in Lower Saxony that Schröder first really made his mark. In 1984 he was SPD candidate for minister-president (i.e. regional head of government); two years later, in June 1986, he became a deputy in the State Parliament (Landtag), for which he had to give up his Federal Assembly seat; and he finally became minister-president after the 1990 state election by forming a 'red–green' coalition with the environmentalist Greens.

During this period Schröder moved away from the radical stance of his early years in politics, alienating some on the left of his own party but cultivating broader contacts and, importantly, winning the confidence of key business figures. The conservative daily *Frankfurter Allgemeine Zeitung* wrote that he had "undergone an astonishing personality change" after coming to power in Lower Saxony. "The wounded aggressiveness of the opposition leader has become relaxed joviality, the stilted wish to impress has been replaced by the cool, governing style of an unassailable office holder." He dropped the Greens from government in Lower Saxony when the SPD gained a majority of one seat in the 1994 state election.

Although he joined the SPD presidium in 1989, he had an ambivalent relationship with the party apparatus and especially with his contemporaries and rivals, Oskar Lafontaine, the former minister-president of Saarland who was later to become his minister of finance, and Rudolf Scharping, who was leader of the SPD group in the Federal Assembly and later became defence minister. By turning the tide of a run of poor party results in state elections, and winning 47.9% of the vote and an absolute majority of seats in the Lower Saxony poll on 1 March 1998, Schröder demonstrated that he had the credentials to succeed at federal level, and he secured election the following day as the SPD candidate for chancellor.

The federal election on 27 September 1998 was Schröder's hour of triumph. As a proponent of the 'new centre' he campaigned as a 1990s politician seeking a 'third way' between old conservative and socialist values. Having determinedly made this move to the centre ground to gain electoral support, like his UK counterpart Tony Blair, he encountered criticism during the campaign from observers who questioned where the substance of his policies lay. His detractors portrayed him as a wheeler-dealer and telegenic showman, who had discarded his radical image in favour of centrist rhetoric, fashionable Italian designer clothes and a penchant for fine cigars and champagne. His image as a modern leader, however, capable of both bold and pragmatic decisions and seeking to reconcile liberal capitalism with social values, appealed to an electorate which was eager for change after 16 years of Chancellor Kohl.

The SPD emerged from the 1998 elections as the largest party, but needed a coalition partner to command a majority in parliament. Schröder put together an agreement with the Greens, who thus entered the federal government for the first time. When Schröder's cabinet was formed in October, however, its image was immediately dented by the withdrawal of his most controversial and business-oriented nominee, computer entrepreneur Jost Stollmann, and by debate about the amount of power he had conceded to Lafontaine, the SPD chairman and standard-bearer of the left, as head of a new financial superministry.

In its first six months the Schröder government had a rude awakening. Battered by disagreements with the Greens, particularly over phasing out nuclear power plants, the SPD suffered badly in state elections in Hesse in early 1999. Bigger drama followed when Lafontaine resigned, following disagreements about monetary issues within the new European single currency, about tax policy, and indeed about the overall direction the SPD was taking in government. Although many still regarded Lafontaine as representing the heart and soul of the party, Schröder assumed the SPD chairmanship himself; his formal election in April 1999 was unopposed, but, unusually, a quarter of the delegates still failed to back him. This early hesitation was replaced by overwhelming party support at his re-election to the post in November 2001.

Following the 11 September 2001 attacks in the USA, Schröder's popularity began to fall as he gave his backing to US president George W. Bush's 'war on terrorism'. In November 2001 he survived a parliamentary vote against the deployment of German troops in the 'war' only by turning it into a confidence vote in his government. His stance forced his Green coalition partners to move further away from their traditional pacifistic stance. More important perhaps was the global economic slowdown, which had been accelerated by the 11 September attacks. Unemployment in Germany slipped past the symbolic four million mark in December and continued to hover around that level. In opinion polls leading up to the September 2002 elections Schröder trailed the Christian Democrat candidate Edmund Stoiber.

Floodwaters came to Schröder's rescue. The dramatic inundation of Dresden in August 2002, and his own swift response, was a boon to his popularity, along with his confident handling of television debates. The SPD did lose seats in the election but maintained a majority with the help of its Green partners in the face of an overall swing to the right. When campaigning for re-election he insisted that he would serve for no longer than ten years, unlike his predecessor Helmut Kohl.

In his second term, Schröder began to lean away from alliance with Bush, notably rejecting participation in the US-led invasion of Iraq in March 2003, and turned instead to the, by now historic, Franco-German alliance.

Gerhard Schröder has had four marriages. The first, in 1968, was with librarian Eva Schubach, his childhood sweetheart. After leaving her, he married schoolteacher Anne Taschenbach in 1971. He benefited during his rise to power from his partnership with his third wife, political scientist Hiltrud 'Hillu' Hampel, whom he married in 1984 and whose two daughters he helped to bring up. In early 1997 he married his fourth wife, the Bavarian journalist Doris Köpf, who also has a daughter.

With unemployment at record levels, Schröder attempted to lift the country from its deep economic malaise with a distinctly right-of-centre set of policy proposals, including plans to cut unemployment benefits and to scale back legislation protecting workers from redundancy. This so-called 'agenda 2010' won backing at the SPD party congress in June 2003 only after Schröder had apparently suggested that he would regard its rejection as a resigning matter, and was narrowly passed by the Federal Assembly in October. His confident prediction that tax cuts would boost consumer spending in 2004 failed to spark the anticipated upturn in the economy, however, so he won only the unpopularity of those hit by, or ideologically opposed to, the cuts in welfare.

Amid a series of defeats for his party in regional elections, Schröder handed over the SPD leadership on 21 March 2004 to Franz Müntefering, but remained in post as chancellor. A further SPD defeat in the key state of North Rhine-Westphalia in May 2005 prompted Schröder to gamble on holding a parliamentary confidence vote on 1 July which he did not seek to win, as a mechanism for forcing an early general election in a bid to secure a fresh popular mandate. The success of this manoeuvre backfired, however, as it quickly became taken for granted by political commentators that he and the SPD were heading for defeat in the 18 September poll.

GHANA

Full name: The Republic of Ghana.

Leadership structure: The head of state is a president, directly elected by universal adult suffrage. The president's term of office is four years, renewable once only. A 25-member Council of State, appointed by the president, and a similarly appointed 20-member National Security Council have advisory functions. The head of government is the president, who is responsible to Parliament. The Council of Ministers is appointed by the president.

| *President*: | Jerry Rawlings (seized power on 31 Dec. 1981) | 7 Jan. 1993—7 Jan. 2001 |
| | John **KUFUOR** | Since 7 Jan. 2001 |

Legislature: The legislature is unicameral. The sole chamber, the Parliament, has 230 members, directly elected for a four-year term.

Profile of the President:

John **KUFUOR**

John Kufuor was a founding member of the New Patriotic Party (NPP). The successor from early 2001 to Ghana's head of state for two decades Jerry Rawlings, Kufuor is a lawyer by training who came to political prominence in the 1990s. He ran unsuccessfully against Rawlings in the 1996 presidential elections.

John Agyekum Kufuor was born on 8 December 1938 in Kumasi, to a respected family of chiefs and professionals. After attending Prempeh College in Ghana he travelled to the UK to study law at Lincoln's Inn in London and was called to the Bar in 1961. After this he attended Oxford University, graduating in politics, philosophy and economics (PPE) in 1964. He is married to Theresa Mensah and they now have five children. Kufuor is a Roman Catholic and is known as the 'gentle giant'.

Returning to Ghana (which had experienced an army coup in 1966), Kufuor entered local government as chief legal officer and town clerk in Kumasi in 1967. While the country swung between democracy and military government in the 1960s–80s Kufuor played a humble role in the country's politics as a founding member of the Progress Party in 1969, the Popular Front Party in 1979 and ultimately the NPP in 1992. He was thrown in jail by military regimes on two separate occasions, but during this period also served as deputy foreign minister and secretary for local government. He resigned the latter post after just seven months in 1982 in disillusion with the newly installed government of President Jerry Rawlings. He was instrumental in the establishment in 1994 of the country's district assemblies. These assemblies were designed to defuse certain racial and regional conflicts by granting a measure of decentralization.

Kufuor was defeated by Rawlings in the November 1996 presidential elections, but his real opportunity came with Rawlings's retirement from the presidency four years later. Rawlings's preferred successor was John Atta Mills, whose nomination as candidate of the National Democratic Congress he had approved in 1999, well ahead of the December 2000 ballot. The election campaign, which contained the country's first ever debate between the seven presidential candidates, rapidly resolved itself into a contest between the two leading contenders, Atta Mills and Kufuor. The resulting win for Kufuor (with 48% against 45% for Atta Mills), and the simultaneous albeit narrow victory of Kufuor's NPP in the parliamentary elections, confirmed that Rawlings's popularity had been more of a personal than a party matter. Kufuor took office on 7 January 2001.

During his first term, Kufuor launched a reconciliation commission to investigate past human rights abuses, and a national insurance health scheme designed to offer affordable health care to the entire 21-million population, and subsidized treatment for the poor and vulnerable. Despite poor economic results, Kufuor was re-elected on 7 December 2004 for a second and final term, securing over 52% of the vote, compared to 44% gained by Atta Mills. In the concurrent legislative polls, the NPP enlarged its majority.

Kufuor has been accused of nepotism—his brother holds the defence portfolio and his wife's brother is senior minister. His detractors claim that the total number of 'close' relatives holding government positions makes Kufuor the world record holder, since the toppling of Saddam Hussein in Iraq.

GREECE

Full name: The Hellenic Republic.

Leadership structure: The head of state is a president, elected by Parliament. The president's term of office is five years, renewable once only. The head of government is the prime minister, who is appointed by the president. The cabinet is appointed by the president on the recommendation of the prime minister.

President:	Costas Stephanopoulos	10 March 1995—12 March 2005
	Karolos **PAPOULIAS**	Since 12 March 2005
Prime Minister:	Costas Simitis	22 Jan. 1996—10 March 2004
	Costas **KARAMANLIS**	Since 10 March 2004

Legislature: The legislature is unicameral. The sole chamber, the Parliament (Vouli), has 300 members, directly elected for a four-year term.

Profile of the President:

Karolos **PAPOULIAS**

Karolos Papoulias was elected president of Greece in February 2005 by a huge majority in parliament and was sworn in on 12 March. A lawyer by training, he was also at one time the national pole vault champion, but spent many years in exile before returning to Greece in 1974 and becoming a founder member of the Panhellenic Socialist Movement (Panellinio Socialistiko Kinima—PASOK). Papoulias was first elected to Parliament in 1977 and held ministerial posts at various times in the 1980s and 1990s, notably in charge of foreign affairs.

Karolos Papoulias was born on 4 June 1929 in the city of Ioánnina, Epirus, in northwest Greece. He studied law in the University of Athens, followed by the University of Munich in Germany, and has a doctorate from the University of Cologne. He went into exile in Germany for the seven-year dictatorship of the Colonels from 1967 and was a founder member of PASOK in 1974, becoming a member of the party's central committee. Papoulias is married with three daughters.

Papoulias was elected to Parliament representing his home city of Ioánnina in 1977, and re-elected eight times, serving a total of 27 consecutive years in Parliament. He was deputy minister of foreign affairs from October 1981 until

February 1984, when he moved to alternate minister of foreign affairs. In July 1985 he was appointed minister of foreign affairs, a position he held until just after the 1989 election, when he became alternate minister of national defence until February 1990. In 1993 Papoulias returned to the post of minister of foreign affairs and remained in office until January 1996, when he led Greece's parliamentary representation to the Organization for Security and Co-operation in Europe (OSCE).

During the course of his career, Papoulias had been a pole vault champion, an official of the national volleyball team, and the president of the national athletics association, and in June 2000 he was appointed as a member of the board of directors and executive committee of the International Olympic Truce Foundation.

In 2005 both main parties backed his candidacy as president and he was elected by an unprecedented 279 votes in the 300-seat Parliament on 8 February. He took office on 12 March.

Profile of the Prime Minister:

Costas **KARAMANLIS**

Costas Karamanlis became Greece's youngest ever prime minister at the age of 47 on 10 March 2004 following the victory of his conservative New Democracy (Nea Demokratia—ND) party in a general election three days earlier. He is a member of one of Greece's great political dynasties as a nephew (and namesake) of former president Constantine Karamanlis, who restored Greek democracy in the 1970s and led his country into the European Economic Community (EEC, forerunner to the European Union—EU) in 1981. Costas Karamanlis has been involved in politics since his youth and has studied law, political science and diplomatic history. He has pledged to fight corruption in public life and supports greater European integration.

Constantine (Costas) Karamanlis was born in Athens in September 1956. He studied at the Athens School of Law and at Tufts University in Boston, USA. During this period he was also a leading member of the ND Youth Organization (ONNED) and ND, as well as serving his time in the Greek navy. From 1984 until 1989, he practised law and taught political science, diplomatic history and corporate law at Deree College (the American College of Greece). Karamanlis is married to Anastasia (Natasa) Pazaiti-Karamanlis; they have twins, one son and one daughter.

Karamanlis was first elected as a member of Parliament for the Thessaloniki district in June 1989. The same year he was also elected secretary of the Parliament's Board and ND secretary of political strategy. Karamanlis was re-elected in 1990 after the collapse of an all-party coalition led to fresh elections;

the same year his uncle Constantine Karamanlis became president for the third time. He retained his seat when PASOK won the 1993 election, and was re-elected again in 1996 and 2000. He was elected president of the ND in 1997.

On 7 March 2004 the ND won the general elections with 45.36%, securing a parliamentary majority of 164 seats out of a total of 300. Karamanlis took over from his predecessor, Costas Simitis, at a critical stage in UN-brokered negotiations on a deal to reunite Cyprus. Naming it his first priority, the prime minister vowed to work for "a just, viable and European solution" for the Mediterranean island; however, Greek Cypriots voted 'no' in the subsequent referendum, and only the Greek part of the island effectively acceded to the EU in May. Another pressing issue facing the government was the Athens 2004 Olympics; with building projects running late and security concerns high, the new prime minister chose to take personal charge of the Games by heading the culture ministry. The Games were generally hailed as a resounding success and a personal victory for Karamanlis, who basked in the afterglow, though only briefly, as Greece's budget deficit for 2004 hit around 5.3% of GDP—well above the 3% ceiling for eurozone members.

GRENADA

Full name: Grenada.

Leadership structure: The head of state is the British sovereign, styled 'Queen of the United Kingdom of Great Britain and Northern Ireland and of Grenada and Her other Realms and Territories, Head of the Commonwealth', and represented by a governor-general who is appointed on the advice of the Grenadian prime minister. The head of government is the prime minister, who is responsible to Parliament. The cabinet is appointed by the governor-general on the advice of the prime minister.

Queen:	Elizabeth II	Since 6 Feb. 1952
Governor-General:	Sir Daniel **WILLIAMS**	Since 8 Aug. 1996
Prime Minister:	Keith **MITCHELL**	Since 22 June 1995

Legislature: The legislature, the Parliament, is bicameral. The lower chamber, the House of Representatives, has 15 members, directly elected for a five-year term. The upper chamber, the Senate, has 13 members all appointed by the governor-general after the election of the House of Representatives (seven on the advice of the prime minister, three on the advice of the leader of the opposition and three on the advice of the prime minister after consulting various interests).

Profile of the Governor-General:

Sir Daniel **WILLIAMS**

Sir Daniel Williams, a former teacher and lawyer, was a member of Parliament and government minister in 1984–89, and then returned to legal practice for seven years until being appointed governor-general.

Born on 4 November 1937 in Grenada, Daniel Charles Williams began his working life early, teaching in a school in Grenada from 1952 to 1958, during which time he was promoted to deputy principal. Moving to London in 1959, he was briefly an assistant machine operator before joining the civil service, working in 1960–64 as a postal and telegraph officer. Entering further education, he became a student at London University and graduated in law in 1967. He then entered Lincoln's Inn to train as a barrister, and was called to the Bar in Grenada in 1969, after which he started in private practice. He served as a magistrate in St Lucia between 1970 and 1974 and then returned to private practice for the next ten years. He is married to Lady Gloria Williams née Modeste, and they have one son and three daughters.

Williams first entered politics in 1984, after the US intervention and the removal of the left-wing revolutionary government. He was a successful New National Party (NNP) candidate in the legislative elections of 3 December. Between 1984 and 1989 he served as minister of health, housing and the environment, of community development and women's affairs, and of legal affairs and as attorney general. In 1988 he acted briefly as prime minister, deputizing for the ailing Herbert Blaize.

Retiring from active politics at the time of the NNP's heavy electoral defeat in 1989, he returned to practising law, becoming a Queen's Counsel in 1996. That same year, following his appointment as governor-general, he was made a Knight Grand Cross of the Most Distinguished Order of St Michael and St George. He has published several works on law and public affairs. He also founded the Grenada, Carriacou and Petite Martinique Foundation for Needy Students, registered in 1996.

Profile of the Prime Minister:

Keith **MITCHELL**

Keith Mitchell became prime minister following the general election in June 1995. A former university lecturer in mathematics, and captain of the Grenada national cricket team in 1973, he has been the leader of the centre-right New National Party (NNP) since 1989.

A Roman Catholic like most Grenadians, Keith Claudius Mitchell was born on 12 November 1946 in Happy Hill, St George's. He attended local primary schools and the Presentation Boys' College, and played cricket for Grenada for several years before going to Barbados to study mathematics and chemistry at the University of the West Indies (1968–71). He returned to Grenada to work as a teacher at the Presentation Boys' College for two years, and captain the island's cricket team, before going to Washington D.C. in 1973. He obtained a master's degree in mathematics at Howard University and a doctorate in mathematics and statistics from the American University, and taught at Howard from 1977 to 1983. Mitchell has written several textbooks on mathematics for Caribbean students. He and his wife Marietta have one son.

In Grenada's last pre-independence elections in 1972 Keith Mitchell stood unsuccessfully as a candidate for the Grenada National Party. He set up the Systems Technology and Research consultancy in 1979, running this business for five years and not returning to active politics until 1984. By this time Grenada's experiment with left-wing socialism under the New Jewel Movement had come to a violent end and a US-led force had intervened to oust a self-styled revolutionary council in 1983.

Mitchell was elected to Parliament in December 1984 as a member of the NNP, a merger of a number of centre and conservative parties brought together with US encouragement by their shared hostility to former prime minister Sir Eric Gairy's Grenada United Labour Party. Between 1984 and 1989 Mitchell was secretary of the NNP, becoming its leader in January 1989. He held government office during this period as minister of works, communications and public utilities, and also dealt with civil aviation, energy, community development and women's affairs.

Increasingly at odds with prime minister and former NNP leader Herbert Blaize, Mitchell was dismissed from the government in mid-1989 by Blaize, who then exacerbated the fragmentation which the party had suffered in recent years by forming a new party himself. The election eventually held the following March (after the death of Blaize) left the NNP with only two seats in the 15-member Parliament, one of them held by Mitchell himself as party leader. He built up the party's credibility again in opposition and led it to victory on 20 June 1995, this time winning eight seats. In addition to becoming prime minister, Mitchell took on the portfolios of finance, external affairs, information and national security.

The NNP lost its one-seat majority in November 1998 when one of its parliamentarians, Raphael Fletcher, resigned from the party. Fresh elections were called for January the following year. Mitchell's popularity was confirmed when the NNP won 62% of the vote and all 15 seats in the House of Representatives. In his second term, Mitchell discussed the idea of reintroducing hanging to tackle growing levels of violent crime. He also re-established diplomatic links with communist Cuba, in October 2002.

In early elections in November 2003 the NNP's majority was slashed back down to one seat again. Mitchell was re-inaugurated as prime minister on 29 November. He now holds, in addition to the post of prime minister, the portfolios of national security, information, human resource development, business and private sector development and information communication technology.

The following summer Grenada was hit by Hurricane Ivan, which destroyed much of the vital nutmeg crop and damaged 90% of houses. Mitchell called for national unity to tackle the rebuilding process, and requested international relief assistance, estimating the economic cost of the damage at US$750 million—about twice Grenada's annual GNP.

GUATEMALA

Full name: The Republic of Guatemala.

Leadership structure: The head of state is a president, directly elected by universal adult suffrage. The president's term of office is four years, not renewable. The head of government is the president, who is responsible to the Congress. The cabinet is appointed by the president.

President:	Álvaro Arzú Irigoyen	14 Jan. 1996—14 Jan. 2000
	Alfonso Portillo Cabrera	14 Jan. 2000—14 Jan. 2004
	Óscar **BERGER** Perdomo	Since 14 Jan. 2004

Legislature: The legislature is unicameral. The sole chamber, the Congress of the Republic (Congreso de la República), has 158 members, directly elected for a four-year term.

Profile of the President:

Óscar **BERGER** Perdomo

Óscar Berger Perdomo, a former mayor of Guatemala City, was sworn in as president of Guatemala on 14 January 2004. Following his defeat in the 1999 presidential election, Berger had retired to his farm having vowed to leave politics for good, but was persuaded to stand again in 2003 by Guatemala's traditional power brokers, the agricultural and banking elite. His victory precipitated the flight of his predecessor, Alfonso Portillo, who was no longer protected by immunity from prosecution and was pursued by creditors and several police forces. Berger has slashed the size of the once dominant army, and has promised to fight corruption, crime and poverty.

Óscar José Rafael Berger Perdomo was born in Guatemala City on 11 August 1946. He was educated at the Liceo Javier, and graduated in law from the Rafael Landívar University. Berger excelled in sports, becoming an outstanding baseball player, and served as president of the Commission of Sports on the Guatemala City Municipal Council. A prosperous businessman and farmer, Berger owns an estate on the south coast of the country. He married Wendy Widmann in 1967 and has five children.

Berger was a founder member of the National Advancement Party (Partido de Avanzada Nacional—PAN) in 1984, the same year he was first elected as a councillor for Guatemala City. He served on the council until 1989, taking particular interest in public works, health and agriculture. He was first elected mayor of Guatemala City in 1991, and was re-elected in 1995, his considerable popularity resting on his ability to distance himself from the many public scandals of the day.

Berger first stood for the national presidency in 1999 as the PAN candidate, but was defeated by Alfonso Portillo Cabrera of the Guatemalan Republican Front (Frente Republicano Guatemalteco—FRG). He then announced his retirement from politics to concentrate on his farm and businesses.

Persuaded to make a comeback, he was nominated in 2002 as the PAN's candidate for the forthcoming presidential elections, but found himself at odds with the PAN's leadership. He split from the party and subsequently headed a Grand National Alliance (Gran Alianza Nacional—GANA) of three parties that had been shaved off from the PAN: the Patriotic Party, the Reform Movement and the National Solidarity Party.

President Portillo and the FRG backed the presidential candidacy of former dictator Efraín Ríos Montt, but in the first round in November 2003 Ríos Montt finished a distant third with just 11% of the vote. Berger won the subsequent runoff in December, beating Álvaro Colom of the National Unity of Hope by 54.1% to 45.9%, and Portillo was forced to flee to Mexico.

Berger set out his priorities as fighting crime, corruption and poverty, and implementing the peace accord that had ended Guatemala's 36-year civil war in 1996. Berger has also backed calls for Ríos Montt to be tried for atrocities during the civil war. He lacks a majority in Congress, however, where the FRG is the second-largest party behind the GANA, and his government is hamstrung by a tiny tax take—despite Guatemala having Central America's largest economy—and an underfunded police force which is itself riddled with corruption.

GUINEA

Full name: The Republic of Guinea.

Leadership structure: The head of state is a president, directly elected by universal adult suffrage. The president's term of office is five years. An amendment to the constitution to allow the incumbent president to stand for a third, longer (seven-year) term was approved in a referendum held on 11 November 2001. The president is head of government and appoints the members of the Council of Ministers.

President:	Maj.-Gen. Lansana **CONTÉ** (seized power on 3 April 1984)	Since 5 April 1984
Prime Minister:	Lamine Sidimé	8 March 1999—23 Feb. 2004
	François Lonseny Fall	23 Feb. 2004—29 April 2004
	vacant	29 April 2004—9 Dec. 2004
	Cellou Dalein **DIALLO**	Since 9 Dec. 2004

Legislature: The legislature is unicameral. The sole chamber, the National Assembly (Assemblée Nationale), has 114 members directly elected for a five-year term.

Profile of the President:

Maj.-Gen. Lansana **CONTÉ**

Maj.-Gen. Lansana Conté has been president since April 1984, following a military coup. A soldier in the French army prior to Guinea's independence in 1958, he had risen through the Guinean armed forces to be chief of army staff by 1975, and took power nine years later following the death of the country's leftist and increasingly dictatorial leader since independence, President Sekou Touré. He was confirmed in office at elections in December 1993, and again in 1998 and 2003 (for a seven-year term), despite increasing rumours of his ill health.

Lansana Conté, who is from the Soussou ethnic group, was born in 1934 in Koya. He went to military schools in Bingerville, Côte d'Ivoire, and Senegal, where he graduated from the St Louis Military School, joining the French army in 1955. After Guinea's independence in 1958 he rose to become regional commander in the north and northwest, was promoted to the rank of colonel in 1975, and for the next nine years was chief of army general staff.

In April 1984, ten days after the death in office of President Sekou Touré, Conté and Col. Diarra Traoré led a successful bloodless military coup. Conté assumed the presidency and the portfolios of defence and security, while Traoré became prime minister. They abolished the constitution and set up the Military Committee of National Recovery with Conté as its chairman. Hundreds of political prisoners were released and freedom of speech was restored.

By December 1984 disagreements between Conté and Traoré led to the latter's demotion. Conté's popularity fell amid resentment of tough austerity measures which he had introduced at the instigation of the World Bank and the International Monetary Fund (IMF). In July 1985 Traoré took advantage of Conté's absence abroad to denounce the regime and try to seize power, but the coup was halted within a day and over 200 prisoners were taken. Traoré and other leaders were executed, although this was not officially confirmed for two years. Those prisoners who survived were released in 1988.

In October 1988 Conté agreed to the drafting of a new two-party constitution which would return the country to civilian rule and this was overwhelmingly approved by a referendum in December 1990. Meanwhile he promoted himself to general and in February 1991 a new Transitional Council of National Recovery was established under his chairmanship. More parties were legalized in 1992 but unauthorized public meetings were banned to avoid further violence.

Presidential elections were set for late 1993 and were eventually held on 19 December after riots had resulted in their postponement by two weeks. Conté secured 51.7% of the vote, in a poll marred by violence, at least 12 fatalities and opposition claims of widespread irregularities.

In June 1995, in the country's first multiparty legislative elections, Conté's Party of Unity and Progress (Parti de l'Unité et du Progrès—PUP) won 71 out of 114 seats, although opposition parties again alleged electoral fraud. The same accusations were levelled at Conté's successful re-election on 14 December 1998. He gained 56% of the vote against 25% for Mamadou Bâ and 17% for Alpha Condé. It was Condé who proved to be Conté's biggest subsequent rival and he was charged with plotting a coup soon afterwards.

Opposition anger at electoral irregularities was deflected by the worsening security problem on the country's southern border. Conté accused the country's immigrant Sierra Leonean population of aiding cross-border attacks. Legislative elections were postponed indefinitely due to the 'state of war' in the south of the country. To try and control internal security, Conté launched a new 'pitiless' era in February 2001, bringing back capital punishment after a seven-year absence.

Relative peace was eventually restored in the south and Conté began to look to the future in late 2001. Legislative elections were called and a referendum was organized to approve constitutional changes to allow Conté a third term. The opposition condemned the approval of these changes in the November vote, claiming that the government's estimation of an 87% turnout was a gross exaggeration of the 20% of the electorate that had actually bothered to take part. The PUP increased its majority to 85 seats in legislative elections, which were eventually held in June 2002 and were boycotted by the opposition.

Conté collapsed in December 2002 while performing a pilgrimage at the Ka'aba in Mecca, Saudi Arabia. He is suffering from diabetes and heart problems, but continues to smoke heavily. He won re-election in December 2003 despite rumours that he was not well enough to rule; all major opposition candidates boycotted the vote. The European Union refused to observe the polls, saying that the preparations had failed to meet the basic criteria for free elections. After his re-inauguration he appointed François Lonseny Fall as prime minister, but Fall resigned two months later, while on a trip to Paris, claiming that Conté was blocking all attempts at reform and making his job impossible. The post of prime minister remained vacant for over seven months before Cellou Dalein Diallo was appointed.

In January 2005 Conté's convoy was attacked, but the president was unharmed—the coup attempt was later blamed on Liberian ex-president Charles Taylor who had resented Conté's support for the Liberian rebels that had ousted him from power in 2003. By 2005 rumours were emerging that Conté's diabetes was acute, often sending him into comas and giving him little grasp of the events and people around him, let alone affairs of state. He has two wives, Henriette and Kadiatou Seth, a former Miss Guinea, and several children, but no-one has been groomed as successor.

Profile of the Prime Minister:

Cellou Dalein **DIALLO**

Cellou Dalein Diallo, an economist, was appointed prime minister in December 2004 by the ailing President Lansana Conté. His predecessor had resigned and gone into exile the previous April, frustrated by the president's intervention in reforms, and the post had then remained vacant for over seven months.

Cellou Dalein Diallo was born in 1953 in Dalein village near Labé, in what was then French Guinea. An economist, he was employed by the country's Central Bank before joining the cabinet of President Lansana Conté in 1995. He is widely regarded as a good technocrat and made his mark as minister of public works, overseeing improvements to Guinea's collapsing road system for a number of years before becoming minister of fisheries. He was appointed as prime minister on 9 December 2004. The post had been vacant since April, the previous occupant François Fall having resigned in protest at his reforms being blocked by the presidency.

Diallo is considered by some to be pro-Russian, an important distinction when it comes to Guinea's major resource, bauxite, which accounts for over 90% of export earnings; the Russian group Rusal is the second-largest consortium operating in Guinea. In an effort to win international aid, he has pledged more transparency and has lifted the ban on private radio stations.

Diallo's position is precarious. He was appointed by a president whom many observers, and many Guineans, believe to be dangerously ill. Guinea's relative peacefulness, compared to its turbulent neighbours, has been ascribed to its strong, centralized army, and Conté's predilection for dividing and ruling—in the process preventing the rise of any potentially able successor.

GUINEA-BISSAU

Full name: The Republic of Guinea-Bissau.

Leadership structure: The head of state under the constitution is a president, directly elected by universal adult suffrage for a five-year term. Following a coup in September 2003, a Military Committee for the Restitution of Constitutional and Democratic Order named an interim president. Presidential elections in mid-2005 promised a return to democracy. The president is the head of government, and appoints the Council of Ministers including the prime minister.

***President*:**	Malam Bacai Sanhá (acting)	14 May 1999—17 Feb. 2000
	Kumba Yallá	17 Feb. 2000—14 Sept. 2003
	Gen. Veríssimo Correia Seabra (interim)	14 Sept. 2003—28 Sept. 2003
	Henrique **ROSA** (interim)	Since 28 Sept. 2003
***Prime Minister*:**	Francisco Fadul (acting from 3 Dec.1998)	20 Feb. 1999—19 Feb. 2000
	Caetano N'Tchama	19 Feb. 2000—21 March 2001
	Faustino Imbali	21 March 2001—9 Dec. 2001
	Alamara Nhassé	9 Dec. 2001—17 Nov. 2002
	Mário Pires	17 Nov. 2002—14 Sept. 2003
	vacant	14 Sept. 2003—28 Sept. 2003
	Artur Sanhá	28 Sept. 2003—10 May 2004
	Carlos **GOMES** Jr	Since 10 May 2004

Legislature: The legislature is unicameral. The sole chamber, the National People's Assembly (Assembléia Nacional Popular), has 102 members, directly elected for a four-year term.

Profile of the President:

Henrique **ROSA**

Henrique Rosa became interim president of Guinea-Bissau on 28 September 2003 after a military coup had ousted the erratic President Kumba Yallá from power earlier in the month. The new military authorities asked respected businessman Rosa to head a caretaker government until fresh elections could be held, although coup leader Gen. Veríssimo Correia Seabra retained considerable control as head of the National Transitional Council (until his death in October 2004).

Henrique Pereira Rosa, born in 1946 to a Portuguese father and Guinean mother, is an economist and businessman. He served as the chairman of Guinea-Bissau's National Election Commission during the country's first free elections in 1994.

Rosa was reluctant to accept the post of interim president following Gen. Correia Seabra's 2003 bloodless coup that deposed President Yallá, but was persuaded to do so by the Roman Catholic Bishop of Bissau, José Camnate, who headed a committee appointed by the military to help set up a caretaker civilian government. Rosa's mixed-race background was a key factor in his selection, as the armed forces are dominated by the Balante ethnic group.

Rosa was praised for his immediate achievements, including the reinstatement of Supreme Court judges previously barred and arrested, and pledges to pay civil service salary arrears and promote transparency and sound financial management. Successful legislative elections were held in March 2004. International aid has also been forthcoming, including funds from the European Union (EU) to keep essential services running in the lead-up to the presidential elections held in June–July 2005.

Profile of the President-elect:

João Bernardo 'Nino' **VIEIRA**

Brig.-Gen. (retd) João Bernardo 'Nino' Vieira won presidential elections in Guinea-Bissau in June–July 2005. He had previously been head of state from 1980 to 1999, having seized power in a coup. Vieira had risen within the African Party for the Independence of Guinea and Cape Verde (Partido Africano da Independência da Guiné e Cabo Verde—PAIGC) as a military commander during the struggle for independence from Portugal. His coup in 1980 removed the senior Cape Verdeans from the leadership, and he turned the country away from its leftist orientation to encourage private enterprise, foreign investment and Western aid. His victory in July 1994 in the country's first multiparty election, having belatedly responded to pressure to end single-party rule, gave him a five-year term in office. However, in 1999 he was himself ousted by a coup led by army chief Gen. Ansumane Mané. After six years punctuated by further coups and mutinies, Vieira returned to Guinea-Bissau to stand for the presidency again.

Born on 27 April 1939 in Bissau, João Bernardo 'Nino' Vieira started out as an electrician but then trained as a soldier in China. He joined the PAIGC in 1960, studying at the party school in Conakry, Guinea, where his teacher was the leader and founder of the party, Amílcar Cabral. The following year he was appointed military commander of Catió and political commissioner. In 1964 he was made a member of the PAIGC's political bureau, commander of the southern front in the war for independence from Portugal, and a member of the War Council; he was vice president of the War Council from 1965, and assumed overall responsibility for military operations in 1970. His nom de guerre was 'Kabi', which is still chanted by his supporters at rallies.

Upon independence in 1974, the PAIGC under Luís Cabral (half-brother of Amílcar Cabral who had been assassinated in 1973) formed a single-party government. Vieira, then aged 35, was commander-in-chief and minister for the armed forces, president of the National People's Assembly, and permanent secretary of the party central committee. After elections in 1977 he was also appointed vice president of the republic, and in August 1978 he added to these posts that of prime minister.

On 19 November 1980 Vieira seized power in a coup, capitalizing on the resentment of those from mainland Guinea-Bissau who felt that there were too many Cape Verdeans (like Cabral) in the government, and also claiming that Cabral was failing to follow the socialist ideals of the party. The coup was welcomed by the government of neighbouring Guinea, which spoke of the possibility of forming a 'Greater Guinea'. Vieira, as chair of a new Revolutionary Council of Guinean Officers, also retained for himself the portfolios of defence and the interior.

In May 1984 Vieira re-established the National People's Assembly, replaced the Revolutionary Council with a Council of State, of which he was unanimously elected president, and also took on the post of prime minister. By this stage he was already turning the country away from left-wing policies followed since independence, instead encouraging private enterprise and foreign investment, and receiving support from the International Monetary Fund. Internal opposition to this change of direction was reflected in a number of coup attempts, one of which ended with the execution of the first vice president, Col. Paulo Correia, and five co-conspirators.

Elections to the National People's Assembly were held in 1989, but still with a single PAIGC list, while Vieira was re-elected to the presidency. By 1992 pressure from both within and outside the PAIGC for multiparty elections led Vieira to promise these would be held later in the year, but they were postponed many times and did not take place until 1994.

Vieira resigned from the army so as to be eligible to stand in the presidential poll. He did not obtain an absolute majority of votes in the first round on 3 July, but won the runoff on 7 August even though all the opposition parties rallied behind a single candidate, Kumba Yallá. In the concurrent legislative election the PAIGC secured 62 of the 100 seats, providing Vieira with a secure majority. He was sworn in for a five-year presidential term on 29 September. He sought to improve

Guinea-Bissau's relations with neighbouring countries. In 1997 Guinea-Bissau joined the franc zone, replacing the peso with the CFA franc.

Disunity within the PAIGC reached a head in January 1998 when Vieira dismissed former ally and army chief Gen. Ansumane Mané for allegedly smuggling arms to the Casamance rebels in Senegal. Mané responded by launching a rebellion in June; about half the population was displaced in the months of fighting that ensued. Troops from the Economic Community of West African States (ECOWAS) intervened and a unity government was formed in February 1999, only to be overthrown by a fresh army coup by Mané in May. With the presidential palace set ablaze, Vieira fled first to the French embassy and then to the Portuguese embassy. He went into exile in Portugal and was expelled from the PAIGC.

Several years of instability ensued, due to recurring army mutinies, coups and unrest and the erratic presidency of Kumba Yallá, elected in 2000. A coup in 2003 heralded fresh elections to return the country once more to civilian rule. The PAIGC won the legislative polls in 2004, but the new ruling elite in the party was dismayed by the hero's welcome that greeted Vieira on his return to the country in April 2005. The Supreme Court exempted him and Yallá from the prohibition barring former presidents from standing in the forthcoming presidential poll, and declared that it could find no record of the outstanding charges against him for ordering the deaths of five senior army officers suspected of plotting a coup in 1985.

Vieira finished second in the first round on 19 June, behind official PAIGC candidate Malam Bacai Sanha. He went on to win the runoff on 24 July with 55.75% of the vote, after Yallá (who had finished third) swung his party's support behind him. He will be sworn into office on 1 October.

Profile of the Prime Minister:

Carlos **GOMES** Jr

Carlos Gomes Jr was sworn in as prime minister of Guinea-Bissau on 10 May 2004, after his African Party for the Independence of Guinea and Cape Verde (Partido Africano da Independência da Guiné e Cabo Verde—PAIGC) won general elections. A businessman and banker, Gomes is thought to be the richest man in Guinea-Bissau. He heads a cabinet made up largely of Western-oriented technocrats, but faces a tough struggle against a failing economy and endemic corruption.

Carlos Domingos Gomes Jr was born on 19 December 1949, the son of Carlos Domingos Gomes and Maria Augusta Ramalho, in Bolama, in what was then Portuguese Guinea (now Guinea-Bissau). His nickname is 'Cadogo'. He is married with four children. Gomes's primary education took place at the Dr

Oliveira Salazar School in the capital Bissau, before he was sent from 1963 to 1967 to the Colégio da Parede in Portugal. He returned to Guinea-Bissau in 1967 to spend two years studying at the Commercial Institute in Bissau. He later spent some time studying at the Université Laval in Québec, Canada.

During his business career, Gomes worked in the Central Bank and ran an oil import company. His family has extensive property holdings in the capital, Bissau. He has been involved in politics since his election to parliament in 1994 and he is currently the head of the PAIGC, which ran the country from independence in 1974 until a coup in 1999. The PAIGC won general elections called in March 2004, the first since a bloodless military coup the previous year; Gomes was sworn in as prime minister on 10 May 2004.

Gomes's cabinet is dominated by young technocrats, although he was also forced to appoint five members of the old guard led by Aristide Gomes, the vice president of the PAIGC. Aristide Gomes was close to overthrown PAIGC president João Bernardo 'Nino' Vieira, and heads a faction within the PAIGC that Carlos Gomes cannot hope to control. However, he is a popular choice as prime minister among the aid donor community as well as among potential foreign investors, whose help will be vital in bringing the country's economy back from the brink of collapse.

The return of Vieira in 2005 dismayed Gomes and his faction of the PAIGC, and following Vieira's victory over Gomes's chosen PAIGC candidate in the presidential poll, it is unclear whether Gomes will remain in office after the former dictator's inauguration in October.

GUYANA

Full name: The Co-operative Republic of Guyana.

Leadership structure: The head of state is a president, nominated by the majority party in the National Assembly after legislative elections. The president's term of office is five years. The president appoints the prime minister and the cabinet. The president is head of government.

President:	Bharrat **JAGDEO**	Since 11 Aug. 1999
Prime Minister:	Sam **HINDS** (except 17 March 1997—22 Dec. 1997 and 9 Aug. 1999—11 Aug. 1999)	Since 9 Oct. 1992

Legislature: The legislature is unicameral. The sole chamber, the National Assembly, has 65 members (53 elected and 12 regional representatives) with a five-year term.

Profile of the President:

Bharrat **JAGDEO**

Bharrat Jagdeo first took over the presidency from Janet Jagan when she was taken ill in 1999, and was re-elected to the post on 19 March 2001. Educated in economics in the Soviet Union, Jagdeo has served People's Progressive Party (PPP) governments as Guyana's representative at the World Bank and International Monetary Fund (IMF) among other posts. He was minister of finance between 1995 and 1999 before being handpicked by Jagan as her successor. His appointment prompted dissent from the mostly Afro-Guyanese opposition People's National Congress (PNC) but was considered by many as the start of a new era in Guyanese politics.

Bharrat Jagdeo was born on 23 January 1964 to ethnically Indian-Guyanese parents in the small farming community of Unity, Mahaica, just east of the capital Georgetown. Bharrat means 'India' in Hindi. His father worked on the railways and his mother was a peasant farmer. After attending the local primary and secondary schools, Jagdeo spent a short time as a teacher before winning a scholarship to study economics at the Patrice Lumumba University in Moscow, then the capital of the Soviet Union, in 1984. Having received a master's degree in 1990 he returned to Guyana and began work at the state planning secretariat in

1992. He had joined the PPP's youth wing in 1980 and became a member of the party itself in 1983.

Between October 1992 and 1999 Jagdeo was attached to the ministry of finance, first as a special adviser to the minister, and then as junior minister himself from October 1993. Within this role he was given responsibility in a number of key institutions including the Guyana Water Authority, and as a director of the regional Caribbean Development Bank (CDB). His reputation in these positions earned him postings as Guyana's governor to the World Bank and IMF (which he still holds) and secured his promotion to full minister of finance in March 1995. However, his hard-line attitude to negotiations is credited with prolonging a strike by civil servants in 1999. Bharrat Jagdeo married his wife Varshnie née Singh in 1998.

When President Janet Jagan, herself a controversial appointment, fell increasingly ill with a heart condition in 1999 she turned to Jagdeo as her chosen heir. A few days before the handover of power in August the then Prime Minister Sam Hinds (a member of the Afro-Guyanese community) agreed to resign to allow Jagdeo's nominal appointment to the post to secure his succession as president under Guyana's constitutional practice. This process caused unrest among Afro-Guyanese, led by the PNC which already disputed the validity of the 1997 elections and Jagdeo's consequent selection as head of state. However, from the start Jagdeo has attempted to overcome the country's long history of race-driven politics and unsuccessfully suggested co-operation with the PNC. Coming from a much younger generation of politicians his appointment was accompanied with keen speculation of imminent change.

The presidential term expired in early 2001 and Jagdeo was selected to run for another term by the PPP. His success at the polls in March was again contested by the PNC which initiated a series of violent demonstrations in Georgetown and across the country in the following month. After extensive talks with PNC leader and former president Desmond Hoyte, Jagdeo's government was able to begin its second term in early May.

Profile of the Prime Minister:

Sam **HINDS**

Sam Hinds is an engineer who spent 25 years working in the bauxite industry and came late to politics. He emerged through his involvement in the human rights movement in the last years of the People's National Congress regime, and became prime minister when former president Cheddi Jagan's left-wing People's Progressive Party (PPP) finally won power at the October 1992 elections. Elevated temporarily from the premiership to the presidency in March 1997 when Cheddi Jagan died, he was passed over as the party's presidential candidate for the December 1997 elections in favour of Jagan's wife, Janet.

Samuel Archibald Anthony Hinds was born on 27 December 1943 in Mahaicony, on the east coast in the Demerara region. He was educated at Queen's College in Georgetown, the capital, and then went on to study at the University of New Brunswick in Canada, where he graduated with a degree in chemical engineering in 1967. He worked for DEMBA, the bauxite operations subsidiary of Alcan in Linden, Guyana, from 1967 to 1992.

Hinds, who is married to Yvonne née Burnett with three children, did not enter politics until 1989. He made his name as a prominent member and cofounder of Guyanese Action for Reform and Democracy (GUARD), a pressure group launched in 1990 by the Guyana Human Rights Association to demand free and fair elections. Not formally a member of the PPP, he was elected to the National Assembly on 5 October 1992 as leader of the Civic movement of business and professional people, standing in an electoral alliance with the PPP. He was appointed as first vice president and prime minister when the new PPP/Civic government came to office under President Cheddi Jagan in October 1992.

Hinds's succession to the presidency on Jagan's death on 6 March 1997 was in accordance with the provisions of the constitution, but it was not generally thought likely that he would retain this top political post for long, even if he were to be re-elected on the PPP/Civic ticket in the end-of-year elections. In the event the party turned instead to Jagan's wife Janet (whom Hinds had appointed as his successor as prime minister in March) as its more charismatic standard bearer.

Two days before Janet Jagan's resignation due to ill health in August 1999, Hinds temporarily stepped down from his post as prime minister. This was merely a manoeuvre to allow Bharrat Jagdeo to hold this office momentarily, and then move up to the vacant presidency, as per the constitution.

HAITI

Full name: The Republic of Haiti.

Leadership structure: The head of state is a president, directly elected by universal adult suffrage. The president's term of office is five years, not immediately renewable. Following an armed uprising in February 2004, an interim president was appointed pending fresh elections scheduled for the end of 2005. The president appoints the prime minister, who must be approved by the National Assembly. The prime minister is head of government and chooses the cabinet, in consultation with the president.

President:	René Préval	7 Feb. 1996—7 Feb. 2001
	Jean-Bertrand Aristide	7 Feb. 2001—29 Feb. 2004
	Boniface **ALEXANDRE** (interim) (acting from 29 Feb. 2004)	Since 8 March 2004
Prime Minister:	Jacques Edouard Alexis (nominated on 15 July 1998)	11 Jan. 1999—2 March 2001
	Jean-Marie Chérestal (acting from 21 Jan. 2002)	2 March 2001—15 March 2002
	Yvon Neptune	15 March 2002—12 March 2004
	Gérard **LATORTUE**	Since 12 March 2004

Legislature: Under the 1987 Constitution, the legislature, the National Assembly (Assemblée Nationale), is bicameral. The lower chamber, the Chamber of Deputies (Chambre des Députés), has 83 members, directly elected for a four-year term. The upper chamber, the Senate (Sénat), has 27 members, directly elected for a six-year term, with one-third of senators elected every two years.

Profile of the President:

Boniface **ALEXANDRE**

Boniface Alexandre was nominated as interim president of Haiti on 29 February 2004 after President Jean-Bertrand Aristide was forced out of office by violent opposition and fled the country. As chief justice, Alexandre assumed the presidency hours later, though was not sworn in until 8 March. Having earned a reputation for integrity, he promised to fight corruption in the judicial system.

236

One of his first acts as president was to ask the UN for a peacekeeping force, which has since been employed in providing humanitarian aid to deal with devastating floods as much as it has been in keeping the peace.

Boniface Alexandre was born on 31 July 1936 in Ganthier in the Département de l'Ouest and brought up by his uncle, former prime minister Martial Célestin. He now has four children. He studied at the Lycée Alexandre Pétion in the capital Port-au-Prince and trained as a lawyer at the State University of Haiti. Called to the Bar in 1963, he worked for Cabinet Lamarre, a Port-au-Prince law firm specializing in business contracts and divorce settlements. During his 25 years with the firm, he represented the French embassy among others. He also taught several university law courses and attended seminars in France, the USA and Africa. He joined the Court of Appeals in the late 1980s and the Supreme Court in 1991, becoming a full member in 1995. He was appointed chief justice (president of the Supreme Court) in 2001.

Largely unknown in Haitian politics, he was next in the presidential line of succession when Aristide fell, according to Haiti's 1987 Constitution. His succession lacked the support of parts of the political opposition, however, on the grounds that as an appointee of Aristide (who never fought for the independence of the judiciary), he remained too closely linked with the latter's legacy.

Profile of the Prime Minister:

Gérard **LATORTUE**

Gérard Latortue was born in Gonaïves and worked as a lawyer and law professor until forced to flee the dictatorship of François 'Papa Doc' Duvalier in 1963. He returned to Haiti to join the government of Leslie François Manigat in 1998, but again had to flee when Manigat was deposed by a military coup. Latortue worked for the UN and then hosted a weekly television show in Miami, USA, where he was a prominent member of the Haitian exile community. After Aristide's ouster, Latortue was called on in March 2004 to form an interim government with no political affiliation.

Gérard Latortue was born in Gonaïves on 19 June 1934. After studying in France at the Institute of Political Sciences and the Institute of Economic and Social Development in Paris, he returned to Haiti in 1960 to practise as a lawyer and professor. Latortue is married with three children and is an avid book collector, especially of those on Haitian history.

In 1961 Latortue cofounded the Institute of Higher Commercial and Economic Studies in Port-au-Prince, saying there was nowhere for Haitians to study economics in their own country. However, in 1963 he was forced to flee the regime of François 'Papa Doc' Duvalier. It was to be the beginning of 25 years in exile.

Latortue lived initially in Jamaica and the US capital, Washington D.C., before moving to Puerto Rico and working as an economics teacher. He later joined the UN Industrial Development Organization, living in Togo and Côte d'Ivoire in west Africa before rising to chief negotiator and living in Vienna, Austria. In 1988 Latortue returned to Haiti to join the government of Leslie Manigat as foreign minister. However, the army staged a coup four months later, forcing Latortue to return to the UN. He moved to south Florida in 1994 to work as an international business consultant and radio show host.

Haitian president Jean-Bertrand Aristide offered Latortue a job in his cabinet in 2001, but Latortue turned him down. In 2003 the Haitian Television Network of America (HTN) was launched, featuring Latortue on two talk shows, *Revue de la semaine* and *L'inviter*.

Meanwhile, in January 2004, a loose alliance of opposition parties, civic groups and students began demanding Aristide's resignation. Mounting protests finally led to an armed uprising, and on 29 February anti-government rebels finally ousted Aristide after seizing much of north Haiti. A US-led peacekeeping force arrived to keep order and a transitional government was established; on 9 March 2004 the seven-member Council of Sages named Latortue the new interim prime minister of Haiti. He arrived in Haiti the following day and was sworn in on 12 March 2004.

The security situation in Haiti remained critical. The Brazilian-led UN peacekeeping force, woefully under strength and comprising contingents from 41 nations, came under heavy criticism for its failure to smother a wave of violence in the capital. Promised overseas aid fell badly behind schedule, while Latortue's government failed to show how it planned to spend US$800 million in donors' project money. A commission to oversee bidding for public contracts took a year to set up. Most accept that it will take years of sustained foreign aid to noticeably affect the living conditions of the Haitian people. Latortue will not be in office to see it; his administration in February 2005 announced elections for the end of the year in which members of the interim government will not stand.

HONDURAS

Full name: The Republic of Honduras.

Leadership structure: The head of state is a president, directly elected by universal adult suffrage. The president's term of office is four years, and is not renewable. The head of government is the president, who appoints the cabinet.

President:	Carlos Roberto Flores	27 Jan. 1998—27 Jan. 2002
	Ricardo **MADURO**	Since 27 Jan. 2002

Legislature: The legislature is unicameral. The sole chamber, the National Congress (Congreso Nacional), has 128 members, directly elected for a four-year term.

Profile of the President:

Ricardo **MADURO**

Ricardo Maduro of the right-wing National Party (Partido Nacional—PN) was elected as president in November 2001 and took office in January 2002. Head of the country's Central Bank in the 1990s, he champions the neoliberal economic approach and has spearheaded an effort to crack down on the country's rising levels of violent crime. He was forced to prove his Honduran nationality in order to run for president.

Ricardo Maduro Joest was born on 20 April 1946 in Panama City. His maternal grandmother had been born in Honduras and it was to there that the family moved in 1952. After attending primary school in Tegucigalpa, Maduro travelled to Pennsylvania, USA, to complete his secondary education and graduated in economics from Stanford University, California, in 1969. He married the Salvadoran Miriam Andreu in 1971 and they had one son and three daughters before divorcing in 1996. Six years later he married the Spaniard Aguas Ocaña Navarro; they have adopted five orphaned Honduran children.

Returning to Honduras in the early 1970s, Maduro began his career there as general manager for the photocopying company Xerox. In 1976 he left the multinational to form his own firm, Inversiones La Paz, an investment holding company which financed and bought a variety of different concerns and currently has many interests in the Honduran commercial sector. Maduro's business career was widely praised and he won awards for 'businessman of the year' in 1983 and even 'man of the year' from *El Heraldo* newspaper in 1991.

When Honduras returned to democracy in 1984 Maduro became involved in centre-right politics and finally took on Honduran citizenship. He headed the presidential campaigns of PN candidate Rafael Callejas. Although unsuccessful in 1985, Callejas was victorious in 1989 and was inaugurated in January 1990. On his appointment he rewarded Maduro by nominating him as director of the Honduran Central Bank and as co-ordinator of the government's economic office. From this position Maduro was able to put his economic training into practice and pushed through the country's first major economic reforms, for which he is now vilified by the liberal opposition. At the end of Callejas's term in office and following the PN's electoral defeat in 1994, Maduro returned to his business interests.

In 1997 Maduro's only son, 24-year-old Ricardo Ernesto, was kidnapped and murdered. The attack had a deep effect on the former banker, who had become leader of the PN, and he sought to win the presidential elections in 2001 on the back of a strong anti-crime platform. He also promised to focus on education. The opposition Liberal candidate, Rafael Piñeda, tried to derail Maduro's campaign with a legal challenge to his nationality, and therefore his right to run. The Honduran birth of Maduro's grandmother vindicated his cause and he resumed campaigning after a brief pause. He secured victory in the first round of the vote on 25 November, with 52% against Piñeda's 44%, and was sworn in the following January for a four-year term at the head of a PN government.

HUNGARY

Full name: The Republic of Hungary.

Leadership structure: The head of state is a president, elected by the National Assembly. The president's term of office is five years, renewable once only. The head of government is the prime minister, who is appointed by the president and appoints a cabinet.

President:	Árpád Göncz (acting from 2 May 1990)	3 Aug. 1990—4 Aug. 2000
	Ferenc Mádl	4 Aug. 2000—5 Aug. 2005
	László **SÓLYOM**	Since 5 Aug. 2005
Prime Minister:	Viktor Orbán	6 July 1998—27 May 2002
	Péter Medgyessy	27 May 2002—29 Sept. 2004
	Ferenc **GYURCSÁNY** (acting from 27 Aug. 2004)	Since 29 Sept. 2004

Legislature: The legislature is unicameral. The sole chamber, the National Assembly (Országgyűlés), has 386 members, directly elected for a four-year term.

Profile of the President:

László **SÓLYOM**

László Sólyom, a noted enviromentalist and civil rights campaigner, was sworn in as president of Hungary on 5 August 2005. He was nominated by Protect the Future (Védegylet), a civil rights and environmentalist NGO that he himself had founded. He was elected by parliament following a decision to abstain by most of the members from the junior coalition party, the Alliance of Free Democrats (Szabad Demokraták Szövetsége—SzDSz), who were unwilling to support the candidate of the Hungarian Socialist Party (Magyar Szocialista Párt—MSzP).

László Sólyom was born in Pécs in southern Hungary on 3 January 1942. He graduated in law from the University of Pécs in 1965 and in 1966 became an assistant teacher at the law faculty of the University of Jena in Germany, earning a doctorate in German civilian law. Sólyom then taught at several universities and law institutes in the capital, Budapest. Initially a legal adviser for civil and

241

environmental organizations, he became noted for his involvement in environmental protection issues, particularly the campaign against the Nagymaros Dam. He is married with two children.

In 1987 Sólyom became a founder member of the Hungarian Democratic Forum (Magyar Demokrata Fórum—MDF), a centre-right opposition party that has since split. He became vice president of the Constitutional Court on its establishment in late 1989 and became its first president the following year, remaining in this post until 1998. Several groundbreaking decisions were taken during Sólyom's stewardship of the Court, including rulings on banning capital punishment and the constitutional protection of homosexual partnerships, and annulling laws limiting freedom of speech. He based many of these decisions on the idea of the invisible constitution, whereby decisions could reflect the motivating spirit of the constitution rather than its written form, and advocated the principle of equal human dignity as more important than parliament or politics.

In 2000 Sólyom founded Protect the Future, a civil rights and environmentalist NGO. He was nominated to the presidency by Protect the Future and 110 prominent public figures and intellectuals in 2005. The Federation of Young Democrats—Hungarian Citizens' Party (Fiatal Demokraták Szövetsége—Magyar Polgári Párt, Fidesz–MPP), the largest right-wing opposition party, decided to back Sólyom after a poll commissioned to find the 'people's president' placed him second only to outgoing president Ferenc Mádl, who refused to run again. Assembly members from the junior coalition party, the SzDSz, signalled on 30 May that they would abstain from the parliamentary vote, unwilling to support MSzP nominee Katalin Szili—considering her to be "too much of a party politician"—and regarding Sólyom as an acceptable alternative. In the third and final round of voting on 7 June, Sólyom won narrowly, by 185 to 182 votes. He took office on 5 August.

The role of president is largely ceremonial, though it does include certain rights, not customarily used, such as the ability to send new bills to the Constitutional Court for review—the Court can annul laws it deems unconstitutional. Sólyom told reporters in his acceptance speech that he intended to be a "passive, strict president who speaks little". However, his track record as president of the Constitutional Court suggests he has limited respect for convention.

Profile of the Prime Minister:

Ferenc **GYURCSÁNY**

Dubbed by his critics a 'salon socialist', Ferenc Gyurcsány was an outsider to be chosen as prime minister-designate following the resignation of independent Péter Medgyessy in August 2004. Gyurcsány, who has a degree in economics, made a fortune through buying state assets in the early years of privatization. He began his political career in the communist youth movement before the regime collapsed in 1989. He served as sports minister for the Hungarian Socialist Party (Magyar Szocialista Párt—MSzP) in the coalition government led by Medgyessy. He is said to be both pro-market and sensitive to the needs of the poor, and has been described as Hungary's equivalent to UK prime minister Tony Blair.

Ferenc Gyurcsány was born in the western town of Pápa on 4 June 1961, into a relatively poor family. His third wife is Klára Dobrev and he is the father of four children. He initially studied to become a teacher and then read economics at the Janus Pannonius University of Sciences in Pécs, graduating in 1984 and 1990 respectively. He first entered politics as a member of the Association of Young Communists (KISZ), before becoming vice president in 1989 of its successor, the Democratic Youth Alliance (DEMISZ). In 1990 he abandoned politics to enter business, becoming a consultant with CREDITUM Financial Consulting Ltd.

For the next decade Gyurcsány immersed himself in business, in the process becoming one of the richest men in Hungary. In 1992 he became a director of Eurocorp International Financing Ltd, and founded ALTUS Investment and Assets Management Inc. Snapping up newly privatized state assets in the early 1990s, Gyurcsány discovered a talent for making money.

He returned to politics in 2002 as chief strategic adviser to Prime Minister Péter Medgyessy. Medgyessy was said to have wanted to move Gyurcsány to an important ministry, but in the power struggle with ambitious party rivals he could only get him into the sports ministry: he became minister of sports, youth and children in 2003. During his time in office, Hungary suffered a high-profile athletic doping scandal at the 2004 Olympic Games in Athens, when five Hungarian athletes were disqualified for drug violations, including two who were stripped of their gold medals.

Gyurcsány became a member of the MSzP's executive committee in 2003 and chairman of the MSzP's Győr-Moson-Sopron county organization in 2004. That summer rumours began to spread that Gyurcsány and Medgyessy had become estranged, and Gyurcsány offered his resignation, which was subsequently accepted. A government crisis developed very quickly, triggered by yet another of many cabinet reshuffles, and Medgyessy was himself forced to resign in August. Gyurcsány was named on 27 August as prime minister-designate.

Gyurcsány was reportedly surprised at the large amount of support he received from the MSzP when the National Assembly approved him as Hungary's next prime minister on 29 September. Many observers felt that the delegates' primary reason for choosing Gyurcsány was the belief that he is the only one in the party who can match rhetorically the charismatic right-wing leader, Viktor Orbán (once a near-anarchist anti-establishment rebel, now a conservative with links to the far right). Much of the theoretical basis for Gyurcsány's political vision is modelled on the UK's 'New Labour', trying to combine right-wing privatization with social justice. In contrast to his predecessor, Gyurcsány does not duck conflict and is a clever politician who is happy to use the media to his advantage.

ICELAND

Full name: The Republic of Iceland.

Leadership structure: The head of state is a president, directly elected by universal adult suffrage. The president's term of office is four years. The head of government is the prime minister, appointed by the president, who also appoints a cabinet.

President:	**ÓLAFUR RAGNAR GRÍMSSON**	Since 1 Aug. 1996
Prime Minister:	Davíd Oddsson	30 April 1991—15 Sept. 2004
	HALLDÓR ÁSGRÍMSSON	Since 15 Sept. 2004

Legislature: The legislature is unicameral. The sole chamber, the Parliament (Althing), has 63 members, directly elected for a four-year term.

Profile of the President:

ÓLAFUR RAGNAR GRÍMSSON

Ólafur Ragnar Grímsson originally made his name as a broadcaster and political scientist. He gave up the leadership of the left-wing People's Alliance (Althýdubandalagid—AB) in 1995, the year before he first stood for the state presidency—a post held in the past by nonparty figures, notably Ólafur Ragnar's immediate predecessor, four-term president Vigdís Finnbogadóttir. Ólafur Ragnar's re-election for a third term in 2004 was contested by two other candidates. Opposition is rare in Iceland when an incumbent president is standing for re-election; it followed his use of the first ever presidential veto a few weeks earlier over a media ownership law.

Born on 14 May 1943 in Ísafjördur in northwest Iceland, the son of a barber, Ólafur Ragnar Grímsson went to the capital, Reykjavík, to complete his secondary education and then to university in England. He graduated in economics and political science at Manchester University in 1965 and completed a doctorate there in political science, working on a research project on smaller European democracies, while becoming known at home through radio and television work. He then took up a lectureship at the University of Iceland, where he became professor of political science in 1973. The following year he married Gudrún Katrín Thorbergsdóttir, the executive director of the Icelandic Post Office Workers' Union, and their twin daughters were born in 1975. His wife died of leukaemia in 1998. In 2003, after a three-year engagement, he married Dorrit Moussaieff from Israel.

Initially a member of the Progressive Party, Ólafur Ragnar first stood for Parliament in 1974 for the Liberal and Left Alliance, whose executive board he chaired in 1974–75. Moving over to a prominent role in the left-wing AB, he was an AB member of Parliament from 1978, first for Reykjavík and then for Reykjanes. Between 1980 and 1983 he chaired the AB parliamentary party and in 1987 he was elected as AB leader, a post he held for eight years but relinquished at the 1995 national convention. In 1988–91 he was a member of the coalition government led by Steingrímur Hermannsson, and as minister of finance was credited with having brought the problem of rampant inflation under control.

A member of the parliamentary assembly of the Council of Europe in 1980–84, and again in 1995, Ólafur Ragnar was active particularly on north–south issues. Between 1984 and 1990 he was chairman and later international president of the association of Parliamentarians for Global Action (PGA). In this capacity he was actively involved with the 'six nations peace initiative', which included among others the late premiers Olav Palme of Sweden and Rajiv Gandhi of India. He accepted the Indira Gandhi Peace Prize on behalf of the PGA in 1987.

Ólafur Ragnar was elected on 29 June 1996 as the fifth president of Iceland, heading the nationwide poll with 40.9% of the vote against three other candidates, and taking office in August. He acceded to a second term without having to contest an election, as is the tradition in Iceland for incumbent presidents; it began on 1 August 2000.

In June 2004, just weeks before the end of his first term, Ólafur Ragnar used the presidential veto for the first time ever since Iceland's independence 60 years ago—against a law restricting ownership of media companies, thereby forcing a referendum on the subject. This provoked a bruising controversy over the role of the presidency in relation to the role of the legislature. (The government subsequently withdrew the act, removing the need for a referendum, and alternative legislation was proposed.)

Two candidates stood against Ólafur Ragnar in the subsequent presidential poll, breaking the tradition of unopposed re-elections for incumbent presidents. Nevertheless, he was returned to office on 26 June with 85% of the vote.

Profile of the Prime Minister:

HALLDÓR ÁSGRÍMSSON

Halldór Ásgrímsson has been leader of the Progressive Party (Framsóknarflokkurinn—FSF) since 1994 and took over as prime minister of Iceland on 15 September 2004 from Davíd Oddsson, leader of the centre-right Independence Party (Sjálfstædisflokkurinn—SSF), in a deal struck to maintain the two parties' coalition government. He has been a member of Parliament since 1974, and was previously a university lecturer.

Halldór Ásgrímsson was born on 8 September 1947. He graduated in 1965 from the Co-operative College of Iceland and in 1970 qualified to be a certified public accountant. He is married to Sigurjóna Sigurdardóttir and they have three daughters. Following graduate studies at the Bergen and Copenhagen Universities of Commerce, Halldór Ásgrímsson became a lecturer at the University of Iceland, in the faculty of economics and business administration.

During this period, Halldór Ásgrímsson entered politics for the first time, being elected in 1974 as a member of Parliament for the FSF in the East constituency. He became a member of the board of the Central Bank of Iceland in 1976, and was appointed chairman of the board in 1983. Meanwhile he had been re-elected to Parliament in 1979 as the member for Reykjavik North. In 1983 he became minister of fisheries, a post he retained until 1991, and in 1984 he was made vice chairman of the party. The following year he added the portfolio of Nordic co-operation, which he held until 1987; in 1988 he was made minister of justice and ecclesiastical affairs.

In 1994 Halldór Ásgrímsson became chair of the FSF, and the following year was appointed minister of foreign affairs and external trade, and minister for Nordic co-operation. He gave up the latter in 1999. In 2004, as part of a deal which prolonged the party's coalition with the SSF, Halldór Ásgrímsson became prime minister, and his predecessor, Davíd Oddsson, took over his responsibilities as foreign minister.

INDIA

Full name: The Republic of India.

Leadership structure: The head of state is a president, elected by an electoral college consisting of both Houses of Parliament for a five-year term. The president is head of the Union, and formally exercises all executive power on the advice of the government. In practice, the head of government is the prime minister, who chairs the Council of Ministers and is responsible to the Parliament.

President:	Kocheril Raman Narayanan	25 July 1997—25 July 2002
	A. P. J. Abdul **KALAM**	Since 25 July 2002
Prime Minister:	Atal Bihari Vajpayee (acting from 17 April 1999—13 Oct. 1999)	19 March 1998—22 May 2004
	Manmohan **SINGH**	Since 22 May 2004

Legislature: The legislature, the Houses of Parliament (Sansad), is bicameral. The lower chamber, the House of the People (Lok Sabha), has 545 members, 543 of them directly elected for a five-year term and two nominated by the president to represent the Anglo-Indian community. The upper chamber, the Council of States (Rajya Sabha), has up to 250 members, not more than 238 of them elected by the State Legislative Assemblies for six-year terms (elected as individual terms expire) and the remainder nominated by the president.

Profile of the President:

A. P. J. Abdul **KALAM**

A. P. J. Abdul Kalam, popularly known as the 'Missile Man', was closely associated with India's drive to produce indigenous missiles and other weaponry, both as engineer and as advocate. He is also the 'father' of India's nuclear weapons programme and masterminded the controversial underground tests in 1998. A practising Muslim from southern India, he was nominated as a presidential candidate in 2002 by the ruling Hindu nationalist Bharatiya Janata Party (BJP) in a successful move to win consensus support.

Avul Pakir Jainulabdeen Abdul Kalam was born on 15 October 1931 near the southern port of Rameswaram in what is now the state of Tamil Nadu. Coming from a lower middle-class background he took on part-time jobs to earn enough to pay for his education. He has never married.

He graduated from the Madras Institute of Technology in 1958 with a degree in aeronautical engineering and immediately applied to both the Indian air force (IAF) and the defence ministry's directorate of technical development and production. While the IAF rejected his application to be a pilot, he was successfully assigned to a hovercraft project in the directorate's Defence and Research Development Organization (DRDO). Five years later he moved to Bangalore, to the new Indian Space Research Organization (ISRO).

Throughout the 1960s Kalam was a powerful advocate of India's need to design and produce its own technology. Within the ISRO he was made director of the satellite launch vehicle (SLV) project. The SLV-III carried the first Indian Rohini satellite into near-earth orbit in 1975. He also worked on projects to create an indigenous battle tank (the Arjun) and the still-in-production Light Combat Aircraft. In 1982 he went to Hyderabad to become director of the DRDO itself, overseeing during the next ten years the implementation of his newly created Integrated Guided Missile Development Programme—producing the *Prithvi*, *Trishul*, *Akash* and *Nag* missiles and most notably the *Agni* long-range missile which is capable of delivering a nuclear warhead.

In July 1992 Kalam was appointed scientific adviser to the defence minister and secretary of the department of defence research and development, supervising the programme which led to India's Pokhran-II nuclear tests in May 1998. The controlled underground explosion of nuclear weapons confirmed India as one of the few nuclear-capable countries of the world and seriously threatened already tense relations with neighbouring Pakistan, which carried out its own tests later that year. From December 1999 until November 2001 Kalam served as chief scientific adviser to the Indian government.

Kalam's presidential candidacy in 2002, as the nominee of the ruling BJP, soon received the backing of most major parties. He faced only a single left-wing candidate, Lakshmi Sahgal, and received 90% of the vote in the election held by the Houses of Parliament on 18 July 2002. He took office on 25 July. He pledged to focus on transforming India into a developed nation by 2020. A devout Muslim, he was seen as a figurehead who could help heal some of the scars of the country's recent intercommunal violence, which had flared up in murderous conflict between Hindus and Muslims in Gujarat earlier in the year. His election was also welcomed by Pakistan, despite his intimate connection with the Indian nuclear weapons programme and the ensuing tension between the two countries.

Profile of the Prime Minister:

Manmohan **SINGH**

Manmohan Singh, India's first Sikh prime minister, was sworn in on 22 May 2004 at the head of a Congress (I) government. Singh, a noted economist, is known as the father of India's economic reforms for the five years he spent as finance minister between 1991 and 1996, during which time India's economy was liberalized and transformed, and with it the lives of thousands of middle-class Indians. While making his maiden speech as finance minister, Singh quoted Victor Hugo: "No power on earth can stop an idea whose time has come." Congress (I) won a surprise victory in elections in 2004 on the back of disillusionment on the part of the rural poor that the economic policies of the Bharatiya Janata Party (BJP) had passed them by, but Congress (I) leader Sonia Gandhi unexpectedly declined the post of prime minister. Singh is widely regarded as the cleanest politician in India, and many observers considered it a masterstroke on the part of Gandhi to nominate him to the top job in her stead, relieving fears on the part of investors that the left would have dominance over the new administration.

Manmohan Singh was born on 26 September 1932 in the village of Gah in the western Punjab province of unpartitioned India. He studied first at the Punjab University in Chandigarh and then at St John's College in the University of Cambridge, UK, where he earned a degree in economics in 1957. Singh followed this with a doctorate in economics from Nuffield College at Oxford University in 1962. He has been married to Gursharan Kaur since 1958, and has three daughters. Singh, a Sikh, is India's first non-Hindu prime minister since independence.

Singh returned to the Punjab University in 1957 to take up a post as senior lecturer in economics. He became reader in 1959, and professor in 1963. In 1964 he published *India's Export Trends and Prospects for Self-Sustained Growth*, an early critique of India's inward-oriented trade policy. In 1969 he took up the post of professor of international trade at the Delhi School of Economics.

Singh was appointed as economic adviser to the Indian ministry of foreign trade in 1971. He became chief economic adviser to the ministry of finance in 1972, and was awarded an honorary professorship at Jawaharlal Nehru University in New Delhi in 1976. The same year Singh became a director both of the Reserve Bank of India and of the Industrial Development Bank of India. The many governmental positions that Singh occupied in the following years included secretary in the ministry of finance, deputy chairman of the planning commission, governor of the Reserve Bank of India (RBI), adviser to the prime minister, and chairman of the university grants commission.

The most important period for Singh and for India was probably the five years between 1991 and 1996 that he spent as finance minister in the Congress (I) government of Narasimha Rao. He is credited with being the driving force behind the liberalization of India's economy. When Singh became finance minister, India's economy was in a shambles and the country was on the verge of bankruptcy. Singh slowly started the process of restructuring the economy, instituting deep changes in the institutions of the country. In 1994 the government of India entered into an understanding with the RBI to deny itself the right to 'draw' on the RBI to fund its deficit. This historic step put paid to the unlimited monetization of fiscal deficit. Many controls and regulations on industry were removed, ending the bureaucratic 'Permit Raj', and unleashing an unprecedented growth in productivity in Indian industry.

Although Singh's economic policies won plaudits from entrepreneurs, Congress (I) was voted out of power in 1999. Despite being appointed leader of the opposition in the Council of States (the upper house of Parliament), he kept a determinedly low profile. BJP reforms aimed at India's urban middle classes eventually triggered something of a rural backlash, and a revived Congress (I) party under Sonia Gandhi stormed to a shock election victory in 2004. The stock market went into a tailspin as investors feared that the return of Congress (I) and its left-wing allies would derail economic reforms. Gandhi surprised her supporters by declining the top post, apparently to protect the party from damaging attacks over her Italian birth; the appointment of Singh, father of Indian economic reform, did much to reassure the markets. Since assuming the premiership he has led moves towards redirecting funds to reduce poverty, especially the plight of the rural poor.

INDONESIA

Full name: The Republic of Indonesia.

Leadership structure: The head of state is a president, directly elected for the first time in 2004. The president's term of office is five years. The head of government is the president, who appoints a cabinet.

President:		
	Abdurrahman Wahid	20 Oct. 1999—23 July 2001
	Megawati Sukarnoputri	23 July 2001—20 Oct. 2004
	Susilo Bambang **YUDHOYONO**	Since 20 Oct. 2004

Legislature: The legislature is bicameral. The lower house, the House of Representatives (Dewan Perwakilan Rakyat), has 550 directly elected members. The upper house, the House of Representatives of the Regions (Dewan Perwakilan Daerah), created under constitutional amendments passed in 2001 to deal with regional matters, has 128 members, four representing each province; they were directly elected on a nonpartisan basis for the first time in April 2004. The People's Consultative Assembly (Majlis Permusyawaratan Rakyat—MPR), which comprises all the members of both Houses, is the highest authority of the state, and makes decisions on the constitution. All three bodies have five-year terms of office.

Profile of the President:

Susilo Bambang **YUDHOYONO**

Susilo Bambang Yudhoyono became the first directly elected president of the post-Suharto period in Indonesia on 20 October 2004, having beaten his former boss, Megawati Sukarnoputri, in the second round of elections. A career army officer, Yudhoyono entered politics on his retirement from active service in 2000, winning a reputation for integrity by resigning from the cabinets of two successive presidents within three years. Yudhoyono has pledged to crack down on corruption and to build a culture of religious moderation and tolerance.

Susilo Bambang Yudhoyono was born on 9 September 1949 in Pacitan, east Java, the son of a retired lieutenant. He followed his father's career, graduating from the Indonesian Military Academy in 1973. He is married to the daughter of another Indonesian army officer, Col. Sarwo Edhie. In 1975 he took part in the Indonesian invasion of East Timor, and served several tours of duty there including the command of the Dili-based battalion. This service has led to accusations of war crimes, though no charges have ever been brought against him.

In the 1980s, Yudhoyono studied in the USA, gaining a master's degree in business management from Webster University as well as studying several military courses. During this period he also lectured at the Army Staff Command College. During the following years Yudhoyono travelled widely, including a stint serving as Indonesia's chief military observer in Bosnia from 1995 to 1996. In the mid-1990s he also worked in territorial commands in Jakarta and southern Sumatra. He was appointed chief of the armed forces social and political affairs staff in 1997 and gained a reputation in the Indonesian media as the 'thinking general'. Yudhoyono retired from active service on 1 April 2000, and in 2004 received a doctorate from the Bogor Institute of Agriculture in agricultural economics.

Meanwhile he entered the political stage, being appointed mines minister under President Abdurrahman Wahid in 1999 and co-ordinating minister for politics and security in the reshuffle of August 2000. This role saw him attempt to withdraw the army from day-to-day involvement in the politics of the country, and, under intense international pressure, to eventually try to rein in the East Timor militias operating in West Timor after several Western aid workers were killed. In 2001 Wahid was facing impeachment and asked Yudhoyono to declare a state of emergency; Yudhoyono refused and was promptly sacked. The incident gave him a new reputation as a liberal, and shortly afterwards new president Megawati Sukarnoputri reinstated him.

Following the 2002 Bali bombing, Yudhoyono was in charge of the search for and arrest of those responsible, and gained plaudits both domestically and internationally for the seriousness with which he undertook this task. In March 2004 he fell out with Megawati in a highly public manner and resigned, the timing of his departure rewarding him handsomely as he was perceived by much of the public as a victim of an unpopular government rather than as a member of it. The incident only served to enhance his reputation as a man of integrity, and positioned him well for the July presidential election. Like all the candidates, Yudhoyono offered no real policy details. He won by 61% of the vote in the second round of the election in September and was sworn in on 20 October.

Yudhoyono pledged to crack down on corruption and on terrorism, promising to create a more moderate Indonesian society, but has been studiously vague on detail. He appointed four former generals to his cabinet, but gave the post of defence minister to a civilian, and allocated cabinet seats to nearly all the major opposition parties bar Megawati's Indonesian Democratic Party of Struggle, though he left five of her ministers in place. Some observers have found Yudhoyono's decisions frustratingly ambiguous; others consider them sensibly pragmatic, given that his own Democratic Party holds just 10% of the seats in the House of Representatives and he needs the support of many others if he is to have any chance of enacting his admittedly vague agenda.

IRAN

Full name: The Islamic Republic of Iran.

Leadership structure: The head of state is a president, who is directly elected by universal adult suffrage. The president's term of office is four years, renewable once only. Overall authority is exercised by the country's spiritual leader, the *wali-e faqih*. The president is head of government and appoints the Council of Ministers, subject to approval by the Consultative Council.

Spiritual Leader (Wali-e Faqih):

Ayatollah Ali **KHAMENEI**	Since 4 June 1989

President:

Mohammad Khatami	3 Aug. 1997—3 Aug. 2005
Mahmoud **AHMADINEJAD**	Since 3 August 2005

Legislature: The legislature is a unicameral Consultative Council (Majlis al-Shoura) with 290 members, directly elected for a four-year term, on a nonparty basis. An 83-member Assembly of Experts (Majlis-e Khobregan), also elected by universal suffrage but consisting entirely of clerics, decides on religious and spiritual matters, notably including the election of the *wali-e faqih*. The Council of Guardians of the Constitution (Shura-ye Negahban-e Qanun-e Assassi) is a 12-member judicial body, elected by the Consultative Council, which is empowered among other things to exercise a supervisory role for elections.

Profile of the Spiritual Leader (*Wali-e Faqih*):

Ayatollah Ali **KHAMENEI**

Ali Khamenei, a follower of the Ayatollah Khomeini since the 1960s, became Iranian president in 1981 effectively by default, there being a dearth of potential candidates for a post which combined lack of powers with risk of assassination. He moved up in 1989 to succeed as the country's 'spiritual leader' following Khomeini's death. Khamenei was generally regarded at the time as a comparatively nonpartisan figure. He relinquished the presidency just as that office took on real powers as head of state and government, but he has latterly proven to be a conservative influence, restraining the introduction of a more liberal stance by the 1997–2005 government of President Mohammad Khatami.

Ali Hoseini Khamenei was born on 17 July 1939 in Mashhad, in the northeastern province of Khorasan. He entered a theological school in Mashhad at the age of ten, graduating in 1957 and continuing his studies at Najaf (in Iraq) and in the Iranian holy city of Qom. At the theological school there he studied religious science and came under the influence of Ayatollah Khomeini, who later led the Islamic Revolution of 1979. Becoming an outspoken opponent of the regime of the shah, Khamenei was active in the anti-shah campaigns led by Khomeini in 1962 and 1963, and was first arrested and briefly detained at this time. Involved thereafter in a combination of religious teaching, pro-Islamic agitation and clandestine militant organization, he was arrested several more times in the next 15 years, spending a total of three years in prison, and in 1977–78 he was exiled to the town of Iranshahr in the far southwest. As a religious authority Khamenei had attained the second-rank religious title of *hojatolislam* by the time of the 1979 revolution. He has written several books on Islam and history, such as *The Role of Muslims in the Independence Struggle of India*. He speaks Farsi, Arabic and Azeri, and is married with four sons and two daughters.

From 1978 Khamenei led the anti-government movement in Mashhad. Moving to Tehran early the following year, he was a founder member of the Foundation of the Oppressed, and joined the central council of the Tehran Militant Clergy Association.

After the 1979 revolution Khamenei was appointed Revolutionary Council representative for the army. He was deputy for, and then head of, revolutionary affairs at the national ministry of defence, becoming commander of the Islamic Revolutionary Guard for a relatively brief period (until February 1980). Elected in 1980 to the Consultative Council, he was secretary-general of the government-sponsored, but now defunct, Islamic Republican Party, of which he had been a cofounder, and was increasingly seen as one of Ayatollah Khomeini's closest associates. He also held, from January 1980, the influential position of leader of the Friday prayers in Tehran.

Khamenei was wounded in the right hand in an assassination attempt in June 1981, part of a spate of terrorist violence affecting the Islamic regime. In October of that year, following the ousting of President Abolhassan Bani-Sadr and the assassination of his successor Mohammad Ali Radjai, Khamenei was picked as the regime's candidate to fill the vacant presidency, winning the predictable overwhelming majority against four other candidates in the nationwide poll. He was re-elected, against two opponents, in August 1985.

Generally seen as a conservative rather than a hard-line radical in the context of postrevolutionary Iranian politics, Khamenei on occasion came under strong criticism from radical rivals, but as president he avoided identifying himself with any particular faction. He also managed to distance himself from the 1983 defection of his sister to Iraq, where she joined his estranged brother-in-law Sheikh Ali Tehrani, who had fled to Baghdad in 1981 where he had begun making broadcasts hostile to the Khomeini regime.

In May 1989 Khamenei was made chairman of the secretariat of the *imam* (Khomeini), and on 4 June, the day after Khomeini's death, was elected by the Assembly of Experts to succeed him as Iran's new 'spiritual leader' (*wali-e faqih*). He was also given the religious title of ayatollah, as being more compatible with his status than the less elevated title *hojatolislam*. Constitutional amendments approved the following month removed the requirement that the 'spiritual leader' should hold the religious status of a grand ayatollah or *marja* (source of emulation), Khamenei himself being only a jurist or *motjahed*.

The 'spiritual leader' combines supreme religious power with overall political authority, although since the death of Khomeini it is not the 'spiritual leader' but the president (previously a mainly ceremonial post) who heads the executive and combines the functions of head of state and head of government. Khamenei's elevation to the post of 'spiritual leader' opened the way for the election as president of Ali Akbar Rafsanjani, seen as a relative moderate. Rafsanjani and to a greater extent his successor in 1997, Mohammad Khatami, steered Iran towards a policy of greater liberalization and openness to the West.

Khamenei, for his part, while presenting himself as generally nonpartisan, has on key occasions been identified as more pro-conservative (such as taking a firm stand against the reformist-dominated press in 2000–01). It was Khamenei who reaffirmed and maintained Khomeini's notorious February 1989 *fatwa* or death sentence against the British writer Salman Rushdie over the publication of a novel held to be blasphemous against Islam, in a confrontation with Western liberal values which cast a long shadow until the eventual lifting of the *fatwa* in 1998.

Beneath him the reformists gained strength in the Consultative Council—with significant victories in the February 2000 legislative elections and with Khatami's re-election in June 2001. In October 2002 Khamenei, amid continuing power struggles between the reformist government and the conservative judiciary, grandly announced that Iran would never accept "so-called democracy".

The reformists called a boycott of the 2004 election after the clergy had banned thousands of their candidates from the poll, an issue that recurred in the run-up to the June 2005 presidential election. Khamenei made a dramatic intervention, ordering the Council of Guardians to reassess its disqualification of all but six of the 1,014 candidates. This concession came at a time of intense international pressure over Iran's nuclear ambitions. Two more reformists were allowed to stand in the poll, which was won by hard-liner Mahmoud Ahmadinejad.

Profile of the President:

Mahmoud **AHMADINEJAD**

Mahmoud Ahmadinejad was elected president of Iran in June 2005 and sworn in on 3 August. Previously the hard-line mayor of Tehran, Ahmadinejad served in the Iran–Iraq war and was senior in the Revolutionary Guard Corps. There are persistent rumours of his involvement in the 1979 siege of the US embassy. Ahmadinejad has pledged to distribute Iran's oil wealth to the people, and to defend the values of the Islamic revolution.

Mahmoud Ahmadinejad was born Mahmoud Saborjhian on 28 October 1956, the fourth of seven children, in the farming village of Aradan near Garmsar, southeast of the capital Tehran. The son of a blacksmith, he moved with his family to the capital when he was just a year old, a move that coincided with the changing of the family name—Ahmadinejad means Muhammad's race or virtuous race. He entered the Iran University of Science and Technology (IUST) in 1976 to study civil engineering. In 1979 Ahmadinejad represented IUST in meetings with Ayatollah Khomeini and became a member of the Office of Strengthening Unity (OSU), the student organization involved in the capture of the US embassy in 1979, although he denies any involvement in that incident. During the crackdown on universities in 1980, the OSU played a key role in purging dissidents. Universities remained closed for three years, but he later returned to IUST to undertake his master's degree and ultimately graduated with a doctorate in traffic and transportation engineering and planning.

Ahmadinejad joined the army at the beginning of the Iran–Iraq war and in 1986 joined the special forces of the Revolutionary Guards. He was stationed in Ramazan Garrison near Kermanshah in western Iran, the headquarters of the 'extraterritorial' brigades that operated beyond the Iranian border. Some analysts have linked Ahmadinejad to a series of international political assassinations, in particular that of Iranian Kurdish leader Abdorrahman Qassemlou, who was shot dead by officers of the Revolutionary Guards in a flat in Vienna, Austria, in July 1989. Again, the allegations are denied by Ahmadinejad's supporters, who say he spent this period involved in civil construction work near Maku in northwest Iran.

Ahmadinejad served for four years as the governor of the towns of Maku and Khoy. In 1993 he was appointed as cultural adviser to the minister of Islamic culture and guidance, Ali Larijani, also an officer in the Revolutionary Guards. A few months later, Ahmadinejad was appointed as the governor of the newly created Ardabil province. President Khatami's administration, which came to power in 1997, replaced Ahmadinejad, who returned to teach at IUST.

In 2003 a majority of the newly elected city council of Tehran were members of the Alliance of Builders of Islamic Iran (Abadgaran), within which Ahmadinejad had a powerful political base. He was appointed mayor and immediately began to reverse many of the changes made by previous reformist mayors, banning fast food restaurants and requiring male city employees to grow beards and wear long-sleeved shirts. His disagreements with Khatami led the latter to exclude him from meetings of the Board of Ministers, a privilege usually accorded to Tehran mayors.

Ahmadinejad was elected to the presidency on 24 June 2005 in the second round of voting, beating reformist ex-president Ali Akbar Rafsanjani with 61.69% of the vote; he was sworn in on 3 August. Analysts ascribe Ahmadinejad's success to his image as a man of the people who maintains a simple lifestyle; his victory may also be linked to his willingness to stand up to the West and in particular to the USA. He ran a campaign that stressed the values of the 1979 revolution and has said, "We did not have a revolution in order to have democracy." He has vehemently defended Iran's right to develop its own nuclear programme, calling it an "inalienable right", and has pledged to rid the oil industry of its 'mafias' and to end all favouritism towards foreign investors. However, some observers have pointed out that Ahmadinejad was a pragmatist as mayor, and that social forces and economic prerogatives may temper some of his more revolutionary zeal.

IRAQ

Full name: The Republic of Iraq.

Leadership structure: The head of state for the transitional period is a president, elected by the Transitional National Assembly, together with two vice presidents. The three posts are divided between the three ethno-religious groups: Sunni, Shi'a and Kurd. Presidential elections under a new constitution are expected in 2006. The head of government for the transitional period is the prime minister, nominated by the president and the two vice presidents and approved by parliament.

President:		
	Saddam Hussein	16 July 1979—9 April 2003
	vacant	9 April 2003—28 June 2004
	Ghazi Mashal Ajil al-Yawer (interim)	28 June 2004—7 April 2005
	Jalal **TALABANI** (transitional)	Since 7 April 2005

Prime Minister:

	Saddam Hussein	29 May 1994—9 April 2003
	vacant	9 April 2003—13 July 2003

President of the Governing Council:

	Muhammad Bahr al-Uloom (acting)	13 July 2003—31 July 2003
	Ibrahim al-Jaafari	1 Aug. 2003—31 Aug. 2003
	Ahmed Chalabi	1 Sept. 2003—30 Sept. 2003
	Iyad Allawi	1 Oct. 2003—31 Oct. 2003
	Jalal Talabani	1 Nov. 2003—30 Nov. 2003
	Abd al-Aziz al-Hakim	1 Dec. 2003—31 Dec. 2003
	Adnan Pachachi	1 Jan. 2004—31 Jan. 2004
	Mohsen Abd al-Hamid	1 Feb. 2004—29 Feb. 2004
	Muhammad Bahr al-Uloom	1 March 2004—31 March 2004
	Massoud Barzani	1 April 2004—30 April 2004
	Izzadine Saleem	1 May 2004—17 May 2004
	Ghazi Mashal Ajil al-Yawer	17 May 2004—1 June 2004

Prime Minister: Iyad Allawi (interim)   1 June 2004—3 May 2005

Ibrahim al-**JAAFARI** (transitional)   Since 3 May 2005

Legislature: A 275-member Transitional National Assembly, elected in January 2005, held its first session on 16 March. In April it elected the presidency and approved the new transitional government, which appointed a panel of negotiators from all political and religious groupings to draft a constitution. The Assembly voted to accept the draft of the constitution on 29 August after several delays caused by disagreement over the federal structure proposed, and over ownership of oil resources. The constitution was scheduled to be put to referendum in October.

Profile of the Transitional President:

Jalal **TALABANI**

Jalal Talabani was named president of Iraq by the Transitional National Assembly in April 2005, two years after the US-led invasion. Formerly a lawyer, political activist, journalist and tank commander, Talabani became leader of the Patriotic Union of Kurdistan (PUK) in the late 1970s and helped lead resistance against Iraqi oppression. The establishment of a no-fly zone in the early 1990s following the first Gulf War gave a modicum of autonomy to Iraqi Kurdistan, but internecine conflict prevented any co-ordinated political activity until after a peace accord was signed in 1998. Kurdish assistance to the USA in the invasion of Iraq boosted Talabani's profile further, and he was appointed to the interim Governing Council before his elevation to the presidency.

Jalal Talabani was born in 1933 in the village of Kelkan near Lake Dokan in the Kurdish region of northern Iraq. His early schooling took place in Koya, while his secondary education was received in the cities of Erbil and Kirkuk. In 1946, at the age of 13, he formed a Kurdish student association, and the following year joined the Kurdish Democratic Party (KDP); by the age of 18 he had been elected to the party's central committee. Talabani wanted to study medicine, but was refused entry to medical school by the ruling Hashemite monarchy because of his political activities. Instead he entered law school in 1953. Forced into hiding in 1956 to escape arrest, Talabani did not return to law school until after the overthrow of the Hashemite monarchy in 1958 by Gen. Abdul Karim Kassem. Talabani finally graduated as a barrister the following year, having also worked as a journalist and the editor of two publications, *Khabat* and *Kurdistan*. He was immediately conscripted into the Iraqi army where he served as commander of a tank unit.

In the Kurdish uprising of 1961, Talabani immediately took command of a number of districts, organizing resistance to the Iraqi military. He led diplomatic missions to Europe and across the Middle East representing the Kurdish leadership. In 1964 Talabani was part of the 'political bureau' group that separated from the leadership of Gen. Mustafa Barzani after the latter signed a peace agreement with the Iraqi government; the stated aim of the split was to create what Talabani described as a more educated, democratic and less tribal political faction, which ultimately evolved into the PUK 11 years later. The schism that this move created remains in Iraqi Kurdish politics to this day.

From 1964 until 1975 Barzani was strong enough to maintain a state of sporadic war and peace negotiations. In 1974 the governing Ba'ath party offered the Kurds autonomy, but the Kurds believed that the offer lacked substance and they decided to fight instead, strongly supported and encouraged by Iran. However, in 1975 the shah of Iran, who had supported Barzani, signed the Algiers Accord with the Iraqi government and abandoned the Iraqi Kurds to their fate; as a result the Kurdish resistance virtually collapsed. Jalal Talabani emerged as leader of the newly formed PUK, which continued to engage in low-level guerrilla activity against the central government, intensifying in the 1980s.

Differences between Talabani and the KDP leadership (now headed by Barzani's son, Massoud, following his father's death) benefited the central government, which could manipulate the opposing factions. What it could not afford was to risk the opening of a second hostile front in Kurdistan as long as it was at war with Iran; thus, throughout the 1980s, Baghdad tolerated the growing strength of the Kurdish resistance. In 1988, during the final six months of the eight-year long war with Iran, however, the government unleashed a wave of violence in Iraqi Kurdistan. Villages were levelled and chemical weapons used against the civilian population, and 80,000 Iraqi Kurds fled into the Turkish borderlands. Talabani went into exile until after the 1991 Gulf War when US planes enforced a no-fly zone over the Kurdish north of Iraq.

In 1992 elections were held in Iraqi Kurdistan and a PUK–KDP joint administration was formed, but tensions between the two groups led to armed confrontations in 1994, known as the 'fratricide war'. After concerted efforts by the US and UK administrations, Talabani and Barzani were persuaded to sign a peace accord in Washington D.C. in 1998. The accord was cemented in 2002 with the reconvening of the regional parliament in a session attended by both parties' MPs, Talabani proposing a law banning and criminalizing inter-Kurdish fighting.

In March 2003, ahead of the US-led invasion of Iraq, the KDP and and the PUK created a 'joint higher leadership' in Iraqi Kurdistan under the chairmanship of Barzani and Talabani. Both were later appointed to the Iraqi Governing Council, together with three other Kurds. Talabani distanced himself from independence calls, limiting his demands to that of autonomy with an eye to pragmatism given the international hostility towards Kurdish independence. Following the Iraqi elections on 30 January 2005, Talabani was named president of Iraq by the transitional National Assembly on 6 April and sworn in the following day, while Barzani headed up the Autonomous Kurdish Government in Iraq. Talabani has pledged to work with all ethnic and religious factions and promised that Iraq would never become an Islamic state, but would enshrine federalism, democracy and pluralism.

Profile of the Transitional Prime Minister:

Ibrahim al-**JAAFARI**

Ibrahim al-Jaafari was approved as prime minister by the Transitional National Assembly on 28 April 2005 and sworn in on 3 May. He is a qualified doctor who spent 23 years in exile when members of his Islamic Call (Dawa Islamiya) party were targeted by Saddam Hussein's regime. On his return to Iraq in 2003, he was appointed to the interim Governing Council. He has been consistently rated as one of the most popular politicians in Iraq.

Ibrahim al-Ashaiqir al-Jaafari was born in 1947 in the Shi'a shrine city of Karbala in central Iraq. He studied medicine at Mosul University in the north of the country, and in 1966 joined the Dawa Islamiya party, a Shi'a Islamist political movement. He qualified as a doctor in 1974 but in 1980 was forced to flee the country after Saddam Hussein's Ba'ath party launched a brutal crackdown on Dawa. It is thought that he spent much of this decade in Iran, though Dawa's exact activities during this period are the subject of some controversy. It is known that in 1983 Dawa staged a suicide bomb attack on the US and French embassies in Kuwait. In 1989 Jaafari moved to London, where he became one of the leaders of the Dawa movement. He remained in exile until after the US-led invasion of Iraq in 2003.

On his return to Iraq, Jaafari was appointed to the interim Governing Council, and in 2004 became one of two vice presidents of the interim government. An opinion poll carried out that year indicated that Jaafari was the most popular politician in the country, trailing only Grand Ayatollah Ali al-Sistani, the leading Shi'a cleric, and Muqtada al-Sadr, also a cleric, in the public's esteem. This is partly ascribed to the popularity of the Dawa movement, which earned immense public respect for its campaign of resistance to Saddam Hussein's regime, but also to the consistency of Jaafari's allegiance to the movement and his own suffering and exile for the cause.

Jaafari brought the Dawa movement into the United Iraqi Alliance (UIA) which won 140 seats in parliamentary elections in January 2005. He was designated prime minister on 7 April 2005 and was approved by the Transitional National Assembly on 28 April, taking office on 3 May.

IRELAND

Full name: Ireland.

Leadership structure: The head of state is a president (*uachtarán na hÉireann*), directly elected by universal adult suffrage. The president's term of office is seven years. The head of government is the prime minister (*taoiseach*), who is elected by the House of Representatives and appoints the cabinet. The prime minister and the cabinet are both responsible to the House of Representatives.

President (Uachtarán na hÉireann):   Mary **McALEESE**   Since 11 Nov. 1997

Prime Minister (Taoiseach):   Bertie **AHERN**   Since 26 June 1997

Legislature: The legislature, the National Parliament (Oireachtas), is bicameral. The lower chamber, the House of Representatives (Dáil Éireann), has 166 deputies (Teachtaí Dála or TDs), directly elected for a five-year term. The upper chamber, the Senate (Seanad Éireann), has 60 members with a five-year term. Eleven members are nominated by the prime minister, six elected by the universities and 43 elected from five panels of candidates representing various sectoral interests.

Profile of the President (*Uachtarán na hÉireann*):

Mary **McALEESE**

Mary McAleese became the eighth president of Ireland on 11 November 1997, succeeding Mary Robinson who had held the post since 1990. McAleese, a Belfast-born barrister, broadcaster and academic, was previously pro-vice chancellor at Queen's University, Belfast, and is the first person from Northern Ireland to be elected as Irish head of state. She was nominated by the conservative nationalist Fianna Fáil (FF) party and by the Progressive Democrats (PD) as a candidate for the presidency, which is a largely ceremonial role. She was returned unopposed in 2004 for a second term.

Born on 27 June 1951 in Belfast, Mary Lenaghan (as she was until her marriage to Martin McAleese) was the eldest of nine children in a Roman Catholic family. She and her dentist husband now have one son and two daughters.

She went to secondary school on the Falls Road in Belfast and then read law at Queen's University, Belfast, graduating in 1973. She studied to be a barrister and was called to the Bar in 1974 where she practised mainly in criminal and family law. In 1975 she was appointed Reid professor of criminal law, criminology and penology at Trinity College, Dublin. She held this position until 1979 when she joined the Irish national broadcasting corporation RTE as a journalist and presenter.

In 1981 she returned to the Reid professorship at Trinity, continuing part-time with RTE. In 1987 she was appointed director of the Institute of Professional Legal Studies, which trains barristers and solicitors for the legal profession in Northern Ireland and is regarded as one of the most pioneering departments in Queen's University. In 1994 she was appointed as a pro-vice chancellor of Queen's, the first woman in history to hold such a position at the university.

In 1995 she was a delegate to the conference on trade and investment in Ireland held at the White House, Washington D.C., and then to the Pittsburg conference in 1996. She was also a member of the Roman Catholic Church delegation in 1996 to the North Commission on Contentious Parades, and is a founder member of the Irish Commission for Prisoners Overseas. Before becoming president in 1997 she also held the positions of director of Channel 4 Television, director of Northern Ireland Electricity and director of the Royal Group of Hospitals Trust.

Her election as president of Ireland in October 1997 broke the record for the greatest margin of victory when she took 42.2% of votes in the first round and 58.7% in the second round. She was inaugurated on 11 November. A second term was endorsed in 2004 when no candidates stood against her for election.

Profile of the Prime Minister (*Taoiseach*):

Bertie **AHERN**

Bertie Ahern became Ireland's youngest ever prime minister in June 1997, at the age of 45. A member of parliament since the age of 25 and a prominent figure in Dublin city politics, the man once seen as heir apparent to Charles Haughey as head of the conservative, nationalist Fianna Fáil (FF) party has proven that his elevation to the leadership marked a decisive change of the generations in Irish politics. Having signed the Good Friday agreement on Northern Ireland in April 1998, he has shown both patience and determination through the subsequent difficulties in implementing that historic accord.

Bartholomew 'Bertie' Patrick Ahern was born on 12 September 1951, in a working-class Dublin family. Educated at the local state school and by the Christian Brothers, he became an accountant after graduating from Rathmines College of Commerce and University College, Dublin. Bertie Ahern married Miriam Kelly in 1975 and they have two daughters. Ahern officially separated from his wife in 1992 and lived until 2003 with Celia Larkin, a Fianna Fáil party worker. He refused to divorce his wife, but the situation was highly controversial among Irish Catholics.

He was first elected to the House of Representatives as a FF deputy at the age of only 25, in 1977. From 1979 he combined his career in parliament, where he represents Dublin Central, with membership of Dublin city council. He was lord mayor of Dublin from 1986 to 1987.

Ahern first held government office as an assistant whip from 1980 to 1981. He was then appointed party spokesperson on youth, and in 1982 became minister of state in the office of the prime minister and the department of defence, and government chief whip. After the defeat of FF in the November 1982 general election he became opposition chief whip and FF's leader of the house. Party vice president from 1983 to 1994, Ahern was also director of by-elections for FF in the 1980s and chaired the party's constituency and organization committee from 1987 to 1992.

With FF back in government after the 1987 general election, Ahern began a seven-year spell as a cabinet minister. His first portfolio was as minister of labour, making his name as architect of a social consensus, which was embodied in a programme for national recovery and a programme for economic and social progress. At the European level, Ireland's turn in the rotating presidency of the European Union (EU) Council of Ministers meant that in the first half of 1990 he was president of the EU Council of social affairs ministers.

In November 1991 Ahern moved to the finance ministry, filling a gap caused by the departure of Albert Reynolds, who left the government after challenging the leadership of the then prime minister, Charles Haughey. The resignation the following February of the discredited Haughey gave rise to a leadership contest from which Ahern, hitherto seen as Haughey's heir apparent, withdrew his own candidacy so that the party could unite behind Reynolds. Ahern retained the post of finance minister in the Reynolds government. He was also a member of the board of governors at the European Investment Bank (which he chaired in 1991/92), the International Monetary Fund (IMF), the World Bank and the European Bank for Reconstruction and Development (EBRD).

In the November 1992 general election a poor result made FF's coalition with the Progressive Democrats (PD) unviable. Ahern, adept at bridge building, eventually succeeded in negotiating a new coalition agreement with the greatly strengthened Labour Party. In the resulting government, which took office in January 1993, he once again took up the finance portfolio under Reynolds.

This coalition collapsed in November 1994 when Reynolds ignored Labour objections and pushed through his favoured appointee for the post of president of the High Court (the country's second-highest judicial post). Reynolds was forced to resign in the uproar which followed. Ahern, now free to seek what was widely regarded as his rightful place as party leader, was elected to that post by FF on 19 November, but found himself on the opposition benches rather than in power, because FF was excluded from a new three-party coalition government headed by John Bruton of Fine Gael.

During the ensuing period the Northern Ireland question loomed large in Irish politics. Bruton, as prime minister, was noted for his conciliatory approach. He pursued a joint initiative with the UK government which was intended to bring the representatives of the province's rival political traditions into an inclusive peace process. FF was traditionally more nationalist. Under Haughey in the mid-1980s, its pro-republican stance on Northern Ireland had been a major factor in driving out a group of party dissidents, who had split away to form the PD. Ten years on, Ahern was aware that maintaining such a stance could mean missing an opportunity for a lasting settlement. Thus, although he was frequently critical of Bruton for bending too far towards the British line, he nevertheless led his party into the June 1997 general election declaring that he would seek to form a coalition with the PD.

Ahern's high personal popularity rating helped boost the otherwise lacklustre performance of FF, which emerged from the election with 77 seats in the 166-seat House of Representatives. This was eight more seats than in 1994, although the party won only a fractionally increased share (39.3%) of the vote. After two weeks of negotiations on the formation of a government, Ahern was sworn in on 26 June at the head of an FF–PD coalition, which nevertheless lacked a parliamentary majority.

Declaring it to be his primary objective to work to achieve a settlement in the talks on Northern Ireland, Ahern formed an effective working relationship with the new UK prime minister Tony Blair, both of them being representatives of a younger generation of political leaders. The momentum which they sustained in driving the Northern Ireland peace process forward had its moment of apparent triumph with the Good Friday agreement concluded in April 1998, but became mired in protracted disputes between signature and implementation.

Domestically, Ahern survived a vote of no confidence in June 2000 and weathered the embarrassment of a 'no' vote in a referendum on the EU's crucial Nice Treaty on enlargement in June 2001—Ireland had been the only country to hold a referendum, a vote being necessary under the Irish constitution. Ahern's minority government struggled through to the end of its term, overseeing the introduction of euro notes and coins in January 2002. In the May 2002 general elections FF increased its share of the vote to 41.5% and gained 81 seats. Although it still lacked its long-hoped-for simple majority, it at least gained parliamentary dominance in a renewed coalition with the PD. In October 2002 the Nice Treaty was finally endorsed and Ahern quickly assured the EU that in future only far-reaching treaties would require a referendum to receive Ireland's consent. The draft EU constitution was the next major hurdle, but the planned referendum was shelved in June 2005 after the French and Dutch 'no' votes.

ISRAEL

Full name: The State of Israel.

Leadership structure: The head of state is a president, elected by Parliament. Under an act approved by Parliament on 21 December 1998, the president's term of office, hitherto five years, was extended to a seven-year nonrenewable term. The head of government is the prime minister, who is appointed nominally by the president, but is in practice responsible to Parliament. The prime minister appoints the cabinet. (The present prime minister was first elected directly, in a nationwide ballot separate from the parliamentary elections, but this short-lived innovation was discontinued under an amendment to the Basic Law on Government passed by Parliament in March 2001.)

President:	Ezer Weizman	13 May 1993—10 July 2000
	Avraham Burg (interim)	10 July 2000—1 Aug. 2000
	Moshe **KATSAV**	Since 1 Aug. 2000
Prime Minister:	Ehud Barak (acting from 17 May 1999 until inauguration, and from 9 Dec. 2000)	6 July 1999—6 Feb. 2001
	Ariel **SHARON**	Since 6 Feb. 2001

Legislature: The legislature is unicameral. The sole chamber, the Parliament (Knesset), has 120 members, directly elected for a maximum four-year term.

Profile of the President:

Moshe **KATSAV**

Moshe Katsav surprised even himself when he defeated former prime minister Shimon Peres in the ballot for a successor to President Ezer Weizman in 2000. The presidency had never previously gone to a Sephardic Jew or to a political right-winger. Katsav first joined Likud (Unity) in the 1970s, held cabinet office in Likud-led coalitions of the 1980s and early 1990s, and several times stood unsuccessfully for the party leadership. As president, however, he promised to stay out of contentious politics.

Moshe Katsav was born in Iran as the eldest of eight children on 5 December 1945 and moved to Israel with his parents six years later. His family lived in an immigrant tent camp named Kiryat Malachi, just south of Tel Aviv. Many such communities sprang up amid the large influx of Jews in the first years of the new state. Katsav wrote as a reporter for the locally based *Yediot Aharonot* daily paper from 1966 and was president of the nationalist B'nai B'rith Youth group in 1968 in the camp, which soon grew to become a town. After serving out his national service as a corporal in the Israeli Defence Force he attended the Hebrew University of Jerusalem to study economics and history.

While still a student, Katsav, who was already chairman of the student council of Gahal (forerunner of Likud), won election in 1969 in Kiryat Malachi as Israel's youngest ever mayor. After completing his studies he returned to the mayor's office in 1974 and held the position for another six years. During this time he joined the newly formed Likud and it was under their banner that he turned his attention to the legislative elections in 1977. Likud swept to power under the leadership of Menachem Begin and Katsav sat in Parliament for the first time.

From 1977 to 1984 Likud dominated the Israeli government and Katsav worked on various parliamentary committees before being appointed as deputy minister of housing and construction in 1981. He joined the coalition cabinet as a full minister in 1984 with the labour and social affairs portfolio. Likud's electoral dominance faded throughout the 1980s. Following the 1988 elections the cabinet was reshuffled once more and Katsav was handed the transportation ministry as well as membership of the ministerial committee on defence. In the course of the government's fourth term it became chronically dependent on smaller right-wing groupings and eventually in 1992 it was voted out of office.

In opposition from 1992 to 1996 Katsav served as Likud's parliamentary leader and also chaired the parliamentary friendship league established with China. He was one of the first right-wing politicians to lend his support to the Oslo Peace Accords signed with the Palestine Liberation Organization (PLO) in 1993 by the Labour prime minister Yitzhak Rabin. Direct prime ministerial elections were held for the first time in 1996 and Likud party leader Binyamin Netanyahu was elected on the back of widespread anger at a spate of Palestinian attacks in Israel. Netanyahu appointed Katsav as his deputy and together they headed a broad-party coalition with Katsav doubling up as the minister of tourism and the minister in charge of Arab–Israeli affairs. However the government's dilatory approach to the peace process proved extremely unpopular and Netanyahu's coalition splintered apart in the run-up to general elections in 1999.

Katsav was returned to Parliament for a seventh time but found himself in opposition once again. Up until the middle of 2000 he remained a low-profile politician described by his colleagues as "unassuming" and by the media as "surprisingly normal". It was not until President Ezer Weizman stepped down, following scandalous revelations of huge cash gifts, that Katsav was propelled into the limelight. Running against the former prime minister Shimon Peres in the presidential election seemed to be a hopeless task and Katsav was first to point this out, playing instead on his relaxed, moderate personality. However, Peres's clear intention to use the constitutionally powerless presidency to back the increasingly unpopular peace efforts of Prime Minister Ehud Barak's government proved indigestible in the Parliament. Katsav's very public religious devotion apparently swung the contest in his favour giving him 63 parliamentary votes to Peres's 57 in the July election. On his inauguration on 1 August he pledged to avoid interfering in domestic politics and to serve instead as a figurehead for all Israelis.

Moshe Katsav is married to Gila and they have four sons and one daughter.

Profile of the Prime Minister:

Ariel **SHARON**

Before beginning a political career in 1973, Ariel Sharon spent 25 years in the Israeli Defence Force (IDF), winning especial fame as a tank commander in the 1973 war. He was subsequently notorious for the invasion of southern Lebanon in 1982, while he was defence minister, and the massacres of Palestinians at Sabra and Chatila. Sharon's 'hawkish' right-wing stance as leader of the opposition in 2000 was one of the sparks which began the second Palestinian uprising (intifada) at a time when a lasting peace had seemed to be a possibility. As prime minister since 2001, however, Sharon has combined military force and the building of a controversial defensive 'wall' with a policy of withdrawal from Gaza, leading to a truce with the new Palestinian leadership but divisions within his own Likud (Unity) party.

Ariel Sharon was born as Ariel Scheinerman on 27 September 1928 in Kfar Malal, an impoverished farming community in what was then British-ruled Palestine. He joined the Jewish resistance movement Haganah at the age of 14 and changed his surname to Sharon ('lion of God') during the 1948 Israeli war of independence, in which he led an infantry company. After the war, and the following Arab–Israeli conflict (1948–49), he was promoted into the IDF's newly created intelligence unit. While studying history and oriental studies at the Hebrew University in Jerusalem in 1952, he was appointed to head the specialist anti-terrorist Unit 101 which carried out covert attacks on the Arab fedayeen militia and their supporters. He went on to lead Unit 101 through a series of punitive raids over the next four years. He led a paratroop brigade during the Sinai campaign in 1956, before being sent to Staff College in Camberley, UK, the following year. He received his second degree, in law, from Tel Aviv University in 1962.

From 1958 to 1967 Sharon worked in the infantry as a brigade commander and as head of the IDF's Northern Command and its training school. He led an armoured division during the Six-Day War of 1967 and headed the Southern Command from 1969. In the latter role he worked to secure Israel's new southern border along the Suez Canal. He attempted to enter politics in 1972 but was recalled to the IDF at the outbreak of the Yom Kippur war in 1973. In this conflict he famously defied his superiors and led an armoured division across the Suez Canal into Egypt in a manoeuvre which hastened the end of the war. He resigned from the IDF again after peace returned later that year to launch his career in politics.

As a candidate for Likud, Sharon was elected to Parliament in December 1973 but stepped down a year later to serve as security adviser to Prime Minister Yitzhak Rabin. After Rabin resigned in 1976 Sharon chose to form his own party, Shlomzion ('peace for Zion'), which won two seats in Parliament the following year. However, Likud had been returned to power in the elections and Sharon opted to disband Shlomzion in favour of rejoining the right-wing establishment. In return Prime Minister Menachem Begin appointed him minister of agriculture and chairman of the ministerial committee for settlements. From this vantage point he advanced the cause of the Gush Emunim settlement movement, and backed an extensive building programme.

As minister of defence from 1981, Sharon spearheaded Operation Oranim in June 1982 as part of the 'peace for Galilee' war. The project aimed to end 'terrorist' attacks in northern Israel and to establish a pro-Israeli, anti-Syrian government in Lebanon. On 16 September that year Christian militiamen massacred around 2,000 Palestinian refugees in camps at Sabra and Chatila. The Kahan Inquiry into the killings ruled that Sharon had not done enough to prevent the murders, and consequently found him indirectly responsible for them. He was forced to resign but remained in the cabinet as minister without portfolio.

Political rehabilitation was swift and from 1984 to 1990 Sharon served as trade and industry minister. In 1990 he was appointed housing minister and in this capacity he ordered the biggest settlement construction drive in the Palestinian areas of the West Bank and the Gaza Strip since they had been occupied by Israel in 1967. Between 1992 and 1996 Likud was forced into opposition but Sharon's popularity among the extreme right continued to grow and he came third and second in consecutive party leadership contests. Following the party's electoral success in 1996 Sharon returned to the cabinet under Prime Minister Binyamin Netanyahu after pressure from the extreme right of the party. He was promoted to the foreign ministry in 1998.

The electoral defeat of Likud in 1999 prompted Netanyahu to resign as party chief; Sharon took over the reins in September that year. As leader of the opposition, Sharon was fiercely critical of the peace initiatives pursued by Labour prime minister Ehud Barak. Progress towards peace with the Palestinian National Authority (PNA) led to a steady stream of compromises on control of the occupied areas over the course of 2000, prompting hope of a lasting peace in the international community, but bitterness among the Israeli far right. On 28 September that year Sharon made a high-profile visit to the Temple Mount/al-Haram al-Sharif site in Jerusalem. His visit provoked widespread anger among the Palestinian community which rapidly escalated into a full-blown *intifada*. While Sharon's critics accused him of purposefully inciting the violence in order to destabilize the Labour government's peace initiatives, Sharon himself blamed Palestinian extremists for using it as an excuse to launch the *intifada*.

As violence continued, public support for Barak's government collapsed and he turned to Likud in an effort to form a national unity coalition. This move in itself prompted further anger among the Palestinians. Although initially Sharon rejected the idea, he reversed his stance by November when Barak called a surprise prime ministerial election for the following February. Sharon immediately began his election campaign, boldly announcing that the 1993 Oslo Peace Accords were dead. His cause was boosted when popular former premier Netanyahu refused to challenge him for the Likud leadership. On 6 February 2001 Ehud Barak was forced to accept defeat in the face of 62% support for Sharon. Once elected Sharon secured parliamentary approval for the abolition of the five-year-old system of direct elections for the premiership.

Unable to command a majority alone, Sharon turned to Labour and other parties to form a 'government of national unity'. Immediately Sharon outlined what was to become the backbone of his policy towards the *intifada*: that there could be no talks before all violence by Palestinian militants had ceased. Despite increasingly powerful retaliations against attacks, and pleas from the Palestinian leadership for militants to end suicide bombings, the cycle of violence rapidly became entrenched. The Labour party under Binyamin Ben-Eliezer began to pull away from Sharon's uncompromising approach and put up a final defence in October 2002 when it unsuccessfully resisted a budget which included funding for the controversial Jewish settlements in the Occupied Territories. The unity coalition collapsed and Sharon was forced to call fresh legislative elections for January 2003.

Sharon now faced a leadership challenge within Likud from Netanyahu. On 28 November he was comfortably re-elected, but by the close of the year he was plagued by corruption scandals involving himself and his son Omri, who had been linked by the press to organized crime. Nonetheless, in parliamentary elections held on 27 January 2003, Likud won 37 seats in the 120-seat Parliament, almost double the number it had previously held. Labour refused to join Likud in any kind of unity coalition without serious concessions. By February Sharon had abandoned coalition talks with Labour and had secured a four-party coalition—Likud, the far-right National Religious Party (NRP) and National Union (NU), and the secular Shinui (Change), which had won 15 seats in the election making it the third-largest party in Parliament.

In May 2003, the US government published its much-anticipated 'roadmap' to peace, which was—surprisingly to some—warmly endorsed by Sharon, and also by Palestinian prime minister Mahmoud Abbas. However, Palestinian militant group Hamas immediately rejected the plan, and by August the roadmap appeared to be in shreds following a suicide attack by Palestinian militants on a bus in

Jerusalem, which killed 23 people including seven children, and injured around 130 others. Sharon retaliated by assassinating senior Hamas leader Ismail Abu Shanab and sending tanks into Nablus, Jenin and Tulkarem. Hamas and Islamic Jihad in return called off their ceasefire, and talks with Abbas were broken off. In September Sharon's government indicated that it was considering the targeted assassination of Palestinian leader Yassir Arafat, but Sharon executed a U-turn within a week following widespread international condemnation, including censure from the USA.

In early 2004 Sharon stunned members of his own party and many settlers, for whom he had been a steadfast advocate, by announcing plans to withdraw Israeli settlers and troops from the Gaza Strip. After senior ministers refused to support the proposal, Sharon agreed to hold a referendum on the issue among party members, and was soundly defeated. An amended disengagement plan was eventually accepted by cabinet, but not before two pro-settler ministers were sacked; the approval of the proposal led to the resignation of two ministers from the NRP and the eventual withdrawal of the party from the coalition. Though now in a minority in Parliament, Likud was kept buoyant by a pledge from Labour, which approved of disengagement, to act as a 'safety net' for Likud to keep the government out of any immediate danger.

In July 2004 Sharon began coalition talks with Labour's Shimon Peres. In August 2004, amid fierce international pressure for Israel to halt construction of the security fence eventually intended to encircle Palestinian territories, Sharon approved 1,000 new building tenders for settlements in the West Bank, as a sop for hard-liners angry over the proposed Gaza pullout. However, it was too little to save his coalition hopes and he suffered a humiliating defeat in a ballot of party members on the proposals. A defiant Sharon vowed to press on with the plan regardless of the opposition. In October, Parliament delegates including members of his own party voted against his opening speech, an unprecedented protest, but later in the month Sharon pushed the plan through—though he was forced to rely on Labour to provide him with the necessary support.

The topography of Israeli–Palestinian relations shifted on the death of Arafat in November 2004 and things moved swiftly in its wake. The steadfast refusal of Sharon's government to open discussions with Palestinian officials while Arafat was in charge was now irrelevant; meanwhile, Sharon was scrabbling to form a unity government after the departure of Shinui from his coalition over a budget spat. Parliament backed the new government on 10 January 2005, just five days before the inauguration of Mahmoud Abbas as president of the PNA. By the end of January Hamas and Islamic Jihad had been persuaded by Abbas to call a conditional ceasefire and on 8 February it was announced that Abbas and Sharon had called a truce.

Later in February Parliament approved a compensation package for settlers from Gaza. In March it threw out a ploy to force a referendum on the withdrawal, promoted by rebels from within Sharon's own Likud party. In June, the Supreme

Court upheld the withdrawal plan, rejecting an appeal by a group of settlers that the withdrawal was in violation of their human rights. This removed the last legal barrier to the disengagement and in August 8,500 settlers were removed from their homes in Gaza, some by force. The formal withdrawal was complete by 11 September.

Ariel Sharon is twice a widower. His first wife, Margalit, was killed in a car accident, and his second, Lily, died in 2000. He has two surviving sons, Omri and Gilad, but a third, Gur, was killed in childhood in a shooting accident.

ITALY

Full name: The Italian Republic.

Leadership structure: The head of state is a president elected by an electoral college comprising both houses of Parliament and 58 regional representatives. The president's term of office is seven years. The head of government is the prime minister, who is appointed by the president, as is the cabinet, but on the prime minister's recommendation.

President:	Carlo Azeglio **CIAMPI**	Since 18 May 1999
Prime Minister:	Massimo D'Alema	21 Oct. 1998—26 April 2000
	Giuliano Amato	26 April 2000—11 June 2001
	Silvio **BERLUSCONI**	Since 11 June 2001

Legislature: The legislature, the Parliament (Parlamento), is bicameral. The lower chamber, the Chamber of Deputies (Camera dei Deputati), has 630 members, directly elected for a five-year term. The upper chamber, the Senate of the Republic (Senato della Repubblica), comprises 315 senators directly elected for five years on a regional basis, and a variable number of life senators, who include ex-presidents and senators appointed by incumbent presidents.

Profile of the President of the Republic:

Carlo Azeglio **CIAMPI**

Carlo Ciampi, the governor of the Bank of Italy from 1979 to 1993 and briefly prime minister thereafter, was elected as president in May 1999 as a consensus candidate and a symbol of Italy's much-hoped-for stability. Almost all of the many political parties from right to left backed his nomination. Old enough to have fought in the Italian army in the Second World War, he spent effectively his whole working life in the Bank of Italy.

Carlo Azeglio Ciampi was born on 9 December 1920 in Livorno, Tuscany. He attended university in the nearby city of Pisa, graduating from the Scuola Normale Superiore with a degree in law. He fought in the Italian army from 1941 to 1944. Joining the Bank of Italy in 1946 (the year of his marriage to Franca Pilla, with whom he has one son and one daughter), he spent 14 years in various branches of the bank as an administrator and inspector of commercial banks, until his appointment to the economic research department in 1960.

In the course of the 1970s Ciampi raced up the bank's hierarchy with astonishing speed. In 1970 he was appointed as the head of the research department, in 1973 he became the bank's secretary-general, and in 1976 he was nominated as deputy director-general. Two years later he was full director-general, and in 1979 was made the governor of the Bank of Italy, a position he fulfilled for 14 years until 1993. In his tenure as governor Ciampi has been credited with drastically reducing the public deficit and overseeing Italy's qualification for first-round entry into the European single currency, his most lauded achievement.

Despite a lack of political experience he was nominated as prime minister in 1993 and served as premier for a single year. From prime minister, Ciampi moved on to become vice president of the Bank for International Settlements from 1994 to 1996 before being appointed as minister for the treasury and the budget. In 1998 he was appointed chair of the interim committee of the International Monetary Fund; he was reappointed to the treasury in 1999.

Ciampi is one of the few quickly elected presidents in Italy's history, winning in the first round of the voting in Parliament on 13 May 1999, whereas the selection process has been known to take up to 23 rounds. He won 70% of the available votes from across the political divide, with only the Communist Refoundation Party and the secessionist Northern League voting against him. His popularity lay in his political neutrality and his international renown following his economic accomplishments. He took office on 18 May. With such a broad support base it was thought that work would begin straight away to reform many of Italy's political processes. Two successive referendums called to approve changes, however, met with such public apathy that they were rendered invalid. Ciampi has regularly clashed with Prime Minister Silvio Berlusconi since the latter's return to power in 2001, in late 2004 rejecting a "clearly unconstitutional" judicial reform bill. In 2005 Ciampi was awarded the prestigious Charlemagne prize for distinguished service on behalf of European unification.

Profile of the Prime Minister:

Silvio **BERLUSCONI**

Silvio Berlusconi first made his name as Italy's foremost media magnate, then built a political career on the back of his business success, and first became prime minister in 1994 within months of forming his right-wing Forza Italia party. That government lasted a mere eight months, collapsing in disputes with his neofascist coalition partners. Having presented Forza Italia as a fresh and dynamic alternative to the corrupt old party system, Berlusconi was himself caught up in the web of political-funding corruption and in fighting a conviction for bribery and other criminal charges. His return to power in June 2001 was followed by highly controversial legislation which benefited both his own legal position and his business interests.

Silvio Berlusconi was born on 29 September 1936 in Milan, the son of a banker. His entrepreneurial skills were already evident at school where he did homework for fellow pupils, charging for his services on a sliding scale depending upon the marks awarded. As a student of law at the University of Milan, his close friends included Bettino Craxi, who was later to become leader of the Italian Socialist Party and prime minister. Milan remains Berlusconi's home, where he now lives with his second wife, the actress Veronica Lario (formerly Miriam Bartolini); he has a son and two daughters by this marriage and a son and a daughter from his first marriage to Carla Dell'Oglio.

After graduation Berlusconi established his own construction and property companies, Cantieri Riuniti Milanesi and Edilnord, in the early 1960s. With these he built up significant property holdings, including the Milan suburb known as Milano 2, on which he began construction in 1969 and which eventually housed 10,000 people.

In the 1970s Berlusconi's business career began to focus increasingly on the media interests for which he was to become best known. In 1974 he founded the cable television company Telemilano, which serviced Milano 2, and the following year he set up Fininvest as the holding company for his growing empire. To circumvent legislation under which only the state-run television service RAI was permitted to broadcast nationally, he set up a network of regional companies, which achieved de facto nationwide coverage by broadcasting the same programmes simultaneously. His own television channel, Canale 5, began broadcasting in 1980. He bought Italy's other two main private television stations, Italia 1 and Rete 4, in 1983 and 1984 respectively.

Having also moved successfully into the advertising business and built up Publitalia to make it the largest advertising agency in Europe, Berlusconi diversified his holdings during the 1980s to include the print media, publishing (including the country's largest publishing concern, Mondadori), the film industry (including the largest cinema chain, Cinema 5), retailing (including the largest chain of department stores, La Standa), insurance, financial services and the football team A.C. Milan. His success in business was based on the combination of commercial acumen and ruthlessness, backed up by an ability to operate the political system to advantage and good high-level connections. His opponents allege that this extended to exploiting links with the freemasons and the Mafia. Berlusconi was a member of the notorious clandestine P-2 masonic lodge, uncovered in 1981 and subsequently outlawed, although he has denied being actively involved in its dealings.

The opportunity for Berlusconi the business phenomenon to become Berlusconi the political leader came with the upheavals of the early 1990s. Ever-widening judicial investigations, mounted by magistrates into kickback payments and related scandals, began to unravel the web of endemic corruption and bribery through which the traditional parties, both socialist and Christian democratic, had wielded power at the local and national level. The impact of the so-called *mani pulite* (clean hands) operation was to discredit the old parties and thus to transform the political landscape. Berlusconi entered the fray with the formation in January 1994 of Forza Italia, a political party named after the Italian football supporters' chant, which translates loosely as "Come on, Italy!". He proceeded to form a right-wing Freedom Alliance for the March 1994 general election, embracing Forza Italia, the separatist Northern League, the neofascist National Alliance and other smaller right-wing parties.

Berlusconi's successful populist campaign was greatly strengthened by his ownership of 85% of commercial television and 20% of the domestic publishing market. The Freedom Alliance secured a majority of seats in the Chamber of Deputies and Berlusconi, as leader of its largest party, was able to form a coalition government in May 1994. His coalition proved divisive and short-lived, however. He was criticized for appointing his own nominees to key public positions. In July he was obliged after a public outcry to withdraw a decree which ended the preventive detention of corruption and bribery suspects (who by then included Berlusconi's brother and a Fininvest director).

Berlusconi also failed to tackle economic problems, including reducing the public debt and reorganizing the public sector. The draft budget, which focused on cuts in pensions and health care and thus penalized the lower paid, provoked widespread protests and a sharp fall in the value of the lira and of the Milan stock exchange in November. Further, Berlusconi received a summons in November in connection with his alleged bribery of tax inspectors, finally prompting the increasingly disaffected Northern League to withdraw from the coalition and obliging Berlusconi to resign in December 1994, leaving office the following month. He remained at the head of Forza Italia, whose support fell slightly in the April 1996 general election, which brought to power a centre-left coalition of the Olive Tree Alliance led by the moderate Romano Prodi.

Berlusconi's political position was undermined further by the progress of corruption investigations implicating him personally. In December 1997 he was convicted on charges of false accounting over a 1987 film company deal and given a 16-month suspended sentence. In two judgements delivered in July 1998 he was found guilty of bribing tax inspectors and of illegally funding Craxi's socialists during the 1980s to the tune of 22,000 million lire (US$13 million). He was sentenced to over five years' imprisonment and a fine of 10,000 million lire (US$6 million) but remained free pending the outcome of appeals—and still faced other corruption charges, as well as allegations of money laundering for the Mafia. In 2000 accusations had spread abroad with a Spanish judge demanding the lifting of the immunity from prosecution enjoyed by Berlusconi as a member of the European parliament (since 1999) in order to press charges over fraud at a Spanish television station. He was saved by his victory in general elections in Italy on 13 May 2001.

Heading a new right-wing coalition, the so-called House of Liberties (Casa delle Libertà) which again included the National Alliance and the Northern League,

Berlusconi was inaugurated for his second term as prime minister on 11 June 2001. Immediately he began preparing bills to effectively quash outstanding charges against him. One law halved the period before a statute of limitations prevents prosecution on charges of false accounting. A number of bribery charges were dropped in October 2001. Another law in July 2002 eliminated the conflict of interest debate over his media empire. Perhaps most significantly in November 2002 a law was passed allowing defendants to move their trial if they can prove a bias in the court. Using this bill Berlusconi hoped to switch a Milan-based trial against him to another court, but failed in his attempt and in May 2003 became the first serving Italian prime minister to appear at his own trial. The trial collapsed after legislation passed which granted Berlusconi immunity, although the Constitutional Court ruled the new law illegal.

Such manipulations and Berlusconi's full support for the USA's 'war on terrorism' produced a rapid drop in his popularity. Rallies against the pro-war stance, labour reforms and immigration laws attracted up to two million people at a time. Nonetheless in May 2004 Berlusconi's government became Italy's longest-serving administration since the Second World War. Protests against Italy's involvement in Iraq grew following the kidnapping of four Italian hostages by Iraqi insurgents in April 2004, but it eventually took the death of an Italian intelligence agent in Iraq, shot by US forces, to trigger the announcement in March 2005 that Italy would withdraw its forces by autumn.

Berlusconi's government was plunged into crisis in April 2005 when disastrous local election results prompted the centre-right Union of Christian and Centre Democrats to withdraw from the governing coalition. However, with typical chutzpah, Berlusconi resigned while stating his intention to immediately form a new government. Had he failed, fresh elections would have been called; three days later Berlusconi submitted a new cabinet with just seven changes.

Italy's richest man, Berlusconi is an opportunist entrepreneur whose risk-taking approach to business has won him control of a vast commercial empire encompassing media, sport, food and drink and construction. However, those same instincts have seen him sail perilously close to the wire in his political career. Always just a few paces ahead of the latest court case, Berlusconi has nonetheless become one of Italy's longest-serving leaders and his willingness to push through legislation to shore up his position has been an effective tool in keeping legal challenges at bay.

JAMAICA

Full name: Jamaica.

Leadership structure: The head of state is the British sovereign, styled 'of Jamaica, and of Her other Realms and Territories Queen, Head of the Commonwealth', and represented by a governor-general who is appointed on the advice of the Jamaican prime minister. The head of government is the prime minister, the leader of the majority party in the House of Representatives. The cabinet is appointed by the governor-general on the advice of the prime minister.

Queen:	Elizabeth II	Since 6 Feb. 1952
Governor-General:	Sir Howard **COOKE**	Since 1 Aug. 1991
Prime Minister:	Percival J. **PATTERSON**	Since 30 March 1992

Legislature: The legislature, the Parliament, is bicameral. The lower chamber, the House of Representatives, has 60 members, directly elected for a five-year term. The upper chamber, the Senate, has 21 members, appointed by the governor-general, 13 on the advice of the prime minister and eight on that of the leader of the opposition.

Profile of the Governor-General:

Sir Howard **COOKE**

Sir Howard Cooke, a teacher by profession, was a founding member of the People's National Party (PNP) before the Second World War, and a government minister in the 1970s. He took office as governor-general on 1 August 1991.

Born on 13 November 1915 at Goodwill in the parish of St James, Howard Felix Hanlan Cooke was educated at Mico College and at London University. During his long teaching career he spent over 20 years at Mico College, was headmaster at Belle Castle All-Age School, Port Antonio Upper School and Montego Bay Boys' School, and was at one time president of the Jamaica Union of Teachers. Cooke has also held various managerial positions in the insurance industry with Standard Life, Jamaica Mutual Life, and the American Life Insurance Company (ALICO).

Cooke's political career began in 1938, when he was a founding member of the PNP. Within the party he has been a member of the national executive, chairman of the regional executive and chairman of the party. He sat in the West Indies Federal Parliament as the representative for St James from 1958 until 1962, was a senator in the Jamaican Parliament in 1962–67, and a member of the House of Representatives in 1972–80. His government posts included ministerial responsibilities for pensions and social security, education, public service and labour. He also served on the executive of the Commonwealth Parliamentary Association. He was appointed governor-general of Jamaica in 1991.

An accomplished cricketer and footballer in his youth, Cooke has also been group scoutmaster and secretary of the St Andrew Boys' Scout Association, and is chief scout of the Scout Association of Jamaica. He is a lay pastor, a senior elder of the United Church of Jamaica and Grand Cayman, and a member of the Ancient and Accepted Order of Masons.

Cooke married Ivy Tai in 1939, and they have two sons and one daughter.

Profile of the Prime Minister:

Percival J. **PATTERSON**

Before becoming Jamaica's first black prime minister in 1992, Percival Patterson, a lawyer who became a Queen's Counsel in 1984, had been for 14 years the loyal deputy to Michael Manley, both in government and in opposition. Securing his position by leading the People's National Party (PNP) to a convincing victory in the March 1993 general elections, Patterson moved the party further away from the radical socialism of the 1970s. His government struggled to bring inflation under control and to reduce the fiscal deficit, and remained preoccupied with the high rate of violent crime, but was re-elected in December 1997 and October 2002.

Percival Noel James Patterson was born on 10 April 1935 at Cross Roads in the parish of St Andrew. He studied English at the University College of the West Indies (UCWI, later renamed the University of the West Indies), graduating in 1958, and went on in 1960 to study law in the UK at the London School of Economics. He was called to the Bar in 1963, and returned to Jamaica to practise as a lawyer. He is now divorced and has one son and one daughter.

Patterson began his political career while he was still at UCWI, as founder and first president of the UCWI's political club. He joined the PNP in 1958 and was a member of the party executive between 1964 and 1969. In 1967 he was nominated to the Senate, and between 1970 and 1980 he held a seat in the House of Representatives, representing South East Westmoreland as a PNP member. He was campaign director for the PNP for the general elections of 1972, 1976 and 1989.

Starting his cabinet career in 1972 as minister of industry, foreign trade and tourism, Patterson became deputy prime minister and minister of foreign trade in

1978. The government was decisively rejected by the electorate in 1980 and the PNP was in opposition for over eight years thereafter, during which time Patterson returned to his legal career, becoming a Queen's Counsel in 1984. He was also engaged as a consultant by the Commonwealth Secretariat to assist in drafting the constitution under which Belize became independent in 1981.

The PNP boycotted the 1983 elections, but swept back to power in February 1989, when Patterson was appointed deputy prime minister and minister of development, planning and production. As minister of finance and planning from 1990 to 1991, he supervised the drafting of a new Banking Act, modernized the tax system, and introduced a general consumption tax (GCT).

Having succeeded Michael Manley as prime minister in March 1992, Patterson led the PNP to victory in the 1993 general election. In the ensuing years his government became embroiled in a lengthy dispute over whether it was appropriate, in a state which was not a UK dependency, to continue to have legal appeal procedures going ultimately to the UK's Privy Council. The issue arose over a Privy Council recommendation that death sentences on two convicted murderers should be commuted because they had spent so long on 'death row'; it thus touched not only on Jamaica's independent status but also on the government's determination to fight violent crime. An agreement with the USA in May 1997 allowed greater scope for action in Jamaica by US drug enforcement officers in the battle against trafficking.

Patterson, who was one of the main protagonists of a free trade agreement covering the Caribbean, is acknowledged to have been during his ministerial career one of the chief architects of the Lomé Convention, governing relations between the European Union (EU) and the African, Caribbean and Pacific countries (ACP). After becoming prime minister he sought to introduce more stable relationships between key sectors in the economic sphere, proposing in early 1996 a tripartite 'social contract' between workers, employers and the government.

A mysterious scandal enveloped the government in October 2000 when Patterson announced that he had not authorized the 'bugging' of his own and other ministers' offices, and that an investigation into police connections to the drugs trade was "interlocked" with the bugging plot. However, it was the unsolved problem of increasing political violence on the streets of Kingston which did most to undermine his popularity. The PNP was returned for a fourth term with a much-reduced majority in the October 2002 elections, now holding just 34 seats in the 60-seat House of Representatives.

In 2004 he controversially refused to recognize the new government of Haiti after the ousting of Jean-Bertrand Aristide. Aristide was given shelter in Jamaica while he launched a lawsuit against the USA and France for "kidnapping" him and the Caribbean Community (Caricom) negotiated his exile to Africa.

Patterson has pledged to make Jamaica a republic by the time his current term expires in 2007. While he favours an executive president to replace Queen Elizabeth II as head of state, the opposition Jamaica Labour Party supports a more ceremonial figurehead. He is also keen for Jamaica to join the Caribbean Court of Justice, thus ending its subjugation to the UK's Privy Council. He has steered the country to the forefront of readiness for the Caribbean Single Market and Economy, due to come into effect in 2006, and a major stepping stone towards a Free Trade Association of the Americas.

Patterson has announced that he will not lead the PNP into the 2007 general election, but has not set a date for his retirement—potential successors within the PNP are gearing up for the leadership race, though this is now not expected to be held before summer 2006.

JAPAN

Full name: Japan.

Leadership structure: The head of state is a constitutional monarch. The head of government is the prime minister, formally elected by the House of Representatives, who appoints the cabinet.

Emperor:	**AKIHITO**	Since 7 Jan. 1989
Prime Minister:	Keizo Obuchi	30 July 1998—5 April 2000
	Mikio Aoki (acting)	3 April 2000—5 April 2000
	Yoshiro Mori	5 April 2000—26 April 2001
	Junichiro **KOIZUMI**	Since 26 April 2001

Legislature: The legislature, the Diet (Kokkai), is bicameral. The lower chamber, the House of Representatives (Shugiin), has 480 members, directly elected by universal adult suffrage for a maximum four-year term. The upper chamber, the House of Councillors (Sangiin), has 242 members, elected for six-year terms, with half due for re-election every three years.

Profile of the Emperor:

AKIHITO

Emperor Akihito has been head of state since January 1989. The role of emperor, while accorded the highest respect, is primarily a ceremonial one, and in all political matters he acts only as advised by the government. Before his accession Akihito had been crown prince for nearly four decades during the long reign of his father, Emperor Hirohito.

Akihito Tsegu no Miya was born in Tokyo on 23 December 1933. He is the fourth child, and eldest son, of Emperor Hirohito and Empress Nagako. His education, interrupted by evacuation to provincial cities during the Second World War, was partly by private tutors. Akihito also attended the Gakushuin School, which covers the whole range from kindergarten to university, and was originally set up specifically for the imperial family and aristocracy, but opened to the public from 1947. He graduated from Gakushuin University in politics and economics in 1956.

In 1952 Akihito was officially named crown prince, and spent the years before his accession engaged in a mixture of official duties and private interests. His public duties included many overseas visits and tours within Japan. In private life a keen ichthyologist, he is a particular expert on the goby fish, and has made numerous contributions to the journal of the Ichthyological Society of Japan; he has also been a research associate at the Australian Museum, and in 1985 he was honorary secretary at the International Conference on Indo-Pacific Fish.

In 1987 Akihito became acting head of state. Acceding to the throne on 7 January 1989, he was formally crowned on 12 November 1990.

In 1959 Akihito married Michiko Shoda, the first nonaristocrat to be elevated to royal status. The couple have two sons and one daughter: Naruhito (born in 1960, invested as crown prince in 1991), Fumihito (born in 1965, now known as Prince Akishino) and Sayako (born in 1969). The three grandchildren are all girls, which has prompted a proposal to amend the constitution to allow women to accede to the Japanese throne.

Profile of the Prime Minister:

Junichiro KOIZUMI

Junichiro Koizumi, who became prime minister in April 2001 following the premature resignation of his deeply unpopular predecessor Yoshiro Mori, is himself exceptionally popular with the Japanese public, although his nationalistic tendencies have led to a cooling in relations with the country's east Asian neighbours. A 'maverick' with an unconventionally enthusiastic style, Koizumi comes from a political family background, and has sat in the House of Representatives as a member of the Liberal Democratic Party (LDP) since 1972.

Junichiro Koizumi was born on 8 January 1942 in Yokosuka, just southwest of Tokyo. His grandfather, Matajiro Koizumi, and his father, Junya Koizumi, both held ministerial posts. Junya was minister of defence in the 1960s. Junichiro graduated from Tokyo's Keio University in 1967 with a degree in economics and travelled to the UK to further his studies at the London School of Economics. However, he returned to Japan after only a year following his father's death from cancer. He unsuccessfully campaigned for his father's seat in the House of Representatives and found work instead as secretary for the LDP member, and future prime minister, Takeo Fukuda.

After two years as a junior secretary Koizumi campaigned again in 1972 for election in the Kanagawa-11 constituency, which covers his home city of Yokosuka. This time he won the seat, and he has been re-elected ever since. Between 1980 and 1988 he served on several parliamentary committees before entering the reshuffled cabinet of Prime Minister Noboru Takeshita as minister of health and welfare. In 1992 he was moved to the posts and telecommunications ministry by Prime Minister Kiichi Miyazawa.

It was during the 1990s that Koizumi was given his 'weirdo' tag. His unusually outspoken rhetorical style was backed by treatises suggesting radical reforms, such as the privatization of the postal savings system. At the same time he was careful not to talk himself out of favour within the guarded and strongly traditional Japanese political system. He even headed one of the internal factions of which the LDP has traditionally consisted, despite later pledging as premier to do away with this patronage-based system.

When the LDP was knocked from its almost permanent position as the ruling party in 1993 by a seven-party coalition led by Shinshinto, it continued its internal wrangling in opposition. Koizumi stood as a candidate for the party leadership in 1995 and 1998—the latter competition was effectively for prime minister as the LDP had returned to power in 1994. In the meantime Koizumi had been returned to the health and welfare ministry in 1996 by Prime Minister Ryutaro Hashimoto.

Prime Minister Keizo Obuchi, who had defeated Koizumi to the party presidency in 1998, led the country through a period of worsening economic prospects and attempted to stave off the trend with record public spending. On his sudden death in April 2000 he was replaced by Yoshiro Mori who stuck closely to Obuchi's policies. The economy did not recover and Mori, not helped by a proneness to public gaffes, eventually stepped down from the party leadership, and consequently the premiership, after just one year. In the complex internal voting system, former prime minister Hashimoto appeared to be the main contender in the race but Koizumi capitalized on massive grass-roots appeal to score an impressive and unexpected victory. His plain-speaking reformist agenda centred on the promise of "change the LDP, change Japan".

Initially Koizumi's promises of wide-ranging economic and political reform kept his popularity soaring. Although he gave offence internationally by visiting the controversial Yasukuni Shrine, which commemorates Japan's war dead, including posthumously convicted war criminals, and by backing revisionist school history text books, this brand of nationalism did him no harm at home. It was his record-breaking inclusion of five women in his opening cabinet that, in one sense, contained the seeds of trouble for his popularity, which began to slide when he was forced to dismiss one of them, his firebrand foreign minister, the popular Makiko Tanaka, in January 2002.

The downward momentum gathered as the lacklustre pace of his economic reforms became apparent. In August 2002 he admitted that his timescale for reform had been overambitious. Unemployment rose, exacerbated by falling consumer spending, By the end of the year the restructuring of banks had put many of Japan's major financial institutions on the rocks. In politics critics suggested that, rather than 'changing' the faction system within the LDP,

Koizumi had been forced to pander to it, further retarding his reforms. Nonetheless, after being re-elected as head of the LDP in September 2003 Koizumi dissolved parliament and called fresh elections, which the LDP won. Though it lost the simple majority that it had held since the last election, within a month it regained a majority by absorbing the New Conservative Party.

By 2005 Koizumi had tied his colours inextricably to the mast of the reform of Japan Post. The postal savings bank, a bloated monster and the world's biggest financial institution, had been responsible for huge distortions in the allocation of funds across the Japanese economy, and with it a great deal of political corruption. Koizumi could have begun his modernization programme elsewhere, but Japan Post had become symbolic of decades of patronage and of factionalism frustrating any attempts at restructuring the domestic economy.

To outface opposition to his reform plans within his own party, he called early elections for September and handpicked a group of high-profile 'assassins' to stand against the rebels. Though only nine of the 'assassin' candidates defeated their opponents, overall the LDP won a landslide victory with a two-thirds' majority in the 480-seat lower house.

Junichiro Koizumi has publicly vowed not to remarry, having decided that he is "better off alone" since his 1982 divorce from Kayoko Miyamoto, a woman 14 years his junior and the daughter of a pharmaceuticals magnate. He took custody of his two eldest sons, who were raised by his sisters, while he has never met his third son, with whom Kayoko had been pregnant when they divorced. His reputation as a keen socialite has not dented his public appeal in the slightest. Indeed his unkempt hairstyle and casual attire have served to improve his popularity. Among his interests he cites *kabuki* (traditional Japanese theatre) as well as karaoke.

JORDAN

Full name: The Hashemite Kingdom of Jordan.

Leadership structure: The head of state is a king. The head of government is the prime minister, who is usually appointed by the king. However, in August 1998, power to appoint and dismiss the prime minister was also given to the crown prince in the event of the king's illness. The Council of Ministers is chosen by the prime minister.

King:	**ABDULLAH II** bin al-Hussein (regent from 5 Feb. 1999)	Since 7 Feb. 1999
Prime Minister:	Abd al-Rauf al-Rawabdeh	4 March 1999—18 June 2000
	Ali Abu al-Ragheb	19 June 2000—25 Oct. 2003
	Faisal al-Fayez (acting until 7 April 2005)	25 Oct. 2003—5 April 2005
	Adnan **BADRAN**	Since 7 April 2005

Legislature: The legislature, the National Assembly (Majlis al-Umma), is bicameral. The lower chamber, the House of Deputies (Majlis al-Nuwaab), has 110 members, at least six of whom must be women, directly elected for a four-year term. The upper chamber, the Senate (Majlis al-Aayan—literally 'House of Notables'), has 55 members, appointed by the king for a four-year term.

Profile of the King:

ABDULLAH II bin al-Hussein

Abdullah II succeeded to the Hashemite throne of Jordan on the death of his father King Hussein. The son of Hussein's English second wife and educated largely in England, Abdullah is seen as very much in the pro-Western mould of his father with close links to many high-level Israelis giving him an obvious role as peacemaker in the Middle East region. His appointment as heir came only two weeks before Hussein's death, replacing the late king's younger brother Hassan as crown prince and causing brief controversy in Jordan. His succession received praise from across the international community and his continuation of his father's moderate policies has so far proved popular in Jordan.

Abdullah bin al-Hussein was born in Amman on 30 January 1962, the eldest son of 11 children born to the reigning monarch King Hussein and his English second wife Queen Muna. His uncle Hassan was named crown prince and heir to the throne in 1965. After a brief period of preschooling in Amman he was sent to England to be educated at St Edmund's School in Surrey in 1966 and then to Eaglebrook School in Massachusetts, USA. For his secondary education he attended the Deerfield Academy in the USA before returning to England to enrol in the Royal Military Academy at Sandhurst in 1980. After receiving his commission as a lieutenant in 1981 he studied for a degree in international affairs at Oxford University.

Pursuing a military career interspersed with further studies abroad, he qualified as a helicopter pilot in 1986 while attached to the Royal Jordanian Air Force, then went to Georgetown University in Washington D.C., USA, where he again studied international relations. Returning to Jordan, he commanded tank battalions as a major from 1989. In 1990 he attended the Command and Staff College in Camberley, England. On his return he became armour representative in the office of the inspector-general in 1991 and was promoted in the same year to lieutenant-colonel. In 1993 Abdullah crossed over to the Jordanian special forces as a full colonel, and assumed control of the Royal Jordanian Special Forces as a brigadier-general the following year. In 1997 he was appointed as commander of the Special Operations Command and in 1998 he was promoted to major-general.

In early 1999 the health of Abdullah's father King Hussein deteriorated rapidly. Flying home from hospital in the USA after the failure of a bone marrow operation, he startled Jordanian politics on 24 January by naming his son Abdullah as his heir in place of Prince Hassan.

Abdullah was not a complete stranger to royal duties. He had accompanied his father on many international visits and had made acquaintance with numerous high-ranking regional politicians. However, in Jordan he was largely an unknown quantity. After his father's death on 7 February, he was quickly accepted by the international community. In Jordan he soon won over the stunned population with promises to maintain Jordan's role as Middle East peace broker and a clear desire to continue in his father's populist vein. His first royal decree complied with his father's wishes and nominated his younger half-brother Prince Hamzah, born on 29 March 1980, as crown prince and heir apparent. However, the title was revoked in November 2004, in order to allow Hamzah to "assume more responsibilities", and no new crown prince was nominated.

As king, Abdullah convened a special parliamentary session to examine possible changes to the controversial press law introduced under his father in September 1998. However, his regime has been criticized for restrictions on freedom of speech and its treatment of Islamic dissidents. He has continued the reforms initiated by his father, and promoted Jordan as a hub of information technology. Six seats in the House of Deputies are now reserved for women, and he has appointed an enlarged Senate, comprising former ministers, journalists and women. In 2005 plans were announced to set up elected councils to oversee political development. His changes of prime minister have also indicated a shift towards modernization and reform.

Abdullah condemned the US-led invasion of Iraq in 2003, but the following year became the first Arab leader to admit his readiness to send troops to Iraq. In an interview with the BBC, Abdullah said that if the interim government of Iraq were to ask for help directly "it would be very difficult to say no", although he doubted that Jordanians would be the "right people" for the job. Earlier that year he had snubbed US president George W. Bush by postponing talks after Bush had condoned Israel's intention to keep most of its settlements in the West Bank.

King Abdullah married Rania al-Yassin on 10 June 1993. Crowned with him on 9 June 1999, Queen Rania was born in Kuwait in 1970 to a notable Jordanian family of Palestinian descent. She had a brief career in private sector banking and information technology before marrying Abdullah, and has since overseen the creation of the Arab world's first child abuse protection project. Together they have two sons and two daughters: Prince Hussein born in 1994, Princess Iman born in 1996, Princess Salma born in 2000 and Prince Hashem born in 2005.

Profile of the Prime Minister:

Adnan **BADRAN**

Adnan Badran was appointed as prime minister on 7 April 2005 to push forward King Abdullah's reformist agenda. He is a well-respected scientist and educationalist who is currently president of Philadelphia University and from 1990 to 1998 worked for the UN Educational, Scientific and Cultural Organization (UNESCO) based in Paris. He has previously served in government as minister of agriculture and minister of education.

Adnan Badran was born on 15 December 1935 in Jarash in Jordan. He attended Oklahoma State University in the USA where he received a degree in 1959, followed by a master's degree and doctorate from Michigan State University in 1961 and 1963 respectively. He worked as a research assistant at Michigan State before joining the United Fruit Research Laboratories as a senior research plant physiologist and biochemist and a member of the board of management. He is married with several children.

In 1966 Badran returned to Jordan as an assistant professor at the faculty of science in the University of Jordan. He became associate professor in 1968 and was made dean of the faculty in 1971. In 1974 he became professor of molecular biology and physiology at the University of Jordan, and in 1976 became professor of biology at Yarmouk University, where he also became university president. A decade later Badran founded the science and engineering campus at the Jordan

University of Science and Technology (JUST). During these years he was heavily involved in the development of a secondary school curriculum for biology education in Jordan and other Arab states.

In 1986 a number of Jordanian students took to the streets to protest over an increase in fees. Rather than negotiate with the protestors, Badran as president of Yarmouk University called in the police and the army. Three students were killed in the resultant violence and at least 15 injured. Badran was removed from his post, though no charges were ever filed against him. Shortly afterwards he was appointed as secretary-general of the Higher Council for Science and Technology, and in 1988 served as minister of agriculture. The following year he became minister of education.

In 1990 Badran moved to Paris to work for UNESCO where he remained for eight years, becoming deputy director-general in 1993. In 1998 he returned to Jordan to become president of Philadelphia University. He was appointed as prime minister on 7 April 2005 by King Abdullah II to replace Faisal al-Fayez who was thought not to be sufficiently reformist. He is also minister of defence. Speculation was rife among opposition activists that the appointment was at the recommendation of US president George W. Bush, whose secretary of state Condoleezza Rice had just completed a visit to Jordan.

KAZAKHSTAN

Full name: The Republic of Kazakhstan.

Leadership structure: The head of state is a president, directly elected by universal adult suffrage. The president's term of office was extended from five to seven years under constitutional amendments approved by the legislature in October 1998, on the same day as it approved the holding of early presidential elections in 1999. The Parliament on 27 June 2000, granted President Nazarbayev special powers for life to address the Parliament and the nation and advise future presidents. The head of government is the prime minister, who is appointed by the president. The deputy prime ministers and the ministers of foreign affairs, defence, finance and internal affairs are also appointed by the president. The remaining ministers are nominated by the prime minister.

President:	Nursultan **NAZARBAYEV**	Since 24 April 1990
	(chairman of the Supreme Soviet from 22 Feb. 1990)	
Prime Minister:	Kasymzhomart Tokayev	12 Oct. 1999—28 Jan. 2002
	(acting from 1 Oct. 1999)	
	Imangali Tasmagambetov	28 Jan. 2002—13 June 2003
	Daniyal **AKHMETOV**	Since 13 June 2003

Legislature: The legislature, the Parliament (Parlament), is bicameral. The lower chamber, the Assembly (Majlis), has 77 members, 67 of them directly elected on a single constituency basis, and ten seats allocated proportionately, for five-year terms. The upper chamber, the Senate, has 39 members, 32 indirectly elected and seven appointed, for six-year terms, with half elected every three years.

Profile of the President:

Nursultan **NAZARBAYEV**

Nursultan Nazarbayev rose through the Soviet system to the top post in Kazakhstan before it became independent and has been the country's president ever since. Despite his communist party background, he became an advocate of transforming the economy on free-market lines, strongly influenced by the advice of the Korean-American economist Chan Young Bang. The dominant political personality, he runs an authoritarian regime and has resorted to ruling by decree for substantial periods.

Nursultan Abishevich Nazarbayev was born on 6 July 1940 in the village of Chemolgan, near Almaty. He attended the higher technology course at the Karaganda Metallurgical Combine, and then worked there until 1969, apart from some time spent in Moscow at the Higher Party School of the Communist Party of the Soviet Union (CPSU), which he had joined in 1962. He is married to Sara Alpysovna née Kunakayeva and they have three daughters.

In 1969 Nazarbayev began a career as a party functionary, which took him via district level posts to membership of the CPSU central committee in 1986, and appointment in June 1989 as first secretary of the Communist Party of Kazakhstan (CPK).

Meanwhile, within the government structure, he had been chairman of the Kazakh Council of Ministers since 1984. Changes to the political structure in 1989 saw the creation of a permanent legislature whose chairman took on many of the functions formerly held by the CPK first secretary. Nazarbayev was elected as the first chairman of this reformed body in February 1990—and then in April was elected by the new legislature as the first president of the Kazakh Soviet Socialist Republic.

Nazarbayev was appointed to the CPSU politburo in 1990, but resigned from both the politburo and the central committee in 1991 in protest over the attempted coup in Moscow that August. Independence soon followed and Nazarbayev became first president of the independent Kazakhstan, with the endorsement of a popular vote that December.

As president, Nazarbayev advocated an independent stance while insisting on the importance of relations with the Russian Federation. He committed Kazakhstan to becoming a non-nuclear state, dismantling nuclear warheads and also signing the Nuclear Non-Proliferation Treaty in 1994.

On 29 April 1995 95% of the electorate approved Nazarbayev in office for a further five-year term. He then went on to better establish his position with a new constitution which was approved by referendum in August that year and abolished the post of vice president among other measures.

Nazarbayev agreed in October 1998 to hold early presidential elections in January 1999 for a chance at a new, and extended, seven-year term. Several prominent opposition figures were barred from standing in the poll due to prior political infractions. Nazarbayev easily won re-election with around 80% of the vote. The Organization for Security and Co-operation in Europe (OSCE) was in the front line of international critics of the election. On 27 June 2000 Nazarbayev was given special powers for life to address the Parliament and the nation, and advise future presidents after his term expires in 2006. Accusations of increasing authoritarianism forced him to appoint a consultative National Council in 2002, however, to draft proposals and make policy recommendations.

In internal affairs, he has used presidential powers to rule by decree to overcome obstacles in the legislature, particularly over the transformation of the economy to a free enterprise model. Opposition and human rights groups have accused him of harassing those who express dissent. However, Nazarbayev vetoed new laws in 2004 that would have placed severe restrictions on the media.

Nazarbayev's Fatherland Republican Party of Kazakhstan (Otan) won the 2004 Assembly elections, while the party led by his daughter Dariga finished second, and main opposition party Ak Zhol won just one seat. Opposition leaders threatened to take the electoral commission to court, following widespread doubts about the fairness of the elections.

Profile of the Prime Minister:

Daniyal **AKHMETOV**

Daniyal Akhmetov, former governor of Pavlodar, was appointed as prime minister of Kazakhstan on 13 June 2003. Akhmetov promised continuity, indicating a minimum of ministerial and policy changes. Although known for a certain severity, and a hostility towards political liberalism, Akhmetov is also respected for his ability to connect with ordinary MPs and build consensus across the political spectrum; one of his first acts of office was to push through the land reform bill over which his predecessor had resigned.

Daniyal Akhmetov was born on 15 June 1954, in the city of Pavlodar in Kazakhstan. He is married to Guliya Koyshibekovna and they have one daughter and one son. Akhmetov studied in his home city and graduated from the Pavlodar Industrial Institute in 1976 with a degree in economic sciences. His first job, which lasted five years, was as a repairman at the home-building company Pavlodarzhilstroi.

From 1981 to 1983 Akhmetov was an instructor with the Ekibastuz city council. From there he was promoted to deputy chief engineer and secretary of the local party committee. In 1987 he became deputy chairman of the city's executive committee and in 1993 Akhmetov was appointed as governor of Pavlodar oblast (region), a post in which he served initially until 1997, when he became governor of North Kazakhstan oblast for two years.

In 1999 Akhmetov was appointed to his first post in central government, as deputy prime minister in charge of industry, energy, agriculture, transportation, communications, and migration and demographic policies. The next year he was appointed as first deputy prime minister, before returning to the governorship of Pavlodar oblast in 2001, where he earned the nickname 'Terminator' for conducting a tough cleanup campaign against supporters of his predecessor, who had become a leader of the opposition democratic movement.

In June 2003 Prime Minister Imangali Tasmagambetov resigned over a dispute over a proposed new law on private land ownership, and Akhmetov was sworn in two days later. He brought with him a reputation as an administrator with little tolerance for opposition, although tempered by a taste for building consensus. Opposition leaders protested Akhmetov's appointment, accusing him of closing down and harassing independent media outlets when he was governor of Pavlodar. He is known to be absolutely loyal to President Nursultan Nazarbayev, and in order to prove this loyalty, he is willing to act ruthlessly against opponents of the leadership.

KENYA

Full name: The Republic of Kenya.

Leadership structure: The head of state is a president, directly elected by universal adult suffrage. The president's term of office is five years. The head of government is the president, who is responsible to the National Assembly. The cabinet is appointed by the president.

President:	Daniel arap Moi (acting from 22 Aug. 1978)	14 Oct. 1978—30 Dec. 2002
	Mwai **KIBAKI**	Since 30 Dec. 2002

Legislature: The legislature is unicameral. The sole chamber, the National Assembly (Bunge), has 224 members (210 directly elected for a five-year term, 12 nominated by the president and two, the attorney general and the speaker, ex officio).

Profile of the President:

Mwai **KIBAKI**

Mwai Kibaki is the leader of the National Alliance Party of Kenya (NAK) which forms the core of the National Rainbow Coalition (NARC). A veteran politician who had been an integral part of the regime during the 1970s and 1980s, Kibaki left the then ruling Kenya African National Union (KANU) when the country moved to multipartyism in 1991. Twice a failed presidential candidate in the 1990s, he unified opposition against KANU in 2002 and secured the presidency in December that year with a convincing 63% of the vote in the first round.

Emilio Mwai Kibaki was born into a wealthy family from the Kikuyu tribe, Kenya's largest single ethnic group, on 15 November 1931. He is married to Lucy Muthoni and has three sons and one daughter; he reportedly entered a traditional second marriage with Mary Wambui in 1972, with whom he had one daughter, though in 2004 he denied the marriage.

After a relatively prestigious education in Kenya, Kibaki went to neighbouring Uganda in 1950 to study economics at Makerere University in Kampala. He then worked briefly for Shell Oil in Uganda, until 1956, when he went to the UK on a Commonwealth scholarship to study public finance at the London School of Economics. He returned to Uganda in 1959 to begin lecturing in economics at Makerere University.

At the height of the Kenyan independence movement Kibaki returned home in 1960 to join the emerging KANU and to help draft the first constitution. He won a seat in the new parliament in 1963, and has been re-elected to the chamber in every successive election, making him the country's second-longest serving deputy after former president Daniel arap Moi.

Kibaki entered government in 1964 when Kenya's first president, Jomo Kenyatta, appointed him assistant minister of economic planning and development. Two years later he was made full minister of commerce and industry and in 1969 began what was to become the longest term in office for a Kenyan minister of finance (1969–82). In this role he oversaw a period of relative economic prosperity. He was also minister of economic planning from 1970 until 1978 and home affairs minister from 1978 to 1988.

In addition to his ministerial posts Kibaki was chosen by Moi to be vice president in 1978, when Moi himself succeeded Kenyatta in the presidency. Kibaki's relationship with Moi began to deteriorate during the 1980s, however. Having lost his responsibilities for the finance portfolio in 1982, he was dismissed as vice president in 1988 and also shunted from the ministry of home affairs to the health ministry, where he remained until 1991.

The introduction of multipartyism in Kenya was forced by popular discontent in 1991 and Kibaki, despite being a former vice president of KANU, took his cue to leave the ruling party. Instead he established the Democratic Party (DP) in December 1991, but was viewed with great suspicion by some who suggested that he was part of a government plot to split the opposition vote. Indeed, opposition rivalries boosted Moi in his successful re-election bids in 1992 and 1997. In the first of these elections Kibaki came a disappointing third, but rose to a surprising second in 1997, gaining over 30% of the vote. From 1998 he was the official leader of the opposition.

Corruption became the watchword of Moi's final term in office and the one-time popularity of the president and the ruling KANU slumped. Kibaki used his 'clean' image to capitalize on the situation. He renamed the DP as the NAK and drew opposition forces into his umbrella NARC just months before the December 2002 elections. In this poll he faced Uhuru Kenyatta, the son of founding president Jomo Kenyatta, whose selection as KANU candidate had been forced through by President Moi to the chagrin of many prominent party members. Kibaki gained a clear 63% victory in the first round and NARC won a majority in simultaneous legislative elections. He was inaugurated on 30 December and promised an end to the country's everyday corruption as his first priority.

Within a month the civil service had been purged of many of Moi's appointees, and in September a committee investigating the judiciary reported that half of all judges and a third of magistrates were corrupt. Kibaki suspended several senior judges, including two-thirds of the Court of Appeals, Kenya's highest court. However, Kibaki's credibility suffered a severe blow in December when he announced that despite estimates that Moi's regime had embezzled as much as US$4,000 million, Moi himself would not be prosecuted, in recognition of the peaceful transfer of power.

A process of constitutional review, begun under Moi, caused internal rifts in the NARC when Liberal Democratic Party (LDP) members backed proposals to reduce the executive powers of the presidency and introduce the post of prime minister. The 30 June 2004 deadline for the introduction of the new constitution had to be postponed—and on that day, Kibaki announced a new cabinet, demoting several LDP ministers and bringing in a few opposition ministers from KANU and the two wings of the Forum for the Restoration of Democracy. The draft constitution was finally approved by legislators in July 2005—still with provision for a prime minister, though the president would retain most power. The constitution will be put to referendum in November 2005.

Meanwhile, Kibaki's own government was becoming mired in corruption allegations. In July 2004 the European Union, USA and Japan threatened to cut off aid. Kibaki responded by creating a national committee to fight corruption. The International Monetary Fund (IMF) subsequently released a loan that had been withheld, but the UK high commissioner in November launched another stinging attack, alleging that Kenyan officials were collaborating with foreigners in the "massive looting" of funds. A further blow came in February 2005 when anti-corruption campaigner John Githongo resigned from the committee in frustration over a perceived lack of co-operation from government officials. A week later Kibaki sacked several ministers, but the country has made little progress towards his electoral pledge to clean up on graft.

KIRIBATI

Full name: The Republic of Kiribati.

Leadership structure: The head of state is a president (*beretitenti*), directly elected by universal adult suffrage from candidates selected by and from members of the legislature. The president's term of office is four years, with a maximum of three terms. In the event of a no-confidence vote in the president, a Council of State (composed of the chair of the Public Service Commission, the chief justice and the speaker of the House of Assembly) is formed and holds executive power until a new president is elected. The head of government is the president, who is responsible to the House of Assembly. The cabinet is appointed by the president.

President:		
	Teburoro Tito	1 Oct. 1994—28 March 2003
	Tion Otang (chair of the Council of State)	28 March 2003—10 July 2003
	Anote **TONG**	Since 10 July 2003

Legislature: The legislature is unicameral. The sole chamber, the House of Assembly (Maneaba ni Maungatabu), has 40 members directly elected for a four-year term, one appointed representative of the Banaban community (who live on Rabi Island, Fiji), and the attorney general.

Profile of the President:

Anote **TONG**

Anote Tong was elected president of Kiribati on 4 July 2003, beating his brother Harry Tong. He was sworn into office on 10 July. The son of a Chinese immigrant and a Gilbertese mother, he is a graduate of the London School of Economics.

Anote Tong was born in 1952, the son of a Chinese migrant who settled in the islands after the Second World War and a Gilbertese mother. He graduated from the London School of Economics with a master's degree in sea use law in 1988. Tong won the presidential election representing the opposition Pillars of Truth (Boutokaan Te Koaua—BTK) party in 2003 with a slim majority having stood against his brother, Harry Tong, of Protect the Maneaba (Maneaba Te Mauri—MTM), and Banuera Berina of the Protect Kiribati Party (Maurin Kiribati Pati—MKP).

The main issue during the campaign had been the respective roles of China and Taiwan, which had been competing for official UN recognition from the tiny island. Anote and Harry Tong's father had helped Chinese officials settle on the island when diplomatic relations were established in 1980. However, after Harry, a long-time MP, made repeated unheeded complaints about a Chinese satellite tracking station, both brothers drifted closer to Taiwan, not least because of the amount of cash offered by Taiwanese officials towards their campaign budgets. Harry had been passed over by his own party and had switched allegiance in order to run for the presidency, while Anote, remaining in Harry's old party, decided to run against him. The campaign got quite personal, with Anote criticizing Harry's lifestyle; Harry countered by freely admitting that he had had several wives and a large number of children.

Following his victory on 4 July 2003 Anote Tong established formal relations with Taiwan in November; China severed relations and vacated the tracking centre in December, also abandoning an unfinished sports facility, pulling out six doctors from the local hospital, and halting funding for i-Kiribati students in Beijing. Taiwan immediately stepped up to fill the gaps left by China's withdrawal. "As far as the people of Kiribati are concerned," said Tong, "they don't really care whether it's Taiwan or China…but they do care how it affects them, how it impacts their lives."

NORTH KOREA

Full name: The Democratic People's Republic of Korea.

Leadership structure: After the death of Kim Il Sung in 1994, the presidency remained vacant until an amendment to the constitution was approved by the legislature on 5 September 1998. While naming the dead Kim Il Sung as 'eternal president', and designating the chairmanship of the National Defence Commission as 'the highest post of the state', it provided that the chairman of the presidium of the Supreme People's Assembly would represent the state on formal occasions. The premier, elected by the Assembly, is head of government. The other members of the cabinet are appointed by the Assembly on the recommendation of the premier.

'Eternal President': Kim Il Sung   (deceased)

Chairman of the National Defence Commission:

     KIM Jong Il   Since 5 Sept. 1998

Chairman of the Presidium of the Supreme People's Assembly:

     KIM Yong Nam   Since 5 Sept. 1998

Premier: Hong Song Nam   5 Sept. 1998—3 Sept. 2003
      (acting from 21 Feb. 1997)

     PAK Pong Chu   Since 3 Sept. 2003

General Secretary of the Korean Workers' Party (KWP):

     KIM Jong Il   Since 8 Oct. 1997

Legislature: The legislature is unicameral. The sole chamber, the Supreme People's Assembly (Choe Go In Min Hoe Ui), has 687 members, elected from a single list of candidates for a five-year term.

Profile of the Chairman of the National Defence Commission:

KIM Jong Il

Kim Jong Il is the eldest son of the now deceased 'eternal president' Kim Il Sung. His presumed leadership role, following the death of his father in July 1994, was not immediately reflected in his formal assumption of top posts. It was not until

October 1997 that he became general secretary of the ruling Korean Workers'
Party (KWP) and nearly a year later that his post as chairman of the National
Defence Commission was formally designated as 'the highest post of the state'.
Kim Jong Il has championed 'Red Flag ideology', a loosely defined popularist
development of the juche *ideology which emphasizes national self-reliance and*
the special role of the leadership.

Kim Jong Il, the eldest son of Kim Il Sung, was born on 16 February 1942. There
are two versions of where this took place. The official version is that he was born
in an anti-Japanese guerrilla camp at Mount Paektu in North Korea (the site of
which is now visited as part of his cult of personality), and grew up lonely
because of his father's frequent absences owing to the duties of political
leadership. Others say he was born at a Soviet army camp in Vyatsk, near
Khabarovsk, the far-eastern region of the former Soviet Union, where his father
was being groomed by the Soviet military to set up and lead a communist party in
Korea.

Kim Jong Il is said to have attended several schools, including two in China
where he was taken for safety during the Korean War. In 1960 he graduated from
Namsan Senior High School. He learned to fly in East Germany, graduated in
political and economic sciences from Kim Il Sung University in Pyongyang in
1964, and entered politics after spending some time as a guidance worker.

Kim Jong Il's rise was predictably rapid as he was prepared for the succession by
his father, who was venerated in the North Korean state and party system as the
'great leader'. Starting as his father's personal secretary, he moved on to the
propaganda and agitation department and the party headquarters, was made
deputy director of culture and art, and secretary for organization and propaganda
in 1973. He was officially designated heir to Kim Il Sung in 1974 when he was
put in charge of party operations against South Korea.

In 1975 Kim Jong Il acquired the title 'dear leader'. This remains the best known
of his epithets abroad (where he also has a reputation as a playboy), although
North Koreans have been encouraged successively to regard him as 'guiding
leader' (1983), 'great guiding leader' (1986), 'unprecedented great man' (1994)
and latterly 'outstanding leader'.

In October 1980, after the conclusion of what was believed to have been a power
struggle over the succession, Kim Jong Il's position was confirmed by his
election to a new presidium of the KWP politburo, the innermost leadership
circle. He also joined the party secretariat (headed by his father as general
secretary) and the military commission, although it was generally believed that he
could not rely on the strength of his support within the armed forces. In
confusingly vague terminology, he was named in 1991 as leader of the party (and
supreme commander of the armed forces, with the rank of marshal).

During the 1980s in particular, Kim Jong Il was linked directly with a number of
acts of state-sponsored terrorism, notably the bombing in 1983 which killed 17

members of a top-level South Korean government delegation in Burma (now Myanmar), and the 1987 bombing of a Korean Airlines plane. There was speculation at this time about his health and stability, and suggestions that Kim Il Sung was displeased by unpredictable actions which he had not himself approved.

When Kim Il Sung died in July 1994, the expectation of a dynastic succession was apparently confirmed by the announcement that Kim Jong Il was taking over all his functions. However, there were no formal appointments until he became party general secretary in October 1997, and his public appearances were unexpectedly infrequent. This encouraged the suggestion that he was ill and that a power struggle was under way, masked by the official explanation that posts were not being filled formally out of respect and mourning for Kim Il Sung. The situation was not clarified until September 1998, when the Supreme People's Assembly formally designated his post as chairman of the National Defence Commission as the 'highest post of the state' (although it also provided that the state would be 'represented on formal occasions' not by him but by the chairman of the Assembly's presidium).

Known increasingly as a recluse, Kim Jong Il has had mixed success in his dealings with the outside world. Relations with South Korea entered what at first promised to be a new era in 2000 when Kim met his South Korean counterpart, President Kim Dae-jung, in June in the first North–South summit since the Korean War. Kim Dae-jung was surprised by a personal reception given by Kim Jong Il at a lavish ceremony at Pyongyang airport and the two leaders signed a landmark agreement which stated eventual reunification to be the ultimate goal and set out plans to reunite separated families, and initiate economic and diplomatic ties. However, the path to peace since then has become confused, with meetings cancelled and projects halted through lack of finance and commitment. In 2001 and 2002 Kim Jong Il made two trips to neighbouring Russia on board special trains; prior to this he had made only one foreign visit (to China) since 1997. He has made two subsequent trips, also to China,

The USA has characterized Kim Jong Il as an erratic and dangerous leader, and has become increasingly perturbed by North Korea's missile development programme and its nuclear research efforts. Relations with the USA sank to a new low following the inauguration of US president George W. Bush in 2001. Kim Jong Il and the North Korean government were horrified to be included in Bush's infamous identification of an 'axis of evil' states sponsoring international terrorism. As tensions mounted, Kim Jong Il reacted with a growing attitude of defiance.

The issue of North Korea's nuclear power programme and the link to nuclear weapons proliferation continued to overshadow all previous advances in opening up the north of the traditional 'hermit kingdom'. Tensions heightened at the beginning of 2005: South Korea in December 2004 had fired on North Korean ships that had entered its waters; Japan threatened economic sanctions over the North's failure to co-operate with the investigation into the fate of Japanese citizens kidnapped in the 1970s and 1980s—North Korea retorted that it would treat the imposition of sanctions as a declaration of war; incoming US secretary of state Condoleezza Rice listed North Korea as an 'outpost of tyranny'; and in February North Korea confirmed to the world that it did possess nuclear weapons. However, by the time six-nation talks reopened in mid-2005 there was a much more conciliatory air. Kim announced that he wanted to rid the peninsula of nuclear weapons and requested a full peace treaty with the USA, which responded by recognizing North Korea as a sovereign state and pledging that it had no intention of invading. Meanwhile, South Korea promised to supply desperately needed electricity if the nuclear weapons programme was ended.

Kim Jong Il married Kim Yong Suk in 1973, and they had one son and two daughters before becoming estranged. He is also rumoured to have a daughter by a previous marriage. He then had a long-term relationship with Ko Yong Hi, whom he may have married. They had two sons, who are likely contenders for the succession along with an older half-brother by a former mistress, Sung Hye Rim; her reported presence in Europe in 1996 contributed to press speculation about the impact of defections on the ruling elite. Ko died in 2004, since when Kim has become even more reclusive.

Profile of the Chairman of the Presidium of the Supreme People's Assembly:

KIM Yong Nam

Kim Yong Nam has worked in the foreign affairs department of the ruling Korean Workers' Party (KWP) since 1970. A reclusive and media-shy figure, he was appointed as chairman of the presidium of the Supreme People's Assembly in September 1998, making him North Korea's representative on official occasions. However, he is entirely overshadowed by Kim Jong Il.

Kim Yong Nam was born on 4 February 1928 in North Korea. He graduated from the Kim Il Sung University and then continued his studies in Moscow. He joined the KWP in November 1970 and was appointed chairman of the committee for cultural relations and foreign countries. In 1972 he became vice minister of foreign affairs. Rising steadily through the party hierarchy, he became a secretary in 1975, a political commissar in 1977 and a politburo member in October 1980. He then became director of international development in the KWP and chairman of the committee for Korean reunification.

In 1982 he led the country's delegation to the General Assembly of the UN, and in December 1983 he was appointed as deputy prime minister and minister of foreign affairs. He was also chairman of the central committee of the General Federation of Trade Unions of Korea. In July 1997 at a memorial service to mark the third anniversary of the death of Kim Il Sung, it was Kim Yong Nam who announced that the period of mourning was now over. A recluse who rarely gives interviews, he was seen making frequent domestic speeches at this time, and also made a number of foreign visits in an attempt to secure food and aid for the country. His election by the Supreme People's Assembly in September 1998, to chair its presidium, made him the country's representative on formal occasions. He travelled widely as North Korea's envoy to the outside world, but his visits were rarely remarked upon, in contrast to the attention given to Kim Jong Il's rare trips beyond North Korea.

Profile of the Premier:

PAK Pong Chu

Pak Pong Chu is a former chemicals minister who was appointed prime minister on 3 September 2003. Many analysts say that his appointment could indicate a willingness on the part of the North Korean elite to begin to undertake serious economic reform.

Pak Pong Chu, born in 1939, started out as the manager of a food company in Ryongchon in North Pyongan province, and then became vice minister of light industry. After his appointment as chemicals minister, he took part in an economic study tour to South Korea in 2002 where he impressed his hosts with his keenness and willingness to learn.

Pak was appointed prime minister on 3 September 2003, replacing Hong Song Nam, leading to international hopes that North Korea had finally appointed a technocrat to high office. However, Pak has been constrained by the prioritization of military requirements and an economy that has yet to recover from the systemic shocks of the 1990s and an industrial infrastructure still little more than rust belt in huge swathes of the northeast.

Nonetheless, Pak's influence appears to be growing. Seasoned North Korea watchers noted that Pak appeared alongside Kim Jong Il on a recent trip to the Russian embassy and on several appearances of the 'dear leader' at cultural events. It is highly unusual in North Korea for a bureaucrat such as Pak to accompany Kim at public events, real power being retained by the military and the Korean Workers' Party. However, Kim appears to have decided to pursue economic development and to have chosen Pak as his 'chief economic policymaker'; this interpretation was reinforced in 2005 when Pak paid an official visit to China's financial hub, Shanghai.

SOUTH KOREA

Full name: The Republic of Korea.

Leadership structure: The head of state is a president, directly elected by universal adult suffrage. The president's term of office is five years, not renewable. The president appoints the prime minister, with the approval of the National Assembly, and the other members of the State Council (cabinet). The prime minister is head of government.

President:	Kim Dae-jung	25 Feb. 1998—25 Feb. 2003
	ROH Moo-hyun	Since 25 Feb. 2003
	Goh Kun (acting)	12 March 2004—14 May 2004
Prime Minister:	Kim Jong-pil (acting from 3 March 1998)	17 Aug. 1998—13 Jan. 2000
	Park Tae-joon	13 Jan. 2000—19 May 2000
	vacant	19 May 2000—22 May 2000
	Lee Han-dong (acting from 23 May 2000)	29 June 2000—11 July 2002
	Chang Sang (acting)	11 July 2002—31 July 2002
	vacant	31 July 2002—9 Aug. 2002
	Chang Dae-whan (acting)	9 Aug. 2002—28 Aug. 2002
	vacant	28 Aug. 2002—10 Sept. 2002
	Kim Suk-soo (acting from 10 Sept. 2002)	5 Oct. 2002—26 Feb. 2003
	Goh Kun	26 Feb. 2003—25 May 2004
	Lee Hun-jai (acting)	25 May 2004—30 June 2004
	LEE Hae-chan	Since 30 June 2004

Legislature: The legislature is unicameral. The sole chamber, the National Assembly (Kuk Hoe), has 299 members, directly elected for a four-year term.

Profile of the President:

ROH Moo-hyun

Roh Moo-hyun succeeded Kim Dae-jung as president of South Korea in February 2003, following his election the previous December as candidate of the Millennium Democratic Party (MDP). Popularly seen as a champion of the poor, he won renown as a human rights lawyer when he prosecuted former top officials during televised corruption trials in 1988. He has continued Kim's policy of negotiation with the erratic North Korean government but has lost popularity for taking an independent line, branching away from the US position, and over his management of the economy. He spent two months suspended from office in 2004 while the National Assembly tried to impeach him for violating his political neutrality.

Roh Moo-hyun was born on 6 August 1946 in rural Gimhae, in southeastern Korea, to a poor peasant family. After graduating from high school in 1966 he was unable to afford formal tertiary education and instead supported himself with menial labour through self-study. He married his childhood sweetheart Gwon Yang-suk in 1971 and they have one son and one daughter. In 1975 he passed his Bar exam and began his own law practice in Busan in 1978.

In 1981 Roh took on the case of one of over 20 students who had been arrested and brutally tortured by the military authorities. Known as the Boolim Incident, the case confirmed Roh as a prominent human rights advocate and as a member of the strengthening pro-democracy movement. In 1987 he was arrested and jailed for three weeks for aiding striking workers during the 'June Struggle' at the Daewoo docks. He moved into the country's newly democratized political sphere in 1988 when he was elected to parliament for the Unified Democratic Party of future president Kim Young Sam. The televised trials that year of former military officials brought Roh to political and public attention for his detailed and thorough questioning. During the 1990s he moved between parliamentary and legal work as he lost his seat in the 1992 election but returned to the chamber in a 1998 by-election.

Despite failing to win a parliamentary seat in the 2000 legislative elections, Roh was made a member of the MDP's Supreme Council and served as maritime affairs and fisheries minister in the cabinet of President Kim Dae-jung between August 2000 and March 2001. Six months later he declared his bid to gain the MDP nomination for the 2002 presidential elections. Once selected, his campaign was boosted when he proved the popular victor of a televised debate with fellow contender Chung Mung-joon and was accepted as the single liberal candidate. However, Chung withdrew his support just hours before polling began in protest over Roh's suggestion that if elected he would seek to mediate between the USA and North Korea, rather than simply backing the USA. In the event Roh won 49% of the vote.

His presidency quickly faced attacks for his indeterminate stance on North Korea and the struggling economy—Roh himself even admitted that others could do his job better. A close friend and former adviser was accused of accepting a million-dollar bribe, and Roh was condemned for vetoing an independent probe into his electoral funding—though he pledged to co-operate fully with the official investigation. Within a year of his election he proposed a referendum to endorse his mandate; this was not held, but Roh announced instead that he would resign if the sum of his party's illegal funds was found to be more than one-tenth of those of the opposition Grand National Party.

Meanwhile, his supporters had broken away from the MDP and formed the Uri (Our) Party, which became the ruling party. Roh himself resigned from the MDP in September 2003, but did not join the Uri Party. However, his involvement in electioneering for the Uri Party ahead of the April 2004 legislative election provoked his suspension from office by the National Assembly in March for up to six months pending a ruling by the Constitutional Court on his impeachment. Prime Minister Goh Kun became acting head of state. The following night as many as 35,000 people gathered for a candle-lit protest in the capital Seoul in support of Roh. Two months later the Constitutional Court ruled that Roh had violated his political neutrality, but that the charges were not sufficiently grave to remove him from office. Roh was reinstated, his position strengthened by electoral success for the Uri Party, which had become the first liberal party in the country's history to win a majority in the National Assembly. Roh joined the Uri Party a few days later.

Though Roh has deviated from staunchly following US policy in relations with North Korea, he did send troops to Iraq in February 2004, making South Korea the third-largest contributor to the occupying force there, behind the USA and the UK. He stressed that it was important for South Korea to act on its close diplomatic relationship with the USA.

Profile of the Prime Minister:

LEE Hae-chan

A former student activist, Lee Hae-chan was nominated as prime minister following his Uri (Our) Party's victory in general elections in 2004 and was confirmed on 30 June. He had previously served as minister of education, pushing through unpopular reforms that his opponents believe still cripple the public education system. The post of premier is usually toothless, but many commentators feel that President Roh Moo-hyun's decision to nominate Lee indicates that he may have more freedom to act.

Lee Hae-chan was born on 10 July 1952 in Cheonyang, South Chungcheong province. He graduated from Yongsan High School in Seoul in 1971. A student activist, he was jailed twice within the next ten years. He finally graduated with a degree in sociology from Seoul National University in 1985. Lee is married to Kim Jung-ok and they have one daughter.

In 1987 Lee became one of the cofounders of the Peace and Democracy Party (PDP), which became the main opposition party under Kim Dae-jung following the 1988 elections to the National Assembly—the first under South Korea's new, democratic constitution. He was elected as a delegate to the Assembly and became deputy floor leader for the PDP, though by 1991 the party had reorganized itself into the New Democratic Party (NDP). He was re-elected in 1992; later that year the NDP merged with the Democratic Party and took the latter's name.

In 1995 most of the Democratic Party followed Kim Dae-jung into the National Congress for New Politics (NCNP) and the Democratic Party disappeared. Lee became vice mayor for political affairs for Seoul, and a year later became the chief of the general election planning team of the NCNP. He was re-elected once again that year and was appointed chairman of the NCNP's policy committee. In 1997 the party succeeded in getting Kim Dae-jung elected as president in the first peaceful transfer of power to the opposition in South Korea's history.

The following year Lee was appointed as minister of education. During his term he forced through several unpopular reforms intended to reduce private education spending. He also cut the teachers' retirement age from 65 to 62. In 2000 his party changed its name yet again, to the Millennium Democratic Party (MDP), and Lee was re-elected for the fourth term in succession. Following the victory of MDP candidate Roh Moo-hyun in presidential elections in December 2002, Lee and many others of Roh's followers left the party to form the Uri Party. In April 2004 Lee was re-elected for the fifth time to the National Assembly, and the Uri Party became the first liberal party in South Korea ever to win a majority. He was nominated as prime minister on 9 June, following the resignation of Goh Kun who no longer felt able to work under Roh, having served as acting head of state during Roh's two-month suspension on impeachment charges. Lee was confirmed in post by the National Assembly on 29 June and took office the following day.

The premiership had long been considered a merely ceremonial post under the traditionally strong presidency, but Roh has pledged to give Lee much more autonomy than most prime ministers have enjoyed. Lee is likely to prefer being number two in any case; throughout his career he has been known as a back-room strategist, though unafraid to push through unpopular measures. A populist Lee is not; Roh's choice of premier could indicate serious intention of domestic reforms.

KUWAIT

Full name: The State of Kuwait.

Leadership structure: The head of state is an amir, chosen from among the ruling family. The amir exercises executive power through the Council of Ministers, which is headed by the prime minister.

Amir:	Sheikh **JABER** al-Ahmad al-Jaber al-Sabah	Since 31 Dec. 1977
Crown Prince:	Sheikh **SAAD** al-Abdullah al-Salem al-Sabah	Since 31 Jan. 1978
Prime Minister:	Sheikh Saad al-Abdullah al-Salem al-Sabah	8 Feb. 1978—13 July 2003
	Sheikh **SABAH** al-Ahmad al-Jaber al-Sabah	Since 13 July 2003

Legislature: The legislature is unicameral. The sole chamber, the National Assembly (Majlis al-Umma), has 50 members, directly elected for a four-year term. Women were granted the right to vote in elections for the National Assembly and to stand as candidates in May 2005. Cabinet ministers who are not already members of the National Assembly are ex officio members of it.

Profile of the Amir:

Sheikh **JABER** al-Ahmad al-Jaber al-Sabah

Sheikh Jaber is the 13th amir from the al-Sabah family, the Sunni Muslim ruling dynasty since 1756. Ousted by the Iraqi invasion of August 1990, he was restored to power seven months later by the forces of the US-led alliance in the Gulf War. He agreed to an element of liberalization in his autocratic regime, holding legislative elections and bringing some opposition National Assembly members into a cabinet previously made up entirely of members of the royal family.

Jaber al-Ahmad al-Jaber al-Sabah was born on 29 June 1928, educated at the Mubarakiya, Ahmadiya and Sharqiya schools, and tutored privately in English, religion and the sciences. He started his public life in 1949 as chief of public security in the oilfields area, a post he held until 1959, when he was made head of the finance department. After Kuwait gained its independence in 1961, the finance department became the ministry of finance and economy, and Sheikh Jaber was appointed its first minister. In 1965 he was appointed prime minister, and on 31 May 1966 he was elected crown prince by the National Assembly. Proclaimed amir of Kuwait on 31 December 1977, he was unanimously given the pledge of allegiance on 1 January 1978.

In the late 1980s the amir became a member of the board of directors of the Kuwait Investment Authority, a member of the higher planning council and chairman of the committee for measures to activate the economy.

When Kuwait was invaded by Iraq in August 1990 the al-Sabah family went into exile, returning on 14 March 1991 after the country had been liberated and Iraqi forces defeated by a US-led alliance. On 20 April the first cabinet since the liberation of Kuwait was announced by amiri decree, and on 9 July the amir opened the second session of the advisory National Council, relaying his thanks to those countries which had come to Kuwait's aid. In response to pressure for a measure of democratization, elections were held (on a nonparty basis) in October 1992 to the National Assembly, which had been in abeyance since the amir dissolved the previous Assembly in 1986. Some opposition Assembly members were then brought in to the Council of Ministers.

The amir issued a decree in 1999 to give women the vote, but it was repeatedly rejected by the National Assembly. A bill was finally passed in 2005, and the country's first female cabinet minister was appointed.

When the USA decided in 2003 to topple the regime of Saddam Hussein in Iraq, the amir supported the coalition and Kuwait's military bases were used to launch the invasion—a symbolic reversal of the 1990 invasion of Kuwait.

Sheikh Jaber has had about 13 wives, 21 sons and 18 daughters. Some concern about the succession was raised in September 2001 when the amir was flown to the UK to receive treatment for a mild brain haemorrhage. However, he soon returned and made a full recovery. In 2005 he travelled to the USA for two operations on his leg. Power traditionally alternates between the al-Jaber and al-Salem branches of the al-Sabah dynasty, but the succession could pass directly from the amir to his half-brother Sheikh Sabah, who is currently prime minister and handling day-to-day affairs—though he is already in his mid-seventies.

Profile of the Crown Prince:

Sheikh **SAAD** al-Abdullah al-Salem al-Sabah

Sheikh Saad, second cousin of the current amir, has been crown prince of Kuwait since January 1978, and was appointed prime minister the following month. Due to ill health he was relieved of the post of prime minister in July 2003, the first time that the role had been separated from that of the crown prince since independence in 1961.

Saad al-Abdullah al-Salem al-Sabah was born in 1929, the eldest son of Sheikh Abdullah al-Salem al-Sabah. He was educated at government schools in Kuwait, and in 1951 went to the UK to attend Hendon College to take a postgraduate course on police and security affairs. Returning to Kuwait in 1954, he held various posts in the police and public security department and was later appointed deputy chief of police and public security. Sheikh Saad is married to Sheikha Latifah Fahd al-Sabah, and has one son and four daughters.

Kuwait became fully independent from the UK in June 1961, with Sheikh Saad's father as amir, and Sheikh Saad entered the new cabinet as interior minister in January 1962. In 1964 he also became defence minister, retaining both posts on the accession of his uncle Sheikh Sabah the following year. His election as crown prince in 1978, and his appointment as prime minister, followed the accession of his second cousin Sheikh Jaber, only one year his senior, as amir.

Sheikh Saad was reappointed prime minister on 3 March 1985 after the election of a new Assembly. This Assembly was dissolved the following year, reinforcing the concentration of power in the hands of the ruling al-Sabah family, after disputes between elected and ex officio Assembly members over internal security and fiscal issues.

When Kuwait was invaded by Iraq in August 1990 the al-Sabah family went into exile, returning on 14 March 1991 after the country had been liberated and the Iraqi forces defeated by a US-led alliance. Sheikh Saad was consistently reappointed after elections in October 1992 and 1996 and July 1999, to the disappointment of Kuwaitis hoping for fresh leadership to reflect the election of government opponents to the Assembly and their inclusion in the cabinet. He was also reinstated after he resigned in March 1998 during conflict with the Assembly. Such confrontations have become more regular as the Assembly has voiced its lack of confidence in the ruling family's government.

However, since an operation on his colon in 1997, his health has continued deteriorating, and following the elections in July 2003 he was replaced as prime minister by the amir's half-brother Sheikh Sabah. He was hospitalized again in June 2005 for a blood condition. He retains the position of crown prince, but given his ailing condition it is possible that the succession could bypass Sheikh Saad and go directly to the amir's half-brother, despite the tradition of it alternating between the al-Jaber and al-Salem branches of the al-Sabah dynasty.

Profile of the Prime Minister:

Sheikh **SABAH** al-Ahmad al-Jaber al-Sabah

Sheikh Sabah al-Ahmad al-Jaber al-Sabah was appointed prime minister of Kuwait on 13 July 2003, the first time that the role had been separated from that of crown prince since independence in 1961. Sheikh Sabah is considered to be something of a progressive, favouring privatization, globalization and improving relations with other Arab states. His appointment, and the separation of the two roles, was considered an important step towards political reform.

Sheikh Sabah al-Ahmad al-Jaber al-Sabah was born on 6 June 1929 and was the fourth son of the former amir of Kuwait Sheikh Ahmad al-Jaber al-Sabah. He is half-brother to the current amir and a widower, the father of three sons and one daughter. Sheikh Sabah was educated at the al-Mubarakiya school in Kuwait and by various private tutors in the palace. The outbreak of the Second World War prevented Sheikh Sabah from completing his studies as planned in the UK under which Kuwait then functioned as a protectorate.

Sheikh Sabah joined the department of press and publications in 1955 and became minister of guidance and information in January 1962. A year later he was appointed foreign minister, a post in which he was to remain until the 1991 Gulf War. From December 1965 to February 1967 he was also minister of finance and acting minister of oil; in 1978 he served as minister of the interior, after which he was appointed deputy prime minister, a post which he also retained until 1991. Between 1982 and 1985 Sheikh Sabah was minister of information in addition to his other posts. At the end of the Gulf War he was briefly left out of the cabinet, but returned in 1992 as first deputy prime minister and minister of foreign affairs.

In 2003 the amir named Sheikh Sabah as the new prime minister. His predecessor, Sheikh Saad al-Abdullah al-Salem al-Sabah retained the title of crown prince, the first time that the two titles had been separated. Sheikh Sabah was already the country's de facto leader, as both the amir and the crown prince were in poor health. Observers speculated that the move was a first response to continued calls for political liberalization in the kingdom; though Kuwait was the first country in the Gulf to hold parliamentary elections four decades ago, political parties are still banned. Sheikh Sabah supports privatization and globalization and is keen to improve relations with other Arab nations, even those that supported the 1990 Iraqi invasion of Kuwait.

KYRGYZSTAN

Full name: The Kyrgyz Republic.

Leadership structure: The head of state is a president, directly elected by universal adult suffrage. The president's term of office is five years and is renewable once only, according to the 1994 Constitution. The prime minister is head of government. The president nominates the prime minister (who must be approved by the Supreme Council) and the other members of the government.

President: Askar Akayev   28 Oct. 1990—11 April 2005
(de facto deposed 24 March 2005)

Ishenbay Kadyrbekov (acting)   24 March 2005—25 March 2005

Kurmanbek **BAKIYEV**   Since 14 August 2005
(acting from 25 March 2005)

Prime Minister: Amangeldy Muraliyev   21 April 1999—21 Dec. 2000
(acting from 12 April 1999, and from 11 Dec. 2000)

Kurmanbek Bakiyev   21 Dec. 2000—22 May 2002

Nikolay Tanayev   30 May 2002—24 March 2005
(acting from 22 May 2002)

Kurmanbek Bakiyev   28 March 2005—15 Aug. 2005
(acting from 25 March 2005)

Medetbek Kerimkulov (acting) 20 June 2005—10 July 2005

Felix **KULOV**   Since 1 Sept. 2005
(acting from 15 Aug. 2005)

Legislature: The legislature, the Supreme Council (Jogorku Kenesh), is unicameral. It has 75 members directly elected for a five-year term.

Profile of the President:

Kurmanbek **BAKIYEV**

Kurmanbek Bakiyev became interim president of Kyrgyzstan on 25 March 2005 and was confirmed in this post following elections in July. He was chosen as interim leader by the country's parliament following the departure of President Askar Akayev, who fled after a wave of political demonstrations against alleged vote rigging. Formerly prime minister under Akayev, Bakiyev had resigned in 2002 in protest over the shooting of opposition demonstrators, and subsequently emerged as leader of the opposition movement which toppled Akayev.

Kurmanbek Saliyevich Bakiyev was born on 1 August 1949 in Masadan (now Teyit) in the Dzhalal-Abad region of what was then the Kyrgyz Soviet Socialist Republic. He graduated from the Kuybyshev Polytechnic Institute in 1972, having specialized in electrical engineering; after military service, he worked in various electronics factories across Kyrgyzstan. He is married with two children.

Bakiyev first entered politics as Kyrgyzstan approached independence. From 1990 until 1991 he was committee secretary for the Kok-Jangak city Communist Party and chairman of the city council, going on to become deputy chairman of the Dzhalal-Abad regional Council of People's Deputies. He rose quickly over the next decade of Kyrgyz independence to become head of the Toguz-Torouz regional administration and deputy chairman of the national State Property Fund. In 1995 he was appointed governor of the Dzhalal-Abad oblast (region), and was governor of Chui oblast from April 1997 until December 2000.

Bakiyev was appointed prime minister on 21 December 2000. He settled in comfortably to his new role, reversing his predecessor's decision to privatize the state-run energy company Kyrgyzenergo. However, in 2002 he resigned after riot police shot dead a number of protestors who were demonstrating against President Askar Akayev in the southern city of Aksy. Following the incident he joined the opposition People's Movement of Kyrgyzstan.

In February 2005 the first round of parliamentary elections sparked countrywide protests over government interference. The demonstrations began in the south, separated from the capital Bishkek physically by a mountain range and culturally by ethnic and religious differences. After the second round in March, the protests finally reached the capital and demonstrators seized government buildings and unleashed a wave of looting, initially aimed at businesses thought to be owned by Akayev and his family, who had fled to Russia. As the chaos died down Bakiyev emerged as leader of the uprising and was appointed by the outgoing parliament as acting president and prime minister on 25 March. An emerging standoff was ended by the decision of the incoming parliament to confirm Bakiyev in both posts. His cabinet was sworn in on 28 March, and shortly afterwards Akayev resigned. New presidential elections confirmed Bakiyev in his post on 10 July, and he was sworn in on 14 August.

Profile of the Prime Minister:

Felix **KULOV**

Felix Kulov is a political activist and politician who played a key role in the tumultuous events surrounding Kyrgyz independence. Having resigned from the government in the late 1990s he was arrested and sentenced to a total of 17 years in prison. However, the revolution of March 2005 saw him freed; following some initial jousting with interim president Kurmanbek Bakiyev, Kulov threw his weight behind Bakiyev's presidential bid, in return for which Bakiyev pledged to appoint him prime minister. He was appointed on 15 August and confirmed on 1 September.

Felix Sharshenbayevich Kulov was born on 29 October 1948 in Frunze, now Bishkek, in northern Kyrgyzstan. His mother worked in the theatre while his father was a colonel in the army. He joined the police force in 1967, and graduated from the Omsk School of Police in 1971 and the police academy in 1978. He went on to work in various positions in the department of the interior, and in 1987 was appointed as deputy minister of the interior. Kulov is married with two daughters.

In 1990 he was appointed military commander of Frunze, and the same year he lost a bid to become chairman of the Supreme Soviet. Nonetheless he played a key role in the turbulent years of the early 1990s; as interior minister he helped hold the country together during the abortive putsch against then-Soviet leader Mikhail Gorbachev and against a constant backdrop of incipient civil war. He was appointed vice president in 1992, overseeing the launch of the new Kyrgyz currency, the som. He became national security minister in 1997 and mayor of Bishkek in 1998, but the following year resigned in an open letter to President Askar Akayev accusing the latter of connivance in acts incompatible with democracy and the rule of law.

In July 1999, with other like-minded Kyrgyz politicians, Kulov formed the 'Ar-Namys' (Dignity) movement and the following February announced his intention to run for president. He was quickly arrested and charged with abetting a crime, exceeding authority and abuse of office, though he was acquitted in August. Following the presidential election of October 2000, he was again arrested, this time on charges of abuse of office, and in January 2001 was sentenced to seven years' imprisonment. The following December he was sentenced to another ten years for embezzlement and barred from public office for three years after the completion of his sentence.

Following the Kyrgyz revolution of March 2005 and the ouster of Akayev, Kulov was released from prison and immediately appointed head of national security in the interim government, though he resigned the position almost as quickly, saying that order had been restored. Observers regarded this as a shrewd political move, intended to distance himself from the interim administration of Kurmanbek Bakiyev while positioning himself for a potential presidential bid. In the event, however, the two men struck a deal to avoid a divisive campaign, and Kulov pledged his support to Bakiyev's presidential bid in return for the latter's pledge to appoint Kulov as prime minister. Bakiyev won the election in July, was sworn in the following month, and Kulov was confirmed as prime minister by the Kyrgyz parliament on 1 September.

LAOS

Full name: The Lao People's Democratic Republic.

Leadership structure: The head of state is a president, elected by the National Assembly. The president's term of office is five years. The head of government is the prime minister, who is appointed by the president, although it is the sole and ruling party, the Lao People's Revolutionary Party (LPRP), which is described as the 'leading nucleus' of the political system. The Council of Ministers is appointed by the president.

President: Gen. **KHAMTAY** Siphandone   Since 24 Feb. 1998

Prime Minister: Gen. Sisavat Keobounphanh   24 Feb. 1998—27 March 2001

                 BOUNNHANG Vorachit   Since 27 March 2001

President of the Lao People's Revolutionary Party (LPRP):

                 Gen. **KHAMTAY** Siphandone   Since 24 Nov. 1992

Legislature: The legislature is unicameral. The sole chamber, the National Assembly (Sapha Heng Xat), has 109 members directly elected in single-party elections for a five-year term.

Profile of the President:

Gen. **KHAMTAY** Siphandone

Gen. Khamtay Siphandone, a veteran communist fighter and stalwart of the Lao People's Revolutionary Party (LPRP), was elected as prime minister by the National Assembly in 1991. He greatly strengthened his position in the leadership the following year when he became party chairman. It was evident that his authority surpassed that of the then state president, Nouhak Phoumsavanh, and since 1998 Khamtay has combined the party chairmanship with the state presidency.

Khamtay Siphandone was born on 8 February 1924 in Houa Khong village, Champasak Province. He is married to Thongvanh Siphandone; they have two sons and three daughters. From the early 1950s he was a prominent member of the insurgent Lao Patriotic Front (LPF), chairing its control committee from 1952 until 1954. Between 1955 and 1956 he was a member of the general staff of the Pathet Lao, the LPF's armed forces, and in 1960 he became its commander-in-chief, leading the military struggle in the protracted civil war until the establishment of the communist People's Democratic Republic in late 1975. Between 1975 and 1991 he was deputy prime minister and minister of national defence.

In 1982 Khamtay became part of the nine-member secretariat of the LPRP, the former Lao People's Party which had been the dominant force in the LPF. His position on the 11-member politburo was confirmed at the party's fifth congress in March 1991. Upon the adoption of the new constitution that August, veteran leader Khaysone Phomvihane moved up from chairing the Council of Ministers to the new executive presidency, leaving the way open for Khamtay to succeed him as prime minister and head of government.

When Khaysone died in November 1992, creating vacancies in both the state and party presidency, the state presidency went to the erstwhile 'number three', Nouhak Phoumsavanh, while Khamtay became LPRP president. Khamtay was re-elected unanimously to the party presidency at the sixth LPRP congress in March 1996 and became vice president, whereas Nouhak Phoumsavanh was relegated from the politburo to the advisory council of 'old guard' leaders. Khamtay's ascendancy was confirmed in February 1998 when the newly re-elected National Assembly voted him state president. He was reappointed party chairman in March 2001 and state president in April 2002.

Khamtay represents the continuing importance of the civil war generation, holding the top posts while younger cadres compete for position and the country faces the immense challenges of economic restructuring. Khamtay's cautious leadership, and the determination that economic liberalization should not be accompanied by any relaxation of the party's political grip, have not prevented major moves towards opening up the economy to market forces.

Profile of the Prime Minister:

BOUNNHANG Vorachit

Bounnhang Vorachit was a prominent member of the Pathet Lao armed independence movement, having joined the liberation struggle in 1952 at the age of 14. Later becoming a regional governor and then mayor of the capital, Vientiane, in the mid-1990s, he became a member of the politburo of the ruling Lao People's Revolutionary Party (LPRP) in 1996 and was appointed to the cabinet at the same time. His elevation to the premiership was decided at the LPRP's seventh congress in March 2001.

Bounnhang Vorachit was born on 15 August 1937 in Na village in the Savannakhet region of southern Laos which was then under French colonial rule. Dropping out of school, he joined the burgeoning communist Lao People's Party in 1952 and was immediately drafted into its armed wing (the basis for the future

Pathet Lao). For the rest of the violent struggle to create a communist state in Laos, Bounnhang divided his time between serving in the command structure of the Pathet Lao and studying at military colleges in communist Viet Nam. He is married to Khammeung Vorachit and they have three sons and two daughters.

In 1980 Bounnhang returned from his last study trip to Viet Nam and capped his military career by being appointed political chief of the Central Armed Force. Two years later he switched to civilian administration when he was made governor of Savannakhet province and was promoted to the LPRP's central committee. He held the governorship for ten years before becoming mayor of Vientiane in 1993. In 1996 he climbed further up the LPRP hierarchy and was admitted to the party's politburo as deputy prime minister and chairman of the Laos–Viet Nam co-operation committee. In 1999 he was awarded the additional finance portfolio, confirming his importance within the government structure. At the LPRP's seventh congress in March 2001 Bounnhang was appointed prime minister.

LATVIA

Full name: The Republic of Latvia.

Leadership structure: The head of state is a president, indirectly elected by Parliament. The president's term of office is four years, renewable once only. The head of government is the prime minister, who is responsible to Parliament. The cabinet is appointed by the prime minister.

President:	Vaira **VIKE-FREIBERGA**	Since 8 July 1999
Prime Minister:	Andris Škele	16 June 1999—5 May 2000
	Andris Berzinš	5 May 2000—7 Nov. 2002
	Einars Repše (acting until 9 March 2004)	7 Nov. 2002—5 Feb. 2004
	Indulis Emsis (acting until 2 Dec. 2004)	9 March 2004—28 Oct. 2004
	Aigars **KALVITIS**	Since 2 Dec. 2004

Legislature: The legislature is unicameral. The sole chamber, the Parliament (Saeima), has 100 members, directly elected for a four-year term.

Profile of the President:

Vaira **VIKE-FREIBERGA**

Vaira Vike-Freiberga is the first female president of Latvia, and indeed of any former-Soviet east European state. Although born in Riga she became a refugee at the end of the Second World War and spent most of her life abroad, mainly in Canada where she emigrated in 1954 and became a psychology professor. She was first elected president in 1999, and was re-elected unopposed in 2003.

Vaira Vike (who added the Freiberga suffix once married) was born on 1 December 1937 in Riga. At the end of the Second World War her family fled the Soviet advance through Latvia and she spent her early life in a refugee camp in Lübeck, West Germany. Her family moved on from Germany to Morocco, then under French administration, in 1949 and she attended college in Casablanca from 1950. Four years later she emigrated to Canada.

She studied for a degree in English language at Victoria College, University of Toronto, graduating in 1958. Along with Latvian and English she is fluent in five other European languages. She put her knowledge of Spanish to use as a part-time translator and Spanish teacher at Ontario Ladies' College while continuing her studies. She gained a master's degree in psychology at the University of Toronto in 1960. She is married to Imants Freibergs, a Latvian-born professor of computer science, whom she met while helping to organize a Latvian Youth Festival in Toronto (and with whom she published a book on Latvian folk songs, their shared passion, in 1988). They have a son and a daughter.

She worked as a clinical psychologist in Toronto's Psychiatric Hospital for a year before returning to full-time education to study for her doctorate in experimental psychology at McGill University in Montréal, Québec, in 1961. In 1965, as a qualified doctor of psychology, she was appointed as an assistant professor at the Université de Montréal, where she worked for the next 33 years until her return to Latvia in 1998. She has published eight books and over 250 articles and speeches on psychology and research.

Since gaining full professorship in 1979 Vike-Freiberga has served as president of the Social Science Federation of Canada (1980), president of the Canadian Psychological Association, and vice chairman of the Canadian Science Council (1984–89). She was also president of the US-based Association for the Advancement of Baltic Studies in 1984–86.

In 1998 Vike-Freiberga returned to Latvia to become director of the Latvian Institute in Riga. One year later she stood as an independent in the presidential election, defeating six other better-known candidates in seven rounds of voting in the Parliament, eventually gaining 53 of the 100 votes. She took office on 8 July 1999. One of her first acts as president was to return to the Parliament a controversial bill to protect and overtly promote the use of Latvian. She also voiced concern over the new aggressive foreign policy seemingly emerging in neighbouring Russia following the election there of President Vladimir Putin in 2000. Relations between the two countries remain strained.

In June 2003 she stood for re-election and was unopposed. She was accepted by Parliament by 88 votes to six. The following year Latvia achieved membership of the European Union, negotiation for which had begun during her first term.

Profile of the Prime Minister:

Aigars **KALVITIS**

Aigars Kalvitis was appointed prime minister of Latvia on 2 December 2004 following the resignation of Indulis Emsis. He is an agriculturist and a founder member of the People's Party (Tautas Partija—TP).

Aigars Kalvitis was born on 27 June 1966 in Riga. He was educated at Riga Secondary School No. 41 before attending the Latvian University of Agriculture, where he graduated from the faculty of economics in 1992 with a degree in agricultural economics. During this time he spent some time working as a tractor driver and a milkman on a Swedish farm. In 1992 he became a director of the company Agro Biznesa Centrs. He is married and has three sons.

Kalvitis studied for a year at University College, in Cork, Ireland, where he graduated with a master's degree in food industry business administration, and in 1994 became chairman of the commission of the central union of Latvian dairying. He also got a second master's degree from the Latvian University of Agriculture, this time in agricultural economics. In 1995 Kalvitis travelled to Wisconsin, USA, where he worked for the Holstein Association, the world's largest dairy cattle breed organization.

Kalvitis was a founder member of the TP in 1997, and was first elected to Parliament in 1998. He served as a member of the budget and finance (taxation) committee and the public expenditure and audit committee. In 1999 he was appointed minister of agriculture and from May 2000 until 2002 he was minister of economics. Kalvitis was re-elected to Parliament in 2002, and chaired the parliamentary group of the TP until appointed prime minister in October 2004 following the resignation of Indulis Emsis. Kalvitis's new government contained nine of the same ministers, and he quickly promised to retain most of Emsis's policies.

LEBANON

Full name: The Republic of Lebanon.

Leadership structure: The head of state is a president, elected by the National Assembly. The president's term of office is six years, nonrenewable, under the constitution. Parliament voted on 3 September 2004 to extend President Lahoud's term for a further three years. The head of government is the prime minister, who is appointed by the president following consultations with the members of the National Assembly.

President:	Gen. Emile **LAHOUD**	Since 24 Nov. 1998
Prime Minister:	Salim al-Hoss	2 Dec. 1998—23 Oct. 2000
	Rafiq al-Hariri	23 Oct. 2000—20 Oct. 2004
	Omar Karameh	21 Oct. 2004—19 April 2005
	(acting 28 Feb.—10 March 2005 and from 13 April 2005)	
	Najib Mikati	19 April 2005—19 July 2005
	Fouad **SINIORA**	Since 19 July 2005

Legislature: The legislature is unicameral. The sole chamber, the National Assembly (Majlis al-Nawab), has 128 members, divided equally between Christians and Muslims, directly elected for a maximum four-year term.

Profile of the President:

Gen. Emile **LAHOUD**

Gen. Emile Lahoud is a Maronite Christian and the son of the prominent pro-independence leader Jamil Lahoud. A naval officer who rose to head the armed forces from the end of the civil war in 1989 until his election as president nine years later, he is credited with having reformed the military after the destructive conflict. His election as president required a change in the constitution to allow a state official to hold the office, but was assured after he received Syrian backing.

Emile Jamil Lahoud was born a member of the Maronite Christian community of Beirut on 12 January 1936. His father Gen. Jamil Lahoud is popularly seen as the creator of the national army and a key figure in the country's struggle for independence from France in the 1940s. Jamil Lahoud went on to serve as labour and social welfare minister and earned the nickname 'the Red General' for his concern for the working classes.

Emile Lahoud was educated in Lebanon and joined the country's military academy as a naval cadet in 1956. Two years later he began the first of a number of military training courses abroad, starting with studies in naval engineering in the UK. Foreign training was interspersed with visits home and promotion in the navy. In 1959 he was appointed to command his first ship, the *Beirut*, and by 1966 he had been placed in command of the 2nd Division of ships before heading to the USA for further training. He was assigned to the Fourth Bureau of the Army Command as a lieutenant in 1970 and, after attending staff college in Rhode Island, USA, became chief of staff in the office of the Lebanese army in 1973. Meanwhile, in 1967 he had married Andrée Amadouny, with whom he has three children.

Following the outbreak of civil war in Lebanon in 1975, Lahoud was promoted to the rank of commander and was sent back to Rhode Island to complete his training. He returned in 1980 as a captain and was immediately appointed director of personnel in Army Command, later moving to the military office in the embattled government's ministry of defence in 1983. After six more years of destructive conflict, during which the army disintegrated into Muslim and Christian militias, the Syrian-brokered Taïf Agreement brought a long-awaited peace to the country. Lahoud was elevated to commander of the armed forces in November 1989 and took charge of the fractious army, navy and air force with a clear vision of reconstruction in mind.

Early in 1990 Lahoud constituted an emergency plan for the armed forces based on three main principles: that the army be rebuilt with the aid of Syria, that Lebanon concentrate its foreign policy on resisting Israeli aggression, and above all that the army stay firmly out of politics. The restoration of relative stability to the country has been popularly credited to the success of his plan and the unified, apolitical military machine it created. Lahoud's popularity coupled with his proven obedience to Syria and his staunch creed of apoliticism made him a perfect candidate for president (an office traditionally held by a Christian) in 1998, based on the perception that what was achieved in the armed forces could be achieved for the country.

To enable Lahoud's election, his predecessor urged the National Assembly to adopt the necessary alterations to the constitution, which at that time barred military figures (and all other state officials) from standing for the office. The passage of the necessary amendment was assured after Lahoud received the political backing of the Syrian government and he took office in November 1998. Under his presidency Lebanon has battled with corruption and introduced moderate economic liberalization with relative success.

Elections in 2000 toppled the government of Prime Minister Salim al-Hoss. The elections were won by supporters of Rafiq al-Hariri, who had refused in 1998 to continue as prime minister under Lahoud's presidency. Now Hariri was reappointed, leading to an uncomfortable period of 'cohabitation' between the two men. In May 2000 Israel fulfilled its earlier promises and comprehensively withdrew from southern Lebanon although Lahoud protested at the minor infractions of the border still being committed by the former occupiers.

Lahoud indicated in 2004 that he would like to stay on in office after the end of his six-year term. The National Assembly amended the constitution to extend his term for a further three years, which Hariri begrudgingly supported under intense pressure from Syria, though several of his ministers resigned in protest. The issue continued to split the government, and finally in October Hariri and his whole government resigned. Lahoud appointed a pro-Syrian candidate, Omar Karameh, as prime minister.

Meanwhile, international pressure for Syria to release its grip on Lebanon was mounting, and when Hariri was assassinated in February 2005 anti-Syrian demonstrations flooded the streets of Beirut. Lahoud was forced to negotiate with Syrian president Bashar al-Assad for troop withdrawal, initially agreeing a half measure of withdrawal to the Beqaa Valley though Syria was soon forced to agree to a full withdrawal.

Karameh was struggling to hold a government together in the face of the popular protests, and resigned two weeks after the assassination, but Lahoud reappointed him charged with forming a government of national unity to run the country until elections due in May–June. However, the opposition refused to join, and Karameh resigned again in April. Lahoud chose another pro-Syrian candidate to fill the post for the remaining few weeks.

Lahoud himself was also coming under pressure to resign, accused of protecting a network of security and intelligence agents responsible for a series of political assassinations, including the killings of prominent journalist Samir Qasir and former Communist Party leader George Hawi. Lahoud's position deteriorated further when the anti-Syrian alliance led by Hariri's son won the legislative elections and he found himself back in 'cohabitation'.

Profile of the Prime Minister:

Fouad **SINIORA**

Fouad Siniora was nominated as prime minister of Lebanon on 30 June 2005 by the anti-Syrian parties that had triumphed in the recent elections on the back of a wave of public resentment of the level of Syrian influence in Lebanese politics, crystallized by the assassination of former prime minister Rafiq al-Hariri in February. Siniora, a Sunni Muslim, had been a close friend of Hariri, and remains involved in his business empire.

Fouad Abdul Basset Siniora was born into a Sunni Muslim family in the southern coastal city of Sidon in 1943. He attended the American School for Boys and the American University of Beirut, where he graduated in business administration. After working for Citibank and teaching at the American University, Siniora worked for the Central Bank of Lebanon from 1977 until 1982, when he joined the business empire of Rafiq al-Hariri, a long-time friend. Since Hariri's death, he has retained his links with Hariri's estate and is currently the chairman and managing director of Groupe Méditerranée, which includes four Hariri-owned banks. He is married to Huda al-Busat and they have one son and two daughters.

Siniora served as finance minister in Hariri's governments from 1992 until 1998 and again from 2000 until 2004. Though he was accused of corruption and mismanagement following Hariri's removal from office in 1998, the allegations were widely regarded as trumped up and he was cleared of all charges by the National Assembly in 2003.

Hariri was assassinated by a car bombing in February 2005. Following the victory of anti-Syrian politicians in elections in May–June, Siniora was asked to form a government on 30 June, nominated by Hariri's son Saad al-Hariri. After long and involved negotiations, Siniora finally named a cabinet on 19 July, including both pro- and anti-Syrian ministers and a senior member of the militant group Hezbollah. Siniora's anti-Syrian coalition holds roughly two-thirds of the posts. The line-up also included Lebanon's first female minister.

LESOTHO

Full name: The Kingdom of Lesotho.

Leadership structure: The head of state is a hereditary monarch. The head of government is the prime minister, leader of the majority parliamentary party, who appoints the cabinet.

King:	**LETSIE III**	Since 7 Feb. 1996
Prime Minister:	Bethuel Pakalitha **MOSISILI**	Since 29 May 1998

Legislature: The legislature, the Parliament, is bicameral. The lower chamber, the National Assembly, has 120 members, elected for a five-year term. The upper chamber, the Senate, has 33 members, comprising 22 principal chiefs and 11 other members named by the king.

Profile of the King:

LETSIE III

King Letsie III replaced his father, King Moshoeshoe II, as head of state of Lesotho after Moshoeshoe's death in a car crash in January 1996. Letsie had already ruled for four years in the early 1990s, but had then abdicated to allow the return to the throne of his father, who had been head of state from the time of Lesotho's full independence within the Commonwealth in 1966 until he was deposed in 1990.

The future King Letsie was born Prince David Mohato Bereng Seeiso on 17 July 1963 in Morija. He went to Iketsetseng private primary school in Maseru in 1968 and then to primary and secondary school in the UK, returning to Lesotho for vacations and spending much time at his father's cattle posts in the mountains. He attended the National University of Lesotho, graduating in 1984 with a degree in law. He then continued his studies in the UK at the universities of Bristol, Cambridge and London, studying English law, development and agricultural economics.

He became principal chief of Matsieng in 1989, and was installed by the military government as King Letsie III in November 1990 following the dethronement of his father. Moshoeshoe had been effectively ousted in March, since when he had been ostensibly on sabbatical leave in the UK. Two years later, when Moshoeshoe returned to Lesotho, Letsie offered to step down in his favour, but this was opposed by the ruling military council. In a compromise formula Moshoeshoe was accorded the status of head of the royal family, but with Letsie still designated as monarch.

A return to civilian rule, and the holding of elections in March 1993, brought the Basotho Congress Party to power under Ntsu Mokhehle. Amid unrest and continuing coup rumours, Letsie attempted a decisive intervention, announcing on 17 August 1994 that he had removed the Mokhehle government and was calling fresh elections. He was immediately challenged by the mobilization of a large protest demonstration, precipitating a crisis which was eventually resolved only with mediation by Botswana, Zimbabwe and South Africa. Letsie agreed in September to reinstate Mokhehle and to abdicate in favour of his father. The necessary legislation was approved and Moshoeshoe returned to the throne on 25 January 1995, with Letsie reverting to the status of crown prince. However, a year later Moshoeshoe was killed in a car crash. Letsie succeeded to the throne three weeks after his death on 7 February 1996, and his coronation took place on 31 October 1997.

In 2000 Letsie married South African commoner Anna Karabo Motšoeneng, now known as Queen Masenate, and they have two daughters. He announced before his wedding that, unlike many other African kings and chiefs, he intends to have only one wife.

Profile of the Prime Minister:

Bethuel Pakalitha **MOSISILI**

Bethuel Pakalitha Mosisili leads the ruling Lesotho Congress for Democracy (LCD). A career academic and examiner for a number of universities in the southern African region, he has been a member of the National Assembly and a cabinet minister since 1993. He was appointed prime minister in May 1998.

Bethuel Pakalitha Mosisili was born on 14 March 1945 near Qacha's Nek, eastern Lesotho. He married Mathalo Mosisili and they had two daughters and two sons, one of whom was shot and killed in 2002. He began his studies in 1966 at the University of Botswana, Lesotho and Swaziland (UBLS) in Roma, near the capital Maseru. A year into his course he joined the Basotho Congress Party (BCP). In July 1970, soon after graduating, he was imprisoned for his political affiliations.

Released from the maximum-security prison in November 1971, Mosisili was ordered not to leave the Mafeteng Reserve in the west of the country for a year. While under this restriction he found work teaching at local schools and was deputy headmaster at one until June 1973. His freedom restored, he went back to Roma to become an assistant lecturer in African languages at UBLS.

To further his training, Mosisili travelled to the USA in 1975 to study education at the University of Wisconsin, to South Africa in 1977 to gain another degree from the University of South Africa, and finally to Simon Fraser University, Canada, where he received a master's degree in 1982. In the meantime he had become a full lecturer in Lesotho in 1976 when UBLS had transformed into the National University of Lesotho. During the 1980s he travelled the region as a senior lecturer and external examiner, working at a number of universities in Lesotho and South Africa until 1992.

Direct military rule ended in Lesotho in 1993 and Mosisili took the opportunity to move from academia into politics. He was elected to the National Assembly to represent the Qacha's Nek constituency. The BCP had won a landslide victory and Mosisili was appointed minister of education and training, sports, culture and youth affairs (the portfolio was later restyled as education and manpower development). In February 1995 he was promoted to deputy prime minister—a post which had been vacant since the assassination of Selometsi Baholo in 1994—and minister of home affairs and local government.

Divisions within the ruling BCP prompted Prime Minister Ntsu Mokhehle in 1997 to form the LCD as the new ruling party. Mosisili was elected to replace Mokhehle as leader of the LCD in February 1998 and led the party to a landslide victory in the 1998 elections. He was appointed prime minister and minister of defence and public service in May. The party's success provoked mass unrest which led to the intervention of South African troops in September. Mosisili clashed with King Letsie over their arrival, and suggested that the king had sheltered opposition activists in the palace grounds during the disturbances, adding to the air of instability. In three days of violence 47 civilians were killed. The government agreed to hold early elections within 18 months.

Over the course of the next four years Mosisili oversaw the prosecution of those involved in the September 1998 violence, charging the opposition leaders of the time with high treason. The elections originally scheduled for mid-2000 were persistently postponed and were finally held in May 2002. The LCD won a sizable majority, securing 61 of the first 62 seats to declare for the 120-seat National Assembly. Mosisili was appointed for a new term on 4 June 2002.

Mosisili's government has established a new National AIDS Commission to replace the existing, and much-criticized, Lesotho AIDS Programme Co-ordinating Authority (LAPCA) and has pushed AIDS to the centre of all government policy—the problem being so acute that life expectancy in the country has fallen from 60 years to 35 years since 1997. Anxious to end the stigma surrounding the virus, in 2005 he became one of the first African leaders to be tested publicly for HIV, as he launched a free national testing programme.

LIBERIA

Full name: The Republic of Liberia.

Leadership structure: Under the 1986 Constitution the head of state is a directly elected president, with a six-year term of office, renewable once only. Under the Accra agreement in 2003, President Taylor handed over power to his vice president, who in turn handed power to a chosen chair of the national transitional government. The head of government under the constitution is the president, who appoints the cabinet. Under the Accra agreement, the head of government is the chair of the national transitional government, who nominates members of the government to the transitional parliament for approval.

President:	Charles Taylor	3 Aug. 1997—11 Aug. 2003
	Moses Blah	11 Aug. 2003—14 Oct. 2003

Chair of the National Transitional Government:

	Gyude **BRYANT**	Since 14 Oct. 2003

Legislature: Under the 1986 Constitution the legislature, the National Assembly, is bicameral. The lower chamber, the House of Representatives, has 64 members, directly elected for a six-year term. The upper chamber, the Senate, has 30 members, two from each of the 15 counties, elected for a nine-year term. Both chambers were elected for the first time in July 1997. The 76-member National Transitional Legislative Assembly (NTLA) inaugurated on 14 October 2003 will be replaced by the National Assembly to be elected in October 2005.

Profile of the Chair of the National Transitional Government:

Gyude **BRYANT**

Gyude Bryant was appointed chair of the National Transitional Government (interim president) of Liberia on 14 October 2003 with the backing of ousted president Charles Taylor and rebel leader Sekou Conneh. A businessman who remained in Liberia throughout its 13-year civil war, Bryant was seen by all sides in the conflict as a neutral party. He promised to focus on elections, disarmament and reducing corruption.

Charles Gyude Bryant was born on 17 January 1949 and initially educated at the B. W. Harris Episcopal High School in the capital Monrovia. He graduated from Liberia's Cuttington University College in economics and in 1972 he was hired by the Mesurado Group of Companies as fleet manager of a fishing company. A year later Bryant joined the National Port Authority as its head of planning and development. He comes from the southern Grebo ethnic group, which has played little part in Liberia's long conflict. Bryant is a devout Christian, prominent in the Episcopalian movement, and is married to Rosie Lee-Bryant, with whom he has three children.

In 1977, Bryant formed the Liberia Machinery and Supply Company, which distributes mining and port handling equipment. He remained in the country despite all its subsequent upheavals and conflict, beginning with the 1980 coup in which President William Tolbert was assassinated and Samuel Kanyon Doe first came to power. Shortly after the 1984 lifting of the ban on political activity, Bryant helped to found the Liberian Action Party (LAP). The LAP claimed victory in the presidential and legislative elections held the following year, but Doe declared himself the winner of the polls and his administration went on to persecute and imprison many LAP members. Bryant spent much of this period providing support to the families of those incarcerated.

In 1990, a many-sided civil conflict erupted in Liberia. Two years later, Bryant was elected chair of the LAP, and eventually in 1997 brought six opposition parties into an alliance to contest elections. The polls were won by former warlord Charles Taylor who ruled the country until 2003, by which time rebel movements had control of most of the country and he was under intense international pressure to resign. Taylor fled the country in August 2003, and was temporarily replaced by his deputy Moses Blah. Bryant was chosen to take over from Blah and to head up an interim government until elections in October– November 2005.

Chosen for his political neutrality, Bryant was such an unknown on the international stage that his biography at the US embassy said simply that he had chaired the LAP. He had been the least likely of several contenders for the post. Bryant pledged to focus on elections, disarmament and restoring order and basic services, saying, "Liberians have spent a lot of resources on retribution…and we can't continue with that." Although the regime was plagued by corruption allegations, Bryant was seen to be attempting to crack down on graft, and won popularity for this among ordinary Liberians.

LIBYA

Full name: The Great Socialist People's Libyan Arab Jamahariyah.

Leadership structure: The head of state is the 'leader of the revolution'. Executive power is held by the General People's Committee. The General People's Congress appoints the Committee's members, and decides on its structure. The Congress also has its own administrative secretariat.

'Leader of the Revolution':

Col. Moamer al-**KADHAFI**	Since 2 March 1979
(seized power on 1 Sept. 1969)	

Secretary-General of the General People's Committee:

Mohammad Ahmed al-Manqoush	29 Dec. 1997—1 March 2000
Mubarak al-Shamikh	1 March 2000—14 June 2003
Shukri Muhammad **GHANIM**	Since 14 June 2003

Legislature: The legislature is unicameral. The sole chamber, the General People's Congress (Mu'tamar al-Sha'ab al-'Am), has 750 members, appointed by local 'basic people's congresses' for a three-year term.

Profile of the 'Leader of the Revolution':

Col. Moamer al-**KADHAFI**

Moamer al-Kadhafi is a maverick pan-Arabist, quick to attack anything he sees as Western imperialism and Zionism, and with a special talent for the inflammatory gesture. His regime attracted particularly strong condemnation from the USA because of Kadhafi's support for foreign liberation, anti-government and terrorist groups. An Islamic reformist as opposed to a fundamentalist, he sees himself as an innovative thinker, aiming to develop a new kind of model for participative democracy in Libya—but retaining the apparatus for strict control of dissident activity. Latterly he has been less in the spotlight and has forged a rapprochement with the West, aiming for Libya's reacceptance by the international community.

Moamer al-Kadhafi was born in the Sirte region on 1 June 1942, one of three children in a bedouin family. He attended a Koranic elementary school and the high school at Sebha, where his early involvement in politics led to his expulsion.

He used a false birth certificate to enrol in another school in Misrata, then studied history and politics at university in Benghazi.

Kadhafi's enthusiasm for the pan-Arabist cause was fired by President Nasser in neighbouring Egypt. In 1963, despite being known as a political activist, he was nevertheless accepted into the Royal Libyan Military Academy in Benghazi. Graduating in 1965, he was commissioned as an officer in the signals corps in Benghazi. A four-month training course in Beaconsfield, England, increased his knowledge of military signalling and armoured vehicle gunnery—and his dislike of the British.

Within the armed forces Kadhafi built up his clandestine Free Officers' Movement, the group that he would lead in a coup in 1969 to overthrow the conservative regime of King Idris. The intended coup date, twice deferred, was finally set for the early morning of 1 September. Kadhafi was already known to Western intelligence agencies and there has been speculation that they must have known something of his plans. When the date came the preparations worked smoothly and efficiently, and military and governmental installations in Benghazi and Tripoli were taken over with little bloodshed. Kadhafi made his first broadcast as head of the new regime within a few hours, and King Idris went into exile. Kadhafi's take-over reportedly preempted plans by more senior officers for a coup of their own.

Kadhafi became commander-in-chief of the armed forces, set up a Revolutionary Command Council with himself as president, and, from 1970 to 1972, also held the posts of prime minister and minister of defence. In 1976 he took the military rank of major-general but continued to use the title of colonel. He relinquished all official positions in 1979, styling himself thereafter 'leader of the revolution'.

Economic, social and political changes after the coup, based on Kadhafi's brand of 'natural socialism', included attempts to redistribute the country's oil wealth more equitably, and nationalization of foreign-owned banks, insurance companies, factories and oil companies. (Some liberalization of the economy did begin in the late 1980s, as did the development of steel manufacturing to reduce the country's near-total dependence on oil revenue.) Wage labour was declared to be abolished and workers were instead deemed to be partners in industrial ventures.

Instead of building a single-party state through mass membership of the Arab Socialist Union, Kadhafi embarked on the more idiosyncratic project of creating a structure for popular participation through a system of basic people's congresses and committees, with the parliament or General People's Congress at the centre. This was embodied in the 1977 Constitution of what was henceforth known officially as the Great Socialist People's Libyan Arab Jamahariyah. The *Green Book*, published in three volumes between 1976 and 1979, contains Kadhafi's thoughts on what he describes as his "third universal theory" spanning socialism, Islam, development and political systems.

Kadhafi's pan-Arabist aspirations, and his inclination to seek solidarity and involvement with regimes elsewhere which he identified as progressive, led him into several declarations of union between Libya and other Arab and African states. Pan-Arabism also underlay his initial enthusiasm for the Arab Maghreb Union, formed in 1989 with Algeria, Mauritania, Morocco and Tunisia. His relations with neighbouring Egypt in particular have been tense, while his commitment to the Palestinian cause, something of an article of faith, has involved supporting 'rejectionist' factions and criticizing the mainstream Palestine Liberation Organization's 'sell-outs' to Israel.

Palestinian groups are only some among many causes to receive his backing, others including the British miners' union in its long strike in 1985, the Irish Republican Army, and leftist radicals in many African countries. Kadhafi has himself survived a number of assassination attempts and attempted coups, and has withstood (and bolstered his own defiant image as a result of) actions to 'punish' his regime on more than one occasion. The UK broke off diplomatic relations in 1984 over the shooting of a woman police officer at the Libyan embassy in London, and in 1986 the USA launched an air strike on Tripoli and Benghazi after a bomb attack on a West Berlin nightclub frequented by US servicemen. The bomb explosion on a Pan Am airliner over Lockerbie in Scotland in December 1988 was also laid at Kadhafi's door, leading to a long dispute about the extradition of suspects from Libya and the imposition of UN sanctions. This eventually was resolved with a complex arrangement in 1999 under which two Libyans were tried under Scottish law in the Netherlands.

Kadhafi is married to Safiya al-Kadhafi. They have four sons and one daughter, and their family also includes a number of adopted children, one of whom was killed in the 1986 US air strike against Tripoli. Kadhafi has a reclusive aspect in his character and has been prone to spending long periods in a tent in the desert.

During the 1990s Kadhafi kept a lower profile, notably remaining relatively silent during the Gulf War in 1991. He has attempted to forge a role as the champion of pan-Africanism. Since the 1990s Kadhafi's regime has been displaced by others as the main targets of Western hostility, and in April 1999 Libya was even taken off the US government's list of countries deemed to support international terrorism. However US president George W. Bush did add Libya to his nebulous 'axis of evil' states sponsoring terrorism in May 2002.

The US-led invasion of Iraq in 2003 was a wake-up call to Kadhafi. He agreed to pay millions of dollars in compensation to the victims' families from the 1988 Lockerbie bombing and in December declared that his regime would abandon its programme to develop 'weapons of mass destruction' and would allow snap inspections of its nuclear facilities in co-operation with the UN. Further compensation payments followed for the actions of other Libyan terrorists in the 1980s and 1990s.

In response, the international community began Libya's rehabilitation. The UN and the USA removed or eased sanctions; a plan was agreed to dismantle the weapons programme and destroy stockpiles of chemical weapons; and diplomatic contacts were restored. UK prime minister Tony Blair made a landmark visit to meet Kadhafi in Libya in March 2004, followed in April by Kadhafi's first official visit to Europe for 15 years. In June the first shipment of Libyan oil was en route for the USA, in July the World Trade Organization gave the go-ahead for membership negotiations, and in October the European Union lifted its arms embargo. By 2005 US oil firms were returning to Libya to explore for oil.

Profile of the Secretary-General of the General People's Committee:

Shukri Muhammad **GHANIM**

Shukri Muhammad Ghanim is an economist with extensive experience in the oil and petroleum industry who was appointed Libyan prime minister by Col. Moamer al-Kadhafi on 14 June 2003. He has been instrumental in disposing of the country's stocks of weapons of mass destruction that had led to the imposition of international sanctions and the strangling of Libya's economic growth.

Shukri Muhammad Ghanim was born in Tripoli in 1942. He graduated with a degree in economics from the University of Libya in Benghazi before taking two master's degrees, in economics and in law and diplomacy, at the Fletcher School at Harvard University in the USA. He later earned his doctorate in international economics in 1975, also from the Fletcher School. Ghanim has written a number of books and articles in both Arabic and English on the petrochemical industry, including *The Rise and Fall of an Exclusive Club*.

Ghanim served as head of American and European affairs at the ministry of economics from 1963 until 1965. The following year he joined the Jamahiriyah News Agency as deputy manager of the translation department. In 1968 he moved to the National Oil Corporation, where he worked as the director of marketing and sat on the board of directors. Two years later he returned to the civil service in the ministry of petroleum, as the general manager of economic management, a position in which he remained until 1975.

That year he was appointed as acting minister of oil and chief adviser. He stayed at the ministry until 1977, when he joined the Arab Development Institute as chief economist and director of the energy studies department. In 1982 he spent two years in London as an academic visitor at the School of Oriental and African Studies (SOAS); on his return he was appointed director of the Economic Studies Centre in Tripoli. He remained in academia for some years, in 1987 moving to al-Jabal al-Gharbi University in Gharyan where he stayed until 1993.

Ghanim went from Gharyan to Vienna to work for the Organization of the Petroleum Exporting Countries (OPEC) in 1993, first as director of the research division, and then in 1998 as the acting deputy to the OPEC secretary-general. He returned to Libya in 2001 to take up the post of minister of economics and trade. One of his major tasks was to reform the system; unemployment then stood at 30% and many international sanctions remained in place, while oil revenues had largely been spent on maintaining the daily budget. On 14 June 2003 Ghanim was appointed prime minister, and tasked with rescuing Libya's economy.

His first job was to rid the country of the millstone of international sanctions, which meant getting rid of Libya's weapons of mass destruction. "They are not making it safe," he told reporters, "they are making us poorer... [Better] to spend this money on butter rather than guns." He helped negotiate a US$2,700 million settlement with the families of those killed in the Lockerbie bombing, and began to rehabilitate his country on the international stage. "It's better to come [in] from the cold than staying in the cold," he said.

LIECHTENSTEIN

Full name: The Principality of Liechtenstein.

Leadership structure: The head of state is a constitutional and hereditary prince. The head of government is the leader of the cabinet, which is appointed by the prince, on the proposal of the Parliament.

Reigning Prince:	**HANS-ADAM II** von und zu Liechtenstein (regent from 26 Aug. 1984)	Since 13 Nov. 1989
Regent:	**ALOIS** von und zu Liechtenstein	Since 15 Aug. 2004
Head of Government:	Mario Frick	15 Dec. 1993—5 April 2001
	Otmar **HASLER**	Since 5 April 2001

Legislature: The legislature is unicameral. The sole chamber, the Parliament (Landtag), has 25 members, directly elected for a four-year term.

Profile of the Reigning Prince:

HANS-ADAM II von und zu Liechtenstein

Prince Hans-Adam II succeeded formally as 'reigning prince' of Liechtenstein upon the death of his father Prince Franz Josef II in 1989. An economics graduate with a business management background, he had already exercised the official powers of head of state, but without the title, for five years. In 2004, he similarly delegated his powers to his son Alois.

Hereditary Prince Hans-Adam was born on 14 February 1945. He went to the Schottengymnasium in Vienna, Austria, and completed his education in Switzerland, obtaining a diploma in national economy from the University of St Gallen in 1969. He worked briefly for a bank in London, before moving on to act as manager of the Prince of Liechtenstein Foundation from 1970 to 1981, during which time he was entrusted with the management and administration of the Royal House's property.

On 26 August 1984 Hans-Adam's elderly father passed all his official duties over to him as the representative of the head of state. When Franz Josef died on 13 November 1989 Hans-Adam became head of state in his own right.

A referendum in March 2003 approved greater powers for the reigning prince, giving him the ability to appoint and dismiss the government, choose judges and veto laws. Hans-Adam had threatened to leave the country if he was not granted these powers. The changes were endorsed by 60% of the voters.

Prince Hans-Adam married Countess Marie Kinsky von Wchinitz und Tettau in 1967. They have three sons and one daughter. In August 2004 Prince Hans-Adam delegated his powers to his eldest son and heir apparent Prince Alois, as a precursor to the formal succession.

Profile of the Regent:

ALOIS von und zu Liechtenstein

Alois von und zu Liechtenstein is the eldest son of Prince Hans-Adam II, who handed over day-to-day responsibility for the running of the tiny country on 15 August 2004 as a precursor to succession. Alois is seen as less combative than his father.

Hereditary Prince Alois Philipp Maria von und zu Liechtenstein was born in Zürich, Switzerland, on 11 June 1968 and is the eldest son of Prince Hans-Adam II and his wife, formerly Countess Marie Kinsky von Wchinitz und Tettau. He was educated at the Liechtenstein Grammar School in Vaduz-Ebenholz before attending the Royal Military Academy at Sandhurst, in the UK. He served in the Coldstream Guards in London and Hong Kong for six months before enrolling at the University of Salzburg, Austria, in October 1988. He graduated with a master's degree in jurisprudence in 1993. He then spent three years working in London for an auditing company before returning to Liechtenstein to live.

Alois married Duchess Sophie of Bavaria in 1993, and they have three sons and one daughter, the eldest son being Hereditary Prince Joseph Wenzel, born in 1995.

Profile of the Head of Government:

Otmar **HASLER**

Otmar Hasler is a former secondary school teacher, and is a leading figure in the centre-left Progressive Citizens' Party (Fortschrittliche Bürgerpartei—FBP). On his inauguration as prime minister in April 2001 he pledged to continue many of the policies of his centre-right predecessor, Mario Frick.

Otmar Hasler was born on 28 September 1953. He graduated in teaching from the University of Fribourg, Switzerland, and began teaching at the secondary school in Eschen, northern Liechtenstein, in 1979. He is married to Traudi née Hilti and they have four children.

Hasler began his political career in 1989 when he was elected to Parliament for the FBP. Four years later, in 1993, he was appointed as a vice president of the legislature, a role he retained until becoming prime minister in 2001, apart from a two-year term as president of the legislature in 1995–97.

In 1993 he was also elected president of the FBP, a post he held for two years, after which he remained a member of the party's presidium. Following the 1997 elections his party had its first spell out of government for 59 years, but after a four-year period in opposition it won an overall (albeit narrow) majority in legislative elections held in February 2001. Hasler was invited to form a government, and secured parliamentary approval two months later for his cabinet, which was drawn entirely from his own party in view of the decision by the rival centre-right Patriotic Union (Vaterländische Union—VU) not to join a coalition.

The FBP lost its majority at the April 2005 elections, but remained the largest party. This time a coalition was successfully negotiated with the VU and Hasler took office on 21 April for a second term as prime minister.

LITHUANIA

Full name: The Republic of Lithuania.

Leadership structure: The head of state is a president, directly elected by universal adult suffrage. The president's term of office is five years, renewable once only. The head of government is the prime minister, who is appointed by the president with the approval of the Parliament.

President:	Valdas Adamkus	26 Feb. 1998—25 Feb. 2003
	Rolandas Paksas	26 Feb. 2003—6 April 2004
	Arturas Paulauskas (acting)	6 April 2004—12 July 2004
	Valdas **ADAMKUS**	Since 12 July 2004
Prime Minister:	Andrius Kubilius	3 Nov. 1999—26 Oct. 2000
	Rolandas Paksas	26 Oct. 2000—20 June 2001
	Eugenijus Gentvilas (acting)	20 June 2001—3 July 2001
	Algirdas **BRAZAUSKAS**	Since 3 July 2001

Legislature: The legislature is unicameral. The sole chamber, the Parliament (Seimas), has 141 members, directly elected for a four-year term.

Profile of the President:

Valdas ADAMKUS

Valdas Adamkus was returned to office as president of Lithuania in July 2004. He had only just taken up residence in Lithuania at the time of his first election to the presidency in 1998, having spent most of his adult life in the USA where he worked in the Environmental Protection Agency (EPA). In each election he has stood as a pro-market, independent candidate, with his nomination supported by right-of-centre political parties.

Valdas Adamkus was born on 3 November 1926 in Kaunas, Lithuania. As a teenager he joined the nationalist resistance, opposing both his country's forcible absorption into the Soviet Union in 1940, and its subsequent wartime occupation by Nazi Germany. During the Nazi occupation he ran an underground newspaper, but as Soviet troops advanced once again from the east he joined an anti-Soviet detachment supplied by the Nazis which fought for Lithuanian independence. When the Red Army took control of the country in 1944, he left Lithuania and fled to Germany.

Five years later he emigrated to the USA, where he found a job teaching Lithuanian, German, Polish and Russian at a US army school in Kansas. In 1951 he married another Lithuanian-born exile, Alma Adamkiene, née Nutautaite; they have no children.

Having moved to Chicago (where there is the largest Lithuanian community outside Lithuania), Adamkus completed a degree in civil engineering at the Illinois Institute of Technology. He joined the Republican Party and campaigned to prevent US recognition of the Soviet annexation of Lithuania, but had to cease party political activity when he started working for the US EPA in 1971. The following year he was on an EPA delegation to Lithuania, his first of a number of such visits to Eastern Europe. In 1981 he was promoted to EPA district administrator for the Mid-West region.

During his time in the USA Adamkus was a leading member of the Lithuanian–American literary group Santara-Sviesa. In 1991, after Lithuania had gained independence from the Soviet Union, he applied for Lithuanian citizenship, and in 1994 he registered as a resident of the town of Šiauliai.

In October 1997 Adamkus gave up his job at the EPA and returned permanently to Lithuania, having been chosen in July as presidential candidate for the Lithuanian Centre Union (although he was not himself a member of any political party). During the three-month campaign he toured much of the country, seeking to demonstrate that he had sufficient experience of Lithuanian affairs. He received greatest support outside Vilnius, whereas in the capital academics disliked his anglicized language and he was criticized for being too pro-Western, giving rise to concerns that he would upset relations with neighbouring Russia.

The first round of voting, contested by seven candidates on 21 December 1997, saw Adamkus take second place with 28% of the vote, against 45% for Arturas Paulauskas, who was backed by the former communists including outgoing president Algirdas Brazauskas. In the runoff on 4 January 1998, Adamkus, supported by a broad centre-right coalition, secured a narrow victory with just 50.4% of the vote. Paulauskas claimed that irregularities had occurred but the electoral commission was satisfied, and Adamkus was duly sworn in on 26 February. As required by Lithuanian law, he immediately began the procedure to give up his US citizenship.

Although he proved to be a popular president—with his rating occasionally reaching an unprecedented 90%—Adamkus had to handle a delicate political situation when a Social Democratic coalition headed by Brazauskas gained ground to become the largest bloc in the legislative elections of October 2000. Having initially invited the centre-right to form a minority government under Rolandas Paksas, he had to go back to the Social Democrats when Paksas's coalition collapsed the following June, and invite Brazauskas to form a government instead.

Seeking a second term as president, Adamkus headed the poll on the first round on 22 December 2002, although he faced an unexpectedly strong challenge from Paksas, and ultimately lost to him in the second round on 5 January 2003. However, a year later Paksas was accused of having links to organized crime gangs in neighbouring Russia, and was impeached in April 2004 for leaking classified material and giving citizenship to a Russian businessman in return for financial support.

Fresh elections were held in June and Adamkus put forward his candidacy, pledging to reunite the country after the divisive period of fractious argument over Paksas's impeachment. Again standing as an independent, this time with the backing of the centre liberals and the conservatives, he won the first round with 30% of the vote. He faced former prime minister Kazimeira Prunskiene in the second round, whom he beat with 52% of the vote. He was sworn into office for his second term on 12 July.

Profile of the Prime Minister:

Algirdas **BRAZAUSKAS**

Algirdas Brazauskas steered Lithuania to independence from the Soviet Union in 1990 as the country's last Communist ruler and went on to be elected its first democratic president (1993–98). He returned to power as prime minister in 2001 at the head of the Lithuanian Social Democratic Party (Lietuvos Socialdemokratu Partija—LSDP) at a time of worsening economic problems, after the collapse of a minority right-of-centre government created after the October 2000 elections to keep his party out of power. He pledged to continue his predecessor's economic reforms, while also pursuing more socially oriented policies.

Algirdas Mykolas Brazauskas was born in Rokiškis on 22 September 1932, in what was then the nominally independent republic of Lithuania. He moved with his family to the town of Kaisiadorys, just east of Kaunas, soon after. Lithuania became a part of the Soviet Union in 1940 and Brazauskas attended the Soviet Kaunas Polytechnic Institute, graduating in 1956 having specialized in hydrotechnology. His first assignment was as senior engineer on the Kaunas hydroelectric power project. In 1958 he married Julia Styraite, a medical doctor, and they had two daughters before divorcing in the late 1990s. In 2002 he married hotelier Kristina Butrimiene.

Having spent eight years chairing the Energy Building Trust Board, Brazauskas shifted directly into the Soviet administration when he was appointed minister for the building material industry in 1965. Two years later he was made deputy chairman of the state planning committee. With the backing of a degree in economics gained in 1974, he was made secretary for economic affairs to the central committee of the ruling Communist Party of Lithuania (Lietuvos Komunistu Partijos—LKP) in 1977 where he stayed for a further ten years.

As the movement for democratization swept the Soviet Union Brazauskas, notwithstanding his association with the regime, was at the forefront of the awakening of Lithuanian nationalism, and initially received the backing of the popular Sajudis independence movement. During a decisive split within the LKP in 1988, Brazauskas was elected first secretary—the most senior position in Lithuania. In this role he led the LKP, and the country at large, away from its ties to Moscow and established an independent Lithuanian party in 1989, retaining the position of first secretary. In the final days of Lithuania's communist era in 1990 Brazauskas transformed the party into the Lithuanian Democratic Labour Party (Lietuvos Demokratine Darbo Partija—LDDP). He was duly elected its chairman, as well as becoming deputy prime minister of the newly independent Lithuania.

In the country's first legislative elections for the new Parliament in 1992 the LDDP scored a surprise victory to emerge as the largest single party. From November of that year Brazauskas served as chairman of the Parliament and thus acting president of Lithuania. In the first direct elections for a head of state Brazauskas emerged the victor with 60% of the vote and was sworn in as president on 25 February 1993. In accordance with the new constitution he suspended his membership of the LDDP. As president he presided over the government's decisions to seek closer ties with the West and to undertake the painful process of market reforms. During his five-year term Lithuania's economy became one of the success stories of the post-Soviet Baltic, although public support for the left-wing government deteriorated.

The LDDP was heavily defeated at the polls in 1996 by the new Homeland Union (Lithuanian Conservatives), and in 1997 Brazauskas announced he would not stand for re-election. His chosen successor was beaten in the subsequent presidential election in 1997–98 by the right-of-centre candidate Valdas Adamkus. In opposition Brazauskas returned to lead the LDDP. As a series of right-wing coalitions came and went between 1998 and 2000 Brazauskas rallied the left-wing opposition behind his own popular image. The A. Brazauskas Social Democratic Coalition won the greatest share of seats in the October 2000 legislative elections but was controversially overlooked by President Adamkus who turned instead to a multiparty minority coalition of the centre right.

In 2001 Prime Minister Rolandas Paksas was compelled to resign by a revolt within his coalition over his privatization and pension reform plans. Brazauskas was called on in June to form a government based on his LSDP—formed from the merger of a party of the same name and the LDDP in January 2001—and the centre-left New Union (Social Liberals). It took office on 3 July. Reflecting the concerns of industry chiefs, President Adamkus warned Brazauskas that he would be watching the leftist government closely, and would intervene if it appeared to be jeopardizing the country's chances of joining the European Union (EU) and the North Atlantic Treaty Organization (NATO). Membership of both these organizations was smoothly achieved in 2004.

Brazauskas spearheaded the campaign to impeach President Rolandas Paksas (who had taken office in February 2003) on allegations of links between the presidential office and international crime rings based in Russia. Several months of bitter debate followed, climaxing with the successful impeachment in April 2004, leaving Lithuanian politics deeply scarred. Voters found themselves turning towards new parties in the legislative elections later that year, which were won by the pro-Russian Labour Party. Brazauskas's For a Working Lithuania alliance of the LSDP and the New Union (Social Liberals) came second.

Brazauskas at first tried to form a 'rainbow' coalition with the Fatherland Union and Liberal and Centre Union—excluding Labour in fear of a resurgence of Russian influence in Lithuania. Agreement could not be reached, however, on how the parties would split the cabinet posts. So in early November a new centre-left government was formed with Labour and the Union of Farmers and New Democracy Party, with Brazauskas remaining as prime minister.

LUXEMBOURG

Full name: The Grand Duchy of Luxembourg.

Leadership structure: The head of state is a hereditary grand duke. The head of government is the prime minister, chosen by the grand duke on the basis of the election results. The prime minister must command the support of the Chamber of Deputies, and appoints the Council of Ministers.

Grand Duke:	Jean	12 Nov. 1964—7 Oct. 2000
	(lieutenant-representative from 4 May 1961)	
	HENRI	Since 7 Oct. 2000
	(lieutenant-representative from 4 March 1998)	
Prime Minister:	Jean-Claude **JUNCKER**	Since 20 Jan. 1995

Legislature: The legislature is unicameral. The sole chamber, the Chamber of Deputies (Chambre des Députés/Châmber vun Députéirten), has 60 members, directly elected for a five-year term. There is also a Council of State, nominated by the monarch and comprising 21 members, which acts as the supreme administrative tribunal and has some legislative functions.

Profile of the Grand Duke:

HENRI

Henri succeeded as grand duke of Luxembourg on 7 October 2000, after the abdication of his father, Grand Duke Jean. Educated in political sciences, Henri follows his father's lead in championing the environment and social causes. As head of state he is constitutional monarch and executive authority is exercised on his behalf by the prime minister.

Henri Albert Gabriel Félix Marie Guillaume d'Aviano was born in Betzdorf in southeast Luxembourg on 16 April 1955, the second child of Crown Prince Jean and Princess Joséphine-Charlotte of Belgium. His father became grand duke after the voluntary abdication of the popular Grand Duchess Charlotte in 1964, making Henri, as his eldest son, the heir apparent. Henri attended primary school in Luxembourg and speaks English, French and German, as well as Luxembourgish. He passed the European baccalaureate in France in 1974 before travelling to the UK where he entered the Royal Military Academy at Sandhurst in 1975.

On passing out of Sandhurst Henri went to Switzerland where he studied political sciences at the University of Geneva. Having graduated in 1980, he married Cuban-born fellow student Maria Teresa Mestre on 14 February 1981; they have four sons and one daughter; the eldest son, Prince Guillaume, born on 11 November 1981, is heir apparent.

Henri's studies also took him to the USA and he continued to travel extensively thereafter, promoting Luxembourg's economy as an honorary chairman of the Board of Economic Development. He served as a member of the Council of State from 1980 to 1998, accustoming himself to the working of the country's government, and since 1998 has been a member of the International Olympic Committee.

The prince's interest in social issues led him to create the Mentor Foundation, in co-operation with the World Health Organization (WHO), to help combat solvent abuse among the young. He is also a member of the Charles Darwin Foundation for the Galapagos Islands, and chairman of its Luxembourg branch. Like his father, Henri is a keen sportsman with a particular interest in outdoor pursuits. He enjoys skiing, sailing, swimming and shooting, in particular.

In March 1998 Henri's father appointed him lieutenant-representative to take over his active duties as head of state and announced in December 1999 that he would abdicate in favour of his son in the following year. At an abdication ceremony on 7 October 2000 Henri was named grand duke.

Profile of the Prime Minister:

Jean-Claude **JUNCKER**

Jean-Claude Juncker, who trained as a lawyer, has been active throughout his career as a member of the Christian Social People's Party (Chrëschtlech Sozial Vollekspartei—CSV), which ruled in coalition with the Luxembourg Socialist Workers' Party (Lëtzebuergesch Sozialistesch Arbechterpartei—LSAP) from 1984 to 1999 and again from 2004. He held a variety of ministerial posts before becoming prime minister in 1995.

Born in Redange-sur-Attert, Luxembourg, on 9 December 1954, Jean-Claude Juncker received his secondary education in Clairefontaine, Belgium. He attended the University of Strasbourg, France, from 1975 and graduated with a degree in public law in 1979, gaining admittance to the Luxembourg Bar in February 1980. He is married to Christiane Frising; they have no children.

From 1979 until 1985 he was president of the youth wing of the CSV and was also the party's parliamentary secretary from October 1979 until December 1982, when he was appointed state secretary for labour and social affairs.

Following the June 1984 general election, which brought the CSV–LSAP coalition to power under Jacques Santer's premiership, Juncker was named as minister of labour and minister in charge of the budget from July. As a result he presided over meetings of social affairs and budget ministers, during Luxembourg's presidency of the European Communities (forerunner of the European Union, EU) for six months in 1985.

Re-elected to parliament in the June 1989 general election he was given responsibility for labour and finance in Santer's cabinet. As such he was instrumental in preparing a draft treaty on economic and monetary union during Luxembourg's presidency of the European Communities in the first half of 1991 which was later to form part of the Maastricht Treaty on European Union. The July 1991 collapse of the Bank of Credit and Commerce International, the holding company and a subsidiary of which were incorporated in Luxembourg, focused attention on Luxembourg's banking secrecy laws. In response to these concerns Juncker introduced legislation two years later requiring banks to notify cases of suspected money laundering and permitting such deposits to be seized.

Juncker retained his cabinet posts after the June 1994 general election. He was also elected president of the CSV in 1990 and president of the European Union of Christian Democratic Workers in 1993, retaining both posts until his appointment as prime minister on 20 January 1995. As prime minister he also holds the key post of minister of finance, although he has gradually relinquished his other ministerial responsibilities, notably for labour and employment.

The June 1999 elections saw both the existing governing coalition parties lose seats, although Juncker's CSV remained the largest party in the Chamber of Deputies, and on 7 August 1999, having formed a new right-of-centre coalition with the Democratic Party of Luxembourg, he was sworn in for a further term as prime minister.

Juncker was a governor of the World Bank from 1989 until 1995 and, as minister of finance, is currently a governor of the European Investment Bank, the European Bank for Reconstruction and Development and the International Monetary Fund. In 2002 he began to be mentioned as a possible successor to Wim Duisenberg as governor of the European Central Bank, though the job went as expected to Jean-Claude Trichet.

The June 2004 election saw victory again for the CSV, though still without an absolute majority. The coalition was re-formed with the LSAP, and Juncker's new cabinet was sworn in on 31 July.

A firm believer in European integration, Juncker has also been a vice president of the European People's Party. Despite the rejection of the EU constitution by the French and the Dutch in 2005, Juncker declared that the treaty was not dead after Luxembourg ratified the proposals by referendum six weeks later.

THE FORMER YUGOSLAV REPUBLIC OF MACEDONIA

Full name: The Republic of Macedonia.

Leadership structure: The head of state is the president, directly elected by universal adult suffrage. The president's term of office is five years. The head of government is the prime minister, who is appointed by the president. Ministers are elected by, but not members of, the Assembly.

President:	Boris Trajkovski	15 Dec. 1999—26 Feb. 2004
	Ljupco Jordanovski (acting)	26 Feb. 2004—12 May 2004
	Branko **CRVENKOVSKI**	Since 12 May 2004
Prime Minister:	Ljubčo Georgievski	30 Nov. 1998—1 Nov. 2002
	Branko Crvenkovski	1 Nov. 2002—12 May 2004
	Radmila Sekerinska (acting)	12 May 2004—2 June 2004
	Hari Kostov	2 June 2004—18 Nov. 2004
	Radmila Sekerinska (acting)	18 Nov. 2004—17 Dec. 2004
	Vlado **BUCKOVSKI**	Since 17 Dec. 2004

Legislature: The legislature is unicameral. The sole chamber, the Assembly (Sobranie), has 120 members, directly elected for a four-year term.

Profile of the President:

Branko **CRVENKOVSKI**

Formerly prime minister and leader of the centre-left Social Democratic Union of Macedonia (Socijaldemokratski Sojuz na Makedonija—SDSM), Branko Crvenkovski became president on 12 May 2004, three months after his predecessor, Boris Trajkovski, had died in a plane crash. Despite his depth of experience, holding the post of prime minister for most of the 1990s and again from 2002, he was still only 41 when he assumed the presidency. Crvenkovski promised to redouble Trajkovski's efforts to consolidate stability in a country riven just three years earlier by ethnic conflict between Macedonians and ethnic Albanians. He is seen as a strong force for peace—despite the largely ceremonial nature of his post—having done much towards reconciliation as prime minister.

However, the peace deal signed by his predecessor promises electoral reforms that are highly unpopular among the ethnic Macedonian majority.

Born on 12 October 1962 in Sarajevo, where his father was serving in the Yugoslav National Army, Branko Crvenkovski graduated in 1986 with a degree in computer science and automation from the faculty of electrical engineering at the St Cyril and Methodius University in Skopje. He is married to Jasmina Crvenkovska with one son and one daughter.

After a period as head of department at the computer engineering company Semos in Skopje, in 1990 Crvenkovski was elected member of the Assembly of the Republic of Macedonia at the first multiparty elections in what was then the Socialist Federal Republic of Yugoslavia. He was elected president of its commission for foreign political affairs and relations, and therefore was closely involved in Macedonia's moves towards independence from Yugoslavia, signing the initiative for a referendum on the issue. The League of Communists was reborn as the SDSM at its party congress in April 1991, and Crvenkovski was elected as its president. Independence was declared in November, though not fully recognized until April 1993 when the country secured membership of the UN under the name of the Former Yugoslav Republic of Macedonia (FYRM).

In August 1992 Crvenkovski was put forward by the SDSM as the new country's first prime minister. His government was formally elected by the Assembly on 4 September, at which time he was the youngest government leader in Europe at just 29 years old. He headed a coalition of his own SDSM, the Alliance of Reform Forces of Macedonia (later the Liberal Party), the ethnic Albanian Party for Democratic Prosperity and the Socialist Party of Macedonia. Immediately after independence, the country was faced with a difficult economic and political situation, with high inflation rates and considerable social instability. The new coalition government managed to stabilize the economy and embarked upon the process of privatization.

He was reappointed as prime minister on 20 December 1994, following the general election held in October–November that year that saw victory for the Union of Macedonia, an alliance of the SDSM, the Liberals and the Socialists. He re-formed the same coalition as before, though the Liberals left the government in 1996. During this term Macedonia became a member of the UN, the Organization for Security and Co-operation in Europe (OSCE) and the Council of Europe, signed agreements with the International Monetary Fund (IMF) and the World Bank, and made its first steps towards Euro-Atlantic integration by becoming a member of the Partnership for Peace initiative with the North Atlantic Treaty Organization (NATO).

An increase in tensions between the majority Macedonian population and the ethnic Albanian minority, and a barely avoided financial scandal involving a 'pyramid investment scheme', resulted in Crvenkovski's coalition losing elections four years later to the political right. Crvenkovski himself was, however, re-elected to the Assembly. Over the next few years ethnic tensions increased dramatically and boiled over into outright civil war in 2001 as ethnic Albanian insurgents demanded greater autonomy and equal rights. Crvenkovski took the SDSM into a 'government of national unity' in May, which was maintained for long enough to achieve the signing of a Framework Agreement. with the Albanian rebels which ushered in a new constitution and guarantees on minority rights. The unity government fell apart in November when Crvenkovski's SDSM withdrew in a calculated strategy to win votes from people critical of the slow pace of the government in its implementation of the accord.

In elections held on 15 September 2002 Crvenkovski led the SDSM, under the Together for Macedonia (Za Makedonija Zaedno—ZMZ) coalition, back into power. The ten-party umbrella group gained 41% of the vote and formed a new government with the Democratic Union for Integration, an ethnic Albanian party that had been deeply involved with the insurgency. He was lauded by the international community for his role in encouraging reconciliation, but his economic record was less favourable. Unemployment rose to record levels and the country remains very poor. He also failed to achieve much progress in tackling corruption, thought to be a factor deterring foreign investment.

Early presidential elections were held in April 2004, following the death in February of President Trajkovski in a plane crash. Crvenkovski secured over 60% of the votes in second-round balloting against Sashko Kedev to become the new president, just after the country formally submitted its application to join the European Union.

Profile of the Prime Minister:

Vlado **BUCKOVSKI**

Vlado Buckovski took office as prime minister of Macedonia on 17 December 2004. Previously a professor of law, he first entered the Macedonian Assembly in 1998, and was minister of defence for several months in 2001 and again after the victory of his Together for Macedonia (Za Makedonija Zaedno—ZMZ) coalition in 2002. The priority for his government is rescuing the Macedonian economy; in the long term it needs to carry out the necessary political and economic reforms to allow Macedonia to pursue membership of the European Union (EU).

Vlado Buckovski was born on 2 December 1962 in Skopje. He studied law at the University of Skopje, graduating in 1986, and went to work at the Macedonian Assembly as a legal assistant. From 1988 until 2002, he worked as an assistant and then a lecturer at the faculty of law at the University of Skopje, gaining his master's degree in 1991 and his doctorate in 1998; he became an associate professor in 2003.

Buckovski only entered politics at the 1998 election, which sent his party, the Social Democratic Union of Macedonia (Socijaldemokratski Sojuz na Makedonija—SDSM), into opposition. He became a member of the State Election Commission, and was chairman of Skopje city council from 2000 to 2001. In May 2001 he was appointed minister of defence in the broad coalition government set up to deal with the country's nascent ethnic conflict as ethnic Albanians demanded more rights. The unity government fell apart in November, when the SDSM withdrew from the coalition, but the centre-left ZMZ coalition led by the SDSM went on to win the 2002 elections; Buckovski was reappointed to the defence portfolio. He was elected vice president of the SDSM in 2003, and became prime minister in December 2004 following the resignation of Hari Kostov.

MADAGASCAR

Full name: The Republic of Madagascar.

Leadership structure: The head of state is a president, directly elected by universal adult suffrage. The president's term of office is five years. The president appoints the prime minister. Under the 1998 amendments to the constitution, the prime minister may be selected from a party which has a minority of seats in the National Assembly. The prime minister is head of government and appoints the other members of the Council of Ministers.

***President*:**	Adml. Didier Ratsiraka	9 Feb. 1997—5 July 2002
	(presidency in dispute between 22 Feb. and 5 July 2002)	
	Marc **RAVALOMANANA**	Since 22 Feb. 2002

***Prime Ministers under Ratsiraka*:**

Tantely René Gabrio Andrianarivo	23 July 1998—31 May 2002
Jean-Jacques Rasolondraibe (interim)	31 May 2002—5 July 2002

***Prime Minister under Ravalomanana*:**

Jacques **SYLLA**	Since 26 Feb. 2002

Legislature: The legislature, the Parliament, is bicameral. The lower chamber, the National Assembly (Antenimierampirenena), has 160 members, directly elected for a five-year term. The upper chamber, the Senate (Antenimieramdoholana), has 90 members, two-thirds of them elected by an electoral college, the remainder nominated by the president, all for a six-year term.

Profile of the President:

Marc **RAVALOMANANA**

Marc Ravalomanana became one of Madagascar's wealthiest businessmen thanks to the success of the dairy produce company he founded in the 1970s. Mayor of the capital from 1999, he challenged long-time president and former dictator Didier Ratsiraka in the presidential elections two years later. Accusations of poll-rigging in Ratsiraka's favour, and Ravalomanana's assertion that he had won in the first round, led to a six-month political struggle which often threatened to spiral into full-scale civil war. Although he was officially sworn in as president on 6 May 2002, it took two more months for his victory to be fully accepted.

Marc Ravalomanana was born on 12 December 1949 in Imerinkasinina near the capital, Antananarivo. His family was part of the country's minority Protestant community and he attended religious schools in his home village before travelling to Sweden to attend secondary school at another religious institution. He is now vice president of Madagascar's Protestant Church of Jesus Christ.

When he returned to Madagascar in the 1970s he set up his own small-scale business, producing home-made yoghurt which he sold from the back of a bicycle with the help of his wife Lalao. Within two years he had successfully applied for a loan from the World Bank, with the support of the Protestant Church, to build his first factory. His company, Tiko, became Madagascar's biggest home-grown business, with a virtual monopoly on dairy and vegetable oil products, and Ravalomanana himself is a dollar millionaire. He has set up other businesses in public works, construction, storage and an airline. He has one daughter and three sons.

In 1999 Ravalomanana decided to divert his energies into politics, and ran successfully as an independent candidate in the mayoral elections for Antananarivo. Famously deriding the city's "filth and anarchy", he set about a massive sanitation and centralization campaign. His policies were exceptionally popular in the capital. Buoyed by this experience he registered to compete in the presidential elections in 2001.

Official results from the first round in December stated that a second round was necessary between Ravalomanana and incumbent president Ratsiraka. Claiming that he had in fact won outright, Ravalomanana rejected this count and refused to participate in the second round, which had been scheduled for February 2002.

A six-month conflict began, in which over 30 people were killed in violent clashes between rival supporters. Ratsiraka retreated to his coastal stronghold of Toamasina while Ravalomanana was blockaded in Antananarivo, where he declared himself president on 22 February 2002. In April a recount of the disputed vote showed that Ravalomanana was indeed the rightful winner, and he was officially inaugurated on 6 May. By late June he had received international recognition; Toamasina, the last city claiming allegiance to Ratsiraka, was taken in early July and the former president fled into self-exile in France.

Ravalomanana's "I Love Madagascar" (Tiako'i Madagasikara—TIM) party went on to win a clear majority in the legislative elections in December. Among Ravalomanana's immediate tasks as head of state was to tackle government corruption. To this end he raised the pay of his ministers tenfold and promised similar raises to other civil servants "bit by bit". He also focused on rehabilitating the country's dilapidated road network, and has scrapped primary school fees and improved access to education.

Profile of the Prime Minister:

Jacques **SYLLA**

Jacques Sylla is an independent lawyer. He served as foreign minister in the 1990s under Madagascar's then president Albert Zafy. Appointed prime minister by presidential claimant Marc Ravalomanana on 26 February 2002, he was confirmed in the post in May, and again in January 2003 after the legislative elections.

Jacques Hugues Sylla was born in 1946 on the island of Sainte-Marie (Nosy Boraha) which lies off the coast of eastern Toamasina province. He trained as a lawyer in the late 1960s. Sylla is married to Yvette Rakoto and they have four children.

He began his political career in earnest in August 1993, when the opposition Forces Vives won legislative elections, allowing the country's first democratically elected president, Albert Zafy, to appoint a new cabinet. Sylla was nominated foreign minister and held that post until Zafy was impeached and failed to win re-election in 1996. Former dictator Didier Ratsiraka's return to power ended Sylla's role in government for the next five years.

When a fresh power struggle gripped the island following the presidential elections in December 2001, Sylla played an important role in the associated legal process, as head of the Toamasina section of the National Committee of Election Observers. Already appointed prime minister in the alternative cabinet drawn up by Ravalomanana in February 2002, he was among the 15 lawyers who attested in April to Ravalomanana's first-round victory. He remained head of Ravalomanana's cabinet once the latter's victory was legitimized in May, and was confirmed again in January 2003 after the sweeping victory of Ravalomanana's "I Love Madagascar" (Tiako'i Madagasikara—TIM) party in the December legislative polls.

Sylla is from the same ethnic *côtier* group as ousted president Ratsiraka, thereby helping to provide Ravalomanana's regime with a sense of truly national representation.

MALAWI

Full name: The Republic of Malawi.

Leadership structure: The head of state is a president, directly elected by universal adult suffrage. The president's term of office is five years, renewable once only. The head of government is the president.

President:	Bakili Muluzi	21 May 1994—24 May 2004
	Bingu wa **MUTHARIKA**	Since 24 May 2004

Legislature: The legislature is unicameral. The sole chamber, the National Assembly, has 193 members (expanded from 177 at the 1999 elections), directly elected for a five-year term.

Profile of the President:

Bingu wa **MUTHARIKA**

Economist Bingu wa Mutharika was the hand-picked successor of Bakili Muluzi and was sworn in as president on 24 May 2004 after winning disputed elections. A trained economist, he was one of the founders of the United Democratic Front (UDF) under Muluzi in 1994. However, the two men fell out, and Mutharika's rehabilitation took ten years. Since his elevation to the presidency Mutharika and Muluzi have fallen out once again and in February 2005 Mutharika left the UDF to form his own party.

Bingu wa Mutharika was born on 24 February 1934, the son of a Roman Catholic primary school teacher, and raised in Kamoto village in Thyolo, the southern tea-growing district of Malawi. He was named Brightson Thom at birth, and was called Webster Ryson Thom for much of his youth, but later changed his name to Bingu wa Mutharika. He graduated from the University of Delhi, India, with a master's degree in economics, and later studied for a doctorate in developmental economics at the Pacific Western University in Los Angeles, USA. He returned to Malawi to join the civil service, and also spent some time working for the government of Zambia.

In 1978 Mutharika went to work for the UN, eventually rising to become the director for trade and development finance for Africa, and in 1991 he was appointed secretary-general of the Common Market for Eastern and Southern Africa (COMESA). One reason for this move was his long-time dislike of the regime of then-president Hastings Banda. Mutharika was one of the founders of the UDF, set up following a referendum which forced Banda to introduce multiparty politics in 1994. Initially he was a supporter of Bakili Muluzi, the leader of the UDF, who ousted Banda in presidential elections that year. On taking office, however, Muluzi's administration ensured that Mutharika lost his job at COMESA and cast him as a failure and a fraud.

Mutharika finally left the UDF to form the United Party (UP) in 1997 and campaigned unsuccessfully against Muluzi in the 1999 presidential elections. He dissolved the UP and rejoined the UDF only after being offered the deputy governorship at the Reserve Bank of Malawi. Muluzi appointed Mutharika as minister of economic planning and development in 2002, and his rehabilitation in the eyes of the party seemed complete when he was nominated by Muluzi as his successor once the latter's attempt to run for a third term was thwarted.

Mutharika won a disputed presidential election and was sworn in as president of Malawi on 24 May 2004. His stated intention to stay on good terms with Muluzi, who remained as head of the UDF, disintegrated quickly and the two men soon found themselves at odds, not least because of Mutharika's campaign against corruption in Malawi. Threatened with expulsion from the party, Mutharika took the initiative himself in February 2005, leaving to set up a new Democratic Progressive Party (DPP).

MALAYSIA

Full name: The Federation of Malaysia.

Leadership structure: The head of state is the *yang di-pertuan agong* (supreme head of state), elected by the nine hereditary Malay rulers of Peninsular Malaysia from among their own number. The head of state's term of office is five years. The head of government is the prime minister, who is appointed, with the cabinet, by the head of state.

Supreme Head of State (Yang di-Pertuan Agong):

Salehuddin Abdul Aziz ibni al-Marhum Hisamuddin Alam	26 April 1999—21 Nov. 2001
Mizan Zainal Abidin ibni al-Marhum Sultan Mahmud (acting from 8 Oct. 2001)	21 Nov. 2001—13 Dec. 2001
Syed **SIRAJUDDIN** ibni al-Marhum Syed Putra Jamalullail	Since 13 Dec. 2001

Prime Minister:		
	Mahathir Mohamed	16 July 1981—31 Oct. 2003
	Abdullah Ahmad **BADAWI**	Since 31 Oct. 2003

Legislature: The legislature, the Parliament (Parlimen), is bicameral. The lower chamber, the House of Representatives (Dewan Rakyat), has 219 members, directly elected for a five-year term. The upper chamber, the Senate (Dewan Negara), has 70 members, serving a six-year term; each of the Legislative Assemblies of the states of Malaysia elects two members of the Senate, and the remaining 44 members are nominated by the head of state.

Profile of the Supreme Head of State (*Yang di-Pertuan Agong*):

Syed **SIRAJUDDIN** ibni al-Marhum Syed Putra Jamalullail

Tuanku Syed Sirajuddin was raja of the Malay state of Perlis before being elevated on 13 December 2001 to yang di-pertuan agong *(supreme ruler of Malaysia). Having received education and military training in the UK, he abandoned a career in the army to concentrate on administration in Perlis. Although as head of state he is also commander-in-chief of the Malaysian armed forces, his role is purely ceremonial.*

Syed Sirajuddin ibni al-Marhum Syed Putra Jamalullail was born on 16 May 1943 in Arau, Perlis, in the far northwest of Malaysia, the second of the ten children of the raja of Perlis. He began his education at a local preparatory school before entering the British colonial education system in 1950. Nine years later he travelled to the UK to complete his studies at the private Wellingborough School near Leicester. He was inaugurated as *raja muda* (crown prince) on 30 October 1960, while still at school.

After secondary school Sirajuddin began officer training in the UK in January 1964, at the Royal Military Academy in Sandhurst, from which he passed out as a second lieutenant in December 1965. He immediately returned to Malaysia and served in the reconnaissance force in Sabah, Sarawak and Pahang. Although he retired from active military service in December 1969, having attained the rank of lieutenant, he continued to serve in the army reserves in Perlis, as a captain from 1970 to 1972. As well as now being commander-in-chief of the national forces, he is also colonel of the Perlis reserve regiment.

His father died on 16 April 2000 and Sirajuddin, who had been acting as regent, was made full raja the next day. He was officially inaugurated in this office on 7 May. His role in Perlis is effectively as a figurehead and traditional leader and as such he is patron of various nongovernmental organizations there. Among them is the Tuanku Syed Putra Foundation which helps students from the state to pursue higher education. He takes an active interest in sport in the region and is president of the Putra Golf Club and was chairman of the Perlis Football Association for 18 years until 1995.

When the ruling *yang di-pertuan agong*, the sultan of Selangor, died in November 2001, the traditional conference of rulers from the nine Malay kingdoms elected Sirajuddin to be his replacement on 13 December. His official coronation as the 12th *yang di-pertuan agong* of Malaysia took place on 25 April 2002.

Sirajuddin married Tengku Fauziah binti Tengku Abdul Rashid, a princess from the ruling houses of Terengganu and Kelantan, on 15 February 1967. She is now chancellor of Universiti Sains Malaysia. Their son, Tuanku Syed Faizuddin Putra, born on 30 December 1967, was on 12 October 2000 made *raja muda* of Perlis, where he is currently acting as regent. They also have a daughter Sharifah Fazira, born on 5 June 1973.

Profile of the Prime Minister:

Abdullah Ahmad **BADAWI**

Abdullah Ahmad Badawi succeeded Mahathir Mohamed as Malaysian prime minister on 31 October 2003. Sacked from the cabinet in the late 1980s due to his association with Tengku Razaleigh, he was rehabilitated in the 1990s. His reputation was fully restored when he was appointed deputy prime minister in

1999. Badawi has managed to neutralize potential opposition since his appointment with a clever combination of impeccable Islamic credentials and a campaign to wipe out corruption, thus stealing the thunder of his opponents, and even his friends warn of confusing his affability for weakness; Badawi is described as the iron fist in the velvet glove.

Dato' Seri Abdullah bin Haji Ahmad Badawi was born on 26 November 1939 in Kampung Perlis, Bayan Lepas, on Pinang island. His father was a founding member of the ruling United Malays National Organization (UMNO). He is informally known as Pak Lah (the Malay diminutive for 'Uncle Abdullah'). The Malaysian government has issued a statement that the prime minister should not be referred to by this nickname in official articles and in the press, but the nickname is still used informally. He has been married to Datin Seri Endon bint Dato' Mahmood since 1965, and they have a son and a daughter. His wife was diagnosed with terminal breast cancer in 2002.

Badawi first attended Pematang Bertam National School. He later attended Bukit Mertajam High School, Pinang Methodist Boys' School and an Islamic religious school started by his family. Badawi pursued his tertiary education at the University of Malaya where he graduated in Islamic studies in 1964.

Upon graduating, Badawi joined the civil service, where he started his career as assistant secretary in the public services department. In 1969, he moved to the National Operations Council, a body given emergency powers following the May 1969 racial riots. He was later promoted to the ministry of culture, youth and sports as director-general from 1971 until 1973 and deputy secretary-general in 1974.

Badawi resigned from the civil service in 1978 to pursue a political career. A loyal UMNO member since 1965, he was elected UMNO Supreme Council member in 1981, UMNO vice president in 1984 and (the higher rank of) UMNO deputy president in 1999.

Badawi won his first election in 1978 for the parliamentary seat of the Kepala Batas constituency (a seat he has retained since). In the same year, he was appointed as the parliamentary secretary to the federal territory ministry. He was then promoted to deputy minister in the same ministry in 1980. Badawi later held the post of minister in the prime minister's department from 1981 to 1984; minister of education from 1984 to 1986; and minister of defence from 1986 to 1987.

In 1987 Tengku Razaleigh Hamzah challenged Prime Minister Mahathir Mohamed for the presidency of UMNO. Mahathir prevailed, but the contest split the party into two rival camps. Badawi, who had backed Razaleigh, was expelled from UMNO and spent several years in the political wilderness before being rehabilitated and appointed minister of foreign affairs in 1991. In January 1999 he was appointed deputy prime minister and minister of home affairs.

Malaysia: *Abdullah Ahmad Badawi*

Badawi succeeded Mahathir Mohamed as prime minister in October 2003, when Asia's longest-serving elected leader retired after 22 years in power. He promised to continue the policies of his predecessor. On taking office he faced a strong political challenge from opposition Islamic fundamentalists and inherited the task of overseeing one of the region's most vibrant economies.

In March 2004 Badawi was sworn in for a new, five-year term after his coalition government won a landslide victory in parliamentary and regional elections. Since becoming prime minister he has clamped down on corruption, giving more power to anti-graft agencies. He has also arrested several Mahathir-era cronies on charges of corruption, a move which has been widely popular. He has advocated an interpretation of Islam known as Islam Hadhari, which maintains that Islam and economic and technological development are not incompatible, and has delivered the kind of pointed criticisms of both the West and the Islamic world for which Mahathir was noted, but without the racial overtones which had made many of Mahathir's statements especially controversial internationally.

MALDIVES

Full name: The Republic of Maldives.

Leadership structure: The head of state is a president, elected by the People's Assembly and confirmed by national referendum. The president's term of office is five years. The head of government is the president, who appoints and presides over the cabinet.

President: Maumoon Abdul **GAYOOM**   Since 11 Nov. 1978

Legislature: The legislature is unicameral. The sole chamber, the People's Assembly (People's Majlis), has 50 members. Two members are directly elected from each of the provinces (atolls) and from Malé, the capital, and the remaining eight members are appointed by the president, all for a five-year term.

Profile of the President:

Maumoon Abdul **GAYOOM**

Maumoon Abdul Gayoom, a former lecturer in Islamic studies, became president of the Maldives in November 1978 and has been re-elected on five successive occasions for further five-year terms, most recently in 2003. Gayoom's dominance in the family-based nonparty political system was challenged, however, by a coup attempt in 1988 and a bid by his brother-in-law Ilyas Ibrahim for nomination for the presidency in 1993, while an educated younger generation is pressing for increased freedoms. In 2005 constitutional changes were approved to steer the country towards multiparty democracy.

Maumoon Gayoom was born in the capital, Malé, on 29 December 1937. Following early schooling in Malé he went to al-Azhar University in Cairo, Egypt, where he graduated with a degree in Islamic studies and a diploma in education, going on to gain a master's degree in Islamic studies in 1966. He then embarked on an academic career, becoming a lecturer in Islamic studies and philosophy at Abdullahi Bayero College, Nigeria, and returning to the Maldives to teach at Aminiya School from 1971 to 1972.

In the 1970s he became successively manager of the government's shipping department, director of the telecommunications department, special undersecretary in the office of the prime minister, deputy ambassador to Sri Lanka and undersecretary at the ministry of external affairs. In June 1976 he was appointed permanent representative at the UN. He then took on a cabinet post as minister of transport, holding this job until the 1978 presidential elections when long-serving president Ibrahim Nasir stood down.

Nominated by the People's Assembly, Gayoom was endorsed by a 92.9% vote in the popular ballot in that election. His nomination for successive terms has usually been uncontested, although in 1993 Ilyas Ibrahim's rival candidacy attracted some support in the Assembly. He was re-elected most recently with a 90.3% endorsement in a national referendum held on 17 October 2003, having been unanimously selected by the Assembly in September from among four candidates.

In addition to the presidency, Gayoom held the defence and national security portfolios for more than two decades, and from November 1993 he was also minister of finance and of the treasury. His dependence on good relations with India was underlined when he had to be rescued by Indian intervention after a coup attempt in 1988. From the 1990s onward he became better known internationally for drawing attention to the threat posed by global warming to small island states.

In recent years calls have increased for political reform and greater democracy in the Maldives, especially from a young Westernized elite. The 1998 Constitution relaxed the rules for presidential candidates challenging for the nomination of the Assembly, but the pace of greater reform has been slow. In 2004 as pressure on Gayoom increased, he proposed to the Assembly that political parties should be allowed, and a constitutional assembly was set up, but its activities were suspended and a state of emergency was imposed in August following a crackdown on pro-democracy protestors. In September 2004 he reshuffled the government, yielding at last his personal control of the defence and finance portfolios.

Although the January 2005 Assembly elections were held, as previously, on a nonparty basis, several of the seats were won by candidates backed by the Sri Lanka-based Maldivian Democratic Party. Gayoom applauded the results as showing the election was "free and fair" and promised to accelerate the constitutional reform process already in motion to introduce a multiparty political system with an elected president and a prime minister. In June the Assembly voted unanimously in favour of multipartyism, and the following month Gayoom was chosen as leader of the newly registered Maldives People's Party (Dhivehi Rayyithunge Party—DRP), which he instated as the ruling party.

Gayoom, who was made a Knight Grand Cross of the Order of St Michael and St George in October 1997, is married to Nasreena Ibrahim and they have two sons and twin daughters.

MALI

Full name: The Republic of Mali.

Leadership structure: The head of state is a president, directly elected by universal adult suffrage. The president's term of office is five years. The president appoints the prime minister, who is head of government and appoints the other members of the Council of Ministers.

President:	Alpha Oumar Konaré	8 June 1992—8 June 2002
	Amadou **TOUMANI TOURÉ**	Since 8 June 2002
Prime Minister:	Ibraham Boubacar Keita	4 Feb. 1994—15 Feb. 2000
	Mandé Sidibé	15 Feb. 2000—18 March 2002
	Modibo Keita	18 March 2002—9 June 2002
	Ahmed Mohamed Ag Hamani	9 June 2002—30 April 2004
	Ousmane Issoufi **MAÏGA**	Since 30 April 2004

Legislature: The legislature is unicameral. The sole chamber, the National Assembly (Assemblée Nationale), has 147 members, directly elected for a five-year term, renewable once only.

Profile of the President:

Amadou **TOUMANI TOURÉ**

Gen. (retd) Amadou Toumani Touré is an independent who led the country to multiparty democracy in 1992 in the wake of a coup. He turned to international politics and conflict resolution after handing power over to his democratically elected successor, Alpha Oumar Konaré, but returned to office in 2002, winning a landslide victory with the backing of over 40 political parties.

Amadou Toumani Touré, now popularly known as 'ATT', was born on 4 November 1948 in Mopti in what was then colonial French Sudan. After a local education, Touré joined the Malian armed forces in 1969, a year after a successful coup by Gen. Moussa Traoré. Toumani Touré is married to Touré Lobbo Traoré and they have two daughters.

Rising through the ranks of the army, Toumani Touré became a lieutenant in 1972 and a captain in the parachute battalion in 1978. In that year he was also appointed commander of Traoré's presidential guard. He stepped down from the guard and attained the rank of lieutenant-colonel in 1986. A rising tide of popular discontent with Traoré was sparked in 1991 by his attempt to suppress an uprising by the northern Tuareg people, and by heavy-handed policing of growing political demonstrations. On 26 March 1991 Toumani Touré organized a coup to overthrow the aging president and placed himself at the head of a Transitional Committee for the Salvation of the People—effectively president.

Keen to relinquish his hold on power, Toumani Touré organized a National Reconciliation Council which approved a new multiparty democratic constitution. In April 1991 he also appointed a civilian, Soumana Sacko, as prime minister. Surviving a failed countercoup in July his government convened fresh presidential and legislative elections in early 1992. On 8 June 1992 Toumani Touré handed over power to Konaré and the Alliance for Democracy in Mali (Alliance pour la Démocratie au Mali—ADEMA) which had won a majority in the National Assembly. For the next ten years Toumani Touré stayed away from Malian politics, acting instead as a prominent mediator in regional conflicts, notably in Burundi and the Central African Republic. He was also involved in charities promoting children's welfare.

By 2001 the ADEMA government had become mired in accusations of corruption. Opposition parties began to flourish and Toumani Touré resigned his army commission (by now he had become a general) in September in order to qualify for the May 2002 presidential contest. He was elected in the second round with an overwhelming 65% majority, having received the backing of around 40 political parties, many of which coalesced in the Hope 2002 movement (Espoir 2002) which went on to gain the largest single share of seats in the July elections.

Having traded heavily on his political independence, Toumani Touré hinted that he would largely follow the policies of Konaré. He remains popular in Mali and is respected by many in the international community, who praise the country's lack of corruption and improvements in social provision, despite its deep poverty exacerbated by locust plagues in 2004 which brought the region to the brink of famine.

Profile of the Prime Minister:

Ousmane Issoufi **MAÏGA**

Ousmane Issoufi Maïga, an independent technocrat, was appointed prime minister of Mali on 30 April 2004. He had worked as an economist before entering government as minister of finance in 2002.

Ousmane Issoufi Maïga was born in 1946 in northern Mali, a member of the Songhai people who once controlled an empire. Maïga became an economist, studying financial management in the former Soviet Union before returning to

Mali to work at the national debt management office and at the public procurement office. During the 1980s he spent a period working for the African Development Foundation (ADF) as its country representative in Mali. Maïga speaks Russian, English, French, Bambara and Songhai, and is nicknamed 'Pinochet' after the Chilean dictator, though nobody seems precisely sure why.

He is regarded as a hard-working technocrat with a reputation for being anti corruption, and is unaligned with any of Mali's many political parties despite being first appointed to government as minister of finance by President Amadou Toumani Touré in 2002. That same year he was chosen to manage the hosting of the African Cup of Nations, an event that was generally lauded as a huge success. He went on to be appointed minister of equipment and transport from 2003 to 2004 before being appointed as prime minister on 30 April 2004 on the resignation of Ahmed Mohamed Ag Hamani.

MALTA

Full name: The Republic of Malta.

Leadership structure: The head of state is a president, elected by the House of Representatives. The president's term of office is five years, renewable once only. The president appoints the prime minister and, on the latter's advice, the other members of the government. The prime minister is head of government. The cabinet is responsible to parliament.

President:	Guido de Marco	4 April 1999—4 April 2004
	Eddie **FENECH-ADAMI**	Since 4 April 2004
Prime Minister:	Eddie Fenech-Adami	6 Sept. 1998—23 March 2004
	Lawrence **GONZI**	Since 23 March 2004

Legislature: The legislature is unicameral. The sole chamber, the House of Representatives (Kamra Tad-Deputati), has 65 members, directly elected for a five-year term by universal adult suffrage. However, if a party gains a majority of votes in a general election, without winning a majority of seats in the House, extra seats are created until that party holds a majority of one seat.

Profile of the President:

Eddie **FENECH-ADAMI**

Eddie Fenech-Adami was elected as president of Malta in March 2004, and took office in April. He had been prime minister from 1987 to 1996 and again from 1998 until he stood for the presidency. A lawyer by training, he was elected to the House of Representatives in 1969 and led the Nationalist Party (Partit Nazzjonalista—PN) from 1977 until 2004. When he first came into government he undertook to overturn years of socialist policies in Malta, steering the country on a path towards eventual European Union (EU) membership.

Edward Fenech-Adami was born in Birkirkara on 7 February 1934, the son of a customs officer. He was educated at St Aloysius College before attending the Royal University of Malta in the 1950s. He graduated with a degree in economics and classics before returning to study law. He was called to the Bar in 1959. A keen journalist, he edited the weekly *Il-Poplu* from 1962 to 1969. In 1965 he married Mary Sciberras, and they have four sons and one daughter.

In 1961 Fenech-Adami joined the PN national executive and served as assistant secretary-general from 1962 to 1975. He was elected to parliament in 1969 and held a seat continually until his retirement from parliament in 2004. From 1975 he acted as president of the administrative and general councils of the PN. Elected to lead the party in 1977 after its second consecutive electoral defeat by the Malta Labour Party (MLP), he set about reforming the PN during a period in opposition which was to last for ten years.

Seeking to adapt to a more socially conscious electorate, Fenech-Adami's reforms attracted a new party membership that was notably more youthful. His support grew to the extent that in the general election of 1981 the PN won a majority of votes but a minority of seats. This bitter defeat caused years of disruption in parliament with Fenech-Adami leading a campaign of civil disobedience and repeated boycotts of parliamentary sessions from 1981 to 1983. A constitutional amendment agreed in 1987 enabled a party with a popular majority to assume 'bonus' seats in the House of Representatives if necessary to form a majority. In that year's election the PN won 31 out of 65 elected seats, and acquired four bonus seats, allowing it to form a government.

As leader of the party, Fenech-Adami was appointed as prime minister and began a series of political reforms to restructure Malta after 16 years of socialist government. Industries were deregulated and some privatized. The government was able to record nine successive years of positive economic growth, during which it was returned for a second term in 1992. Fenech-Adami brought the country ever closer to the EU and as part of this drive introduced value-added tax (VAT) in 1996. It proved an unpopular move and the PN found itself back in opposition after defeat in an early election in that year.

Fenech-Adami was returned to the premiership after only two years in opposition following unwelcome increases in taxation by the MLP government, whose decision to call a snap election in September 1998 backfired when the PN won by a margin of 4.8% of the vote. Enjoying the luxury of the biggest PN majority since the Second World War (albeit only with 35 seats in the 65-seat House of Representatives), Fenech-Adami promptly reinstated VAT, and he and the then foreign minister Guido de Marco reactivated Malta's application for EU membership, which had been frozen under the MLP. In December 2002 Malta was among ten countries invited to join the EU in May 2004, and Malta was the first of the ten aspirant countries to hold a referendum on membership, voting in favour in March 2003.

Riding high on this success, the PN won 52% of the vote in the April 2003 election, retaining its 35 seats, and days later Fenech-Adami signed the accession treaty to the EU. In recognition of his efforts to integrate Malta into Europe he was named 'European of the year' for 2003 by Brussels-based newspaper *European Voice*.

On 7 February 2004—his 70th birthday—he resigned as PN leader, and the following month stepped down as prime minister and gave up his parliamentary seat. Six days later, on 29 March, he was elected to the more ceremonial post of president, and he took office on 4 April.

Profile of the Prime Minister:

Lawrence **GONZI**

Lawrence Gonzi became prime minister of Malta on 23 March 2004, when Eddie Fenech-Adami moved up to become president. Gonzi had previously held the posts of deputy leader of the Nationalist Party (Partit Nazzjonalista—PN) and deputy prime minister. Both Gonzi and Fenech-Adami are ardent pro-Europeans and together steered their country into the European Union (EU) in May 2004. Gonzi's stated priorities for Malta include cutting bureaucracy, reducing the ballooning budget deficit and creating employment, but he is often seen as weak and indecisive and his reputation was badly damaged in August 2004 by a property scandal.

Lawrence Gonzi was born in Valletta on 1 July 1953 to Louis Gonzi and Inez Gonzi (née Galea). He is married to Catherine Gonzi (née Callus); they have two sons and a daughter. He graduated as a doctor of law from the University of Malta in 1975 and practised law between 1975 and 1988.

Gonzi was chairman of a leading commercial company in the private sector between 1989 and 1997, and has been actively involved in the voluntary and NGO sectors since 1976, particularly in the fields of disability and mental health. He occupied the position of general president of Malta Catholic Action between 1976 and 1986. Having failed to win a seat in the 1987 elections, Gonzi was appointed ex officio speaker of the House of Representatives in October 1988 and in 1992 was reappointed with a unanimous vote. He successfully stood for election in 1996, and again in 1998 and 2003. He was appointed opposition party whip, secretary to the parliamentary group and shadow minister of social policy in 1996. Following the PN's electoral victory in September 1998, he became minister of social policy and leader of the House of Representatives.

Gonzi was elected deputy leader of the party in 1999 and was subsequently appointed deputy prime minister. He held this position as well as those of minister of social policy and leader of the House until March 2004, when he was elected as head of the ruling PN after veteran leader Edward Fenech-Adami announced his retirement. Gonzi took office weeks ahead of Malta's entry into the EU. A committed Roman Catholic, Gonzi pushed for the phrase 'Christian heritage' to be included in the new EU constitution. He promised to boost tourism and to create favourable conditions for investment, but most believe that his first priority must be job creation.

MARSHALL ISLANDS

Full name: The Republic of the Marshall Islands.

Leadership structure: The head of state is a president, elected by the Parliament from among its members for a four-year term. The president is also head of government and appoints the cabinet.

| *President*: | Imata Kabua | 22 Jan. 1997—10 Jan. 2000 |
| | Kessai **NOTE** | Since 10 Jan. 2000 |

Legislature: The legislature is unicameral. The sole chamber, the Parliament (Nitijela), has 33 members, directly elected for a four-year term. There is also a 12-member Council of Chiefs (Council of Iroij), composed of traditional leaders (*iroijlaplap*), which has consultative authority on matters relating to land and custom and which advises the cabinet.

Profile of the President:

Kessai **NOTE**

Kessai Note, the third president of the Marshall Islands, has a long record as a member of the Parliament, and was elected as its speaker three times. An influential critic of the previous heads of state, Amata and Imata Kabua, he was elected president in 2000. He is supported in government by the United Democratic Party (UDP), whose majority was significantly increased at the 2003 elections.

Kessai Hesa Note was born on 7 August 1950 on Jabat, one of the smallest of the 24 inhabited atolls that make up the Marshall Islands. At that time the islands were part of the UN Trust Territory of the Pacific. Note went to school first on Ebeye and then to the Marshall Islands' High School on Majuro, before attending Vudal College of Agriculture, Papua New Guinea, between 1971 and 1974, where he witnessed much of that country's transition to independence, achieved in 1975.

Returning to Majuro, he worked in the agriculture office of the Trust Territory administration, but did not become involved in the Marshalls' separation movement until his election to the Constitutional Convention in 1977. This body oversaw the drafting of the new constitution, which came into effect in 1979.

Note then was recommended to be the parliamentary candidate for his home island of Jabat. With an area of only 0.22 sq km, Jabat has a population recorded in 1999 as just 95, and Note has faced no opposition in holding on to its seat since his first election in 1980. He is married to Mary Neimoj Note and they have five children.

The Marshall Islands was dominated for almost two decades by Amata Kabua, the high-ranking traditional chief of Majuro atoll, who held the presidency from 1979 until his death in 1996 when he was succeeded by his cousin, the chief of Kwajalein atoll, Imata Kabua. Note was a strong critic of their rule and a thorn in the executive's side, serving on both the High Court and the Supreme Court. His ability to oppose the government increased greatly in his three terms from 1987 as speaker of the Parliament. From this position he became an active counterweight to both of the Kabua administrations, successfully pushing through a proposal to outlaw gambling. In September 1999 Note oversaw the country's very first no-confidence vote against a head of state. Although the motion failed, Kabua's days in power were numbered. In the run-up to the presidential elections on 3 January 2000, in which Note proposed to stand, the newly elected Parliament had first to choose a new speaker. The resounding defeat of Kabua's preferred candidate sent shock waves through the executive and Kabua declined to stand in the presidential contest. Note's election, all the more spectacular as he thus became the first commoner to win the presidency, was achieved on a strong anti-corruption platform calling for a major reform of government.

Among Note's policies is opposition to the storage of nuclear or other toxic wastes on the uninhabited atolls. He is also keen to increase productivity among civil servants, who, he complained, often work for only an hour and a half a day. His government has started to cut bureaucracy for businesses, injected funds into NGOs to assist with social provision, and improved education.

A year into his administration Note survived the country's second no-confidence vote, brought by opposition senators led by Kabua, winning 19 votes in his favour in the 33-seat Parliament. Among his opponents' complaints was Note's apparent unwillingness to tackle the delicate subject of land rental with the USA, despite the expiry that year of the Compact of Free Association with the USA. The Compact was eventually renegotiated in 2003, providing the basis of the two countries' relationship for the next 20 years. Under the new deal a trust fund will be established to provide financial aid after 2023, though agreement was not reached on the rent for the US missile base, and this needs to be settled by 2008.

Note also faces strong criticism for his relationship with the controversial Reverend Sun Myung Moon, self-proclaimed messiah and founder of the Unification Church (Moonies).

Elections in November 2003 gave a significant victory to the UDP, with 20 of the 33 seats. At the new parliament's opening session in January 2004 Note was duly re-elected as president.

MAURITANIA

Full name: The Islamic Republic of Mauritania.

Leadership structure: The head of state is a president, directly elected by universal adult suffrage for a term of six years according to the constitution. Col. Maaouya ould Sid' Ahmed Taya was overthrown in a bloodless coup on 3 August 2005. The leader of the newly formed Military Council for Justice and Democracy (Conseil Militaire pour la Justice et la Démocratie—CMJD) was appointed head of state. Presidential elections were promised within two years. The head of state appoints the prime minister, who is designated head of government.

President:	Maaouya ould Sid' Ahmed Taya (seized power on 12 Dec. 1984)	18 April 1992—3 Aug. 2005
	Ely ould Mohamed **VALL**	Since 3 Aug. 2005
Prime Minister:	Cheikh el-Avia ould Mohamed Khouna	16 Nov. 1998—6 July 2003
	Sghair ould M'Bareck	6 July 2003—7 Aug. 2005
	Sidi Mohamed ould **BOUBACAR**	Since 7 Aug. 2005

Legislature: The legislature, the Parliament (Barlamane), is bicameral. The lower chamber, the National Assembly (Jamiya-al-Wataniya), has 81 members, directly elected for a five-year term. The upper chamber, the Senate (Majlis al-Chouyoukh), has 56 members (of whom three represent Mauritanians living abroad), indirectly elected for a six-year term, one-third renewed every two years.

Profile of the President:

Ely ould Mohamed **VALL**

Ely ould Mohamed Vall was born in the capital Nouakchott in 1950. He was head of national security from 1987, but on 3 August 2005 he led a military coup that ousted his erstwhile ally President Maaouya ould Sid' Ahmed Taya. He was named president immediately. Though the coup was initially condemned by the international community, it has since been tacitly accepted on the understanding that Vall honours his commitment to hold early elections in which none of the current junta will stand.

Profile of the Prime Minister:

Sidi Mohamed ould **BOUBACAR**

Sidi Mohamed ould Boubacar was born in 1945. An experienced politician, and a member of the Democratic and Social Republican Party (Parti Républicain Démocratique et Social—PRDS), he was prime minister from 1992 until 1996 under President Maaouya ould Sid' Ahmed Taya. He was then appointed as Mauritania's ambassador to France. Following the bloodless military coup which overthrew Taya in August 2005, the junta headed by newly appointed president Ely ould Mohamed Vall nominated Boubacar as prime minister on 7 August. The choice was controversial in some quarters because of his previous association with the unpopular Taya regime.

MAURITIUS

Full name: Republic of Mauritius.

Leadership structure: The head of state is a president, elected by the National Assembly. The president's term of office is five years. The head of government is the prime minister, the leader of the majority party in parliament. The Council of Ministers is appointed by the president on the advice of the prime minister.

President:	Cassam Uteem	1 July 1992—15 Feb. 2002
	Angidi Chettiar (acting)	15 Feb. 2002—18 Feb. 2002
	Arianga Pillay (interim)	18 Feb. 2002—25 Feb. 2002
	Karl Offmann	25 Feb. 2002—1 Oct. 2003
	Raouf Bundhun (acting)	1 Oct. 2003—7 Oct. 2003
	Sir Anerood **JUGNAUTH**	Since 7 Oct. 2003
Prime Minister:	Navinchandra Ramgoolam	27 Dec. 1995—15 Sept. 2000
	Sir Anerood Jugnauth	16 Sept. 2000—30 Sept. 2003
	Paul Bérenger	30 Sept. 2003
	Navinchandra **RAMGOOLAM**	Since 5 July 2005

Legislature: The legislature is unicameral. The sole chamber, the National Assembly, has 62 directly elected members, plus eight 'best losers' in the general election. The members serve for a five-year term.

Profile of the President:

Sir Anerood JUGNAUTH

Anerood Jugnauth is a barrister and veteran politician, who was prime minister from 1982 to 1995 and from 2000 until his election to the presidency in 2003. Made a member of the (UK) Privy Council in 1987, he was knighted in 1988, and received the French Legion of Honour in 1990.

Anerood Jugnauth was born on 29 March 1930 in Palma. He was educated at the Church of England School in Palma, and then at Regent College, Quatre Bornes. He studied at Lincoln's Inn in the UK from 1951 and was called to the Bar in

1954. He is married to Sarojini Devi Ballah, with two children, and he speaks English, French, Hindi, Bhojpuri and Creole.

In 1963 Jugnauth first became a member of the Legislative Assembly (redesignated as the National Assembly in 1992 when Mauritius became a republic within the Commonwealth). In 1965 he was appointed minister of state for development, a post he occupied until 1967, when he became minister of labour. Between 1967 and 1969 he was a district magistrate, becoming Crown Counsel in 1969, Senior Crown Counsel in 1971 and Queen's Counsel in 1980.

In 1969 he was a cofounder, along with Paul Bérenger, of the Mauritian Militant Movement (Mouvement Militant Mauricien—MMM), and as president of the MMM between 1973 and 1982 became leader of the opposition in 1976. In 1982 the MMM formed a coalition government with the Mauritian Socialist Party (Parti Socialiste Mauricien—PSM) and Jugnauth became prime minister, with Bérenger as minister of finance. In 1983 he broke with Bérenger and the MMM to form the Militant Socialist Movement (Mouvement Socialiste Militant— MSM), which incorporated the PSM. This break in the coalition ended the government's majority and fresh elections were held in August. The MSM remained the dominant party in the coalition governments of 1983–87 and 1987– 91, and 1991–95, and Jugnauth retained the premiership. In addition, during the 1980s he at various times held the ministerial portfolios of finance, defence, internal security and reform institutions, information, interior and exterior communications with the outer islands, justice and was attorney general. Two attempts were made on Jugnauth's life, one in November 1988 and the other in March 1989, which he attributed to narcotics traffickers.

In November 1995 the government was defeated in a vote in the National Assembly on a constitutional amendment to provide primary education in oriental languages. Jugnauth dissolved the Assembly, elections were held in December, and a new government was formed by an alliance of the MMM and the Labour Party of Navinchandra Ramgoolam, with the MSM completely unrepresented in the Assembly. Within five years this catastrophic defeat was reversed, and the MSM returned to power in alliance with the MMM in September 2000, winning over three-quarters of the seats. Jugnauth was duly called upon to form another government, although under the electoral pact between the two parties he pledged to step down in favour of Bérenger half way though his term.

In April 2003 he passed the party leadership to his son Pravind, and then on 30 September he stepped down from the premiership as promised. A week later, the final part of the planned reorganization was followed through when Jugnauth was elected by the National Assembly to the ceremonial post of president. Critics questioned whether Jugnauth would be able to maintain the constitutional independence of the presidency, given his son's appointment as Bérenger's deputy prime minister. The situation was resolved in 2005 by electoral defeat for the MSM–MMM alliance.

Profile of the Prime Minister:

Navinchandra **RAMGOOLAM**

Navinchandra Ramgoolam took office for a second term as prime minister of Mauritius in July 2005, when an alliance led by his Labour Party (Parti Travailliste—PT) won the general election. Qualified as both a medical doctor and a barrister, he trained in Dublin, Ireland, and has spent much of his adult life working in the UK. His father, Sir Seewoosagur Ramgoolam, was the first prime minister of Mauritius from independence in 1968 until 1982 and also leader of the PT, a moderate democratic socialist party drawing its support mainly from the majority Hindus of Indian descent. Navinchandra's first appointment as prime minister had come in 1995, after winning elections in alliance with the Mauritian Militant Movement (Mouvement Militant Mauricien—MMM), but he had lost power in 2000 when corruption scandals forced early elections.

Born on 14 July 1947, Navinchandra (Navin) Ramgoolam completed his secondary schooling at the Royal College, Curepipe, and then studied at the Royal College of Surgeons in Dublin from 1968, qualifying as a medical doctor in 1975. From 1976 until 1985 he worked in the UK at the University College Hospital in London and at a clinic in West Yorkshire. Returning to Mauritius in 1985, he was a general medical practitioner there until 1987, when he went back to the UK to study law at the London School of Economics. Graduating in 1990, he enrolled at the Inns of Court in 1993 and was called to the Bar that same year. He is married to Veena Ramgoolam.

Ramgoolam's active involvement in politics began in 1990 when he took over the Labour leadership. He entered parliament for the first time as one of only three successful opposition candidates in the September 1991 general election. Splits within the ruling coalition, however, led to the dismissal of MMM leader Paul Bérenger from the government and the formation in 1994 of an opposition alliance between Labour and the MMM. This alliance won 60 of the 66 seats in the National Assembly at the general election of 21 December 1995. Ramgoolam was sworn in as prime minister on 27 December; he also took on several other portfolios including defence and internal security.

Ramgoolam pledged to continue the outgoing government's free-market economic policies, which had made the country's economy one of the most successful in Africa. He also undertook to legislate for equal opportunities and to ensure a fairer distribution of wealth. His promises of better economic management and an end to corruption, while attractive to the largely white-run business sector, were however constrained by resistance among his party's traditional supporters to reductions in job opportunities in the government bureaucracy. In June 1997 Bérenger pulled the MMM out of the governing coalition, leaving Ramgoolam to announce a new Labour-only cabinet the following month.

In August 2000 President Cassam Uteem unexpectedly dissolved the National Assembly after a number of high-profile corruption scandals. A general election was held on 11 September, several months ahead of schedule, and the Labour Party in alliance with the Mauritian Party of Xavier Duval won just eight seats in the Assembly. Five years in opposition followed for Ramgoolam, facing a government of Bérenger's MMM and Sir Anerood Jugnauth's Militant Socialist Movement. However, by the end of their term in 2005 rising inflation and unemployment had revived support for the Labour Party, which led a six-party Social Alliance (Alliance Sociale) to victory in the July election. Ramgoolam took office as prime minister again on 5 July.

MEXICO

Full name: The United Mexican States.

Leadership structure: The head of state is a president, directly elected by universal adult suffrage. The president's term of office is six years; presidential candidates must not have held public office in the six months prior to the election. The head of government is the president, who appoints the cabinet.

President:	Ernesto Zedillo	1 Dec. 1994—30 Nov. 2000
	Vicente **FOX**	Since 1 Dec. 2000

Legislature: The legislature, the Congress of the Union (Congreso de la Unión), is bicameral. The lower chamber, the Chamber of Deputies (Cámara de Diputados), has 500 members, directly elected for a three-year term. The upper chamber, the Senate of the Republic (Senado de la República), has 128 members, directly elected for a six-year term.

Profile of the President:

Vicente **FOX**

Vicente Fox's election as president in 2000 ended 71 years of rule by the Institutional Revolutionary Party (Partido Revolucionario Institucional—PRI), while his centrist National Action Party (Partido Acción Nacional—PAN) swept the PRI from power in concurrent legislative elections. He is a rural businessman who received his commercial training when he headed Coca-Cola's operations in Latin America in the late 1970s and his political education as governor of Guanajuato state. Fox's plain talking, cowboy-dressing style was much criticized by opponents as lacking in substance. He promised to soften the country's 'harsh' capitalism with a 'third way'.

Vicente Fox Quesada was born in Mexico City on 2 July 1942 but was soon taken home to the San Cristóbal ranch in Guanajuato state in central Mexico. He was raised in the rural community and has kept closely in touch with his agricultural roots throughout his career. He studied business administration at the Ibero-American University, in Mexico City, then went to Harvard University in the USA to get a diploma in management skills, and returned to Mexico in 1965 to work for the Coca-Cola Company as a 'route supervisor'.

After three years of travelling around the country on delivery trucks Fox was appointed as the company's youngest ever regional manager. He continued to work his way up the ranks, to become manager for the company's operations in Mexico and Latin America in 1975. During his four years in this position Fox ensured that Coca-Cola replaced its main international rival, Pepsi, as the dominant supplier of soft drinks in Mexico.

In 1979 Fox abandoned management in the multinational to direct his family's Guanajuato-based agricultural enterprise, Gruppo Fox (GF). As well as ranching, GF engaged in various types of agro-industrial activities, and even shoe making, a speciality of the area. Fox has maintained an active role in agriculture and his family farm in the central state exports vegetables to Europe, Japan and the USA, as well as rearing cattle and ostriches for the domestic market. While managing GF, Fox developed an association with the opposition PAN, and began to write political articles for national and state newspapers.

In elections in 1988 Fox won a seat in the Federal Chamber of Deputies as a PAN candidate. Three years later he stood in gubernatorial elections for Guanajuato state but was defeated by PRI candidate Ramón Aguirre. However, popular discontent with the result forced Aguirre from office, leaving a PAN member as interim governor. Fox won fresh elections in 1995. His governorship of Guanajuato was widely seen as a major success and provided the training ground for his later bid for the presidency. Under his leadership there was greater investment in the state and a marked improvement in education.

Fox, who has married twice (most recently to Marta Sahagún Jiménez in July 2001) and has four adopted children (two sons and two daughters), made much of his rural roots during his campaign for president in 1999–2000, even pledging to continue wearing cowboy boots and jeans if elected. His abrasive manner towards his opponents, labelling the PRI candidate Francisco Labastida a "sissy", won support among the rural voters. However, his detractors accused him of carrying no real conviction with his pledge to perform a "new economic miracle". Although he was an extremely popular candidate, there can be little doubt that dissatisfaction with 71 years of PRI rule played a major role in his electoral victory in the July 2000 poll. He gained a convincing 43.4% of the vote, ahead of Labastida with only 36.9%.

Promises of an inclusive consensus government were confounded when the PRI rejected Fox's invitation to join a broad-based coalition, and political rivalry between the PRI and PAN has dominated elections at all levels. The PAN lost 40 seats in mid-term congressional elections in July 2003, half of which went to the PRI, which increased Fox's difficulties in trying to pass legislation through Congress, notably his proposed changes to the 2005 budget. In 2005, with presidential elections looming the following year, two key state governorships were also lost to the PRI, though the front-runner for the presidency is in fact Mexico City mayor Andrés Manuel López Obrador, the candidate of the third-ranking Party of the Democratic Revolution. Protests erupted when he was charged with contempt of court in early 2005 and Fox's government came under intense pressure to backtrack on what was seen as a politically motivated action by the state prosecutor.

Among Fox's campaign pledges had been a promise to recommence negotiations with Zapatista rebels from the southern state of Chiapas and within weeks of his inauguration he ordered the first major troop withdrawals from the state. Despite this gesture, however, the Zapatistas continued to press for further concessions. However, a breakthrough appeared to come in July 2005 when the Zapatistas made an unprecedented statement promising a new political initiative, raising the expectation that they would join mainstream politics.

Elsewhere Fox's popularity has begun to fall as he has done little to achieve his "economic miracle", stymied by the global economic slowdown which particularly affected the USA, Mexico's main trading partner. In January 2002 he dismantled the now defunct agrarian policy which had once been the cornerstone of the PRI regime, and promised to properly codify land claims to end decades of disputes. Plans to extend (a reduced) value-added tax (VAT) to medicines and food, and to allow private investment in the energy sector, which many suspect is the beginning of full privatization, provoked mass protests in 2003. Violent crime levels have also remained high, despite Fox's stand against organized crime in particular.

Going against the traditionally good ties between Mexico and Cuba, Fox publicly questioned the Castro regime in 2004, and in the ensuing diplomatic spat ambassadors were withdrawn temporarily. However, he has also been keenly aware of the unpopularity of following US foreign policy, notably in 2003 ahead of the invasion of Iraq, when Mexico was one of the temporary members of the UN Security Council and was under intense pressure from the USA to back a resolution for war.

FEDERATED STATES OF MICRONESIA

Full name: The Federated States of Micronesia.

Leadership structure: The head of state is a president, elected by the Congress. The president's term of office is four years. The head of government is the president, who is responsible to the Congress. The cabinet is appointed by the president, and confirmed by the Congress.

| *President*: | Leo Falcam | 12 May 1999—10 May 2003 |
| | Joseph **URUSEMAL** | Since 10 May 2003 |

Legislature: The legislature is unicameral. The sole chamber, the Congress of the Federated States of Micronesia (FSM), has 14 members, ten senators directly elected for a two-year term and four 'at large' senators (one from each state) who are elected for a four-year term. Both president and vice president must be chosen from among the 'at large' senators.

Profile of the President:

Joseph **URUSEMAL**

Joseph Urusemal was elected president of Micronesia in May 2003, having served as the 'at-large' senator for Yap since 1987. He had studied administration of justice in the USA and worked in the US prison administration service before returning to Micronesia as a teacher.

Joseph J. Urusemal was born on Woleai, one of the outer islands in the state of Yap in Micronesia, on 19 March 1952. His early education took place on Woleai before he left for Chuuk state to attend Xavier High School. On graduating in 1973, Urusemal left for Kansas City, Missouri, USA, where he attended Rockhurst College to study administration of justice. He worked for the department of correction in Jackson County, Missouri, for the next six years.

In 1982 Urusemal returned to Micronesia where he worked as a teacher in Yap at the Outer Islands High School. He is married to Olania Latileilam and they have four children. In 1987 he was elected as Yap state's 'at-large' senator for a four-year term, and has remained in Congress since. In 1991 he was chosen as floor leader. On 10 May 2003 Urusemal was elected president by Congress; he immediately took the oath of office, though his official inauguration was held on 14 July. He has stated his main goals as the expansion of strategic partnerships with Japan, Australia and other Pacific Island nations.

MOLDOVA

Full name: The Republic of Moldova.

Leadership structure: The head of state is a president, hitherto directly elected by universal adult suffrage, but, under the constitutional amendment of 2000, now elected by the Parliament. The president's term of office is four years. The president nominates a prime minister and a government. The prime minister is head of government, although the president may preside over Council of Ministers meetings on matters of particular importance. A referendum held on 23 May 1999, under the terms of which the president would also be head of government, was ruled invalid on 3 November 1999 by the Constitutional Court. In July 2000 Parliament overruled the president to amend the constitution to increase the powers of the executive.

President:	Petru Lucinschi	15 Jan. 1997—7 April 2001
	Vladimir **VORONIN**	Since 7 April 2001
Prime Minister:	Dumitru Braghiş	21 Dec. 1999—19 April 2001
	Vasile **TARLEV**	Since 19 April 2001

Legislature: The legislature is unicameral. The sole chamber, the Parliament (Parlamentul), has 101 members, directly elected for a four-year term.

Profile of the President:

Vladimir **VORONIN**

Vladimir Voronin is a charismatic former baker, who worked his way up through the ranks of the Moldovan Communist hierarchy for 30 years, reaching the presidency (to the considerable alarm of foreign investors) in 2001 ten years after the country had gained independence upon the breakup of the Soviet Union. Despite campaigning against the presidential system in the late 1990s, he attempted to increase the position's power after his election. The failure of his proposals of federalization, aimed at breaking the deadlock over the separatist Transdniestria region where he himself was born, and the increasing interference of Russia in Moldovan affairs have led Voronin to a complete U-turn on foreign policy. He has exchanged his staunchly pro-Russian platform for a pro-Western stance, aiming for European integration.

Vladimir Nikolayevich Voronin was born on 25 May 1941 in Corjova (Korzhevo), a village in the Chişinau (Kishinev) district but now within the breakaway Transdniestrian Republic. At the time, Moldova had been incorporated into the Soviet Union, as it was once again in 1944 (after a period of Soviet retreat before Hitler's armies). In 1958 Voronin enrolled at the Chişinau Consumer Co-operation College and graduated in 1961 to become manager of a bakery in Criuleni, on the Dniester River. He moved on in 1966 to become the director of a municipal bakery in the town of Dubossary across the river.

Voronin, who is married to Taissia Voronina with one son and one daughter, retrained in 1971 as an economist at the Moscow Food Industry Institute and then returned to Moldova to begin work within the republican branch of the Communist Party. Between then and 1989 he was an active party official in Dubossary, in the western border town of Ungeny, and in Bendery (back on the Dniester). He also became a deputy in the Moldovan Supreme Soviet (parliament) in 1980 and retrained as a political scientist at the Academy of Social Sciences, graduating in 1983.

Entering the Moldovan government as minister of internal affairs in 1989 (and given the rank of major-general), he left the government before it declared Moldovan independence in 1991 and spent two years out of the limelight, studying law. During this time he was also a reservist in the Russian police force. In 1993 he returned to mainstream Moldovan politics. He helped to co-ordinate the rebirth of the Moldovan Communist Party (Partidul Comunistilor din Republica Moldova—PCRM) and was elected its first secretary at the December 1994 party congress.

When Voronin stood as the party's candidate in the 1996 presidential elections, he came third out of nine with just over 10% of the vote. Two years later, in the country's third legislative elections, the PCRM secured 40 seats in Parliament, Voronin's among them. Within Parliament, Voronin led the PCRM in campaigns against the weak presidential system and the country's increasingly painful economic reforms. Constitutional amendments in 2000 saw Parliament take over responsibility for electing the president, but after repeated failures by any candidate to gain a victory, the legislature was dissolved. Legislative elections in February 2001 produced a dramatic and overwhelming PCRM victory. With 71 seats in the 101-seat chamber, the party's deputies had no difficulty in electing Voronin to the presidency in a ballot held on 4 April.

At the start of his presidency, Voronin personally led renewed negotiations with the self-proclaimed president of separatist Transdniestria, Igor Smirnov, although these talks achieved few tangible results to match their many headlines. Voronin was also eager to expand his own constitutional powers. It was even suggested that he intended to merge the presidency with the premiership. His appointment of the independent businessman Vasile Tarlev as prime minister left him as the most influential member of the PCRM in government. The choice of Tarlev, coupled with his own pledges of commitment to a market economy, went some way to placate reformists and foreign investors alarmed by his postelection proclamation that "I have been, am, and will remain a Communist". Nevertheless, during this period his government distanced Moldova from Western Europe and he even expressed interest in making the country a third member of a proposed Russia–Belarus union. His government's failure to hold referendums on Moldova's application for membership of the EU and NATO caused opposition parties to boycott Parliament.

In 2003 Voronin staked his office on plans for a new federal constitution, backed by Russia, proposing that Transdniestria should be a fully autonomous region with its own national symbols and budget, and that Russian would be an equal official language. Popular protests, arguing that the plans aimed to cement Moldova in the Russian sphere of influence, forced him to backtrack in December in favour of a more vague US-sponsored plan involving the deployment of international—rather than just Russian—peacekeepers ahead of a political reorganization of the country.

Relations with the Transdniestrian government and with Russia soured during 2004. Voronin labelled the Transdniestrian authorities a "transnational criminal group" and a dispute over the Transdniestrian closure of schools using the Latin script spiralled into mutual recriminations, an economic blockade, and Voronin's snubbing of Russia by refusing to attend a CIS summit. By the run-up to the 2005 elections Voronin had turned firmly towards the West, repeatedly accusing Russia of interfering in Moldova, and he pledged to continue the impoverished country's push towards European integration. The PCRM won a reduced majority in the poll in March 2005, and Voronin was safely re-elected by the new Parliament on 4 April, and re-inaugurated three days later.

Profile of the Prime Minister:

Vasile **TARLEV**

Vasile Tarlev was inaugurated as prime minister of Moldova on 19 April 2001. Five times the Chişinau 'businessman of the year' at the head of the sweet and chocolate giant Bucuria, he had no affiliation to any political party, and his appointment signalled the new Communist Party government's intention to maintain a free-market economy after its sweeping electoral victory in early 2001. His position is somewhat undermined by the efforts of President Vladimir Voronin to strengthen his own role.

Vasile Petru Tarlev, who is now married with two children, was born into the ethnic Bulgarian community in Bascalia in the extreme south of Soviet-controlled Moldova on 9 October 1963, and worked in the village as a tractor and goods vehicle driver before being conscripted into the Soviet army in 1981. He returned to work as a driver, moving in this capacity to the Pushkin Theatre in the capital

Chişinau (Kishinev), until 1985 when he enrolled with the technology faculty of the Chişinau Polytechnic Institute.

On graduation Tarlev found employment in the capital with the Bucuria confectionery firm as a mechanic, and steadily worked his way up the company. By the time of Moldovan independence in 1991 he was chief engineer, and within a further four years he had become director-general of Bucuria and been elected chairman of the National Producers' Association. He was first awarded the accolade of 'businessman of the year' by the Chişinau city authorities in 1996 and held the title for four successive years.

In 1998 Tarlev was awarded a doctorate in technical studies and entered government service as a member of President Petru Lucinschi's Supreme Economic Council. This experience, along with his prominent role at the head of Bucuria, made Tarlev an attractive choice for prime minister in April 2001 for the newly elected President Voronin, eager to convince foreign donors that his Communist Party government would not derail the country's post-Soviet economic reforms. Tarlev's lack of political affiliation also helped counter the concern that the Communists' parliamentary majority would be used to swamp the government with party apparatchiks. His lack of a power base in the party was another reason for Voronin to favour him, avoiding the emergence of a powerful party rival.

As prime minister, Tarlev has continued the free-market policies of his predecessors but did criticize the method of previous privatizations. Under his stewardship the country has been welcomed into the World Trade Organization (WTO) and the Balkan Security Pact. Tarlev was re-elected to Parliament in the March 2005 elections on the Communist Party list, and Voronin reappointed him as prime minister, giving him a mandate to form a cabinet that would focus on modernizing the country, rooting out corruption, reforming education, and paving the way towards European integration.

MONACO

Full name: The Principality of Monaco.

Leadership structure: The head of state is a hereditary prince. The head of government is the minister of state, nominated by the prince from a list of three French diplomats submitted by the French government.

Prince:	Rainier III	9 May 1949—6 April 2005
	ALBERT II (regent from 31 March 2005)	Since 6 April 2005
Minister of State:	Michel Lévêque	3 Feb. 1997—5 Jan. 2000
	Patrick Leclercq	5 Jan. 2000—1 June 2005
	Jean-Paul **PROUST**	Since 1 June 2005

Legislature: The legislature is unicameral. The sole chamber, the National Council (Conseil National), has 24 members, directly elected by universal adult suffrage for a maximum five-year term.

Profile of the Prince:

ALBERT II

Prince Albert of Monaco inherited the throne on 6 April 2005 following the death of his father, Prince Rainier III. Albert is a quiet, sports-loving man who has been groomed for the succession for most of his life. He has been president of the Monégasque delegation to the UN since 1993 and for the final decade of his father's life regularly consulted with him on the day-to-day running of the principality.

Prince Albert of Monaco was born on 14 March 1958, the second child (and only son) of Prince Rainier III and his wife, the US film star Grace Kelly. He attended the Lycée Albert I in Monaco, receiving a baccalaureate with distinction in 1976. In 1977 he enrolled at Amherst College, Massachusetts, USA, where he studied political science, economics, English literature and music, graduating in 1981 with a degree in political science.

In September 1981 Albert enlisted with the French navy as a second-grade sublieutenant on board the helicopter carrier *Jeanne d'Arc*. He remained in the navy until the following year. In early 1983, he served a finance administration internship at the Morgan Guaranty Trust in New York, from where he went on to work for Moët-Hennessy in Paris. In January 1984 he returned to the Morgan Guaranty Trust to participate in its marketing training scheme, this time in Paris again.

In the meantime Albert was steadily gaining a reputation as a connoisseur of sports. By 1984 he was president of the Monégasque Swimming Federation, the Monaco Yacht Club, and the Monégasque Athletic Federation. He took part in the Paris-Dakar rally of 1985 and that same year was co-opted into the International Olympic Committee; the poverty he saw in north Africa prompted him to set up the Monaco Aid and Presence Association, which now has aid projects in several developing countries. In 1988 he participated as a member of the bobsleigh team in the winter Olympics, and again in 1992 and 1994.

During this period Albert was also being prepared for his eventual succession. In 1993, when Monaco finally joined the UN, Albert was designated president of the Monégasque delegation, and he consulted daily with his father over the next decade on the day-to-day running of the principality as well as, in effect, serving as Monaco's ambassador to the world. Albert's failure to marry and produce children became a concern for his father in his later years, and in 2002 a law was passed to ensure that the throne would pass to his sisters and their children should he die without an heir. In March 2005 Rainier was admitted to hospital and Albert was named as prince regent; on 6 April 2005 Rainier died and Albert became prince. Shy and quiet compared to his flamboyant sisters, Albert nevertheless hit the headlines just days before his investiture on 12 July when revelations broke of an illegitimate son by a French air hostess, originally from Togo.

Profile of the Minister of State:

Jean-Paul **PROUST**

Jean-Paul Proust, a French career civil servant, was appointed minister of state for Monaco on 1 June 2005. Like all Monaco's ministers of state, he neither grew up nor lives in the principality. He had previously been Paris's police commissioner.

Jean-Paul Proust was born on 3 March 1940 in Vaas in the French *département* of Sarthe. He graduated from France's elite public administration university, the Ecole Nationale d'Administration, and in 1967 embarked on a career in the French civil service, holding several senior posts both at home and in the French overseas territories, including serving as the administrator of Guadeloupe from 1989 to 1991.

He then returned to various prefectures on the French mainland, including Haute-Normandie and Provence-Alpes-Côte d'Azur, before heading the office of the minister of the interior from 1999 to 2000 under Jean-Pierre Chevènement.

However, his most prominent position was as the police commissioner for the City of Paris, in which he oversaw 19,000 officers from March 2000 until 6 December 2004.

Then he was assigned to the position of 'state counsellor on special duty' in order to allow him to be nominated for the post of minister of state for Monaco. He succeeded Patrick Leclercq on 1 June 2005—a month later than intended due to the death of Prince Rainier III in April. Proust is married with two children.

MONGOLIA

Full name: Mongolia.

Leadership structure: The head of state is a president, directly elected by universal adult suffrage. The president's term of office is four years. The head of government is the prime minister, who is elected by the State Great Hural and appoints a cabinet.

President:	Natsagyn Bagabandi	20 June 1997—24 June 2005
	Nambariyn **ENKHBAYAR**	Since 24 June 2005
Prime Minister:	Rinchinnyamyn Amarjargal	30 July 1999—26 July 2000
	Nambariyn Enkhbayar	26 July 2000—13 Aug. 2004
	Chultem Ulaan (acting)	13 Aug. 2004—20 Aug. 2004
	Tsakhiagiyn **ELBEGDORJ**	Since 20 Aug. 2004

Legislature: The legislature is unicameral. The sole chamber, the State Great Hural (Ulsyn Ikh Khural), has 76 members, directly elected for a four-year term.

Profile of the President:

Nambariyn **ENKHBAYAR**

Nambariyn Enkhbayar became president of Mongolia in June 2005, during a period of uncomfortable coalition between his Mongolian People's Revolutionary Party (MPRP) and the Motherland–Democratic Coalition (MDC) that had emerged from the deadlock of the 2004 legislative elections. Prior to that poll Enkhbayar had held office as prime minister, having returned the MPRP to power in 2000 with a sweeping victory after its first four years in opposition. To achieve that victory he had transformed the MPRP (the former ruling communists) into a modernist centre-left party, distancing it from its Soviet heritage. His style is often likened to that of UK prime minister Tony Blair.

Nambariyn Enkhbayar was born on 1 June 1958 in Ulan Bator, the capital of what was then the Mongolian People's Republic. He went to school in the city before travelling to the neighbouring Soviet Union to attend the prestigious Moscow Institute of Literature. After graduating in 1980 he returned to Mongolia and joined the Mongolian Writers' Union (MWU) as an interpreter–editor.

During the course of the 1980s Enkhbayar rose up the hierarchy of the MWU, becoming chief secretary in 1990 as well as vice president of the Mongolian Interpreters' Union. He is married to Onon Tsolmon and they have three children. He is fluent in Russian and English and took a year out in 1986 to study English literature at the University of Leeds in the UK; he has translated into Mongolian some of the works of, among others, Charles Dickens, Aldous Huxley and Virginia Woolf.

In 1985 he joined the MPRP, and made the transition to a government role with relative ease, serving in 1990–92 as the first deputy chairman of the government committee on culture and art. In the country's first democratic elections in 1992 Enkhbayar won a seat in the State Great Hural, and was appointed minister of culture.

The MPRP suffered a crushing defeat at the hands of the Democratic Union Coalition (DUC) in the general elections of June 1996. Enkhbayar lost his parliamentary seat, as did many of his colleagues. Splits then began to emerge within the MPRP between the communist old guard and the reformist faction eager to reinvent the party. As a reformist, Enkhbayar was elected as general secretary in July, and after the election of the party chairman Natsagyn Bagabandi as president in 1997, he was appointed to succeed him as chairman. He re-entered the Hural through a by-election for Bagabandi's vacant seat. One of his first actions as leader of the opposition was to initiate a motion of censure against the DUC government, setting the tone for the next three years. In 1998 he led the MPRP in a boycott of the Hural, returning only to pass a motion of no confidence in the beleaguered administration. In all, Enkhbayar faced three successive prime ministers across the parliamentary floor before general elections in July 2000 returned the transformed MPRP to power with an overwhelming majority, controlling 95% of the seats in the Hural.

On winning the election, Enkhbayar made it clear that he and his party were not 'communist monsters' and would press ahead with a 'third way' of industrial privatizations coupled with generous social spending. However, his grand programme of modernization depended heavily on international aid, and in reality the country was struggling to recover from the crippling winter of 1999/2000.

The June 2004 election resulted in a dead heat between the MPRP and the new MDC opposition, with both sides just short of controlling the 39 seats constitutionally required to form a government. After weeks of political confusion an agreement was reached in August to form a power-sharing government with the MDC taking over the post of prime minister while Enkhbayar was switched to become speaker of the Hural.

The fragility of the arrangement laid greater importance on the formerly largely ceremonial presidency. Enkhbayar stood as the MPRP candidate in presidential elections on 22 May 2005 and won outright in the first round with 53.4% of the vote. He took office on 24 June.

Mongolia: Nambariyn Enkhbayar

Enkhbayar has tried consciously to emulate modern Western leaders in style. He associates with popular musicians and dresses according to modern fashion in an attempt to shake off the dusty image of communist-era bureaucrats. To this end he has even hired an image consultant from a UK firm.

Profile of the Prime Minister:

Tsakhiagiyn **ELBEGDORJ**

Tsakhiagiyn Elbegdorj of the Motherland–Democratic Coalition (MDC) was finally appointed Mongolian prime minister on 20 August 2004 after nearly two months of political deadlock followed a general election that was initially called as a dead heat between the MDC and the former communist Mongolian People's Revolutionary Party (MPRP). An ex-journalist, and an enthusiast for neoliberal economics, Elbegdorj, who previously held the post of premier for a few months in 1998, has vowed to continue with economic reforms despite rising unemployment and shrinking demand for Mongolia's primary commodities.

Tsakhiagiyn Elbegdorj, known as 'EB' to his friends, was born on 30 March 1963 in Zereg district in the western province of Hovd, the son of a herdsman. His first job was as a machinist in the Erdenet copper mine from 1981 until he began his army service in 1982. Elbegdorj is married and has four children.

During his military service, Elbegdorj submitted poetry to the army newspaper, and his skills came to the attention of senior officers, who sent him on a scholarship to become a military reporter at the military school in Lvov in the Ukraine, where he remained until 1988. On his return to Mongolia he began working as a journalist for the ministry of defence newspaper, *Ulaan-Od* (Red Star), where he remained for two years.

He was elected in December 1989 as a member of the presidium of the General Co-ordinating Council of the Mongolian Democratic Union (MDU), a new anti-MPRP grouping with a separate political wing—the Mongolian Democratic Party (MDP). He became editor-in-chief of the MDU's paper, which he founded, called *Ardchilal* (Democracy). He became general co-ordinator of the MDU from January 1991 until November 1993, and its chairman from then until May 1999. In 1990 he was first elected to political office and rose quickly through the ranks of the MDP, until in 1996 he was elected president of the Mongolian National Democratic Party (MNDP), which had been formed four years earlier from a merger of the MDP with three other opposition parties.

Two years later in April 1998 he was elected prime minister at the age of just 35. A strong advocate of political and economic liberalization, Elbegdorj quickly moved to allow freedom of the press and freedom to travel, and began to privatize the vast majority of state-owned enterprises and housing. However, the massive economic dislocation caused by the abolition of price controls led to him losing a vote of no confidence in July. He remained in office in an acting capacity as a replacement was not finally approved until December.

Following his defeat, Elbegdorj travelled to the USA, where he studied at the Kennedy School of Governance, Harvard University. He has since established the Liberty Center, which promotes political and legal reform, and is overseeing translations of the works of Milton Friedman and Friedrich Hayek into Mongolian.

In July 2004 Elbegdorj's MDC (a regrouping of the Democrats in alliance with the Motherland party) shocked observers by overturning the overwhelming majority of the MPRP, which after the previous election in 2000 had held 72 out of 76 seats. A hung parliament and a two-month political crisis followed the surprise result, during which the MPRP and the MDC held separate sessions of parliament. Ultimately, the MDC entered into a power-sharing agreement with the MPRP, in which the chairman of the MPRP, Nambariyn Enkhbayar, became speaker of the State Great Hural while Elbegdorj was named prime minister. He has memorably described holding the current coalition together as akin to trying to hold together a raw egg.

MOROCCO

Full name: The Kingdom of Morocco.

Leadership structure: The head of state is a hereditary constitutional monarch. The head of government is the prime minister, appointed by the king. The prime minister appoints the cabinet.

King:	**MOHAMMED VI**	Since 23 July 1999
Prime Minister:	Abderrahmane el-Youssoufi	4 Feb. 1998—9 Oct. 2002
	Driss **JETTOU**	Since 9 Oct. 2002

Legislature: The legislature, the Parliament (Barlaman), is bicameral. The lower house, the House of Representatives (Majlis al-Nuwab), has 325 members, directly elected for a five-year term. The upper house, the House of Councillors (Majlis al-Mustasharin), has 270 representatives from local authorities, professional organizations and the 'salaried classes', indirectly elected for nine years, with one-third of its members elected every three years.

Profile of the King:

MOHAMMED VI

Mohammed succeeded to the throne on the death of his father King Hassan II in July 1999. Although royal iconography is prevalent everywhere in Morocco, he stated his intention of pursuing a constitutional monarchy, taking King Juan Carlos of Spain as a model for his own role. Although he has fostered his image as a modernizer and a reformer, he has proceeded cautiously, while sometimes using the more traditional direct means of government to introduce reforms.

Sidi Mohammed ben Hassan was born on 21 August 1963, in Rabat, and educated at the Collège Royale, and the faculty of judicial, economic and social sciences at the University Mohammed V, Rabat. Under his father he had very limited direct political involvement, although he did chair the organizing committee for the Ninth Mediterranean Games, held in Casablanca in 1982, and the following year led the Moroccan delegation to both the Seventh Summit of Non-Aligned Nations in New Delhi (India) and the Tenth Franco-African Conference at Vittel (France). In 1985 he was appointed co-ordinator of administration and services for the armed forces, and he was promoted to the rank of general in 1994.

Propelled into the centre of political life by the death of King Hassan in mid-1999, Mohammed concentrated on fulfilling public engagements during the first few months of his reign, but did mark a departure from his father's policy by meeting the son of the former Berber leader Abdelkarim Khattari during a visit to the north in October. The first real indication of major change came in November when he dismissed the authoritarian minister of the interior, Driss Basri, who had been close to King Hassan. The following March he launched his National Action Plan, which included provision for extending the rights of women. Despite fierce opposition from Islamic fundamentalists, proposed changes to the *mudawana* code on family life were passed by parliament in January 2004, effectively ending the practice of polygamy, giving women greater access to divorce, raising the legal age for women to marry from 15 to 18, and granting women equality of responsibility over family matters.

While some of Mohammed's efforts in the sphere of human rights promotion have been applauded, such as his opening of the first Arab human rights training centre in Rabat in April 2000, his intolerance of criticism in the media has caused concern. In late 2000 journalists and newspapers were prosecuted for printing stories critical of the military and the ruling socialist government. Similarly, he inaugurated the Royal Institute for Amazigh (Berber) Culture in July 2001 and approved the use of the Berber language in primary schools in 2003, but has been forthright in restating his country's claim to Western Sahara. He withdrew the Moroccan ambassador to South Africa following that country's recognition of Western Sahara in 2004, and the following year he pulled out of the first summit of heads of state of the Arab Maghreb Union since 1994 after Algeria voiced its support for the annexed region's independence struggle.

In a notable break with tradition Mohammed publicly announced his July 2002 marriage to computer engineer Salma Bennani, now Princess Lalla Salma, before it happened, and agreed to stage a televised public ceremony. Their son Crown Prince Moulay al-Hassan was born on 8 May 2003.

Profile of the Prime Minister:

Driss **JETTOU**

Driss Jettou is an independent technocrat and a career politician. Having served as commerce and industry minister with varying responsibilities throughout much of the 1990s, he was appointed prime minister by King Mohammed VI on 9 October 2002 following general elections.

Driss Jettou was born on 24 May 1945 in El Jadida on the Atlantic coast of Morocco. After studying in nearby Casablanca he graduated in physics and chemistry in 1966, and completed his education in 1968 with a diploma in business management from Cordwainers College in London, UK. He has headed a number of commercial federations, including the Moroccan Federation of

Leather Industries and the Moroccan Association of Exporters. He is married and has four children.

When King Hassan II appointed a nonparty government in 1993, he included Jettou as commerce and industry minister. Jettou held this portfolio for five years, adding in July 1994 the portfolios of foreign trade (although only until February 1995) and artisans.

In 1998, when the Socialist Union of Popular Forces (Union Socialiste des Forces Populaires—USFP) formed a government after the legislative elections, Jettou was excluded from office, but he returned to the cabinet on 19 September 2001, this time as interior minister under USFP prime minister Abderrahmane el-Youssoufi.

In legislative elections held on 27 September 2002 the USFP and its right-of-centre ally Istiqlal remained the largest parties in the House of Representatives despite an increase in support for Islamist parties. However, King Mohammed VI retired the veteran Youssoufi and turned instead to Jettou as a prominent nonpartisan figure to head his new government.

MOZAMBIQUE

Full name: The Republic of Mozambique.

Leadership structure: The head of state is a president, directly elected by universal adult suffrage. The president's term of office is five years, renewable only once (under the 2004 Constitution). The president is head of government, and appoints the Council of Ministers, including a prime minister to assist the president in the leadership of the government.

President:	Joaquim Alberto Chissano	6 Nov. 1986—2 Feb. 2005
	Armando **GUEBUZA**	Since 2 Feb. 2005
Prime Minister:	Pascoal Mocumbi	16 Dec. 1994—17 Feb. 2004
	Luisa Dias **DIOGO**	Since 17 Feb. 2004

Legislature: The legislature is unicameral. The sole chamber, the Assembly of the Republic (Assembléia da República), has 250 members, directly elected for a five-year term.

Profile of the President:

Armando **GUEBUZA**

Armando Guebuza succeeded Mozambique's long-term leader Joaquim Chissano in February 2005. Politically active with the Mozambique Liberation Front (Frente da Libertação de Moçambique—FRELIMO) from an early age, he shadowed Chissano throughout his career, and has been a member of the various Mozambican governments since independence in 1975. Profiting from the abandonment of socialism and the privatization of state assets, Guebuza is now one of the richest men in Mozambique. He has promised to tackle corruption, but critics say that his wealth coupled with his long history among Mozambique's political elite will cripple any real effort to do so.

Armando Emilio Guebuza was born on 20 January 1943 in the town of Murrupula, in the northern province of Nampula. His father, Miguel Guebuza, worked as a male nurse, while his mother, Marta Bocota Guebuza, was a housewife. At the age of five the family moved to Lourenço Marques (now Maputu) where Guebuza went to school at the Centro Associativo dos Negros da Colónia de Moçambique. At secondary school he joined the Núcleo dos Estudantes Secundários Africanos de Moçambique (NESAM), a civic organization created by the historical leader of Mozambique's fight for independence, Eduardo Mondlane, in 1949. He was elected president of NESAM in 1953, the same year he joined FRELIMO.

Guebuza was jailed and tortured for five months in 1964 and arrested by the British authorities in what is now Botswana the following year. By 1965 he was a member of both the central and executive committees of FRELIMO, which by this time was based in Tanzania. In 1966 he was transferred from Nachingwea to Dar es Salaam to become private secretary to Mondlane, then president of FRELIMO, and two years later was appointed inspector of FRELIMO schools. By the early 1970s, FRELIMO's 7,000-strong guerrilla force had wrested control of much of the central and northern parts of Mozambique from the Portuguese authorities.

After the signing of the Lusaka Agreement in 1974, which opened the way for Mozambique's independence from Portugal, Guebuza was appointed minister of internal administration in the transitional government that led the country to independence in 1975. He has remained a member of Mozambique's various governments ever since. From 1975 until 1977 he was interior minister and again from 1983 until 1985. He was responsible for some of the most controversial decisions of the FRELIMO government during these periods. In his first period in office he ordered the evacuation of Portuguese settlers within 24 hours carrying only 20 kg of luggage; around 90% of settlers fled, including most of the doctors and professionals in the country. In Guebuza's second term, he oversaw the implementation of 'Operation Production', under which thousands of unemployed city-dwellers were sent to 're-education camps' in the isolated northern province of Niassa with little more than the clothes they were wearing if they were perceived to be insufficiently compliant to the authorities or engaged in anti-social practices, such as prostitution.

In 1986 Guebuza was appointed head of the Inquiry Commission responsible for investigating the strange circumstances surrounding the death of President Samora Machel in an air crash. By this time the leadership of FRELIMO had largely conceded the failure of the socialist experiment and moved towards political and economic reforms. Machel's successor, Joaquim Chissano, opened negotiations with the South African-backed rebel guerrilla movement, the Mozambique National Resistance Movement (Resistência Nacional Moçambicana—RENAMO). Guebuza headed the government's delegation in charge of negotiating a peace settlement. The new constitution enacted in 1990 provided for a multiparty political system, market-based economy and free elections, and led to the signing of the Rome Peace Agreement in October 1992. He then led the government delegation on the Supervision and Control Commission, the UN body overseeing the implementation of the agreement and guiding the country towards its first multiparty elections in 1994. He was elected as a member of the Assembly in 1994 and head of the FRELIMO parliamentary group, and re-elected in 1999.

In 2002 Guebuza was elected FRELIMO secretary-general and he stood as the party's presidential candidate in the 2004 elections, after a long and difficult nomination process. He won the national poll with 64% of the vote—though the result was challenged by the opposition—and was sworn in on 2 February 2005, pledging to wage an "unrelenting war on poverty". Guebuza had been one of the first Mozambican politicians to recognize the need to establish links with the World Bank and the International Monetary Fund (IMF), and to advocate the creation of a 'national bourgeois' of local capitalists and middle classes.

Guebuza himself has been described as a leading exponent of black-Mozambican economic empowerment, personally benefiting from the privatization of many state-owned assets in the late 1980s and early 1990s. Today he is considered to be one of the wealthiest, if not the wealthiest, Mozambican citizen, and has earned the nickname of 'Mr Gue-Business'. His two big challenges will be eradicating the gap between the north and the south—the southern capital Maputo accounts for one-third of Mozambique's wealth, and Guebuza is deeply unpopular in the north for his deportations in the 1980s—and tackling the endemic corruption that pervades every aspect of Mozambican life.

Profile of the Prime Minister:

Luisa Dias **DIOGO**

Luisa Dias Diogo was appointed prime minister of Mozambique in February 2004, after many years of experience in governmental and intergovernmental finance roles. She is the country's first female prime minister.

Luisa Dias Diogo was born on 11 April 1958 in the district of Màgoe in Tete. She was educated at the Eduardo Mondlane University in Mozambique and the University of London in the UK. She is married to António Albana Silva and has two sons and a daughter.

In 1980 Diogo joined the ministry of planning and finance, before switching to the department of economics and investment, and then associate head of department in 1984. She became programme officer in the study department in 1986 and was made head of the department of budget in 1989, then promoted to national director of budget in 1993. One year later Diogo moved to the World Bank as a programme officer in Maputo. That year Diogo joined the government as vice minister of planning and finance, where she remained for six years before becoming minister. She was appointed prime minister by President Joaquim Chissano in February 2004, retaining the planning and finance portfolios.

She was reappointed by newly elected president Armando Guebuza in February 2005, although with many new faces in the government in an attempt by Guebuza to tackle corruption. She retained policy control of finance and planning.

MYANMAR

Full name: Union of Myanmar (formerly Burma).

Leadership structure: The de facto head of state under the military regime is the chair of the State Peace and Development Council (SPDC), formerly the State Law and Order Restoration Council (SLORC) until 15 November 1997. The head of government is the prime minister, who appoints the members of the government.

Chairman of SLORC/SPDC: Senior Gen. **THAN** Shwe   Since 23 April 1992

Prime Minister:	Senior Gen. Than Shwe	24 April 1992—25 Aug. 2003
	Lt.-Gen. Khin Nyunt	25 Aug. 2003—19 Oct. 2004
	Lt.-Gen. **SOE** Win	Since 19 Oct. 2004

Legislature: The unicameral 485-member Constituent Assembly elected in 1990 has not been allowed to meet.

Profile of the Chairman of the SPDC:

Senior Gen. **THAN** Shwe

Senior Gen. Than Shwe, a career soldier from the generation which joined the military after Burma's independence in 1948, is head of state by virtue of his office as chairman of the ruling military council which seized power in 1988. He also held the post of prime minister from 1992 to 2003. It was he who announced in April 1991 the military regime's refusal to accept the results of the 1990 elections, declaring the election winners, the National League for Democracy (NLD), "subversive" and "unfit to rule".

Born on 2 February 1933, in Kyaukse, Mandalay division, Than Shwe attended secondary school before becoming a postal clerk. Joining the military officers training school in 1953, he rose to the position of army general.

In 1985 he became deputy commander-in-chief of the army under Gen. Saw Maung. After Saw Maung seized power in 1988 and became chairman of the State Law and Order Restoration Council (SLORC), Than Shwe became deputy chairman and commander-in-chief of the army. Burma was officially renamed the Union of Myanmar in 1989.

Than Shwe took over the defence ministry in March 1992 and was appointed on 23 April of that year to head the ruling military council in succession to Saw Maung, who was replaced on grounds of health. Than Shwe was in addition named as prime minister the following day, and retained control of the defence portfolio.

He is generally seen as a hard-liner, although in recent years he has ordered the release of a number of political prisoners, including members of the pro-democracy NLD. The release in 2001 of its leader, Aung San Suu Kyi, the winner of the 1991 Nobel Peace Prize, allowed hopes of some form of dialogue which were dashed when she was placed back under house arrest in May 2003.

Than Shwe delegated the role of prime minister to intelligence chief Gen. Khin Nyunt in August 2003. Khin, seen as a moderate, promised that free elections would be convened, and soon the military junta's seven-point 'roadmap' to democracy was being implemented and contacts were established with all major political parties, including the NLD. However, Khin's downfall in 2004 amid a scandal over illegally imported luxury cars was a victory for the more hard-line elements. In February 2005, when the junta reopened talks on a new constitution, there was international criticism that the convention was unrepresentative, and it was boycotted by several opposition parties.

Increasingly pragmatic in his approach, Than Shwe realizes that Myanmar can only receive foreign aid if it is willing to make some changes—hence his redesignation of the SLORC in 1997 as a State Peace and Development Council (SPDC). By accepting the need for some reform, however, his regime risks encouraging stronger opposition from pro-democracy supporters. In the meantime, with a military government and no officially recognized opposition party, most opposition is met with heavy repression.

Profile of the Prime Minister:

Lt.-Gen. **SOE** Win

Lt.-Gen. Soe Win is thought to have been born in 1948. He is a career infantry officer in the Burmese army and graduated from the Defence Services Academy, where apparently he was described as an average student. During his academy years he was thought by his contemporaries to be very left wing. He rose to the rank of colonel in the early 1990s and was appointed as chairman of the regional State Law and Order Restoration Council in Chin. Promoted to brigadier-general, he assumed the Northwest Command in 1997 and was made a full member of the State Peace and Development Council (SPDC). Promoted to the post of air defence general in 2001 and first secretary of the SPDC in 2003, he was appointed prime minister on 19 October 2004, replacing the moderate Khin Nyunt. Soe is regarded as a hard-liner and is reportedly a close ally of SPDC chair Than Shwe.

NAMIBIA

Full name: The Republic of Namibia.

Leadership structure: The head of state is a president, directly elected by universal adult suffrage. The president's term of office is five years, renewable once only. The president is also head of government. The president appoints the prime minister and other members of the cabinet.

President:	Sam Nujoma	21 March 1990—21 March 2005
	Hifikepunye **POHAMBA**	Since 21 March 2005
Prime Minister:	Hage Geingob	21 March 1990—28 Aug. 2002
	Theo-Ben Gurirab	28 Aug. 2002—21 March 2005
	Nahas **ANGULA**	Since 21 March 2005

Legislature: The legislature, the Parliament, is bicameral. The lower chamber, the National Assembly, has 72 members, directly elected for a five-year term. Six additional nonvoting members may be appointed by the president. The upper chamber, the National Council, has 26 members, indirectly elected by the Regional Councils from among their members for a six-year term.

Profile of the President:

Hifikepunye **POHAMBA**

Hifikepunye Pohamba succeeded Sam Nujoma as president of Namibia at the age of 69 on 21 March 2005. He first joined the fight for Namibia's independence as a young man and became a full-time worker for the South West Africa People's Organization (SWAPO) in the early 1960s. Detained and deported several times for his activities, he was rewarded by being appointed the first minister of home affairs on the country's independence in 1990. As lands minister he accelerated the process of land reform and is expected to be more ardent on the topic than his predecessor.

Hifikepunye Pohamba was born on 18 August 1935 in Okanghudi in northern Namibia (then known as South West Africa and ruled by South Africa under a mandate from the League of Nations), where he was educated by missionaries. He is married with six children. As a young man he joined the Ovamboland People's Organization (OPO), agitating against South African rule, and when it was dissolved in 1960 he became a founder member of the new SWAPO movement. At the time he had been working in the Tsumeb gold mines; he left the area to return to what was then Ovamboland in order to become a full-time mobilizer for SWAPO.

Pohamba was first arrested a year later and charged with political agitation. He was flogged and ordered to leave the area. Along with two colleagues he left the country, making his way to Dar es Salaam, Tanzania, where he spent a year before being ordered back by the SWAPO leadership. He was arrested by the Southern Rhodesian authorities on the way and imprisoned for two months before being deported to South Africa, where in turn he was given 48 hours to leave the country.

Within a week of Pohamba's arrival in Windhoek, he was arrested for political agitation and having left the country illegally, and sentenced to six months' imprisonment. Released early on appeal, he was then deported to his home area in the north, where he joined the regional party leadership of SWAPO and resumed his activism. In 1964 Pohambo and other members of the party leadership were forced to flee the country again. By September he had been sent to open a regional office in Zambia, where he remained for five years.

In 1969 Pohamba was elected as a member of SWAPO's central committee and as deputy administrative secretary, and the following year was assigned to open a regional office in Algeria. He returned to Tanzania in 1973 to become SWAPO's chief representative in east Africa, just as the UN decided to recognize SWAPO as the sole legitimate representative of the people of Namibia. He was elected a member of the politburo and secretary of finance in 1977. Appointed as head of SWAPO affairs in Zambia two years later, he was transferred to SWAPO headquarters in Angola in 1981.

The years of guerrilla struggle finally ended when independence was promised under a settlement signed in New York in December 1988, between South Africa, Western powers, the UN and SWAPO. The following year Pohamba returned to Namibia as head of administration at the newly established SWAPO headquarters in Windhoek. Elections were held that year and Pohamba became a member of the Constituent Assembly, which became the National Assembly in 1990, whereupon he was appointed the first minister of home affairs for the new Republic of Namibia.

Pohamba subsequently served as minister of fisheries and marine resources and as minister of lands, resettlement and rehabilitation. In 1997 he was elected secretary-general of SWAPO and in 2002 as SWAPO vice president. As lands minister, Pohamba strongly advocated the government's attempt to speed up land reform and redistribute lands from the white minority to the black majority. Pohamba was President Sam Nujoma's favoured candidate to succeed him and was chosen as SWAPO's candidate in June 2004; he won election by a landslide in September and was sworn in on 21 March 2005.

Profile of the Prime Minister:

Nahas **ANGULA**

Nahas Angula was appointed prime minister of Namibia on 21 March 2005. He has been involved for many years both in the South West Africa People's Organization (SWAPO) and in education, and held the position of minister of higher education, training and employment creation for a decade before his promotion.

Nahas Gideon Angula was born on 22 August 1943 in Onyaanya in Oshikoto province. He graduated from the University of Zambia with a degree in education and went on to do two master's degrees in education at Columbia University in New York, USA. He is married with two daughters and a son.

Angula founded the Namibia Education Centre for refugees in Zambia in 1974 and was headteacher, before becoming an international civil servant at UN headquarters in Angola from 1976 to 1980. He then became SWAPO's secretary for information and publicity and from 1981 secretary for education and culture in Luanda, Angola.

On his return to Namibia in 1989 he led the voter registration and education section of SWAPO's election directorate while continuing his postgraduate studies in education by distance learning from the University of Manchester in the UK. He was minister of higher education, training and employment creation from 1995 until 2005, when he was appointed prime minister following the election of Hifikepunye Pohamba as president.

NAURU

Full name: The Republic of Nauru.

Leadership structure: The head of state is a president, elected by Parliament from among its members for a three-year term. The head of government is the president, who is responsible to Parliament. The cabinet is appointed by the president.

President:	Rene Harris	28 April 1999—19 April 2000
	Bernard Dowiyogo	19 April 2000—30 March 2001
	Rene Harris	30 March 2001—8 Jan. 2003
	Bernard Dowiyogo	9 Jan. 2003—17 Jan. 2003
	Rene Harris	17 Jan. 2003—18 Jan. 2003
	Bernard Dowiyogo	18 Jan. 2003—9 March 2003
	Derog Gioura (acting from 9 March 2003)	20 March 2003—29 May 2003
	Ludwig Scotty	29 May 2003—8 Aug. 2003
	Rene Harris	8 Aug. 2003—22 June 2004
	Ludwig **SCOTTY**	Since 22 June 2004

Legislature: The legislature is unicameral. The sole chamber, the Parliament, has 18 members, directly elected for a three-year term.

Profile of the President:

Ludwig **SCOTTY**

Following a period of high turnover of presidents in Nauru in 2003–04, Ludwig Scotty emerged as a longer-lasting incumbent, charged with steering the economy out of even more turbulent times as the nation's earnings from phosphate mining dry up.

Ludwig Derangadage Scotty was born on 20 June 1948 in Anabar, a northeastern district of Nauru. He was first elected to Parliament in 1983 and served as speaker of the house from the late 1990s until 2000. In May 2003 he was elected president with a parliamentary vote of 10–7, defeating ex-president Kinza Clodumar. He was ousted in August and replaced by Rene Harris; however he returned as president in June 2004 when Clodumar defected to the opposition while Harris was out of the country.

Fresh elections in October strengthened Scotty's position and gave a much-needed sense of political stability. Nauru is almost bankrupt, and its once-prosperous economy is currently one of the poorest in the region, the profits from years of fruitful phosphate mining having been invested badly. Scotty is moving to squeeze the last possible revenues from the defunct mines and is undertaking some delicate manoeuvres between Taiwan and China to ensure the largest possible aid revenues for his people.

NEPAL

Full name: The Kingdom of Nepal.

Leadership structure: The head of state is the king. Executive power is vested in the king and the Council of Ministers. The prime minister is formally appointed by the king, but must be able to command a parliamentary majority. However, there has been no prime minister since King Gyanendra imposed direct rule in February 2005, and took the position of chair of the Council of Ministers.

King:	Birendra Bir Bikram Shah Dev	31 Jan. 1972—1 June 2001
	Dipendra Bir Bikram Shah Dev	1 June 2001—4 June 2001
	GYANENDRA Bir Bikram Shah Dev (regent from 2 June 2001; chair of Council of Ministers from 2 February 2005)	Since 4 June 2001

Prime Minister:	Krishna Prasad Bhattarai	31 May 1999—22 March 2000
	Girija Prasad Koirala	22 March 2000—26 July 2001
	Sher Bahadur Deuba	26 July 2001—4 Oct. 2002
	vacant	4 Oct. 2002— 11 Oct. 2002
	Lokendra Bahadur Chand	11 Oct. 2002—4 June 2003
	Surya Bahadur Thapa	4 June 2003—2 June 2004
	Sher Bahadur Deuba	2 June 2004—1 Feb. 2005
	vacant	Since 1 Feb. 2005

Legislature: The legislature, the Parliament (Sansad), is bicameral. The lower chamber, the House of Representatives (Pratinidhi Sabha), has 205 members, directly elected for a five-year term. The upper chamber, the National Council (Rastriya Sabha), has 60 members, ten of them nominated by the king, and 50 indirectly elected, for a six-year term, with one-third renewed every two years. The House of Representatives was dissolved by the king in May 2002, but 'special sessions' were held in June and July 2003 to debate restrictions on the king's powers.

Profile of the King:

GYANENDRA Bir Bikram Shah Dev

King Gyanendra has a reputation as a conservative hard-liner but became more widely known before he ascended the throne as the champion of conservation programmes. He also has various commercial interests. He came to power on 4 June 2001 after the massacre of the reigning royal family by the then crown prince, Dipendra. He has already used the authority which the constitution allows him, but which his predecessor Birendra had not used since the democratization of 1990, to take on executive powers briefly in October 2002 and again from February 2005.

Prince Gyanendra Bir Bikram Shah Dev was born on 7 July 1947 in Kathmandu. He was briefly crowned king in November 1950, when he was just three years old, during a power struggle between his own grandfather, King Tribhuvan, and the government of Prime Minister Mohan Shamsher Rana. He was removed from the throne on 7 January 1951 when Tribhuvan returned from exile in India. Gyanendra graduated from St Joseph's College, India, in 1966 and from the Tribhuvan University, Kathmandu, in 1969. He married Komal Rajya Laxmi Rana on 2 May 1970. They have two children. Their controversy-seeking son Prince Paras was declared crown prince and heir to the throne in November 2001.

Once a keen hunter, Gyanendra became chairman in 1982 of the King Mahendra Trust for Nature Conservation, whose most important responsibility is for the Annapurna Conservation Area Project, created in 1986 at the centre of the Himalayas as the country's largest nature conservation area. He is now the Trust's patron and is also an honorary member of the World Wide Fund for Nature (WWF) and a member of the WWF's 1001: Nature Trust. Along with his conservation work he has a number of commercial interests, including stakes in a hotel in Kathmandu, a tea estate in the east of the country and a cigarette factory. He was a key opponent of King Birendra's failed attempt to have the members of the royal family shed their business interests.

On 1 June 2001 Crown Prince Dipendra gunned down his father King Birendra, his mother Queen Aishwarya and seven other family members in an apparent drunken rage before turning his automatic weapon on himself. Although fatally injured, Dipendra became king under the rules of succession upon Birendra's death. Gyanendra, whose own wife was one of only two survivors of the Narayanhiti Palace massacre, was not present at the time and now found himself next in line to the throne. He was rushed to Kathmandu to act as regent for Dipendra, who died three days later, whereupon Gyanendra was automatically named as the next monarch. Confusion over the details of the massacre, and the deep popularity of Birendra, in contrast to the general mistrust cast on Gyanendra, led to an overflow of conspiracy theories and days of widespread unrest.

In the face of an intensifying Maoist guerrilla campaign, Gyanendra's conservative leanings have been accompanied by a willingness to become personally engaged in politics. For a week in early October 2002 Gyanendra assumed executive powers for himself after his prime minister had called for a postponement of general elections. Although the move was strictly in line with the constitution it represented an unprecedented interference from the throne since the implementation of democracy in 1990. His imposition of a succession of appointed—rather than elected—prime ministers provoked frequent demonstrations against his authoritarian rule and demands for a return to democracy. With the Maoist insurgency escalating and strikes crippling the economy the country became mired in political turmoil. Even the reappointment of the ousted prime minister Sher Bahadur Deuba in 2004 did nothing to improve the situation.

On 1 February 2005 Gyanendra declared a state of emergency, sacked the government and resumed direct power. He installed himself at the head of the Council of Ministers the following day, imposing a ban on media criticism of these moves. Phone lines and Internet links were cut, and opposition politicians were reportedly placed under arrest. The international community condemned Gyanendra's actions, ambassadors were withdrawn and aid was suspended.

Gyanendra pledged to crack down on the Maoists and set up a commission against corruption, but set no date for legislative elections. Protests continued against his authoritarian regime and opposition parties combined in their fight to have democracy restored, though stopped short of accepting the offer of an alliance with the Maoists.

NETHERLANDS

Full name: The Kingdom of the Netherlands.

Leadership structure: The head of state is a constitutional monarch. The head of government is the prime minister, who is responsible to the States-General. The Council of Ministers is appointed by royal decree, on the advice of the prime minister.

Queen:	**BEATRIX**	Since 30 April 1980
Prime Minister:	Wim Kok	22 Aug. 1994—22 July 2002
	Jan Peter **BALKENENDE**	Since 22 July 2002

Legislature: The legislature, the States-General (Staten-Generaal), is bicameral. The lower chamber, the Second Chamber (Tweede Kamer), has 150 members, directly elected for a four-year term. The upper chamber, the First Chamber (Eerste Kamer), has 75 members, indirectly elected for a four-year term.

Profile of the Queen:

BEATRIX

Queen Beatrix of the Netherlands succeeded to the throne at the age of 42 following the abdication of her mother, Queen Juliana, in April 1980. As queen she is also head of state of Aruba and of the Netherlands Antilles, represented on each by a governor. Her role is ceremonial, although views which she has expressed on environmental and social issues in particular have had some political impact.

Beatrix Wilhelmina Armgard was born at the Soestdijk Palace in Baarn on 31 January 1938, the eldest of the three daughters of Juliana and Prince Bernhard. Following the German invasion in May 1940 she was taken to England and on to Ottawa, Canada, for the duration of the Second World War. On her return to the Netherlands she continued her primary education, and received her grammar school certificate in 1956. When she had reached her 18th birthday earlier that year, she had become a member of the Council of State. In the same year she entered the University of Leiden, studying sociology, jurisprudence, economics, constitutional law and international affairs. She passed her final doctoral degree examination in July 1961.

Beatrix's interests include sculpture, painting, dramatic art and ballet. She enjoys riding and sailing, is patron of the National Fund for the Prevention of Poliomyelitis and also supports, among others, charities assisting handicapped children. Queen Beatrix married Claus von Amsberg, a former German diplomat, on 10 March 1966, the nationality of her husband causing adverse reactions in some circles at the time. They had three sons, the heir to the throne being Prince Willem-Alexander, born in 1967. Prince Claus died in October 2002. Beatrix's mother and father, Queen Juliana and Prince Bernhard, both died in 2004.

Profile of the Prime Minister:

Jan Peter **BALKENENDE**

Jan Peter Balkenende, of the conservative Christian Democratic Appeal (Christen Democratisch Appèl—CDA), is a graduate in law and a university teacher who began his political career in local government, and only entered parliament in 1998. Prime minister from July 2002, he headed the shortest-lived government in the country's postwar history, a three-party coalition which included the anti-immigrant Pim Fortuyn List (Lijst Pim Fortuyn—LPF), and which collapsed in October. The CDA remained the largest party after fresh elections in January 2003, and Balkenende formed a new coalition after five months of negotiations.

Jan Peter (also spelled Pieter) Balkenende was born on 7 May 1956 in the southwestern Dutch town of Kapelle, near Goes. He graduated in history and then law from the Free University of Amsterdam in 1982. For the next two years he advised the Netherlands Universities Council on legal affairs. He was awarded his doctorate in law in 1992 and from 1993 taught Christian social thought on society and economics at the university. Brought up in the Dutch Reformed Church, he has chaired the Association of Christian Lawyers and has held executive positions in Christian broadcasting companies. He married Bianca Hoogendijk in 1996 and they now have one daughter.

Balkenende began his political career after graduating in 1982, on the municipal council of Amstelveen, on the outskirts of Amsterdam. His association with the Christian democrats was formalized in 1984 when he began working in the CDA's policy institute. He became leader of the Amstelveen CDA group in 1994. These roles were left behind in May 1998 when he was successfully elected to the Second Chamber. His rise within the party was then meteoric. He emerged victorious in October 2001 from an internal leadership contest. Just seven months later he led the party to its first election win in eight years. After two months of negotiations he formed a somewhat unlikely coalition with the populist LPF and the liberal People's Party for Freedom and Democracy (Volkspartij voor Vrijheid en Democratie—VVD) in July 2002.

Netherlands: *Jan Peter Balkenende*

Balkenende's dramatic rise to power was rapidly overshadowed by an even more dramatic fall. The LPF, which had been boosted by a big sympathy vote due to the assassination nine days before polling of its charismatic founder Pim Fortuyn, quickly became mired in internal disputes which prompted the coalition's premature collapse just three months later on 16 October. It had been the shortest-lived government in recent Dutch history.

Balkenende remained in office as caretaker pending fresh elections, held in January 2003. The CDA remained the largest party, but the LPF saw its support plummet. Balkenende began negotiations to form a 'grand' coalition with the opposition Labour Party, despite the 'considerable' differences between the parties. By April these talks had failed, and a coalition was finally formed in mid-May between the CDA, the VVD and the centrist Democrats 66. On 27 May Balkenende was sworn in for his second term.

The murder of controversial filmmaker Theo van Gogh by a Dutch-Moroccan Muslim in 2004 coincided with the Dutch period of presidency over the EU, at a time when talks over membership for the first Islamic country—Turkey—were on the agenda. Balkenende had warned the European parliament in July that Islamophobia must not be allowed to affect Turkey's chances of joining. Concerns about immigration and EU enlargement were key issues that brought about the 'no' vote in the referendum on the EU constitution in June 2005. Balkenende reluctantly agreed to abide by the decision, even though it was not legally binding on the government.

NEW ZEALAND

Full name: New Zealand.

Leadership structure: The head of state is the British sovereign, styled 'Queen of New Zealand, and of Her other Realms and Territories, head of the Commonwealth, Defender of the Faith', and represented by a governor-general who is a New Zealander appointed on the advice of the New Zealand government. The head of government is the prime minister, who, with the cabinet, is appointed by the governor-general on the advice of the House of Representatives and responsible to it.

Queen:	Elizabeth II	Since 6 Feb. 1952
Governor-General:	Sir Michael Hardie Boys	21 March 1996—22 March 2001
	Dame Sian Elias (acting)	22 March 2001—4 April 2001
	Dame Silvia **CARTWRIGHT**	Since 4 April 2001
Prime Minister:	Helen **CLARK**	Since 10 Dec. 1999

Legislature: The legislature is unicameral. The sole chamber, the House of Representatives, has 120 members, directly elected for a three-year term. Under a new electoral system first implemented in October 1996, there are 61 members from single-member constituencies, six from Maori constituencies, and 53 allocated from party lists.

Profile of the Governor-General:

Dame Silvia **CARTWRIGHT**

Dame Silvia Cartwright is a qualified lawyer and prominent advocate for women's rights. She was New Zealand's first female High Court judge in 1993 and is the second woman (following Dame Cath Tizard in 1990–96) to hold the post of governor-general.

Silvia Rose Poulter was born on 7 November 1943 in Dunedin on the southeast coast of New Zealand's South Island. She graduated in law from the local University of Otago in 1966, was admitted as a solicitor in 1967 and as a barrister in 1968. She married fellow lawyer Peter Cartwright in 1969. He is now an appeal authority for New Zealand's public accident compensation system and a member of the Film and Literature Board of Review.

Silvia Cartwright joined the private law firm Harkness Henry & Co. in 1971 where she specialized in family law. She was made a district and family court judge in 1981; eight years later she became the country's first ever female chief district court judge, and was also made a dame commander of the order of the British Empire. In 1993 she moved up to be a High Court judge, another groundbreaking step for a woman.

Concurrent with her judicial career, Cartwright championed the cause of female equality. She reached the national consciousness in 1987 when she headed an inquiry into treatment for cervical cancer at the National Women's Hospital in Auckland. The inquiry prompted widespread reforms in treatment and has since become known by her name. She also sought to promote equality in the judicial system as convenor of the Judicial Working Group on Gender Equity. From 1993 to 2000 she raised her profile to the international level when she was a member of the UN committee seeking to oversee compliance with the UN Convention on the Elimination of All Forms of Discrimination Against Women (CEDAW).

In August 2000 Dame Sylvia Cartwright was nominated by Queen Elizabeth II to be her next representative as head of state in New Zealand. She took over accordingly as governor-general following the retirement of Sir Michael Hardie Boys on 22 March 2001. (During the brief period between his retirement and her inauguration on 4 April, the functions of the governor-general were formally exercised in an acting capacity by the chief justice, Dame Sian Elias.) It attracted considerable attention internationally that at this time women held the five highest offices in New Zealand (head of state, governor-general, chief justice, prime minister and leader of the opposition).

Profile of the Prime Minister:

Helen **CLARK**

Helen Clark has led two minority governments since first becoming prime minister—coalitions of her New Zealand Labour Party first with the Alliance party from 1999 to 2002, and since the July 2002 elections with the Progressive Coalition (renamed the Progressive Party in 2003). A farmer's daughter and former student activist, she was a university lecturer in politics before entering parliament in 1981. Although she can point to a career in which she has held responsibility at every level in Labour, her approach to politics has been described as lacking in charisma and strongly academic.

Helen Elizabeth Clark was born in Hamilton on 26 February 1950, the daughter of a farmer from the rural Waikato district on North Island. She was educated at boarding school in Auckland, where she admits to having been painfully shy, before attending the University of Auckland to study politics.

She began her active involvement in politics by joining the Labour Party in 1971 and was active in student societies against the Viet Nam War and apartheid in South Africa. She graduated with a master's degree in 1974 with a thesis on rural political behaviour. She lectured on political studies at the university from 1973 until her election to the House of Representatives on behalf of the Mount Albert constituency in 1981.

Clark became a member of the Labour executive in 1978 and represented the party at congresses of the Socialist International in 1976, 1978, 1983 and 1986. Following Labour's electoral victory in 1984 Clark was convenor of a government committee on external affairs and security. Further success at the polls in 1987 led to her appointment as minister, holding the conservation and housing portfolios. Two years later she switched these for the ministries of health and labour and was promoted to deputy prime minister in August 1989. Through this influential position Clark chaired numerous cabinet committees until in 1990 Labour's disastrous economic experiments led to defeat at the polls and a return to opposition.

From 1990 until 1993 Clark was deputy leader of the opposition. When she replaced Mike Moore in December 1993 as leader of the Labour Party, she thereby became leader of the opposition in parliament.

The 1996 elections, held under a newly introduced system of proportional representation, almost saw a return to power for Labour. This was forestalled when a coalition was put together at the last moment by the incumbent New Zealand National Party and its small splinter party New Zealand First (NZ First)—but not before the holding of premature celebrations in the Labour camp, and the publication of an issue of *Time* magazine featuring Clark on the cover as New Zealand's first female prime minister. This distinction went instead, the following year, to the National Party's Jenny Shipley.

By the time of the next elections, in November 1999, the government's difficulties and the internal fractiousness of the National–NZ First coalition had provoked a swing of popular support back to Labour. The party took 38.7% of the national vote and secured 49 of the 120 seats in the House of Representatives, enabling Clark to form a minority government in coalition with the Alliance party. In addition to the prime ministership she also took on the arts, culture and heritage portfolio.

Clark pledged to return the nation to "basic New Zealand values" of fairness, opportunity and social equality, along with increases in taxation. Although never an outspoken republican, in the months following her election she stated that for New Zealand replacing the monarchy was inevitable. She has also backtracked on years of opposition to the idea of a single Australian–New Zealand dollar, suggesting that, like republican status, this too might be merely a matter of time.

Among other policies she has cut the New Zealand armed forces—grounding the combat wing of the air force altogether.

Splits within the Alliance party over the government's support for the war in Afghanistan in late 2001 prompted Clark to call early legislative elections for 27 July 2002. Labour increased its share of the vote to 41.3%, giving it 52 seats. Clark formed a new minority coalition with the left-of-centre Progressive Coalition, receiving support from the liberal United Future party and co-operation from the Green Party.

Clark refused to take New Zealand into the 'coalition of the willing' in the run-up to the US-led invasion of Iraq in 2003, and subsequently politically battled the USA over the country's nuclear-free status.

Her government also became mired in controversy over the issue of ownership of the seabed and shore. The government announced legislation to define it as belonging to the state but permitting the Maoris consultation over its use. The Maoris, sensitive to any erosion of their historic land rights, viewed this as a fresh wave of confiscation, and Maori members quit Labour; the conservative National Party on the other hand decried the legislation as unfair discrimination in favour of Maoris, a stance which greatly restored that party's popularity among the non-Maori population. The legislation was passed in 2004 and gradually support for Labour was restored, but Clark postponed the calling of the 2005 election until the last possible moment to give her party the best chance of a historic third term. The poll was set for 17 September, and taxation and student loans became key issues alongside relations with the USA and the continuance of the nuclear ban.

Helen Clark is married to Peter Davis but made a conscious decision not to have children, stating that she valued her "personal space and privacy too highly". Her personal space is occupied with studying politics, classical music, cross-country skiing, and an appreciation of good Chardonnay wine.

NICARAGUA

Full name: The Republic of Nicaragua.

Leadership structure: The head of state is a president, directly elected by universal adult suffrage. The president's term of office is five years. A president may not serve two consecutive terms, but may stand for re-election in a later election. Close relatives of the incumbent president may not stand for election as president. The head of government is the president, who is responsible to the National Assembly. The cabinet is appointed by the president.

| *President*: | Arnoldo Alemán | 10 Jan. 1997—10 Jan. 2002 |
| | Enrique **BOLAÑOS** Geyer | Since 10 Jan. 2002 |

Legislature: The legislature is unicameral. The sole chamber, the National Assembly (Asamblea Nacional), has 90 members directly elected for a five-year term. In addition, any presidential or vice-presidential candidate who receives nationally at least as many votes as the average of the winning percentages in each regional electoral district, but is not successful in being elected president or vice president, instead becomes a member of the National Assembly.

Profile of the President:

Enrique **BOLAÑOS** Geyer

Enrique Bolaños is a successful businessman and a former leader of the conservative Liberal Constitutionalist Party (Partido Liberal Constitucionalista—PLC). An outspoken critic of the left-wing 1980s Sandinista regime, he was persecuted and imprisoned but refused to leave the country. Since running for the presidency in November 2001 he has distanced himself from his former running mate and scandal-tainted predecessor Arnoldo Alemán.

Enrique Bolaños Geyer was born on 13 May 1928 in Masaya, near Managua. His younger brother Nicolas is now a member of the rival Conservative Party of Nicaragua. Enrique married Lila T. Abaúnza, also from Masaya, in 1949 and they had four sons and one daughter, although one son has since died. Bolaños graduated in industrial engineering from the Jesuit-run St Louis University in Missouri, USA.

Back in Nicaragua from 1952, Bolaños developed the family farming business, creating one of the country's largest cotton-growing firms. By 1978 the Bolaños-Geyer family company was producing 5% of the country's cotton. In 1979 the

413

revolutionary Sandinista regime confiscated the company and nationalized the cotton industry. Bolaños refused to go into exile, as many of the previous regime's entrepreneurs had done, and instead faced the wrath of the left-wing government for his voluble criticism. He spent a period in jail. During the 1980s, while civil war raged, he headed various business groups, including the Nicaragua Chamber of Industry and the Central American Institute of Business Administration, where he had also previously studied management. He took to writing, producing critical articles and books including *How are we doing?* (1982) and the *Ideas for All* column.

In 1996 Bolaños was chosen as the PLC's candidate for vice president, as the running mate of Managua mayor Arnoldo Alemán. The pair were successfully elected in October, and took office in January 1997. As vice president he struggled to promote government transparency. By the end of its term in 2001 the Alemán regime had become embroiled in corruption scandals, raising the prospect of a Sandinista victory at the polls. Bolaños resigned as vice president and began to distance himself from Alemán in order to take on the PLC nomination for president. In the November election he defeated the Sandinista candidate, former president Daniel Ortega, by taking 56% of the vote. He took office on 10 January 2002.

As president, Bolaños opened a corruption investigation into his predecessor. His efforts were lambasted by the PLC in August 2002 when it accused him of pursuing a personal vendetta against Alemán, which was splitting the party into factions. In March 2003 the PLC cut its ties to Bolaños, and he was left with the support of just nine PLC parliamentarians. Later that year Alemán was jailed for 20 years. The opposition launched a congressional corruption inquiry against Bolaños himself in 2004, though it was portrayed as a politically motivated attempt to force him out of office.

More pressing calls for his resignation were voiced in April 2005 as thousands of demonstrators took to the streets after bus fares were hiked by 20% in response to rising world oil prices. The following month a state of economic emergency was declared to enable Bolaños to raise electricity prices. Meanwhile the Congress, dominated by the opposition, had passed constitutional reforms in 2004 to take control of key public works agencies away from the presidency. The increasing impasse between the president and the Congress and judiciary looked set to head the country even deeper into political crisis.

NIGER

Full name: The Republic of Niger.

Leadership structure: The head of state is a president, directly elected by universal adult suffrage. The president's term of office is five years, renewable once only. The head of government is the prime minister, who is appointed from the parliamentary majority.

President:	Mamadou **TANDJA**	Since 22 Dec. 1999
Prime Minister:	Ibrahim Hassane Mayaki	27 Nov. 1997—3 Jan. 2000
	HAMA Amadou	Since 3 Jan. 2000

Legislature: The legislature is unicameral. The sole chamber, the National Assembly (Assemblée Nationale), has 83 members, directly elected for a five-year term.

Profile of the President:

Mamadou **TANDJA**

Mamadou Tandja started his career as a professional soldier, and came into government as a result of the military coup against President Hamani Diori in April 1974. He was twice an unsuccessful candidate in presidential elections, in 1993 and 1996, before his victory in 1999. He was the first elected president to complete a term in office, and was re-elected in 2004. He has a reputation for being both thorough and hardworking.

Mamadou Tandja was born in 1938 in the southeastern part of the country. He joined the armed forces and took part in the 1974 coup, after which he became interior minister. He rose to the rank of lieutenant-general before retiring to civilian life. He is married to Laraba Tandja.

In July 1991 he became leader of the National Movement for a Development Society (Mouvement National pour la Société de Développement—MNSD-Nassara) in succession to President Ali Saïbou, and stood as the MNSD-Nassara candidate in the 1993 presidential elections when Saïbou himself declined to take part. Despite winning the greatest share of the vote in the first round, he lost in the runoff to Mahamane Ousmane.

The 1990s were a time of considerable unrest, and in April 1994 Tandja was briefly detained after an anti-government protest, when many members of the opposition were arrested and prosecuted. In the next election, held in 1996 (following a coup in January and the formation of a transitional government), Tandja was again an unsuccessful candidate, this time losing to Brig.-Gen. Ibrahim Barre Maïnassara, the coup leader and head of the transitional government.

In 1999 the pattern of military coup followed by a return to elected government was repeated, but on this occasion without the coup leader himself being a candidate for the presidency. Polling took place in two rounds, on 17 October and 24 November. Tandja, standing once again as the MNSD-Nassara candidate, won the runoff against Mahamadou Issoufou of the Nigerien Party for Democracy and Socialism, and the MNSD-Nassara also gained a majority in the concurrent election to the National Assembly. He took office on 22 December.

The economy dominated the political agenda in Tandja's first term. The country had been starved of foreign aid due to the recent coups, and efforts to rein in government spending brought Tandja's government into conflict with students who objected to cuts in scholarship funding and civil servants who were subject to pay cuts and pay delays. The issue of pay caused soldiers to mutiny in 2002, but the rebellion was quickly quelled.

Tandja completed his term in office in December 2004—the country's first elected president to do so. He was re-elected for a second term, having again faced Issoufou in the runoff in December. (Constitutionally this is his final term, though it is rumoured that he may attempt to change the constitution to allow a further term.) The MNSD-Nassara remained the largest party in the concurrent legislative elections, though it lost its overall majority. Tandja faced immediate problems to steer the country through a severe food crisis—not uncommon in Niger, but exacerbated by drought and a plague of locusts.

Profile of the Prime Minister:

HAMA Amadou

Hama Amadou had a career in broadcasting before becoming private secretary to successive presidents in the 1980s and early 1990s. A leading figure in the National Movement for a Development Society (Mouvement National pour la Société de Développement—MNSD-Nassara), he was first appointed as prime minister in February 1995. Ousted in the military coup the following January, he returned to office four years later following his party's success in the presidential and legislative elections of November 1999.

Hama Amadou was born in 1950 and is married to Hama Zeinabou. A former managing director of the Niger Broadcasting Board, he established himself as an influential political figure as a result of his posts as private secretary to Presidents Seyni Kountché (1974–87) and Ali Saïbou (1987–93) and also secretary-general, and then president, of MNSD-Nassara, the pro-military party originally founded by Saïbou prior to the adoption of a multiparty constitution.

Hama was out of government from 1993 as a result of the electoral victory that year of the Democratic and Social Convention (Convention Démocratique et Sociale—CDS-Rahama). He was reluctantly appointed as prime minister on 17 February 1995, however, by the CDS-Rahama leader President Mahamane Ousmane, who had resorted to calling early legislative elections only to see his party suffer losses at the hands of the MNSD-Nassara. The turbulent period of 'cohabitation' which ensued was brought to an end by the military coup of January 1996. A constitutional referendum held in May 1996 prepared for a return to elected government, but, with the MNSD-Nassara out of power for nearly four years, Hama did not return to office until after its November 1999 election victory. In the intervening period, he was briefly detained after being arrested on 1 January 1998 and accused of involvement in a coup attempt. He was appointed prime minister by the incoming President Tandja in January 2000.

Following the re-election of Tandja and the MNSD-Nassara in 2004, Hama was reappointed as prime minister. He responded to the country's food crisis of 2005 by appealing to the international community for aid to ease the famine. Tandja, however, viewed labelling the crisis as a famine as an overstatement; this difference in reaction was thought to underline a growing rift between the two men.

NIGERIA

Full name: The Federal Republic of Nigeria.

Leadership structure: The head of state is an elected president. The president's term of office is four years, renewable once only. The head of government under the 1999 Constitution is the president, who names a cabinet or Federal Executive Council, which must be approved by the Senate.

President: Gen. (retd) Olusegun **OBASANJO**   Since 29 May 1999

Legislature: The legislature, the National Assembly, is bicameral. The lower chamber, the House of Representatives, has 360 members and the upper chamber, the Senate, has 109 members, both elected for four-year terms.

Profile of the President:

Gen. (retd) Olusegun **OBASANJO**

Olusegun Obasanjo was a leading figure in the 1975 coup which ousted Gen. Gowon. He won credit by returning the country to civilian rule in 1979. Concentrating thereafter on an international role, he was nevertheless arrested under the autocratic regime of Gen. Sani Abacha in 1995 and spent three years in prison, emerging to campaign for, and win, the presidency in the 1999 elections. He has tried to steer his federal government away from direct confrontation with Islamists in the north; he is himself a Christian southerner from the Yoruba ethnic group.

Olusegun Obasanjo was born on 6 March 1937 in Abeokuta, Ogun State, in the southwest of the country, and was educated at the Baptist Boys' High School in Abeokuta. He enlisted in the Nigerian army in 1958, and trained in the UK at Mons Officers Cadet School, Aldershot, the Royal College of Military Engineering, Chatham, and the School of Survey, Newbury. In 1958 and 1959 he served in the fifth battalion, Nigerian army, in Kaduna and the Cameroons, and in the 1960s he was posted to the UN peacekeeping force in Congo. Promoted through the ranks to colonel by 1969, he fought in the civil war against the Biafra secessionists, and received the surrender from the Biafran army in 1970.

He first entered the government in January 1975, as federal commissioner for works and housing, and the same year was appointed chief of staff. He was a member of the Supreme Military Council which took control of the country in July 1975, after the incumbent president Gen. Gowon had refused to set any agenda for a return to civilian rule. The Supreme Military Council appointed Brig. Murtala Mohammed as president, but in February 1976 he was assassinated and replaced by Obasanjo as both head of state and commander-in-chief of the armed forces. Obasanjo presided over the return to civilian elected government in September 1979, when he retired from the army (with the rank of general) to his poultry farm.

Although appointed a member of the advisory Council of State in 1979, he pursued a more international role for the next two decades, with a series of appointments notably at the UN Educational, Scientific and Cultural Organization (UNESCO) and the World Health Organization (WHO). In 1980 he was a member of the Independent Commission on Disarmament and Security, and in 1985 he cochaired the Eminent Persons Group on South Africa. He also founded the Africa Leadership Forum in 1987 and was involved in mediation efforts in Namibia, Angola, Sudan, South Africa, Mozambique and Burundi. In 1991 he was a candidate for the post of secretary-general of the UN. He served as an official observer in elections in Angola (1992) and Mozambique (1994), and until 1999 was chairman of the advisory council of Transparency International, the organization campaigning against corruption in business and public life.

In 1995 he became involved in domestic politics once more when he was among 43 people arrested and charged with treason, for an alleged plot against the then military ruler, President Sani Abacha. Obasanjo was given a 15-year prison sentence, but was released in 1998. Selected as the presidential candidate of the People's Democratic Party (PDP) for elections in 1999, he emerged as the victor in the 27 February poll, his party having won a parliamentary majority in the legislative elections the previous week. He took office at the end of May, and a month later he swore in a new civilian government, leaving northerners aggrieved at the loss of the preponderance of power they had enjoyed under military rule.

His presidency has had to contend with a marked rise in Islamic fundamentalist influence in the Muslim north, where eight states adopted *shari'a* (Islamic law), a divisive issue over which Obasanjo has been very guarded in his public responses. Ethnic and religious clashes have been frequent, and have killed thousands and displaced hundreds of thousands since Obasanjo took office. Riots have also been recurrent over the contentious issue of the price of fuel.

Religion was a factor in the April 2003 presidential election when Obasanjo faced Muslim former military ruler Gen. Muhammadu Buhari. Obasanjo won over 60% of the vote, and the PDP secured a majority in both houses, but the opposition alleged fraud in many states. It was not until 2005 that the Supreme Court finally ruled that, though there had been some fraud, the result should stand.

The key issue of Obasanjo's presidency has been the fight against corruption. Obasanjo has been well aware of the importance of presenting a clean image to the international community in order to win debt relief. He has formed an anti-corruption commission, introduced ID cards to counter fraud and striven to rid the legislature and the government of corrupt members. Allegations have even been levelled at Obasanjo himself, despite his long-standing reputation as one of the least corrupt people in Nigerian political circles. He declared in 2004 an income of US$250,000 a month from his farm to allay claims of embezzlement from public funds, and in 2005 he agreed to be investigated by the corruption commission after the governor of Abia state, already under investigation himself, accused Obasanjo of accepting bribes.

Obasanjo's published works include *My Command* (an account of the Nigerian civil war, published in 1979), *Africa Embattled* (1988), *Constitution for National Integration and Development* (1989), *Africa: Rise to Challenge* (1993) and *This Animal Called Man* (1999). He had two sons and four daughters by his first wife, Oluremi Akinbwon, and is now married to Stella Abebe.

NORWAY

Full name: The Kingdom of Norway.

Leadership structure: The head of state is a constitutional monarch. The head of government is the prime minister, who is responsible to Parliament. The Council of State is appointed by the prime minister.

King:	**HARALD V**	Since 17 Jan. 1991
Regent:	Crown Prince Håkon	25 Nov. 2003—13 April 2004 and 29 March 2005—7 June 2005
Prime Minister:	Kjell Magne Bondevik	17 Oct. 1997—17 March 2000
	Jens Stoltenberg	17 March 2000—19 Oct. 2001
	Kjell Magne **BONDEVIK**	Since 19 Oct. 2001

Legislature: The legislature is unicameral. The sole chamber, the Parliament (Storting), has 165 members, directly elected for a four-year term. When dealing with legislative matters, the Parliament divides itself into two bodies, the upper chamber (Lagting) and the lower chamber (Odelsting).

Profile of the King:

HARALD V

King Harald V came to the throne in 1991 following the death of his father King Olav V, having taken over his official duties the previous year, and having served a 33-year apprenticeship as crown prince. As a young man he studied political science at Balliol College, Oxford, and he is noted as an Olympic sailor. His marriage to Sonja Haraldsen, a commoner, in 1968 was extremely popular with the Norwegian people.

Harald was born on 21 February 1937, at Skaugum, the estate which is still the home of the royal family. He was baptized on 31 March 1937 in the palace chapel. With the Nazi invasion in 1940, the royal family fled into exile and he spent most of the war years living in the USA near Washington D.C. He returned to Norway after liberation in 1945, attending Smestad primary school until 1950 and the Oslo cathedral school until 1955, taking his upper secondary diploma in science. Between 1956 and 1957 he attended the cavalry officers' candidate school at Trandum, and then the military academy where he remained until graduation in 1959. He has the rank of general in the army and the air force and admiral in the navy.

On 21 September 1957 he took his place beside his father, King Olav V, in the Council of State following the death of his grandfather, King Håkon VII. He was made crown prince, taking the oath to the constitution on 21 February 1958.

Harald studied political science at Balliol College, Oxford, UK, between 1960 and 1962, and subsequently devoted much time to foreign visits and the promotion of Norwegian business interests abroad. He took over his father's official duties after King Olav suffered a stroke in June 1990. He came to the throne on his father's death on 17 January 1991, and was sworn in as king four days later.

Harald continues to hold weekly meetings of the Council of State and receives new ambassadors. He is also commander-in-chief of the armed forces, and head of the Norwegian Church. He enjoys outdoor life, especially fishing, shooting, hunting, skiing, and is a keen yachtsman both in competitive and noncompetitive sailing.

King Harald married Sonja Haraldsen on 29 August 1968. They have one daughter, Princess Märtha Louise, born in 1971, and one son, Crown Prince Håkon, who was born in 1973. Håkon is the heir to the throne, although legislation passed in May 1990 gives equal succession rights to both sexes thereafter.

Profile of the Prime Minister:

Kjell Magne **BONDEVIK**

Kjell Magne Bondevik, a priest in the (Lutheran) Church of Norway, first became prime minister of Norway in October 1997, heading a minority coalition government including his right-of-centre Christian Democratic Party (Kristelig Folkeparti—KrF). Out of office between March 2000 and October 2001, he then formed another minority coalition government. Bondevik himself has retained a seat in parliament since 1973 and held cabinet office in the mid-1980s and in 1989–90, when he was foreign minister.

Kjell Magne Bondevik was born on 3 September 1947 in Molde, a coastal town west of Trondheim. He was active in the KrF party youth movement, the Young Christian Democrats (Kristelig Folkepartis Ungdom—KrFU), becoming its deputy leader in 1968 and leader from 1970 to 1973. From 1972 to 1973 he was a municipal councillor in Nesodden and a member of the municipal school board. He was also state secretary in the office of the prime minister during the same period. He entered the Parliament for the first time in 1973, after four years as an alternate member, and has represented his native county, Møre and Romsdal, ever since.

Pursuing his theological studies, Bondevik gained a degree from the free faculty of theology at the University of Oslo in 1975. In 1979 he was ordained as priest in the (Lutheran) Church of Norway. Kjell Magne Bondevik is married to Bjørg née Rasmussen, and they have three children.

Within the KrF he was party deputy chairman between 1975 and 1983, and in addition leader of the parliamentary party between 1981 and 1983, in which year he became party chairman. He retained the party chairmanship for 12 years (being succeeded in 1995 by Valgerd Svarstad Haugland), and was in addition leader of the parliamentary party between 1986 and 1989 and again from 1993 onward. In the course of his career, when not holding a ministerial post, he has sat on the parliamentary standing committees on the Church and education (1973–77), on finance (1977–83), on foreign affairs (1986–89), on defence affairs (1990–93) and once again on foreign affairs (1993–97). Between 1983 and 1986 he was minister of Church and education, and in 1989 he became minister of foreign affairs in the short-lived centre-right minority coalition government of the conservative Jan Syse, which held power until October 1990. As foreign minister, Bondevik, an opponent of membership of the European Union (EU), conducted Norway's negotiations with the EU on the formation of the European Economic Area (EEA), which were eventually concluded in October 1991.

Bondevik became prime minister in the government appointed on 17 October 1997 as a result of lengthy coalition negotiations in the aftermath of the election held on 15 September. The KrF and its Agrarian and Liberal coalition partners had won an aggregate of only 26.1% of the vote and held less than a quarter of the seats in the Parliament, and Bondevik's prime ministership thus began amid much speculation as to how long his government might survive. Concerns were heightened when he took three weeks' leave at the end of August 1998 for 'stress'. Lacking a parliamentary majority, Bondevik was forced by the far-right Progress Party (Fremskrittspartiet—FrP) to abandon tax increases in order to pass the 1999 budget.

In March 2000 Bondevik became the first Norwegian prime minister to resign over an environmental issue. His government had lost a no-confidence motion over the proposed postponement of plans to build new gas-fired power stations. Bondevik nominated the Norwegian Labour Party (Det Norske Arbeiderparti—DNA), the largest party in Parliament, to take over in a single-party minority government.

However, public sympathies were steadily swinging to the right and by the time of the September 2001 legislative elections the DNA recorded its worst result in over 100 years while the parties of the right performed well—although the KrF itself slightly decreased its representation. After a tentative DNA minority government collapsed, Bondevik was asked to head a right-wing minority coalition from 19 October. His KrF dominates, but is supported by the conservative Høyre (now the second-biggest party) and the liberal Venstre, with parliamentary backing again from the FrP (the third-biggest party). The influence of the FrP forced Bondevik in December 2002 to introduce tax cuts in the 2003 budget in the face of a threatened vote of no confidence.

The race for the September 2005 election showed the ruling coalition lagging behind a red–green alliance, signalling a desire for change among the Norwegian electorate. Bondevik promised tax cuts, based on increased oil prices, but the opposition decried this pledge as benefiting only the rich, campaigning instead for extending Norway's generous welfare system for the benefit of all.

OMAN

Full name: The Sultanate of Oman.

Leadership structure: The head of state is the sultan, who is also head of government, advised by the cabinet and the Consultative Council.

Sultan:	**QABOOS** bin Said al-Said (prime minister from 2 Jan. 1972)	Since 23 July 1970

Legislature: Legislation is by decree of the sultan, advised by the 83-member Consultative Council (Majlis al-Shoura). The Council was directly elected for the first time in September 2000, when successful candidates included two women. Election is by electoral college in each province, with a total of over 200,000 electors, made up of men and women 'of standing' in the community. The Council has a three-year mandate. On 16 December 1997 Sultan Qaboos appointed for the first time the 41 members of a new Council of State (Majlis al-Dawlah), which was intended to serve as "a positive contributor to constructive co-operation between the government and the citizens".

Profile of the Sultan:

QABOOS bin Said al-Said

Sultan Qaboos has ruled Oman since July 1970, when, at the age of 29, he deposed his father Said bin Taimur. Qaboos took control with the support of the armed forces and several members of the royal family after the alleged deterioration in the former sultan's health. As sultan he is in effect an absolute monarch, and his rule is authoritarian but paternalistic, combining a conservative perspective with cautious modernization to the extent of holding direct elections to the advisory Consultative Council from 2000.

Qaboos bin Said al-Said was born in Şalalah, in the southern province of Dhofar, on 18 November 1940. He is the latest heir to the Bu Said dynasty, the Ibadi Muslim clan which has ruled Oman since the 18th century; the sultanate of Muscat and Oman formally gained independence from the UK in 1951. Qaboos was educated privately in England and trained as an officer at the Royal Military Academy, Sandhurst, from 1960, including a one-year tour of duty with a British infantry battalion stationed in West Germany. Before returning to Oman he studied local government with Bedfordshire County Council for almost 12 months. In Şalalah, from 1966, he studied Islamic history and culture under the guidance of his father.

Qaboos justified the 1970 coup in Ṣalalah with reference to a need to modernize and develop Oman's international relations, and has maintained a consistently pro-Western stance, while also developing contacts within the Arab world and among the other conservative Gulf sheikhdoms. He framed a series of five-year plans, designed to create a modern infrastructure in Oman, which nevertheless remains relatively little developed and dependent on oil for its prosperity. He has also held the role of prime minister since 1972.

In tentative moves towards wider participation in public affairs, Qaboos established in 1981 an appointed Consultative Council, which in 1991 became an indirectly elected body and in 2000 was directly elected for the first time. In the 2003 election women were allowed to vote, and that year the first female minister was appointed.

The creation of a second chamber, the advisory Council of State, took effect with appointments made by Qaboos at the end of 1997, pursuant to a decree he had issued on 6 November 1996 which forms the Basic Statute of the State, and which, among other things, also clarifies the royal succession. As Qaboos has never married and has no children, his heir is likely to be one of his cousins; the Statute states that the sultan will name his preferred successor in a letter to the royal family to be read on his death.

PAKISTAN

Full name: The Islamic Republic of Pakistan.

Leadership structure: Under the 1973 Constitution, the head of state is a president, elected by Parliament, for a five-year term of office. Although the October 1999 coup did not entail any change in this nominal position, Gen. Pervez Musharraf dismissed Muhammad Rafiq Tarar on 20 June 2001 and assumed the presidency himself.

Musharraf also retained until November 2002 the position of chief executive, which he had assumed at the time of the coup. Following the October 2002 elections the post of head of government passed to the newly appointed prime minister. The prime minister is nominated by and responsible to Parliament, and appoints the cabinet.

Prior to those elections the extension of Musharraf's presidency for a further five years had been approved in a referendum on 30 April 2002, and on 21 August 2002 Musharraf announced changes to the constitution giving him the right to dismiss an elected Parliament. More changes to the constitution were made in November 2002 giving the president the power to take legislative powers if no party could achieve a majority in Parliament.

President:	Muhammad Rafiq Tarar	1 Jan. 1998—20 June 2001
	Gen. Pervez **MUSHARRAF**	Since 20 June 2001
Chief Executive:	Gen. Pervez Musharraf (seized power on 12 Oct. 1999)	15 Oct. 1999—23 Nov. 2002
Prime Minister:	Mir Zafarullah Jamali (acting until 30 June 2004)	23 Nov. 2002—26 June 2004
	Chaudhry Shujaat Hussain	30 June 2004—28 Aug. 2004
	Shaukat **AZIZ**	Since 28 Aug. 2004

Legislature: Under the constitution, the Parliament (Majlis al-Shoura) is bicameral. The National Assembly has 342 members (including ten elected by non-Muslim minorities and 60 elected women), increased from 237 by the Legal Framework Order; the Senate has 100 members, 88 of them elected by the provincial assemblies, eight chosen by tribal agencies, and four elected by the National Assembly. The term of the Assembly is five years; the term of the Senate is six years.

Profile of the President:

Gen. Pervez **MUSHARRAF**

Gen. Pervez Musharraf was head of the Pakistani army before staging the bloodless coup which brought him to power as 'chief executive' in October 1999. His reputation in the armed services and his vow to sweep away 'sham' democracy initially gave him high approval ratings. However, by the time he assumed the role of president in June 2001, his support in the country had dropped to less than 25%. He met a self-imposed deadline to reintroduce a democratically elected parliament by October 2002, while guaranteeing his own position by extending his mandate and increasing his constitutional powers.

Pervez Musharraf was born on 11 August 1943 in New Delhi, the capital of what was then British-controlled India. His family was relatively wealthy and his father served in the colonial government's foreign service. As Muslims they migrated to Karachi, in what had become West Pakistan, soon after the partition of India in 1947, managing to avoid the violent scenes that accompanied the later exodus. As an Urdu-speaking migrant from India, Musharraf is known in Pakistan as a *mohajir.* His father, Syed Musharraf-ud-Din, transferred to the foreign ministry of the fledgling Pakistani state and was despatched to Turkey in 1949, taking his family with him. Musharraf spent seven years in Ankara and is consequently fluent in Turkish, as well as professing great admiration for that country's military founder, Gen. Mustafa Kemal Atatürk.

The family returned to Pakistan in 1956 and Musharraf was educated at two prestigious, and originally Christian-run, schools before travelling to the UK to attend the Royal College of Defence Studies. He received a commission in the artillery in 1964 having graduated finally from the Pakistan Military Academy. He first saw action on the field during the first India–Pakistan war of 1965, for which he received a medal for gallantry. After that war he volunteered to join the Special Service Group 'commandos', and he led a commando company during the second India–Pakistan war in 1971. Meanwhile he had married Sehba Fareed in 1968; they have one son and one daughter.

Over the next 20 years Musharraf held various positions in the army, including leading artillery regiments, infantry brigades and an armoured artillery division. In 1991 he was promoted to major-general and given command of an infantry division. Four years later he rose to be lieutenant-general and took control of a prestigious strike corps.

In October 1998 Musharraf achieved the rank of full general and was appointed chief of army staff. He is only the second *mohajir* to head the Pakistani army. Some observers suggested that the then prime minister Nawaz Sharif had specifically appointed Musharraf because of his background; reasoning that a *mohajir* would find it harder to build up popular support and would consequently pose no threat to the government. However, the very next year Musharraf and Sharif quarrelled over Pakistan's military activities in the disputed region of

428

Kashmir. When Sharif attempted to dismiss Musharraf in October 1999, the general responded by staging a military coup on 12 October. He had Sharif imprisoned before suspending multiparty politics and the country's constitution, installing himself as chief executive on 15 October.

In the beginning the coup received widespread public support as it was seen to overthrow a corrupt regime. On 20 June 2001 Musharraf assumed the presidency, while maintaining his role as chief executive and head of the armed forces. His term was extended for five years following the approval of a controversial referendum held in April 2002, and later that year he reinstated the constitutional powers of the presidency, just two months before legislative elections. Under these changes he has the power to dissolve Parliament and alter the constitution.

Legislative elections held on 10 October 2002 were won by the pro-presidential Pakistan Muslim League/Quaid-e-Azam (PML/Q) but saw significant support go to the previous ruling parties and Islamists. Making sure that he would avoid 'cohabitation' with an opposition-led government, Musharraf stretched out the period for coalition talks by over a month and then, to ensure the accession of Mir Zafarullah Jamali of the PML/Q, altered the boundaries for prime ministerial qualification by suddenly including previous state premiers, as long as they had only ruled in an 'acting' capacity. Musharraf himself was inaugurated for another five-year presidential term on 16 November 2002. Although he officially handed over the reins of government to Jamali a week later, he remained firmly in control of the regime.

Parties opposed to Musharraf effectively paralyzed the National Assembly for over a year. The deadlock ended in December 2003, when Musharraf made a deal with the Muttahida Majlis-e-Amal (MMA), agreeing to resign as head of the army by the end of 2004. With the support of the MMA, Musharraf was able to muster the two-thirds' majority required to pass an amendment which retroactively legalized the 1999 coup, and in January 2004 Musharraf won votes of confidence which confirmed him in office until 2007. In late 2004, however, pro-Musharraf MPs passed a bill allowing Musharraf to retain his position as head of the army as well as that of president, and Musharraf said that he intended to remain in both posts, breaking his earlier promise to the MMA.

Following the terrorist attacks on the USA on 11 September 2001, Musharraf controversially threw his weight behind US President George W. Bush's 'war on terrorism', against a strong current of Islamist opinion in the country. Musharraf's aid was critical in the US-led assault on neighbouring Afghanistan which ultimately saw the overthrow of the *taliban* and in 2002 he gave a speech denouncing Islamic extremism and all forms of terrorism, including that carried out by those enraged by India's control over parts of Muslim Kashmir. Among other things, this contributed to the easing of relations with India. Brought to the brink of war several times in recent years, including in 2002, the peace process has since accelerated and has been described as "irreversible". Musharraf has visited India to watch a cricket match between the two countries' national teams.

Profile of the Prime Minister:

Shaukat **AZIZ**

Shaukat Aziz was sworn in as prime minister on 28 August 2004, days after winning the requisite by-election needed to enter parliament. The personal choice of President Pervez Musharraf, he had previously served as finance minister, and is credited with turning the Pakistani economy round from recession to rapid growth, undoubtedly aided by his 30 years of experience in global finance and international banking and the contacts he made during this period. While campaigning for the by-election that allowed him to take up the premiership, Aziz survived a suicide bomb attack in which his driver and eight other people died.

Shaukat Aziz was born in Karachi on 6 March 1949 and was educated at St Patrick's School, Karachi, and Abbottabad Public School. He graduated from Gordon College in Rawalpindi in 1967, going on to do a master's degree at the Institute of Business Administration at the University of Karachi. He is married to Rukhsana Aziz and they have three children.

On graduation, Aziz joined Citibank in Karachi. He left Pakistan in 1975 and worked overseas for many years, including in the UK, the USA, Greece, Saudi Arabia and the Philippines. He was appointed executive vice president of Citibank in 1992, reporting directly to the chairman. Before taking leave from Citigroup, he was the head of its global private banking division.

In November 1999, a month after Musharraf's bloodless coup, Aziz was appointed as Pakistani minister of finance. He oversaw a period of economic recovery and was declared 'finance minister of the year' in 2001 by *Euromoney* and *Bankers Magazine*. Aziz was elected as a senator in 2002.

Aziz was named by the Pakistan Muslim League/Quaid-e-Azam (PML/Q) as the next prime minister after the resignation of Mir Zafarullah Jamali on 26 June 2004. The post was held by Chaudhry Shujaat Hussain while Aziz secured a seat in the lower house of parliament. He was elected prime minister by parliament on 27 August 2004 by a vote of 191 to 151, and sworn in the following day. He retained his position as minister of finance.

PALAU

Full name: Republic of Palau.

Leadership structure: The head of state is a president, directly elected by universal adult suffrage. The president's term of office is four years, renewable once only. The constitution also provides for an advisory body to the president which is composed of the paramount chief of each of the country's 16 separate states. The head of government is the president. The cabinet is appointed by the president.

President:	Kuniwo Nakamura	1 Jan. 1993—19 Jan. 2001
	Tommy **REMENGESAU**	Since 19 Jan. 2001

Legislature: The legislature, the National Congress (Olbiil era Kelulau), is bicameral. The lower chamber, the House of Delegates, has 16 members, directly elected for a four-year term. The upper chamber, the Senate, has 14 members, elected for a four-year term. Members of both houses are elected as independents.

Profile of the President:

Tommy **REMENGESAU**

Tommy Remengesau's inauguration as president of Palau in January 2001 followed his election on 7 November 2000 when he was backed by outgoing president Kuniwo Nakamura. Educated in the USA, he had been vice president since 1993, and his appointment represents little change in previous policy, seeking greater economic development for Palau.

Thomas Esang Remengesau Jr was born in Palau, then a district of the UN Trust Territory of the Pacific Islands, on 28 February 1956. His father Thomas Remengesau Sr was Palau's first district administrator, and served as vice president under Lazarus Salii from 1985, completing Salii's term in 1988. Thomas Jr studied as a postgraduate at the Michigan State University, USA, after graduating from the state's Grand Valley University in the late 1970s. He returned to the Micronesian islands in 1980 and began work as an administrator and planner at the Palau Bureau of Health Services. He married Debbie Mineich and they have two sons and two daughters. He is a keen fisherman and has been All-Micronesian Grand Champion twice.

In 1981 Remengesau was appointed public information officer at the newly created autonomous Palau legislature, the National Congress. In 1984, though still only in his twenties, he decided to run for a seat in the Senate. He surprisingly received the most votes out of the 14 candidates vying for the three seats of the northeastern Badelboab constituency. He spent eight years in the Senate, gradually earning the respect of the older generation of politicians.

In popular elections held in November 1992 Remengesau was elected vice president, and he took on the role of administration minister. Two years later the country entered into a Compact of Free Association with the USA and became fully independent, the last of the US-administered Trust Territories to make this step. He served a second elected term as vice president from 1997 to 2001.

President Nakamura, whose second term was due to end in January 2001, could not stand for re-election and strongly supported Remengesau's candidacy to replace him. Remengesau won the November 2000 election with 52% of the vote, defeating his only rival, Peter Sugiyama. He inherited a determined policy to rescue the country from its dependence on US financial assistance, and focused on developing tourism, agriculture and aquaculture, while preserving the country's environment and culture. He also made many reforms to the institutional structure of government. He clashed with Congress in 2003 over the budget; Remengesau claimed that the version passed by Congress infringed his powers by limiting his spending and his executive right to control foreign affairs policy.

Remengesau easily won re-election in November 2004, defeating Polycarp Basilius with 66% of the vote. The major challenge for his second term will be preparation for the end of the current Compact, which expires in 2009.

PALESTINE

Leadership structure: Mahmoud Abbas was elected as executive president in January 2005, and sworn in on 15 January. He is generally accorded the status of head of state internationally, although a formal declaration of Palestinian statehood has not been made. The head of government is the prime minister, who is appointed by the president. The prime minister appoints the Palestinian National Authority (PNA), or cabinet, which must be approved by the Palestinian Legislative Council.

President:	Yassir Arafat (chairman of PNA from 5 July 1994)	12 Feb. 1996—11 Nov. 2004
	Ahmed Qurei (acting)	29 Oct. 2004—11 Nov. 2004
	Rauhi Fattouh (acting)	11 Nov. 2004—15 Jan. 2005
	Mahmoud **ABBAS**	Since 15 Jan. 2005
Prime Minister:	Mahmoud Abbas (acting until 7 Oct. 2003)	30 April 2003—6 Sept. 2003
	Ahmed **QUREI**	Since 7 Oct. 2003

Legislature: The legislature is unicameral. The sole chamber, the Palestinian Legislative Council (PLC, Majlis al-Tashri'i), has one seat reserved for the Palestinian president, and 88 constituency members. On election in 1996 all members of the PLC were given automatic membership of the Palestine National Council (PNC), which is the governing body of the Palestine Liberation Organization (PLO).

Profile of the President:

Mahmoud **ABBAS**

Mahmoud Abbas (also known as Abu Mazen) became Palestinian leader in January 2005 following the death of Yassir Arafat. Regarded as a moderate by many Israelis as well as Palestinians, he has been a member of Fatah and the Palestine Liberation Organization (PLO) since their inception, and was one of the chief architects of the 1993 Oslo Accords.

Mahmoud Abbas was born in 1935 in Safed in Palestine, then part of the British Mandate. In 1948 Israel was recognized as an independent state in its own right by the UN and was immediately attacked by several Arab nations. Abbas and his

433

family, along with an estimated 750,000 compatriots, became refugees following the war and eventually settled in Syria, where Abbas taught in an elementary school. He later graduated from Damascus University before travelling to Egypt to study law.

In the 1950s Abbas became heavily involved in underground Palestinian politics in Qatar, where he became director of personnel for the country's civil service. Abbas recruited a number of people who would later become key members of the PLO and in 1957 was a founder member of the militant group Fatah. He became a member of the Palestine National Council in 1968 and was widely regarded as one of the most powerful people behind the scenes in the PLO. After the PLO's expulsion from Jordan, Abbas spent the next three decades travelling with Yassir Arafat and the rest of the PLO leadership in exile.

An early advocate of negotiations with the Israelis, Abbas began a dialogue with various Jewish and pacifist movements in the 1970s. As early as January 1977, he worked out a declaration of 'principles of peace' with Israeli Maj.-Gen. Mattityahu Peled. It was the first time a leading Palestinian figure had signed a document calling for a 'two-state solution' under which Israel would continue to exist. In 1980 he was appointed to the PLO department for national and international relations.

When the PLO leadership moved from Lebanon to Tunis in 1982, Abbas moved to Moscow where he studied at the Oriental College for a doctorate in history, on alleged contacts between the Zionist movement and the Nazis. His doctoral dissertation was published in Arabic in 1984; it later returned to haunt him and he was forced to disown the implications of holocaust denial in the book. In 1988 Abbas was elected to the PLO executive committee to replace the assassinated Abu Jihad.

By 1991 the PLO was conducting open negotiations—co-ordinated by Abbas—for the first time. His long history of contacts with Israelis on the left meant he was the natural choice to oversee the Palestinian negotiating team during the Oslo talks, and he is considered by many to be one of the major architects of the subsequent accords, travelling with Arafat to Washington D.C. to sign them in 1993. A year later he became head of the PLO negotiating affairs department and signed the Interim Agreement in September 1995—also the year he published a memoir *Through Secret Channels: The Road to Oslo* and returned to the Occupied Territories for the first time after 47 years of exile. In May 1996 Abbas headed, with Uri Savir, the first session of the Israeli–Palestinian Final Status talks. Earlier that year, Abbas had been elected to the Palestinian Legislative Council, the new legislature set up under the 1993 Accords—he had also served as head of the central election commission that had allowed the Council to take shape.

In March 2003 Abbas was nominated to be the first prime minister of the Palestinian National Authority, and finally took office at the end of April.

Initially, Arafat resented the international pressure that had been brought to bear on him to appoint a prime minister, and he tried to avoid devolving any real authority to Abbas, whose term in office was dominated by this ongoing tussle over the distribution of power; in particular Arafat refused to relinquish control of the security services. Abbas resigned as prime minister in frustration on 6 September 2003, citing continual opposition from Arafat and others in the PNA and a lack of support from the international community. He was replaced by Ahmed Qurei a month later. Abbas said afterwards that he had felt his life to be in danger from fellow Palestinians and that he had had no relationship with Arafat from the moment of his resignation.

Arafat died on 11 November 2004 and Abbas was seen by some, though certainly not all, as his natural successor; he was quickly endorsed by Fatah as its preferred candidate for the Palestinian presidential election. Following the withdrawal of his main rival, Marwan Barghouti, Abbas was elected with 62% of the vote on 9 January 2005 and sworn in on 15 January. Just eight days later it was reported that Abbas had secured a temporary ceasefire from Hamas and Islamic Jihad, and by 8 February Abbas had engaged in talks in Cairo with Israeli prime minister Ariel Sharon and the two sides had called a truce, ending more than four years of violence. Abbas then secured an agreement from the main militant groups to extend their temporary cessation of violence until the end of the year.

Profile of the Prime Minister:

Ahmed **QUREI**

Ahmed Qurei (also known as Abu Ala) was nominated as Palestinian prime minister on 7 September 2003, and took office a month later. Regarded as a moderate and a pragmatist, Qurei, a banker by trade, had gradually gained influence as many other Palestinian leaders fell by the wayside, imprisoned or assassinated by the Israelis. As a member of Fatah's central committee, Qurei had been involved in negotiating the 1993 Oslo Accords, and retains the support of the USA and the European Union (EU) as long as he demonstrates a willingness to cope with the Palestinians' numerous security problems. On the death of Yassir Arafat in 2004, and Mahmoud Abbas's subsequent victory in the Palestinian presidential election of 2005, Qurei was asked to continue in his post and form a new cabinet.

Ahmed Ali Mohammed Qurei was born in 1937 to a relatively wealthy merchant family in Abu Dis (near Jerusalem) where he now lives with his wife and five children. In the wake of the Israeli occupation of the West Bank in 1967, Qurei, a banker by trade, left Abu Dis for the Persian Gulf, moving to Beirut, Cyprus and Tunis.

Qurei joined the Fatah wing of the Palestine Liberation Organization (PLO) in 1968 but did not come to prominence within the organization until the mid-1970s, when he took over its economic and production enterprises in Lebanon. By 1980 the PLO's business enterprises generated an income estimated at around US$40 million a year and, with over 6,000 employees, had become one of the largest employers in the country.

When the PLO was expelled from Lebanon by the Israeli army in 1982, Qurei went to Tunis with Arafat. He gradually rose within the PLO, partly because he survived while several of his colleagues were incarcerated or assassinated. He was elected a member of the Fatah central committee in 1989. That marked the start of his political career, and he began to play an increasing role in peace negotiations. In 1993 Qurei headed the Palestinian delegation to the secret talks in Norway that led to the Oslo Accords. Around the same time, Qurei was instrumental in drafting a Palestinian development plan, which became a central document in the PLO development strategy for the Palestinian territories.

He returned to Gaza with Arafat in 1994. In January 1996, when Palestinians voted for their first parliament, Qurei was elected speaker of the 88-member Palestinian Legislative Council (PLC), a position he held until 2003. A day after the resignation of Mahmoud Abbas as prime minister on 6 September 2003, Arafat appointed Qurei as his replacement. He took office a month later on 7 October.

In 2004 Qurei became embroiled in a scandal over accusations that a company owned by his family, the Al-Quds Cement Company, was supplying materials used in building Israeli settlements and for the construction of the West Bank Barrier. However, a parliamentary inquiry came to nothing, and on Arafat's death in 2004, and Abbas's subsequent victory in the Palestinian presidential election of 2005, Qurei was asked to continue in his post and form a new cabinet. Due to demands by Fatah officials and PLC members to make the new cabinet more reform-minded, the vote of confidence in the new cabinet was repeatedly delayed. It was finally passed on 24 February 2005 after Qurei revised the list of ministers to accommodate these demands.

Qurei is a man of substantial personal charm, which has contributed to his success as a negotiator. His easy-going style has won him friendships with his Israeli counterparts and he is seen as having a rare understanding of Israeli concerns. There are, however, some concerns about his health; he has suffered badly from heart problems since the mid-1990s, and has undergone surgery to unblock a coronary artery.

PANAMA

Full name: The Republic of Panama.

Leadership structure: The head of state is a president, directly elected by universal adult suffrage. The president's term of office is five years, not renewable. The head of government is the president, who is responsible to the Legislative Assembly. The cabinet is appointed by the president.

| *President*: | Mireya Moscoso | 1 Sept. 1999—1 Sept. 2004 |
| | Martín **TORRIJOS** | Since 1 Sept. 2004 |

Legislature: The legislature is unicameral. The sole chamber, the Legislative Assembly (Asamblea Legislativa), has 78 members, directly elected for a five-year term.

Profile of the President:

Martín **TORRIJOS**

Martín Torrijos Espino, son of former military leader Omar Torrijos, won the May 2004 presidential elections in Panama and took office on 1 September 2004. Leader of the Democratic Revolutionary Party (Partido Revolucionario Democrática—PRD), Torrijos played heavily on his father's reputation as the hero who negotiated the 1977 treaty with US president Jimmy Carter that led to the eventual handover of the Panama Canal to Panamanian control in 1999. Torrijos studied in the USA, and holds degrees in political science and economics. Just 18 when his father died in a plane crash, Torrijos joined the party that his father founded and rose to deputy minister of the interior and justice. He was defeated in the 1999 presidential election by Mireya Moscoso, whose husband had been deposed by Omar Torrijos in his 1968 coup.

Martín Erasto Torrijos Espino was born on 18 July 1963 in Panama City, the illegitimate son of former military leader Omar Torrijos, who fathered six children by four different women. He was raised by maternal grandparents and a working mother. In 1977 his father took him to the USA for the signing of the Panama Canal treaty, and then sent him to St John's Military Academy in Wisconsin. Martín was just 18 when his father died in a 1981 plane crash. Mentored by a friend of his father, he went on to graduate from Texas A&M University with degrees in political science and economics. He later worked as a manager at McDonald's in Chicago from 1988 until he returned to Panama in

1992. Torrijos owns several construction and export businesses. He is married to Vivian Fernández de Torrijos and they have three children.

His first government post was as deputy minister of government (the interior) and justice under the administration of Ernesto Pérez Balladares (1994–99). He became leader of the PRD, the party founded by his father, in 1999, when he was defeated in the presidential elections by Mireya Moscoso. Moscoso's government ended with an approval rate of about 15%, mostly because of corruption scandals and incompetence.

Torrijos capitalized successfully on Moscoso's unpopularity in his 2004 presidential election campaign, setting out three top priorities: fight corruption, create more jobs and improve security. He also harnessed the reputation of his father, whom many Panamanians revere as the father of modern Panama. However, he also made it clear that he stood for a different agenda, of strengthening democracy, cleaning up corruption and examining the human rights legacies of his predecessors, as well as economic liberalization.

Torrijos won the election with about 47% of the vote, against 30% for his closest challenger, former president Guillermo Endara of the Solidarity Party. Torrijos has supported talks for free trade with the USA, and has spoken of setting up an independent auditor-general to oversee the public accounts and an ombudsman for human rights.

PAPUA NEW GUINEA

Full name: Independent State of Papua New Guinea.

Leadership structure: The head of state is the British sovereign, styled 'Queen of Papua New Guinea, and of Her other Realms and Territories, head of the Commonwealth'. She is represented by a governor-general elected by Parliament and formally appointed by the queen as head of state for a six-year term. The head of government is the prime minister, appointed by the governor-general on the proposal of the National Parliament. The National Executive Council is appointed on the proposal of the prime minister.

Queen:	Elizabeth II	Since 6 Feb. 1952
Governor-General:	Sir Silas Atopare	20 Nov. 1997—20 Nov. 2003
	Bill Skate (acting)	20 Nov. 2003—3 March 2004
	vacant	3 March 2004—5 March 2004
	Bill Skate (acting)	5 March 2004—26 May 2004
	vacant	26 May 2004—28 May 2004
	Jeffery Nape (acting)	28 May 2004—29 June 2004
	Sir Paulias **MATANE**	Since 29 June 2004
Prime Minister:	Sir Mekere Morauta	14 July 1999—5 Aug. 2002
	Sir Michael **SOMARE**	Since 5 Aug. 2002

Legislature: The legislature is unicameral. The sole chamber, the National Parliament, has 109 members, directly elected for a five-year term.

Profile of the Governor-General:

Sir Paulius **MATANE**

Sir Paulius Matane was elected as governor-general of Papua New Guinea in May 2004 and took office on 29 June. He had worked as a teacher and headmaster before joining the government in various roles to do with education and foreign affairs.

Paulius Matane was born in 1931 in East New Britain into traditional society, but was later educated at missionary school, gained a scholarship to be trained as a teacher, and then rose to headteacher. In 1986 he authored the *Ministerial Committee Report on a Philosophy of Education*, which became known as the Matane Report. It proposed a move away from the colonial-style education system in favour of 'integral human development'—an education system that fitted with Papuan cultures. In particular he stressed the need for more early childhood education opportunities, and that children should be taught in their native language—a major challenge to the government of a country with over 800 different dialects. Parliament adopted all his proposals except vernacular teaching, and the report remains a keystone of the country's education structure.

Among other governmental roles, he worked as a diplomat and as foreign affairs secretary. He was elected governor-general after a series of parliamentary ballots between 20 and 27 May 2004. He was sworn into office on 29 June.

He is a popular newspaper columnist and author of the autobiographical *My Childhood in New Guinea*, in which he charts his lifetime journey from 'stone age to computer age'. It gives an insight into his childhood growing up in the men's house, surrounded by magic and the world of spirits, and the cultural upheaval engendered by the Westernization of traditional New Guinean life.

Profile of the Prime Minister:

Sir Michael **SOMARE**

Sir Michael Somare, a former teacher, heads the National Alliance Party (NAP) after years as a prominent member of the Papua New Guinea United Party (Pangu Pati). He is known in Papua New Guinea (PNG) variously as 'the chief', 'the old man', and the 'father of the nation' as he led the country to independence in 1975 and became its first prime minister thereafter. His face can now even be found on the 50 kina bank note, the country's largest denomination bill. He has held the post of premier a total of three times—in 1975–80, in 1982–85 and since August 2002.

Michael Thomas Somare was born in Rabaul on the eastern tip of New Britain Island on 9 April 1936, although his family had originally come from the East Sepik region of the northern PNG mainland. He learnt basic Japanese when the country was partially occupied by Japanese forces in the Second World War. He trained to be a teacher at Sogeri Education Centre in the 1950s and taught at various schools from 1956 before becoming deputy headmaster at Talidig Primary School in Madang after further training.

Switching from teaching in 1962, Somare joined the department of information at Wewak as a broadcast officer. In 1965 he married Veronica Bula Kaiap and they have three sons and two daughters. In the same year he received further education at the Port Moresby Staff College before going on air in 1966 as a radio journalist. In 1967 he joined Pangu Pati, standing as the party's candidate the following year for the East Sepik constituency, which he won and which he has held in every subsequent election. Pangu emerged victorious in the 1972 elections and Somare, by now its leader, was charged with putting together the country's first coalition government with himself as chief minister.

Independence from Australia was achieved in 1975, with Somare becoming the first prime minister. He remained in office for most of the following decade, with a two-year break in 1980–82 when he was leader of the opposition following a vote of no confidence. The objectives of cutting back government spending, and introducing a fairer distribution of the country's considerable potential wealth, were goals which he (in common with all prime ministers since that time) signally failed to achieve, obstructed by the political hierarchy's ingrained business interests and the exploitation of the country's resources by foreign firms.

In the elections of 1982 Pangu gained the largest parliamentary majority ever attained in PNG. The lack of a structured opposition, however, actually hindered Somare's government, as rival factions within Pangu itself arose to counter the government's policies. Somare was eventually ousted as prime minister in 1985 after a protracted leadership struggle and his second no-confidence vote.

Once again leader of the opposition, he failed to lead Pangu back to power in the 1987 elections and was forced out as party leader in 1988. However, shifts in the precarious balance of power in Papuan politics enabled Somare to return to government as foreign minister to the man who had succeeded him as Pangu leader, Prime Minister Rabbie Namaliu. He was knighted in 1991 and in 1995 he was appointed governor of his home province of East Sepik.

In and out of the party leadership in the 1990s, he was definitively ousted in 1997 when his party membership was terminated by the Pangu parliamentary caucus. In response he formed his own party, the NAP. Two years later in July 1999 the party was brought into the ruling coalition, and Somare returned to the foreign ministry. However, the relationship between Prime Minister Sir Mekere Morauta and Somare was far from smooth. By the end of 1999 he had been made Bougainville minister (in which capacity he concluded the March 2000 Loloata Understanding, consolidating the two-year-old ceasefire with guarantees of the island's autonomy), but had lost the foreign ministry and instead now doubled as mines minister.

As Somare's rivalries with Morauta became increasingly overt, he ceased to be a member of the cabinet in late 2000, and a complete breach between them in May 2001 saw the NAP return to opposition. In June 2002, after 12 days of chaotic legislative elections, the NAP emerged as the largest single party (although with only 19 out of the 109 seats) and Somare was asked to become prime minister for a third time. He took office on 5 August heading a ten-party coalition.

His first policy moves were to call a halt to the previous administration's privatization programme and to cancel PNG's involvement in the Australian government's 'Pacific Solution' to its own immigration problem. Despite having campaigned against Morauta's austerity programme, Somare's government quickly admitted that the country was near to bankruptcy and declared that spending must be drastically reduced, in line with reforms backed by the International Monetary Fund. A year later the Central Bank warned that the once vibrant copra-exporting industry was now close to collapse, and a report by the Australian Strategic Policy Institute in 2004 said the country was heading towards social and economic collapse and could fall "off a cliff into full-scale state failure".

Somare appointed his son Arthur as a minister in the first cabinet reshuffle, in August 2003. By February 2004 the government's constitutional 18-month 'honeymoon' period had expired and the fragile coalition was under threat of a vote of no confidence—from within its own ranks. Somare had attempted twice to amend the constitution to give a new government a three-year 'honeymoon period' during which motions of no confidence could not be tabled. Opposition to these moves had caused splits in several of the coalition's parties. Somare then tried to adjourn Parliament for six months to avoid a no-confidence vote, but the Supreme Court ruled that it had to reconvene to elect a new governor-general. In May he brought Morauta's party into the coalition in an attempt to improve political stability, but the need to redistribute ministerial portfolios provoked further ructions and resulted in the removal of all ministers from the People's National Congress (PNC) and the People's Action Party, both of which had refused to back the constitutional amendment. Somare then proceeded to oust PNC leader Bill Skate from his post as speaker in order to adjourn Parliament again and preempt his threatened no-confidence motion.

PARAGUAY

Full name: The Republic of Paraguay.

Leadership structure: The head of state is a president, elected directly by universal adult suffrage. The president's term of office is five years, not renewable. The head of government is the president, who is responsible to Congress. The Council of Ministers is appointed by the president.

President:	Luis González Macchi	28 March 1999—15 Aug. 2003
	Nicanor **DUARTE FRUTOS**	Since 15 Aug. 2003

Legislature: The legislature, Congress (Congreso), is bicameral. The lower chamber, the Chamber of Deputies (Cámara de Diputados), has 80 members, directly elected for a five-year term. The upper chamber, the Senate (Senado or Cámara de Senadores), has 45 members, also directly elected for a five-year term.

Profile of the President:

Nicanor **DUARTE FRUTOS**

Nicanor Duarte Frutos is a member of Paraguay's dominant National Republican Association/Colorado Party (Asociación Nacional Republicana/ Partido Colorado) and was inaugurated as the country's president on 15 August 2003. Duarte Frutos has deliberately distanced himself somewhat from the USA; he won much admiration in the region in March 2004 for refusing to meet White House Special Adviser for Latin American Affairs Otto Reich, a Cuban-American right-wing ideologue infamous for his involvement in the Iran-Contra scandal. Duarte Frutos stood on an anti-corruption platform, pledging to purge his own party and the military, and to kick-start Paraguay's ailing economy with the social security system on the verge of bankruptcy and the tax base devastated by the dominance of the black economy. A year after his election he had the highest popularity rating in the Americas.

Óscar Nicanor Duarte Frutos was born on 11 October 1956 in the agricultural town of Coronel Oviedo, east of the capital Asunción. He is married to María Gloria Penayo; they have five children. Duarte Frutos studied law first at the Catholic University of Asunción, graduating in 1984, then at the National University, from which he graduated in 1989, before studying as a postgraduate in political sciences at the National University and the Hans Seidel Foundation.

During this period he worked as a journalist and editor of the newspaper *Última Hora* in Asunción.

Duarte Frutos first joined the Colorado Party in 1971 at the age of 14. He served as education minister from 1993 until 1997, and again from 1999 until 2001, having formerly held the position of professor of sociology and ethics in the faculty of philosophy at the National University of Asunción. He was elected party leader in 2001.

A seasoned politician, Duarte Frutos is seen as something of a populist. Throughout his presidential campaign, he promised to attack crime and corruption, to create new jobs and to slim down the bloated civil service, upon whose loyalty the Colorados have often depended. He won presidential elections in April 2003 with 38% of the vote, well ahead of his nearest rivals; Julio César Franco of the Authentic Radical Liberal Party polled 23%, while Pedro Fadul, a conservative businessman running for the Beloved Fatherland Movement, polled 22%.

Since his inauguration on 15 August 2003 he has earned consistently high public approval ratings through his vigorous—and to date successful—efforts to overhaul some of Paraguay's public institutions, such as the reform of the Supreme Court and the dismissal of officials tainted by corruption, including some personal friends.

PERU

Full name: The Republic of Peru.

Leadership structure: The head of state is a president, directly elected by universal adult suffrage. The president's term of office is five years, renewable once only. The constitution also provides for two vice presidents. The head of government is the president, who is responsible to the Congress of the Republic. The Council of Ministers is appointed by the president.

President:	Alberto Fujimori	1 July 1990—21 Nov. 2000
	Valentín Paniagua	22 Nov. 2000—28 July 2001
	Alejandro **TOLEDO**	Since 28 July 2001

President of the Council of Ministers:		
	Alberto Bustamante Belaúnde	10 Oct. 1999—29 July 2000
	Federico Salas Guevara	29 July 2000—19 Nov. 2000
	vacant	19 Nov. 2000—25 Nov. 2000
	Javier Pérez de Cuéllar	25 Nov. 2000—28 July 2001
	Roberto Dañino	28 July 2001—12 July 2002
	Luis Solari	12 July 2002—28 June 2003
	Beatriz Merino	28 June 2003—15 Dec. 2003
	Carlos Ferrero Costa	15 Dec. 2003—16 Aug. 2005
	Pedro Pablo **KUCZYNSKI**	Since 16 Aug. 2005

Legislature: The legislature is unicameral. The sole chamber, the Congress of the Republic (Congreso de la República), has 120 members, directly elected for a five-year term. The term of the Congress elected in April 2000 was reduced on 5 October 2000, so as to expire on 26 July 2001, and thus enable early legislative elections to be held at the same time as the presidential elections.

Profile of the President:

Alejandro **TOLEDO**

Alejandro Toledo, leader of the Perú Posible (PP) party, is Peru's first president of Amerindian descent. His life has been a real rags-to-riches story. A soccer

445

scholarship to the USA lifted him from poverty and opened a path leading eventually to international consulting. He failed to make much of an impact in presidential elections in 1995, but in 2000 he led opposition to the corruption of President Alberto Fujimori, and the following year he won the presidential election on the second round in June. Since then his promises of an economic turnaround have not been fulfilled and his popularity has sunk dramatically.

Alejandro Celestino Toledo Manrique was born on 28 March 1946 in the small Andean village of Cabana in Ancash province. He was one of 16 children in a poor family of mixed Amerindian descent. The Toledo family joined the migration of Amerindians to Peru's developing ports in the 1950s and settled in Chimbote. The economic migrants became known as *cholo*, a name Toledo now bears with pride. He was put to work polishing shoes and selling soft drinks. He eventually found employment as a newspaper correspondent on *La Prensa* in Chimbote, where he interviewed many high-ranking politicians of the day. His intelligence was noted and he was helped by the US Peace Corps to gain a soccer scholarship to Stanford University, California, in 1965.

Toledo's studies in economics were supported by part-time jobs including teaching and semiprofessional soccer playing. His undergraduate studies were completed at the University of San Francisco and he returned to Stanford in 1970 where he obtained a doctorate in human resources economics in 1976. While at Stanford he met Eliane Karp, a Belgian-born Jewish American who had studied the Amerindian people of Peru, and they married in 1979. They have one daughter. From his time in the USA Toledo is now fluent in English while, from her studies, Eliane is fluent in the Amerindian language Quechua.

Between 1976 and 1985 Toledo took on various jobs around the world. Moving from the USA to Paris, France, and then to Geneva, Switzerland, he found employment as an academic and as an adviser to the UN, the World Bank, the International Labour Organization (ILO) and the Organization for Co-operation and Economic Development (OECD) among others. He returned to Peru in 1985 and took up a position as director of the government-run Sur Medio y Callao bank. He also taught at the Business Management School for Graduates in Lima. Six years later he became a visiting researcher at the Institute for International Development at Harvard University.

Toledo's political career began in 1994 when he established País Posible, the forerunner to PP. He stood in the next year's presidential elections against incumbent President Fujimori but came a poor third behind Fujimori and the popular former UN chief Javier Pérez de Cuéllar, receiving barely 3% of the vote. Stung by the defeat, he returned to the Business Management School and nurtured plans for a comeback in 2000, reforming his party into the PP in 1999. His reinvigorated campaign in that year was based on a more populist platform. His appeal as a successful *cholo* was aided by the prominence given to his wife Eliane, and the popular association of European brides with social advancement. His fiery, populist rhetoric was also enhanced by Eliane's ability to give campaign speeches in Quechua. He encountered vilification, however, from Fujimori, who accused him of abusing cocaine in the 1980s as well as fathering an illegitimate child.

In the first round of voting in April 2000, Fujimori claimed to have taken 49% of the vote, fractionally short of a simple majority. Accusing his rival of blatant fraud, Toledo withdrew from the second round held in May, which Fujimori therefore won uncontested. Toledo fomented popular anger at such a 'victory' and formed the opposition Democratic Alliance for National Unity in July. Domestic unrest, international pressure and high-profile corruption scandals forced Fujimori to offer to step down from office, and fresh elections were scheduled. In November he fled into self-exile in Japan and announced his immediate resignation.

Toledo only narrowly won the ensuing presidential election on the second round in June 2001, taking 52% of the vote against former president Alan García Pérez. He took office on 28 July. Within months he was facing popular protest over the continuing poor state of the economy and from highland Amerindian farmers over the US-backed programme to eradicate coca crops. He pursued his liberal economic agenda, although he tempered it with the announcement in October of an ambitious public works scheme called 'To Work', and himself took a voluntary 33% pay cut the following month. However, his unsuccessful privatization policies provoked such violent protest in June 2002 that he was forced to declare a state of emergency in the southern city of Arequipa.

In October 2002 Toledo finally admitted that he had indeed fathered an illegitimate child in the late 1980s and agreed to pay US$100,000 to his second daughter, Zarai. The paternity suit actually increased the president's flagging popularity in macho-oriented Peruvian society.

However, the failure to deliver promised wage increases, due to pressure from the International Monetary Fund, provoked more demonstrations in 2003. These were not appeased by further ministerial pay cuts—Toledo's salary decreasing from its original US$18,000 to just US$3,660 a month. Two new prime ministers were appointed in the next six months amid various reshuffles, but protests and strikes over economic policies and the coca eradication programme continued, and by 2004 Toledo's popularity rating had fallen to just 7%. That July *Caretas* magazine accused him of accepting bribes, though Toledo denied the charges.

In May 2005 a congressional commission found Toledo guilty of electoral fraud for helping his PP to forge almost 80% of the 520,000 signatures it needed to register for the 2000 legislative elections.

Toledo gave way to coca growers' demands in June 2005 and approved limited cultivation. He followed this move by appointing his ally Fernando Olivera as foreign minister, a move opposed by Prime Minister Carlos Ferrero Costa, who feared it would lead to an increase in cocaine production. Ferrero resigned shortly afterwards, prompting yet another reshuffle.

Profile of the President of the Council of Ministers:

Pedro Pablo **KUCZYNSKI**

Pedro Pablo Kuczynski was appointed prime minister of Peru in August 2005. He had worked for national and international financial institutions before he joined newly elected President Alejandro Toledo's government as economy and finance minister in 2001.

Pedro Pablo Kuczynski was born in 1938 and is of Polish descent. He graduated from Oxford University in the UK in 1959 with a degree in politics, philosophy and economics (PPE), and went on to do a master's degree in public administration at Princeton University in the USA.

Kuczynski was just 29 when he was appointed deputy director of the Peruvian Central Bank. He went on to work for the International Monetary Fund and the World Bank. In 1980 he was appointed minister of energy and mines, and remained in that post until 1982, when he became managing director of First Boston International.

A political independent, he was appointed economy and finance minister by Toledo in 2001, but resigned in July 2002 following violent protests over electricity privatization proposals. He was reappointed in February 2004. On 16 August 2005 he was appointed prime minister.

Kuczynski is the author of several books on the economics of Latin America. He has let it be known that he is interested in the presidency of Peru at some future date.

PHILIPPINES

Full name: The Republic of the Philippines.

Leadership structure: The head of state is a president, directly elected by universal adult suffrage. The president's term of office is six years, not renewable. The head of government is the president. The cabinet is appointed by the president.

President:	Joseph Estrada	30 June 1998—19 Jan. 2001
	Gloria Macapagal **ARROYO**	Since 20 Jan. 2001

Legislature: The legislature, the Congress (Kongreso), is bicameral. The lower chamber, the House of Representatives (Kapulungan ng mga Kinatawan), currently has 236 members, 212 directly elected and the rest from party and minority-group lists, all for a three-year term. The upper chamber, the Senate (Senado), has 24 members, directly elected for a six-year term (with half re-elected every three years).

Profile of the President:

Gloria Macapagal **ARROYO**

Gloria Arroyo is the daughter of former president Diosdado Macapagal. She was popular enough to win the greatest personal majority in Philippine history when she was re-elected to the Senate in 1995. Vice president from 1998, she led the opposition to the corruption of President Joseph Estrada in 2000 and replaced him after the country's second demonstration of 'people power' in January 2001. She has made herself a key US ally in southeast Asia and has attempted to reinvigorate the country's liberal economic reforms. She faces strong political opposition and has had to move to preempt attempts to oust her by force. Allegations of electoral fraud and financial scandals involving members of her family brought her to the brink of impeachment proceedings in 2005.

Gloria Macaraeg Macapagal was born on 5 April 1947 in Manila and voluntarily split her childhood between there and her grandmother's home town of Iligan, on the southern island of Mindanao. She was 14 when her father became president. She began her further education with a two-year course at Georgetown University, USA, where she was a contemporary of future US president Bill Clinton. Returning to the Philippines, she graduated with a degree in commercial science from the Assumption Convent in Manila and then a master's degree in economics from the Ateneo de Manila University. Her working life began as a teacher at the Assumption Convent. She is married to the lawyer and businessman Jose Miguel Tuason Arroyo and they have two sons and a daughter.

In the early 1980s, persuaded to develop her career further, Arroyo returned to university to study for a doctorate in economics at the University of the Philippines. Following the first 'people power' movement in 1986, Arroyo entered the government of President Corazon Aquino as an assistant secretary in the ministry of trade and industry. She was later promoted to undersecretary. In 1992 she ran successfully for a seat in the Senate and in 1995 she was re-elected with 16 million votes—the largest personal mandate in Philippine history.

After considering seeking the presidency in the 1998 elections, Arroyo decided instead to set her sights on the vice presidency (for which there is a separate ballot under the Philippine system), standing as an independent. The 13 million votes she received was the highest number ever cast for a vice-presidential or presidential candidate. Her victory gave her the post of vice president in the administration headed by Joseph Estrada, the former action-movie star whose populist campaign had brought him success in the presidential poll. Although their politics were quite markedly at odds, Estrada also appointed her secretary of social welfare and development in his cabinet.

As serious accusations of corruption began to emerge against Estrada, his position became increasingly untenable, despite his immense popularity especially in rural areas. He was finally accused outright in 2000 of accepting US$8.5 million from illegal gambling syndicates.

Arroyo distanced herself from his regime at this point by resigning from the social welfare and development department, but voiced concern that her support for impeachment would be improper, as she would clearly gain politically from the president's removal. However, in October 2000 she cast her doubts aside and formed the anti-Estrada United Opposition. Estrada was impeached in December, found guilty and dismissed from office on 19 January 2001 after a massive protest against him on the streets of Manila. Arroyo was inaugurated as president the following day. In 2002 she joined the ruling Lakas ng (Power of) EDSA–National Union of Christian Democrats (Lakas–NUCD), becoming party co-chairman.

Arroyo's main policy platforms have been based on her contrast to Estrada's populist flamboyance. She has targeted cronyism and corruption while reinstating the economic liberalization programmes of Estrada's predecessor, Fidel Ramos. Her support for the USA after the 11 September 2001 terrorist attacks gained her that country's increased backing, while her attempts to deal firmly and diplomatically with Muslim separatists in Mindanao have won praise from the international community as a whole. However, extremists pose a big threat to her administration, with ongoing bombing campaigns in Mindanao and across the country. The presence of US troops to assist Filipino soldiers against the extremists has also been highly contentious, causing a lasting rift in 2002 with Vice President Teofisto Guingona, who resigned from the foreign affairs portfolio.

Arroyo supported the US-led invasion of Iraq in 2003 and later that year US president George W. Bush designated the Philippines as a "major non-NATO ally", paving the way for a further increase in military co-operation. However, a small contingent of soldiers, sent to assist with peacekeeping in Iraq, was pulled out ahead of schedule when a Filipino civilian was taken hostage in July 2004.

Despite the strong showing of support for her in the capital, Arroyo's position was far from secure. Within a week of her inauguration there were rumours of an imminent military coup. In May, following Estrada's eventual arrest, violent demonstrations forced Arroyo to declare a week-long 'state of rebellion' in the capital. Three senators were arrested for plotting to overthrow her. Less than a year later, in January 2002, Arroyo warned that unnamed groups were actively attempting to destabilize her government. In July 2003 around 300 soldiers staged a mutiny that was rebuffed by Arroyo in a televised address; Estrada was accused of being behind it but the link was never proven. The following February the defence minister warned that anti-government rebels were actively attempting to recruit soldiers for another uprising.

Despite her announcement in December 2002 that she would not stand for re-election as president, ten months later Arroyo bowed to pressure and announced her candidacy. The May 2004 poll between Arroyo and movie star Fernando Poe Jr, a close friend of Estrada, was viewed as a test of her presidency's legitimacy, and Arroyo emerged with a 3% margin of victory. Poe filed allegations of massive electoral fraud, but these were eventually overturned by the Supreme Court.

However, within a year Arroyo was under siege when tapes were disclosed allegedly of a phone conversation between her and an election official at the time of the 2004 poll count. Her popularity sank to an all-time low, also due to the poor state of the economy and proposed reforms, and another controversial allegation that her husband and relations had accepted bribes from illegal gambling syndicates. Arroyo apologized in a televised speech in June 2005 for making the phone call, although she denied any intent to influence the election result, and her husband agreed to move abroad to take the pressure off the corruption allegations. The pressure did not ease, however, and ten cabinet ministers resigned in July, requesting her to follow suit. Large demonstrations also demanded her resignation, and were not appeased by her establishment of a "truth commission". The opposition swiftly launched impeachment proceedings in July, but several motions were rejected by Congress in late August.

POLAND

Full name: The Republic of Poland.

Leadership structure: The head of state is a president, directly elected by universal adult suffrage. The president's term of office is five years, renewable once only. The head of government is the chairman of the Council of Ministers (prime minister), who is appointed by the Diet on the basis of a motion made by the president. The Council of Ministers is appointed by the Diet.

President:	Aleksander **KWAŚNIEWSKI**	Since 23 Dec. 1995
Prime Minister:	Jerzy Buzek	31 Oct. 1997—19 Oct. 2001
	Leszek Miller	19 Oct. 2001—2 May 2004
	Marek **BELKA** (acting from 2 May 2004)	Since 24 June 2004

Legislature: The legislature, the National Assembly (Zgromadzenie Narodowe), is bicameral. The lower chamber, the Diet (Sejm), has 460 members, directly elected for a four-year term. The upper chamber, the Senate (Senat), has 100 members, elected for a four-year term.

Profile of the President:

Aleksander **KWAŚNIEWSKI**

The election of ex-communist Aleksander Kwaśniewski to the Polish presidency in 1995 caused some alarm, especially in the USA. However, he represented a younger generation of pragmatic reformers in the party, the heir of which had become a part of the Democratic Left Alliance (Sojusz Lewicy Demokratycznej— SLD). An economist by training and editor of party youth publications, he was a junior minister in the last communist governments of the late 1980s and was active in the 1989 round-table debates on introducing a multiparty system. He led the reformed communist party from 1990 until his election as president.

Aleksander Kwaśniewski was born in the northwestern town of Białogard on 15 November 1954. After attending high school in Białogard, he graduated from the University of Gdańsk with a degree in transport economics. He was an energetic political activist in the student socialist youth union, joined the then ruling communist party, the Polish United Workers' Party (Polska Zjednoczona Partia Robotnicza—PZPR), in 1977, edited the official student weekly paper in 1981–84 and was editor-in-chief of the youth daily *Sztandar Mlodych* in 1984–85. He is married to Jolanta Kwaśniewska née Konty and they have one daughter.

In November 1985 Kwaśniewski joined the Council of Ministers and had special responsibility for youth affairs. By 1987 he had become chairman of the committee for youth and physical education and in October 1988 he was appointed head of the government sociopolitical committee. The following year he took part in the round-table debates on the creation of a pluralist system, held between February and April. After these talks had opened the way for partially free elections, and the PZPR had entered a Solidarity-led coalition government, the party held an extraordinary congress in January 1990 and reconstituted itself as the Social Democracy of the Republic of Poland (Socjaldemokracja Rzeczypospolitej Polskiej—SdRP), with the youthful Kwaśniewski a forward-looking choice as its first chairman.

Kwaśniewski was elected in 1991 to sit as a deputy in the Diet, the lower chamber in what had become a bicameral parliament. For two years from November 1993 he chaired the parliamentary constitutional committee and gained a reputation for seeking consensus in the interests of political unity. This even extended to giving his initial support to the conclusion of a concordat between Poland and the Vatican, to which many in his party were openly hostile. Kwaśniewski also sat as a member of the foreign affairs committee and the economic policy, budget and finance committee.

In the November 1995 presidential election, Kwaśniewski led in the first round with just over 35% of the vote, narrowly ahead of the incumbent Lech Wałęsa in a field of 13 candidates. The runoff was again close, Kwaśniewski winning with 51.7%. He was sworn in on 23 December, after the constitutional tribunal had ruled against Wałęsa's attempt to have him disqualified for allegedly misleading the voters about his electoral qualifications by claiming a postgraduate degree.

As president, Kwaśniewski committed himself to promoting national consensus—a promise sorely tested the following year by the issue of abortion. (He eventually signed into law a bill permitting terminations but only within the early period of a pregnancy.) He also expressed his support for continuing economic reforms and concluding the formulation of a democratic constitution (which finally took effect in October 1997), and backed Poland's applications for membership of the European Union (EU) and the North Atlantic Treaty Organization (NATO). Although both membership quests ultimately proved successful in 2002, with accession to both in 2004, Kwaśniewski has strongly argued the case for preventing foreigners from buying Polish agricultural land.

In August 2000 Kwaśniewski was exonerated of any involvement with the communist-era secret police, clearing his candidature for the October presidential election. He was successfully re-elected in the first round of voting on 9 October with 53.9% of the vote against 11 opponents. As he neared the end of his second term in late 2005, he was eyed as a possible future UN secretary-general.

Profile of the Prime Minister:

Marek **BELKA**

Marek Belka, an economist by training, succeeded Leszek Miller as prime minister of Poland in May 2004, and was confirmed in office in June. He belonged to no party but headed a government of the ex-communist Democratic Left Alliance (Sojusz Lewicy Demokratycznej—SLD). He had previously been an economic consultant to government and intergovernmental organizations, and had served as finance minister in Poland. He is viewed more as a technocrat than a politician, and the neoliberal policies of his ministerial team have brought him into conflict with more traditional SLD members.

Marek Belka was born on 9 January 1952 in Łódź and graduated from the department of socioeconomics in Łódź University in 1972. He later studied in the USA and UK at Columbia University, the University of Chicago and the London School of Economics, before becoming a professor of economics at Łódź University in 1994. From 1990 until 1996 Belka acted as a consultant for the Polish ministry of finance, the World Bank and JP Morgan & Co. During this time he resigned from the SLD. He is married to Krystyna, with two children.

In 1997 he was finance minister and deputy prime minister and again in 2001–02, in between serving as economic consultant to President Aleksander Kwaśniewski (in 1996–97 and again from November 1997 to October 2001). In 2003 he spent some time working for the interim coalition administration in Iraq, first as the head of the Coalition Council for International Co-ordination, then as director responsible for economic policy. He has written a dozen books and over 100 scholarly articles, largely on macroeconomics and monetary theory and policy.

In March 2004, faced with a slump in popularity for the SLD and the defection of several SLD Assembly members, Prime Minister Leszek Miller announced he would resign on 2 May, the day after Poland's accession to the European Union. Belka's nomination as Miller's successor was initially rejected by parliament on 14 May, but he was nominated again on 11 June and finally confirmed on 24 June. Several of his ministers are neoliberal technocrats, whose appointments caused tensions within the ruling SLD. The new government pledged to fight poverty and unemployment, to improve health care and to reduce the Polish deployment in Iraq, though Belka's firsthand experiences in the Coalition administration made him promise that soldiers would remain while they were needed.

However, with unemployment remaining high and corruption scandals continuing to plague the government—though Belka faced down allegations of involvement with the communist-era secret police—in March 2005 he called for early elections. The Democratic Party (Partia Demokratyczna—PD) was founded, based on the liberal Freedom Union but including liberal members of the SLD. Belka joined the party in May, but with popular discontent for the existing regime plummeting, centre-right parties looked favourites to win the September poll.

PORTUGAL

Full name: The Republic of Portugal.

Leadership structure: The head of state is a president, directly elected by universal adult suffrage. The president's term of office is five years, renewable once only. The head of government is the prime minister, who is appointed by the president. The Council of Ministers is appointed by the president on the advice of the prime minister.

President:	Jorge **SAMPAIO**	Since 9 March 1996
Prime Minister:	António Guterres	29 Oct. 1995—6 April 2002
	José Manuel Durão Barroso	6 April 2002—17 July 2004
	Pedro Santana Lopes	17 July 2004—12 March 2005
	José **SÓCRATES**	Since 12 March 2005

Legislature: The legislature is unicameral. The sole chamber, the Assembly of the Republic (Assembléia da República), has 230 members, directly elected for a four-year term.

Profile of the President:

Jorge **SAMPAIO**

Jorge Sampaio is a lawyer and former mayor of Lisbon, and a one-time student activist agitating for an end to the Salazar regime. He began his second five-year term as president of Portugal in March 2001, having been re-elected with an increased majority as the candidate of the Socialist Party (Partido Socialista— PS).

Jorge Fernando Branco de Sampaio was born on 18 September 1939 in Lisbon. The son of a doctor, he spent part of his schooldays in England, and went to Lisbon University in 1956 to study law. His political career began at this time and he led student protests against the dictatorship of António de Oliveira Salazar. He went on to defend other opponents of the regime as a young lawyer in Lisbon.

After the 'carnation revolution' in 1974 he initially supported the small Movement of the Socialist Left, but distanced himself from the movement when it began to adopt Marxist policies. In 1978 he joined the PS, led by Mário Soares, and was elected as a parliamentary deputy in the 1979 general election and in subsequent elections. Throughout, Sampaio has maintained a strong commitment to the defence of human rights and from 1979 to 1984 served on the Council of Europe's Commission for Human Rights in Strasbourg. In 1987 he was elected president of the PS parliamentary party; he became PS secretary-general in 1989, but was replaced in 1992 by António Guterres.

In December 1989 Sampaio was elected mayor of Lisbon, a post to which he was re-elected in 1994. He lives in Lisbon with his second wife Maria José Ritta, and they have one son and one daughter.

The election of a socialist government in October 1995, and Sampaio's election as president on 14 January 1996, when he won 53.8% of the vote, brought to an end a decade of Portuguese politics dominated by socialist Soares as president and centre-right Social Democratic Party (Partido Social Democrata—PSD) leader Aníbal Cavaco Silva as prime minister. However, while Sampaio remained highly popular, the PS government rapidly lost support as the country's economy failed to improve.

Sampaio easily won re-election in the January 2001 presidential election, gaining 55.8% of the vote in the first round, but he found himself in 'cohabitation' with a PSD government from April 2002. However, after the resignation of Prime Minister José Manuel Durão Barroso in July 2004 to head the European Commission, Sampaio surprisingly chose not to call early elections but to appoint a new PSD government, stating that the country needed continuity at that time in order to cope with economic recession. The popularity of this PSD government fell as Barroso's successor struggled with a shaky coalition. In December Sampaio called early elections for February 2005, telling the nation that the need for structural reforms to the economy meant that a fresh mandate was needed. A landslide PS victory ended the 'cohabitation' period.

Profile of the Prime Minister:

José **SÓCRATES**

José Sócrates was sworn in as prime minister of Portugal on 12 March 2005 following a landslide election victory for his Socialist Party (Partido Socialista— PS). He is a civil engineer by training, though he has been involved in politics since he was a young man, and first entered parliament at the age of 30. His victory in the general election was hailed as bringing a measure of political stability to Portugal after nearly a year of volatility following the resignation of José Manuel Durão Barroso to head up the European Commission.

José Sócrates Carvalho Pinto de Sousa was born on 6 September 1957 in Vilar de Maçada, in Alijó in the Vila Real district, and grew up in Covilhã. He trained as a civil engineer, and holds postgraduate qualifications in sanitary engineering from the National School for Public Health. Sócrates joined the PS in 1981 at the age of 24, and was elected to the Assembly in 1987, where he sat in opposition to the ruling Social Democratic Party (Partido Social Democrata—PSD), then led by Aníbal Cavaco Silva. From 1991 he was the party's spokesman on environmental affairs and a member of its national secretariat. From 1989 to 1996 he was also a member of the Covilhã municipal council.

When the Socialists returned to power in 1995, Sócrates joined the environment ministry as state secretary assisting the minister in the first government of António Guterres. Two years later he became an assistant minister to the prime minister responsible for youth, drug addiction and sport. In this capacity, he was chosen as president of the first World Conference of Ministers responsible for Youth, held in Lisbon in 1998, and led the campaign to bring the Euro 2004 football competition to Portugal. In 1999 Guterres was returned to power and Sócrates became minister of the environment. He set up a network of landfills and launched the POLIS programme, a scheme to rehabilitate Portugal's inner cities. However, he was returned to opposition with the rest of the Socialist Party in 2002 by the electoral victory of José Manuel Durão Barroso and his PSD.

Barroso announced in July 2004 that he would step down from office in order to be appointed president of the European Commission. The decision of President Jorge Sampaio (of the PS) to appoint a new PSD premier rather than call early elections led to the resignation of PS leader Ferro Rodrigues. Sampaio maintained that his decision was predicated by the need to ensure political stability in a time when the country was facing economic recession.

The PS party leadership contest occasioned by Rodrigues's resignation was held on 24 September 2004 and won by Sócrates with 80% of the vote of party members. The PSD government meanwhile lurched from crisis to crisis, and by December it was clear that the hoped-for stability had never materialized. Sampaio accordingly dissolved the government and called early elections for February, which the PS won in a landslide, with their first absolute majority in parliament since the overthrow of the military regime in 1974. José Sócrates was sworn in as prime minister on 12 March.

Despite his strong majority, which presages four years of political stability, Sócrates faces serious challenges. Unemployment is over 7% and the economy is only just limping out of recession. Sócrates plans to emulate the success of the Nordic countries and Ireland by investing in research, in English-language teaching and in subsidizing science graduates to create a 'technological shock' to catapult Portugal into a lean, IT-based future.

QATAR

Full name: The State of Qatar.

Leadership structure: The head of state is an amir. The amir is head of government and appoints the members of the Council of Ministers, including the prime minister.

Amir: Sheikh **HAMAD** bin Khalifa al-Thani Since 27 June 1995

Prime Minister: Sheikh **ABDULLAH** bin Khalifa al-Thani Since 29 Oct. 1996

Legislature: There is no legislature. There is a 35-member Advisory Council, which is appointed by the amir. Under the terms of the 2005 constitution, 30 members of a new Shura Council will be elected, and 15 appointed by the amir. The council will have legislative powers.

Profile of the Amir:

Sheikh **HAMAD** bin Khalifa al-Thani

Sheikh Hamad acceded to power on 27 June 1995, ousting his father, Sheikh Khalifa, in a bloodless coup to become amir of Qatar. A Sandhurst-trained officer and head of his country's armed forces since 1972, he had played a major role in modernizing army units and in increasing armed forces personnel.

Born in 1952 in Doha, Hamad bin Khalifa al-Thani attended primary and secondary schools there before joining the Royal Military Academy, Sandhurst, UK, from which he passed out in 1971. He joined the Qatari armed forces and was appointed commander of the First Mobile Battalion with the rank of major, a rank he held until his promotion to major-general and appointment as commander-in-chief of the armed forces in February 1972.

On 31 May 1977 he was named as heir apparent and first entered the government as minister of defence, while remaining as commander-in-chief of the armed forces. In May 1989 he was appointed chairman of the Higher Council for Planning, a position considered to be vital in the building of a modern state. He also chaired the Higher Council for Youth Welfare from its establishment in 1979 until September 1991, when the General Authority for Youth and Sports was established and a full-time chairman appointed.

Sheikh Hamad's takeover of power on 27 June 1995, while his father was abroad, was overwhelmingly supported by the armed forces and cabinet, and welcomed by neighbouring states. It was apparently motivated by disagreements when Sheikh Khalifa sought to resume closer control of the government, having effectively passed over its management to Sheikh Hamad three years earlier.

On becoming amir, Sheikh Hamad also became prime minister, but held this post for only a year. In 1996 he issued an amiri decree to amend the Basic Temporary Amended Statutes of the Rule of the State, in order to separate the role of amir and the post of prime minister, to which he then appointed his brother Sheikh Abdullah.

Sheikh Hamad has married three times and has 11 sons and six daughters. His second wife and consort Sheikha Mozah bint Nasser al-Missned works to promote education and family affairs; she was appointed a special envoy for basic and higher education for the UN Educational, Scientific and Cultural Organization (UNESCO) in 2003. Her second son (and Sheikh Hamad's fourth son) Tamim was appointed heir apparent in 2003, replacing his elder brother Jassem, who stepped down from the post.

Sheikh Hamad's father returned to Qatar in 2004 for the first time since he was deposed, in order to attend his wife's funeral. He was greeted by Sheikh Hamad on his arrival.

In 2005 Qatar adopted its first written constitution, which guarantees freedom of expression, assembly and religion, equal rights for women, and allows for a partially elected legislative body of 45 seats, a third of which will be appointed by the amir.

Profile of the Prime Minister:

Sheikh **ABDULLAH** bin Khalifa al-Thani

Sheikh Abdullah is the younger brother of Qatar's ruling amir, Sheikh Hamad. Prior to the creation of the post of prime minister in October 1996, he had headed the country's Olympic committee from 1979 and run the interior ministry from 1989.

Abdullah bin Khalifa al-Thani was born in Doha on 25 December 1959 into Qatar's ruling Thani clan. His father, Sheikh Khalifa, became amir in 1972, and Sheikh Abdullah's elder brother Sheikh Hamad took the title for himself in 1995. As a member of the ruling royal family, Sheikh Abdullah had a privileged upbringing. After a local education, he went to the UK to attend the prestigious Royal Military Academy at Sandhurst, from which he passed out as an officer in December 1976.

On his return to Qatar, Sheikh Abdullah served in the military in various senior posts until 1989. By the end of his military career he had achieved the rank of lieutenant-colonel and was assistant commander-in-chief of the armed forces. He also sought to foster the country's sporting aspirations, establishing the Qatar Olympic Committee in March 1979 and heading it for the next ten years.

In 1989 Sheikh Abdullah was appointed to his father's government as interior minister. In July 1995 he took on the additional role of deputy prime minister in the new government formed after his brother's coup. The following year Amir Sheikh Hamad amended the constitution to separate the roles of head of state and head of government. He appointed Sheikh Abdullah as prime minister on 29 October 1996, while retaining him also as interior minister (although he relinquished the latter post in January 2001). Sheikh Abdullah chairs the cabinet, but real power remains with his brother.

ROMANIA

Full name: Romania.

Leadership structure: The head of state is a president, directly elected by universal adult suffrage. The president's term of office is five years, renewable once only. The head of government is the prime minister, who is appointed by the president. The cabinet is appointed by the prime minister.

President:	Emil Constantinescu	29 Nov. 1996—20 Dec. 2000
	Ion Iliescu	20 Dec. 2000—20 Dec. 2004
	Traian **BASESCU**	Since 20 Dec. 2004
Prime Minister:	Mugur Isarescu	21 Dec. 1999—28 Dec. 2000
	Adrian Nastase	28 Dec. 2000—21 Dec. 2004
	Eugen Bejinariu (acting)	21 Dec. 2004—29 Dec. 2004
	Calin **POPESCU-TARICEANU**	Since 29 Dec. 2004

Legislature: The legislature, the Parliament of Romania (Parlamentul României), is bicameral. The lower chamber, the House of Deputies (Camera Deputaților), has 345 members (with 18 seats reserved for minorities), directly elected for a four-year term. The upper chamber, the Senate (Senatul), has 140 members, directly elected for a four-year term.

Profile of the President:

Traian **BASESCU**

Traian Basescu was an officer in the Romanian merchant navy who entered politics only in the postcommunist era. A former mayor of the capital Bucharest, he is credited with ridding the city of stray dogs and improving its infrastructure. He was elected president on 12 December 2004 as a candidate of the Justice and Truth Alliance (Alianța Dreptate si Adevar—DA) and sworn in on 20 December.

Traian Basescu was born on 4 November 1951 in Basarabi, a small town in southeastern Romania near the port city of Constanța. He graduated from the Navy Institute in Constanța in 1976 and joined the merchant navy, working for the state-owned shipping company Navrom. From 1981 to 1987 he captained the country's flagship oil tanker *Biruinta* before heading the Navrom Agency office in the Belgian port of Antwerp.

461

Though a member of the Communist Party, Basescu did not seriously enter politics until after the Romanian revolution of December 1989. He first joined the National Salvation Front, then on its demise joined the Democratic Party (Partidul Democrat—PD). He served as minister of transport from 1991 to 1992 as a PD representative in the coalition government of Theodor Stolojan, and held the post again in the succession of governments from 1996 until 2000; that year he was narrowly elected mayor of Bucharest. He was re-elected as mayor with a larger majority in 2004. Basescu is credited with ridding the city of its packs of stray dogs and improving its infrastructure despite the efforts of some government officials to frustrate him.

When Stolojan withdrew from the 2004 presidential elections, Basescu stood on behalf of the DA, formed by the PD and Stolojan's National Liberal Party (Partidul Naţional Liberal—PNL). In an unexpected result, he won the presidential runoff on 12 December and was sworn in on 20 December. He is regarded as a thick-skinned populist with a pro-Western bent who is willing to undertake controversial reforms.

Profile of the Prime Minister:

Calin **POPESCU-TARICEANU**

An engineering professor, Calin Popescu-Tariceanu helped found the National Liberal Party (Partidul Naţional Liberal—PNL) in the 1990s and was first elected to parliament in 1996, becoming minister of industry and trade and deputy prime minister in the administration of Victor Ciorbea until 1997. The PNL joined with the Democratic Party (Partidul Democrat—PD) in 2003 to form the Justice and Truth Alliance (Alianţa Dreptate si Adevar—DA); following the surprise victory of the PD's Traian Basescu in presidential elections in 2004, Popescu-Tariceanu was asked to form a government and was sworn in on 29 December 2004. He threatened to resign in July 2005, following a ruling by the Constitutional Court that blocked judicial reforms necessary for accession to the European Union (EU).

Calin Constantin Anton Popescu-Tariceanu was born on 14 January 1952 in Bucharest. He graduated from the Institute of Civil Engineering in Bucharest, and then took a master's degree in mathematics and informatics. In 1976 he joined the National Water Administration in Argeş county as an engineer and later worked for a construction company in Bucharest; in 1980 he became a professor at the faculty of hydrotechnics in Bucharest, a position he held until 1991.

In 1990 Popescu-Tariceanu founded Radio Contact, the first independent private radio network in Romania. He became general manager of the network and remained in this post until 1996. In the meantime, he became a founding member of the PNL in early 1990 and was the party's secretary until 1992 and deputy chairman from 1993. In 1994 he helped found the Automobile Manufacturers and Importers Association.

He was first elected to Parliament in 1996 for the constituency of Bucharest, and was appointed as minister of industry and trade as well as deputy prime minister in the cabinet of Prime Minister Victor Ciorbea until 1997; he is credited with the restructuring of the country's mining industry and oil sector. In 2003 the PNL joined with Traian Basescu's PD to form the DA. Theodor Stolojan stepped down as president of the PNL in October 2004, and Popescu-Tariceanu took over this party post on an interim basis. The December 2004 presidential victory of Basescu opened the way for a DA government, which Popescu-Tariceanu was invited to lead, and he was sworn in as prime minister on 29 December 2004.

In office, Popescu-Tariceanu lowered income and business taxes to a flat 16% to encourage investment, but by July 2005 the administration had been derailed by the Constitutional Court's decision to block a set of laws for the reformation of the judicial system—reforms necessary for Romania to proceed with its bid to accede to the EU. Popescu-Tariceanu and his cabinet offered their resignations. Basescu had in any case been pushing for early elections since his victory in the 2004 elections, in order to secure a more comfortable majority for his alliance. However, on 17 July Popescu-Tariceanu withdrew his resignation, saying that it would be wrong to leave office at that moment because of the need to deal with a flood emergency in which 66 people had been killed.

RUSSIAN FEDERATION

Full name: The Russian Federation (Russia).

Leadership structure: The head of state is a president, directly elected by universal adult suffrage. The president's term of office is four years, renewable only once consecutively. The president appoints (subject to parliamentary approval) the chairman of the Council of Ministers. The president is, however, entitled to chair sessions of the Council.

President:	Vladimir **PUTIN** (acting from 31 Dec. 1999)	Since 7 May 2000

Chairman of the Council of Ministers:

Vladimir Putin (acting from 9 Aug. 1999)	16 Aug. 1999—7 May 2000
Mikhail Kasyanov (acting from 7 May 2000)	17 May 2000—24 Feb. 2004
Viktor Khristenko (acting)	24 Feb. 2004—5 March 2004
Mikhail **FRADKOV** (acting 7 May 2004—12 May 2004)	Since 5 March 2004

Legislature: The legislature, the Federal Assembly (Federalnoye Sobraniye), is bicameral. The lower chamber, the State Duma (Gossudarstvennaya Duma), has 450 members, directly elected for a four-year term. The upper chamber, the Council of the Federation (Soviet Federatsii), has 178 members (two representatives from each constituent of the Russian Federation). The individual members' terms vary according to the electing region.

Profile of the President:

Vladimir **PUTIN**

Vladimir Putin was little known when Boris Yeltsin made him prime minister in 1999, and was then propelled into the presidency by Yeltsin's unexpected resignation that December. He had spent the majority of his career working as a KGB agent, and had no political affiliation in the post-Soviet era. As acting head of state he pursued the war in Chechnya with determined ferocity, and with the Russian economy in an apparent state of recovery he won a convincing first-round victory in presidential elections in March 2000. Despite criticism of his behaviour at the time of the sinking of the Kursk *submarine and draconian security measures following the Beslan school siege, Putin has retained his popularity—and his grip on the Russian media—and he won his second election in 2004 with 71.3% of the vote. He has pushed for greater centralization of power from the regions to Moscow.*

Vladimir Vladimirovich Putin was born on 7 October 1952 in Leningrad (now St Petersburg). His grandfather was Lenin's cook and from a young age Putin expressed a desire to serve the state by working as a spy. In 1975 he graduated from the law department of Leningrad's State University and was immediately recruited by the Committee for State Security (Komitet Gosudarstvennoy Bezopasnosti—KGB). Little is known of the details of his secret service career other than that he spent most of his time in East Germany following his transfer there in 1984. By the time he left active service in 1990 he had reached the rank of colonel. He is married to Lyudmila, and they have two children.

Returning to Leningrad (renamed St Petersburg the following year), Putin began work as an adviser on international affairs to the State University and the city council in 1990 and quickly made his name in city politics under his old law professor and mentor, the reformist mayor Anatoly Sobchak. Putin became a deputy mayor and worked as the chairman of the committee on foreign relations from 1994 to 1996. He instigated a series of successful export quotas designed to generate funds to tackle the city's acute shortages, which had followed hard on the heels of the Soviet Union's collapse in 1991. After Sobchak was defeated in mayoral elections in 1996, Putin moved to Moscow to pursue a governmental career in the Kremlin. In 1997 he was appointed as head of the control department, deputy manager of property and deputy administrator for the presidential department; in the latter role he was an influential adviser to President Yeltsin on matters concerning Russia's regional policy.

In July 1998 Yeltsin promoted Putin to be head of the KGB's successor, the Federal Security Service (Federal'naya Sluzhba Bezopasnosti—FSB). In this role his main mandate was economic espionage and cracking down on illegal foreign trading. By March 1999 he had added the role of secretary of Yeltsin's security council and was heavily involved in the dispute with the North Atlantic Treaty Organization (NATO) over Kosovo.

On 9 August 1999 Yeltsin named Putin as his new prime minister and endorsed him as his preferred presidential heir. Putin's lack of high-powered political experience made him an unusual choice for the role of prime minister, the fourth since March 1998. From his first day Putin showed what his approach would be, taking a hard line on separatism in the Caucasus, no matter the international response, while leaving the economic policies of his predecessor largely unchanged to minimize domestic upheaval. Rebels in Dagestan were crushed with remorseless swiftness, and in October Putin masterminded an invasion of Chechnya. Despite initial media cynicism, this soon won him the rating of Russia's most popular politician, as Russian troops made steady advances on the

Chechen capital Grozny. He was also building an impressive base of support in the State Duma, with the newly formed pro-Putin grouping Unity making sizable gains in legislative elections in December.

The drama climaxed on 31 December 1999 when Yeltsin publicly announced his resignation and personally nominated Putin as his interim replacement. As acting president, Putin became solely responsible in the public's eye for the continuing Chechen war which persistently overran its 'imminent' end, and he quickly sought to soften his authoritarian image. A hastily drawn together collection of interviews was published as an autobiography, and much was made of his concerns for animal welfare with the release of his email correspondence with the famous ex-film-star activist Brigitte Bardot. Despite mounting international criticism of the war, Putin retained his lead over other Russian politicians and clinched the presidency in the first round of elections in March 2000 with 52.9% of the vote. His nearest rival, the Communist Gennady Zyuganov, received less than 30%.

One of his first acts as president-elect was to talk of the "dictatorship of the law" while recommitting his administration to the Chechen war. While some Russian writers talked of a "modernized Stalinism", others suggested that in Russia "dictatorship" was not seen as inherently bad. Fears abroad were allayed when Putin assembled an economic think tank comprising the four men considered the most liberal and pro-market on the Russian scene. He also rejected outright the Communist Party's demand that it be included in the new cabinet in proportion to its size in the Duma. Confirming his nonparty style of politics, Putin made it clear that his chosen ministers would have to leave their party affiliations at the door when they entered his government. Putin was inaugurated on 7 May.

Domestically, Putin consolidated his power beginning with a fierce assault on the 'oligarchs' of the Yeltsin era and a concerted attempt to centralize control over the country's vast infrastructure. In the Duma he enabled the growth of Unity Party into a full political party which, through mergers and defections, became a rival in size to the Communists. In April 2001 the Unity Party of Russia merged with the Fatherland–All Russia party to form the United Russia party.

Putin's political popularity was jolted in August 2000 with the sinking of the *Kursk* nuclear-powered submarine with the loss of all 118 sailors aboard. His hesitation over whether to involve foreign countries in the ultimately doomed rescue effort, and his failure to cancel a vacation on hearing the news, severely damaged his personal standing in Russian eyes. Despite this setback, however, a noticeable cult of personality began forming around the president.

Internationally, Putin's position was revolutionized by the 11 September 2001 terrorist attacks on the USA. Where once he was openly criticized by the West over the war in Chechnya (which he grandly and somewhat disingenuously declared to be "over" in April 2002), Putin was suddenly welcomed by US president George W. Bush and his allies as a fellow combatant against terrorism.

Putin quickly capitalized on this change, toning down previous criticism of the USA's controversial National Missile Defence system, and shelving suspicion of NATO expansion in the Baltic States to move instead to participation, through the NATO–Russia Council, from May 2002. His publicly cordial relations with Bush became less convincing towards the end of 2002, however, as Putin joined a chorus of doubters over the justification for a US-led war on Iraq.

The United Russia party won a landslide victory in the 2003 parliamentary elections, helped by a media that barely acknowledged other contenders. Putin increased the pressure on the Yeltsin-era oligarchs, with such former luminaries as Boris Berezovsky and Vladimir Gusinsky subject to government investigations into their business interests. On 24 February 2004, just ahead of presidential elections, Putin sacked his entire cabinet and appointed Viktor Khristenko as prime minister.

Putin won the presidential poll with 71.3% of the vote—his nearest rival, Nikolai Kharitonov, could muster just 13.7%. His political opponents again claimed media bias, and indeed most Russian television channels were by this stage owned or controlled by Putin and his supporters, and they made little attempt at even-handedness. Nevertheless, the Organization for Security and Co-operation in Europe (OSCE) declared the election and the balloting as free and fair. Putin appointed a technocrat, Mikhail Fradkov, as prime minister.

In September 2004 the Putin presidency faced its second major shock after armed terrorists took hundreds of schoolchildren and their families hostage in Beslan in North Ossetia. In the bloody resolution of the siege, more than 300 people were killed, most of them children. Controversy raged over whether government special forces precipitated the storming of the school and caused booby-trapped explosives to be detonated, and why the number of hostages being held was consistently underestimated by official sources.

Putin responded to the crisis by suggesting a series of draconian reforms of the country's political and security systems. A crackdown on people without identity papers was ordered, while plans were announced to replace directly elected regional governors with appointees from the Kremlin. Reintroduction of the death penalty was mooted. These suggestions were generally received well within Russia, with some opinion polls suggesting that they did not go far enough. In response to international criticisms of his proposals, Putin told Western leaders to sit down and negotiate with Osama bin Laden before they told him to negotiate with child-killers.

In November 2004 Putin caused some controversy by endorsing US president George W. Bush ahead of that country's parliamentary elections, though in the event he picked a winner. However, he was not so successful in personally backing Ukrainian presidential candidate Viktor Yanukovych. It was even suggested that his unconditional support for Yanukovych in the face of allegations of electoral fraud contributed to provoking Ukraine's 'orange revolution'. Putin was subsequently more circumspect in offering his endorsements during political upheaval in Kyrgyzstan in 2005.

Putin is constitutionally barred from seeking a third consecutive term in office, leading to speculation that he is already considering potential successors.

Profile of the Chairman of the Council of Ministers:

Mikhail **FRADKOV**

Mikhail Fradkov was a surprise appointment as Russian prime minister, recalled from his post as special envoy to the European Union (EU) to be sworn in on 5 March 2004. He was a former minister of trade and a deputy minister for foreign economic relations, but little was known about Fradkov's political or economic views. He belonged neither to President Vladimir Putin's inner circle of former security officials, nor to the pro-oligarch faction that was dominant under ex-President Boris Yeltsin. However, observers speculated that it was just this 'outsider' status that won him Putin's nomination, giving him an aura of independence from any of the factions within the Kremlin.

Mikhail Yefimovich Fradkov was born on 1 September 1950 in a small town near the city of Krasnoyarsk in the Kuybyshev region. He is married with two children. Fradkov was initially educated at the Moscow Machine-Tool Institute, before going on to the Foreign Trade Academy. His long career as a bureaucrat and diplomat began in 1973, when he worked in the economic section of the Soviet embassy in India.

From 1975 he served in various executive positions at the Soviet state committee/ministry of foreign economic relations, including a stint with the foreign trade agency. From 1991 to 1992 he served as deputy resident representative of the Russian Federation to the General Agreement on Tariffs and Trade (GATT). In 1992 Fradkov was appointed not only as the senior advisor to Russia's permanent mission to the UN, but also as deputy minister of foreign trade, putting him very close to the helm of the country's growing oil economy.

He was made director of the federal tax police by President Vladimir Putin in 2001, having previously been deputy secretary of the security council, and in 2003 he went to Brussels as Russia's envoy to the EU. On 1 March 2004 he was nominated by Putin as the next prime minister, and the appointment was approved by the State Duma on 5 March.

Putin and his allies have praised Fradkov as experienced, professional and honest. When he was named as prime minister, much was made in the press of his background as a technocrat and that his appointment represented a change from his predecessor Mikhail Kasyanov, who had often become involved in public disputes with his own ministers and the Kremlin. Fradkov, however, has turned out to be just as adept at political infighting and well able to defend his own turf.

RWANDA

Full name: The Republic of Rwanda.

Leadership structure: The head of state is a president, directly elected by universal adult suffrage. Under the 2003 Constitution the president's term of office is seven years, renewable once only. The president appoints the Council of Ministers, whose head is the prime minister.

President:	Pasteur Bizimungu	19 July 1994—23 March 2000
	Maj.-Gen. Paul **KAGAME** (interim from 23 March 2000)	Since 22 April 2000
Prime Minister:	Pierre-Célestin Rwigyema	31 Aug. 1995—8 March 2000
	Bernard **MAKUZA**	Since 8 March 2000

Legislature: The legislature, the Parliament (Inteko Ishinga Amategeko), is bicameral. The lower chamber, the Chamber of Deputies (Umutwe w'Abadepite), has 80 members, of whom 53 are directly elected. Each province also elects two women members (a total of 24); in addition, two members represent youth organizations and one member represents organizations of disabled people. The term of office for all members is five years. The upper house, the Senate (Umutwe wa Sena), has 26 members indirectly elected for an eight-year term. Former heads of state can be additional members of the Senate.

Profile of the President:

Maj.-Gen. Paul **KAGAME**

Paul Kagame grew up in Uganda and has close connections with the Ugandan president Yoweri Museveni. He fought in the guerrilla struggle through which Museveni came to power, and then with the Rwandan Patriotic Front (Front Patriotique Rwandais—FPR) which finally overthrew the ethnic Hutu-dominated genocidal regime in the Rwandan capital Kigali in 1994. He himself is a Tutsi, but has stated his preference for being called Rwandan rather than Tutsi. In power he has retained a reputation for not being associated with corruption.

Paul Kagame was born on 23 October 1957 in Gitarama prefecture, central Rwanda, to Deogratius and Asteria Rutagambwa. In 1960 his family went into exile to avoid growing Hutu violence towards the Tutsi people. Kagame went to primary and secondary school in Uganda, and from there to Makerere University, where he joined Yoweri Museveni in the overthrow of Milton Obote, and was appointed Museveni's chief of intelligence.

Kagame stayed in Uganda, becoming a senior officer in the Ugandan army in the late 1980s. In 1990 he attended staff and command courses at Fort Leavenworth, Kansas, USA, and then returned to Uganda to take up his role as military chief of the largely Tutsi FPR.

The FPR launched its military campaign from Uganda in October 1990. Almost four years of fighting followed before the FPR made its final assault on the Rwandan capital, Kigali, in June–July 1994. The FPR was included in the 'government of national unity' sworn into office in July, and Kagame was appointed vice president and minister of defence, and was viewed as the real power holder in the country. In 1998 he was elected FPR chairman.

President Pasteur Bizimungu resigned from office on 23 March 2000 after disagreeing with Kagame over the number of portfolios given to the FPR in a new cabinet. Kagame, as his deputy, was appointed interim president by the Supreme Court. He was formally elected president by the Transitional National Assembly just under a month later, with 81 of the 86 votes cast. He was inaugurated on 22 April, the first Tutsi head of state since 1959. Bizimungu tried to form an opposition party and was subsequently arrested and sentenced to 15 years in jail for embezzlement, associating with criminals and inciting violence.

The adoption of a new constitution in 2003 paved the way for Rwanda's first elections since 1988. Kagame won the presidential ballot on 25 August with 94% of the vote, and his FPR subsequently won three-quarters of the directly elected seats in the new Chamber of Deputies.

In March 2004 a French judge accused Kagame of personally ordering the downing in 1994 of President Habyarimana's plane, the event which triggered the start of the 1994 genocide. However, other investigators believe that militant Hutus shot down the plane as a deliberate pretext for the slaughter. Kagame refuted the allegation, and accused France of having had "direct involvement" in the genocide, alleging that it had provided weapons and training and given orders to those involved in the slaughter.

Kagame holds a diploma in professional management and business studies from the Open University (UK). He married Jeanette Nyiramongi in 1989, and they have four children.

Profile of the Prime Minister:

Bernard **MAKUZA**

Hutu politician Bernard Makuza was appointed prime minister in 2000, in a reshuffle of the government of national unity that had been ruling in Rwanda since the end of the 1994 genocide. He was reappointed to the post following the 2003 elections that ended the country's transitional period. He had formerly served as ambassador to Burundi and Germany.

Bernard Makuza, who was born on 30 September 1961, is married with three children. In the late 1980s he worked for various firms including Petrorwanda. Following the 1994 genocide, during which he was himself a target of the extremist Hutu Interahamwe, he worked with the special investigation mission of the UN Assistance Mission for Rwanda (UNAMIR). He was then chosen as one of the Hutu representatives appointed to head diplomatic missions, posted to the key embassy in neighbouring Burundi. However, a few years later he was transferred to the more distant posting of Germany.

Makuza was a member of the Hutu-dominated Democratic Republican Movement (Mouvement Démocratique Républicain—MDR), which had been given control of the post of prime minister in the government of national unity. Following the resignation of Pierre-Célestin Rwigyema, Makuza was the party's choice to succeed him, taking office on 8 March 2000.

Makuza's new government, announced on 19 March, was the first since 1994 in which the parties were not represented in accordance with the 1993 Arusha peace accords. This controversial lineup provoked the resignation on 23 March of President Pasteur Bizimungu, who clashed with his deputy Paul Kagame, the dominant leader of the Rwandan Patriotic Front (Front Patriotique Rwandais—FPR). Kagame succeeded Bizimungu and Makuza remained in post.

The MDR struggled with internal factionalism over the next few years, as some members decried the sway of the FPR over Makuza and the party. A cross-party parliamentary committee set up to consider the 'divisive ideology and activities' of the MDR recommended in April 2003 that the party should be banned and reprimanded Makuza for not having given sufficient consideration to the disunity the party was causing among Rwandans. The committee's conclusions were seen as an attempt by the FPR to destroy the MDR. Makuza responded that the MDR had suffered from internal divisions for decades, long before the FPR had even existed. A month later the government approved the party's dissolution, but Makuza remained in post as an independent.

Rwanda held elections for the first time for 15 years in September–October 2003. Makuza was reappointed as prime minister on 11 October, and a reshuffled cabinet was named on 19 October. The government coalition is dominated by the FPR, but includes several smaller parties and independents.

ST KITTS AND NEVIS

Full name: The Federation of St Kitts and Nevis (also known as St Christopher and Nevis).

Leadership structure: The head of state is the British sovereign, styled 'Queen of St Christopher and Nevis, and of Her other Realms and Territories, Head of the Commonwealth', and represented by a governor-general who is appointed on the advice of the St Kitts prime minister. The head of government is the prime minister, who is responsible to the National Assembly and is appointed by the governor-general. The cabinet is appointed by the governor-general.

Queen:	Elizabeth II	Since 6 Feb. 1952
Governor-General:	Sir Cuthbert **SEBASTIAN**	Since 1 Jan. 1996
Prime Minister:	Denzil **DOUGLAS**	Since 4 July 1995

Legislature: The legislature is unicameral. The sole chamber, the National Assembly, has 15 members, 11 directly elected for a five-year term, a speaker and three members appointed by the governor-general in accordance with the wishes of the prime minister and leader of the opposition.

Profile of the Governor-General:

Sir Cuthbert **SEBASTIAN**

Sir Cuthbert Sebastian is the second governor-general of St Kitts and Nevis. He trained in Canada as a doctor, later specializing in obstetrics and gynaecology (for which he trained in Scotland), and was for many years the chief medical officer at the general hospital in St Kitts.

Cuthbert Montraville Sebastian was born on 22 October 1921 and was educated at Basseterre Boys' Elementary School, teaching the younger boys for the last few years he was there. In 1939 he joined the St Kitts-Nevis Defence Force and started work as a learner dispenser at Cunningham hospital. Four years later he finished his training as a chemist and druggist and was promoted to medical sergeant. In 1944 he qualified as a laboratory technician. He then joined the UK's Royal Air Force, serving as a rear gunner until the end of the war.

In 1945 Sebastian was appointed senior dispenser and steward (hospital administrator) at Cunningham hospital, where he remained for the next five years.

He then went to study medicine in Canada, graduating from Mount Allison University and going on to Dalhousie Medical School, where he gained his doctorate in 1958 as well as a master's degree in surgery. Having obtained licences from the Nova Scotia Medical Board and the Canadian Medical Council, he returned to St Kitts, becoming captain-surgeon of the Defence Force and working as a general practitioner for four years in many parts of St Kitts, Nevis and Anguilla.

In 1962 he decided to specialize in obstetrics and gynaecology and he attended the Dundee Royal Infirmary in Scotland for the next four years. On his return to St Kitts in 1966 he was appointed medical superintendent and obstetrician gynaecologist at Cunningham hospital and again took up the post of captain-surgeon of the Defence Force, which he held until 1980. In 1967 he moved to the new Joseph N. France general hospital and was made chief medical officer three years later.

In 1975, during a visit by the prince of Wales to St Kitts, Sebastian was appointed as his local physician. Two years later he accompanied the then prime minister, Robert L. Bradshaw, to London for Queen Elizabeth II's Silver Jubilee, acting as his aide-de-camp and personal physician. He continued to practise medicine until he was appointed to the governor-generalship on 1 January 1996. In 2001 he published *St Kitts—100 Years of Medicine*.

Profile of the Prime Minister:

Denzil **DOUGLAS**

Denzil Douglas became prime minister of St Kitts and Nevis following the general election in July 1995, and won further terms in March 2000 and October 2004. A doctor and former president of the country's medical association, he is the leader of the moderate left-of-centre Labour Party.

Born on 14 January 1953, Denzil Llewellyn Douglas holds three degrees—in medicine, surgery and science—from the University of the West Indies (UWI). After a two-year internship at the General Hospital in Port of Spain, Trinidad, he returned to St Kitts and Nevis in 1986 to practise as a family physician. He served as president of the St Kitts-Nevis Medical Association until 1989. In March of that year he was elected to the National Assembly as one of only two successful candidates of the Labour Party (which had been the dominant party for decades under British rule but had lost its majority at the last pre-independence elections, held in 1980). Shortly after the 1989 election Douglas took over as party leader.

Within the broader regional context, the situation on Haiti was a major issue in 1990, in which Douglas became involved through his participation in a National Democratic Institute, sending a delegation to Haiti to demonstrate international support for its transition to democracy. Later that year he joined the mission led by former US president Jimmy Carter which acted as an international observer group at the Haitian general election.

Under Douglas's leadership the Labour Party in the early 1990s recovered much of its former support on St Kitts, the main island, and won four of the eight St Kitts seats at the November 1993 general election, but was kept in opposition by a coalition which included the three members from Nevis. (Labour has consistently been critical of the overrepresentation of Nevis proportional to its population, an attitude which made secession appear a more attractive option to the inhabitants of the smaller island when a Labour government did come to power in 1995.)

An early general election was held in 1995, the government having been severely weakened by the political repercussions of a crime wave related to drugs trafficking, to the extent that a 'national unity forum' had provided for all-party involvement in key decision-making in an interim pre-election period. The poll in July was a major victory for Douglas, with his Labour Party winning 58.8% of the vote and a clear parliamentary majority, and he was sworn in as prime minister on 4 July 1995.

In his first term of office, the Douglas government was preoccupied largely with the Nevis secession issue, which became particularly acute when the prime minister's initiative on constitutional reform was rebuffed by the Nevis legislature in a unanimous vote for secession in October 1997. The issue was only silenced when a referendum on secession failed on 10 August 1998 when the vote in favour fell just short of the necessary two-thirds' majority.

Hoping to capitalize on a historic corruption scandal concerning the previous government, Douglas called early legislative elections for March 2000. Labour won all eight seats on St Kitts although its overall share of the vote fell slightly, to 53.9%. The biggest issue in his second term in office was the international community's perception that St Kitts and Nevis had become a centre for money laundering. A tightening of financial regulations saw the country removed from a blacklist of suspect states in June 2002.

Douglas's Labour Party gained a third term in early parliamentary elections on 25 October 2004, winning 50.6% of the vote and seven seats in the National Assembly. The election campaign was largely fought over the economy—the islands had been badly hit by the downturn in tourism that followed the 11 September 2001 terrorist attacks on the USA.

ST LUCIA

Full name: St Lucia.

Leadership structure: The head of state is the British sovereign, styled 'Queen of St Lucia, and of Her other Realms and Territories, Head of the Commonwealth', and represented by a governor-general who is appointed on the advice of the St Lucian prime minister. The head of government is the prime minister, who is responsible to Parliament and is appointed by the governor-general on the advice of Parliament. The cabinet is appointed by the governor-general.

Queen:	Elizabeth II	Since 6 Feb. 1952
Governor-General:	Dame Pearlette **LOUISY**	Since 17 Sept. 1997
Prime Minister:	Kenny D. **ANTHONY**	Since 24 May 1997

Legislature: The legislature, the Parliament, is bicameral. The lower chamber, the House of Assembly, has 17 directly elected members and an appointed speaker, all serving a five-year term. The upper chamber, the Senate, has 11 members, six nominated by the government, three by the opposition and two by the governor-general.

Profile of the Governor-General:

Dame Pearlette **LOUISY**

Dame Pearlette Louisy, the first woman governor-general of St Lucia, is a former teacher and principal of a tertiary education college in the capital, Castries. She took office as governor-general on 17 September 1997.

Calliopa Pearlette Louisy was born on 8 June 1946 in the small village of Laborie on the south coast of the island. She attended St Joseph's Convent School in Castries and went on to the University of the West Indies (UWI) in Barbados, graduating in English and French in 1969. By 1975 she had obtained a master's degree in linguistics from the Université Laval in Québec, Canada. Between periods of study she taught in Castries, where she was a college principal in the 1980s and also national correspondent to the Agence de Coopération Culturelle et Technique, a position she held for ten years.

In 1986 she moved to the Sir Arthur Lewis Community College at The Morne, Castries, as dean of the division of arts, science and general studies, a position she held for six years before her promotion to vice principal and (in 1996) principal of the college. By 1994 she had obtained a doctoral degree in higher education from the University of Bristol, UK. From 1996, until her appointment as governor-general the following year, she was secretary and treasurer of the Association of Caribbean Tertiary Institutions in addition to her role as college principal.

During her career Louisy has written a number of papers and spoken frequently on a range of issues in tertiary education; she has also written several publications on learning the Creole language.

Profile of the Prime Minister:

Kenny D. **ANTHONY**

Kenny Anthony, a teacher and barrister, taught law at the University of the West Indies (UWI) before being elected leader of the St Lucia Labour Party (SLP) in 1996. He led his left-of-centre party to victory in the election the following year, and won a second term at elections in December 2001.

Kenny Davis Anthony was born on 8 January 1951. Educated at the Vieux Fort Senior Secondary School and then the St Lucia Teachers' College, he went on to study government and history at UWI, graduating in 1976. He began a teaching career at the Castries Anglican Primary School, moving later to the Vieux Fort Senior Secondary School. From 1978 to 1979 he was a part-time tutor at the St Augustine Campus of the UWI in Trinidad.

Anthony held ministerial office briefly in the SLP government of Allan Louisy between 1980 and 1981. He was initially appointed, in July 1979, as a special adviser in the ministry of education and culture, but was not able to take the post of minister at this stage because he held no seat in the House of Assembly, and was too young to be eligible for appointment to the Senate. Legislation to reduce the qualifying age from 30 to 21 was passed in time for him to take office as minister of education from December 1980, but he resigned the following March, disillusioned with the rampant factional disputes within the ruling party.

Resuming his studies, this time in law, Anthony completed his degree and master's degree at UWI and studied for his doctorate (awarded in 1988) at the University of Birmingham in the UK. Called to the Bars of St Lucia and Barbados, he was lecturer in law at the Cave Hill campus of UWI in Barbados and head of the law teaching department there from 1989 to 1993. In October 1993 he was appointed director of the Caribbean justice improvement project in the faculty of law at Cave Hill. He is married to Rose Marie Belle Antoine-Anthony, a Trinidadian and senior law lecturer at UWI, and has three children.

In March 1996 Anthony was seconded from UWI as general counsel to the secretariat of the Caribbean Community (Caricom) at Georgetown, Guyana, but resigned a month later to contest the election for the leadership of the SLP at the party convention in April and took up the party leadership in May. In a landslide victory at the general election on 23 May 1997 the SLP (in opposition since 1982) won 16 of the 17 elected seats in the House of Assembly. Anthony thereupon took office as prime minister.

Four-and-a-half years later the party slipped slightly, to 14 seats, after elections held on 3 December 2001. A key issue of Anthony's second term of office was the growing international pressure to reform St Lucia's financial regulations following criticism that the country was a centre for money laundering. Anthony accused elements in the international community of orchestrating the destruction of the region's financial industries, but also took steps to tighten up controls; a money laundering (prevention) act was passed in 2003, with amendments the following year. He was also an eager participant in the creation of the Caribbean Court of Justice to provide the region's Commonwealth members with a highest court of appeal separate from the Privy Council in London.

ST VINCENT AND THE GRENADINES

Full name: St Vincent and the Grenadines.

Leadership structure: The head of state is the British sovereign, styled 'Queen of St Vincent and the Grenadines, and of Her other Realms and Territories, Head of the Commonwealth', and represented by a governor-general who is appointed on the advice of the prime minister. The head of government is the prime minister, who is responsible to the House of Assembly and is appointed by the governor-general on the advice of the House of Assembly. The cabinet is appointed by the governor-general on the advice of the prime minister.

Queen:	Elizabeth II	Since 6 Feb. 1952
Governor-General:	Sir Charles Antrobus	1 June 1996—3 June 2002
	Monica Dacon (acting)	3 June 2002—2 Sept. 2002
	Sir Frederick **BALLANTYNE**	Since 2 Sept. 2002
Prime Minister:	James Mitchell	30 July 1984—27 Oct. 2000
	Arnhim Eustace	27 Oct. 2000—29 March 2001
	Ralph **GONSALVES**	Since 29 March 2001

Legislature: The legislature is unicameral. The sole chamber, the House of Assembly, has 21 members, 15 directly elected for a five-year term and six senators appointed by the governor-general.

Profile of the Governor-General:

Sir Frederick **BALLANTYNE**

Sir Frederick Ballantyne is a US-trained doctor, leading hotelier and entrepreneur. He was appointed governor-general of St Vincent and the Grenadines on 2 September 2002 after the sudden death of his predecessor.

Frederick Nathaniel Ballantyne was an only child born to one of St Vincent's first hoteliers. He became an integral part of the family business and in 1974, while still in his early twenties, he and his compatriot Vidal Browne amassed US$370,000 to buy the 14-hectare Young Island and its luxury hotel complex, off the St Vincent coast. He continues to own and run Young Island as well as a number of other tourist ventures.

Travelling to the USA, Ballantyne was trained as a medical doctor at Syracuse University in New York. After graduating he found work at Montréal General Hospital, Canada, and Rochester General Hospital in New York. He returned to the Caribbean to serve as chief of medicine and medical director for the newly built Kingstown General Hospital in St Vincent. He worked at the hospital for 14 years, while also acting as assistant dean of clinical studies at the medical school at St George's University in Grenada. Although now retired from medical practice he continues to volunteer at Kingstown and remains in charge of visiting medical specialists, whom he accommodates on Young Island.

Moving from general practice to public life, Ballantyne served as chief medical officer for St Vincent and the Grenadines for seven years into the mid-1990s. In February 1998 he was appointed president of the international branch of Dimethaid, a Canadian-based company specializing in developing methods for the 'transdermal delivery' of drugs. A member of the scientific advisory board of the Windward Islands Research and Education Foundation, he was also appointed deputy director of its new St Vincent office in 2001.

In June 2002 Governor-General Sir Charles Antrobus died, leaving the position vacant. Three months later Ballantyne was appointed in his place after the interim administration of Monica Dacon, the country's first female governor-general. He was knighted two months after taking office.

Profile of the Prime Minister:

Ralph **GONSALVES**

Ralph Gonsalves leads the centre-left Unity Labour Party (ULP). A former university lecturer who retrained as a lawyer, he is popularly known as 'Comrade Ralph' for his left-wing views. He entered the House of Assembly in 1994 and became prime minister in March 2001 after the ULP won a landslide victory in elections.

Ralph Everard Gonsalves was born on 8 August 1946 in Colonarie, St Vincent. His ancestors had arrived in St Vincent in the 19th century as indentured servants from the Portuguese island of Madeira. He graduated in economics from the University of the West Indies (UWI) in 1969 and stayed on for a master's degree in government studies, completed in 1971. He continued his university career by completing a doctorate in government studies at the University of Manchester in the UK in 1974.

Returning to the Caribbean to lecture in government and politics at UWI, he also became directly involved in politics, leading the United People's Movement in 1979–82. Meanwhile studying law, he was called to the Bar at Gray's Inn,

479

London, in 1981. Gonsalves is married to Eloise née Harris and they have five children.

For almost two decades Gonsalves combined an active career as a lawyer at the Eastern Caribbean Supreme Court with work as an activist for the political opposition to the ruling conservative New Democratic Party (NDP). He raised his public profile as a weekly columnist and writer on political issues.

In 1994 Gonsalves was elected to the House of Assembly as deputy leader of the resurgent ULP. Four years later he was elected to head the party, and in 1999 he became leader of the opposition. Two years later a ULP electoral victory ended 17 years of NDP rule, and Gonsalves became prime minister in March 2001. He has launched initiatives to modernize the government and economy and restructure the banana industry, which will lose its preferential access to the EU market in 2006, and strongly advocates closer integration among east Caribbean states.

SAMOA

Full name: The Independent State of Samoa (formerly Western Samoa).

Leadership structure: The head of state is an elective monarch or *o le ao o le malo*. The next *o le ao o le malo* will be elected by the Legislative Assembly and will have a five-year term of office. The head of government is the prime minister, who is appointed by the *o le ao o le malo* on the recommendation of the Legislative Assembly. The cabinet is appointed by the prime minister.

O le Ao o le Malo: Susuga Malietoa **TANUMAFILI II**   Since 1 Jan. 1962
(ruling jointly until 5 April 1963)

Prime Minister: **TUILAEPA** Sailele Malielegaoi   Since 24 Nov. 1998

Legislature: The legislature is unicameral. The sole chamber, the Legislative Assembly (Fono), has 49 members, elected for a five-year term. The right to stand for election is confined to members of the *matai* (elected clan leaders).

Profile of the *o le Ao o le Malo*:

Susuga Malietoa **TANUMAFILI II**

Malietoa Tanumafili II has been monarch since independence in 1962. Although his office is an elective one, he holds it for life, unaffected by the constitutional amendment defining the term of future monarchs as five years.

Tanumafili was born on 4 January 1913 and was educated in New Zealand at St Stephen's College, Auckland, and Wesley College, Pukekohe. He succeeded to the title of Malietoa (head of one of the four Samoan royal families) on the death of his father in 1940. In the same year he was appointed *fautua* (adviser) to the New Zealand governor of Western Samoa.

Tanumafili was one of the prominent Samoan leaders in the period leading up to independence in 1962. In 1958 he joined the New Zealand delegation to the UN, and was joint chairman of the working committee on independence and the constitutional convention in 1959. At the end of 1961, when the country achieved independence from New Zealand administration, he was appointed joint head of state. The death of Tupua Tamasese Mea'ole the following year left him as sole head of state, a post he holds for life. Celebrations held in 1990 marked his 50-year jubilee of continuous service to the government and people of the country.

Tanumafili has been married twice. With his first wife Lili Tunu, whom he married in 1940, he had five children, one of whom died in 1985. He has no children with Tiresa Patu Tauvela Hunter, whom he married in 1962.

Profile of the Prime Minister:

TUILAEPA Sailele Malielegaoi

Tuilaepa Sailele Malielegaoi leads the Human Rights Protection Party (HRPP). A career politician, he trained as an economist and briefly represented Samoa at the European Economic Community. He first entered government in 1982 and was appointed prime minister in November 1998 after veteran leader Tofilau Eti Alesana resigned. Tuilaepa has sought to strengthen the economy through modernization.

Tuilaepa Aiono Sailele Malielegaoi was born on 14 April 1945 in Lepa, on the southeastern tip of 'Upolu. At that time the islands constituted the New Zealand-controlled colony of Western Samoa. After a local early education, Tuilaepa travelled to New Zealand to attend St Paul's College in Auckland. He stayed in that city throughout the 1960s and attended Auckland University where he studied commerce. He obtained a degree in 1968, and the following year he became the first Samoan to receive a master's degree.

Returning to what was now independent Western Samoa, Tuilaepa worked in the treasury department based in Apia in the 1970s. In 1972 he married Gillian Meredith (now Gillian Malielegaoi) and the couple have eight children. In 1978 he departed for Brussels, Belgium, to take up a financial position in the European Economic Community, but returned two years later when he was elected to the Legislative Assembly for the first time, representing the Lepa constituency for the newly created HRPP. Initially he also continued to work for a private accountancy firm.

Under Prime Minister Tofilau, the first HRPP premier, Tuilaepa was appointed as minister of economic affairs, transport and civil aviation, and as associate minister of finance in 1982. In 1984 he was promoted to head the finance ministry. Although removed from office in 1985, he returned as finance minister in 1988. Three years later he was appointed deputy prime minister, as well as minister of finance, tourism, trade, commerce and industry.

Through the 1990s resentment over Tofilau's increasingly autocratic and self-serving administration began to erode the HRPP's popularity. Under great pressure to resign, Tofilau eventually stepped down in 1998, officially citing health concerns. Tuilaepa was appointed in his place. He also took on the foreign affairs and treasury, inland revenue and customs portfolios.

As prime minister, Tuilaepa has sought to sweep away the cronyism which had blossomed under Tofilau, and has taken a firm grip of the economy. The HRPP was re-elected in 2001 and the government outraged the opposition by getting itself reappointed without the usual parliamentary debate. In a reshuffle in 2003 the number of ministries was streamlined from 27 to 14. In the new line-up Tuilaepa retained responsibility for foreign affairs and foreign trade.

SAN MARINO

Full name: The Republic of San Marino.

Leadership structure: The heads of state are two captains-regent, elected by the Great and General Council for a term of just six months. The captains-regent are also joint heads of government, responsible to the Great and General Council. The Congress of State is elected by the Great and General Council.

Captains-Regent:	Marino Bollini & Giuseppe Arzilli	1 Oct. 1999—1 April 2000
	Gian Marco Marcucci & Maria Domenica Michelotti	1 April 2000—1 Oct. 2000
	Enzo Colombini & Gianfranco Terenzi	1 Oct. 2000—1 April 2001
	Luigi Lonfernini & Fabio Berardi	1 April 2001—1 Oct. 2001
	Alberto Cecchetti & Gino Giovagnoli	1 Oct. 2001—1 April 2002
	Antonio Lazzaro Volpinari & Giovanni Francesco Ugolini	1 April 2002—1 Oct. 2002
	Giuseppe Maria Morganti & Mauro Chiaruzzi	1 Oct. 2002—1 April 2003
	Pier Marino Menicucci & Giovanni Giannoni	1 April 2003—1 Oct. 2003
	Giovanni Lonfernini & Valeria Ciavatta	1 Oct. 2003—1 April 2004
	Paolo Bollini & Marino Riccardi	1 April 2004—1 Oct. 2004
	Giuseppe Arzilli & Roberto Raschi	1 Oct. 2004—1 April 2005
	Fausta **MORGANTI** & Cesare **GASPERONI**	Since 1 April 2005

Legislature: The legislature is unicameral. The sole chamber, the Great and General Council (Consiglio Grande e Generale), has 60 members, directly elected for a five-year term.

Profiles of the Captains-Regent:

Fausta **MORGANTI**

Fausta Morganti was appointed to a six-month term as captain-regent of San Marino on 1 April 2005. She was one of the first women to be elected to the Great and General Council, representing the San Marino Communist Party (Partito Comunista Sammarinese—PCS) and its successors. She has also held ministerial office, making education a speciality.

Fausta Simona Morganti was born on 20 August 1944. She studied languages at university and taught for many years at the Scuole Superiori di San Marino. In 1974 she became one of the first three women to be elected to the Great and General Council and joined the central committee of the PCS, on which she remained until the party re-formed itself in 1990 into the San Marino Progressive Democratic Party (Partito Progressista Democratico Sammarinese—PPDS).

She served on the Congress of State as deputy for culture, education and justice from 1978 until 1983, and again for education and culture from 1988 until 1992. She led the parliamentary group from 1997 to 2002, during which time the PPDS merged into the Party of Democrats (Partito dei Democratici—PD). When a new coalition government was formed in mid-2002, Morganti was appointed secretary of state for education, university and cultural institutions. This coalition only lasted until December, when the PD were ejected from government and Morganti returned to leading the parliamentary faction until 2004.

She was elected as one of the two captains-regent of San Marino to serve from 1 April 2005 until 1 October 2005. Their first official duties included attending the funeral of Prince Rainier III of Monaco and the inauguration of Pope Benedict XVI. She has also been a delegate to the Organization for Security and Co-operation in Europe (OSCE) and the International Monetary Fund (IMF).

Cesare **GASPERONI**

Cesare Gasperoni is secretary-general of the San Marino Christian Democratic Party (Partito Democratico Cristiano Sammarinese—PCDS). He was elected as captain-regent for the second time from April to October 2005, having previously held the post in 1990–91.

Cesare Antonio Gasperoni worked as a surveyor for the office of tourism, the council and the office of heritage. He is now retired. He joined the PCDS in 1968 and was the party's political secretary from 1993 to 1998, becoming its secretary-general in 2002.

Gasperoni was first elected to the office of captain-regent from October 1990 to April 1991 (alongside Roberto Bucci). He served on the Congress of State from 1998 to 2001 as secretary for relations with the castles' councils and the state companies. During this time he was made an honorary citizen of the Free Commune of L'Ilot Sacré in Brussels, Belgium, on the occasion of the signing of a friendship treaty between the commune and the nine castles of San Marino.

Gasperoni was elected captain-regent for a second six-month term lasting from 1 April 2005 to 1 October 2005, along with Fausta Morganti. Their first official duties included attending the funeral of Prince Rainier III of Monaco and the inauguration of Pope Benedict XVI. Gasperoni is also on the town planning commission and the permanent council commission for health and heritage.

SÃO TOMÉ AND PRÍNCIPE

Full name: The Democratic Republic of São Tomé and Príncipe.

Leadership structure: The head of state is a president, directly elected by universal adult suffrage. The president's term of office is five years, renewable once only. The president appoints the prime minister, who is head of government and who proposes the other members of the cabinet.

President:	Miguel Trovoada (deposed temporarily in Aug. 1995)	3 April 1991—3 Sept. 2001
	Fradique **DE MENEZES** (deposed temporarily in July 2003)	Since 3 Sept. 2001
Prime Minister:	Guilherme Pósser da Costa	30 Dec. 1998—18 Sept. 2001
	Evaristo Carvalho	26 Sept. 2001—26 March 2002
	Gabriel Costa	26 March 2002—7 Oct. 2002
	Maria das Neves	7 Oct. 2002—16 July 2003
	vacant	16 July 2003—23 July 2003
	Maria das Neves	23 July 2003—18 Sept. 2004
	Damião Vaz d'Almeida	18 Sept. 2004—8 June 2005
	Maria **DO CARMO SILVEIRA**	Since 8 June 2005

Legislature: The legislature is unicameral. The sole chamber, the National Assembly (Assembléia Nacional), has 55 members, directly elected for a four-year term. An eight-member regional council, established in April 1995, looks after the affairs of the island of Príncipe.

Profile of the President:

Fradique **DE MENEZES**

Fradique de Menezes is a successful businessman and former diplomat. Once a member of what was then the sole and ruling party, the Movement for the Liberation of São Tomé and Príncipe (Movimento de Libertação de São Tomé e Príncipe—MLSTP), he was briefly foreign minister, but left the party in 1990 claiming growing ideological differences. He defeated its candidate in the second round of presidential elections in July 2001, but the MLSTP remains the largest party in the National Assembly, forcing de Menezes to cohabit with an opposition-led government. Frequent clashes have ensued, six prime ministers have held office, and de Menezes was even briefly ousted by a coup in July 2003.

Fradique Bandeira Melo de Menezes was born in Água-Têlha on 21 March 1942 to a Portuguese father and a São Toméan mother. Until 2001 he held the citizenship of both countries, potentially jeopardizing his future political aspirations. He was educated abroad and, after a year's military service, graduated from the Higher Institute of Applied Psychology in Lisbon, Portugal, and in human sciences from the University of Brussels, Belgium. He is a widower, with one stepdaughter.

When São Tomé gained independence in 1975 as a Marxist single-party state, de Menezes returned and found work as a teacher, and later in the ministry of agriculture. His experience of living and working in Europe inclined him towards diplomacy and in 1981 he was despatched to London to head the São Tomé and Príncipe commercial delegation. Two years later he switched to Brussels as São Tomé's ambassador to Belgium, Germany, Holland, Italy, Luxembourg, Norway, Sweden, the European Communities, the Food and Agriculture Organization (FAO) and the UN Educational, Scientific and Cultural Organization (UNESCO).

De Menezes returned to São Tomé once again in 1986, when he was appointed foreign and co-operation minister by the Marxist president Manuel Pinto da Costa. He remained co-operation minister when the portfolios were split the following year, but soon handed in his resignation, citing "incompatibility" with the government. He left the cabinet in a reshuffle in January 1988 and in 1990 he left the MLSTP altogether.

For the rest of the 1980s and 1990s, as the country emerged as a multiparty democracy, de Menezes headed a successful cocoa-producing company. As president, he has retained the idea that agriculture forms the basis of the country's economy, despite the potential from new-found oil wealth. Between 1987 and 1994 he chaired the São Tomé chamber of commerce.

In presidential elections in 2001 de Menezes challenged the ruling MLSTP–Social Democratic Party (Partido Social Democrata—PSD), which had been returned to power in legislative elections in 1994, and held a majority in the National Assembly. He received the backing of the main opposition Independent Democratic Action (Acção Democrática Independente—ADI), which had supported his predecessor, outgoing president Miguel Trovoada. During the campaign the MLSTP–PSD unsuccessfully challenged his candidature on the grounds of his former dual citizenship. Although there was some confusion in the close-run first round, de Menezes won a clear but slim majority in the second stage, despite an all-time low voter turnout of only 62%. He was inaugurated as the country's third president on 3 September 2001.

His supporters soon formed the Force for Change Democratic Movement (Movimento Democrático Força da Mudança—MDFM), which contested the

2002 elections in alliance with the Democratic Convergence Party. It finished a close second, robbing the MLSTP–PSD of its overall majority, but de Menezes had to continue to ask the MLSTP–PSD to head the government.

Disputes were common between the president and the ministerial teams, not helped by de Menezes's volatility and irascibility and his continual interference in government business; within his first two years in office he dismissed three prime ministers. On 16 July 2003, while de Menezes was on a visit to Nigeria, Maj. Fernando 'Cobo' Pereira led a bloodless coup. International mediators negotiated the return of de Menezes a week later, and an accord was signed granting amnesty to the putschists and restoring de Menezes as president. For his part de Menezes promised to respect the separation of powers between presidency and government. Just under two years later, in June 2005, however, de Menezes's fifth prime minister resigned, citing a lack of support from the president.

Profile of the Prime Minister:

Maria **DO CARMO SILVEIRA**

Maria do Carmo Silveira, governor of the Central Bank, was appointed as prime minister in June 2005, the second woman to hold this office in São Tomé and Príncipe. Her appointment was the sixth change of prime minister in the country in four years, a reflection of an uncomfortable period of political cohabitation between a president and successive governments of different political affiliation.

Maria do Carmo Trovoado Pires de Carvalho Silveira was born in 1960 and trained as an economist at Donetsk University in the former Soviet republic of Ukraine. She has been governor of the Central Bank since 1999, a post she still holds though her deputy is currently fulfilling her duties in an acting capacity.

She is a member of the politburo of the Movement for the Liberation of São Tomé and Príncipe—Social Democratic Party (Movimento de Libertação de São Tomé e Príncipe—Partido Social Democrata, MLSTP–PSD), the successor to the single-party Marxist regime of 1975–1990. The MLSTP–PSD is the largest party in the National Assembly, just ahead of the Force for Change Democratic Movement—Democratic Convergence Party that backs President Fradique de Menezes. Do Carmo Silveira's appointment as prime minister on 7 June 2005 followed the resignation of Damião Vaz d'Almeida, also from the MLSTP–PSD, due to a dispute with de Menezes over the process of allocation of oil exploration licences and the handling of a lengthy public sector strike.

Her government was sworn in the following day, and she also took on the finance and planning portfolios. The previous four governments since the 2002 elections had been coalitions led by the MLSTP, but do Carmo Silveira's government comprises only MLSTP members and independents. Her first objective is to work with the International Monetary Fund to secure debt relief.

SAUDI ARABIA

Full name: The Kingdom of Saudi Arabia.

Leadership structure: The head of state is a king, who is also head of government in his capacity as prime minister, and who appoints the Council of Ministers. Under a royal decree of 20 August 1993, the Council's term of office and that of each member was fixed at four years.

King, Prime Minister and Custodian of the Two Holy Mosques:

Fahd ibn Abdul Aziz al-Saud   13 June 1982—1 Aug. 2005
(custodian of the two holy mosques since 1986)
ABDULLAH ibn Abdul Aziz al-Saud   Since 1 Aug. 2005

Legislature: There is no legislative assembly. The Consultative Council (Majlis al-Shoura), appointed every four years, now has 150 members. Three women were appointed to the Consultative Council on 26 June 2003.

Profile of the King:

ABDULLAH ibn Abdul Aziz al-Saud

Abdullah ibn Abdul Aziz al-Saud is one of the 37 sons of King Abdul Aziz al-Saud and succeeded to the throne of Saudi Arabia upon the death of his half-brother King Fahd on 1 August 2005. King Abdullah is perceived as being less pro-Western than his predecessor and enjoys considerable popularity in the country; however, he must contend with a nascent pro-democracy movement, a continuing terror threat and the difficulties entailed in ordering his own succession.

Abdullah ibn Abdul Aziz al-Saud was born in the capital Riyadh to Fahda, eighth wife to King Abdul Aziz ibn Abdul Rahman al-Saud, the founder of modern Saudi Arabia. His exact birth date is unknown, but 1924 is often quoted; succession in the Saudi royal family is restricted to the 37 sons of King Abdul Aziz, some of whom are flexible with their date of birth in order to give the impression of youth and vigour. He received a traditional religious education, and is thought to enjoy the Saudi tribal way of life, spending periods of time in the desert. Abdullah has four wives, seven sons and 15 daughters.

In 1962 Abdullah was appointed as the head of the National Guard, an internal security force forged from those tribal elements loyal to the al-Saud family. The National Guard's mission is to protect the royal family from internal rebellion and the other branches of the Saudi army; however, following Abdullah's assumption of control, the National Guard gradually modernized and became an integral part of the Saudi military establishment.

In 1975 Abdullah's half-brother King Khaled appointed him as second deputy premier. On King Fahd's accession to the throne in 1982, he appointed Abdullah as crown prince. After Fahd suffered a stroke in 1996, Abdullah took on a greater share of responsibility, becoming de facto leader and running the day-to-day affairs of the kingdom.

As crown prince, Abdullah developed a reputation as being less pro-Western than King Fahd; in 2001 he repeatedly refused to make an official visit to Washington D.C. in protest at the US refusal to condemn Israeli violence against Palestinians. This autonomy, coupled with his image as an Arab nationalist and a good Muslim, did much to ensure his popularity in the country. Abdullah consolidated his position with strategic allegiances with other members of the royal family to offset the influence of the 'Sudayri Seven', a group of his half-brothers— including King Fahd—whose mother was a member of the Sudayri tribe.

King Abdullah acceded to the throne on the death of King Fahd in August 2005, and chose to appoint Fahd's full brother Prince Sultan as crown prince. Abdullah faces a number of challenges: the growth of Islamic militancy, a small but increasingly vocal movement for democratization, growing resentment at the perceived corruption and extravagance among the royal princes—who number over a thousand—and the lack of employment available for young Saudis. Also important is to consider his own long-term succession; all of Abdullah's half-brothers are now in their seventies and eighties, and if the kingdom is to look forward to any continuity then the third generation must begin to play a more important role in the running of the country.

SENEGAL

Full name: The Republic of Senegal.

Leadership structure: The head of state is a president, directly elected by universal adult suffrage for a five-year term (reduced from seven years under the 2001 constitutional amendments), with a limit of two terms. The president appoints the prime minister, who then proposes the other members of the Council of Ministers. The president is designated head of government.

President:	Abdou Diouf	1 Jan. 1981—1 April 2000
	Abdoulaye **WADE**	Since 1 April 2000
Prime Minister:	Mamadou Lemine Loum	3 July 1998—1 April 2000
	Moustapha Niasse	1 April 2000—3 March 2001
	Mame Madior Boye (acting)	3 March 2001—5 Nov. 2002
	Idrissa Seck	5 Nov. 2002—21 April 2004
	Macky **SALL**	Since 21 April 2004

Legislature: The legislature is unicameral, since the abolition of the upper house, the Senate, under the 2001 constitutional amendments. The sole chamber, the National Assembly (Assemblée Nationale), has 120 members, directly elected for a five-year term.

Profile of the President:

Abdoulaye **WADE**

Abdoulaye Wade is a veteran opposition politician, who was elected president for a seven-year term in 2000, at his fifth attempt. His main policy has been opposition to the Socialist Party (Parti Socialiste—PS), in power since independence in 1960, and in particular to its former leader, ex-president Abdou Diouf. He is known as a devout Muslim, a political liberal and a free marketeer, and he describes himself as a "committed pan-Africanist".

Abdoulaye Wade was born on 29 May 1926 in St Louis and was educated in Senegal and France. He graduated in law from the faculty of law and economics in Dijon, France, in 1955, trained at the Bar in Besançon between 1955 and 1957, and gained a doctorate in law and economics from Grenoble in 1959. In 1960 he

492

was appointed assistant lecturer at the University of Dakar, a post he left in 1966, and he spent the following year in research in Boston, USA. He returned to France in 1967 for university posts in Paris, before becoming professor and later dean of the law and economics faculty at the University of Dakar. He also worked as a barrister at the Court of Appeal in Dakar, and is a member of the International Academy of Comparative Law in Stockholm, Sweden, and the International Academy of Trial Lawyers. He is married to Viviane, a French-born Catholic, and they have two children.

In 1974 he founded the Senegalese Democratic Party (Parti Démocratique Sénégalais—PDS), and has been the party's secretary-general ever since. He was elected to parliament in 1978, and was the unsuccessful PDS candidate in the presidential elections of 1978, 1983, 1988 and 1993. During the 1980s Wade was in outright conflict with the government: he was arrested in July 1985 and held for several days for taking part in an 'unauthorized demonstration', and again after the February 1988 elections, when public protests over the election results led to charges relating to the country's internal security, and he was given a one-year suspended sentence. The following year he left Senegal for France, returning in February 1990.

In the 1990s he continued to oppose Diouf and the PS, but in April 1991 accepted the post of minister of state as one of four PDS representatives in the government. He resigned in October 1992 in order to contest the 1993 presidential elections. In October 1993 he was charged with complicity in the murder earlier that year of Babacar Sèye, president of the Constitutional Council, and a few months later he was also facing charges in connection with violence at a demonstration protesting against the January 1994 devaluation. He was taken into custody awaiting trial. The charges in connection with Sèye's murder were dropped in May, but he remained in detention. He began a hunger strike in June, was released in July, and the charges in connection with the riots were subsequently dropped.

In January 1995 he held a private meeting with Diouf, at which he and the PDS were invited to rejoin the government, and he became minister of state to the president. In the presidential election held in February 2000 the first round was inconclusive, although Diouf emerged as the leading contender. In the runoff election in March five of the original eight candidates transferred their support to Wade, including Moustapha Niasse, who later became Wade's first prime minister, and Wade gained a 17% margin over Diouf. Traditionally Wade and the PDS drew the major part of their support from urban areas, but the 2000 elections, in which Wade's main campaign promise was simply for "change", indicated that they had made inroads into the rural vote as well. During his first year in office Wade presided over the drafting of a new constitution, which was endorsed in a referendum. In April 2001 fresh legislative elections were held, and the newly formed Sopi (Change) coalition, in which the PDS was the largest party, won 89 of the 120 seats in the National Assembly. The PS gained only ten seats, behind the Alliance of Progressive Forces, led by Niasse, with 11.

Wade has chaired many international conferences on law and the problems of development, and has written many publications on economics, law and politics, with a special interest in development issues.

In 2003 he was awarded Liberal International's Prize for Freedom in recognition of his lifelong struggle for democracy in Senegal. As president, he continues to promote human rights—Senegal abolished the death penalty in 2004 and press freedom is generally respected. Wade's 'Plan Omega' for economic development was one of the foundation blocks behind the New Partnership for Africa's Development (Nepad), a continent-wide programme to eradicate poverty and promote sustainable development.

Profile of the Prime Minister:

Macky **SALL**

Macky Sall became prime minister of Senegal on 21 April 2004 following the departure of Idrissa Seck. A well-known loyalist of President Abdoulaye Wade, Sall is a technocrat with a background in energy and mining. He was first brought into government in 2001 and has held various portfolios including that of government spokesman.

Macky Sall was born on 11 December 1961 in Fatick, in western Senegal. He attended the Lycée Gaston Berger in the city of Kaolack, graduating with his baccalauréat in 1982, before attending the Université Cheikh Anta Diop (UCAD) in the capital Dakar, where he studied geological and hydrological engineering. Sall then went on to the Institut Français du Pétrole in Paris, graduating in 1993.

Sall returned to Senegal to take up the position of head of the databank division in the Société des Pétroles du Sénégal (PETROSEN), where he remained until 2000, when he was made director-general. Earlier in the same year he had become a special adviser to new President Abdoulaye Wade on energy and mining. In May 2001 he was appointed minister of energy, mining and hydraulics, adding the transport portfolio in 2002—also the year he became mayor of his home town of Fatick. From 2003 until 2004 Sall was minister of state, minister of the interior and local communities, and government spokesman.

Sall was appointed prime minister on 21 April 2004, following the dismissal of Idrissa Seck, who had begun to make noises about standing for president and was regarded by some as 'getting too big for his boots'. Sall, the fourth prime minister since Wade came to power, has by contrast made the most of his humility and his loyalty to Wade, praising him as the man who taught him the art of politics and describing his own role as merely that of a technocrat giving shape to Wade's larger vision.

SERBIA AND MONTENEGRO

Full name: Serbia and Montenegro.

Leadership structure: The Federal Republic of Yugoslavia became the looser union of its two remaining republics, Serbia and Montenegro, in February 2003. The president of Serbia and Montenegro is elected by the Serbia-Montenegro union parliament for a four-year term. The union government consists of a council of three Serb and two Montenegrin ministers with the president as ex officio chair. Serbia and Montenegro also each have an elected president and their own governments, each led by a prime minister.

Federal President:	Slobodan Milošević	23 July 1997—7 Oct. 2000
	Vojislav Koštunica	7 Oct. 2000—7 March 2003
Union President:	Svetozar **MAROVIĆ**	Since 7 March 2003

Federal Prime Minister:

Momir Bulatović	20 May 1998—4 Nov. 2000
Zoran Zizić	4 Nov. 2000—24 July 2001
Dragiša Pešić	24 July 2001—17 March 2003

(post abolished under union constitution)

President of Serbia:

Milan Milutinović	29 Dec. 1997—29 Dec. 2002
Nataša Mićić (acting)	29 Dec. 2002—4 Feb. 2004
Dragan Marsicanin (acting)	4 Feb. 2004—3 March 2004
Vojislav Mihailović (acting)	3 March 2004—4 March 2004
Predrag Marković (acting)	4 March 2004—11 July 2004
Boris **TADIĆ**	Since 11 July 2004

Prime Minister of Serbia:

Mirko Marjanović	18 March 1994—24 Oct. 2000
Milomir Minić	24 Oct. 2000—25 Jan. 2001
Zoran Djindjić	25 Jan. 2001—12 March 2003

Nebojsa Ćović (acting)	12 March 2003—16 March 2003
Zarko Korać (acting)	17 March 2003—18 March 2003
Zoran Zivković	18 March 2003—3 March 2004
Vojislav **KOŠTUNICA**	Since 3 March 2004

President of Montenegro:

Milo Djukanović	15 Jan. 1998—25 Nov. 2002
Filip Vujanović (acting)	25 Nov. 2002—19 May 2003
Rifat Rastoder & Dragan Kujović (acting)	19 May 2003—22 May 2003
Filip **VUJANOVIĆ**	Since 22 May 2003

Prime Minister of Montenegro:

Filip Vujanović	5 Feb. 1998—25 Nov. 2002
Milo **DJUKANOVIĆ**	Since 26 Nov. 2002

Legislature: The legislature of Serbia and Montenegro is unicameral. The sole chamber, the Assembly of Serbia and Montenegro (Skupština Srbije i Crne Gore), has 126 members elected by the republican assemblies, 91 from Serbia and 35 from Montenegro, for a four-year term. The two republics each have their own parliament. The legislature of the Republic of Serbia, the Serbian National Assembly (Narodna Skupština Srbije) has 250 members, the Assembly of the Republic of Montenegro (Skupština Republike Crne Gore) has 77 members, all elected for a four-year term.

Profile of the Union President:

Svetozar **MAROVIĆ**

Svetozar Marović, cofounder of the pro-independence Democratic Party of Socialists of Montenegro (Demokratska Partija Socijalista Crne Gore—DPSCG), became the first president of Serbia and Montenegro on 7 March 2003. Involved in politics from an early age, Marović became a member of the Montenegrin parliament in 1990 and has been its speaker three times. In November 2003 he won international plaudits for issuing on behalf of his country an apology to Bosnia and Herzegovina for atrocities committed during the war.

Svetozar Marović was born on 21 March 1955 in Kotor in Montenegro. He graduated from the faculty of law in Podgorica University, Montenegro. As well as his career in politics, Marović has written for a number of newspapers and magazines, including *Ideje* (Ideas), *Praksa* (Practice) and *NIN* and the daily *Pobjeda* (Victory). Marović was also the man behind the 'Theatre City' Festival in the city of Budva, and wrote the book *Times of Temptation*. He speaks English and Russian, and is also a keen volleyball player. He is married to Djina née Prelević and they have a son and a daughter.

Marović became involved in politics very early in life and held several important positions in the days of the former socialist Yugoslavia, including the presidency of the central committee of the League of Communists of Montenegro. He is cofounder and deputy chairman of the Montenegrin pro-independence DPSCG, formed as a successor to the League of Communists. Marović was first elected a member of Montenegro's parliament in 1990. He was elected its speaker three times between 1994 and 2001, and has also headed its foreign affairs commission. He has served as secretary-general and vice president of the DPSCG, and as a federal and Montenegrin MP.

Marović was elected the first president of the new union of Serbia and Montenegro on 7 March 2003, less than a month after the former Yugoslav federation was abolished. He was the only candidate. In his inaugural speech, Marović described the agreement that led to the creation of the new union as "the first democratic agreement between Serbia and Montenegro ever", and said that his main focus during the three years before the two republics can opt out of the union would be on improving living standards. Marović also pledged co-operation with the UN war crimes tribunal in The Hague. In November 2003 he issued on behalf of his country an apology to Bosnia and Herzegovina for atrocities committed during the war.

Profile of the President of Serbia:

Boris **TADIĆ**

Serbian reformist Boris Tadić of the Democratic Party (Demokratska Stranka—DS) beat his nationalist rival Tomislav Nikolić to win the second round of Serbia's 2004 presidential election, taking office on 11 July. A psychologist and lifelong political activist, Tadić is known as a pragmatic man and is popular among young and professional Serbs. As union minister of defence from March 2003 until April 2004, he won plaudits for modernizing the armed forces: one of his first moves was to give soldiers better food and allow them to have showers more than once a week. The presidency is largely ceremonial.

Boris Tadić was born on 15 January 1958 in Sarajevo. His father, Ljuba Tadić, was a prominent dissident who was dismissed from his post as philosophy professor at Belgrade University by Yugoslav leader Josip Broz Tito. Boris Tadić attended elementary and high school in Belgrade. He was convicted for his opposition activities while studying social psychology at the University of Belgrade under Communist rule, though he went on to teach psychology at the

First Belgrade High School after graduation. Tadić is married to Tatjana and they have two children.

Tadić has been a research worker on various projects in the area of development and social psychology, a clinical psychologist in the armed forces, and a professor of psychology. He has also worked in a hospital and as a freelance radio journalist. In 2003 he was appointed professor of politics and advertising at the University of Arts in Belgrade.

Tadić joined the fledgling DS in 1990. Since then he has performed several roles, including acting secretary of the general committee and vice president and acting president of the executive board. He was twice elected vice president of the party. In 1996 Tadić was first elected to the Serbian National Assembly. The following year he founded and was the first director of the Centre for Development of Democracy and Political Skills.

In 2002 he became minister of telecommunications in the federal government; in March 2003 he became minister of defence in the new union's Council of Ministers. He won a reputation for his army reforms and became widely known for his plan to send a Serbian contingent on a mission to Afghanistan in a bid to warm his country's relations with NATO—stymied only by the collapse of the Serbian government in late 2003. He strengthened the powers of politicians and civil administration over the general staff, and launched a modernization plan aimed at readying the armed forces for membership in NATO's Partnership for Peace programme.

Politics in Serbia, in upheaval for much of 2003, took a new turn with the results of elections held in the republic in December of that year. The defeated DS, of which Tadić was by now president, did not join the government coalition. In February 2004 the Serbian parliament finally voted to scrap the minimum 50% election turnout threshold which had invalidated three previous elections for the republic's head of state, and in May Tadić won 53.7% of the vote in the second round, beating Serbian nationalist Tomislav Nikolić. Tadić was sworn in on 11 July, pledging to continue the policies of his former party colleague, the assassinated Zoran Djindjić.

Profile of the Prime Minister of Serbia:

Vojislav **KOŠTUNICA**

Vojislav Koštunica, head of the Democratic Party of Serbia (Demokratska Stranka Srbije—DSS), emerged from relative obscurity as the standard bearer of the Democratic Opposition of Serbia (Demokratska Opozicija Srbije—DOS) for presidential elections in 2000 and became president of the Federal Republic of Yugoslavia after a popular uprising prevented the incumbent, Slobodan Milošević, from 'stealing' victory. Free from any connection with the Milošević regime, he was described as a 'soft' nationalist in the 1970s. He had, however, sided with the extreme right during the early 1990s, and in 1999 loudly condemned the West's bombing of Yugoslavia over oppression in Kosovo. When Yugoslavia was transformed into the confederal state of Serbia and Montenegro in 2003, Koštunica stepped down from the presidency, a post that no longer wielded much political power. A year later, however, he secured the high-profile position of Serbian prime minister, heading a centrist minority coalition. On his appointment he immediately antagonized the West by declaring that co-operation with the International Criminal Tribunal for the former Yugoslavia (ICTY) would not be a top priority for his government.

Vojislav Koštunica was born in Belgrade, Serbia, on 24 April 1944. A year after his birth Marshal Tito established a communist federal republic in Yugoslavia. Koštunica attended the University of Belgrade's faculty of law from the mid-1960s, achieving a master's degree in 1970 and a doctorate in 1974. He is married to fellow lawyer Zorica Radović; they have no children.

Koštunica's nationalist politics jarred with the Tito regime. He was eventually dismissed from the Belgrade law faculty over his support for prominent critics of Tito's 1974 federal constitution, which Serb nationalists resented for giving Kosovo and Vojvodina autonomous status within Serbia. When offered a professorship at the same institute in 1989 he famously refused.

From 1974 Koštunica worked at the Institute for Social Sciences in Belgrade and was briefly its director in the mid-1980s. During this period he also edited several well-respected political and legal journals including *Law and Social Sciences Archive* and *Philosophy and Society*. His doctoral thesis, on institutionalized opposition in capitalist political systems, was also published as a book along with further writings on law and politics. He mixed nationalism with advocacy of human rights and was prominent on the Board for the Protection of the Freedom of Thought and Expression. In 1989, with civil unrest mounting and nationalism gaining popularity, Koštunica put his theories into practice and cofounded the Democratic Party (Demokratska Stranka—DS). In elections in 1990 he won a seat in the lower house of the Federal Assembly which he held through consecutive elections until 1997.

He left the DS in 1992, considering its stance during Yugoslavia's civil war to be insufficiently pro-Serb. Instead he created the DSS and has been its president ever since. By 1993 the DSS was on the very fringe of Serbian politics, becoming known as the 'van party' on the basis that all of its supporters could fit in one van. Koštunica earned the dubious honour of being lumped among the pro-war bloc in parliament for his continual attacks on the various Western-proposed peace plans, and for his support for the extreme nationalist Radovan Karadžić and the rebellious Bosnian Serbs, although he condemned the excessive violence of the various paramilitary groups.

Hostility to Milošević grew in strength after the Yugoslav defeat in Kosovo in 1999, and when Milošević unexpectedly called a presidential election the disparate opposition parties turned to Koštunica in July 2000 as a unifying candidate free from the taint of the corrupt regime. He proved himself an able politician, despite lacking the charisma of the other candidates, and under the slogan "no to the White House [USA], no to the White Castle [Milošević government]" he won popularity among Serbia's dissatisfied but still proudly nationalistic populace. After the electoral commission admitted having been ordered to falsify the results of the elections, a wave of mass demonstrations on 5 October forced Milošević to resign. Final results confirmed Koštunica's first-round victory with 50% of the vote ahead of Milošević's 37%.

This 'October revolution' opened the way for Yugoslavia to rejoin the international community and Koštunica was hailed as a champion of democracy. Famously eschewing the trappings of power, he could still be seen driving through the streets of Belgrade in his battered old Yugo car. The old pro-Milošević infrastructure slowly dissolved and a new government was formed in November. However, Koštunica proved to be as consistent as ever and continued to condemn outside interference. With Montenegro no longer effectively participating in the federal structure, Koštunica attempted to establish his role as the pre-eminent power in Serbia. He easily overshadowed the Milošević-era Serbian president, Milan Milutinović, but found himself unable to dominate the Serbian government formed by Zoran Djindjić after the DOS won the December 2000 elections to the republican legislature.

In January 2001 Koštunica sent shock waves through the DOS when he met with Milošević to discuss the issues of the day, and openly condemned the ICTY as a "monstrous institution". His most important political relationship, with the Serbian government, worsened considerably. The main bone of contention between Koštunica and Djindjić became the Serbian government's level of co-operation with the West, particularly over the indictment of suspected war criminals. When Milošević himself was arrested on 1 April, and extradited on 28 June, tensions were magnified. Divisions were played out in the machinations of the Serbian parliament.

In June 2002 Koštunica took his DSS out of the DOS coalition altogether after its members were expelled from the Serbian parliament for failing to attend sessions. Formally cut off from the Serbian government (which wielded much more importance in Yugoslavia than the federal authority), Koštunica multiplied his opposition to Djindjić. He horrified the international community when he reportedly said that the ethnic Serb Republic (Republika Srpska) in neighbouring Bosnia was only temporarily separated from Serbia.

As the constituent parts of the Federal Republic of Yugoslavia voted over the course of the year to dissolve the union in favour of a looser confederation of 'Serbia and Montenegro', Koštunica's position became somewhat that of a lame duck. Eager to remain influential in the new state's political life, he declared on

26 August 2002 that he would stand in the forthcoming Serbian presidential election.

Although Koštunica led in both rounds of the elections, held on 30 September and 13 October, voter turnout failed to pass the necessary 50% barrier, making the poll null and void. Again he led the field in the rerun on 8 December, but again fewer than half of the electorate bothered to cast their ballots. By the end of the year the Serbian presidency had passed to the speaker of the Serbian parliament, Nataša Mićić, while Koštunica's position as Yugoslav president looked set to have only a few more months of relevance.

Koštunica did not stand for the ceremonial presidency of the new confederation, following its formation in February 2003, and found himself out of political office. However, a month later his arch-rival Djindjić was assassinated; the new DS leader succeeded as prime minister, but the assassination had undermined the stability of the Serbian government. With the DOS coalition disintegrating, early elections were called in November in order to avoid a no-confidence vote.

In the December poll Koštunica's DSS finished second behind the far-right Serbian Radical Party, led by indicted war criminal Vojislav Seselj. Protracted coalition talks began as parties manoeuvred to overcome their differences in order to avoid allowing the SRS into office. DSS member Dragan Maršićanin was elected speaker of the new parliament in February 2004—and therefore acting president, following the third failure of presidential elections the previous November—and from this position nominated Koštunica to form the new government.

A coalition comprising the DSS, the moderate G17 Plus and the New Serbia—Serbian Renewal Movement alliance, and backed in parliament by Milošević's Socialist Party of Serbia, took office on 3 March 2004. Koštunica confirmed the fears of the international community when he proclaimed that co-operation with the ICTY would not be a top priority for his government. The voluntary surrender in 2005 of a few indicted suspects has helped to vindicate Koštunica's policy of relying on persuasion rather than arrest. In April the European Commission recommended that talks should begin with Serbia and Montenegro on eventual membership of the European Union, following the handover of another 13 war crimes suspects.

Profile of the President of Montenegro:

Filip VUJANOVIĆ

Filip Vujanović is a moderate member of the centre-left Democratic Party of Socialists of Montenegro (Demokratska Partija Socijalista Crne Gore—DPSCG). He served in the Montenegrin government as justice minister and interior minister before becoming prime minister in 1998 in succession to Milo

Djukanović. When the latter then sought to reclaim his role in late 2002, Vujanović became acting president and won presidential elections in May 2003.

Filip Vujanović was born on 1 September 1954 in Belgrade. He graduated in law from the city's university in 1978 and began work in the district attorney's office in Belgrade before moving to Podgorica, the capital of his ancestral homeland, Montenegro, in 1981. He is married to Svetlana, and has two daughters and a son.

After working in the city's district court in the 1980s, Vujanović was registered as the youngest lawyer in the attorney's chamber in 1989. He became a well-known figure in 1992 when he represented the then president of Montenegro, Momir Bulatović, in his lawsuit against detractors.

In March 1993 he was appointed to Djukanović's cabinet as justice minister and later moved to the interior ministry in 1996, in which position he remained in the next Djukanović cabinet inaugurated later that year. Following Djukanović's electoral success as president in January 1998, he was appointed prime minister of Montenegro on 5 February and was reconfirmed in the post on 2 July 2001.

As the demise of Yugoslavia loomed in late 2002, Djukanović sought to maintain a position of power in the new confederal structure and preemptively resigned as president on 25 November in order to take over from Vujanović as prime minister. In his role as speaker of the Montenegrin parliament, Vujanović took over as acting president, and stood for the post in early elections on 22 December.

Despite his decisive majority of 86% of the vote, the poll was ultimately rejected as it had failed to attract the necessary minimum of 50% of the electorate. A second poll in February met with a similar fate, so the turnout condition was abolished, and a third election was held on 11 May. Vujanović gained over 65% of the vote (on a turnout of 48%). Shortly thereafter he stepped down from the acting presidency and on 22 May he was sworn into office.

As president he continued to support moves towards Montenegrin independence, arguing that the union with Serbia was not functioning, and that EU membership could be achieved much earlier if Montenegro were a separate state. Serbian prime minister Vojislav Koštunica has rebuffed such discussions for breaching the 2002 Belgrade accord that precludes either republic from holding a referendum on the issue until 2006.

Profile of the Prime Minister of Montenegro:

Milo DJUKANOVIĆ

In November 2002 Milo Djukanović resumed the post of prime minister of Montenegro, having stood down from the presidency, a position he had held for almost five years. He did so because the presidency was about to lose its significance, in structural changes accompanying the passage from federal

Yugoslavia to a looser confederation of 'Serbia and Montenegro'. He had previously held the post of Montenegrin prime minister from 1991 to early 1998. Although he belongs to the former communist Democratic Party of Socialists of Montenegro (Demokratska Partija Socijalista Crne Gore—DPSCG), Djukanović is generally considered a pro-Western reformer.

Milo Djukanović is the son of a High Court judge and was born on 15 February 1962 in the industrial town of Nikšić where he went to school. He studied economics at Titograd University (now the University of Montenegro), where he first became involved in politics, joining the League of Communists of Yugoslavia (LCY) in 1979. He is married to Lidija née Kuć and they have one son.

By the age of 24 Djukanović had been appointed to the party's central committee. In 1989–90, when Slobodan Milošević secured first the chairmanship of the collective presidency of Serbia and then in 1990 the Serbian presidency itself, Djukanović at first supported him, and was rewarded with the post of prime minister of Montenegro in January 1991.

However, over the course of the wars in the ensuing five years, Djukanović became a firm opponent of Milošević, accusing the Serbian dictator of corruption and the destruction of Yugoslavia for his own ends. In 1996 he gave his support to the Serbian protest movement and the DPSCG (the successor to the LCY in Montenegro) split into two factions, one led by him and the other by the then Montenegrin president, Momir Bulatović. Djukanović reportedly blamed Milošević for the continuation of international sanctions against Yugoslavia, and wanted to improve Montenegro's relations with Western countries to ensure that they were lifted.

In the first round of the October 1997 presidential election in Montenegro none of the eight candidates achieved an absolute majority, although both Djukanović and Bulatović secured well over 40%. When Djukanović won the 19 October runoff by a narrow margin, Bulatović claimed that irregularities had occurred, demanded new elections, and threatened not to stand down as president, but international observers declared the elections valid.

As president, Djukanović slowly began the process of wresting control of the republic away from the federal authorities in Belgrade. His desire for full independence for Montenegro has been openly opposed by the West, which fears sparking a further round of pro-independence violence in other parts of the Balkans. During the 1999 Kosovo conflict Djukanović declared Montenegro's neutrality, sparing the country from bombardment by Western warplanes. In the aftermath there was widespread fear that Milošević would punish Djukanović by engineering his overthrow.

The hope that the ouster of Milošević in October 2000 would dampen Djukanović's separatist ambitions was dashed when he rejected the plans of the new Yugoslav president Vojislav Koštunica to reform the existing federation. In

November that year he confidently declared that "Yugoslavia does not exist", echoing the famous statement by the Croat leader Stipe Mesić which heralded the collapse of the former socialist state in 1991. However, support for secession in Montenegro is finely balanced, and coupled with the international community's reluctance, Djukanović has had to accept a compromise reform of Yugoslavia. Conjoined for three years as the new state of 'Serbia and Montenegro', the smaller republic will have the option to vote for full secession from 2006 and Djukanović has made it clear that he intends to exercise this option.

In order to remain relevant in the structure of the new state, Djukanović resigned as Montenegrin president on 25 November 2002. Instead he became the republic's constitutionally more powerful prime minister. The incumbent premier, Filip Vujanović, became acting president in his capacity as speaker of the Montenegrin parliament. Both leaders have continued to press the case for independence; Djukanović responded to a lawsuit filed against him by the European Union in 2003 for involvement in cigarette smuggling as just another move by the West to pressure his government away from its commitment to independence.

SEYCHELLES

Full name: The Republic of Seychelles.

Leadership structure: The head of state is a president, directly elected by universal adult suffrage. The president's term of office is five years, with a maximum of three consecutive terms. The head of government is the president. The Council of Ministers is appointed by the president.

| *President*: | France Albert René | 5 June 1977—14 April 2004 |
| | James **MICHEL** | Since 14 April 2004 |

Legislature: The legislature is unicameral. The sole chamber, the National Assembly, has up to 34 members, 23 members directly elected for a five-year term and up to 11 members allocated on a proportional basis.

Profile of the President:

James **MICHEL**

James Michel became president of the Seychelles on 14 April 2004. A teacher by training, he spent most of his career working in the tourism industry before joining the post-coup government in 1977 under President France Albert René. In government ever since, he was René's chosen successor.

James Michel was born on 16 August 1944. He trained as a teacher at the Seychelles teacher training college before leaving the profession to work for Cable and Wireless Telecommunications. In 1971 he began his involvement with the archipelago's burgeoning tourism industry when he went to work for the Hotel des Seychelles, eventually becoming its manager.

By 1974 Michel had joined the Seychelles People's Progressive Front (SPPF) of France Albert René. He was a member of its executive committee when René staged a coup against the islands' first president James Mancham just a year after the Seychelles gained independence in 1976. He served under President René throughout the 16-year one-party socialist dictatorship that followed, in a range of political posts including minister of education, of finance, of information and as chief of staff of the Seychelles People's Defence Forces from 1979 to 1993.

Michel has played a role in the country's slow process of democratization, which began with multiparty elections in 1993. He has promised new openness and dialogue, particularly with regard to the national economy, and to open more of the economy to the private sector. Identified by René as his chosen successor, he was sworn in as president on 14 April 2004 when René stepped down. Opposition politicians pledged to co-operate with Michel despite deploring the manner of his elevation.

SIERRA LEONE

Full name: The Republic of Sierra Leone.

Leadership structure: Under the 1991 Constitution the head of state is a president, directly elected by universal adult suffrage for a four-year term. The president is also the head of government and appoints the cabinet.

President: Ahmed Tejan **KABBAH**   Since 29 March 1996
                (in exile from 25 May 1997 to 10 March 1998)

Legislature: The legislature is unicameral. The sole chamber, the Parliament, has 112 members directly elected for a five-year term, and 12 members indirectly elected to represent the 12 provincial districts.

Profile of the President:

Ahmed Tejan **KABBAH**

Ahmed Kabbah is a barrister and former UN official. He won the 1996 presidential elections as the candidate of the Sierra Leone People's Party (SLPP). Forced into exile by a coup in May 1997 but restored to office the following March, he entered a power-sharing agreement with the rebel Revolutionary United Front (RUF) in 1999 in an attempt to end the decade-long civil war, but the violence continued and he found himself dependent on UK military intervention to repel advancing RUF forces the following year. A ceasefire in 2001 allowed him to confirm his position at the polls in May 2002.

Ahmed Tejan Kabbah was born on 16 February 1932 in Pendembu, Kailahun district. Although he is himself a Muslim, he went to the country's oldest Roman Catholic school, St Edward's in Freetown. He completed his education in Wales, first at Cardiff College of Technology and Commerce and then at University College, Aberystwyth, where he gained a degree in economics before joining the colonial administrative service in 1959.

Kabbah was an assistant district commissioner in the Bombali, Moyamba, Kono and Kambia districts before transferring to Freetown as deputy permanent secretary in the ministry of social welfare. Promoted to permanent secretary, he then worked at the ministry of trade and industry and the ministry of education. In 1965 he married Patricia Lucy Tucker, a Catholic former teacher from southern Sierra Leone who was working in the prime minister's office, and together they went to London in 1968 to study law. They subsequently had a daughter and three sons. Patricia died in May 1998.

Called to the Bar at Gray's Inn in London, Kabbah moved to the UN in New York on completion of his barrister's examinations, as deputy chief of its West African division. He headed the UN Development Programme (UNDP) missions in several southern African states between 1973 and 1981, when he was promoted to deputy personnel director, then director of UNDP's division of administration and management.

In the 1996 presidential elections he won 35.8% of the vote in the first round on 26–27 February and 59.5% in the runoff on 15 March. Polling was disrupted by the rebel RUF and some 27 people were killed. Kabbah was sworn in on 29 March.

Kabbah was forced to flee to Guinea on 25 May 1997 following a coup led by Lt.-Gen. Johnny Koroma. Kabbah, however, retained recognition internationally as the lawful president, representing Sierra Leone in this capacity at the Commonwealth heads of government meeting in Edinburgh in October 1997. The Economic Community of West African States (ECOWAS) dispatched to Sierra Leone an Economic Community Ceasefire Monitoring Group (ECOMOG) peacekeeping force. Its intervention eventually resulted in his restoration as president on 10 March 1998.

Back in power, Kabbah returned his attention to peace negotiations with the RUF. He signed the Lomé peace deal with RUF leader Foday Sankoh in July 1999, but this was undermined by a return to full-scale violence in May 2000. Peace was finally achieved in January 2002 after the intervention in 2001 of the UK armed forces on the side of the government. Kabbah was resoundingly re-elected on 14 May 2002 with 70.1% of the vote, and was inaugurated for his second full term six days later. In parallel legislative elections the SLPP gained a commanding majority while the RUF's new political party failed to win a single seat.

In 2004 the UN-backed War Crimes Tribunal began hearing trials, and UN peacekeepers reduced their presence, handing over security to local forces in Freetown and other parts of the country. However, a report published by the Truth and Reconciliation Commission in October stated that many of the "dire conditions" that had given rise to the brutal civil war were still present and were hampering efforts to rebuild the country. The report warned that while security had improved, corruption remained rampant, discouraging investment and dooming young adults to a "twilight zone" of unemployment, frustration and despair.

SINGAPORE

Full name: The Republic of Singapore.

Leadership structure: The head of state is a president, directly elected by universal adult suffrage. The president's term of office is six years. The head of government is the prime minister, who is appointed by the president. The cabinet is appointed by the president.

President:	Sellapan Rama **NATHAN**	Since 1 Sept. 1999
Prime Minister:	Goh Chok Tong	28 Nov. 1990—12 Aug. 2004
	LEE Hsien Loong	Since 12 Aug. 2004

Legislature: The legislature is unicameral. The sole chamber, the Parliament, has 84 directly elected members, and up to six extra members from opposition parties (depending on their share of the vote) elected for a five-year term. Up to nine members may also be nominated for two-year terms by the government.

Profile of the President:

Sellapan Rama **NATHAN**

S. R. Nathan was declared the winner of the 1999 presidential election on 18 August after all other candidates had been deemed ineligible to run. A long-serving government minister and former head of the state media empire, the Straits Times Press, Nathan is the second ethnic Indian to be president of the city-state since its independence from Malaysia in 1965. Under constitutional changes in 1991 the office of president became a mostly ceremonial role, but with powers to check government actions including the use of the state's vast financial reserves.

Sellapan Rama Nathan was born in Singapore on 3 July 1924 and was educated in the city. Before he had completed his primary studies he began working and put himself through secondary education on a self-study course. In 1954 he graduated from the University of Malaya, which was then based in Singapore, with a diploma in social studies. He is a Hindu and has been prominent in Singapore–India relations, cofounding the Singapore Indian Development Association. Nathan is married to Urmila née Nandey and they have one daughter and one son.

In 1955 Nathan began working for the civil service as a medical social worker and the following year he was appointed seamen's welfare officer at the ministry of labour. From 1962 he began a long association with the labour research unit when he was appointed as assistant director. He went on to become a full director of the unit until February 1966 when he was transferred to the foreign ministry of the newly independent state. There he rose rapidly to become deputy secretary before being transferred to the ministry of home affairs, where he was appointed acting permanent secretary in 1971. Later that year he switched to become permanent secretary in the defence ministry, in which role he was noted for taking part in a commando operation to disarm hijackers on board a ship in Singaporean waters in 1974. For his actions he was awarded the meritorious service medal. In 1979 he returned to the foreign ministry as its first permanent secretary.

Nathan switched from politics to the press in February 1982 when he left the foreign ministry to become executive chairman of the Straits Times Press, at the behest of the then prime minister, Lee Kuan Yew. Over the next six years he spread his commercial activities wide, acting as director for a number of publishing and media companies in Singapore, as well as continuing his connection with the Japanese engineering company Mitsubishi, for which he had begun working in 1973.

In 1988 Nathan was appointed high commissioner to Malaysia. Two years later he went to the USA as ambassador, and remained there until June 1996. When he returned he was appointed ambassador-at-large and also became director of the Institute of Defence and Strategic Studies, a defence think tank based at the Nanyang Technological University. He resigned from both positions to stand as president in 1999, and was elected to that office on 18 August 1999, as the only candidate, with the full support of Lee Kuan Yew (who had stepped down as prime minister in 1990, but remained powerful as senior minister). Nathan was inaugurated on 1 September.

He was sworn in for a second six-year term on 1 September 2005 after being declared re-elected unopposed on 17 August, ten days ahead of the scheduled poll. Three challengers had been ruled ineligible to stand by the authorities, triggering stirrings of discontent in a populace that rarely criticizes the ruling elite of the People's Action Party.

Profile of the Prime Minister:

LEE Hsien Loong

Lee Hsien Loong, the eldest son of Singapore's first prime minister Lee Kuan Yew, took over from Goh Chok Tong on 12 August 2004. Lee, who was aware that he was destined for high office since boyhood, graduated in mathematics from the University of Cambridge in the UK and achieved a master's degree in public administration from Harvard University in the USA. He then served in the Singapore armed forces, rising quickly to the rank of brigadier-general, before becoming a member of Parliament in 1984 and then deputy prime minister in 1990. Lee faces criticism over his family's monopolization of Singapore's power structure—the elder Lee intends to retain an important role in government, as an official 'minister mentor' to his son. He also faces the challenge of coping with Singapore's aging population, and the desire of his people to see some political liberalization, conspicuously absent under his father's rule.

Lee Hsien Loong was born on 10 February 1952 to Singapore's first prime minister Lee Kuan Yew and his wife Kwa Geok Choo. He was educated first at Singapore's Catholic High School, which required students to be proficient in both English and Mandarin. In addition to these two languages, he was proficient in Malay and had also studied Russian. Lee went on to the National Junior College, before joining the Singapore armed forces in 1971 for his national service. Lee spent part of his service at Cambridge University, UK, from which he graduated with first-class honours in mathematics and a diploma in computer science. He remained in the army until 1984, though in 1979 he attended the Mid-Career Programme at the Kennedy School of Government, Harvard University, USA, for a master's degree in public administration. Lee's first wife, with whom he had one son and one daughter, died of a heart attack in 1982. He married businesswoman Ho Ching in 1985 and they have had a further two sons.

Lee left the army in 1984 with the rank of brigadier-general in order to enter politics. He was elected member of Parliament in 1984, and re-elected in 1988, 1991, 1997 and 2001. He was elected to the central executive committee of the People's Action Party (PAP) in 1986 and was appointed deputy prime minister by Prime Minister Goh Chok Tong on 26 November 1990. He became chairman of the Monetary Authority of Singapore in January 1998, and minister of finance in November 2001, in which post he was credited with helping to secure Singapore's competitive edge amidst growing competition from China.

In 2003 Goh made it known that Lee would be his successor, and the members of the ruling PAP, which controls all but two seats in Parliament, duly selected him unanimously as prime minister, as did the party's executive committee and the cabinet. On 12 August 2004 Lee was sworn in as prime minister. He remains minister of finance but has handed the chairmanship of the Monetary Authority to Senior Minister Goh. Lee vowed to continue the careful liberalization of Singaporean society and its economy.

Critics of the administration note how tightly the net of the Lee family has wound itself around Singapore's governing apparatus; Lee senior, although over 80 years old, still sits in the cabinet as 'minister mentor' and supervises the Government Investment Corporation (GIC), which manages Singapore's foreign reserves. Meanwhile, Lee junior's wife, Ho Ching, runs Temasek, a government holding company that owns shares in many of Singapore's largest firms, and his brother, Lee Hsien Yang, runs Singapore Telecommunications. What most observers agree upon is that Lee must meet the expectations of three disparate social groups: blue-collar workers, the older middle classes and the professional elite.

SLOVAKIA

Full name: The Slovak Republic.

Leadership structure: The head of state is a president, directly elected for the first time in May 1999. The president's term of office is five years, renewable once only. The head of government is the prime minister, who is appointed by the president. The cabinet is appointed by the president on the recommendation of the prime minister.

President:	Rudolf Schuster	15 June 1999—15 June 2004
	Ivan **GAŠPAROVIČ**	Since 15 June 2004
Prime Minister:	Mikuláš **DZURINDA**	Since 30 Oct. 1998

Legislature: The legislature is unicameral. The sole chamber, the National Council of the Slovak Republic (Národná Rada Slovenskej Republiky), has 150 members, directly elected for a four-year term.

Profile of the President:

Ivan **GAŠPAROVIČ**

Ivan Gašparovič defeated former prime minister Vladimír Mečiar in the second round of the presidential elections in April 2004 on the eve of entry to the European Union (EU), taking office on 15 June 2004. A former colleague of Mečiar, he left the Movement for a Democratic Slovakia (Hnutie za Demokratické Slovensko—HZDS) in 2002 along with several other members in protest at Mečiar's autocratic leadership, despite having supported many of Mečiar's more controversial policies. Gašparovič apologized for past actions and overtook Mečiar in the second round of the elections after the candidates eliminated in the first round came out in his favour.

Ivan Gašparovič was born on 27 March 1941 in the town of Poltár near Lučenec and Banská Bystrica in south-central Slovakia. His father had migrated to Slovakia from Rijeka, Croatia, at the end of the First World War, and worked as a teacher at a secondary school in Bratislava. Ivan was educated at Komenský University, Bratislava, where he studied law. Upon graduation in 1964, he entered the public prosecutor's office in Martin. Between 1966 and 1989 he served as the vice chairman of the Czechoslovak Ice Hockey Federation

International Commission. He married Silvia Gašparovičová née Beníková in 1964 and they have one son and one daughter.

By 1966 Gašparovič had become Bratislava's municipal public prosecutor. Two years later he joined the Communist Party of Slovakia to support Alexander Dubček's reforms, but he was deprived of his party membership after the Warsaw Pact invasion of Czechoslovakia in August 1968. That year he acquired his doctorate and returned to Komenský University as a lecturer in the faculty of law, where he remained until 1990.

Gašparovič was appointed pro-rector in 1990, the year after the 'velvet revolution' that brought down the communist regime. He was chosen by President Václav Havel to become the prosecutor-general of Czechoslovakia based in Prague from July 1990 to March 1992, through a period of significant political upheaval. Then Gašparovič briefly became vice president of the Legislative Council of Czechoslovakia, before the country ceased to exist in January 1993; he was one of the authors of the new Slovakia's constitution.

In 1992 Gašparovič became a member of the HZDS, led by the charismatic and controversial Vladimír Mečiar. Prime minister from 1992 to 1998, Mečiar was constantly criticized by his opponents and the West for corruption, autocracy and the manner in which state assets were privatized under his rule. In 2002 Gašparovič resigned from the party after an internal split—his name did not appear on the ballot for that year's general election—and several others joined him from the HZDS to set up the Movement for Democracy (Hnutie za Demokraciu—HZD) party, of which he became the first leader. In the September election the HZD polled just 3.3% of the vote, not enough to win a seat, and Gašparovič returned to Komenský University and wrote several university textbooks as well as working papers and studies on criminal law.

Gašparovič apologized for his past support for Mečiar's controversial policies in the area of minority rights and tight controls on the media, and announced that he would stand against Mečiar in presidential elections in 2004. Mečiar won 32.7% of the first-round vote on 3 April in a surprise result that saw the government-backed favourite, Foreign Minister Eduard Kukan, trail in third place with just 22.1%. Mečiar and Gašparovič, who came second, went forward to the second round on 17 April. Gašparovič won the rerun with 59.9% of the vote after receiving the support of the eliminated candidates. He stepped down as HZD leader and pledged to remain above politics while in office.

Profile of the Prime Minister:

Mikuláš **DZURINDA**

Mikuláš Dzurinda has been prime minister of Slovakia since 30 October 1998. An ardent advocate of pro-market economics, he was brought to power at the head of a broad-based right-of-centre coalition which set integration with the West among its top priorities. Rifts within the coalition led Dzurinda to form a new party, the Slovak Democratic and Christian Union (Slovenská Demokratická a Krestanská Únia—SDKÚ), which went on to form a new conservative coalition after the September 2002 elections. He briefly held executive powers prior to the election of President Rudolf Schuster in 1999 and during his serious illness in 2000.

Mikuláš Dzurinda was born in Spišský Štvrtok, in the central mountain district of Spišská Nová Ves, on 4 February 1955. A student at the University of Transport and Communications in Žilina from 1974, he began working at the city's transport research institute in 1979, having graduated the previous year. In 1980 he moved to the Slovak capital, Bratislava, to work in the information technologies section of the Czechoslovak State Transport agency. From 1988 he headed the agency's automated controls section. He is married to Eva Dzurindová and they have two daughters.

In 1991 Dzurinda began his political career in the emergent democracy and was appointed deputy transport minister in the Slovakian government. In elections in 1992, preceding independence, Dzurinda entered the National Council. He was affiliated to the Christian Democratic Movement and was appointed its vice chairman in 1993 with responsibility for economic policy. Strong resistance to attempts by the authoritarian Prime Minister Vladimír Mečiar to weaken opposition parties led to the formation of the Slovak Democratic Coalition (Slovenská Demokratická Koalícia—SDK) in 1997, with Dzurinda as its unofficial head, a role formalized in July 1998. Mečiar's Movement for a Democratic Slovakia (Hnutie za Demokratické Slovensko—HZDS) remained the largest single party in parliament by just one seat in elections held that October. Unable to find coalition partners it was left to Dzurinda and the SDK to form a new broad centre-right coalition and Dzurinda was duly appointed prime minister. One of his first tasks was to sweep away the Mečiar regime. The corruption-prone police force was overhauled and amnesties granted to those involved in high-level scandals were quickly withdrawn (although the Constitutional Court later overruled Dzurinda's right to revoke the amnesties).

With an eye constantly on the objective of European integration, Dzurinda was quick to start reforming the economy to meet international criteria and 'catch up' with neighbouring states already in membership discussions with the European Union (EU). In November 1998 he secured an agreement establishing a committee to identify the key areas in need of reform. Negotiations for Slovakia's entry began in March 2000, and the country was invited in December 2002 to become a full member from May 2004, the same year that it also became a member of the North Atlantic Treaty Organization (NATO).

Along with changes to the economy, a priority for the new government was the introduction of direct elections for the presidency. Since early 1998 the post had been left vacant due to parliamentary disagreements, with the prime minister wielding executive powers in the interim. The election of the pro-Western Rudolf Schuster in May 1999 was seen as a positive step towards integration. However, when Schuster fell seriously ill in 2000 Dzurinda was roundly criticized by the opposition, and Schuster himself, for quickly adopting executive powers along with the speaker of the National Council. Schuster resumed his full duties towards the end of the year.

The disunity of the SDK government quickly became a cause for concern. Tensions were heightened when Dzurinda's ardent pro-NATO stance forced colleagues to give grudging support to the bombing campaign against Yugoslavia in 1999. The cracks in the coalition deepened and in January 2000 Dzurinda spearheaded the formation of a new political group, the SDKÚ, but insisted it would not become a separate group in parliament for the rest of its term. Despite vocal opposition from within and without the ruling coalition, Dzurinda survived a vote of no confidence in April 2000, and a referendum calling for early elections failed to attract sufficient public support in November. The SDKÚ was finally transformed into a full party in November 2001 and Dzurinda was elected its leader.

Although the HZDS still retained its position as the largest single party after the September 2002 elections, it again failed to form a ruling coalition. Dzurinda's SDKÚ came in second in a field dominated by new parties. He cobbled together a new conservative four-party coalition, successfully excluding both the authoritarian HZDS and the populist Direction Party–Third Way, which had taken the third-largest share of seats on its electoral debut.

SLOVENIA

Full name: The Republic of Slovenia.

Leadership structure: The head of state is a president, directly elected by universal adult suffrage. The president's term of office is five years. The head of government is the prime minister, who is nominated by the president, and elected by the National Assembly. The prime minister appoints a cabinet, which must be approved by the National Assembly.

President:	Milan Kučan	Since 10 May 1990
	(president of the state presidency until 22 Dec. 1992)	
	Janez **DRNOVŠEK**	Since 23 Dec. 2002
Prime Minister:	Janez Drnovšek	14 May 1992—3 May 2000
	Andrej Bajuk	3 May 2000—1 Dec. 2000
	Janez Drnovšek	1 Dec. 2000—23 Dec. 2002
	Anton Rop	23 Dec. 2002—9 Nov. 2004
	Janez **JANŠA**	Since 9 Nov. 2004

Legislature: The legislature is unicameral. The sole chamber, the National Assembly (Državni Zbor), has 90 members, directly elected for a four-year term. The National Council (Državni Svet), with 40 indirectly elected members, has an advisory role.

Profile of the President:

Janez **DRNOVŠEK**

Before his election as president at the end of 2002, Janez Drnovšek had been prime minister for almost the whole decade of Slovenia's existence as an independent state. An economist by training, he led the Liberal Democracy of Slovenia (Liberalna Demokracija Slovenije—LDS) party, which was a major element in successive coalition governments. He stepped down as party leader in order to become president.

Janez Drnovšek was born on 17 May 1950 in Celje, some 60 km northeast of Ljubljana. He obtained a doctorate in economics at the University of Maribor, near the Austrian border, in 1986, with a thesis entitled *The International Monetary Fund and Yugoslavia*. Having completed his education, he worked first with a construction company, then as chief executive of a branch of Ljubljanska Bank and finally as adviser on economic affairs at the Yugoslav embassy in Egypt. He is the author of numerous articles in the area of finance, and speaks many languages including English, German, Italian, French and Spanish. He is divorced and has two children.

Drnovšek first emerged as a prominent political figure in 1989, as the then Socialist Federal Republic of Yugoslavia (SFRY) began to enter the period of its fragmentation into its constituent republics. He was elected as the Slovenian representative to the collective SFRY presidency, standing as an independent and defeating the communist candidate in the first genuinely contested election of its kind. Between 1989 and 1990 he was president of the presidency under its principle of annual rotation between republics. In this capacity he headed the Non-Aligned Movement and chaired the Non-Aligned Summit in Belgrade in September 1989. In October 1990, however, he withdrew from the SFRY presidency, protesting over its manipulation by its new Serbian president.

The progressive disintegration of Yugoslavia from the late 1980s was dramatically accelerated when Slovenia and Croatia simultaneously declared independence on 25 June 1991; federal Yugoslav troops failed in their attempt to reverse these declarations by military action. Drnovšek was the main Slovenian negotiator with the Yugoslav People's Army in talks brokered by European Community intermediaries, which resulted in a ceasefire agreement in July and the international recognition of independent Slovenia (and Croatia) by early 1992.

Drnovšek was a founder of the LDS, a secular centre-left party which, in the December 1992 general election, won the highest number of seats in parliament. Drnovšek had by this time already been prime minister for seven months, having been appointed after the collapse in April of Slovenia's first postindependence government led by Lojze Peterle. He required the support of four other parties to form a coalition in January 1993. During his first period in office Drnovšek focused on the economic transformation of the country to a free-market system.

A general election in November 1996 increased the parliamentary representation of the LDS from 22 to 25 out of 90 seats but gave the centre-right opposition Slovenian Spring grouping control of 45 seats. It was only in March 1997 that Drnovšek eventually succeeded in forming a four-party coalition, having failed in his bid to create a 'national unity' government. However, this was then undermined in March 2000 when two of the parties agreed to merge and withdraw from the government. Without a parliamentary majority Drnovšek was forced to resign. In opposition he gained in popularity, especially as the replacement government of Andrej Bajuk struggled against a hostile parliament.

In legislative elections held on 15 October 2000 the LDS won an impressive 34 seats becoming by far the biggest party in the National Assembly. Weeks of negotiations led to the formation of a new four-party coalition.

Throughout Drnovšek's career as prime minister, Slovenia's closer integration with western Europe was the key priority. In March 1994 Slovenia joined the Partnership for Peace programme of the North Atlantic Treaty Organization (NATO), but was left out of the first round of NATO expansion announced in mid-1997. In June 1996 Drnovšek signed an association agreement with the European Union (EU) and negotiations for membership began in November 1998. Accession to both bodies was achieved in 2004.

Amid growing speculation Drnovšek confirmed in October 2002 that he would seek the presidency in elections held on 10 November. Campaigning while still in office as prime minister, he was forced to a runoff on 1 December against former chief prosecutor, and independent candidate, Barbara Brezigar. In the event, Drnovšek was victorious, gaining 56.5% of the vote. He handed over the role of prime minister, and leadership of the LDS, to his finance minister Anton Rop and was inaugurated on 23 December.

Profile of the Prime Minister:

Janez **JANŠA**

Janez Janša was a youth activist whose arrest in the late 1980s helped to trigger the Slovenian Spring that ultimately led to the country's independence from Yugoslavia in 1991. He served as minister of defence following the first democratic elections in 1990 and is credited with helping to reconstitute the Slovenian Armed Forces from the rump of the Territorial Defence Force, the efficiency of which contributed to the war for Slovenia's independence from Yugoslavia lasting just ten days. Janša's Slovenian Democratic Party (Slovenska Demokratska Stranka—SDS) won legislative elections in 2004 and he was elected prime minister of Slovenia by parliament on 9 November 2004.

Janez Janša was born Ivan Janša on 17 September 1958 in the city of Ljubljana. He graduated with a degree in defence studies from the University of Ljubljana in 1982 before sitting professional exams at the Republican Secretariat for Defence. He was appointed president of the Committee for Basic People's Defence, part of the Alliance of Socialist Youth of Slovenia, and the following year drafted a paper highly critical of conditions within Yugoslavia's army that set his reputation as a dissident; the security forces were ordered to confiscate and destroy all copies of the paper. Janša was put under surveillance and he was prevented from standing for re-election to his post.

By 1985 Janša's passport had been confiscated and his prospects of employment had withered. Supporting himself by computer programming, he became increasingly politically active, and in 1986 became secretary of the *Journal for the Criticism of Science*, writing and publishing articles on democracy, sovereignty and liberalization.

In May 1988 Janša was arrested and detained in solitary confinement in the military prison of Metelkova in Ljubljana. Three others were detained and prosecuted along with him in what became known as the 'Trial of the Four'. Janša was eventually sentenced to 18 months' imprisonment but not before the trial, held in a military court in Serbo-Croat, had sparked mass demonstrations and the start of the Slovenian Spring; tens of thousands of people joined the new Committee for the Protection of Human Rights and public pressure forced Janša's transfer from a maximum-security jail to an open prison. It was at one of these demonstrations that the May Declaration of 1989—demanding democracy and Slovenian sovereignty—was first read, and by the summer of that year Janša had been released after serving just a third of his sentence.

On his release Janša became the editor of the weekly *Demokracija* which became the unofficial voice of Demos, the united opposition. He also helped found the Slovene Democratic Alliance (Slovenska Demokratična Zveza—SDZ), the country's first true opposition party. In Slovenia's first democratic elections in April 1990 he was elected to parliament representing the SDZ. Janša became minister of defence for the united Demos coalition government, and was partly responsible for turning the Territorial Defence Force into the Slovenian Armed Forces. Following a referendum on independence in December 1990, Slovenia formally seceded from Yugoslavia in 1991 sparking a ten-day war; the newly reconstituted army proving invaluable in minimizing casualties and allowing the country to proclaim full independence.

The SDZ disintegrated by the autumn of 1991 and Janša joined the SDS in 1992. Janša was dismissed as minister of defence in March 1994 after allegations that army officials had beaten up an employee of the interior ministry. Though the situation was unclear, it was obvious that the interior and defence ministries had been effectively spying on one another. Nonetheless, Janša's dismissal sparked large demonstrations and the SDS gained over 5,000 new members.

Janša was re-elected in the legislative elections of 1996 following which the SDS became the main Slovenian opposition party. He was appointed minister of defence again in the short-lived government of Andrej Bajuk in 2000, and in October of that year was re-elected in legislative elections once again.

In the October 2004 election, the SDS took just over 30% of the vote making it the largest party in the National Assembly, and Janša was elected prime minister by the legislature with 57 of 90 votes.

Janša has written several books and hundreds of articles and has spoken at several high-level conferences on defence and geostrategic issues. He has pledged that the focus of his administration will be consolidating Slovenia's good international standing and ensuring that a balance is struck between a market orientation and social values.

SOLOMON ISLANDS

Full name: The Solomon Islands.

Leadership structure: The head of state is the British sovereign, styled 'Queen of the Solomon Islands, and of Her other Realms and Territories, Head of the Commonwealth', and represented by a governor-general who is chosen by Parliament. The head of government is the prime minister, who is elected by members of Parliament from among their number. The cabinet is appointed by the governor-general on the recommendation of the prime minister.

Queen:	Elizabeth II	Since 6 Feb. 1952
Governor-General:	Sir John Lapli	7 July 1999—7 July 2004
	Sir Nathaniel **WAENA**	Since 7 July 2004
Prime Minister:	Bartholomew Ulufa'alu	30 Aug. 1997—30 June 2000
	Manasseh Sogavare	30 June 2000—17 Dec. 2001
	Sir Allan **KEMAKEZA**	Since 17 Dec. 2001

Legislature: The legislature is unicameral. The sole chamber, the National Parliament, has 50 members, directly elected for a four-year term.

Profile of the Governor-General:

Sir Nathaniel **WAENA**

Sir Nathaniel Waena was elected as governor-general of the Solomon Islands in June 2004, and took office on 7 July. He had previously held senior government posts, most recently as minister for peace and national reconciliation.

Nathaniel Rahumaea Waena was born on Ulawa Island in the Makira-Ulawa province of the Solomon Islands and was a member of parliament for the Ulawa-Ugi constituency from its inception in the mid-1980s until his election as governor-general. In June 2000, following the ousting of Prime Minister Bartholomew Ulufa'alu, Waena was appointed as assistant prime minister and minister of provincial government and rural development in the national unity government headed by Manasseh Sogavare. During this time he promoted trade links between the outlying provinces and other nearby Pacific island nations. Following the December 2001 legislative elections he was appointed minister for peace and national reconciliation in the government of Sir Allan Kemakeza, and oversaw the arrival of the Australian-led Regional Assistance Mission to Solomon Islands (RAMSI) to quell continuing civil unrest.

Waena was elected as the fifth governor-general of the Solomon Islands by Parliament on 15 June 2004, with 27 of 41 votes, against six for incumbent Sir John Lapli and eight for former prime minister Sir Peter Kenilorea. He was sworn in for a five-year term on 7 July 2004, the 26th anniversary of the country's independence. Shortly afterwards he received a knighthood, though he wasn't officially invested with it until May 2005 when he made his first official visit to the UK, accompanied by Lady Waena.

He has called for action to address social problems such as population pressure, illiteracy and youth unemployment, as well as other issues such as deforestation and the use of aid.

Profile of the Prime Minister:

Sir Allan **KEMAKEZA**

Sir Allan Kemakeza has led the ruling People's Alliance Party (PAP) since 2001. Originally a policeman, he entered politics in 1989 and has represented his home constituency of Savo/Russells ever since. Despite controversy over the destination of compensation payments for the two-year civil conflict, which saw him sacked as deputy prime minister in August 2001, he was elected prime minister four months later after the PAP was victorious in general elections. The issue of compensation still plagues Kemakeza and threatens to bankrupt the country.

Allan Kemakeza was born in 1951 in Panueli village on Savo Island, to the north of Honiara. After a local education he enlisted in the Royal Solomon Islands Police Force in 1972 when the country was still a colony of the UK. (Independence was achieved in 1978.) He remained in the force for 17 years, rising to the rank of assistant superintendent. During his police career he attended policing courses in the UK and Australia. In the late 1980s he worked closely with the Solomons' first governor-general, Sir Baddeley Devesi.

In 1989 Kemakeza resigned his commission and entered politics. He won a seat in the National Parliament representing Savo and the Russell Islands. Solomon Mamaloni, the leader of the PAP, was elected prime minister for a second time and he appointed Kemakeza as minister of housing and government services. Kemakeza's political career remained linked to that of Mamaloni throughout the 1990s. The government coalition was defeated in 1993, but Mamaloni returned in 1995 and Kemakeza was appointed minister of forests, environment and conservation. Mamaloni was defeated again in elections held in 1997 and Kemakeza found himself out of ministerial office once more.

Ethnic tensions between the indigenous Guadalcanal, or Isatabu, islanders and immigrants from neighbouring Malaita Island exploded in 1998 into full-scale civil war. In June 2000 the conflict came to a head when the Malaita Eagle Force kidnapped Prime Minister Bartholomew Ulufa'alu, and a new unity government was formed under opposition leader and former finance minister Manasseh Sogavare. Kemakeza was reappointed to the cabinet, this time as deputy prime minister and, most importantly, minister for peace and national reconciliation. He approached the role with gusto, falling back on his experience in the police and engaging the rebels face-to-face. He proved pivotal in organizing peace talks, which eventually produced the breakthrough Townsville Peace Accord, and he received a knighthood for his efforts, his wife becoming Lady Jocelyn Kemakeza.

Under the terms of the accord, Kemakeza supervised the creation of a fund to pay compensation for damages caused during the conflict. In August 2001 Kemakeza was publicly sacked by Sogavare for paying himself compensation for property on Savo which had been looted by rebels. He had already been forced to admit in July that claims had outstripped the US$25 million fund provided by Taiwan. Nonetheless, he denied any wrongdoing and suggested that Sogavare was instead attempting to secure his own position in government. In elections in December the PAP, of which Kemakeza had become party leader, regained its position as one of the Solomon Islands' main political parties, emerging as the largest single party in the National Parliament. Kemakeza was duly elected prime minister.

Faced with continuing unrest and economic problems exacerbated by the mounting compensation claims, Kemakeza's government brought in the Australian-led Regional Assistance Mission to Solomon Islands (RAMSI) in 2003 to disarm rebels and root out corruption in order to rebuild stability. Several ministers have been arrested, though Kemakeza himself has not been targeted, despite plenty of accusations against him from both home and abroad. Criticism of RAMSI's 'takeover' of the Solomon Islands' internal administrative affairs has also provoked ministerial resignations and a motion of no confidence in the government in February 2005, which Kemakeza survived.

A new draft federation constitution was presented to the government by the advisory committee in July 2005; it proposes decentralization and the replacement of the British monarch as head of state with an elected president.

That same month, while visiting Expo 2005 in Japan, Kemakeza paid a controversial visit to the Yasukuni Shrine, which honours Japan's war dead, including several people judged as war criminals. He said, "Solomon Islands and Japan [have] the common culture to appreciate their ancestors. I want to see the place where souls are enshrined."

SOMALIA

Full name: Somalia.

Leadership structure: Dominated through the 1990s by conflict between rival warlords, Somalia in August 2000 established a Transitional National Assembly (inaugurated in Djibouti but later moved to the Somali capital, Mogadishu), and a president was elected by that assembly. The president named a prime minister in October, and the prime minister in turn named an interim government a month later. Powerful warlords refused to recognize this regime, as did secessionists in Somaliland, which had declared independence in 1991, and in Puntland, which had declared its autonomy in 1998 pending the formation of a federal system of national government. In March 2001 the main warlords held a reconciliation conference and named a rival Council. An internationally backed conference was called in October 2002 in Kenya. The president refused to attend unless he was fully recognized as head of state, but representatives of his interim government did take part. A deal was reached on 5 July 2003 under which a new transitional parliament would be appointed and a new national government set up to hold power until elections in 2007. An agreement, which was based on a new federal structure, was eventually signed in January 2004 by representatives of the president and of the regional regime in Puntland, and by many of the warlords. The new Transitional National Assembly was sworn in, still in Kenya, in August and it elected a national president in October, who appointed a prime minister a month later. The prime minister nominated a cabinet, approved by the Assembly.

Transitional President:

vacant (since overthrow of Siyad Barre regime)	26 Jan. 1991—27 Aug. 2000
Abdulkassim Salat Hassan	27 Aug. 2000—14 Oct. 2004
Abdullahi Yusuf **AHMED**	Since 14 Oct. 2004

Transitional Prime Minister:

vacant (since overthrow of Siyad Barre regime)	26 Jan. 1991—8 Oct. 2000
Ali Khalif Galayadh	8 Oct. 2000—28 Oct. 2001
Osman Jama Ali (acting)	28 Oct. 2001—12 Nov. 2001
Hassan Abshir Farah	12 Nov. 2001—9 Aug. 2003
vacant	9 Aug. 2003—8 Dec. 2003

Muhammad Abdi Yusuf	8 Dec. 2003—3 Nov. 2004
Ali Muhammad **GHEDI**	Since 3 Nov. 2004

Legislature: The Transitional National Assembly inaugurated in Djibouti on 13 August 2000, which later transferred to Mogadishu, had 245 members. The new Transitional National Assembly inaugurated in Kenya on 29 August 2004 has 275 members.

Profile of the Transitional President:

Abdullahi Yusuf **AHMED**

Abdullahi Yusuf Ahmed was elected transitional president of Somalia on 10 October 2004 by the transitional government sitting in exile in Nairobi, Kenya, and was sworn in four days later. Originally a commander in the Somali national army, Ahmed fled to Kenya following an unsuccessful coup against President Siyad Barre in 1978 and launched a guerrilla war. He returned to Somalia in 1991 after Siyad Barre was ousted, rising to pre-eminence in his native Puntland, which he declared autonomous in 1998. As Somali president he has appointed a prime minister whose clan has connections in the Somali capital Mogadishu.

Abdullahi Yusuf Ahmed was born on 15 December 1934 in Gaalkacyo in the now autonomous region of Puntland, Somalia. He is the leader of the Darod clan, one of the five main clans in the country. Ahmed was educated in Italy and in the Soviet Union. He neither smokes nor drinks and is married with four children.

Ahmed became a commander in the army in the 1960s, but was jailed by fellow clansman and officer Gen. Siyad Barre in 1969 for refusing to take part in the military coup that brought the latter to power. He spent some time while in jail with Somali warlord Mohammed Farah Aydid. Ahmed was released in 1975, but three years later unsuccessfully attempted to overthrow Siyad Barre and was forced to flee to Kenya.

While in Kenya, Ahmed began a guerrilla movement aimed at unseating Siyad Barre, backed by the Ethiopian government—then at war with Somalia. However, he broke with Ethiopia over the government's claim to Somali territory, and in 1985 found himself imprisoned once again, this time in the Ethiopian capital Addis Ababa. He languished in jail for six years, until the disintegration of the Mengistu regime in 1991. On his release he returned to his native Puntland, where he soon came to pre-eminence. After the ouster of Siyad Barre in 1991, Somalia was plunged into civil war and chaos, with mass starvation. Ahmed declared Puntland autonomous of Somalia in 1998 and became its president.

Ahmed, along with other warlords outside Mogadishu, opposed the transitional national government formed in 2000, which effectively became just another faction among the many battling for a share of power in Somalia. Ahmed asked for his term as Puntland president to be lengthened in 2001, but instead Jama Ali Jama was elected by the traditional elders to replace him, and Ahmed launched a war for power, claiming that he was fighting terrorism. He seized control of Jama's last stronghold Boosaaso in May 2002, reportedly with the backing of Ethiopian forces.

Having joined the internationally backed conference on Somalia held in Kenya from October 2002, two years later on 10 October 2004 Ahmed won 179 of 270 parliamentary votes in the third round of elections for the transitional presidency of Somalia. He has since formed a government under Prime Minister Ali Muhammad Ghedi. Known for his authoritarian leadership style, Ahmed surprised many by beginning his presidency by asking forgiveness from his opponents. The security situation in Somalia remains volatile and the government infrastructure nonexistent.

Profile of the Prime Minister:

Ali Muhammad **GHEDI**

Ali Muhammad Ghedi, a former vet and university lecturer, was chosen in late 2004 as prime minister in Somalia's transitional government, then based in Kenya. A Hawiye clan member from Mogadishu, he provides a useful balance to President Abdullahi Yusuf Ahmed (a member of the Darod clan from the Puntland region) in the ethnic makeup of the transitional regime.

Ali Muhammad Ghedi was born in 1952 in Mogadishu where he was educated before studying veterinary medicine in universities in Somalia and in Italy. He worked as a lecturer and researcher at the Somali National University until the outbreak of the civil war in 1991, when the university was destroyed. Ghedi then concentrated on acting as a special adviser to bodies working with the livestock trade, which is crucial to Somalia's economy and which was devastated by the conflict. He also supervised an internationally funded animal disease control programme from exile in Nairobi in Kenya. He is married with several children.

Ghedi was not linked to any armed groups during the war; he is a member of Mogadishu's Hawiye clan, and observers say that his appointment as prime minister is part of a delicate balancing attempt by President Ahmed, who is a member of the Darod clan which is unpopular in the capital. Ghedi was nominated for the post of prime minister on 3 November 2004. However, on 11 December the parliament-in-exile in Kenya dismissed Ghedi and his government for not having been formally approved by them, as well as complaining that the new cabinet did not share power equally among the five major clans. The president renominated Ghedi three days later, requesting a vote of confidence in a revised cabinet. He was finally confirmed as prime minister by the parliament-in-exile on 13 January 2005.

SOUTH AFRICA

Full name: The Republic of South Africa.

Leadership structure: The head of state is a president, elected by the National Assembly. The president's term of office is five years, renewable once only. The head of government is the president, who is responsible to Parliament. The cabinet is appointed by the president.

President:　　　　　　　Thabo **MBEKI**　　　　　　Since 16 June 1999

Legislature: The legislature, the Parliament, is bicameral. The lower chamber, the National Assembly (Volksraad), has 400 members, directly elected for a five-year term. The upper chamber, the National Council of Provinces (Nationale Raad van Provinses), has 90 members, indirectly elected (ten for each of the nine provinces) for a five-year term.

Profile of the President:

Thabo **MBEKI**

Thabo Mbeki, who succeeded the renowned South African leader Nelson Mandela in 1999 and thus became his country's second post-apartheid president, had worked in exile during the apartheid years as a representative of the African National Congress (ANC), and was central to the negotiations which brought the apartheid regime to an end in 1990. A one-time student activist and lifelong socialist who completed his university education in the UK in the mid-1960s, Mbeki benefited from Mandela's endorsement. As president he has faced a rising tide of crime and lawlessness in the country's inner cities, and the serious threat of the AIDS epidemic.

Thabo Mvuyelwa Mbeki was born on 18 June 1942 in Idutywa, Transkei. His parents were both civil rights activists. His father, Govan Mbeki, was a leading figure in the local ANC and headed the movement's Youth League (ANCYL) which Thabo joined in 1956. After receiving his primary education in Idutywa and Butterworth, Thabo went on to high school in Alice, Ciskei, from where he was expelled in 1959 for taking part in student strikes. He completed his secondary education from home and studied for British 'A-level' qualifications between 1960 and 1961. His British education extended to include a correspondence degree course in economics with the University of London, from 1961 to 1962, and eventually full enrolment at the University of Sussex, where he received a master's degree in economics in 1966.

Mbeki's political radicalism began when he joined the ANCYL. In the early 1960s he was actively involved in various underground activities, including a student strike against the move to take South Africa out of the Commonwealth in 1961. In the same year he was elected as secretary of the African Students' Association (ASA). With the apartheid government stepping up its counterinsurgency measures (which dealt the ASA a fatal blow, and led to the arrest and life imprisonment of Govan Mbeki), Thabo Mbeki, along with many other young activists, was urged to leave the country by the ANC. In 1962 he travelled first to Southern Rhodesia (modern Zimbabwe) and then via Tanganyika (modern Tanzania) to the UK.

After completing his master's degree in 1966, Mbeki formalized his activism by working for the ANC's London office for three years from 1967. In 1970 the ANC, which was still essentially a revolutionary organization, sent Mbeki to undergo military training with its international ally, the Soviet Union. The following year Mbeki returned to Africa to work at the office of the revolutionary council of the ANC in Lusaka, Zambia, as an assistant secretary.

For the next seven years Mbeki travelled through southern Africa as a representative of the ANC and worked to establish foreign departments, earning himself the unofficial title of ANC 'foreign minister'. During this period he married the businesswoman and active feminist Zanele Dlamini in 1974. Together they have two children; a third child born before 1974 was reported as missing in the 1980s.

From 1973 to 1974 Mbeki worked in Botswana, before moving on to Swaziland. In both countries he worked to strengthen the ANC infrastructure in southern Africa, and in 1975 he was appointed to the movement's National Executive Committee (NEC). From 1976 to 1978 he played the same role in Nigeria until returning to Lusaka to work in the office of the ANC president, Oliver Tambo.

From 1984 to 1990 Mbeki was deeply involved in the ANC's transition from revolutionary force to democratic movement, and was vital in the discussions with the white minority government. In these years he worked through various ANC roles: as the director of the movement's department of information and publicity, secretary for presidential affairs, and member of the political and military councils. He has been credited with doing much to turn the international community against apartheid, and so to facilitate the regime's crippling isolation. He also led ANC delegations in significant communication with South African representatives, including a meeting with members of the country's business community at Mfuwe, Zambia, in 1985, and with the Institute for a Democratic Alternative for South Africa at Dakar, Senegal, in 1987. The crowning achievement of this period of tense negotiation came in 1989 when Mbeki joined other high-level members of the ANC in direct secret talks with the South African government which led to the lifting of the ban on the ANC.

From that point onward, Mbeki worked closely on the negotiations leading to the adoption of South Africa's interim nonracial constitution in 1993, in which year he was also elected as chairman of the ANC. After the first democratic elections in 1994, newly elected President Mandela appointed Mbeki as his deputy and thereby singled him out as his ultimate successor. Three years later Mbeki took over the presidency of the ANC and his position seemed set, although to the public he was still largely an unknown. To win hearts as well as minds, Mbeki embarked on a process to humanize the public's image of him as a cold efficient ruler whose only known habits were pipe smoking and reading English poetry and economic tomes. Obliged to engage the populace, he swapped formal suits for the more colourful approach already used by Mandela.

Mbeki had sufficient success in cultivating this new image to see the ANC under his leadership reaffirmed as the dominant power in South Africa at the June 1999 elections, when it won two-thirds of the vote and 266 seats in the 400-seat National Assembly. The Assembly duly elected Mbeki as president and he was inaugurated on 16 June 1999. As president he confirmed his commitment to the ANC's policy of steady reform, while urging a faster pace to combat social and economic crises.

Mbeki's international image suffered greatly following a speech in April 2000 in which he expressed personal doubt over the accepted connection between the HIV virus and AIDS, an enormous problem in southern Africa where 50% of young people are expected ultimately to succumb to the disease. Mbeki vociferously opposed what he called "Western solutions" to a "uniquely African catastrophe". Critics have claimed that his opinions led to the South African government's failure to respond adequately to the epidemic, and in April 2002 the cabinet appeared to overrule the president when it issued a statement saying that its starting point in dealing with the epidemic was the premise that HIV causes AIDS.

He has also lost face with the West through his support for Zimbabwean president Robert Mugabe; his steadfast refusal to condemn the regime led to tensions even with other African leaders. Nonetheless, Mbeki is highly regarded among political elites across the continent and has led peace talks within Kenya, Sudan, the Democratic Republic of the Congo, Gabon and Côte d'Ivoire. With an earnest, rather academic mien, Mbeki is not a traditional 'big man' and lacks the charismatic authority of his predecessor—and many of his counterparts—trading instead on South Africa's political and economic dominance of the continent.

Nevertheless, in elections in April 2004, Mbeki's ANC scooped a record 70% of the vote, a huge landslide that gave it the two-thirds' majority needed to change the constitution should it choose—though the party has said it has no intention of doing so. Some high-profile domestic critics are concerned that Mbeki's unfettered authority may undermine the democracy won at such cost. In November 2004 Archbishop Desmond Tutu delivered a stinging attack on Mbeki, warning that a culture of "sycophantic, obsequious conformity" was emerging around the president, as he surrounded himself with "yes-men". Mbeki returned that Tutu was a "creation of the media", and an "icon of the white people".

Despite these concerns over his democratic pedigree, Mbeki has retained the respect of many for his stewardship of the economy. His reforms are finally beginning to show results, with sustained growth and low inflation holding out the prospect of delivering the reduction of poverty which has long been Mbeki's desired legacy to South Africa.

Mbeki, who is required by the constitution to step down at the end of his current term, sacked his expected successor, Vice President Jacob Zuma, in June 2005 after he was implicated in corruption. The dismissal shocked many of his supporters and caused something of a schism within the ANC.

SPAIN

Full name: The Kingdom of Spain.

Leadership structure: The head of state is a constitutional monarch. The head of government is the president of the government (prime minister), who is appointed by the king. The Council of Ministers is appointed by the king on the recommendation of the president of the government.

King:	**JUAN CARLOS I** de Borbón	Since 22 Nov. 1975
	(acting from 30 Oct. 1975)	

President of the Government:

José María Aznar López	6 May 1996—17 April 2004
José Luis **RODRÍGUEZ ZAPATERO**	Since 17 April 2004

Legislature: The legislature, the Cortes (Cortes Generales), is bicameral. The lower chamber, the Congress of Deputies (Congreso de los Diputados), has 350 members, directly elected for a four-year term. The upper chamber, the Senate (Senado), has 259 members, 208 directly elected and 51 indirectly elected, for a four-year term.

Profile of the King:

JUAN CARLOS I de Borbón

Juan Carlos I was proclaimed king of Spain in November 1975, following the death of Gen. Francisco Franco, whose right-wing dictatorship dated from his military uprising in 1936 at the onset of the civil war. The country had become a republic in 1931, but Franco declared it in 1947 to be a monarchy (without a monarch), and designated Juan Carlos as heir to the throne in 1969. Spain is now a parliamentary monarchy, and the duties of the king are mainly ceremonial, although Juan Carlos has gained considerable moral authority by showing his commitment on occasions of crisis to upholding the constitution.

Juan Carlos de Borbón y Borbón was born on 5 January 1938 in Rome. Initially educated in Italy, Switzerland and Portugal, Juan Carlos first went to Spain at the age of ten, when Franco announced his wish to groom him as his successor. He completed his schooling at the San Isidro School in Madrid in 1954, then studied at the army, navy and air force academies, and finally in 1961 studied law and economics at Madrid's Complutense University. In 1962 he went to live at the

Palacio de la Zarzuela, on the outskirts of Madrid. In July 1969 Franco officially designated the prince as his successor.

Juan Carlos became provisional head of state on 30 October 1975, in the last weeks of Franco's terminal illness, and was formally declared king on 22 November, becoming also commander-in-chief of the armed forces and head of the Supreme Council of Defence. In his first message to the nation as king he expressed his intent to restore democracy and to become king of all Spaniards, without exception. He hastened reform in July 1976 by appointing a new head of government, Adolfo Suárez, and supporting him at critical junctures thereafter. Multiparty elections in June 1977 were followed by a referendum in December 1978 to approve a new constitution. This constitution was ratified by the king, who also supported the progressive devolution of powers to the regions.

Meanwhile in May 1977 his father, the count of Barcelona, transferred his dynastic rights to Juan Carlos, together with his position as head of the Royal Household. (He had ruled out his own reinstatement by refusing to swear allegiance to the principles of the Franco period.)

In February 1981, when a group of Civil Guards stormed the parliament building, Juan Carlos acted swiftly to secure the loyalty of other branches of the armed forces and thus restore the democratic process. His actions earned him widespread respect both within the armed forces and among the wider population. Since then he has assumed a more traditional role as constitutional monarch, touring every continent and addressing many international organizations, including the UN. He has had a particular impact in relations with Latin America, emphasizing the common cultural community.

Juan Carlos married Princess Sofía of Greece on 14 May 1962 in Athens. They have three children, Princess Elena, Princess Cristina and Prince Felipe.

Profile of the President of the Government:

José Luis **RODRÍGUEZ ZAPATERO**

José Luis Rodríguez Zapatero was sworn in as president of the government (prime minister) of Spain on 17 April 2004 following the surprise general election victory in March of his Spanish Socialist Workers' Party (Partido Socialista Obrero Español—PSOE). The election had taken place in the shadow of Spain's worst terrorist atrocity in recent years, the Madrid train bombings that killed more than 200 people on 11 March. The government of José María Aznar initially insisted that Basque separatist movement ETA was responsible for the bombings, despite growing suspicions that al-Qaida was involved. Criticism of the government's handling of events grew vociferous and protests were staged in many cities against both terrorism and Aznar's government. Meanwhile Zapatero reiterated his party's promise to withdraw Spanish troops from their widely unpopular deployment in Iraq, a vow he fulfilled upon election despite howls of protest from other politicians and governments, who accused him of capitulation. Zapatero immediately began to help establish an alternative axis of European power, hosting a mini-summit of French and German leaders in September 2004.

José Luis Rodríguez Zapatero was born on 4 August 1960 in Valladolid, though he grew up in León from where his family originates. Zapatero (as he is known in Spain, though his surname is Rodríguez) is the son of a prominent lawyer; his grandfather, a freemason and a Republican captain, was executed in León in 1936 by Nationalists during the Spanish Civil War. José became a member of the PSOE in 1979, despite being legally too young to do so, after hearing then Prime Minister Felipe González speak at a political rally in Gijón. Zapatero married Sonsoles Espinosa, a lawyer and opera singer, in 1990, and the couple have two daughters, Laura and Alba.

After studying law at the University of León, in 1982 he became head of the socialist youth organization in the province of León. In 1986 he was elected to represent the province of León, becoming, at 26, the youngest member of the Cortes. In 1988 he was elected to head the regional chapter of the PSOE in León, and in 1997 he was appointed to the party's governing body.

Economic crisis, scandals of corruption and alleged state terrorism against Basque separatists had gradually eroded the popularity both of Felipe González and his party. By 2000 the PSOE had lost its second successive election to the People's Party (Partido Popular—PP) of José María Aznar by an embarrassing margin, and an opportunity was open to a young modernizer; Zapatero, representing a faction known as 'Nueva Vía' (New Way), was elected leader of the PSOE in the same year. Four years followed as leader of the opposition, during which period the PSOE could make little headway against Aznar, who appeared to be riding a European-wide wave of centre-right popularity. The 2004 general election, though far from a foregone conclusion, appeared to be weighted in favour of Aznar's governing PP, though his decision to send troops to Iraq remained massively unpopular.

On 11 March 2004, only days before the election, more than 200 people were killed and around a thousand injured when a series of bombs exploded in Madrid. Aznar's government immediately claimed that the attacks were the work of the Basque separatist group ETA, despite evidence pointing to Islamic extremism. The Spanish public, shocked and angry, turned on Aznar's administration; street protests accused the government of lying about who was responsible for the bombings for fear that any links to militant Islam would reflect on Aznar's unpopular decision to deploy Spanish troops to Iraq.

Zapatero's PSOE won a surprise victory on the back of the protests, though with just 164 seats it was 12 short of an absolute majority in the Cortes. Zapatero eventually won parliamentary backing on 16 April as head of a minority government by securing the support of 19 non-Socialist legislators, mainly from radical Catalan nationalists and the hard left. He was sworn in the following day. He moved quickly to break with his predecessor, pledging to allow the Spanish crown to be inherited by a woman, to relax abortion laws and to improve gay rights. He also tore up the national hydrology plan to siphon water from the River Ebro in northeast Spain to the parched south. Zapatero described both the invasion and the occupation of Iraq as a "huge disaster" and, in line with his election pledge, withdrew Spanish forces within two months. A year later he was riding high in the opinion polls, but US president George W. Bush was still not speaking to him.

SRI LANKA

Full name: The Democratic Socialist Republic of Sri Lanka.

Leadership structure: The head of state is a president, directly elected by universal adult suffrage. The president's term of office is six years. The president appoints the cabinet, may choose to hold any portfolio in it, and presides over its meetings. The prime minister, a member of the cabinet, needs to command a majority in Parliament, and wields considerable executive powers, but is formally appointed by (and may be dismissed by) the president.

President: Chandrika Bandaranaike **KUMARATUNGA** Since 12 Nov. 1994

Prime Minister: Sirimavo Bandaranaike 14 Nov. 1994—10 Aug. 2000

Ratnasiri Wickremanayake 10 Aug. 2000—9 Dec. 2001

Ranil Wickremasinghe 9 Dec. 2001—6 April 2004

Mahinda **RAJAPAKSE** Since 6 April 2004

Legislature: The legislature is unicameral. The sole chamber, the Parliament, has 225 members, directly elected for a six-year term.

Profile of the President:

Chandrika Bandaranaike **KUMARATUNGA**

Chandrika Bandaranaike Kumaratunga is, uniquely, the daughter of two former prime ministers—and also the widow of an assassinated 'rising star'. In office as prime minister from August 1994, but switching within months to the executive presidency, she modified the leftist agenda of her People's Alliance (PA) to promote neoliberal policies, but failed to deliver her promise of ending Sri Lanka's protracted ethnic conflict with the rebel Tamil Tigers (Liberation Tigers of Tamil Eelam—LTTE). She later became a critic of the peace process as pursued by the government of the rival United National Party (UNP), with which she was forced to 'cohabit' after the December 2001 legislative elections. The victory of her electoral alliance, the United People's Freedom Alliance (UPFA), in 2004 ended the period of cohabitation, though controversy over the peace process continued.

Chandrika Bandaranaike was born in Colombo on 29 June 1945, and was educated initially at St Bridget's Convent in the capital. Her father Solomon

Bandaranaike founded the Sri Lanka Freedom Party (SLFP), leading it to electoral success and becoming prime minister, but was assassinated in 1959. Her mother Sirimavo Bandaranaike, propelled into politics as his widow, took over the party leadership prior to an election campaign in 1960 which resulted in her becoming the first woman in the world to be elected as prime minister. Sirimavo Bandaranaike held that office from 1960 to 1965 and from 1970 to 1977, but was later banned from taking any active part in politics on grounds of abuse of power; she nevertheless remained the power behind the scenes at the SLFP throughout its nearly two decades in opposition.

Chandrika, meanwhile, spent the latter part of the 1960s in France, training in political journalism with *Le Monde* in Paris, completing degrees in law and political science, and going on to gain a doctorate in development economics. This served as preparation for a subsequent career which encompassed teaching and lecturing, research and work in land reform. Between 1972 and 1976, while her mother was head of government, she helped run the Land Reforms Commission of Sri Lanka, and she then worked as an expert consultant for the UN Food and Agriculture Organization (FAO) until 1979. During this period she published a book entitled *The Janawasa Movement: Future Strategies for Development in Sri Lanka*. She chaired the Janawasa Commission in the late 1970s and carried out research projects in the fields of food policy, political violence and agrarian reform. In 1974 she became a member of the executive committee of the SLFP's Women's League.

After 1977, with the SLFP cast out into the political wilderness, Chandrika Bandaranaike pursued her press and publishing career, as chairman and managing director from 1977 to 1985 of the Sinhalese daily newspaper *Dinakara*. By 1980, the year in which her mother was deprived of her political rights, Chandrika was playing a greater role in working to rebuild the fortunes of the SLFP, as a member of both its executive and its working committee. Factional disputes, however, conducted in an atmosphere of heightened tension following the outbreak of what was to become a protracted civil war with the minority ethnic Tamil separatists in the north and east, led to the formation of a separate left-wing socialist Sri Lanka People's Party (Sri Lanka Mahajana Pakshaya—SLMP) in January 1984. Chandrika was closely involved with this new party, whose moving spirit was the film idol Vijaya Kumaranatunga whom she had married in 1978. While he was its national organizer, she was the party's first vice president, and from 1986 to 1988 its president. Together they had two children.

On 16 February 1988 Vijaya Kumaranatunga was shot dead in Colombo. His killing, like other political attacks at this time, was attributed not to Tamil separatists but to Sinhalese extremists. The widowed Chandrika (who later dropped one of the syllables of her late husband's name, calling herself Chandrika Bandaranaike Kumaratunga) went abroad for three years, attending the Institute of Commonwealth Studies at the University of London as a research fellow, but returned once again to Sri Lanka in 1991.

Realizing the futility of an opposition weakened by factional divisions, Chandrika Kumaratunga was instrumental in forming in early 1993 a broader left-wing PA, encompassing both the SLFP and the United Socialist Alliance (a grouping of which Chandrika's SLMP had been a member since 1988). In May 1993 this PA recorded a notable victory in Western province (which included the capital, Colombo) when elections were held for provincial councils. Chandrika Kumaratunga was sworn in on 21 May as chief minister of Western province. Another of the obstacles to effective opposition unity was removed later that year when her brother and sometime rival Anura Bandaranaike resigned from the SLFP. The general election in August 1994 saw her campaigning as the PA leader, with the leadership of the SLFP itself being retained by her mother (whose political rights had been restored in 1986). Their victory on 16 August opened the way for Kumaratunga to become prime minister, and she was duly sworn in three days later.

Following on her general election victory, Kumaratunga secured the PA's nomination to stand three months later in elections for the country's presidency, the top executive post since a constitutional change in 1978. She won a record 62% of the vote in the November 1994 presidential poll, and was inaugurated for a six-year term on 12 November. Her mother Sirimavo Bandaranaike, despite having harboured her own ambitions for the top job, instead accepted the subordinate role of prime minister. Kumaratunga has since postponed the idea of abolishing the executive presidency and reverting to a prime ministerial form of government.

Kumaratunga based her 1994 presidential campaign, like the PA's general election campaign, around her pledge to restore peace to Sri Lanka. This entailed seeking a rapid end to the ethnic conflict which had divided the majority Sinhalese and minority Tamil populations for over a decade. She launched several initiatives over the succeeding years in efforts to negotiate with the Tamil separatists, pursuing a far-reaching devolution policy to assist in this. However, the initial optimism encouraged by a truce in January 1995 was soon lost amid renewed violence, and, beginning with a major army offensive in July 1995, Kumaratunga has repeatedly shown herself prepared to use force in efforts to break the Tamil separatists' military resistance in the north. In 1998, with the fighting still continuing, her government attempted to tighten its grip with the imposition of a formal ban on the main Tamil separatist organization, followed by press controls on reporting of the war and, later in the year, the declaration of a state of emergency.

Early presidential elections were called for 21 December 1999 amid a worsening in the conflict. On 18 December Kumaratunga survived an assassination attempt by a suspected Tamil suicide bomber, in which 21 people were killed and 150 injured; she herself suffered damage to her right eye. Her subsequent victory in the presidential election, with 51.1% of the vote, was partly attributed to public sympathy, while the opposition also claimed widespread fraud and intimidation.

Kumaratunga's mother stepped down as prime minister in August 2000, and died that October. Kumaratunga's personal loss was compounded by the loss of a key and powerful ally in Parliament. Nonetheless, public sympathy was again on the president's side and, along with a breakthrough military victory in the ongoing war, the PA won the greatest share of seats in Parliament in the 13 October 2000 poll. Kumaratunga was forced to form a government with moderate Tamil and Muslim parties while the opposition complained bitterly once more of electoral fraud and state-sponsored violence.

From then on Kumaratunga's position was increasingly undermined. Her relatively weak parliamentary base was exacerbated by the failure of her peace plans offering limited autonomy for the Tamils. She was forced to dissolve Parliament altogether from July 2001 in order to avoid a vote of no confidence. Her parliamentary majority crumbled when 12 members of the PA defected as soon as the house was reconvened in October. Snap elections were called for December 2001.

In that poll, conducted amid serious violence, the opposition UNP fell just short of winning an outright majority. It formed a coalition with the main Muslim party, and Kumaratunga was forced to enter into 'cohabitation' with UNP leader Ranil Wickremasinghe as prime minister. The two were immediately at loggerheads, with Wickremasinghe scoring a massive early victory by negotiating a permanent ceasefire with the Tamil Tigers on 21 February 2002. This left Kumaratunga apparently sidelined, with the prime minister taking on near executive powers.

Wickremasinghe's government agreed with the Tigers in December 2002 that the two sides should share power, with the north and east of the country gaining some autonomy. In May 2003 Kumaratunga warned that she would not hesitate to sack Wickremasinghe's government if she felt it was conceding too much to the Tigers. That November, while Wickremasinghe was out of the country, Kumaratunga dismissed three ministers and suspended Parliament. Deploying troops, she imposed in effect a state of emergency.

In January 2004 Kumaratunga's PA and the Marxist People's Liberation Front (Janatha Vimukthi Peramuna—JVP) entered into a coalition known as the UPFA. Kumaratunga announced that her abbreviated first term entitled her to an extra period in office the second time around, claiming a mandate to rule until December 2006. Parliamentary elections in April 2004 left the pro-presidential UPFA coalition short of an absolute majority, but able to form a government with the backing of the Sinhala extremist National Heritage Party. Mahinda Rajapakse was appointed premier.

Following the devastating Asian tsunami of December 2004, the UPFA began negotiations with the Tamil Tigers over the distribution of aid to northern and eastern regions of Sri Lanka. The JVP, incandescent over what it saw as concessions to terrorists, left the alliance in high dudgeon, effectively leaving

Kumaratunga's PA as a minority government. Meanwhile, in August the Supreme Court ruled that Kumaratunga had no mandate beyond December 2005 and presidential elections were set for November.

Profile of the Prime Minister:

Mahinda **RAJAPAKSE**

Mahinda Rajapakse became prime minister of Sri Lanka on 6 April 2004, following the victory of the United People's Freedom Alliance (UPFA) in elections four days earlier. A long-time ally of President Chandrika Kumaratunga, whose Sri Lanka Freedom Party (SLFP) is the largest party in the UPFA, Rajapakse is thought to have been chosen for the post ahead of rival Lakshman Kadirgamar partly because of his popular credentials. He first entered Parliament in 1970 at the age of 24, representing the southern district of Beliatta—his father having represented the same area until 1965—and he is well known for his attempt as minister of labour to push through a Workers' Charter. Rajapakse is believed to strongly support the resumption of stalled peace talks with Tamil Tiger rebels.

Mahinda Rajapakse was born on 18 November 1945 in Weeraketiya, in the district of Hambantota in rural Sri Lanka, the son of prominent local politician D. A. Rajapakse. He was educated at Richmond College, Galle, later moving to Nalanda College and Thurstan College, Colombo, where he studied law. Rajapakse was first elected to Parliament in 1970 for his father's old constituency of Beliatta, the youngest member of the house at just 24 years old. A Sinhalese Buddhist, he is married with three children.

Rajapakse lost his seat in 1977, but returned to Parliament in 1989, this time representing Hambantota. By this time he had been appointed the assistant secretary of the SLFP. Throughout this period Rajapakse maintained his law practice in Tangalle, until his elevation to government ministry in 1994, in which year he became both vice president of the SLFP and minister of labour and vocational training in the People's Alliance (PA) government.

Rajapakse came to the post intending to bring his Workers' Charter into law. The charter would have established trade union rights, social security and a wages commission, but it ran into sharp opposition from the International Monetary Fund (IMF) and World Bank, which were demanding the reduction of protection for workers' jobs and conditions. President Kumaratunga demoted Rajapakse to fisheries minister in 1997. In this new post he initiated the first ever University for Oceanography, and oversaw the establishment of a coastguard. In 2001 he became senior vice president of the SLFP and was appointed leader of the opposition following the defeat of the SLFP and its allies in the December 2001 elections.

Kumaratunga called snap legislative elections for April 2004, which were won by the UPFA—an alliance of the SLFP, several smaller parties from the PA and the People's Liberation Front (Janatha Vimukthi Peramuna—JVP). Rajapakse had strongly opposed the coalition agreement with the Sinhala chauvinist JVP, arguing instead for a grand alliance with the United National Party (UNP) in order to advance peace negotiations with the Tamil Tigers. In order to make the deal with the JVP, the SLFP had agreed that ex-foreign minister Lakshman Kadirgamar rather than Rajapakse would be prime minister in any UPFA government.

However, the SLFP found itself in a precarious position. It had just 60 seats of the 105 won by the whole coalition, which itself was eight seats short of an overall majority. This meant it needed the support not only of the JVP but also of the Sinhala extremist National Heritage Party (Jathika Hela Urumaya—JHU), which put up Buddhist monks as candidates and won nine seats. Kumaratunga found herself needing a premier who could manage to restart the peace process and at the same time placate the JHU who were against it. Rajapakse seemed the only candidate to be all things to all men.

SUDAN

Full name: The Republic of the Sudan.

Leadership structure: The head of state is a president, usually directly elected by universal adult suffrage. The president's term of office is five years. The incumbent president was re-inaugurated under the new 2005 Constitution for a transitional three-year term. The head of government is the president. The cabinet is appointed by the president.

President: Lt.-Gen. Omar Hassan Ahmad al-**BASHIR**   Since 16 Oct. 1993
                 (seized power on 30 June 1989)

Legislature: Under the 1999 Constitution the legislature was unicameral. The sole chamber, the National Assembly (Majlis Watani), had 400 members directly elected for a four-year term. The Assembly extended its own term when elections were due in December 2004. Under the 2005 peace accord, a transitional bicameral legislature was established in August. The Transitional National Assembly has 450 members, allocated as agreed in the peace accord to the ruling National Congress party (234 members), Sudan People's Liberation Movement (126 members), opposition groups in the north (63 members), and equivalent opposition groups from the south (27 members); the Transitional Council of States has two members from each of the 26 states. The Assembly met for the first time on 31 August 2005. Elections are promised for 2008.

Profile of the President:

Lt.-Gen. Omar Hassan Ahmad al-**BASHIR**

Lt.-Gen. Bashir, a career soldier from the north, was a major-general when he launched his 1989 coup. He sought democratic legitimacy for his rule in a nonparty presidential election in March 1996, defeating a large number of relatively unknown opponents, and held elections again in December 2000, when he secured a further term. His regime is dominated by Islamic fundamentalists through the ruling party, which recently changed its name from National Islamic Front (NIF) to National Congress (NC). Bashir's expressions of desire for an end to conflict with the (mainly Christian) south gradually translated into a peace process, with an accord finally signed in January 2005 ending 21 years of civil war.

Omar Hassan Ahmad al-Bashir was born on 1 January 1944 in Hoshe Bannaga and was educated in Khartoum, the capital, where he worked part-time in a

540

garage. He enrolled as a pilot at the Sudanese military academy from 1960. He fought for the Egyptians in the Yom Kippur war against Israel in 1973, and was involved also in the Sudanese government's long conflict with southern rebels, who were resisting attempts to make Sudan an Islamic state ruled by *shari'a* (Islamic law). In 1981 he achieved a master's degree in science from the Military Staff College, and two years later gained a master's in military sciences in Malaysia. By 1987 he had been awarded a fellowship of the Sudan Academy of Administrative Sciences.

On 30 June 1989 Bashir staged a coup, ousting the government of Sadiq al-Mahdi and dissolving parliament. He appointed himself chairman of the Revolutionary Command Council for National Salvation (RCC), prime minister (a position he still holds) and minister of defence. He also banned political parties and suspended the constitution, imprisoning many government members and releasing soldiers implicated in previous military coup attempts. Still at war with rebel groups in southern Sudan, his regime became increasingly committed to the introduction of *shari'a* throughout the country, an objective kept in the forefront by the political dominance of the NIF.

In 1993 the RCC announced a return to civilian rule, after appointing Bashir as president and consolidating the power of the National Islamic Front. Nonparty elections for a president and a new National Assembly were held in March 1996 but were boycotted by the major opposition factions which had formed a National Democratic Alliance (NDA) based in Asmara, Eritrea. Forty independent candidates stood and, amid outcries of irregularities, Bashir was elected president for a five-year term with 76% of the vote. The NIF won the majority of seats in the Assembly. Elections in December 2000 produced a similar outcome. Bashir was re-elected with 86.5% of the vote and the newly renamed NC gained a majority of over 75% in the Assembly. Again the opposition boycotted the polls, although Bashir had made overtures to the NDA and the Umma party (led by Mahdi), which he had allowed back into the country in March 2000. A splinter of Umma then joined the government outright in July 2002.

Arguably the greatest challenge to Bashir has been the ongoing civil war with the rebel Sudan People's Liberation Army (SPLA) in the south. A number of peace agreements were drafted and rejected, while innumerable ceasefires were implemented only to be broken within days. A state of emergency declared by Bashir in December 1999 was consistently extended in what became an annual event. Nonetheless, a breakthrough was eventually achieved under proposals formulated in July 2002, whereby the south of the country would gain legislative autonomy for six years prior to holding a referendum on possible independence, and during that time *shari'a* would not be extended to non-Muslims. The final peace deal was signed with the SPLA in January 2005, swiftly followed by an accord with the NDA. The state of emergency was lifted in July but the death of former rebel leader and new vice president John Garang in a helicopter crash later that month threatened to destabilize the process. However, a new Parliament was constituted in September with a prescribed division of seats, and a national unity government was agreed. Meanwhile, on 30 June, Bashir announced that the state of emergency would be lifted, and that Islamist opposition leader Hassan al-Turabi, a former ally of Bashir whom he had ousted from the government in 1999, would be released from prison, having been held on charges of plotting a coup.

Under the Bashir regime, diplomatic links have been severed with neighbouring countries which Sudan accused of aiding the southern rebels, among them Eritrea. Other states have offered assistance in providing a base for peace talks, including Ethiopia, Kenya and, from 2001, Egypt.

Bashir was among the first world leaders to offer condolences after the 11 September 2001 attacks on the USA. The same month saw the lifting of the five-year-old UN sanctions against Sudan, which had been accused by the USA and other countries of harbouring Islamist terrorists. Later that year, however, Bashir was quick to condemn the US-led war in Afghanistan as unfairly targeting Muslims.

Bashir's regime again attracted international censure from 2003 onward over savage attacks in the western region of Darfur by government-backed Arab militias against the black African population. Bashir claimed that the militias were crushing rebels and that the West was interfering in order to exploit Sudan's oil and gold resources. His government eventually agreed to comply with a UN resolution on ending the crisis. A UN inquiry reported in January 2005 that the violence in Darfur could not be characterized as genocide, but did find that the Sudanese government and its militias had systematically abused civilians—more than 70,000 people had been killed and an estimated two million people displaced over two years.

SURINAME

Full name: The Republic of Suriname.

Leadership structure: The head of state is a president, elected (along with the vice president) by the National Assembly or, if the required two-thirds' majority is not achieved, by a broader United Peoples' Conference (UPC) convened for the purpose and including district and local council representatives. The president's term of office is five years. The head of government is the president. The Council of Ministers is appointed by the president, and chaired by the vice president.

President:	Jules Wijdenbosch	15 Sept. 1996—12 Aug. 2000
	Ronald **VENETIAAN**	Since 12 Aug. 2000
Vice President:	Pretaapnarian Radhakishun	15 Sept. 1996—12 Aug. 2000
	Jules Ajodhia	12 Aug. 2000—12 Aug. 2005
	Ram **SARDJOE**	Since 12 Aug. 2005

Legislature: The legislature is unicameral. The sole chamber, the National Assembly (Nationale Assemblee), has 51 members, directly elected for a five-year term.

Profile of the President:

Ronald **VENETIAAN**

Ronald Venetiaan leads the New Front for Democracy and Development (Nieuwe Front voor Democratie en Ontwikkeling) four-party coalition. A prominent figure in Suriname's relatively recent return to democracy, he was president for the first time from 1991 to 1996. He was re-elected to the post in August 2000 after a landslide victory at the polls for the New Front, and again in 2005, although without the same strong parliamentary support.

Runaldo Ronald Venetiaan was born on 18 June 1936 in Paramaribo. He went to the Netherlands in the 1950s to study mathematics and physics at the University of Leiden, receiving a doctorate in mathematics in 1964. He is married to Liesbeth Vanenburg and they have four children.

In 1964 Venetiaan returned to Suriname, where he worked as a mathematics teacher at the University Preparatory and Teacher Training Colleges. He ran the mathematics department from 1965 and in 1969 he was appointed headmaster of

Algemene Middelbare School. During his teaching career he had begun working with the political left and in 1973 he was called to government as minister of education under Prime Minister Henck Arron.

After the military coup led by Lt.-Col. Desi Bouterse in 1980, Venetiaan returned to full-time teaching as a lecturer in mathematics. He re-engaged with politics as a research adviser to the general statistics bureau in 1985 and as chairman of the advisory board of the Suriname National Party (Nationale Partij Suriname—NPS) from 1987. He was returned to the education ministry following the reappointment of Arron after fresh elections in 1988.

Venetiaan remained education minister through the second military coup and until fresh elections were held in 1991. These were won by the New Front coalition, which included the NPS, and after the poll Venetiaan was nominated as the coalition's candidate for president; he was successfully elected in September. As president he consolidated the country's democracy, purging the government of military control and replacing Bouterse, who had become commander-in-chief of the armed forces. He also instituted a Structural Adjustment Programme which involved unpopular but largely successful economic austerity measures. In addition he oversaw the end of the six-year Maroon insurgency in 1992.

Legislative polls in 1996 saw the New Front lose its majority in the National Assembly, although it remained the largest party. Amid protracted coalition talks, Venetiaan faced Jules Wijdenbosch in presidential elections. Neither candidate could achieve the two-thirds' majority to secure election so a United People's Conference was convened, which elected Wijdenbosch as president. Two factions then split from the New Front and agreed to join Wijdenbosch's coalition on condition that Bouterse was excluded from the government.

For the next four years Venetiaan led the New Front in opposition. The grouping rode to a significant victory in early elections held in 2000, retaking a majority in the National Assembly, and Venetiaan was once again elected president. Elections in 2005 were a replay of 1996, with the New Front losing its majority and neither Venetiaan nor rival presidential candidate Rabin Parmessar achieving a two-thirds' majority to secure election. This time the United People's Conference backed Venetiaan's bid to remain in office with 560 votes to 215, and he was sworn in on 12 August.

Profile of the Vice President:

Ram **SARDJOE**

Ram Sardjoe is a member of Suriname's south Asian community, which makes up about one-third of the total population. He was first elected to the National Assembly over 40 years ago, and was speaker from 2002 until his election as vice president in August 2005 (in which capacity he also chairs the Council of Ministers).

Ramdien Sardjoe was born on 10 October 1935. He first became a member of the National Assembly in July 1964 and has held a seat almost continually since then, except for the period between August 1980 and November 1987. He represents the constituency of Paramaribo, the capital of Suriname.

Since 2003 he has led the Progressive Reform Party (Vooruitstrevende Hervormings Partij—VHP), which is mainly backed by the Hindu population of Suriname. It is the second-largest party in the ruling New Front for Democracy and Development (Nieuwe Front voor Democratie en Ontwikkeling) coalition. Sardjoe served as speaker of the National Assembly from 2002 until July 2005, and in 2003–04 was one of the two co-presidents of the Joint Parliamentary Assembly of the European Union (EU) and the African, Caribbean and Pacific (ACP) group of states.

Sardjoe was chosen as running mate by incumbent president Ronald Venetiaan in July 2005. Neither Venetiaan nor his main opponent Rabin Parmessar were able to garner the necessary two-thirds' majority of the 51-member National Assembly in two rounds of voting, and the vote eventually went in August to the United People's Conference, when Venetiaan was elected as president and Sardjoe as vice president (by 591 votes against 285 for his rival Wilfried Roseval). He was sworn in on 12 August.

His distinctions include officer in the Order of the Netherlands Lion, officer in the Order of the Yellow Star, and grand officer in the Order of the Yellow Star.

SWAZILAND

Full name: The Kingdom of Swaziland.

Leadership structure: The head of state is the king. The head of government is the prime minister who is appointed by the king. The king also appoints the cabinet, in consultation with the prime minister.

King:	**MSWATI III**	Since 25 April 1986
Prime Minister:	Barnabas Sibusiso Dlamini	26 July 1996—30 Sept. 2003
	Paul Shabangu (acting)	30 Sept. 2003—26 Nov. 2003
	Themba **DLAMINI**	Since 26 Nov. 2003

Legislature: The legislature, the Parliament (Libandla), is bicameral. The lower chamber, the House of Assembly, has 65 members (55 directly elected, ten appointed by the king), serving for a five-year term. The upper chamber, the Senate, has 30 members (ten elected by the House of Assembly, 20 appointed by the king), also serving for a five-year term.

Profile of the King:

MSWATI III

Mswati III was crowned king of Swaziland on 25 April 1986, becoming the youngest reigning monarch in the world at the age of 18. His father, King Sobhuza II, had died four years previously and a power struggle had ensued during the regency, with the result that Mswati was invested as king earlier than planned. He has strengthened the royal powers and rules mainly by decree, despite pressure for democratization and criticism of his flamboyant lifestyle.

Prince Makhosetive (as he was known before his coronation) was born on 19 April 1968. He was educated in Swaziland and then in England, at Sherborne public school and the Royal Military Academy, Sandhurst. His father died when he was 14 and Queen Dzeliwe, one of the royal wives, was appointed regent with the task of governing together with the Liqoqo, the traditional advisory council. No heir was announced but speculation singled out Makhosetive as the likely successor.

The following year Dzeliwe was ousted by members of the Liqoqo and replaced by Queen Ntombi, Makhosetive's mother. On the same day, 10 August 1983,

Makhosetive was declared heir to the throne which, according to custom, he could not ascend until he was 21. A month later the Liqoqo requested that he return from school in England in the hope that his presence would reduce the unrest in the country.

Over the next three years the power struggle continued, with the result that the coronation was brought forward and held on 25 April 1986. The following month the newly enthroned King Mswati abolished the Liqoqo, and in May 1987 he charged 12 government officials with sedition for their alleged involvement in the dethronement of Queen Dzeliwe and the subsequent intrigue. In September of that year he dissolved Parliament. Fresh elections were held in November under a system whereby the electorate could vote for candidates nominated by local councils.

On his 21st birthday Mswati assumed the full powers and responsibilities of the paramount chief, but there were already demands for multiparty elections and the restriction of the monarchy to a ceremonial position. In October 1992 he again dissolved Parliament, appointed a Council of Ministers and with their help agreed to rule by decree until multiparty elections could be held. However, political parties have still not been legalized. Elections were held to the House of Assembly in September–October 1993 and again in October 1998, but the Assembly did not have full legislative powers and could only debate government policy and advise the king.

Mswati's response to growing pressure within the region for a degree of democratization has been limited. After an eight-day protest in January 1996 he agreed to begin talks on the future of the monarchy but refused to consider giving up his powers. Delays on political reforms caused significant social unrest again in 1997, when he appointed a constitutional review commission. The conclusion of this commission, published in August 2001, was that the majority of Swazis actually wanted to see the king's powers extended rather than restricted—a conclusion fiercely contested by pro-democracy groups and trade unions. In 2003 Mswati denounced democracy and multipartyism, and reiterated his claim to absolute rule based on the principle of divine right. His comments preceded the publication of a draft new constitution which guaranteed fundamental human rights of equality and freedom of expression but still banned multipartyism. A Big Inbada consultation with leaders of civil society and commerce in July 2003, asking for suggestions on how to solve the country's problems, did little to appease his opponents. Under pressure from the African Commission on Human and Peoples' Rights to make reforms in order to make Swaziland conform to the African Charter, the new constitution was finally approved and signed by the king in 2005, but only after parliament had made amendments on taxing members of his family. Mswati retained veto powers over anything he deemed to be against the public interest.

Mswati's lavish and autocratic lifestyle frequently draws criticism, both internally and abroad. In 2001 he delayed the start of the school term, while schoolchildren assisted with a week's weeding duty on his own personal fields. The House of Assembly prevented him from purchasing a US$50 million private jet in 2002, while in 2004 he asked for US$15 million to be spent on renovating his existing three palaces and building eight new ones, to accommodate his many wives. The annual Reed Dance Ceremony, during which tens of thousands of bare-breasted women dance in front of the king for him to choose a new wife, is anathema to women's rights activists worldwide. In 2001 Mswati imposed a five-year chastity order on all girls under 18 to help combat the spread of AIDS—but promptly broke the ban himself when he chose a 17-year-old bride from that year's Reed Dance (and paid the fine of one cow). The order was repealed in 2005, days before he chose a 13th wife at the annual ceremony. As is customary, he will marry her when she becomes pregnant: he has so far fathered 27 children.

Profile of the Prime Minister:

Themba **DLAMINI**

Themba Dlamini, a member of the royal Dlamini clan, was appointed as prime minister on 14 November 2003 and took office on 26 November. He is a well-respected businessman who had spent ten years running the Tibiyo Taka Ngwane investment company, which is owned by the royal family and has links with almost all of Swaziland's businesses.

Absalom Themba Dlamini was born on 1 December 1950. He graduated from the then University of Botswana and Swaziland in 1978 with a degree in commerce, and later gained a master's in business administration from the University of Nairobi in Kenya.

He has worked in a wide range of private-sector jobs, including managerial positions with the Swaziland National Provident Fund, the Central Bank of Swaziland and the Swaziland Industrial Development Company. In 1991 he became managing director and chief executive officer of Tibiyo Taka Ngwane, an investment company controlled by the Swazi royal family, which claims to promote development as well as "undertake commercial and strategic investment" and "preserve traditional and cultural values and heritage".

Dlamini was appointed as Swaziland's prime minister on 14 November 2003; as he was not a member of the House of Assembly, he was nominated to the Senate to enable him to take up the post. He has emphasized the importance of upholding the rule of law, a stance that helped to end a two-year walkout by High Court judges over the government's refusal to abide by their judgements. However, the post of prime minister has little power, as its main function is to administer the policies laid down by the palace.

SWEDEN

Full name: The Kingdom of Sweden.

Leadership structure: The head of state is a constitutional monarch. The head of government is the prime minister, who is responsible to Parliament. The cabinet is appointed by the prime minister.

King:	**CARL XVI GUSTAF**	Since 15 Sept. 1973
Prime Minister:	Göran **PERSSON**	Since 17 March 1996

Legislature: The legislature is unicameral. The sole chamber, the Parliament (Riksdag), has 349 members, directly elected for a four-year term.

Profile of the King:

CARL XVI GUSTAF

Carl XVI Gustaf, the 74th king of Sweden, belongs to the Bernadotte dynasty, which has been on the throne since 1818. At the time of his accession in 1973 he was only 27, the youngest ever Bernadotte monarch. His style is unostentatious, in the manner of Scandinavian constitutional monarchies, and he is noted for his commitment to environmental protection, exemplified by his presidency of the Swedish branch of the World Wide Fund for Nature (WWF).

Carl XVI Gustaf was born on 30 April 1946 at the Haga Palace, the fifth child and only son of Hereditary Prince Gustaf Adolf, who was killed in a plane crash the following year. Carl Gustaf was educated privately, initially at the royal palace in Stockholm, after which he went on to Broms school and Sigtuna boarding school, where he matriculated in 1966. He then did two-and-a-half years of military service, training in the army, navy and air force. He passed his naval officer examination in 1968. His military training was later supplemented by a management course at the national defence college and commissioned service on board ships of the Swedish navy. In 1968 and 1969 the crown prince studied history, sociology, political science, financial law and economics at Uppsala University. Later he also studied economics at Stockholm University.

Under a programme designed to give him experience of the local, national, and international political scene, he was attached to Sweden's permanent mission to the UN in New York and then spent time in London, UK, at Hambros Bank and at the Swedish embassy and chamber of commerce. When his grandfather King Gustaf VI Adolf died on 15 September 1973, Carl Gustaf became king.

In addition to his interest in conservation and environmental protection, he has been active representing Sweden at international events, and was made honorary president of the World Scout Foundation in 1977. He also presents the Nobel prizes each year.

King Carl XVI Gustaf is married to Queen Silvia, née Sommerlath, the daughter of a German businessman. They met at the 1972 Munich Olympic Games where she was working as an interpreter and hostess. They have two daughters and one son. Their eldest child, Crown Princess Victoria, born in 1977, is heir to the throne under the 1980 Act of Succession, which now stipulates that the title passes to the monarch's eldest child regardless of sex.

Profile of the Prime Minister:

Göran **PERSSON**

Göran Persson became prime minister in 1996 in succession to his social-democratic colleague Ingvar Carlsson, whom he had previously served as finance minister. Two days before becoming prime minister, Persson also assumed the leadership of the Swedish Social Democrats (Socialdemokraterna or Socialdemokratiska Arbetarepartiet—SAP). He worked as an administrator in adult education before entering Parliament in 1979, since when his political career has involved him in a variety of posts at both the national and local level.

Göran Persson was born on 20 January 1949 in Vingåker. He left secondary school with a certificate in engineering in 1969, and went on to the University College of Örebro until 1971. In that year he took up the first of a number of administrative posts in adult education, and became organizing secretary of the SAP youth league, having first joined the party's youth wing at the age of 15. Between 1972 and 1975 he was a member of the board of the SAP youth league. He did his military service between 1973 and 1974.

He was first elected to Parliament in 1979, after two years as full-time chairman of the Katrineholm board of education. He left Parliament in 1985 to return to local politics, as municipal commissioner in Katrineholm, a post he held for four years. Between 1989 and 1991 he was minister at the ministry of education with responsibility for comprehensive and upper schools, adult education and public education.

Re-elected to Parliament in 1991, he was chairman of the parliamentary standing committee on agriculture from 1991 to 1992, a member of the parliamentary standing committee on industry from 1992 to 1993 (and also party spokesperson for industrial policy issues), and vice chairman of the parliamentary standing committee on finance (1993–94). He was chairman of the SAP district organization in Sörmland from 1992 to 1996, and between 1993 and 1996 he was a deputy member of the SAP executive committee.

The September 1994 general election returned the SAP to power, in a minority government, and Persson was appointed minister of finance. In this post he introduced tough austerity measures in 1995 to tackle the economic recession which had beset the country since the early 1990s. He was also a strong supporter of Swedish participation in the single European currency, following Sweden's accession to the European Union in January 1995.

Persson became prime minister on 17 March 1996, his predecessor Carlsson having announced in August 1995 his intention of resigning the premiership which he had held for most of the last ten years. Persson's government's first major controversy came over the commitment to the decommissioning of all nuclear power stations in Sweden by 2010, as had been approved by referendum in 1980. Persson confirmed in early 1997 that his government would close two of Sweden's 12 nuclear reactors by 2001. The first closed in 1999, but a second one did not come offline until 2005, and it looked unlikely that the country would meet the 2010 target. In May 2001 Persson became the first Western leader to travel to North Korea to meet that isolated country's leader, Kim Jong Il.

The SAP lost ground in the 1998 elections, though it remained the largest party in Parliament. The 2002 polls saw the party bounce back, but still short of a majority, relying again on support in Parliament from the Left Party and the Greens. Adopting the euro has been part of the SAP's official party policy since 2000, but Persson declined from holding a referendum on the issue until September 2003. The vote was overshadowed by the stabbing of the high-profile 'yes' campaigner and foreign minister, Anna Lindh, but 56% of voters rejected joining the eurozone.

Göran Persson has two daughters from his first marriage. He divorced his second wife Annika in December 2002 after seven years of marriage. A year later he married Anitra Steen, who manages Systembolaget, the Swedish national alcohol-retailing monopoly.

SWITZERLAND

Full name: The Swiss Confederation.

Leadership structure: The head of state is a president, elected annually by the Federal Assembly from the members of the Federal Council. The president's term of office is one year. The president chairs the Federal Council (Bundesrat; Conseil Fédéral; Consiglio Federale), which has joint responsibility for government. The Federal Council is chosen by the Assembly from its members after every general election, and serves for four years.

President:	Adolf Ogi	1 Jan. 2000—31 Dec. 2000
	Moritz Leuenberger	1 Jan. 2001—31 Dec. 2001
	Kaspar Villiger	1 Jan. 2002—31 Dec. 2002
	Pascal Couchepin	1 Jan. 2003—31 Dec. 2003
	Joseph Deiss	1 Jan. 2004—31 Dec. 2004
	Samuel **SCHMID**	Since 1 Jan. 2005

Legislature: The legislature, the Federal Assembly (Bundesversammlung; Assemblée Fédérale; Assemblea Federale), is bicameral. The lower chamber, the National Council (Nationalrat; Conseil National; Consiglio Nazionale), has 200 members, directly elected for a four-year term. The upper chamber, the Council of States (Ständerat; Conseil des Etats; Consiglio degli Stati), has 46 representatives directly elected within each canton for a four-year term.

Profile of the President:

Samuel **SCHMID**

Samuel Schmid is a lawyer affiliated to the right-wing Swiss People's Party/Democratic Union of the Centre (Schweizerische Volkspartei/Union Démocratique du Centre—SVP/UDC). He became a national councillor in 1994 and a state councillor in 1998. He was elected as a member of the Federal Council in December 2000, holding the defence portfolio, and took over the rotating presidency on 1 January 2005.

Samuel Schmid was born on 8 January 1947 and studied law at the University of Berne. He graduated as a lawyer in 1973 and went to work at the Swiss Federal Finance Administration for a short period before joining a Berne firm of

552

solicitors. He was a member of the town council of Rüti near Büren from 1972 until 1974 when he was elected president of the council. He graduated as a notary in 1978 and set up in private practice in the town of Lyss.

In 1982 he became a member of the Cantonal Council of Berne and sat on various committees before becoming a national councillor in 1994 until 1998. That year he also became a legal consultant to Kellerhals and Partners, a firm of solicitors based in Berne. He became a state councillor in 1999 and a member of the foreign affairs committee, the committee for economic affairs and taxation, and the social security and health committee. On 6 December 2000, he was elected as a member of the Federal Council, heading the department of defence, civil protection and sports.

Under the Swiss system the presidency rotates every year. Schmid held the vice presidency in 2004 under Joseph Deiss, and took office as president on 1 January 2005.

SYRIA

Full name: The Syrian Arab Republic.

Leadership structure: The head of state is a president, elected by parliament for a seven-year term and confirmed by referendum. The head of government is the president. The Council of Ministers is appointed by the president.

President:	Hafez al-Assad (seized power on 15 Oct. 1970)	14 March 1971—10 June 2000
	Abd al-Halim Khaddam (acting)	10 June 2000—17 July 2000
	Bashar al-**ASSAD**	Since 17 July 2000
Prime Minister:	Mahmoud al-Zubi (acting from 7 March 2000)	1 Nov. 1987—20 March 2000
	Mohammad Mustafa Miro (acting from 10 Sept. 2003)	20 March 2000—18 Sept. 2003
	Mohammad Naji al-**OTARI**	Since 18 Sept. 2003

Legislature: The legislature is unicameral. The sole chamber, the People's Council (Majlis al-Sha'ab), has 250 members, directly elected for a four-year term.

Profile of the President:

Bashar al-**ASSAD**

Bashar al-Assad was proclaimed president of Syria in 2000 following the death of his father, President Hafez al-Assad, who had ruled the country since 1970. An ophthalmologist by training, Bashar had only been groomed for the succession after the accidental death of his elder brother Basil in 1994. Since then he has proceeded through a crash course in leadership. Under his presidency, liberalization has been slow, with the focus on economic rather than political reform. His administration is supported by the all-powerful Renaissance Arab Socialist Party (Hizb al-Ba'ath al-Arabi al-Ishtriraki—Ba'ath), of which he is also leader.

Bashar al-Assad was born in Damascus on 11 September 1965. He was the third child of Gen. Hafez al-Assad and was educated at one of the city's elite Franco-

Arab schools, al-Hurriyet. From 1982 he began his studies in medicine at Damascus University; he graduated as a general practitioner six years later. He first specialized in ophthalmology at a military hospital before going to the UK in 1992 to pursue his professional qualifications in London.

The death of Bashar's elder brother Basil in a car crash in 1994 changed Bashar's life dramatically. The fast-living Basil had long been brought up as Hafez's successor and was a man much in his father's mould. Bashar, on the other hand, is described as shy and reserved, and at first refused his father's demands to return from the UK to prepare as the future leader of his country.

Processed through the military academy at Homs, a necessary measure in view of the domination of Syrian politics by the military, Bashar was a colonel by January 1999. Meanwhile he also began to be sent on official visits to neighbouring states. He is thought to have played a key role in the accession of Gen. Emile Lahoud as president in Lebanon in 1998, and reportedly referred to Iraqi dictator Saddam Hussein as a "beast", while on a tour of Kuwait. At home he spearheaded a 'clean hands' campaign to root out corruption in the regime. Many senior army officers and members of the intelligence organization, all possible obstacles to his succession, were forced to resign. His role in politics was formalized in March 2000 when he advised his ailing father on the formation of a new government under Prime Minister Mohammad Mustafa Miro.

Throughout this period Bashar insisted that he had no presidential ambitions. However, when Hafez eventually died on 10 June 2000, Bashar was immediately nominated as the new leader of the Ba'ath party, the constitution was hastily altered lowering the minimum age for a president from 40 to 34 (Bashar's age), and he was promptly promoted to lieutenant-general and chief of staff of the armed forces. His succession as president was endorsed by an overwhelming 97% of the electorate in a popular referendum held on 10 July and he was sworn in a week later.

Modernization of the economy has ranked high on Bashar's agenda. A raft of reforms issued in December 2000 included the reintroduction of private banks for the first time since 1963, and the creation of a stock market. He is also keen to promote new media. As chairman of the Syrian Computer Society he encouraged the growth of Internet usage in the country despite the hesitations of his father. In November 2000 he also promised to modernize the press laws and permitted the circulation of political papers by parties other than the Ba'ath. A general air of new freedoms has evoked small-scale criticism of the regime in the People's Council and has encouraged some unusually outspoken journalism. Initially, Bashar encouraged the formation of forums to enhance political discussion, but key members of the last-remaining forum were arrested in 2005 for using it "to disseminate the ideas of the Muslim Brotherhood", an organization that is banned in Syria. However, in June of that year the Ba'ath party voted to ease the 40-year state of emergency, limiting its scope to national security violations, and to allow new political parties to be formed. The moves fell short of the radical reforms that many had hoped for, but were generally welcomed by observers. The proposals, which also included media liberalization and economic reform, required approval by the legislature.

Hopes for a quick thawing of relations with Israel were soon dispelled when Bashar reiterated his father's demands for the return of the Golan Heights as a precondition for any talks. However, before the situation deteriorated on the West Bank in late 2000, he did suggest he was willing to restart negotiations when the Israeli government was ready. Relations suffered a further setback in October 2003 when Israel made retaliatory strikes on Palestinian terrorist training camps in Syria. It was the first attack by Israel on Syria in over 20 years.

Earlier that year Syria had been accused of assisting Saddam Hussein's crumbling regime in Iraq in the face of the US-led invasion. Its own supposed chemical weapons programme was also drawing international condemnation, but in January 2004 Bashar declared that his country would not give up its weapons of mass destruction unless there was a similar move by Israel and other regional powers. He made the statement during a historic visit to Turkey, the first by a Syrian leader after years of mutual suspicion. The USA imposed economic sanctions in May 2004, which the Syrian authorities called "unjust and unjustified".

Meanwhile, Syria's pervasive influence and troop presence in Lebanon was receiving strong criticism. A UN Security Council resolution in September elicited a partial withdrawal. Suspected Syrian involvement in the assassination of Lebanese former prime minister Rafiq al-Hariri in February 2005 provoked an international outcry, with countries such as Russia and Saudi Arabia joining demands from the West for a complete withdrawal, which was completed in April.

Known affectionately as 'Doctor', Bashar is noted for his close physical resemblance to his father, but his personality is very different. Described as bookish, his interests include photography and cycling. Bashar al-Assad married Asma al-Akhras, a computer specialist born in the UK to Syrian parents, at a secret ceremony at the end of December 2000. They now have two sons and a daughter.

Profile of the Prime Minister:

Mohammad Naji al-**OTARI**

Mohammad Naji al-Otari was appointed prime minister of Syria in September 2003. An engineer and former provincial governor, he only entered the higher echelons of the ruling Renaissance Arab Socialist Party (Hizb al-Ba'ath al-Arabi al-Ishtriraki—Ba'ath) in 2000. He is the maternal uncle of President Bashar al-Assad's wife.

Mohammad Naji al-Otari was born in Aleppo in 1944. He studied civil engineering at Aleppo University, and obtained a diploma in town planning from the Netherlands. Otari was head of Aleppo city council from 1983 to 1987; he is also a former governor of Homs. He was president of Aleppo's engineering association from 1989 to 1993.

Otari joined the Ba'ath party's central committee only in 2000, at the same time as he became a member of the Regional Command and was made deputy prime minister for services affairs. He became speaker of the People's Council in 2003 for a brief period, before being nominated as Syrian prime minister on 10 September 2003 to succeed Mohammad Mustafa Miro. His cabinet was approved eight days later. More reform-minded than his predecessor, he is an advocate of modernization.

TAIWAN

Full name: The Republic of China.

Leadership structure: The head of state is a president, directly elected by universal adult suffrage. The president's term of office is four years, renewable only once. The head of government is the premier, who is appointed by the president. The ministers are appointed by the president on the advice of the premier.

President:	Lee Teng-hui	13 Jan. 1988—20 May 2000
	CHEN Shui-bian	Since 20 May 2000
Premier:	Vincent Siew	1 Sept. 1997—20 May 2000
	Tang Fei	20 May 2000—3 Oct. 2000
	Chang Chun-hsiung (acting from 4 Oct. 2000)	6 Oct. 2000—1 Feb. 2002
	Yu Shyi-kun	1 Feb. 2002—1 Feb. 2005
	Frank **HSIEH**	Since 1 Feb. 2005

Legislature: The legislature is unicameral. The Legislative Yuan (Li-fa Yuan) has 225 members (176 directly elected, 49 elected proportionately by party) serving a three-year term.

Profile of the President:

CHEN Shui-bian

Chen Shui-bian's inauguration in 2000 as the tenth president of Taiwan broke 50 years of domination by the nationalist Kuomintang (KMT). As a major opposition figure he was mayor of Taipei from 1994 to 1998. Determined to succeed from humble origins, he is intolerant of ideology, and his authoritarian nature led to serious conflict in late 2000 with the Legislative Yuan, which was at that time dominated by the KMT. The 2001 legislative elections changed this situation to Chen's advantage, with the KMT losing ground and his Democratic Progressive Party (DPP) becoming the largest party. Since 2002, however, the rapprochement of the KMT with the breakaway People First Party (PFP) has given a narrow majority to the opposition again.

Chen Shui-bian was born in 1950 to poor native tenant farmers in Hsi-chuang, Tainan province, in the south of the island (known then as Formosa). He was a weak infant so his parents did not immediately register his birth; his identification certificate shows his date of birth as 18 February 1951. Chen's family borrowed money to send him through school and he is famed for his remarkable academic achievements, reportedly coming first at every level from primary school to university. He entered the National University in 1969 and, after changing course the following year, graduated with a degree in law in 1974. He went on to join the Formosan International Marine and Commercial Law Office as an attorney specializing in maritime law.

Chen Shui-bian met Wu Sue-jen, the daughter of wealthy doctors, while at university, and they eloped to marry in 1975. Wu followed her own political career and won great public sympathy when she was knocked down by a farm vehicle in 1985 in what is rumoured to have been a politically motivated assassination attempt. Since then she has been paralyzed from the waist down. She is a close adviser to her husband and often makes appearances at political rallies. They have one son and one daughter.

It was the Kaohsiung Incident of 1979 which provided Chen with his first taste of politics. The editors of *Formosa* magazine, to which he was affiliated, were charged with sedition and rioting after their attempts to hold an anti-KMT rally erupted in violence in Kaohsiung. Chen defended them in court, despite his lack of relevant experience and the heavy odds against them. He lost the case in 1980 but was inspired to enter politics as an opponent of the KMT's prolific use of martial law. He became the youngest ever city councillor in Taipei in 1981 and stayed on the council for four years.

The tables turned against Chen in 1985 when *Formosa* magazine, of which he was now chairman, was sued for libel; on losing the case, he left the magazine and resigned from the city council. He was defeated in an attempt to seek office in his rural birthplace and an appeal against the libel conviction failed. He was sent to Tucheng penitentiary for eight months. On release from prison Chen joined the DPP, which had emerged following a relaxation in martial law in 1987. His wife Wu had entered the Legislative Yuan in 1986 on the back of popular anger at his own imprisonment, and Chen served as her office manager. In 1989 he was elected to the Legislative Yuan himself and was a leading member of the DPP's parliamentary bloc. He became the first opposition politician to hold the chairmanship of the National Defence Committee.

After two terms in the Legislative Yuan, Chen became the first democratically elected mayor of Taipei in 1994, having benefited greatly from a divisive split of traditional votes between the KMT and the New Party (NP). Despite his strong anti-KMT image, Chen showed himself to value pragmatism above consistency and chose to work alongside proven KMT administrators. As mayor, Chen is remembered for greatly improving the city's transport network and business profile, but also for pursuing unpopular and ruthless right-wing cleanup campaigns. A crackdown on Taipei's sex industry was harshly executed, with no provisions for the welfare of the many sex workers, while in the creation of two city parks Chen evicted all the residents of 'Kangleh village'. The justifications for some of the measures implemented by his administration were overturned later in courts of appeal. An alliance between the KMT and the NP led to Chen being voted from office in 1998.

Losing the post of mayor proved fortuitous for Chen in that it freed him to run for the presidency at a time when the DPP had been struggling to find a high-profile representative. Moreover, the ruling KMT's support was being drained by the defection of the popular James Soong, who then stood as an independent candidate. Chen campaigned on a platform of opposition to years of KMT corruption and he countered mainland Chinese threats of imminent war with reassurances to his supporters that he no longer advocated immediate sovereignty. He was elected the first non-KMT president of Taiwan in March 2000 with 39.3% of the vote. The KMT's Lien Chan came a poor third. Chen took office on 20 May.

For the first 18 months of his presidency, Chen had to face the hostility of a KMT-dominated Legislative Yuan. An attempt to promote a sense of national consensus failed when his KMT prime minister Tang Fei resigned after four months. The nationalists were particularly angered by Chen's proposal to scrap a KMT-initiated nuclear power plant project. However, massive displays of anti-nuclear feeling, and popular support for Chen, muted opposition calls for his recall.

Legislative elections on 1 December 2001 put Chen in a far more commanding position when the KMT lost its majority for the first time in Taiwanese history. Although the DPP became the largest single party, it failed to secure an outright majority and the KMT and other opposition groups were unmoved by Chen's call for a 'unity' coalition. In an effort to 'stabilize' democracy, Chen took over as leader of the DPP in July 2002. However, after the December 2004 legislative elections left the opposition KMT–PFP alliance with a slim overall majority, he resigned from the leadership, taking full responsibility for the party's poor showing.

Two days before the presidential elections in March 2004, Chen and Vice President Annette Lu were shot and injured during an election rally. The subsequent poll resulted in a slim win for Chen, with a majority of just 29,000 out of 13 million votes cast. Opposition demonstrators took to the streets demanding a recount, which Chen hastened to approve as the instability was impacting on the stock market. While the result was upheld, an opposition inquiry into the shootings later concluded that the episode had been faked in order to win sympathy votes. Chen was sworn in for his second term on 20 May, calling for dialogue with mainland China to establish stability and promising to press ahead with plans to adopt a new constitution by 2008, which in itself could be viewed by China as tantamount to a declaration of independence.

Relations with China have been a major focus of Chen's presidency. Contacts grew in the period after he took office, but in 2003, when Parliament passed a bill allowing a future referendum on the island's formal independence from China if the island is attacked, the Chinese government responded with a warning that the new law contained "a time bomb". In December of that year Chen threatened to retract his electoral promise to avoid pushing for the island's formal independence, if China were to add to the arsenal of missiles he says are aimed at his country from across the Taiwan Strait. In February 2004 Chen organized a human chain of 1.2 million people running the length of Taiwan in protest over Chinese military threats and to draw attention to the situation in Taiwan.

When China carried out a simulated invasion of Taiwan on the nearby island of Dongshan in July 2004, Chen responded with a military exercise to practise the Taiwanese army's response. However, both sides cancelled further exercises in August, and following the resignation of former Chinese president Jiang Zemin, known for his tough stance on Taiwan, from his last official post as head of the armed forces in September, Chen called for arms control talks and the establishment of a "code of conduct" as a guarantee of peace between the two countries. He later also offered to cut Taiwan's troop strength by 100,000 from its current level of 380,000.

Relations with China continued on a roller coaster in 2005. The Chinese New Year was the occasion of the first direct commercial flights for 55 years, and trade between the two countries had risen by 34% over the previous two-year period. However, the funeral of Pope John Paul II in April caused a diplomatic spat: Chen became the first Taiwanese president to visit the Vatican; China, in protest, refused to send a representative. Later that month, Lien Chan became the first KMT chairman to set foot on Chinese soil since 1949—Chen Shui-bian had given cautious backing to the trip.

Profile of the Premier:

Frank **HSIEH**

A former broadcaster and mayor of Kaohsiung city, and one of the founders of the Democratic Progressive Party (DPP), Frank Hsieh was appointed prime minister of Taiwan on 1 February 2005 by President Chen Shui-bian, his long-time political rival (and the man who had succeeded him as DPP chairman). Hsieh has a reputation as a skilled political operative in the face of a hostile legislature, and it is hoped that his renowned pragmatism and flexibility will serve as an advantage when dealing with the ever-present antagonism of the Chinese administration.

Frank Chang-ting Hsieh was born on 18 May 1946 in Dadaocheng, Datong district, Taipei. He studied law at the National Taiwan University and did his master's degree in law at Kyoto University in Japan. In 1969 he became a practising attorney. He is married to Yu Fang-chih, with one son and one daughter.

Hsieh entered politics in 1981 as a city councillor in Taipei and served two terms. In 1986 he helped found the DPP, even suggesting the party's name. He became a member of the central standing committee and in 1989 was elected as a member of the Legislative Yuan. He stood as a vice-presidential candidate in the 1996 presidential election with Peng Ming-min; they finished second, with 21% of the vote, and in 1998 Hsieh was elected mayor of Kaohsiung city.

During this period Hsieh became known as a broadcaster, hosting a TV and radio show. From 2000 to 2002 he was chair of the DPP. On 1 February 2005 he was appointed as prime minister by President Chen Shui-bian, his successor as party chairman—the two are regarded as long-time political rivals. Hsieh had earned a reputation for pragmatism and flexibility as Kaohsiung city mayor, remaining personally popular despite having to work with a council dominated by opposition politicians. Hsieh has described his policy as "co-operation without confrontation", and his appointment as prime minister reflected Chen's hope that he could use the same political skills to navigate legislation through the opposition-dominated legislature.

TAJIKISTAN

Full name: The Republic of Tajikistan.

Leadership structure: The head of state is a president, directly elected by universal adult suffrage. The president's term of office is seven years. Under the 1999 constitutional amendments a president may serve only one term, but the 2003 amendments permit the current incumbent to stand for two further terms after his current term finishes in 2006. The head of government is the president. The Council of Ministers is appointed by the prime minister.

President:	Imomali **RAKHMANOV**	Since 16 Nov. 1994
	(chairman of Supreme Soviet from 19 Nov. 1992)	
Prime Minister:	Akil **AKILOV**	Since 20 Dec. 1999

Legislature: The legislature, the Parliament (Majlisi Oli), is bicameral. The lower chamber, the Assembly of Representatives (Majlisi Namoyandagon), has 63 members, directly elected for a five-year term, and the upper chamber, the National Assembly (Majlisi Milli), has 33 members, 25 indirectly elected and eight appointed by the president, for a five-year term.

Profile of the President:

Imomali **RAKHMANOV**

Imomali Rakhmanov has been in power in Tajikistan, amid conditions of civil war, since late 1992, and was confirmed in office as president by elections held in November 1994, when a new constitution was also adopted by referendum. An ex-communist, he was seen when he came to power as pro-Russian, and is a former ally of ex-president Rakhmon Nabiyev. He has promoted close links with the Karimov regime in neighbouring Uzbekistan.

Imomali Rakhmanov was born on 5 October 1952 in Dangara in the Kulob district of southern Tajikistan. He graduated in economics from Tajik State University, then worked as an electrician, salesman, government secretary and chairman of a trade union committee. Rising up the Communist Party system, from 1988 he was director of collective farms in the Kulob region, and in 1992 became chairman of the executive committee of the Kulob regional soviet (i.e. council). He is married to Azizmo Asadullaeva and they have nine children.

Following Tajikistan's declaration of independence in 1991 and the disintegration of the Soviet Union, the new state faced a period of civil war in which the former communist authorities were ranged against an Islamic fundamentalist opposition. The Islamist forces briefly gained the upper hand in September 1992, but the ex-communists regained control of the capital, Dushanbe, in December. Rakhmanov, chosen the previous month as chairman of the Supreme Soviet, thereupon formed a new government. His authority was effectively preserved by the intervention of a Russian-led peacekeeping force intended to prevent the re-escalation of the conflict.

In the presidential elections of 6 November 1994, held amid conditions of continuing civil war, Rakhmanov won 58.3% of the vote, according to the official results, against 35% for the former prime minister, Abdumalik Abdullajanov, whose supporters complained of alleged vote rigging.

Although he had kept the Islamists from power, Rakhmanov faced the continuing threat of violence, with insurgents operating by infiltration from neighbouring Afghanistan. Amid continuing conflict and the open violation of ceasefire agreements, a proposal to create a National Reconciliation Council was agreed in December 1996. Over the course of the next two years, a stumbling peace process was interrupted by flashes of violence. Rakhmanov himself was wounded in April 1997 when a grenade was thrown at his feet, killing two other people and injuring 60. A final agreement, first drafted in January 1997, led to the eventual return of peace by early 1999, with members of the United Tajik Opposition sitting in a new interim government. A referendum in September 1999 approved the extension of future presidential terms from five to seven years ahead of presidential elections in November.

On 6 November 1999 Rakhmanov claimed to have won 97% of the vote in the presidential election. The opposition expressed profound suspicion at the size of his victory and the Organization for Security and Co-operation in Europe (OSCE), which had refused to observe the poll at all, claimed widespread irregularities. Similar complaints surfaced following legislative elections on 27 February 2000. The pro-presidential People's Democratic Party of Tajikistan (PDPT) won an outright majority, securing Rakhmanov's position. The 2005 legislative polls were no different, with the OSCE condemning the "improbably high" turnout figures and the opposition claiming that the results were "complete falsification"; the PDPT took all but six seats in the Assembly of Representatives.

Human rights organizations continue to accuse Rakhmanov of autocratic practices and of using the international 'war on terrorism' to crack down on political opponents. Constitutional changes in 2003 will allow him to seek two further seven-year terms after his current period in office finishes in 2006, overriding the 1999 amendment that introduced a one-term limit. Economically, the country has suffered from devastating droughts, while prices for basic goods spiralled when Rakhmanov introduced a new currency, the somoni, in October 2000.

Profile of the Prime Minister:

Akil **AKILOV**

*Akil Akilov is a member of the People's Democratic Party of Tajikistan (PDPT).
Trained as an engineer under the Soviet regime, he entered the independent
Tajikistani government in 1994 and was elevated to prime minister in 1999.*

Akil Gaibullayevich Akilov was born on 2 February 1944 in the northern city of
Leninabad (modern-day Khujand) in what was then the Tajik Soviet Socialist
Republic. After qualifying as an engineer from the Moscow Institute of
Construction and Engineering, he found work in Leninabad on a number of
construction projects. From 1976 he also officially worked within the structure of
the ruling Communist Party.

Akilov served the government of the newly independent Tajikistan from 1993 as
construction minister, and also as deputy prime minister from 1994. From 1996 to
1999 he was first deputy governor of the Leninabad region. After the presidential
elections in November 1999, he was brought back into the cabinet in December
as prime minister.

TANZANIA

Full name: The United Republic of Tanzania.

Leadership structure: The head of state is a president, directly elected by universal adult suffrage. The president's term of office is five years, renewable once only. The head of government is the president, who is responsible to the National Assembly. The cabinet is appointed by the president.

President:	Benjamin **MKAPA**	Since 23 Nov. 1995
Prime Minister:	Frederick Tluway **SUMAYE**	Since 28 Nov. 1995

Legislature: The legislature is unicameral. The sole chamber, the National Assembly (Bunge), has 280 directly elected members serving five-year terms and five members chosen by the House of Representatives of Zanzibar. The attorney general has a seat ex officio. Since February 2000 the president has had powers to appoint up to ten members to the National Assembly.

Profile of the President:

Benjamin **MKAPA**

Benjamin Mkapa took office as president of Tanzania in November 1995 after the country's first multiparty presidential and legislative elections the previous month. A former journalist and for many years foreign minister, he was the candidate of the Revolutionary Party (Chama Cha Mapinduzi—CCM), the former sole and ruling party.

Benjamin William Mkapa was born on 12 November 1938 in Ndanda near Masasi in the southeast of what was then Tanganyika. Mkapa was educated locally and then went to Uganda to complete his studies, obtaining a degree in English from Makerere University in 1962. He is married to Anna Joseph Maro and they have two sons.

Mkapa began his career as a civil servant, working briefly as an administrative officer in Dodoma and Dar es Salaam and then as a foreign service officer from 1963. He joined the ruling party, the Tanganyika African National Union, which was later renamed as the CCM after the 1977 merger with the ruling party of Zanzibar.

Switching from the civil service to journalism, Mkapa was managing editor of the party-owned newspapers *The Nationalist* and *Uhuru* from 1966. *The Nationalist* merged with *The Standard* to form the state-owned *Daily News* in 1972 and Mkapa remained as managing editor. He was a founding director of the Tanzania News Agency (Shihata) in 1976.

In 1974 he was appointed press secretary to the president. In 1976 he was made high commissioner to Nigeria. The following year he joined the cabinet as minister of foreign affairs, until 1980 when he was appointed minister of information and culture. Two years later he returned to the diplomatic service as high commissioner to Canada and the USA in 1982–83, before returning to Tanzania, once again to the post of minister of foreign affairs between 1984 and 1990. He was minister of information and broadcasting in 1990–92 and minister of higher education, science and technology in 1992–95.

Mkapa represented Nanyumbu in the National Assembly for ten years from 1985, until his election as president in October 1995. This poll, held concurrently with the legislative elections, was the first since the transition from a single-party state to a multiparty democracy in 1992. Mkapa had only narrowly won the nomination as CCM candidate at the party congress, but the strength of the party was sufficient to ensure him a wide margin of victory in the nationwide poll. Organization of the elections was chaotic at times and opposition parties alleged electoral fraud, but the High Court eventually declared Mkapa to have won with 61.8% of the vote. He was subsequently re-elected on 29 October 2000 with an increased 71.7% of the vote, having narrowly avoided death in a freak traffic accident three weeks previously. In concurrent legislative elections the CCM gained a massive 82% of seats in the National Assembly.

As president, Mkapa has had to contend with political violence in the island province of Zanzibar, and international criticism for the purchase of a US$40 million air traffic system from the UK in 2002. More positively, he has actively promoted the battle against HIV/AIDS, implementing a programme to expand the provision of free anti-retroviral drugs in 2004, and has introduced free primary education. Tanzania was one of the first countries to negotiate a debt swap with the UK in 2005, using the funds for secondary education with a target of 50% enrolment by 2015.

Mkapa is not eligible to stand for a third term in office, so will step down after the presidential election in late 2005.

Profile of the Prime Minister:

Frederick Tluway **SUMAYE**

Frederick Sumaye is a former carpenter whose only governmental experience was in the ministry of agriculture prior to being named as prime minister in 1995. Like President Benjamin Mkapa, who appointed him immediately after winning the presidency, he is a member of the Revolutionary Party (Chama Cha

Mapinduzi—CCM), the former sole party and still the country's dominant political organization. Sumaye, too young to have been involved in the independence movement of the 1950s, has a reputation for competence rather than charisma.

Frederick Tluway Sumaye was born on 29 May 1950 in Hanang in the Arusha region. He attended the Ilboru Secondary School in Arusha and trained as a carpenter, going on later to study agricultural engineering. He is married to Esther Sumaye and they have four children.

A member of the ruling CCM who now holds a seat on the party's national executive, Sumaye first entered parliament at the October 1985 elections, representing his native Hanang constituency. He has been re-elected on successive occasions in 1990, 1995 and, most recently, 2000.

Sumaye's first government post was as deputy minister of agriculture, to which he was appointed in December 1990 by the then president Ali Hassan Mwinyi. He rose to full ministerial rank in the same department before being named in November 1995 as prime minister by the incoming president Benjamin Mkapa in a reorganization of the cabinet following that year's elections.

He was reappointed to the premiership by Mkapa on 17 November 2000, again following the simultaneous presidential and legislative elections held on 29 October. He was one of 11 candidates who were nominated in April 2005 to be the CCM candidate for presidential elections in late 2005. He was knocked out of the race in the second round of screening, however, and the party's nomination was eventually won by Foreign Minister Jakaya Kikwete at the party congress in May.

THAILAND

Full name: The Kingdom of Thailand.

Leadership structure: The head of state is a king. The head of government is the prime minister, who is responsible to the House of Representatives. The cabinet is appointed by the prime minister.

King:	**BHUMIBOL** Adulyadej (Rama IX)	Since 9 June 1946
Prime Minister:	Chuan Leekpai	9 Nov. 1997—18 Feb. 2001
	THAKSIN Shinawatra	Since 18 Feb. 2001

Legislature: The legislature, the National Assembly (Rathasapha), is bicameral. The lower chamber, the House of Representatives (Saphaphuthan-ratsadon), has 500 members, directly elected for a four-year term. Under the 1997 Constitution (which expanded the membership of the House from 393 to 500 members), 400 of them are elected in single-member constituencies and 100 from party lists. The 200-member upper chamber, the Senate (Wuthisapha), which was formerly appointed, is directly elected on a nonparty basis, with a six-year term.

Profile of the King:

BHUMIBOL Adulyadej (Rama IX)

King Bhumibol has been king of Thailand for well over half a century and is the world's longest-reigning current monarch, his official royal title being King Rama IX. He is a highly influential figure, revered as semi-divine by some of his subjects, although he rules as a constitutional monarch.

Bhumibol Adulyadej was born on 5 December 1927 in the USA, in Cambridge, Massachusetts. The youngest of the three children of Prince and Princess Mahidol of Songkla, at the time of his birth he was not expected ever to become king, and there was little mention of his birth in the newspapers in Bangkok. His early education was in Bangkok, but in 1934 his widowed mother took her children to Switzerland to continue their education. He attended the Gymnase Classique Cantonal in Lausanne, Switzerland, and graduated in political science and law from Lausanne University.

Bhumibol acceded to the throne in June 1946, aged 18, succeeding his elder brother, Ananda Mahidol, who had been found shot dead. He was formally crowned on 5 May 1950 as King Rama IX, the ninth ruler of the Chakri Dynasty.

Much of his energy has latterly been devoted to the Chaipattana (Victory in Development) Foundation, which he set up in 1988 and of which he is president. It enables funds to be made immediately available to the king for urgent projects without need for approval by the government, as was formerly necessary. One of the earliest and better known projects funded by the foundation has been the Chaipattana Aerator machine, and in 1993 a patent was granted to the king for the invention of the Chaipattana Aerator Model RX-2. Other projects include the lessening of traffic congestion and better flood control. Aside from his skill in engineering, the king has a keen interest in jazz music and cartography.

He married Mom Rajawongse Sirikit Kitiyakara, daughter of Prince Chandaburi Suranath, on 28 April 1950. He and Queen Sirikit have one son, Crown Prince Maha Vajiralongkorn, born in 1952, and three daughters. In 1977 the constitution was altered to allow women to succeed to the throne; the king's second-oldest daughter Princess Maha Chakri Sirindhorn advises her father and has acted on his behalf on several occasions. The crown prince's second wife gave birth to a boy in April 2005, who is now second-in-line to the throne after his father. He is the king's only legitimate grandson, following the death of Bhumi Jensen, the king's eldest daughter's son, in the Asian tsunami of December 2004.

Profile of the Prime Minister:

THAKSIN Shinawatra

Thaksin Shinawatra is a flamboyant multimillionaire who founded and heads the ruling party Thais Love Thais (Thai Rak Thai—TRT). Trained as a policeman, he began a telecommunications business in 1982 which became one of the country's largest firms, making him one of Thailand's richest men. Brought into government in the mid-1990s, he was ousted in 1997 and formed TRT in 1998. Charges of corruption did not prevent him winning elections in January 2001 and were ultimately dropped. He is noted for initiatives such as the 'million baht village' rural investment scheme and efforts to get government ministers to relax by taking them on train journeys for 'mobile cabinet meetings'.

Thaksin Shinawatra was born on 26 July 1949 in the northern city of Chiang Mai. He has had a close association with the distinct northern cultural movement and has headed a number of groups dedicated to it, including the Northerners' Association of Thailand. His family (the family name is Shinawatra, although he is always referred to by his given name as Thaksin) operated a successful silk firm which diversified into buses and cinemas, giving him a taste of business management from an early age. Nonetheless, he found his vocation in the police force and graduated from the Police Cadet Academy in 1973. He married Khunying Potjaman Damapong in 1974 and the couple have one son and two daughters.

Winning a scholarship from the government, Thaksin travelled to the USA to study for a master's degree in criminal justice at the Eastern Kentucky University in Richmond. After graduating in 1974 he went on to the Sam Houston State University in Huntsville and received his doctorate in the same subject in 1978. He returned to Thailand to teach at the police academy and had risen to the rank of lieutenant-colonel by the time he left in 1987. In the interim he and his wife had founded a telecommunications company in 1982 that would grow eventually into the powerful Shin Corporation.

The company signed a contract with the police department to supply computer software in 1982 and Thaksin was able to resign his commission in 1987 to become full-time head of the firm, which went on to market a pager service and even a homegrown satellite communication system. In 1990 he signed a 20-year contract with the Telephone Organization of Thailand for a monopoly on mobile phone services. He was nominated by the Association of South-East Asian Nations (ASEAN) as 'businessman of the year' in 1992. When he was invited in 1994 to enter the government he undertook to 'cleanse' himself for public service and resigned from all his positions within the Shin Corporation. In April 2001 Thaksin was overtaken as the country's richest man by his own son.

In 1994 he was appointed foreign minister and was affiliated to the Moral Force (Palang Dharma—PD) party. He was elevated to deputy prime minister and PD leader in 1995 and was charged with resolving the terrible traffic problems experienced by Bangkok. Although, somewhat predictably, he failed in his grand aims, he was retained as a deputy prime minister in the next government formed in 1997, but was forced from the cabinet later that year after its collapse. Soon after it had lost its position of power, the PD fell apart.

The following year Thaksin resolved to return to government and formed the enigmatic, populist TRT in July 1998. Promising to lead the country from its financial malaise by investing over US$1,000 million in the rural economy and clearing banks' bad debts, he led the TRT to a massive electoral victory in the polls in January 2001, and formed a coalition with Chart Pattana, Chart Thai and the New Aspiration Party. Soon after he came to power he was almost dramatically removed in March when a plane he was about to board exploded on the runway. Early claims of terrorism were later discounted by proof of a malfunction.

Thaksin's future was also briefly in question owing to a charge of failing to declare his personal assets. His successful defence was that he had forgotten about his decision to divulge his fortune into the hands of trusted family servants. (He was eventually acquitted of the charges in August 2001.)

Thaksin's populist economic policies, which became known as 'Thaksinomics', included a large-scale spending programme for the rural poor, discounted loans for farmers, major public works projects, and the creation of a national asset management company (AMC) to take on the crippling debt incurred by the country's financial sector in 1998. The 'million baht village' scheme was launched in 2001, aiming to boost the rural economy by granting one million baht (US$22,000) to each of the country's estimated 70,000 villages, and a programme to provide health care to the poor for just 30 baht (US$1) per person per annum followed in October. The economy grew rapidly in 2002–04, and the dip in growth in 2005 was blamed on the December 2004 tsunami.

Thaksin's support for US foreign policy, which included sending troops to Iraq in 2003, was shaken when the US State Department criticized his government's human rights record during a crackdown on the illegal drugs trade. He denounced his country's previously close ally as a "useless friend". Over 2,000 people are thought to have died during the crackdown, mainly in early 2003—the government claims most were victims of clashes between gangs. Thailand's own Human Rights Commission has also accused the government of putting its own interests ahead of those of its people and heading towards a culture of authoritarianism. However, the government's war on 'social evils' such as narcotics, organized crime, poverty and corruption has boosted its approval rating as high as 70% in opinion polls.

This popularity—undented by various corruption scandals—coupled with some key party mergers, resulted in a landslide victory for the TRT in February 2005, winning 377 of the 500 seats in the House of Representatives which gave the party a mandate to form Thailand's first democratically elected single-party government. Thaksin was formally re-elected to office by parliament on 9 March.

Thaksin increased his powers to act against terrorism in 2005, especially in relation to the threat of Islamist militant attacks in the south of the country. Martial law had been imposed in 2004, and a US$800 million package of development aid approved by the government to try to reduce poverty in the region.

TOGO

Full name: The Republic of Togo.

Leadership structure: The head of state is a president, directly elected by universal adult suffrage. The president's term of office is five years. In December 2002 the National Assembly passed a constitutional amendment which removed the limit on the number of consecutive terms. The head of government is the prime minister, who is appointed by the president. The prime minister, in consultation with the president, appoints the other members of the Council of Ministers.

President:	Gen. Gnassingbé Eyadema (seized power on 13 Jan. 1967)	14 April 1967—5 Feb. 2005
	Faure Gnassingbé (acting from 21 Feb 2005)	5 Feb. 2005—25 Feb. 2005
	Abass Bonfoh (acting)	25 Feb. 2005—4 May 2005
	Faure **GNASSINGBÉ**	Since 4 May 2005
Prime Minister:	Eugene Koffi Adoboli	21 May 1999—31 Aug. 2000
	Agbéyomè Messan Kodjo	31 Aug. 2000—29 June 2002
	Koffi Sama	29 June 2002—8 June 2005
	Edem **KODJO**	Since 8 June 2005

Legislature: The legislature is unicameral. The sole chamber, the National Assembly (Assemblée Nationale), has 81 members, directly elected for a five-year term.

Profile of the President:

Faure **GNASSINGBÉ**

Faure Gnassingbé was one of over a hundred children of Togo's long-time dictator Gnassingbé Eyadema, who held power from 1967 until 2005. Gnassingbé studied in France and in the USA before returning home to be groomed for a political career. When his father died suddenly in 2005, he was propelled into the presidency by the military, prompting outrage from abroad including sanctions from the African Union (AU). Gnassingbé stepped down and called elections which he went on to win with 60% of the vote as the candidate of the ruling Rally of the Togolese People (Rassemblement du Peuple Togolais— RPT). He was sworn in on 4 May and has since held talks with opposition politicians and promised to work towards national reconciliation.

Faure Essozimna Gnassingbé, also known as Faure Eyadema, was born on 6 June 1966 in the town of Afagnan in the southeast corner of Togo, about 30 km from the border with Benin. His mother was from the Ewe clan from Afagnan; his father was Gnassingbé Eyadema, who took power as president the following year. He is one of Eyadema's estimated 100 children of several wives.

Gnassingbé's childhood was split between the main northern town, Kara, where his father's clan were based, and the southern capital, Lomé; he later travelled to former colonial power France to study management, following which he graduated with a master's degree in business administration from George Washington University in the USA.

On his return to Togo, Gnassingbé began laying the grounds for a political career. He was elected to the National Assembly for the constituency of Blitta in 2002, and the same year the minimum age for the presidency was lowered from 45 to 35 (Gnassingbé was 35 at the time).

The following year he was appointed minister of public works, mines, post and telecommunications—a post that saw him take charge of the country's lucrative phosphate mines, through which Togo makes most of its foreign exchange.

In February 2005 his father, President Gnassingbé Eyadema, died suddenly. While the speaker of parliament, Fambaré Ouattara Natchaba, should have become acting president, he was at the time outside the country and the army moved swiftly to seal off the country's borders. The military summarily installed Gnassingbé as leader, and parliament, which was full of his father's allies, amended the constitution and the electoral code to rubber-stamp the decision. This, accompanied by the sealed border crossings, prompted the African Union (AU) to declare the transition a military coup.

Under pressure from neighbouring countries, in particular Nigeria, Gnassingbé stepped down later that same month in order that elections could be held on 24 April; he went on to win just over 60% of the vote. Though the results were marred by violence, Gnassingbé was sworn in as president on 4 May.

Since his election, sanctions on Togo have been lifted, despite anger among many in the opposition and the exodus of around 40,000 refugees from the electoral violence into neighbouring Benin and Ghana. However, Gnassingbé has moved to curb corruption and child trafficking, has released 14 men jailed for plotting a coup, and has held peace talks with exiled opposition leader Gilchrist Olympio in Rome as part of a wider attempt to achieve national reconciliation.

Profile of the Prime Minister:

Edem **KODJO**

Edem Kodjo took office as prime minister for the second time in June 2005 under new president Faure Gnassingbé; he had previously served under Gnassingbé's father Gen. Gnassingbé Eyadema in the mid-1990s. Kodjo is a committed pan-Africanist who was previously secretary-general of the Organization of African Unity (OAU, now the African Union—AU). He is a moderate and leader of the Patriotic Pan-African Convergence (Convergence Patriotique Panafricaine— CPP), but his critics say he is too close to the ruling Rally of the Togolese People (Rassemblement du Peuple Togolais—RPT) and this undermines his credibility.

Edouard Kodjovi Kodjo (known as Edem) was born on 23 May 1938 in Sokodé in central Togo. He served as finance minister from 1973 until 1976 and as foreign minister from 1976 until 1978 under President Eyadema, whose home town was also Sokodé. In 1978 he was appointed secretary-general of the OAU. He remained in this post until 1983. In 1985 Kodjo published *Africa Tomorrow*, in which he called for the map of the continent to be redrawn, and borders imposed by imperialism reconsidered.

Kodjo broke with Eyadema in the early 1990s, setting up the Togolese Union for Democracy. Kodjo put pressure on Eyadema to hold elections in 1994, which were won by other opposition parties. Nonetheless Eyadema offered the post of prime minister to Kodjo who accepted and formed a government, in the process badly damaging ties with the rest of the Togolese opposition. Kodjo resigned from the job in 1996 after Eyadema's allies took greater control over the government.

In February 2005, Eyadema died suddenly and the military propelled his son, Faure Gnassingbé, into office in his place. The AU moved to declare the transition a military coup and, under pressure from neighbouring countries, Gnassingbé stepped down in order that elections could be held in April; he went on to win just over 60% of the vote. Following the refusal of the main opposition parties to present a list of candidates for prime minister, Kodjo was invited once again to form a coalition government—his Patriotic Pan-African Convergence coalition was so moderate it refused to take sides in the presidential poll. His new government excludes the remainder of the opposition; he took office on 8 June 2005.

TONGA

Full name: The Kingdom of Tonga.

Leadership structure: The king of Tonga is hereditary head of state. An appointed 11-member Privy Council functions as a cabinet, presided over by the king. The prime minister is head of government.

King:	**TAUFA'AHAU** Tupou IV	Since 16 Dec. 1965
Prime Minister:	Baron Vaea	22 Aug. 1991—3 Jan. 2000
	Prince Ulukalala **LAVAKA ATA**	Since 3 Jan. 2000

Legislature: The legislature is unicameral. The sole chamber, the 30-member Legislative Assembly (Fale Alea), consists of the king, Privy Council, nine hereditary nobles (elected by their peers) and nine popularly elected representatives. Elected representatives hold office for three years.

Profile of the King:

TAUFA'AHAU Tupou IV

Taufa'ahau Tupou IV, the son of the late Queen Salote Tupou III, became the king of Tonga in 1965. Australian-educated, a keen mathematician and a Wesleyan lay preacher, he is a direct descendant of King George Tupou I, who is considered to be the founder of modern Tonga.

Crown Prince Siaosi Taufa'ahau Tupoulahi was born on 4 July 1918 in the royal palace in Tonga. He was the first monarch to receive a Western education, attending Newington College and Sydney University in Australia, graduating both in the arts and law. His mother appointed him minister of education in 1943, and soon afterwards he established a teacher training college and revised the Tongan alphabet; in 1947 he founded the Tonga High School. In 1944 he was made minister of health, a post he held until he became premier in 1949. While premier he was also responsible for foreign affairs and for agriculture.

Taufa'ahau succeeded to the throne on 16 December 1965 on the death of his mother. His coronation was held on 4 July 1967. He is a member of the International Mathematics Association. He is a lay preacher of the Free Wesleyan Church, and holds a special position giving him the conditional right to appoint an acting president of the Church. Between 1970 and 1973 he was chancellor of the South Pacific University.

King Taufa'ahau and his wife Queen Halaevalu Mata'aho, who married in 1947, have three sons and one daughter. Their eldest child Crown Prince Tupouto'a is heir to the throne and their third son Prince Ulukalala Lavaka Ata has been prime minister since 2000.

The 21st century has seen increasing calls for democracy, but the king opposes reform. He tried to quash the country's only independent newspaper *Taimi 'o Tonga* in 2003, but the new restrictive media laws were subsequently overturned by the Supreme Court. During this battle, the Legislative Assembly amended the constitution to allow the king to override its own decisions—although all 'commoners' in the Assembly voted against the changes.

In 2005 political parties were legalized, but within weeks the country was crippled by a six-week public-sector strike over pay. Rallies saw more than 10,000 Tongans take to the streets—almost 10% of the population—and the strike was only resolved after the government agreed to consider setting up a commission to review the constitution with a view to allowing a more democratic form of government.

Profile of the Prime Minister:

Ulukalala **LAVAKA ATA**

Prince Ulukalala Lavaka Ata was appointed by his father King Taufa'ahau Tupou IV as Tonga's prime minister for life on 3 January 2000. His appointment took the country by surprise as it was widely expected that his elder brother Crown Prince Tupouto'a would be appointed. A staunch conservative and an opponent of the democratic movement which Tupouto'a has championed, Lavaka Ata is constitutionally subordinate to his father who appoints the cabinet.

Prince 'Aho'eitu' Unuaki'otonga Tuku'aho was born into the ruling Ha'a Havea clan on 12 July 1959. He was the fourth child, and third son, of the then Crown Prince Siaosi Taufa'ahau Tupoulahi, who ascended the throne of Tonga on 16 December 1965. He was granted the titles Ulukalala and Lavaka Ata in 1989. As a member of the royal family he completed a commission as a naval officer. The prince married Heuifanga Nanasipau'u, daughter of Baron Vaea of Houma (who was Tonga's prime minister from 1991 to 2000), on 11 December 1982. They have two sons and one daughter. After a diploma course in strategic studies in the USA in 1988, Lavaka Ata achieved two master's degrees in Australia in the late 1990s, the first in defence studies at the University of New South Wales, and the second in international relations from the small, private University of Bond.

On his return in 1998, Lavaka Ata was appointed to the cabinet by his father to fulfil the role of minister of foreign affairs and defence. This post had been vacated by his elder brother Tupouto'a, who had resigned from politics to pursue his various business interests after quarrelling with the king over proposed democratic reforms, including the abolishment of the permanent premiership.

The continuing dispute left Lavaka Ata in a position, as a supporter of Taufa'ahau's authoritarian rule, to take over the premiership in 2000. Lavaka Ata cancelled his plans to pursue a doctoral degree in Australia when the king finally accepted the long-proffered resignation of the aging Baron Vaea, and appointed Lavaka Ata in his stead. In a reshuffle in August–September 2004, he gave up the foreign affairs and defence portfolios, which he had retained on his initial appointment.

Lavaka Ata's opposition to change is reflected in his connections with the conservative Wesleyan Church, in which he is a lay preacher like his father. Whereas his elder brother looked set to question their father's powers of appointment and rule, Lavaka Ata has been happier to accept the status quo in the country, confounding the hopes of the younger generation, who are becoming increasingly vocal in their demands for reform.

TRINIDAD AND TOBAGO

Full name: The Republic of Trinidad and Tobago.

Leadership structure: The head of state is a president, elected by an electoral college comprising both houses of Parliament. The president's term of office is five years. The head of government is the prime minister, who is responsible to Parliament. The cabinet is appointed by the prime minister.

President:	Arthur N. Robinson	19 March 1997—17 March 2003
	Max **RICHARDS**	Since 17 March 2003
Prime Minister:	Basdeo Panday	9 Nov. 1995—24 Dec. 2001
	Patrick **MANNING**	Since 24 Dec. 2001

Legislature: The legislature, the Parliament of Trinidad and Tobago, is bicameral. The lower chamber, the House of Representatives, has 36 members, directly elected for a five-year term. In 2005 Parliament approved the expansion of the House of Representatives to 41 members at the next election. The upper chamber, the Senate, has 31 members, appointed by the president on the advice of the prime minister and leader of the opposition for a five-year term. Tobago's legislature is a unicameral House of Assembly with 15 members, 12 of them elected and three chosen by the House for a four-year term.

Profile of the President:

Max **RICHARDS**

Max Richards was sworn in as president of Trinidad and Tobago on 17 March 2003. A UK-trained chemical engineer, Richards is the first president of the country not to be an attorney-at-law. He began his working life in the oil business, before joining the University of the West Indies (UWI) as a senior lecturer in chemical engineering in 1965; he was appointed principal in 1985. The post of president in Trinidad and Tobago is largely ceremonial.

George Maxwell Richards (known as Max) was born in 1931 in San Fernando, and went to primary school there before winning a scholarship to Queen's Royal College in Port of Spain. He graduated from the University of Manchester Institute of Science and Technology (UMIST) in the UK in 1957 with a master's degree in chemical engineering. Richards then stayed in the UK to study for a doctorate in the same subject at Cambridge University. Having begun as a staff trainee with United British Oilfields of Trinidad Ltd (later Shell Trinidad), he returned to work for the company in a range of management posts on graduation. He is married to Jean Ramjohn-Richards, a medical doctor who works as an anaesthetist; they have one son and one daughter.

Richards remained with Shell Trinidad until 1965, when he joined UWI as a senior lecturer in chemical engineering. He lectured at the university as professor of chemical engineering until 1985, for the last five years of which he also served as deputy principal and pro vice chancellor. He was then promoted from acting principal to principal, and remained in the position until 1996.

Richards has served on the boards of several companies and service organizations, including the Trinidad and Tobago Oil Company, the National Training Board, the Institute of Marine Affairs, and the Salaries Review Commission; he was elected president of the latter in 1997.

A joint sitting of the two houses of Parliament elected Richards as president of Trinidad and Tobago on 14 February 2003, and he took office on 17 March. He is regarded as an apolitical figure; the presidency is generally ceremonial. However, he has pledged to work to heal racial divisions in the country and is much concerned with tertiary education; Richards wants to raise the level of participation in higher education from its current rate of 10%, and is closely following the development of the new University of Trinidad and Tobago.

Profile of the Prime Minister:

Patrick **MANNING**

Patrick Manning leads the right-of-centre People's National Movement (PNM). Originally trained as a geologist, he entered government service in the early 1970s and went on to have a prominent political career. He was prime minister from 1991 to 1995 and regained power in 2001 amid unprecedented political wrangling.

Patrick Augustus Mervyn Manning was born on 17 August 1946 in San Fernando, western Trinidad. After leaving school in 1965 he spent a year as a refinery operator with the oil giant Texaco in Pointe-à-Pierre, just to the north of San Fernando. He travelled to Jamaica in 1966 to study geology at the University of the West Indies (UWI), and returned to Pointe-à-Pierre in 1969 to apply his new knowledge in the service of his former employer. Two years later he swapped geology for the world of politics and was elected to represent San Fernando East constituency for the PNM. He married Hazel Anne-Marie Kinsale in 1972 and they have two sons.

Between 1971 and 1978 Manning served as a parliamentary secretary for various ministers in the PNM governments of the time. He shuttled between the ministry of petroleum, the prime minister's office and ended at the ministry of works, transport and communications. In 1978 he was appointed to the cabinet as a junior minister in the ministry of finance, and added a position in the prime minister's office in 1979. He became a full minister for the first time in 1981 as minister of information and minister of industry and commerce. He went on to serve as minister of energy and natural resources from 1981 to 1986.

Since 1987 Manning has been leader of the PNM. As such he led it in opposition until its triumphal return to power in 1991. As prime minister his policies of economic liberalization and privatization brought praise and investment from abroad, but failed to captivate the electorate. The PNM was forced from power once again in 1995 and Manning returned to his post as leader of the opposition. The party fared badly in the 2000 elections, as the centre-left United National Congress (UNC) climbed to a simple majority.

The UNC majority proved fragile, however, and in December 2001 fresh elections were held which resulted in an unprecedented tie of 18 seats each for the PNM and the UNC. President Arthur Robinson was left to choose the premier and plumped for Manning, much to the anger of the UNC. Manning agreed to hold fresh elections within the year. In October 2002 the PNM was returned with an indisputable majority of its own (20 out of 36 seats) and Manning was reconfirmed as prime minister.

Manning's current term has been blighted by a spiralling crime wave, especially of murders and kidnaps for ransom; the prime minister has blamed the illegal narcotics trade for creating a "criminal elite" able to bribe public officials and buy weapons and ammunition. Even some of his ministers have been accused of accepting bribes or kickbacks and are under investigation by the Integrity Commission. Manning has also faced criticism for nepotism with the appointment of his wife as a senator and minister of education.

TUNISIA

Full name: The Republic of Tunisia.

Leadership structure: The head of state is a president, directly elected by universal adult suffrage. The president's term of office is five years. A referendum, held on 26 May 2002, approved changes to the constitution to remove the three-term limit and to raise the maximum permitted age of candidates from 70 to 75. The head of government is the president, who is responsible to the Chamber of Deputies. The Council of Ministers is appointed by the president.

President:	Zine el-Abidine **BEN ALI**	Since 7 Nov. 1987
Prime Minister:	Mohammed **GHANNOUCHI**	Since 17 Nov. 1999

Legislature: The legislature is unicameral. The sole chamber, the Chamber of Deputies (Majlis al-Nuwaab), has 189 members, directly elected for a five-year term. The Chamber of Councillors (Majlis al-Mustasharin), elected for the first time in July 2005, has 126 members indirectly elected by regions and professional organizations, and 41 appointed by the president, all for a six-year term.

Profile of the President:

Zine el-Abidine **BEN ALI**

Gen. Zine el-Abidine Ben Ali is a former military and intelligence specialist, and only the second president of Tunisia since independence in 1956. Having taken over in 1987 when Habib Bourguiba was deposed on grounds of senility, he has been confirmed in power in five-yearly direct elections since 1989. In spite of facing opposition in the two most recent elections, he was still credited with well over 90% of the vote.

Zine el-Abidine Ben Ali was born in Hammam Sousse on 3 September 1936. He was expelled from secondary school for political activism. Initially trained in electronics at the military academy in Saint-Cyr in France, he was later educated in all aspects of military intelligence at the artillery school in Châlons-sur-Marne (France) and at the senior intelligence school in Maryland (USA). Unlike Bourguiba, who was an agnostic, Ben Ali is a practising Muslim, even though his training and policies are primarily Western in orientation. He is married to Leila née Trabelsi, with six children, the youngest born in 2005, when Ben Ali was 68. He also has children from a previous marriage.

He began his working career as a military officer, and was the director of Tunisia's military intelligence security department from 1964 to 1974. For the next three years he was attaché to Spain and Morocco with general responsibility for defence, military and naval matters. By 1977 he had risen to the position of director-general of national security and was responsible for curbing protests by striking workers in 1978 and bringing under control an uprising by Islamic fundamentalists in the mining town of Gafsa in January 1980. Later that year, however, he was removed from his post and sent as ambassador to Poland.

In 1984 he entered the cabinet as minister of national security, and in 1986 was appointed secretary-general of the ruling Destour Socialist Party (Parti Socialiste Destourien—PSD), which had been the sole legal political party from 1964 until 1981. From 1986 until he commenced his presidency, Ben Ali was minister of the interior and from October 1987 he was also prime minister. His assumption of the presidency on 7 November 1987, in a move backed by the military, signalled the first change in executive power since Bourguiba had led Tunisia to independence in 1956.

In 1988 Ben Ali changed the name of the PSD to the Constitutional Democratic Rally (Rassemblement Constitutionnel Démocratique—RCD) as part of a process which sought to reflect a climate of increased openness and legitimacy. He has since been re-elected with massive majorities in April 1989, March 1994, October 1999, and most recently in October 2004, while the RCD has consistently won the vast majority of seats in the Chamber of Deputies. The 1999 poll was the first to be contested by other candidates, but nonetheless Ben Ali still secured 99.45% of the vote. The quasi-unanimity of his endorsements has been tainted by the frequent arrest-release-rearrest of opposition pro-democracy activists.

In September 2001 the RCD defied the constitution to nominate the president to stand for a fourth term in office in 2004. In order to legitimize his candidacy, Ben Ali organized the country's first ever referendum on 26 May 2002, in which 99% of voters approved abolishing the three-term limit. The referendum also raised the maximum age for presidents from 70 to 75 years of age, thereby allowing for the possibility of a fifth term, and included provisions to introduce a second parliamentary chamber and pledges to improve human rights. Facing three other candidates in the 2004 vote, Ben Ali polled 94.5%.

Ben Ali has been criticized for failing to introduce a genuinely pluralist form of politics in Tunisia, for the poor treatment of political prisoners, and for clampdowns on Islamic fundamentalist groups. Mindful of the turmoil in neighbouring Algeria, he has maintained a hard line in an attempt to preserve stability and thus ensure continued income from tourism, the country's largest source of foreign currency earnings.

Profile of the Prime Minister:

Mohammed **GHANNOUCHI**

Mohammed Ghannouchi is a leading member of the ruling Constitutional Democratic Rally (Rassemblement Constitutionnel Démocratique—RCD). A career politician and economist, he entered the ministry of planning in 1966 and was first appointed to the cabinet in 1987. His appointment as prime minister in November 1999 was seen as confirming the government's commitment to economic liberalization.

Mohammed Ghannouchi was born near Sousse on 18 August 1941. He graduated from the Tunis University of Law, Political Sciences and Economics (now the University of Tunis III) with a degree in economics in 1966 and went straight to work for the ministry of planning. Ten years later he was appointed general director of planning.

In 1987, after Gen. Zine el-Abidine Ben Ali had assumed power as prime minister, Ghannouchi was inducted into government as minister of planning. From 1989 he was also minister of finance, and minister of national economy and finance from 1990. A year later he was made simply minister of finance and in 1992 his role was specialized as minister of international co-operation and foreign investment. For the rest of the 1990s Ghannouchi was crucial to Tunisia's negotiations with international financial institutions such as the World Bank, the International Monetary Fund (IMF) and the European Union (EU). Consequently he gained international exposure and a reputation for supporting liberal economics. In 1995 he oversaw the signing of a free trade zone agreement with the EU.

Following the re-election of President Ben Ali and the RCD in 1999, Ghannouchi was appointed prime minister on 17 November. His nomination sent a clear message to the international community that Tunisia was eager to embrace the economic policies of the West; key issues are privatization, encouraging foreign investment and reducing trade barriers and bureaucracy, with the target of entering a free trade era with the EU by 2010. Ghannouchi was reappointed with a reshuffled cabinet after the 2004 legislative elections.

TURKEY

Full name: The Republic of Turkey.

Leadership structure: The head of state is a president, elected by the Turkish Grand National Assembly. The president's term of office is seven years, not renewable. Parliament rejected various proposals submitted in February 2000 to make the presidency directly elected, and to enable a president to serve two five-year terms. The head of government is the prime minister, who is appointed by the president. The cabinet is appointed by the prime minister.

President:	Süleyman Demirel	16 May 1993—16 May 2000
	Ahmet Necdet **SEZER**	Since 16 May 2000
Prime Minister:	Bülent Ecevit	11 Jan. 1999—18 Nov. 2002
	Abdullah Gül	18 Nov. 2002—11 March 2003
	Recep Tayyip **ERDOĞAN**	Since 11 March 2003

Legislature: The legislature is unicameral. The sole chamber, the Turkish Grand National Assembly (Türkiye Büyük Millet Meclisi), has 550 members, directly elected for a five-year term.

Profile of the President:

Ahmet Necdet **SEZER**

Ahmet Sezer, a judge by training and chief of the Constitutional Court from 1998 until May 2000, was then chosen as a last-minute apolitical candidate to succeed the popular Süleyman Demirel as president. A reserved and uncharismatic figure, he is only the fourth civilian to hold this largely ceremonial post, and the first holder to be neither a general nor a politician. From the beginning he has stressed his commitment to democracy and urged reforms to help Turkey head towards membership of the European Union (EU).

Ahmet Necdet Sezer was born in Afyon in west-central Anatolia on 13 September 1941. He attended secondary school in the town before heading to Ankara in 1958 to study law. He graduated with a degree from the University of Ankara in 1962 and began his career as a judge in the city in the same year. After completing a period in the Land Forces Academy as part of his military service, he moved to the town of Dicle in the southeast near the border with Syria, where he again worked as a judge. In the 1970s Sezer was back in Ankara after being appointed as a supervisory judge at the High Court of Appeals. He returned to the capital's university and received a master's degree in civil law in 1978. Five years later he was elected to be a full judge at the High Court of Appeals and served in this capacity for a further five years.

Sezer, who is married to Semra with one son and two daughters, was appointed by the president in 1988 to work in the Constitutional Court and by 1998 he was the court's chief justice. His reputation as a no-nonsense advocate of secular democracy was forged in this role when in 1998 he pronounced a ban on the main Islamic party of the time. He has since stressed his strong belief that a secular state is a "must for democracy". He also made a strongly worded speech in April 1999 calling for profound constitutional changes to the military-dictated constitution which has been in place since a coup in 1980. His pleas centred on Turkey's much-condemned policies limiting freedom of speech and expression.

When President Demirel's seven-year term expired in early 2000, the prime minister, Bülent Ecevit, made a last-minute plea to maintain a sense of continuity and harmony in the Grand National Assembly by allowing him to serve on for a second term. Only when this failed did Sezer's name arise as a suitable nonpartisan replacement. Despite his public popularity, a number of politicians questioned his lack of political experience. After failing to win the necessary majorities in the first two votes, due largely to protest voting from deputies, Sezer was eventually elected in May 2000 by 330 of the Assembly's 550 possible votes.

Within hours of his election Sezer made his first public comments and immediately called for further and faster political reform, stating that "democracy and democratic values" were essential in creating a "social state of law". He has also urged greater economic reforms based on an inspection of public spending and rates of inflation in an attempt to redress disparities in income. Essentially Sezer's main task is to help to align Turkey with the policies of the EU to enable the country's eventual admission.

Sezer's secular stance has been strained since the 2002 elections saw the rise of the Islamist-dominated Justice and Development Party (Adalet ve Kalkinma Partisi—AKP). However, the current prime minister Recep Tayyip Erdoğan shares Sezer's desire for EU membership, and necessary reforms of human rights, military involvement in politics and the penal code have been pushed through.

Profile of the Prime Minister:

Recep Tayyip **ERDOĞAN**

Recep Tayyip Erdoğan was finally appointed as Turkish prime minister on 11 March 2003, four months after the sweeping victory of his Islamist-dominated Justice and Development Party (Adalet ve Kalkinma Partisi—AKP) in general elections. He became mayor of Istanbul in 1994, but was convicted of inciting religious hatred in 1998 for publicly reciting an Islamic poem containing military imagery and was sentenced to ten months in jail. Along with former colleagues from the Welfare Party, he formed the Justice and Development Party in 2001 and won a landslide victory in elections in November the following year, but his criminal conviction prevented him from standing himself, until a constitutional amendment and a by-election remedied this problem and allowed his appointment as prime minister. Erdoğan has disavowed the hard-line Islamic views of his past and presented himself as a pro-Western conservative, his pragmatic approach to tendentious issues such as headscarves serving to calm Western fears of a hard-line Islamic state on the edge of Europe.

Recep Tayyip Erdoğan was born on 26 February 1954 in Istanbul, but spent most of his early childhood in Rize on the Black Sea coast where his father worked as a coastguard. The family returned to Istanbul when Erdoğan was 13, in order to give the five children a better upbringing. Erdoğan sold lemonade and *simit* (sesame rings) on the streets as a teenager in order to earn extra money. He was educated at a religious Imam Hatip School and then at Marmara University where he graduated in economics and business. Erdoğan began playing as a semiprofessional footballer at this time for a team sponsored by Istanbul's municipal transport company. He attended his first political meeting at the age of 15, and in the early 1970s became involved with the now defunct Islamist National Salvation Party (Milli Selamet Partisi—MSP), led by Necmettin Erbakan, whom Erdoğan met while at university. In 1978 he married Emine, and they have two sons and two daughters.

Erdoğan left the municipal transport authority and gave up his football career in 1980 following Turkey's military coup; a retired colonel at the authority told him to shave off his moustache, and when Erdoğan refused he was forced out of his job. He then went on to work in the private sector for two years before his mandatory military service in 1982, where he served as a commissioned officer.

Following the 1980 coup, all political parties were disbanded until 1983, when the former members of the MSP founded the Welfare Party (Refah Partisi—RP). In 1985 Erdoğan became the RP's chairman in Istanbul Province, and stood several times as a candidate for the Grand National Assembly in the late 1980s. In 1991 the RP won 17% of the vote. In the local elections of March 1994, the RP did extremely well, and Erdoğan became mayor of Istanbul as well as president of the Greater Istanbul Metropolitan Council.

Even Erdoğan's critics accept that he was a success as mayor. He improved the water supply, cleared slums, fought pollution and planted thousands of trees, beautifying the city as he fixed its infrastructure. He also gained a reputation for honesty. Erdoğan became one of Turkey's most popular politicians, although his decision to ban alcohol from the city's cafés displeased secularists. His pro-Islamic stance also saw him accuse the UN and the North Atlantic Treaty

Organization (NATO) of being lackeys of the USA, and oppose Turkey's moves towards European integration.

In 1996 the RP was declared unconstitutional and was disbanded on the grounds of threatening the secular nature of the state. The party promptly re-formed as the Virtue Party (Fazilet Partisi—FP). The following year, at a public meeting in Siirt in southeast Turkey, Erdoğan read out a poem by Ziya Gökalp, containing the lines: "Mosques are our barracks, domes our helmets, minarets our bayonets, believers our soldiers." He was tried and convicted in 1998 of inciting religious hatred, banned from ever holding public office and sentenced to ten months in prison (though he was freed after serving four months of the sentence). The following year the FP was itself found unconstitutional on the same grounds as the RP had been banned.

The decision prompted a split among former members of the now defunct party. Many, seeking to remain true to Islamic fundamentalism, formed the Felicity Party (Saadet Partisi—SP); Erdoğan, however, led those wishing to adapt Islamist politics into a secular democratic system into the new AKP. The AKP went on to win 34% of the vote in the 2002 general election and an overall majority in the Grand National Assembly. However, Erdoğan's 1998 conviction precluded him from standing for a seat in the Assembly, let alone taking office as prime minister. One of Erdoğan's key supporters, Abdullah Gül, had to act as a stand-in prime minister and hastily push through a constitutional amendment allowing Erdoğan to stand in the next Assembly by-election.

Erdoğan was finally appointed as prime minister on 11 March 2003. He has tried to break from militant Islam, but has provoked some tension with the staunchly secular military elite by seeking to make the qualifications of those attending Islamic schools equal to those attending standard secondary establishments. However, he has maintained close relations with the USA and Israel, and has pursued talks on EU accession. He has neatly sidestepped the troubled issue of headscarves by saying that he would not bring his wife, who wears a headscarf, to secular political occasions. His distrust of the nationalism of the military has however led to a thawing of relations with neighbouring Greece; in May 2004 Erdoğan became the first Turkish leader to visit Greece since 1988. In response, Greek leader Costas Karamanlis offered Turkey his government's backing for the country's EU bid, a huge symbolic concession.

TURKMENISTAN

Full name: Turkmenistan.

Leadership structure: The head of state is a president, directly elected by universal adult suffrage. Under the constitution the president's term of office is five years, renewable once only, but the term of incumbent president Saparmurad Niyazov has been extended indefinitely. The head of government is the president, who appoints the Council of Ministers.

President: Saparmurad **NIYAZOV**   Since 27 Oct. 1990
                (chairman of Supreme Soviet from 19 Jan. 1990)

Legislature: The legislature is bicameral. The Parliament (Majlis) has 50 members, directly elected for a five-year term. The People's Council (Khalk Maslakhaty), which is the supreme representative, legislative and supervisory body, has 2,507 members including the president (who is the chair for life), the Council of Ministers, the 50 members of the Parliament, regional governors, appointed members and ethnic and regional representatives.

Profile of the President:

Saparmurad **NIYAZOV**

Saparmurad Niyazov, the first elected president of the Turkmenistan republic within the Soviet Union, remained in office as the republic moved to independence with the collapse of the Soviet system. An engineer by training, he was previously the first secretary of the Communist Party of Turkmenistan (CPT) in 1985–90. Since independence in 1992 he has promoted a cult of personality, and had his term of office extended first for five years and then indefinitely, though he has promised that he will step down by 2010.

Saparmurad Niyazov was born on 18 February 1940 and grew up in the capital, Ashkhabad. His father died in the Second World War, and in 1948 he lost most of his remaining close family in the Ashkhabad earthquake. He is now married and has one son and one daughter.

Niyazov studied physics and mathematics at the Leningrad Polytechnic School in 1962–66, and graduated as a power engineer. From 1959 to 1967 he was a member of the All-Union Central Trade Union Council, working as an instructor for mineral prospecting works in Turkmenistan. From 1967 to 1970 he worked at the Bezmeinskaya hydroelectric power station.

In 1962 Niyazov joined the CPT, and by 1970 he had risen to the position of instructor, then department head, within its central committee. He was first secretary of the CPT central committee for Ashkhabad in 1980–84, and in 1985 was appointed first secretary for Turkmenistan, the highest party post in the republic. In this capacity, like the 14 other first secretaries of the republics making up the Soviet Union, Niyazov was brought into the politburo of the Communist Party of the Soviet Union (CPSU) in the major restructuring of that organ in July 1990.

Niyazov became chairman of the Turkmenistan Supreme Soviet, in effect the republic's head of state, in January 1990. He held the republic's new directly elective presidency as a result of elections in October 1990 when he won what was recorded as 98.3% of the vote, and became commander-in-chief of the armed forces. The CPT was renamed in 1991 as the Democratic Party of Turkmenistan (DPT), with Niyazov continuing as its chairman. In the first elections held after full independence, in June 1992, he was confirmed in his post as president with 99.5% of the vote.

Closing his grip on power, Niyazov has instituted a grandiose cult of personality. In 1993 the Parliament conferred upon him the title Turkmenbashi—'father of the Turkmen people' and in 2001 debated conferring the additional title of 'prophet' on him. Among the monuments to the president in Ashkhabad is a 12-metre-high construction featuring a revolving gold-plated statue of Niyazov which permanently faces the sun. Niyazov often complains about the number of portraits of him on display, but these complaints are usually the prelude to the installation of even more portraits and statues. His guide to life, the *Ruhnama*, was adopted as a 'national code' in October 2001 and is now required reading for university applicants or driving licence applicants—to ensure that they "are educated in the spirit of high moral values of Turkmenistan's society". He has renamed the days of the week and the months of the year, in honour of himself, his mother and key national symbols

Behind the flamboyance lies an increasingly apparent tendency for authoritarianism and isolation. He has banned young men from wearing beards and long hair—not so much to crack down on overt religious symbols as to avoid displays of individualism. The playing of recorded music at public events, weddings and on television has also been banned in order to protect Turkmen culture from negative influences. Niyazov has dismissed all traffic policemen and several thousand health workers, replacing them with cheaper, but unqualified, conscripted soldiers. Rural libraries have been closed, Niyazov saying they are pointless as villagers do not read. The closure of all regional hospitals outside Ashkhabad and the abolition of free health care has left the country with the lowest life expectancy in Europe and central Asia. Niyazov has furthermore closed nearly all higher education facilities, preventing the training of new medical staff.

Opposition to him is growing. Although political debate is seriously curtailed, certain exiled figures have appeared as potential rivals. On 25 November 2002 gunmen opened fire on the president's motorcade in the capital and Niyazov immediately blamed 'foreign' sources, principally his former foreign minister Boris Shikhmuradov. After a public confession Shikhmuradov was arrested on 29 December.

Politically Niyazov has tried to make his position unassailable. A referendum in January 1994 on a five-year extension (until 2002) of his term in office was approved with a recorded 99.9% endorsement. This was superseded on 28 December 1999 when the Parliament unanimously voted to remove the limit to the length of his term in office altogether. To counterbalance these moves, Niyazov has declared that he would step down before he turns 70 in 2010. The People's Council reconfirmed his life presidency in 2004, but Niyazov has continued to ask for the holding of presidential elections in 2009. Candidates in the December 2004 legislative elections had to swear lifelong loyalty to the 'eternal president' and first-time voters were given copies of the *Ruhnama*.

TUVALU

Full name: Tuvalu.

Leadership structure: The head of state is the British sovereign, styled 'Queen of Tuvalu, and of Her other Realms and Territories, Head of the Commonwealth', and represented by a governor-general who is appointed on the advice of the Tuvaluan prime minister. The head of government is the prime minister, who is elected by MPs from among their number. The cabinet is appointed by the governor-general on the advice of the prime minister.

Queen:	Elizabeth II	Since 6 Feb. 1952
Governor-General:	Sir Tomasi Puapua	26 June 1998—9 Sept. 2003
	Faimalaga Luka	9 Sept. 2003—15 April 2005
	Filoimea **TELITO**	Since 15 April 2005
Prime Minister:	Ionatana Ionatana	27 April 1999—8 Dec. 2000
	Lagitupu Tuilimu (acting)	8 Dec. 2000—24 Feb. 2001
	Faimalaga Luka	24 Feb. 2001—14 Dec. 2001
	Koloa Talake	14 Dec. 2001—2 Aug. 2002
	Saufatu Sopoanga	2 Aug. 2002—27 Aug. 2004
	Maatia **TOAFA** (acting from 27 Aug. 2004)	Since 11 Oct. 2004

Legislature: The legislature is unicameral. The sole chamber, the Parliament of Tuvalu (Palamene o Tuvalu), currently has 15 members, directly elected for a four-year term. The constitution stipulates a minimum of 12 members, with more added by Act of Parliament to account for changes in population and boundaries of each electoral district, and any other special circumstances.

Profile of the Governor-General:

Filoimea **TELITO**

Reverend Filoimea Telitoa is from the island of Vaitupu. He graduated from the Pacific Theological College in Suva, Fiji, in 1982, publishing a thesis on the impacts of social change on the Tuvaluan family. He worked as a school headteacher and as a Protestant church minister until his appointment as governor-general of Tuvalu on 15 April 2005, replacing Faimalaga Luka. As governor-general he also became chief scout of the Tuvalu Scout Association. In the first few months of his term in office he met with Taiwanese president Chen Shui-bian, and officially received the Queen's Baton on its journey to Melbourne for the 2006 Commonwealth Games.

Profile of the Prime Minister:

Maatia **TOAFA**

Maatia Toafa was elected as prime minister of Tuvalu in October 2004, having held office as deputy prime minister for the preceding two years.

Maatia Toafa is the first prime minister of Tuvalu to come from the island of Nanumea, the most northerly of the group that makes up the archipelago. He served as deputy prime minister in the government of Saufatu Sopoanga from 2 August 2002.

Sopoanga lost a confidence vote on 25 August 2005, while one of his government's supporters was receiving medical treatment in New Zealand; Toafa became acting prime minister two days later. Sopoanga also resigned from Parliament, in order to stall the election for a new prime minister as the constitution requires all seats to be filled before Parliament can meet on important issues.

Six weeks later, a by-election was held re-electing Sopoanga, and Parliament then elected Toafa prime minister on 11 October by eight votes to seven; Sopoanga became his deputy. Toafa made a radio broadcast immediately after being sworn in, expressing hope that his government would now bring political stability to the country and be allowed to finish its term. He has pledged a review of the country's constitution with a view to dropping Queen Elizabeth II as head of state.

By mid-2005 the death of one MP and resignations of two others required three by-elections, putting the government's 8–7 majority in doubt. However, two of the successful candidates announced that they would support the government, strengthening Toafa's majority to 9–6.

UGANDA

Full name: The Republic of Uganda.

Leadership structure: The head of state is a president, directly elected by universal adult suffrage. The president's term of office is five years, limited by the constitution to two terms, though Parliament passed a bill in July 2005 to remove this limit. The head of government is the prime minister, who is appointed by the president with the approval of the Parliament. The cabinet is appointed by the president.

President:	Yoweri **MUSEVENI** (took power on 26 Jan. 1986)	Since 29 Jan. 1986
Prime Minister:	Apollo **NSIBAMBI**	Since 6 April 1999

Legislature: The legislature is unicameral. The sole chamber, the Parliament, has 276 members, serving a five-year term. Of these, 214 are elected by constituencies and 62 are elected indirectly to represent particular groups including women, youth and the disabled. Cabinet ministers who are not already members of the Parliament are ex officio members of it, as is the vice president.

Profile of the President:

Yoweri **MUSEVENI**

Yoweri Museveni presides over a nonparty system based on his National Resistance Movement (NRM), and was most recently re-elected as president in March 2001. He originally came to prominence in the Tanzanian-backed intervention in 1979 to remove the regime of Idi Amin. Soon rebelling once more, against the dictatorial rule of Milton Obote, he waged a five-year guerrilla struggle, culminating in the ousting in 1986 of a military regime which had deposed Obote the previous year. Since then Museveni has done much to revive the economy and restore peace in the strife-ridden country, but has persisted in seeking a military solution to the renewed Lord's Resistance Army (LRA) insurgency in the north, where a massive humanitarian crisis has developed.

Yoweri Kaguta Museveni was born in 1944 in Ntungamo in southwest Uganda. He studied locally before reading political science, economics and education at Dar es Salaam University in Tanzania in 1967–70. Closely linked during his student days with the Marxist guerrilla Front for the Liberation of Mozambique, he also chaired the University Students' African Revolutionary Front, a pan-Africanist and anti-colonialist organization.

Returning to Uganda, he worked briefly as a research assistant at the office of President Milton Obote, until Gen. Idi Amin overthrew the government in 1971. Museveni fled back to Tanzania, where in 1973 he married a fellow Ugandan and fellow Christian, Janet Kataaha; they have one son and three daughters. While teaching at Moshi Co-operative College in Tanzania, Museveni set up an exile Front for National Salvation. This organization grew to the point where it could claim a fighting strength of up to 9,000, and in 1979 it was part of the ad hoc coalition which launched a bid to overthrow Amin. Heavily backed by Tanzanian forces, the Uganda National Liberation Front succeeded in driving out Amin. Museveni served briefly as defence minister in an interim government and vice chairman of a subsequent military commission pending the holding of a general election in 1980.

Museveni stood as a candidate of the Uganda Patriotic Movement in the 1980 election, but returned to guerrilla resistance when Obote's Uganda People's Congress hijacked the poll with blatant ballot-rigging to ensure its own victory. Museveni spent the next five years waging a gradually growing insurgency, as founder and leader of the National Resistance Army (NRA), against the Obote regime. Effectively without external support, his guerrilla forces gained ground in the south and west. When the NRA was unable to reach an agreement with the military government that had toppled Obote in mid-1985, it began a rapid advance towards the capital, Kampala, where in January 1986 the government of Gen. Tito Okello collapsed. Museveni took power himself on 26 January, and was sworn in as president and minister of defence three days later.

In power, Museveni continued to project himself as a 'freedom fighter'. While urging national reconciliation, he had also to contend with continuing violence in the north in particular for the first years of his rule. To prevent fresh outbreaks of ethnic violence he instituted a nonparty 'movement' system that did not ban political parties but prevented them from taking part in elections.

Although his NRM-based regime emphasized nonalignment internationally, Museveni established sufficient credibility with foreign aid donors to attract sustained backing from the World Bank for economic reconstruction work. He built up regional links particularly through the southern African Preferential Trade Area, and was chairman in 1990–91 of the Organization of African Unity (OAU, now the African Union—AU).

A new constitution, the product of lengthy consultation over two years, came into effect in 1995, providing for an elective presidency and a mainly elective Parliament. Museveni won the presidential election on 9 May 1996, campaigning with the slogan 'No Change' and taking almost 75% of the vote against two other candidates. The legislative elections held on a nonparty basis in late June of the same year produced an assembly in which the president's supporters held a clear majority. Just over 90% of voters backed the 'No Change' formula again in a referendum held on 29 June 2000, despite opposition calls for a boycott.

The presidential election campaign in 2000–01 was a tense race between Museveni and former ally Kizza Besigye. The opposition accused the government of intimidation. Museveni's campaign was aided by an increase in regional tensions and rumours that Besigye had received illegal funding from the 'hostile' regime in neighbouring Rwanda. In the event, Museveni was resoundingly re-elected with 69.3% of the vote on 12 March 2001, with Besigye receiving only 27.8%. International observers echoed opposition unease over the level of pre-electoral intimidation. Pro-Museveni candidates went on to win a majority in the June legislative elections. By the end of 2001 Museveni had established a committee to evaluate alternatives to the movement system, including full democracy.

Museveni's second term has been dominated by the re-intensification of the conflict in the north of the country with the brutal LRA and a rebellion in the west in 2000. In response Museveni dropped plans to cut defence spending in favour of funding an improvement of the armed forces and a crackdown on corruption in the military. Ceasefires with the LRA were short-lived and peace talks erratic; by 2004 there were over 1.6 million internally displaced persons and the UN warned that Uganda was suffering the most neglected humanitarian crisis in the world. Museveni still favours a military solution despite regular messages from NGOs working in the conflict areas that such an approach is not working. His government's request in 2005 for a joint operation with the neighbouring Democratic Republic of the Congo (DRC) against LRA fighters operating from DRC soil was rejected by the DRC authorities, who were keen to keep Uganda troops out of the country, having finally achieved their withdrawal in 2003 from involvement in the DRC's own civil war. Museveni's own brother had been named by the UN in 2001 on a list of people accused of plundering the DRC's resources under cover of war.

Legal wranglings over the validity of the 2000 referendum result and the legality of the Political Organizations Act 2002 forced Museveni to reconsider multipartyism. He retired from the army on 31 December 2003—ahead of new laws forcing soldiers to refrain from political activity—though constitutionally as head of state he will remain commander of the armed forces. A referendum was held in July 2005 which backed returning the country to multiparty democracy ahead of elections in 2006.

Museveni's support for the 'yes' campaign was seen as a concession to sweeten a controversial constitutional amendment secured earlier that month to remove the two-term presidential limit. This would allow him to stand for a third time in 2006. The move was condemned at home and abroad, offsetting the praise won internationally by Museveni's achievements in economic stability and growth.

Profile of the Prime Minister:

Apollo **NSIBAMBI**

Apollo Nsibambi has an academic background in economics and political science, working on issues of governance and development in Africa. He was one of a key group of Baganda intellectuals whose support for Yoweri Museveni helped swing this ethnic constituency, Uganda's largest, behind the president in the 1996 elections. He joined the cabinet shortly afterwards, rising within three years to the premiership.

Apollo Nsibambi was born on 27 November 1938. He gained a degree in economics from London, UK, in 1964, a master's degree in political science from Chicago, USA, in 1966 and a doctorate from Nairobi, Kenya, in 1984. He taught political science in higher education, becoming a professor, head of department, and in 1993 dean of the faculty of social sciences at Makerere University in Kampala, as well as director of the Makerere Institute of Social Research and vice chairman of the Council of the Christian University of East Africa. It was at Makerere University that he met his wife Rhoda, who taught there for over 30 years; she died in 2001, leaving four daughters.

Unlike many teachers and intellectuals who went into exile during the violence of Idi Amin's regime and the long years of civil war, Nsibambi remained in Uganda, working in higher education, throughout the 1970s and 1980s. He also had some experience in government, as minister of constitutional and political affairs and human rights in the regional government of the kingdom of Buganda, before serving as a delegate on the Uganda Constituent Assembly in 1994. Following the 1996 elections, in which the king of Buganda and intellectual leaders such as Nsibambi were influential in swaying the sizable Baganda vote behind Museveni, he was appointed in July 1996 to the Ugandan government as minister of public service. In May 1998 he became minister of education and sports, and in April 1999 Museveni appointed him prime minister.

UKRAINE

Full name: Ukraine.

Leadership structure: The head of state is a president, directly elected by universal adult suffrage. The president's term of office is five years. The president appoints the Council of Ministers, which is chaired by the prime minister as head of government.

President:	Leonid Kuchma	19 July 1994—23 Jan. 2005
	Viktor **YUSHCHENKO**	Since 23 Jan. 2005
Prime Minister:	Viktor Yushchenko	22 Dec. 1999—29 May 2001
	Anatoliy Kinakh	29 May 2001—21 Nov. 2002
	Viktor Yanukovych	21 Nov. 2002—5 Jan. 2004
	Mykola Azarov (acting)	7 Dec. 2004—28 Dec. 2004
	Mykola Azarov (acting)	5 Jan. 2005—24 Jan. 2005
	Yuliya **TYMOSHENKO** (acting from 24 Jan. 2005)	Since 4 Feb. 2005

Legislature: The legislature is unicameral. The sole chamber, the Supreme Council (Verkhovna Rada), has 450 members, directly elected for a four-year term.

Profile of the President:

Viktor **YUSHCHENKO**

Viktor Yushchenko is a banker who was a surprise choice as prime minister under President Leonid Kuchma in 1999. Removed from office in a confidence vote two years later, he went into opposition to the Kuchma government, setting up the 'Our Ukraine' movement. In 2004, with Kuchma retiring, Yushchenko stood for the presidency against Kuchma's handpicked successor, Viktor Yanukovych. He became seriously ill and was permanently scarred by dioxin poisoning in September of that year. In the October poll Yushchenko came a narrow second, and a runoff was scheduled for November. Accusations of fraud and widespread popular protest, known as the 'orange revolution', led to the results being overturned by the Supreme Court and a new runoff scheduled for 26 December. Yushchenko won the fresh vote and was sworn in on 23 January 2005.

Viktor Yushchenko, the son of two teachers, was born on 23 February 1954 in the village of Khoruzhivka in Sumska Oblast in northern Ukraine. He studied economics at university in Ternopil, graduating in 1975, then trained as a village accountant before national service, after which he moved into the banking system of the then Soviet Union. Yushchenko is married with five children.

Yushchenko worked for the USSR State Bank from 1976, heading the Ulyanovsk department for nine years and then deputy director of the Ukrainian regional office until 1988 when he was promoted to a managerial position in the Ukrainian Agro-Industrial Bank, based in Kiev. He remained at the bank, later named Ukraina, until 1993, when he was invited to join the central National Bank of Ukraine and was swiftly promoted to chairman and governor. Yushchenko played a central role in creating Ukraine's new national currency (the hryvna) and a new regulatory system for commercial banking.

In 1999 Yushchenko was a surprise nomination for prime minister after President Kuchma's previous choice was rejected by parliament by a single vote. Yushchenko by contrast was ratified by 296 votes to 12. However, his government, and in particular Deputy Prime Minister Yuliya Tymoshenko, became involved in a series of bruising confrontations with the 'oligarchs' who had control of the country's gas and coal reserves. Tymoshenko was sacked in January 2001 amid allegations of embezzlement and Yushchenko was removed from office by a vote of no confidence in April, despite last-minute support from Kuchma. The vote was regarded with dismay in many quarters; four million signatures were gathered in support of Yushchenko and 10,000 people rallied in the centre of Kiev to protest over his dismissal.

In July 2001 Yushchenko launched the 'Our Ukraine' coalition, which, by the time of the legislative elections the following year, had built up sufficient support to become the largest single element in parliament. However it proved unable to form a government, and Yushchenko took on the role of heading the anti-Kuchma opposition.

In 2004, as Kuchma's term in office drew to a close, Yushchenko announced his intention to stand for the presidency. With Kuchma constitutionally barred from standing again, Yushchenko faced his chosen successor, Prime Minister Viktor Yanukovych. The election campaign was bitterly contested and split the country both politically and geographically, much of Yanukovych's support coming from the industrialized and largely Russian-speaking east. In September 2004 Yushchenko became seriously ill and was flown to Austria for emergency treatment for what was later diagnosed as dioxin poisoning. The incident left Yushchenko with permanent facial scarring.

The initial presidential poll on 31 October saw Yushchenko garner 39.87% of the vote to Yanukovych's 39.32%, and a second round of voting was scheduled for 21 November. Accusations of vote rigging and intimidation in this second round were rampant, and there were serious discrepancies between exit polls showing

Yushchenko with an 11% lead and the final result indicating that he had lost by 3%. Yushchenko and his supporters refused to recognize the results and so began 13 days of popular protest in the central squares of Kiev; this became known as the 'orange revolution', after the colour of ribbons and scarves worn by protestors. The election results were eventually overturned by the Supreme Court and a rerun of the second round was scheduled for 26 December, which Yushchenko won by an 8% margin.

Yushchenko was sworn in on 23 January 2005 and appointed Tymoshenko as prime minister. The new administration had a distinctly pro-Western bent, as opposed to Kuchma and Yanukovych's pro-Russian orientation. This was prompted at least partly by Russian president Vladimir Putin's steadfast defence of Kuchma and Yanukovych throughout the popular protests against them.

Profile of the Prime Minister:

Yuliya **TYMOSHENKO**

Yuliya Tymoshenko is a successful businesswoman and Ukrainian politician who was appointed prime minister by President Viktor Yushchenko on 24 January 2005. She was one of the foremost leaders of the previous year's popular protests known as the 'orange revolution' that brought the downfall of the old regime.

She was born on 27 November 1960 in the Ukrainian city of Dnipropetrovsk, then part of the Soviet Union. (There is dispute over whether her maiden name was Grigyan or Telegina.) She studied economics at the Dnipropetrovsk State University, graduating in 1984, and going on to gain the equivalent of a doctorate. After graduation she worked as an engineer-economist in Dnipropetrovsk at the Lenin Machinery Plant for five years. Quick to see business opportunities as the communist system began to collapse, she launched a video rental chain in 1989, before founding and directing several energy-related companies in the 1990s with her husband, Oleksandr Tymoshenko, who rose to be one of the wealthiest 'oligarchs' in the country. She is regularly rated the richest woman in Ukraine and in July 2005 was named the third most powerful woman in the world by *Forbes* magazine.

In 1996 Tymoshenko was elected to parliament representing the Kirovohrad oblast, winning over 92% of the vote. She was comfortably re-elected in 1998, becoming chair of the budget committee, and the following year was appointed deputy prime minister for fuel under then prime minister Viktor Yushchenko. She was controversially dismissed by President Leonid Kuchma in January 2001 on charges of fraud and smuggling, and arrested in February, though she was released a few weeks later. Tymoshenko alleged that the charges were trumped up by the Kuchma regime under pressure from those involved in the coal industry who resented her attempts to root out corruption. However, others accuse Tymoshenko herself of having acquired her fortune through dubious if not nefarious means. In particular, her links with Pavlo Lazarenko, a former prime minister who fled the country in 1997 amid allegations of corruption, have returned to haunt her. She was drawn into the scandal that surrounded Lazarenko and accused of giving kickbacks in exchange for her company's gaining control of nearly 20% of Ukraine's GDP. Lazarenko was convicted in the USA in June 2004 on charges of money laundering and extortion.

Following her dismissal, Tymoshenko led street protests against Kuchma for his alleged involvement in the murder of journalist Georgi Gongadze. Never one to hide her light under a bushel, she founded the Yuliya Tymoshenko Bloc to contest the 2002 parliamentary elections, and positioned herself as a rebel leader. In September 2004, she signed a coalition pact with Victor Yushchenko, which reportedly contained an agreement that he would appoint her as premier if he won the imminent presidential elections, despite the fact that the two do not personally get on. Yushchenko became seriously ill and was flown to Austria for emergency treatment for what was later diagnosed as dioxin poisoning, leaving Tymoshenko to campaign across the country for Yushchenko's cause.

The presidential poll on 31 October saw Yushchenko win a narrow lead over his rival, Kuchma's chosen successor Victor Yanukovych. A second round of voting on 21 November was initially declared as a victory for Yanukovych, giving rise to accusations of vote rigging and intimidation, with Yushchenko and his supporters refusing to recognize the results. Tymoshenko was widely seen as one of the leaders of the 13 days of popular protest that followed, known as the 'orange revolution' after the colour of ribbons and scarves worn by protestors. The election results were subsequently overturned by the Supreme Court and a rerun of the second round was scheduled for 26 December, which Yushchenko won by an 8% margin. Tymoshenko was duly appointed prime minister on 24 January 2005 and confirmed in office by parliament on 4 February.

UNITED ARAB EMIRATES

Full name: The United Arab Emirates.

Leadership structure: The head of state is a president. The president and vice president are elected by the Supreme Council of Rulers (comprising the hereditary rulers of the United Arab Emirate's seven constituent emirates) from among its members. The president's term of office is five years. The head of government is the prime minister, who is appointed by the president. The Council of Ministers is appointed by the president.

President:	Sheikh Zayed bin Sultan al-Nahyan	2 Dec. 1971—2 Nov. 2004
	Sheikh Maktoum bin Rashid al-Maktoum (acting)	2 Nov. 2004—3 Nov. 2004
	Sheikh **KHALIFA** bin Zayed al-Nahyan	Since 3 Nov. 2004
Prime Minister:	Sheikh **MAKTOUM** bin Rashid al-Maktoum	Since 20 Nov. 1990

Legislature: The Federal National Council (Majlis Watani Itihad), which is unicameral and has 40 members, appointed for a two-year term, is a consultative body. It considers legislation proposed by the Council of Ministers.

Profile of the President:

Sheikh **KHALIFA** bin Zayed al-Nahyan

Sheikh Khalifa bin Zayed al-Nahyan succeeded his late father as president of the United Arab Emirates (UAE) on 3 November 2004. He had been groomed for the post from a young age, given responsibility for Abu Dhabi's defence force at just 21. He became prime minister of Abu Dhabi two years later in 1971, deputy prime minister for the UAE in 1973, and has been heavily involved in finance, infrastructure and construction.

Khalifa bin Zayed al-Nahyan was born in 1948, in the inland oasis city of Al-Ain, where he went to school. At the age of 18, following the elevation of his father Sheikh Zayed bin Sultan al-Nahyan to ruler of Abu Dhabi, Sheikh Khalifa was appointed as his representative in the eastern region of the country, and as head of the courts department in Al-Ain. Three years later, in 1969, he was nominated as crown prince of Abu Dhabi, and given the portfolio of defence within the emirate's government.

In this capacity, Sheikh Khalifa oversaw the evolution of the Abu Dhabi Defence Force (ADDF), which later became the nucleus of the UAE armed forces. In 1970 the Defence Force was reorganized with two infantry brigades and an artillery brigade. The UK withdrew as a protecting force in 1971 and the UAE federation was declared in December, with Sheikh Zayed as president. That same year, Sheikh Khalifa was appointed prime minister of Abu Dhabi as well as minister of defence and finance, and two years later he became deputy prime minister in the federal UAE cabinet (a post he held for four years). When Abu Dhabi's cabinet was dissolved shortly afterwards and replaced by an executive council, Sheikh Khalifa was appointed its first chairman.

The new council oversaw extensive development including water, housing, roads and general infrastructure in Abu Dhabi, turning the city into a modern metropolis. Meanwhile, the armed forces were unified within the federation in 1976. President Zayed became the supreme commander of the UAE armed forces while Sheikh Khalifa was appointed deputy supreme commander.

In 1981 Sheikh Khalifa established the Abu Dhabi department of social services and commercial buildings, which made loans to citizens for construction. Known as the Khalifa Committee, it followed the decision of Sheikh Khalifa to fix the interest rates on construction loans at 0.5%, with the balance of any interest due to private banks to be paid by the government. A decade later, Sheikh Khalifa established the Private Loans Authority, which loaned US$3,000 million to over 11,000 citizens within months of its formation. The following year Sheikh Khalifa raised the total amount of individual loans available from US$250,000 to US$330,000.

As well as these two areas of responsibility, Sheikh Khalifa has also chaired the Supreme Petroleum Council, and tried to steer the country's economy away from overreliance on oil and gas production. He also chairs the Abu Dhabi Investment Authority, the Environmental Research and Wildlife Development Agency, and the Abu Dhabi Fund for Development, the body overseeing the country's overseas aid programme.

Sheikh Zayed died on 2 November 2004. Sheikh Khalifa immediately became ruler of Abu Dhabi, and the following day the Supreme Council of Rulers elected him as president of the UAE.

Profile of the Prime Minister:

Sheikh **MAKTOUM** bin Rashid al-Maktoum

Sheikh Maktoum was the first prime minister of the United Arab Emirates (UAE), in the 1970s, and resumed this post, as well as becoming UAE vice president and ruler of Dubai—the second-largest of the seven emirates which make up the UAE—upon the death of his father in 1990. The Cambridge-educated Sheikh Maktoum is also known internationally for his involvement in horse racing.

Maktoum bin Rashid al-Maktoum, born in 1943, is the eldest of four brothers. When his grandfather Sheikh Saeed died in 1958, his father became ruler of Dubai and he was made crown prince of Dubai. He was appointed in 1960 as chairman of the Dubai lands department, established to deal with the legalities of land and property ownership. Between 1961 and 1964 he studied in the UK at the University of Cambridge. Sheikh Maktoum married in 1971.

Upon the creation of the UAE in 1971, when Sheikh Zayed al-Nahyan and Sheikh Rashid al-Maktoum (as the rulers of Abu Dhabi and Dubai respectively) were elected as the UAE's first president and vice president, Sheikh Maktoum was appointed as prime minister. They were re-elected, and he was reappointed, at the end of their initial five-year term.

During this period Sheikh Zayed, supported in the main by the smaller emirates, had worked towards greater centralization, giving rise to growing concern in Dubai about Abu Dhabi becoming too dominant. In April 1979 Sheikh Maktoum resigned as prime minister to boost the position of his father, Sheikh Rashid, who took on the post himself with Sheikh Maktoum as his deputy.

As crown prince of Dubai, Sheikh Maktoum succeeded automatically as ruler of Dubai when his father died on 7 October 1990. The following month he was elected formally by the Supreme Council of Rulers as UAE vice president, and appointed by the president, Sheikh Zayed, as prime minister.

Sheikh Maktoum's brother Sheikh Mohammed was appointed crown prince of Dubai in January 1995 and is also minister of defence in the UAE government. Another brother, Sheikh Hamdan, is the UAE minister of finance and industry. The fourth brother, Sheikh Ahmed, is a military commander. The four brothers rule Dubai in what has been described as a collegiate system, though Sheikh Mohammed is in charge of day-to-day affairs.

UNITED KINGDOM

Full name: The United Kingdom of Great Britain and Northern Ireland.

Leadership structure: The head of state is a constitutional monarch. The sovereign is styled 'of the United Kingdom of Great Britain and Northern Ireland and of Her other Realms and Territories Queen, Head of the Commonwealth, Defender of the Faith'. The head of government is the prime minister, who is responsible to Parliament. The cabinet is appointed by the prime minister.

Queen:	**ELIZABETH II**	Since 6 Feb. 1952
Prime Minister:	Tony **BLAIR**	Since 2 May 1997

Legislature: The legislature, the Parliament, is bicameral. The lower chamber, the House of Commons, currently has 659 members, directly elected for a maximum five-year term. The future of the upper chamber, the House of Lords, was the subject of a Royal Commission report published on 20 January 2000. An interim measure approved by the House of Lords on 26 October 1999, provided that some 650 hereditary peers would no longer have seats as of right. On 5 November 1999, they elected 75 of their number to the House, which also includes over 500 life peers, certain senior judges, 26 bishops of the Church of England, two ceremonial posts held by hereditary peers, and 15 deputy speakers elected by the whole House from among the hereditary peers.

Profile of the Queen:

ELIZABETH II

Elizabeth II succeeded to the throne on the death of her father George VI in 1952. Her coronation took place on 2 June 1953. She had been named as heir presumptive in 1936 following the death of her grandfather George V and the abdication of her uncle Edward VIII. She is also the head of the navy, air force and army, head of the Church of England and head of the Commonwealth, in which capacity she is titular head of state of Antigua and Barbuda, Australia, the Bahamas, Barbados, Belize, Canada, Grenada, Jamaica, New Zealand, Papua New Guinea, the Solomon Islands, St Kitts and Nevis, St Lucia, St Vincent and the Grenadines and Tuvalu.

Elizabeth Alexandra Mary of Windsor was born in London on 21 April 1926, the first child of George VI and Queen Elizabeth (who were then the duke and duchess of York). She spent most of her early childhood in the London area, and

605

was educated mainly by private tutors in French, art, music, law and constitutional history. In October 1940 she gave her first public broadcast in a message to the children of Britain and the Commonwealth. In 1944, during the Second World War, she was appointed a counsellor of state and had her first formal experience as future monarch while the king was at the front in Italy. She had joined the war effort as a member of the Auxiliary Territorial Service (ATS).

In 1947 she made her first formal visit abroad, to South Africa. Her special dedication to the Commonwealth was re-emphasized when she came to the throne in 1952, her father's death occurring and being announced while she was on a state visit to Kenya, and a year after her coronation she resumed her tour of the Commonwealth, at a time when many colonies and territories were pushing for independence from British rule.

Her long reign has been characterized by far-reaching changes in the public face of the British monarchy and its relationship with the nation. As an institution, the monarchy has faced increasing scrutiny in terms of the cost to the public and whether it yields 'value for money', accompanied by pressure to streamline the civil list. The queen is present at numerous public occasions, maintains the traditional weekly audience with the prime minister, and sees all cabinet papers and a daily summary of events in Parliament. Besides being head of the Church, she is the patron of many societies and institutions. Her coronation ceremony was the first to be televised, and was broadcast worldwide by radio, and she marked her silver jubilee in 1977 (celebrated in popular events and parties around the country) by an extensive tour of the UK and the Commonwealth. Her golden jubilee, celebrated in 2002, was generally accounted a great popular success.

Elizabeth married Prince Philip in November 1947. The son of Prince and Princess Andrew of Greece and Denmark, he was naturalized a British subject and created duke of Edinburgh. They have three sons and one daughter. Their eldest child, the prince of Wales and heir to the throne, is Prince Charles, born in 1948. The life of the royal family has been conducted under intense, and ever growing, media attention. The wedding of Prince Charles and Lady Diana Spencer in 1981 was immensely popular with the public. Princess Diana's glamour did much to change public expectations of the monarchy away from the family-centred ideal and the concepts of impartial service to the nation with which Elizabeth had grown up. While she herself continued to personify this ideal, it was undermined by the failure of the marriages of three of her children. The separation of Prince Charles and Princess Diana in 1992, the separation of the queen's second son from his wife and the formalization of her daughter's divorce in the same year, and the coincidence of a destructive fire at the queen's Windsor Castle residence, led her to describe 1992 in a famous phrase as her "annus horribilis". In 1997 a wave of public emotion and grieving over the death of Princess Diana in a car crash in Paris fuelled further criticism that the queen and the royal family held too much to tradition in such a moment and were too reserved and out of touch with the 'mood of the nation'.

From this low point the public perception of the monarchy and the queen herself has rebounded. The year 2002, her golden jubilee, began with more personal grief. Her sister Princess Margaret died on 9 February from a stroke and her mother Queen Elizabeth, the enormously popular 'Queen Mum', died on 30 March. The resulting public sympathy added extra significance to the summer's golden jubilee celebrations.

The controversial civil marriage of Prince Charles to his long-term partner Camilla Parker-Bowles in 2005 ended years of speculation over her status. However, it reignited constitutional debate over whether civil marriage was legal for the royal family, what Camilla's title would be, and whether Prince Charles would be able to head the Church of England, which does not recognize civil marriage. The queen, as current head of the Church, did not attend the wedding ceremony, but she joined the church blessing afterwards at Windsor.

As the queen approached her 80th birthday in April 2006, there was press speculation that she might follow other European monarchies and abdicate, but she indicated that she intended to remain in office until her death. She quashed rumours in 2005 of cutting back on international travel by announcing a suitably packed programme of visits planned for the year ahead.

Profile of the Prime Minister:

Tony **BLAIR**

Tony Blair swept to power in the 1997 elections after revamping the old socialist Labour Party into a centrist 'New Labour'. He introduced devolution to the UK, came near to achieving a lasting peace in Northern Ireland and championed the idea of public–private partnerships as a third alternative to nationalization and privatization. In 2005 he secured a third term, unprecedented for a Labour government. His critics accuse him of excessive reliance on presentation and 'spin' and of subservience in his close relationship with right-wing US president George W. Bush.

Anthony Charles Lynton Blair was born on 6 May 1953 in Edinburgh. For three years in the mid-1950s his family lived in Australia. After their return, his father, a law lecturer, industrial tribunal chairman and later a failed candidate for the Conservative (Tory) Party, held a university post in Durham, where the young Blair attended Durham Cathedral School. He finished his education at Fettes College, Edinburgh, before attending Oxford University, where he studied law at St John's College, graduating in 1975.

During his time in Oxford, Blair was lead singer and bass guitarist in a college rock band called Ugly Rumours, and he then worked briefly in Paris as a bartender and insurance clerk before resuming his legal training. Called to the Bar at Lincoln's Inn in 1976, he practised as a barrister until 1983, specializing in employment and industrial law. Tony Blair met Cherie Booth when they were both working in the barristers' chambers headed by Alexander (Derry) Irvine, later the lord chancellor. He and Cherie married in 1980; she is now a Queen's Counsel, and the couple have four children, born in 1984, 1986, 1989 and 2000. The youngest, Leo, was the first child born to a serving UK prime minister in over 150 years. Blair has been a committed Christian since his student days, his religious faith being an integral element in his political beliefs. A member of the Anglican Church, he also frequently attends mass in the Roman Catholic Church to which his wife belongs, and in which their children have been brought up.

Blair joined the Labour Party in 1975 and was elected to Parliament for the first time in June 1983, the year Labour suffered its heaviest defeat in its history. He held his seat, in the traditionally safe Labour constituency of Sedgefield in County Durham, at successive elections in 1987, 1992, 1997, 2001 and 2005.

Between 1984 and 1994, when Blair became Labour Party leader, he held a series of posts as 'shadow' spokesman, representing Labour (as the official opposition in Parliament) on issues dealt with by a specific government department. From 1984 to 1987 he was treasury spokesman, with special responsibility for consumer affairs and the City (London's financial sector). From 1987 to 1988 he was trade and industry spokesman. In 1988 he was elected to the shadow cabinet, becoming shadow secretary of state for energy, and then for employment (1989–92), in which role he forged a new industrial relations policy ending Labour's support for the so-called 'closed shop' or compulsory union membership in particular workplaces. After the Labour defeat in the 1992 election Blair was promoted to shadow secretary of state for home affairs under a new party leader, John Smith.

Shortly after the 1992 election defeat, Blair and Gordon Brown, the then shadow chancellor of the exchequer (i.e. shadow minister of finance), visited the USA on a fact-finding mission, holding discussions with Democratic Party campaign chiefs to discuss tactics for getting the Labour Party elected to government. In September that year Blair was elected to Labour's national executive committee, the ruling body of the party. He led the drive to turn Labour into a mass membership party (whereas in the past the Labour membership had been dominated by affiliated trade unions, wielding 'bloc' votes at party conferences proportionate to their size). By 1997 Labour had more than 400,000 individual members, making it one of the fastest-growing parties in Europe. Since it came to power, however, numbers have fallen significantly.

In May 1994 Labour leader John Smith died suddenly of a heart attack. An election for the leadership and deputy leadership of the party followed. Blair put himself forward as a candidate for the leadership, despite what was reportedly an earlier informal understanding between himself and Gordon Brown that he would back a Brown candidacy. Rumours concerning a so-called 'gentleman's agreement' between the two continue to haunt Blair, prompting a public rejection from him in September 2001 of the idea that he had at one time agreed to step down after one term in office in favour of Brown. In the event, it was Brown who stood aside in the 1994 contest and Blair came top of the poll, ahead of John Prescott (who became deputy leader).

Tony Blair thus became Labour leader on 21 July 1994 at the age of 41, the youngest leader of the party in its history. His youthful image helped him to create the concept of 'New Labour'. The party has been centralized, with discipline tightened ferociously, indeed to such an extent that Blair was labelled a 'control freak' by members of his own party within a year in office. One of his first acts of party reform was to abolish Clause IV in the party constitution, on the nationalization of the key elements of the economy. He went on to lead 'New Labour' to a landslide victory in the 1 May 1997 general election against a tired and scandal-plagued Conservative government. The first Labour administration for 18 years took office amid a wave of optimistic enthusiasm.

In his first term as prime minister Blair made good use of his unprecedented 419-seat majority in Parliament to introduce radical reforms. In Northern Ireland, after a committed negotiation process, the Good Friday Agreement was signed by the various parties in the troubled province in April 1998, and in June that year the Northern Ireland Assembly was inaugurated providing the region with its own government for the first time in 25 years. Though the Assembly was subsequently closed down and the peace process floundered, in 2005 the Provisional Irish Republican Army announced that it had renounced violence and decommissioned all its arms. Elsewhere, a government white paper on devolution for Scotland and Wales was published in July 1997 and elections to a separate Scottish Parliament and a Welsh Assembly were held in May 1999.

Politically, Blair has championed the now global concept of the 'third way', essentially the yoking of free-market economics with social welfare considerations, promoted by public–private sector partnership and guided by consultation with 'stakeholder' groups. With the help of Brown as 'iron chancellor', New Labour's policies have helped the UK maintain relatively high growth and record low unemployment despite a slowdown in the global economy. In Blair's first term this success was partly buoyed by the 'dotcom' bubble of Internet start-up companies. A particular achievement was the introduction of the minimum wage in April 1999.

Despite these successes, the high popularity with which Blair entered government began to fade. Some key election pledges were seen to have been avoided. Businesses complained of an increase in red tape rather than a reduction, while a spontaneous one-week blockade of fuel depots by the so-called 'fuel tax protestors' in September 2000 brought the country to a standstill. Despite public support for the protest, Blair refused to give in to the protestors' demands for fuel tax cuts. This gave a hint of his determination to ride out periods of unpopularity with dogged resistance, although he has shied away from applying subsequent fuel tax increases as too politically sensitive.

The strongest criticism in the first term was reserved for the use of 'spin', which had been mobilized by Blair in order to turn the Labour Party into a modern, media-savvy organization. Far from endearing the government's message to the public, this glossy approach to public relations saw a drop in trust and a rise in scepticism. The Conservative opposition made much of the issue, accusing Blair of hiding behind his media machine in order to evade key issues such as whether the UK should join the eurozone and adopt the euro currency. For his part, Blair has repeatedly stated that he is waiting for the country to pass Chancellor Brown's five economic tests before any vote is held on joining the euro.

Labour won a second term in office on 7 June 2001, winning a slightly reduced majority and 40.7% of the vote. However, the success was tainted by the lowest turnout since 1918—at only 59.4%—and seemed unremarkable in the face of a lacklustre campaign led by the then Conservative leader William Hague.

In Blair's second term in office his support for the principle of public–private partnerships as an alternative to full privatization drew considerable criticism from within the Labour movement and by the end of 2002 he was also facing a critical stand-off with the firefighters' union, one of the last old-style monopoly trade unions, which took high-profile strike action over pay and conditions.

However, by far the biggest criticism Blair drew was for his 'special relationship' with the new US president, the right-wing Republican George W. Bush. Blair had appeared to aspire to equal status on the world stage alongside Bush's predecessor Bill Clinton, despite the huge real power disparity. A genuine friendship between the two men was backed by similar political outlooks, particularly, it then appeared, in foreign policy. This was most evident in Blair's high-profile role in the decision to mount a sustained aerial bombardment of Yugoslavia, in a bid to halt its persecution of ethnic Albanians in Kosovo.

After the 11 September 2001 attacks on the USA, however, Blair promised to stand 'shoulder to shoulder' with the USA. His solidarity with Bush led to fierce criticism from within Labour. Although military intervention in Afghanistan proved more successful than many had anticipated, the hawkish Bush/Blair stance towards Iraq in 2002 over enforcing the elimination of weapons of mass destruction placed Blair at odds with a growing anti-war movement on the left.

Blair had long been a supporter of the idea of invading Iraq to facilitate regime change. Evidence suggests that he had tried to persuade Clinton of this, and that he had been concerned about Saddam Hussein's possible weapons of mass destruction for some years. In early 2003 it became clear that neoconservative hawks in the Bush administration had won the argument about going to war; Blair, keen to remain influential in the US foreign policy debate, is said to have felt that it was not in the UK's interests, nor anyone else's, for the USA to act alone.

However, in the early months of 2003 before the Iraq war, Blair had limited influence over the behaviour of the US administration, and appeared not to fully comprehend the depth of European concern about the US Republican administration's unilateralist behaviour. Though he did convince Bush to push harder for the implementation of the 'roadmap' to peace between Israel and the Palestinians, and to pursue a second UN resolution to strengthen the legitimacy of action against Iraq, he underestimated the intransigence of the French, with President Jacques Chirac, emboldened by recent election victories, prepared to wield a veto "whatever the circumstances". On 20 March, ten days after Chirac's assertion and with the second resolution now recognized as unattainable, UK troops joined with US soldiers to invade Iraq. Baghdad fell on 9 April.

Public approval of the war in Iraq, at a high of 63% in the days after Baghdad's fall, had dropped to around 50% by the summer, and Blair's popularity fell still further amid allegations that false intelligence about the supposed threat from Iraqi weapons of mass destruction had been inserted deliberately into a government 'dossier' used to justify intervention. The negative findings of the Hutton inquiry, set up after the suicide of Dr David Kelly, a government scientist regarded as a source of leaked information on this matter, were predictably dismissed by Blair's critics as a whitewash. On 1 August 2003 Blair became the UK's longest continuously serving Labour prime minister, though in the fallout of Dr Kelly's death the occasion was not marked.

Meanwhile, Blair was pushing through reforms of higher education financing which would introduce variable tuition fees, widely unpopular among students and many members of his own party. The bill eventually scraped through its second reading with a majority of just five. In late 2003 Blair was forced to go to hospital to have an irregular heartbeat treated, and by spring 2004 family problems had placed Blair under what a friend called "colossal strain", prompting rampant speculation that he planned to resign. Before undergoing a catheter ablation to correct his irregular heartbeat in October 2004, Blair told a BBC reporter that he would serve a full third term if elected but would not fight a fourth general election.

Labour won the general election of May 2005 with a heavily reduced majority. This led many to describe Blair as a 'lame duck' and again call for his resignation; however, as he entered the summer, Blair brushed this aside and took on the presidency of the G8 and the European Union (EU) with gusto. He confronted Chirac over EU farm subsidies and refused to give ground on the UK's EU rebate, winning plaudits in the UK press. The 2012 Olympics were awarded to London on 6 July, Blair having been personally involved in the campaign. At the same time he managed to broker a deal on aid to developing countries at the G8 summit, but these successes were overshadowed by four suicide bomb attacks on London's transport system on 7 July, which killed 57 people and injured many more. Blair's response to the bombings was again widely praised; despite most people blaming the invasion of Iraq for the attacks, his approval rating rose to 49%, its highest for months.

UNITED STATES OF AMERICA

Full name: The United States of America.

Leadership structure: The head of state is the president, chosen (technically) by an electoral college which is elected state by state by universal adult suffrage. The president's term of office is four years, with a maximum of two consecutive terms. The head of government is the president. The cabinet is appointed by the president, subject to confirmation by the Senate.

President:	Bill Clinton	20 Jan. 1993—20 Jan. 2001
	George W. **BUSH**	Since 20 Jan. 2001

Legislature: The legislature, the Congress, is bicameral. The lower chamber, the House of Representatives, has 435 members, directly elected for a two-year term. The upper chamber, the Senate, has 100 members, elected for a six-year term; one-third of the membership is up for election every two years.

Profile of the President:

George W. **BUSH**

George W. Bush was inaugurated as the 43rd president of the USA after the most closely fought and hotly contested election in decades, held in November 2000, when he was only the second person in history to win without a majority of the popular vote. Son of the former president George Bush, he had been governor of Texas from 1994, overseeing more executions than occurred in any other state. Ridiculed by opponents during his first election campaign for verbal gaffes and a painful ignorance of international affairs, George 'Dubya' Bush now seeks to lead a global 'war on terrorism' in response to the 11 September 2001 attacks in New York and Washington D.C. He was re-elected to a second term in November 2004.

George Walker Bush was born on 6 July 1946 in New Haven, Connecticut. His father took the family to Odessa in oil-rich Texas after he himself had graduated from the prestigious Yale University in 1948. The Bush dynasty has since been tied to the twin drives of politics and oil. George W. Bush's grandfather, Prescott Bush, who remained in the northeast, was a moderate, pro-civil rights Republican senator for Connecticut between 1952 and 1962.

After primary school George W. Bush was sent to Phillips Academy, an elite high school in Andover, Massachusetts, in 1961. Following in his father's footsteps he then attended Yale, where he studied history from 1964, but did not achieve academic distinction. A staunch conservative, he chose to avoid political debate on the hot issues of the day, including civil rights and the Viet Nam War. Facing the prospect of the draft after graduating in 1968, he enrolled in the elite Texas Air National Guard, an opportunity to spend two years learning to fly fighter planes, as well as to discharge his military service obligations in the comparative safety of Texas.

Having been active in all of his father's political campaigns in the 1960s, George W. Bush drifted thereafter into what he described as his "nomadic" years between 1970 and 1973. Dabbling in politics and mixing various jobs with periods of unemployment, playing sport, partying and flying, he lacked direction until he decided to return to full-time education in 1973 and got into Harvard University in Cambridge, Massachusetts, for an MBA (master's degree in business administration) course. After graduating in 1975, he went back to Texas and the oil business, establishing Bush Exploration that year. The company failed to turn major profits and was rescued from financial ruin on two separate occasions. After the second bailout in 1986, Bush was left as a consultant for the Harken Energy Corporation. In the meantime he had married Laura Welch, a former teacher and librarian from Texas, in 1977 and their twin daughters had been born in 1981.

Bush ran in his first election campaign in 1978, competing unsuccessfully for a seat in the House of Representatives. His father, however, was seeing his political fortunes change for the better. After a spell as head of the Central Intelligence Agency (CIA), Bush Sr was elected in 1980 to be vice president under Ronald Reagan, and (after two terms) was selected by the Republican Party to run for president in 1988. Bush Jr was enrolled to write speeches for his father in this campaign and moved with his young family to Washington D.C.

After his father's election as the 41st US president, Bush returned to Texas. Turning this time not to oil but to his childhood love for baseball, he mobilized support among family friends and oil magnates to form a consortium of investors to purchase the Texas Rangers team in 1989. In the 1990s his fortunes rebounded. He had given up his increasingly prominent vices of drinking and smoking and was 'born again' into the conservative Christian faith. In 1994 he set his eyes upon the gubernatorial elections for Texas. Riding high on the Rangers' success and his father's high approval rating following the 'victorious' conclusion of the Gulf War, he defeated the incumbent, Democrat Ann Richards. His campaign had focused on education and legal reform and he had won a convincing 54% majority. His re-election four years later was even more spectacular, making him the first two-term Republican governor of Texas, with an unprecedented 69% majority.

As governor of Texas, Bush is most famous for the rate of executions in the state—the highest in the country. Almost half of the lethal injections conducted since the death penalty's introduction there in 1977 were carried out under Bush's governorship in the late 1990s. He claims to have only spent an average of 15 minutes considering each case. Generally his terms in Texas were characterized by strict conservatism, with the abolition of parole for violent offenders, a cut in government spending accompanied by large tax cuts and an encouragement to faith-based charities to take up welfare provision. These were policies he was to bring with him to the presidency.

Success in Texas led Bush to the Republican nomination for the presidential campaign of 2000 against the incumbent Democrat vice president, Al Gore. Despite revelations about a previous arrest for drink-driving, several prominent gaffes, and the remarkable US economic boom under outgoing President Bill Clinton, the election proved one of the closest ever fought. It ended in a series of legal claims and counterclaims revolving around hand recounts in the crux state of Florida—the governor of which was Bush's elder brother, Jeb. The Supreme Court finally ruled in favour of the Republicans, banning further recounts and effectively handing Bush the presidency.

The first year of Bush's presidency prompted frustration from liberals around the world. Within days of his inauguration he had stepped firmly into controversy by re-imposing a Reagan-era ban on the government funding of foreign family-planning campaigns which treated abortion as a possible option. He also blurred the divisions between state and religion by proposing direct funding of faith-based charities. In international affairs he made good on his election pledge to refocus the country's foreign policy on the Americas, at the cost of making his administration appear parochial, stepping away from the Kyoto Protocol on greenhouse gas emissions, shunning the formation of an International Criminal Court, and allowing US–Chinese relations to deteriorate badly over the course of 2001.

Even though Bush's cabinet was the most ethnically diverse ever appointed, it was immediately criticized by the political opposition as containing renowned conservative hard-liners, including Condoleezza Rice as national security adviser, Donald Rumsfeld as secretary of defence and, most notably, his father's erstwhile defence secretary Dick Cheney as vice president.

The horror of 11 September 2001, when thousands were killed by terrorists flying hijacked passenger jets into the World Trade Center in New York and the Pentagon in Washington D.C., was to prove the making of George W. Bush's presidency. Despite initial criticism when he was rushed into hiding on the day itself, the president emerged as the nation's champion. Where once his lack of verbal finesse had attracted ridicule, his plain speaking, all-American vocabulary now appeared tailor-made to comfort a shocked and deeply frightened populace. The sense of a nation under siege was boosted by a spate of mysterious anthrax attacks designed to target high-ranking officials. Just nine days after 11 September Bush launched his 'war on terrorism'. Afghanistan, and its Islamic *taliban* regime, became the first target for refusing to hand over suspected terrorist mastermind Osama bin Laden. Bush asserted dramatically on 6

November, in a joint press conference with French president Jacques Chirac, that the nations of the world would be "held accountable for inactivity" and were "either with us or against us in the fight against terror". US-led intervention in Afghanistan tilted the balance decisively against the *taliban* and a new regime was successfully installed, albeit at a cost of more lives than were lost in the 11 September attacks.

Although many countries gave their support for the 'war on terrorism' in its initial stages, many have since expressed reservations, especially over the apparent focus on Islamic extremists rather than terrorism in general. Bush's denunciation of an 'axis of evil' states that sponsored terrorism, the oddly assorted trio of the officially secular (though largely Muslim) Iraq, the Islamic theocracy of Iran and the Stalinist dictatorship of North Korea, did little to change this perception—especially since, with regard to the Israeli–Palestinian conflict, Bush maintained US support for the right-wing Israeli prime minister Ariel Sharon.

Within the USA, however, Bush enjoyed a period where he appeared almost immune to criticism. His domestic political agenda received a major boost when the Republicans achieved historic election victories in the mid-term congressional polls in November 2002. The first president in 50 years to see his party gain in the mid-terms, Bush now had the majority support in both houses of Congress that he needed to implement his ambitious trillion-dollar tax-cutting programme. To many Americans, the serious downturn in the US economy spelled more of a threat to the president's popularity than the looming prospect of a war in Iraq to enforce the elimination of Saddam Hussein's alleged weapons of mass destruction (WMDs).

Under pressure from UK prime minister Tony Blair, the Bush administration sought more explicit UN endorsement before taking action against Iraq for its alleged breaches of previous Security Council resolutions and retention of WMDs. It soon became clear, however, that Russia and France (both of which had the power to veto a second UN resolution) opposed the use of military force. On 10 March 2003 Chirac announced that he would wield the veto "whatever the circumstances", signalling that there was no chance at all that the resolution would be passed. Bent nevertheless on action, the US-led 'coalition of the willing' invaded Iraq on 20 March, and the capital Baghdad fell on 7 April. Hubris over the ease of the initial victory quickly faded as it became clear that the looting and general disorder unleashed by Saddam Hussein's overthrow would necessitate a long-term US presence in Iraq, and that the very fact of that presence would inspire more resentment.

By the end of his first four-year term Bush's popularity had declined from its post-9/11 apex. His administration was struggling with a record deficit, which peaked at US$300,000 million in 2003, and questions were increasingly being raised over the administration's justification for the invasion of Iraq. Public opinion in the USA had become polarized with, on the one side, those who felt that the rationalization for the invasion was at best disingenuous and at worst dishonest, and at the other extreme those who regarded Bush and his administration as the guarantors of US security in the face of an amorphous and vicious threat.

The 2004 election campaign was bitterly fought. Democrat John Kerry, a veteran of the war in Viet Nam, attacked the Bush administration for its failures in Iraq and tried to portray Bush himself as stubbornly clinging on to a failing foreign policy. The Bush camp in turn attacked Kerry as someone unable to make up his mind or stick to a point of view. Most polls had Kerry entering election day with a narrow lead, but in the event Bush won the same states that he had in 2000, but with a larger majority in the vital swing states of Ohio and Florida. The next afternoon Kerry conceded.

Bush began his second term with a trip to Europe to try to mend fractured relationships, though it was unclear to what extent the journey was a success. Domestically, despite Bush's election victory, many Democrats appeared emboldened rather than cowed, and attacked Bush's programmes wherever a weak point appeared. His poll ratings dropped as the public articulated its dislike for his plans for social security reform and its disquiet at the ongoing military losses in Iraq. Bush's nomination of notorious hawk John Bolton as ambassador to the UN was delayed for several months by Democrat and rebel Republican senators, and he was ultimately forced to make a recess appointment.

Meanwhile, two senior aides to Dick Cheney were implicated in a scandal over the revealing of the identity of a CIA agent; Lewis Libby was eventually indicted on perjury charges while Karl Rove remained a subject of investigation. Bush's 2005 summer retreat was overshadowed by a campaign by Cindy Sheehan, mother of a young man killed in Iraq, who mounted a protest outside Bush's ranch near Crawford, Texas; her picket and a competing pro-war protest dominated headlines throughout the summer.

Even more damaging to the administration's ratings was the perceived sluggishness of the federal response to Hurricane Katrina, which devastated much of coastal Louisiana in late August and saw the city of New Orleans flooded and abandoned. As television viewers around the world were shocked by images of tearful and desperate US citizens stranded at the New Orleans convention centre pleading for food and water, Bush appeared to have lost his popular touch, particularly when he flew in to tell the then head of the Federal Emergency Management Agency Michael Brown what a fine job he was doing. Polls in September 2005 recorded satisfaction with Bush's leadership at an all-time low of 40%, and rumblings from the left that he had become a lame-duck president became clamorous.

URUGUAY

Full name: The Eastern Republic of Uruguay.

Leadership structure: The head of state is a president, directly elected by universal adult suffrage for a five-year term. An incumbent president may not stand for immediate re-election. The president is also head of government, responsible to the General Assembly, and appoints the Council of Ministers.

President:	Julio María Sanguinetti	1 March 1995—1 March 2000
	Jorge Batlle Ibáñez	1 March 2000—1 March 2005
	Tabaré **VÁZQUEZ**	Since 1 March 2005

Legislature: The legislature, the General Assembly (Asamblea General), is bicameral. The lower chamber, the Chamber of Representatives (Cámara de Representantes), has 99 members, directly elected for a five-year term. The upper chamber, the Chamber of Senators (Cámara de Senadores), has 31 members, 30 elected for a five-year term and one ex officio member (the vice president).

Profile of the President:

Tabaré **VÁZQUEZ**

Tabaré Vázquez was a medical doctor, specializing in oncology, before entering politics. A former mayor of Montevideo, he won the presidency at the third attempt in 2004 and was sworn in on 1 March 2005. He was the candidate of the left-wing Broad Front (Frente Amplio) coalition, whose full name is now the Progressive Encounter—Broad Front—New Majority (Encuentro Progresista—Frente Amplio—Nueva Mayoría). His first move in office was to restore ties with Cuba.

Tabaré Ramón Vázquez Rosas was born on 17 January 1940 in the La Teja area of the Uruguayan capital Montevideo. Vázquez studied medicine at the Universidad de la República medical school, graduating in 1969, and specialized in oncology and radiation therapy in 1972. He also studied at the Gustave Roussy Institute in Paris, France. Vázquez is a keen football fan and was president of the Club Progreso team from 1979 until 1989. He is married to María Auxiliadora Delgado with four sons, one of whom is adopted.

Vázquez, a member of the left-wing Broad Front, was elected mayor of Montevideo in 1989, taking office for five years in 1990. He made unsuccessful bids for the presidency in 1994 and 1999, again losing in the runoff in 1999 by a narrow margin to Jorge Batlle Ibáñez after leading in the first round. Finally, in the October 2004 elections, Vázquez won 50.45% of the vote in the first round, removing the need for a runoff.

When he was sworn in on 1 March 2005, Vázquez's first moves were to restore full diplomatic relations with Cuba, broken off in 2002 by his pro-US predecessor, and to sign an anti-poverty bill. However, Vázquez resisted pressure to add leftists to his economic team and was expected to maintain a broadly similar economic policy to that of his predecessor.

UZBEKISTAN

Full name: The Republic of Uzbekistan.

Leadership structure: The head of state is a president, directly elected by universal adult suffrage. The president's term of office under the 1992 Constitution was normally five years, renewable once only, but the term was extended to seven years under constitutional amendments in 2002. The president appoints the cabinet, which is defined as the government of the country, but is subordinate to the president. The government is chaired by the prime minister, who is appointed by the president.

President:	Islam **KARIMOV**	Since 24 March 1990
Prime Minister:	Utkir Sultonov	21 Dec. 1995—11 Dec. 2003
	Shavkat **MIRZIYAEV**	Since 11 Dec. 2003

Legislature: The legislature, the Supreme Assembly (Oliy Majlis) is bicameral. The lower house, the Legislative Chamber, has 120 members, directly elected for a five-year term. The upper house, the Senate, has 100 members, 16 of them appointed by the president as distinguished individuals, and the rest elected by regional deputies to represent the regions and the capital, Tashkent, for a five-year term. The incumbent president became a life member of the Senate on its first election in January 2005.

Profile of the President:

Islam **KARIMOV**

Islam Karimov is a former engineer who rose through the Uzbek state planning committee (Gosplan) to senior government and party roles under the communist regime, becoming first secretary of the Communist Party of Uzbekistan in 1989. He has been president of Uzbekistan since March 1990, when it was a republic of the former Soviet Union, and had his position endorsed in a popular vote in December 1991, following the declaration of independence that August. A March 1995 referendum extended his term of office to the year 2000, when he was re-elected against token opposition in a poll dismissed by international observers as neither free nor fair.

Islam Karimov was born on 30 January 1938 in Samarkand and was raised in a Soviet orphanage. After completing his schooling he attended the Central Asian

Polytechnic and Tashkent Economics Institute, gaining diplomas in mechanical engineering and economics. He began his working career in 1960 in the Tashkent agricultural machinery plant. The following year he moved to Tashkent's aviation factory as senior design engineer where he worked for five years. He is married to Tatyana Karimova and they have two daughters.

Having joined the Communist Party of the Soviet Union (CPSU) in 1964, Karimov became a member of the state planning committee (Gosplan) of Uzbekistan in 1966, rising from senior specialist in the scientific department to be its vice chairman. He was appointed finance minister in the Uzbek Council of Ministers in 1983, and by 1986 was its deputy chairman. For the next three years he was first secretary of the Kashkadarinsk region committee. During 1989 to 1991 he was first secretary of the Communist Party of Uzbekistan and also a member of the Congress of People's Deputies of the Soviet Union. In 1990 Karimov, together with the party first secretaries of the other republics, became a member of the CPSU politburo as part of the restructuring of that body.

On 24 March 1990 he was elected by the republican Supreme Soviet as president of the Uzbek Soviet Socialist Republic, a newly created position, as the republics began moving towards independence. However, he supported moves by the then Soviet president Mikhail Gorbachev to prevent the complete disintegration of the Union. When the breakup of the Union became a fait accompli following the August 1991 attempted coup in Moscow, Karimov resigned from the CPSU politburo but was reluctant to see the party itself dissolved.

Uzbekistan followed its neighbouring states by declaring independence on 31 August, and joined the Commonwealth of Independent States (CIS) on 21 December, but it was not until 29 December that a referendum was held to give formal popular confirmation to its independence. On the same day, Karimov was confirmed as president of the new republic for a five-year term. He was credited with winning 86% of the vote against one other candidate, while the main secular nationalist opposition grouping Birlik (Unity) was debarred from contesting the election on the grounds that it was not formally a political party.

On 26 March 1995 a referendum extended Karimov's term of office until 2000, reputedly with 99.6% support from a turnout of 99.3%, and he was subsequently re-elected in the January 2000 poll with an official result of 91.2% of the vote. Both the USA and the Organization for Security and Co-operation in Europe (OSCE) condemned the poll for having no candidates from opposition parties. Two years later, in January 2002, 90% of voters apparently approved the extension of Karimov's term in office even further, from five years to seven, in an equally condemned referendum. The relevant constitutional amendment was passed by the Supreme Assembly in April.

The 1992 Constitution gives formal backing to multipartyism. Karimov resigned the chairmanship of the former communist party—renamed the People's Democratic Party (PDP)—in 1996 to present himself in a nonparty light, but

Birlik remained subject to a ban imposed in 1992. In elections held on 5 and 19 December 1999, while the PDP emerged as the largest single party, nonpartisans took the lion's share of seats in the Supreme Assembly. The two opposition parties in existence had been barred from participating. The country's dismal human rights record and unwillingness to reform prompted suspensions of aid in 2004 by the USA and the European Bank for Reconstruction and Development (EBRD). The 2004–05 elections saw five parties contesting the poll, though all were pro-Karimov, with the anti-Karimov parties again denied registration, despite a glimmer of an opening the previous year when Freedom (Erk) had been allowed to hold its first formal meeting.

Karimov is an advocate of the unification of the former Soviet republics in central Asia, and has seen some progress achieved in this direction with Kazakhstan and Kyrgyzstan. In the economic sphere his regime has retained characteristics of the centrally planned command economies of the communist era rather than pursuing a rapid transition to a free-market system. The development of the oil and gas resources of the region, however, has resulted in the conclusion of a number of joint ventures with foreign companies.

Although Karimov is himself a Muslim, like the majority of the population, his regime has taken a firm stand against Islamic fundamentalists. When thousands of demonstrators protested over the trial of a group of alleged Islamists in Andizhan in May 2005, Karimov, wary of an uprising to mirror the recent regime oustings in Ukraine and Kyrgyzstan, sent in the security forces. Their heavy-handed response killed hundreds, including women and children—almost sparking the very uprising that Karimov had feared, as more outraged protestors took to the streets and called for international assistance to get rid of Karimov. The international community condemned the massacre, including begrudgingly the USA (which valued Uzbekistan as a key ally in its 'war on terrorism'). Karimov responded by demanding the withdrawal of all US personnel from its bases—leaving the USA with a logistical nightmare for supporting its ongoing mission in Afghanistan

Profile of the Prime Minister:

Shavkat **MIRZIYAEV**

Shavkat Mirziyaev was appointed prime minister of Uzbekistan on 11 December 2003. He had previously been governor first of Dzhizak and later of Samarkand. He has a reputation as being a tough manager and an effective administrator, especially with regard to agricultural affairs, but is also accused of brutality and corruption. He is no longer considered as a serious candidate to succeed President Islam Karimov.

Shavkat Mirziyaev was born in the Dzhizak region of Uzbekistan in 1957. He graduated from the Tashkent Institute of Irrigation, Engineering and Agricultural

Mechanization, where he later served as pro-rector. He was governor of the Dzhizak region from 1996 to 2001, where he first gained a reputation for corruption and brutality, and is accused of ordering public beatings of those who displeased him.

As governor of Samarkand from 2001–03 Mirziyaev became respected among fellow politicians as a tough manager and an effective administrator, especially in rural affairs. The Samarkand Centre for Human Rights Initiatives says that this was achieved by using schoolchildren and students as free labour, and is bringing a court case against him over the deaths of ten teenagers during the cotton harvest.

He first entered parliament in 1999 and was appointed prime minister on 11 December 2003. Analysts say he was given the post because of his expertise in internal order and agricultural affairs. He was at one point regarded as a possible successor to President Islam Karimov; however, he lacks the sources of influence available to a number of his rivals, such as access to a private army, and many feel he was drafted into his post merely as a temporary measure to solve an agricultural crisis. Certainly he is no longer spoken of as a successor to Karimov should the president ever choose to step down.

VANUATU

Full name: The Republic of Vanuatu.

Leadership structure: The head of state is a president, elected by an electoral college. The president's term of office is five years. The head of government is the prime minister, who is elected by Parliament. The Council of Ministers is appointed by the prime minister.

President:	Fr John Bani	24 March 1999—24 March 2004
	Roger Abiut (acting)	24 March 2004—12 April 2004
	Alfred Maseng	12 April 2004—10 May 2004
	Roger Abiut (acting)	10 May 2004—29 July 2004
	Josias Moli (acting)	29 July 2004—16 Aug. 2004
	Kalkot **MATASKELEKELE**	Since 16 Aug. 2004
Prime Minister:	Barak Sope	25 Nov. 1999—13 April 2001
	Edward Natapei	13 April 2001—29 July 2004
	Sergei Vohor	29 July 2004—11 Dec. 2004
	Ham **LINI**	Since 11 Dec. 2004

Legislature: The legislature is unicameral. The sole chamber, the Parliament, has 52 members, directly elected for a four-year term.

Profile of the President:

Kalkot **MATASKELEKELE**

Kalkot Mataskelekele is a lawyer who has been involved in politics in Vanuatu since the independence struggle of the 1970s. He became president in August 2004 after the removal from office of his predecessor, Alfred Maseng, who was serving a suspended sentence for corruption.

Kalkot Mataskelekele was born in 1949 on the island of Ifira to an Ifira father and a Tongan mother. His early education took place on the island before he was sent to Melbourne, Australia, to attend secondary school. Mataskelekele then attended the University of Papua New Guinea where he studied law. He is married to

Hanson Lini, the sister of founding prime minister Walter Lini and current prime minister Ham Lini, and has three sons and three daughters.

Mataskelekele was heavily involved in the independence movement, leading some of the first demonstrations against the continuation of Anglo-French colonial rule, and was instrumental in drafting the young country's constitution ahead of independence in 1980. He worked as a legal officer in the office of the attorney general from 1982 until 1987 before entering Parliament for four years. In 1991 he started his own legal practice as well as becoming secretary to the minister of justice.

Mataskelekele stood for president in the election of April 2004, backed by the then government of Edward Natapei, but was eventually defeated by Alfred Maseng after several rounds of voting in the electoral college. Maseng however was impeached by the Supreme Court in May under a rule banning anyone with a criminal record from serving as president—Maseng had been given a two-year suspended sentence on corruption charges the previous year. A new election was held on 13 August, which went to further rounds on 16 August; in the final round Mataskelekele beat Willie David Saul by 49 votes to seven, and was sworn in the same day.

Profile of the Prime Minister:

Ham LINI

Ham Lini, brother of Vanuatu's first postindependence prime minister Walter Lini, was elected as prime minister in December 2004. He leads the National United Party (NUP).

Ham Lini Vanuaroroa was born in 1951 on Pentecost Island in Penama province, the younger brother of Vanuatu's first prime minister Walter Lini. He was a teacher and a carpenter before entering politics, becoming president of the Penama provincial government, and was chosen to stand for Parliament following the death of his brother in 1999.

In the general election of July 2004, the NUP became the largest party in Parliament, but Lini was defeated in elections to the premiership by Serge Vohor of the Union of Moderate Parties (UMP). Lini contested the results and led opposition to Vohor until the two established a national unity administration in August, with Lini becoming deputy prime minister.

However, Vohor in December established diplomatic relations with Taiwan without consultation and he was removed by Parliament in a vote of no confidence. Lini was elected in his place on 11 December and immediately moved to re-establish relations with China.

VATICAN CITY

Full name: The State of the Vatican City.

Leadership structure: The head of state is the pope, who heads the Roman Catholic Church and is elected for life by a conclave comprising members of the Sacred College of Cardinals. The administrative affairs of the Vatican City are conducted by a Pontifical Commission, appointed by the pope.

Pope:	John Paul II	16 Oct. 1978—2 April 2005
	Eduardo Cardinal Martínez Somalo (chamberlain)	2 April 2005—19 April 2005
	BENEDICT XVI	Since 19 April 2005
Secretary of State:	Cardinal Angelo **SODANO**	Since 2 Dec. 1990

Legislature: None.

Profile of the Pope:

BENEDICT XVI

Pope Benedict XVI, previously Cardinal Joseph Alois Ratzinger, was born in Bavaria to devout Catholics who opposed the Nazis, although he himself joined the Hitler Youth under duress at the age of 14. Called up into the armed forces, he was never sent to the front, and soon after the war ended he began studying for the priesthood; he was ordained in 1951. He was named archbishop of Munich and Freising in 1977 but resigned the archdiocese after his appointment as prefect of the Holy Office of the Inquisition, overseeing Roman Catholic Church doctrine. A cardinal from 1993, he was dean of the Sacred College of Cardinals from 2002. On the death of Pope John Paul II in 2005 Ratzinger quickly emerged as a favourite to succeed him and was elected to the papacy on 19 April. He was enthroned on 7 May. Ratzinger is known as an uncompromising traditionalist and was generally expected to continue the conservative legacy of his predecessor.

Pope Benedict XVI was born Joseph Alois Ratzinger on 16 April 1927 in the Bavarian village of Marktl am Inn, Germany. He was the youngest of three children of a police officer and a barmaid. His father, also Joseph, was forced to move his family several times as his opposition to Nazism on grounds of faith led to his demotion and relocation. He eventually retired to the town of Traunstein in 1937.

The young Ratzinger was forced to join the Hitler Youth in 1941 at the age of 14—membership had become mandatory five years earlier. Ratzinger was apparently a reluctant member who refused to attend meetings. He was drafted into the anti-aircraft artillery corps two years later and then transferred to the Austrian border with Hungary to set up anti-tank defences ahead of an expected offensive from the Red Army. In November 1944, after a few weeks at home, he was drafted into the German infantry in Munich; he was never sent to the front, though spent a brief period in a prisoner-of-war camp before returning home in 1945.

In January 1946, with his brother, he began studies for the priesthood firstly in the Munich diocesan seminary and later at the Ludwig-Maximilian University in Munich. He and his brother were ordained by Cardinal Faulhaber of Munich on 29 June 1951. Ratzinger became a professor at the University of Bonn in 1959 before moving on to the University of Münster in 1963. In 1966 he was appointed to the chair of dogmatic theology at the University of Tübingen, but returned to Bavaria three years later to the University of Regensburg.

Ratzinger was named archbishop of Munich and Freising in March 1977 and was made a cardinal in June by Pope Paul VI. In 1981 he became prefect of the Congregation for the Doctrine of the Faith, otherwise known as the Holy Office of the Inquisition, the body that oversees Roman Catholic Church doctrine. He resigned the archdiocese of Munich and Freising the following year and was raised to Cardinal Bishop of Velletri-Segni in 1993. He became vice dean of the Sacred College of Cardinals in 1998, and dean in 2002.

On the death of Pope John Paul II, Ratzinger quickly emerged as a favourite for the succession. He was elected as the 265th reigning pope on 19 April 2005. He celebrated his Papal Inauguration Mass on 24 April and was enthroned in St John's Basilica, the cathedral church of Rome, on 7 May, taking the name of Pope Benedict XVI.

The new pope is a conservative with views similar to those of his predecessor on subjects such as abortion and birth control. He has described homosexuality as a tendency towards an "intrinsic moral evil", and has spoken out against Turkey, a Muslim country, joining the European Union. He also, during the 1980s, played a key role in silencing outspoken liberal clergy in Latin America.

Profile of the Secretary of State:

Cardinal Angelo **SODANO**

Angelo Sodano's career in the Roman Catholic Church has been divided between Latin America and the Vatican. An Italian who was first ordained in 1950, he became a cardinal in May 1991, the year after his appointment as secretary of state—in which capacity he is the papal representative in the civil government of the State of the Vatican City.

Angelo Sodano was born on 23 November 1927 in Isola d'Asti, southwest of Turin, in the family of an Italian parliamentary deputy. He studied theology and canon law in Rome at the Pontifical Gregorian University, the Pontifical Lateran University and the Pontifical Ecclesiastical Academy, and was ordained in 1950. From 1959 to 1968 he worked in the office of the Vatican secretary of state and in papal nunciatures in Ecuador, Uruguay and Chile. From 1968 to 1977 he worked in the Vatican council for the public affairs of the Church, before being nominated by Pope Paul VI in November 1977 as apostolic nuncio in Chile and being invested as titular archbishop of Nova di Cesare in January 1978. Between 1988 and 1989 he was secretary of the council for public affairs of the Church, and for the following year he was secretary for relations with states.

He was appointed secretary of state by Pope John Paul II in December 1990, as successor to Cardinal Casaroli. He became a cardinal on 29 May 1991 and received the church of Santa Maria Nuova. In January 1994 he was made titular bishop of Albano. On 23 April 1997 he was nominated the papal legate for the 46th international eucharistic congress in Wrocław, Poland. He was the pope's personal representative at the funeral of Mother Teresa on 13 September 1997, where he read the funeral mass.

On 30 April 2005, shortly after Benedict XVI was elected pope, Sodano was reconfirmed as secretary of state and approved as dean of the Sacred College of Cardinals (having been vice dean since November 2002).

VENEZUELA

Full name: The Bolivarian Republic of Venezuela.

Leadership structure: The head of state is a president, directly elected by universal adult suffrage. Under the 1999 Constitution, the president's term of office is six years, renewable once consecutively. The head of government is the president. The Council of Ministers is appointed by the president.

President:	Col. (retd) Hugo Chávez Frías	2 Feb. 1999—12 April 2002
	Pedro Carmona Estanga	12 April 2002—13 April 2002
	Diosdado Cabello (acting)	13 April 2002—14 April 2002
	Col. (retd) Hugo **CHÁVEZ** Frías	Since 14 April 2002

Legislature: Under the 1999 Constitution, the new unicameral National Assembly (Asamblea Nacional) has 165 members, directly elected for a five-year term.

Profile of the President:

Col. (retd) Hugo **CHÁVEZ** Frías

Col. Hugo Chávez is a charismatic advocate of the ill-defined 'Bolivarian revolution', and was once jailed for two years following a failed coup attempt in 1992. The winner of the 1998 presidential elections, he pursued his centralizing 'third way' in head-on struggles with the legislature, the Supreme Court and the trade unions. Having rewritten the constitution during his first year in power, he was re-elected for a six-year term on 30 July 2000. With strong parliamentary support from his own Movement of the Fifth Republic (Movimiento V (Quinta) República—MVR) and soaring energy revenues, he has pursued ambitious social programmes and a daring attempt to construct a regional consensus rejecting US-backed models of economic development. This has often put him on a collision course with US officials, a prospect he has welcomed with delight.

Hugo Rafael Chávez Frías was born on 28 July 1954 in Sabaneta in the western state of Barinas. His parents, both schoolteachers, sent him to the Venezuelan Military Academy in Caracas in the mid-1960s. He graduated with a degree in military sciences and the rank of second lieutenant in 1975. Staying on at the academy throughout the next 15 years, he specialized and excelled in the study of engineering and military armour. After receiving a master's degree in politics from the Simón Bolívar University in 1990, he trained to become a commando and reached the rank of colonel in 1992. Hugo Chávez married firstly Nancy Colmenares, with whom he had two daughters and a son. During his first marriage he had a nine-year affair with Herma Marksman, but he did not divorce his first wife until the mid-1990s. He married his second wife, journalist Marisabel Rodríguez de Chávez, in 1997 and they had one daughter; their divorce was finalized in 2004.

In 1982 Chávez formed the Revolutionary Bolivarian Movement (Movimiento Bolivariano Revolucionario—MBR), based on the principles of South American independence hero Simón Bolívar, and dedicated his life to 'redeeming' Venezuela. On 4 February 1992 he led an armed rebellion against the troubled social-democratic regime of President Carlos Andrés Pérez Rodríguez. Hundreds of rebels were killed in the action and Chávez was captured. He spent two years in jail from where he remained a prominent opposition figure but did little to affect the regime. The military hierarchy denounced Chávez for his role in the attempted coup and the US government barred him from ever entering the USA.

President Pérez was forced from office amid charges of corruption in 1993 and his successor, Rafael Caldera Rodríguez, pardoned Chávez the following year. Once free Chávez set about furthering his revolutionary cause, establishing the MVR in 1997 and drawing increasing popular support among the poor. Acquiring political backing from several other leftist parties under the umbrella of the Patriotic Pole (Polo Patriótico—PP), he headed into the November–December 1998 elections confident of victory. His outspoken leftist politics put fear into business leaders and the Caracas stock exchange, which plummeted in the face of pro-Chávez opinion polls. However, he toned down the Bolivarian rhetoric in the run-up to the presidential poll, promising to encourage foreign investment and introduce business-friendly policies such as guarantees for investors' rights and a hard line on government corruption.

The 1998 elections saw the PP gaining 34% of the vote, shattering the traditional pattern of party voting in Venezuela, while Chávez himself won a convincing 56% in the presidential poll—the largest majority since the 1950s. The peaceful conduct of the voting swayed previously hostile opinions. The army, opposition regional governors and the stock market all expressed confidence in the new president, and the USA even offered to extend him a visa should he want to apply.

The honeymoon soon passed as Chávez attempted to realize his promises of rewriting the constitution, with the intention of strengthening the presidency and reorganizing the legislature. He threatened to rule by decree if the Congress did not respond to his calls for its dissolution. A referendum in April 1999 (marred by a low turnout of under 40%) approved his proposal to create a new transitional Constituent Assembly, which by August had voted to strip Congress of its powers. In December Chávez renamed the country the Bolivarian Republic of Venezuela as part of the new constitution.

Chávez began 2000 effectively ruling by decree, with the Constituent Assembly winding up its operations ahead of scheduled elections. His popularity among urbanized Venezuelans ebbed away through the year as continuing low wages and his struggle with the trade unions drew thousands of protestors onto the streets of Caracas. Nonetheless, he was re-elected with 59.5% of the vote in presidential elections held on 30 July 2000, and the MVR entered the newly created National Assembly in August with 76 of its 165 seats. The new Assembly soon approved Chávez's Enabling Act in November 2000, granting him one year's licence to rule by decree in areas of economic, social and technological policy—ostensibly to lighten the burden on the legislature.

Over the course of 2001 opposition to Chávez began to coalesce around the traditionally conservative pillars of Venezuelan society: business leaders, the Roman Catholic Church and the army. Large-scale protests both for and against the president were common sights in the capital and elsewhere. True to his word, Chávez rescinded his emergency powers on 14 November, rushing through a handful of decrees to beat the deadline on the day itself. However, handing power back to the government and parliament, which was increasingly preoccupied with infighting within the PP, failed to quiet his opponents. On 10 December 2001 the country's first general strike in 40 years was called by the Fedecámaras chamber of commerce.

Chávez's position was seriously undermined in March 2002 when trade unions gave their support to the protestors, calling for further industrial action to overthrow Chávez. Several senior military figures had either resigned or given their outspoken support to the opposition. Another general strike was called for 9 April, during which 16 protestors were killed by police, prompting military officers to launch a bloodless coup three days later. Chávez agreed to resign and business leader Pedro Carmona was appointed in his place. However, the coup was brought down by a groundswell of pro-Chávez support in the capital. After massive counterdemonstrations, and the refusal of some sectors of the military to join the coup, Chávez was airlifted back to the presidential palace and reinstated within 48 hours. Aware of the strong support his opponents had been able to marshal, Chávez announced a general amnesty and called for negotiations.

Unbowed by the failure of the April coup, demonstrators returned to the capital's streets and by October competing rallies were drawing around a million people each. Chávez claimed a coup plot had been foiled later that month and took personal control of the police in Caracas in November, on the grounds that the ranks of the municipal security forces had "fallen into anarchy". A one-day general strike on 2 December escalated into a two-month industrial lockdown, crippling the country's vital oil industry amid daily calls for Chávez's resignation. Chávez dismissed the strike out of hand and sat out the action, knowing that another military coup was unlikely, but the economy suffered an estimated loss of US$4,000 million.

The opposition then tried a new tack, circulating a petition calling for fresh presidential elections. A valid petition was finally submitted to the National Electoral Council with 2,436,830 signatures, and a recall referendum was announced on 8 June. Chávez mobilized a huge grass-roots campaign and won the referendum, held on 15 August, with 58% of the vote. The opposition alleged fraud on a grand scale, but international observers led by former US president Jimmy Carter disagreed.

This victory, coupled with soaring oil prices, put Chávez in a position of considerable strength. Armed with several billion dollars in extra foreign exchange reserves, he launched major social programmes as growth forecasts rocketed. In addition, he engaged with a multitude of regional and international leaders, pushing his own vision of alternative economic development and trade policies. He appeared to welcome the fact that this put him firmly on a collision path with the USA, champion of economic liberalism and free market capitalism.

He has called US president George W. Bush a "killer" and a "genocidal madman", and accused Bush of plotting to assassinate him—threatening to cut off Venezuela's oil supplies to the USA if any such scheme was attempted. He has called US Secretary of State Condoleezza Rice "pathetic" and "illiterate". The USA has in turn said that Chávez is a "negative force" in the region and has actively, if ineffectively, worked to isolate him.

Chávez has slashed military ties with the USA, instead procuring weapons from China, Brazil and the European Union, asking all serving US military officers to leave Venezuelan territory, and establishing a 'citizens' militia' against potential US invasion—notwithstanding repeated US assertions that they have never had any intentions of invading.

Chávez has instead pursued trade relations with Cuba and a warm friendship with its leader, Fidel Castro, and pushed for Venezuela to join the South American economic bloc Mercosur, something of a rival to the US-backed Free Trade Area of the Americas. He has offered preferential oil deals to up to 20 nations, including the Mercosur members and Cuba, which in return has supplied teachers and doctors to staff Chávez's ambitious social programmes.

Since the recall referendum the opposition has seemed almost dazed, unsure how Chávez has come to this point and this power. His popularity ratings have soared to over 70%, he has altered the constitution and loaded the courts in his favour, and senior government officials now appear on national television to lambaste individual newspaper articles critical of government policy. Most insidiously, the petition of signatures collected to call the recall referendum has been published on the Internet by Chávez supporters, and rumours abound that if one's name is found on *la lista* it becomes impossible to get a government job or to sign on to social welfare programmes.

VIET NAM

Full name: The Socialist Republic of Viet Nam.

Leadership structure: The head of state is a president, elected by the National Assembly. The president's term of office is five years. The head of government is the prime minister, who is responsible to the National Assembly. The cabinet is appointed by the National Assembly.

President:	Tran Duc **LUONG**	Since 24 Sept. 1997

Prime Minister:	Phan Van **KHAI**	Since 25 Sept. 1997

General Secretary of the Communist Party of Viet Nam:

Le Kha Phieu	29 Dec. 1997—22 April 2001
Nong Duc **MANH**	Since 22 April 2001

Legislature: The legislature is unicameral. The sole chamber, the National Assembly (Quoc-Hoi), has 500 members, directly elected for a five-year term.

Profile of the President:

Tran Duc **LUONG**

Tran Duc Luong, a former engineer who is generally described as a technocrat and pragmatist, came into government only in 1987 and first joined the politburo of the ruling Communist Party of Viet Nam (CPV) in 1996, the year before he became president. His elevation was part of a 'generation change' in the Vietnamese leadership, where the key figures are the triumvirate of president, prime minister and general secretary of the CPV.

Tran Duc Luong was born on 5 May 1937 in the central province of Quang Ngai. He studied engineering at Hanoi Mining and Geology University and in the Soviet Union, and worked in the General Directorate for Geology, where he was general director from 1979 until 1987. He is married to Nguyen Thi Vinh, and they have one son and two daughters.

He chaired the science and technology committee of the National Assembly, and in 1987 was appointed as a vice chairman of the Council of Ministers, with responsibility for industry, external economic relations, capital construction, transport and communications. Luong headed Viet Nam's delegation to the USA in 1994, which laid foundations for the normalization of relations a year later. He joined the CPV politburo in 1996, when he ranked 12th of its 19 members.

With President Le Duc Anh, Prime Minister Vo Van Kiet and CPV General Secretary Do Muoi all due to stand down ahead of the 1997 party congress because of old age and poor health, the renewal of the leadership was a major issue for debate throughout the year. Luong was nominated for the presidency in September 1997 by the CPV central committee, and confirmed as president by the National Assembly the same month.

At the CPV annual congress in April 2001 he was promoted within a revised politburo to be second in the party hierarchy behind the new CPV general secretary, Nong Duc Manh. Later that year, in August, he made a landmark visit to South Korea. On 24 July 2002 Luong was re-elected president of Viet Nam for a second five-year term, receiving 97% of the parliamentary vote. In 2004 he dismissed an appeal for clemency from execution for mafia boss Nam Cam; corruption scandals linked to Nam Cam had reached as high as the 'number ten' member in the politburo.

Profile of the Prime Minister:

Phan Van **KHAI**

Phan Van Khai was a close adviser to Vo Van Kiet, his predecessor as prime minister. His career up to that point had centred more on economics than on politics, especially on the issue of administrative reform. One of two new members of the ruling 'triumvirate' appointed at the September 1997 National Assembly session (together with President Tran Duc Luong), he is a strong advocate of measures to attract foreign investment, and his appointment was generally welcomed in Western business circles as confirming Viet Nam on the path to economic restructuring.

Phan Van Khai was born on 25 December 1933 in the Cu Chi district near Saigon (now Ho Chi Minh City). He is married to Nguyen Thi Sau and they have two children. He took part in the anti-French resistance in the south of the country from 1947 to 1954, and moved to North Viet Nam following the partition of the country.

In 1960 he joined the Communist Party of Viet Nam (CPV) and was sent to Moscow where he studied at the National Institute of Economics. On his return, he worked with North Viet Nam's state planning commission until 1972, before being sent to South Viet Nam as a member of the Liberation Movement, the North's underground provisional government. In 1974 he went to Hanoi as deputy director of the committee for reunification.

On the reunification of Viet Nam in 1976, Khai returned to Ho Chi Minh City, becoming a member of the local CPV committee, and vice president, later president, of the state planning commission for the city. Rising through the ranks of the party, he was promoted to permanent member and then deputy secretary of the local CPV committee. In 1984 Khai was put forward for membership of the central committee of the CPV, and two years later he became president of the people's committee (i.e. mayor) of Ho Chi Minh City.

In 1989 Khai was chosen to head the influential state planning commission, joining the 19-member CPV politburo as its eighth-ranking member. In 1991 he was appointed first deputy prime minister, and as such, was identified as the most likely successor to the old and ailing prime minister, Vo Van Kiet, in speculative discussions which lasted so long that they had the effect of slowing down the country's economic reform process. His nomination for the premiership by the CPV's central committee (the real centre of power) was formally endorsed by a vote of the newly elected National Assembly in September 1997.

Before his elevation to the premiership, Khai had overseen, as minister in charge of the economy, Viet Nam's transition in the late 1980s from a communist, centrally planned economy towards an open market economy, halving to some 6,000 the number of state enterprises as part of a policy known as *doi moi* (renovation). As prime minister, he announced in late October 1997 that the reform of loss-making state-owned enterprises was of "fundamental importance", although a core of 300 companies, either essential utilities or "purely profit-generating enterprises", would continue to receive preferential state support. In his new role Khai also shared the responsibility of dealing with endemic corruption, a major issue in the restructuring process, although there was a history of corruption charges against members of his family.

The Asian economic crisis of 1997–98 reduced the scope of Khai's reforms and his government has since aimed at more moderate growth, although the country continues to perform relatively strongly against its competitors. In 2000 Khai oversaw the introduction of policies designed specifically to boost foreign investment and also the opening of the country's first stock exchange. In February 2002 the CPV voted to allow its members to participate in private business ventures.

At the April 2001 CPV congress Khai was repositioned as the third most powerful member of the party's politburo, behind the new general secretary, Nong Duc Manh, and President Tran Duc Luong. A year later, on 25 July 2002, he was re-elected as prime minister with 90% of the parliamentary vote.

In June 2005, Khai became the first Vietnamese prime minister to visit the USA and Canada since the end of the Viet Nam War in 1975. Diplomatic ties had been restored in 1995, and the USA is Viet Nam's top trading partner; Khai wants US assistance to gain Viet Nam's admittance to the World Trade Organization (WTO). His arrival was met by anti-communist protests.

Profile of the General Secretary of the Communist Party of Viet Nam:

Nong Duc **MANH**

Nong Duc Manh is a former forest ranger who has been a member of the Communist Party of Viet Nam (CPV) since 1963. He first became a member of the ruling politburo in 1991. His election as general secretary in April 2001 was seen as a boost to the reformist wing of the party, although Manh has excelled at keeping out of party infighting.

Nong Duc Manh was born on 11 September 1940 in the far north in what was then known as Bac Thai province (now Bac Can province). A member of the Tay ethnic minority, he was rumoured to be the illegitimate son of revolutionary leader Ho Chi Minh. Whatever his parentage his family background was poor and he is said to have been forced to wait until he was 11 to start his education. He is credited with joining the revolution in 1958, when he also began attending the Hanoi Agro-Forestry High School, and the CPV in 1963, a year after beginning work as a forestry worker in Bac Thai.

Being a party member enabled Manh to serve in administrative positions and from 1963 to 1980 he worked at various levels in the forestry and agricultural industries in the north. During this period he also travelled to Hanoi once more to attend a one-year Russian language course, before studying forestry at the Leningrad Forestry Institute in the then Soviet Union between 1966 and 1971. He also studied at the Nguyen Ai Quoc Party School from 1974 to 1976. By the time he left forestry work in 1980 he had become director of the forestry service in Bac Thai province.

Following the end of the ten-year Viet Nam War with the USA in 1975, Manh entered politics as a member of the provincial CPV committee in Bac Thai. He moved into the CPV machinery on a full-time basis in 1980 when he was elevated to deputy chairman of the Bac Thai People's Committee. Working his way up in the local party, he was elected as a member of the CPV central committee in May 1989. Later that year he entered the National Assembly in a by-election and two years after that he entered the party politburo for the first time as an alternate member.

Manh was re-elected to his politburo post in 1996 and became a full member in 1997. He chaired the National Assembly from 1992 until his election as CPV general secretary at the party congress in April 2001, replacing the more conservative Le Kha Phieu. In this role he became the third member of the country's ruling triumvirate, but ranking higher in the party hierarchy than his colleagues, President Tran Duc Luong and Prime Minister Phan Van Khai, who had both been in post for four years.

YEMEN

Full name: The Republic of Yemen.

Leadership structure: The head of state is a president, directly elected for the first time in September 1999. The president's term of office is seven years under the 2001 constitutional amendments, renewable once only. The head of government is the prime minister, who is appointed by the president. The Council of Ministers is appointed by the president on the advice of the prime minister.

President:	Field Marshal Ali Abdullah **SALEH** (president of Yemen Arab Republic from 18 July 1978 until unification; chairman of presidential council to 1 Oct. 1994)	Since 22 May 1990
Prime Minister:	Abd al-Karim Ali al-Iryani (acting from 29 April 1998)	14 May 1998—31 March 2001
	Abd al-Qadir **BA-JAMMAL**	Since 31 March 2001

Legislature: Under the constitutional amendments approved in February 2001, the legislature remains unicameral. The House of Representatives (Majlis al-Nowab) has 301 members, directly elected for a six-year term under the constitutional amendments. The amendments created in addition a Shura Council, replacing the previous Consultative Council, with 111 members appointed by the president to advise on issues of fundamental importance in Yemeni society.

Profile of the President:

Field Marshal Ali Abdullah **SALEH**

Ali Abdullah Saleh, head of state since unification in 1990, is a soldier from the Sana region who began his army career as a noncommissioned officer (NCO). He took part in the 1974 military coup in the Yemen Arab Republic (YAR) and in 1978 he succeeded to the YAR presidency, in which capacity he was a leading advocate of unification with the People's Democratic Republic of Yemen (PDRY, also South Yemen). The approval of the new constitution in May 1991, and the defeat of a secessionist rebellion in the south in July 1994, enabled him to consolidate his position, and he was re-elected for further terms in 1994 and 1999. His term of office was subsequently extended from five to seven years.

Ali Abdullah Saleh was born on 21 March 1942 in Beit al-Ahmar, near Sana. He is married and has several children. His own primary education took place in a local Koranic school and it was through the armed forces, which he joined in 1958, that he obtained his subsequent training as well as his commitment to republicanism. He began attending the army's NCO school in 1960, and participated in preparations among fellow NCOs for the 1962 revolution, which ousted the ruling Zaidi Islamic theocracy and installed a republican military regime. A year later he entered the Armor school for further military training. He fought, and was wounded several times, in the civil war between Saudi-backed royalists and republicans, which ended in 1970 with a republican victory. He rose to be battalion commander and then Armor brigade commander, and commander in Taiz province.

In 1974 Saleh participated in an army coup in the YAR. Between 1974 and 1978 he was part of the military government of Taiz province. In July 1978, following the assassination of President Ahmed Hussein al-Ghashmi, he was brought into a four-member presidential council and almost immediately elected by the parliament as president of the YAR and commander-in-chief of the armed forces. Promoted in September 1978 to the rank of colonel, he was re-elected in 1983 and 1988 to further terms as president and commander-in-chief.

Upon unification in May 1990 Saleh was elected chairman of the presidential council (i.e. president) of the Republic of Yemen. His initial 30-month transitional term was extended pending delayed parliamentary elections, but in October 1993 the new House of Representatives confirmed his position. Under his leadership the government sought to modernize the country, building schools and hospitals and embarking on a literacy campaign to transform a society hitherto dominated by conservative clan allegiances. His failure to criticize Iraq's invasion of Kuwait in 1990 resulted in a temporary halt to foreign aid, and strained relations with neighbouring Saudi Arabia to the north.

Saleh has had to contend with continuing tensions between Islamist and secular groups, and between regions. A brief but intense civil war erupted in 1994, ending with the defeat of 'southern' secessionists. Saleh was re-elected as president by the House of Representatives in October 1994, the president's powers having been greatly enhanced by amendments to the constitution, and in April 1997 his General People's Congress (GPC) secured an absolute majority of seats in the republic's second general election, thus consolidating his hold on power. In December 1997 he was promoted to the rank of field marshal.

In the first direct presidential elections in Yemen, held on 23 September 1999, Saleh was re-elected with a resounding 96.3% of the vote. Opposition groups decried the lack of a plausible alternative to Saleh—his only opponent was a member of the GPC who stood as an independent. In a referendum held on 20 February 2001 Saleh's term in office was extended from five to seven years as part of constitutional amendments. Two years later in legislative elections the GPC expanded its share of seats in the House of Representatives from 62% to 79%. In 2005 Saleh pledged to step down at the next election in 2006 and urged parties to choose young leaders to run for power. Critics argued that the announcement was a ploy, possibly to pave the way for his eldest son, Ahmed Saleh, to take over

In October 2000 a suicide bomber attacked the USS *Cole* in Aden harbour, killing 17 US personnel. Since that time, in answer to the US suspicion that the state of lawlessness in much of the country's interior was being exploited as a safe haven and fertile recruiting ground by Islamist terrorists, Saleh has made a bold stand in favour of US policy, further alienating Islamist groups. Since late 2001, with the advent of the US-led 'war on terrorism', Saleh has ordered military strikes by Yemeni and US forces against suspected terrorist cells in his own country, has shut down hundreds of *madaris* (Islamic schools), and has made payoffs to tribes that had once sheltered militants. He also offered in 2004 to send Yemeni troops as part of a multinational peacekeeping force to Iraq.

An Islamist revolt in the north was crushed in 2005; its leader had accused Saleh of pleasing the USA "at the expense of his own people". Despite this co-operation, relations with the USA are sensitive, and have been harmed by a number of incidents including an attack on a French tanker in October 2002 and the discovery in December that Saleh's government had purchased Scud missiles from North Korea.

Profile of the Prime Minister:

Abd al-Qadir **BA-JAMMAL**

Abd al-Qadir Ba-Jammal is a senior member of the ruling General People's Congress (GPC). A member of the government of the former People's Democratic Republic of Yemen (PDRY, also South Yemen), he joined the unified administration in 1990 and backed the incumbent government in the 1994 civil war. He was foreign minister before being made prime minister in March 2001.

Abd al-Qadir Abd al-Rahman Ba-Jammal was born on 18 February 1946 in the southern Hadhramaut region. He went to Egypt to study and graduated in commerce from Cairo University in 1974. While at the university he had chaired the Arab Nationalist Students' Union in 1969. He returned to Yemen and taught economics at Aden University between 1978 and 1980, in what was then the PDRY. He was a member of the Yemen Socialist Party.

In 1978 he joined the government of the PDRY as deputy minister of industry and became deputy minister of planning and chairman of the oil and mineral resources authority in 1980. Five years later he was appointed minister of minerals. When the two Yemens were unified in 1990, Ba-Jammal joined the GPC led by the former Yemen Arab Republic leader and now president of the unified state, Ali Abdullah Saleh. From 1991 to 1994 he served as chairman of the Free Zone Authority.

During the 1994 civil war Ba-Jammal backed the Saleh government. In May of that year he was appointed deputy prime minister, a post he retained until 2001, adding the foreign affairs portfolio to his responsibilities from 1998. In March 2001, in the country's first major cabinet reshuffle in four years, Ba-Jammal was appointed prime minister to replace the long-overworked Abd al-Karim Ali al-Iryani. His new cabinet was sworn in on 4 April. After the 2003 elections, in which the GPC greatly increased its majority, Ba-Jammal was reappointed prime minister on 17 May at the head of a reshuffled cabinet.

ZAMBIA

Full name: The Republic of Zambia.

Leadership structure: The head of state is a president, directly elected by universal adult suffrage. Under the 1991 Constitution, the president's term of office is five years, renewable once only. The head of government is the president. The cabinet is appointed by the president.

President:	Frederick Chiluba	2 Nov. 1991—2 Jan. 2002
	Levy **MWANAWASA**	Since 2 Jan. 2002

Legislature: The legislature is unicameral. The sole chamber, the National Assembly, has 150 members directly elected, up to eight nominated by the president, and a speaker, all having a five-year term.

Profile of the President:

Levy **MWANAWASA**

Levy Mwanawasa is a member of the Movement for Multiparty Democracy (MMD). A well-respected lawyer, he is often referred to as 'Mr Injunction' in a reference to his fight against corruption. Although opposition parties admitted that there was no trace of corruption around Mwanawasa himself, his decisive election in December 2001 was viewed with deep suspicion by domestic and international observers. He is a keen farmer who spends the summer months 'on leave' inspecting work on his three farms.

Levy Patrick Mwanawasa, the second of ten children, was born on 3 September 1948 in the city of Mufulira. He graduated in law from the University of Zambia in 1973, having been vice president of its students' union. He worked part-time with the private law firm Jaques & Partners while he completed his training at the Law Practice Institute in Lusaka, and transferred to the firm's Ndola office when he was called to the Zambian Bar in 1975. Two years later he left to form his own practice.

Mwanawasa & Company was tremendously successful and Mwanawasa was made vice chairman of the Zambian Law Association in 1982–83, the first University of Zambia-educated lawyer to head the association. In 1985 he was appointed solicitor general of Zambia. He returned to private practice the following year. In 1988 he married fellow lawyer Maureen Kakubo and they have four children. Mwanawasa also has two children from an earlier marriage. He is a committed Christian, having been baptized again in 1977, while Maureen was a Jehovah's Witness before being excommunicated in 2001 because of the family's involvement in politics.

Operating at the highest level of his profession, Mwanawasa successfully defended Lt.-Gen. Christon Tembo against charges of involvement in a coup plot against the Kaunda regime in 1989. Tembo went on to become a leading member of the MMD and ultimately Zambia's vice president before leading a party split in 2001.

In the meantime, Mwanawasa had joined the MMD on the country's return to multiparty democracy in 1991 and was appointed as the party's deputy leader. He gained a seat in the National Assembly amid the MMD's election victory that year and was nominated as vice president in November. The following month he suffered serious head injuries in a mysterious car accident and was hospitalized in South Africa for three months. Opponents later suggested that his injuries were causing him to slur his speech, giving him the unkind nickname 'Cabbage'.

Mwanawasa's reputation as incorruptible was strengthened greatly in 1994 when he resigned as vice president in disgust at the abuse of power he had witnessed in his own office. Between then and 2001 he avoided mainstream politics and returned to private legal practice, although he made an unsuccessful bid to become MMD leader in 1996.

Over the course of 2001 the MMD was split asunder over the failed attempt by incumbent President Frederick Chiluba to stand for an unconstitutional third term. Mwanawasa was selected as its presidential candidate in August, having been made party leader in March. The official results of the December 2001 elections, giving him the presidency and returning the MMD as the largest party in parliament—though without a majority—were derided by the new and popular opposition and also questioned by observers from the European Union (EU). Since becoming president in January 2002, Mwanawasa has attempted to sweep aside the controversy of his election. As part of this aim, he has distanced himself from his former guardian Chiluba, and removed the former president's immunity from prosecution in order to pursue charges of corruption against him. The Supreme Court finally upheld the validity of the election in 2005.

Low food production due to severe drought plagued the first two years of Mwanawasa's term. The government's focus on agriculture reversed the threat, and by 2004 Zambia was the only country in southern Africa to be exporting grain. Meanwhile, tough austerity measures backed by the International Monetary Fund (IMF) were proving deeply unpopular, as public-sector wages were frozen in the face of income tax rises. Mwanawasa's government even agreed to a 30% pay cut in 2003, reversing an earlier pay rise. The spending cuts did earn Zambia US$3,900 million of debt relief under the Highly Indebted Poor Countries (HIPC) initiative, but left many schools in rural areas severely understaffed as wages for 9,000 recently trained teachers could not be afforded.

The instability of party politics in Zambia caused frequent reshuffles of government, as Mwanawasa manoeuvred to reward opposition defectors and form unity alliances. The MMD regained its majority in the National Assembly in 2003, following several by-elections, but that year Mwanawasa was criticized for appointing too many extraparliamentary (unelected) people to his cabinet, in particular to the vice presidency, which the opposition claimed was unconstitutional. He was also attacked over his initiation of a constitutional review process, despite promises that he would not tailor the new constitution to suit his own needs. The ejection from the MMD of several senior party members in 2005 as part of Mwanawasa's anti-corruption drive provoked a leadership challenge, but Mwanawasa received a huge vote of confidence with 1,211 votes against 68.

ZIMBABWE

Full name: The Republic of Zimbabwe.

Leadership structure: The head of state is a directly elected president. The president's term of office is six years. The head of government is the president. The cabinet is appointed by the president.

President:	Robert **MUGABE**	Since 31 Dec. 1987
	(prime minister from 18 April 1980)	

Legislature: The legislature is currently unicameral. The sole chamber, the Parliament, has 150 members, 120 directly elected for a five-year term, 20 appointed by the president, and ten traditional chiefs. Under the 2005 constitutional amendments, a bicameral Parliament is to be reintroduced. The current sole chamber will become the lower house, the House of Assembly, with 150 members, 120 directly elected, 12 appointed by the president, ten provincial governors and eight traditional chiefs. The upper house, the Senate will have 66 members, five of whom will be elected from each of the ten provinces, six appointed by the president, and ten traditional chiefs, one from each province, including the president and vice president of the Council of Chiefs. All elected or appointed members will serve five-year terms.

Profile of the President:

Robert **MUGABE**

Robert Mugabe is a veteran of the long guerrilla struggle for independence and against white minority rule. He led the more left-wing of the two main African nationalist movements at the 1979 Lancaster House conference, which established the framework for independence and majority rule. In power ever since, he now stands accused of ruthlessness in eliminating opponents, abuse of human rights, large-scale repression and the manipulation of elections. The violence unleashed in a populist drive to redistribute white-owned farmland contributed to his regime being shunned internationally, and to dire problems of food shortage for ordinary Zimbabweans.

Robert Gabriel Mugabe was born on 21 February 1924 at Kutama Mission in Zvimba. A member of the country's majority Shona ethnic group, he had a Christian upbringing in mission schools, where he then became a teacher himself. He obtained a degree in history and English from the University of Fort Hare in South Africa in 1951. Returning to teaching, he worked in mission schools, in government schools in Salisbury (now Harare) and Gwelo, and at teacher training college from 1955. He did an external degree with the University of London at this time, graduating in economics in 1958. In that year he went to Ghana to lecture at St Mary's Teacher Training College in Takoradi, but returned in 1960 to chair the inaugural congress of the National Democratic Party (NDP). Chosen as NDP secretary for information and publicity, he began his long involvement in full-time African nationalist politics. Mugabe married Sarah (Sally) Francesca Hayfron in April 1961. After her death in 1992 he married a second time, in August 1996, to Grace Marufu, his former secretary who is 41 years younger than him. Together they have one son and two daughters; the oldest two were born while he was still married to Sally.

The proscription of the NDP in December 1961 prompted its leaders to reorganize as the Zimbabwe African People's Union (ZAPU). Joshua Nkomo, the erstwhile NDP president, headed the new party, of which Mugabe was a cofounder, acting secretary-general, publicity secretary and editor of *The People's Voice*. ZAPU was soon banned in its turn, however, in September 1962. A split and realignment in the nationalist movement led to Mugabe becoming secretary-general in 1963 of a new Zimbabwe African National Union (ZANU), led by Rev. Ndabaningi Sithole.

Mugabe was detained from December 1963 until March 1964, and then imprisoned for over ten years, from August 1964 until December 1974, for his political activities. Imprisonment reinforced his political solidarity with fellow nationalist detainees, while he also completed three further academic degrees during this period. In 1975 he escaped to Mozambique, where he set about reinvigorating the armed liberation struggle as leader of ZANU's armed wing, the Zimbabwe African National Liberation Army.

Mugabe was at this point isolated in opposing a ceasefire with the white minority regime of Prime Minister Ian Smith, which had unilaterally declared independence, as Rhodesia, ten years previously in 1965. The better known African nationalist leaders—Nkomo of ZAPU and Sithole of ZANU—favoured attending talks with Smith under the umbrella of the African National Council (ANC), formed in 1971 by Bishop Abel Muzorewa to co-ordinate internal opposition when the British government was considering an earlier constitutional proposal. Mugabe's stance split ZANU into internal and external wings, but was vindicated by the failure of the latest round of talks with the Smith regime. Nkomo and he set up a Patriotic Front (PF) alliance in 1976 between ZAPU and ZANU, pledging to fight on to achieve genuine black majority rule. Sithole began to be marginalized, leading a separate faction when Mugabe was elected president of ZANU at the party's congress-in-exile in Mozambique in 1977.

The Patriotic Front held together in rejecting a subsequent internal settlement, in which Smith and Muzorewa were the main participants, and in boycotting the 1978 elections held to legitimize their formula. The guerrilla struggle, backed by Africa's key Cold War-era 'front-line' states, was stepped up, until the internal regime agreed to attend a constitutional conference convened by the British government at Lancaster House in London in September 1979. Mugabe performed impressively as leader of ZANU in a joint Patriotic Front delegation, and the pre-independence general elections held in March 1980 proved a triumph for him and his party (renamed as ZANU–PF). He became prime minister, leading the country to independence as Zimbabwe on 18 April 1980, and announcing a policy of national reconstruction aimed at restoring peace and stability.

In power, Mugabe initially avoided alienating the international business community and the white minority, making only gradual moves towards the redistribution of wealth which he had propounded as a Marxist guerrilla leader, and keeping within the terms of the agreed constitutional settlement (although he launched more far-reaching proposals for the compulsory acquisition of white-owned land in 1992, 1997 and 2000). The main conflict in the 1980s was not with the white minority but with his former allies in ZAPU. Under a state of emergency which remained in force until 1990, Mugabe used troops with great ruthlessness in 1983–84 to crush resistance in Matabeleland, the main Ndebele-populated heartland of ZAPU support. The massacres at this time, and the detention and alleged torture of dissident opponents, were accompanied by the strengthening of ZANU–PF's political dominance. Elections in 1985 gave the party an increased majority, and by the end of the decade the abolition of the reserved white seats in Parliament and the merger of ZAPU into the ruling party left it with little more than nominal opposition. Mugabe himself advocated the creation of a single-party state, but in 1991 he announced that he was abandoning plans to implement this.

Meanwhile Mugabe had moved over from the post of prime minister to the newly created executive presidency on 31 December 1987. Unopposed as first holder of the post, he was re-elected in March 1990 with just under 80% of the vote against one other candidate. In 1991 he hosted the Commonwealth heads of government meeting in Harare. This summit broadened his international profile, Zimbabwe's main role having hitherto been as a front-line state in the anti-apartheid struggle and the confrontation with South African-backed forces in Namibia, Angola and Mozambique. In November 1995 Mugabe became the chairman of the Group of 15 developing countries. His aspiration to an 'elder statesman' role on the international stage was fatally compromised, however, by the criticisms levelled at his regime over human rights and the restriction of political opposition, compounded by his intemperate denunciations of homosexuality on a number of occasions. He was re-elected president on 16–17 March 1996, although his victory was undermined by a turnout of only 31% and no real opposition; both Muzorewa and Sithole, although named on the ballot papers, withdrew in protest over restrictive electoral laws and alleged intimidation.

Domestic opposition to Mugabe crystallized in January 2000 when the Movement for Democratic Change (MDC) held its first party convention. Since then it has risen to become the biggest threat to the Mugabe regime. Its first victory was the defeat of a referendum in February aimed at increasing Mugabe's powers. However, the entire situation in the country was electrified when Mugabe ushered in a revitalized campaign later that month to redistribute the large farm estates owned almost exclusively by wealthy white farmers. The invasion of squatters was led by the semi-official 'war veterans' movement, which used blatant intimidation to force white families and their workers from their farms. This movement prompted the West to turn its back on Mugabe, halting aid and giving open support to the MDC, but it won support from the former African 'front-line' states, particularly South Africa. However, the war veterans themselves appeared to be beyond government control and were occasionally ordered to rein in their violent enthusiasm, which soon included the murders of white farmers and MDC supporters. Mugabe himself declared the country's wealthy white minority as its greatest enemy.

Mugabe held on to power in the 24–25 June 2000 legislative elections, despite a strong showing by the MDC on its electoral debut. The European Union (EU) derided the violent polls as "neither free nor fair" and dropped all development aid in March 2001, before imposing travel restrictions on Mugabe and his ministers in February 2002. Over the course of 2000–02 Mugabe continued to tolerate the violence of the war veterans, while persecuting MDC voters and white farmers. High on his list of enemies was MDC leader Morgan Tsvangirai. During the run-up to presidential elections on 13 March 2002, Tsvangirai was accused of treason in a last ditch effort to derail his growing support. Mugabe's re-election with 54% of the vote was immediately contested by the MDC and split the international community along Western and African lines once again. Later in the month the Commonwealth even suspended Zimbabwe for 12 months after reluctant support from South Africa and Nigeria. By the end of 2002 it was claimed that Mugabe had sanctioned the targeted refusal of food aid to regions which had supported the MDC in elections, and felt compelled to illegalize insulting gestures made towards his motorcade.

In mid-2002 the African Commission on Human Rights sent a mission to Zimbabwe. The subsequent report was eventually adopted by the African Union (AU) in 2004. It criticized the Mugabe regime for the arrests and torture of opposition MPs and human rights campaigners and clampdowns on civil liberties. This was one of the first open criticisms of the Zimbabwean government by fellow Africans, among whom Mugabe remains something of a hero; that same year he came third in a poll of 100 greatest Africans in *New African* magazine, behind Nelson Mandela and Ghanaian independence leader Kwame Nkrumah.

Internationally, Mugabe and his regime have become increasingly isolated. In March 2003 US president George W. Bush pushed through economic sanctions against Mugabe and many senior members of his administration. After the Commonwealth extended the suspension of Zimbabwe in December 2003, Mugabe withdrew the country altogether.

In June 2005 he received yet more condemnation following 'Operation Murambatsvina', Shona for 'Operation Drive Out Trash'. The crackdown saw hundreds of thousands of people evicted from slum dwellings which were then bulldozed, leaving them homeless, and forcing many to attempt the long journey back to rural villages which cannot afford to support them. Critics say that the policy is designed to clear urban areas in which opposition support is strongest out to rural districts where many are more dependent on the government. The AU again refused to intervene, saying that it would be improper for it to interfere with Zimbabwe's "internal legislation", though it later appointed former Mozambican president Joaquim Chissano, who was best man at Mugabe's second wedding, to try to persuade Mugabe to negotiate with the MDC. His appointment was rejected by Mugabe.

In July Mugabe approached China for a substantial loan, having been warned by the International Monetary Fund that the country faced expulsion over a US$300 million debt. China refused, negotiating a smaller package of trade ties instead. South African president Thabo Mbeki had previously offered to help Zimbabwe pay the debt rather than see the country expelled, but its help was said to have conditions attached on economic and political reform. It is not clear where Mugabe will find the money he needs; his people are too impoverished to bear much in the way of tax rises and most donors will no longer consider funding his regime.

APPENDIX: CONTACT DETAILS

Afghanistan

Office of the President
Kabul
Tel.: +93 25889
http://afghangovernment.com/

Albania

Office of the President
Bulevardi Deshmoret e Kombit
Tirana
Tel.: +355 4 228313
Fax: +355 4 233761
Email: presec@presec.tirana.al
http://president.al/

Office of the Prime Minister
Tirana
Tel.: +355 4 228210
Fax: +355 4 227888
www.albgovt.gov.al/

Algeria

Office of the President
Présidence de la République
Place Mohamed Seddik Benyahya
el-Mouradia
BP Alger Gare
Algiers
Tel.: +213 21 691515
Fax: +213 21 606628
www.elmouradia.dz

Office of the Prime Minister
rue Docteur Saâdane
Algiers
Tel.: +213 21 732300
Fax: +213 21 717929

Andorra

Spanish Embassy
   (Delegation of Bishop of Urgel)
Carrer Prat de la Creu 34
Andorra la Vella
Fax: +376 868500

French Embassy
   (Delegation of President of France)
Ave Tarragona 50-78
Edifici Les Columnes
Despatx núm 19
Andorra la Vella
Tel.: +376 803666
Fax: +376 803668
Email: rcpf@andorra.ad
www.coprince-fr.ad/

Presidency of the Executive Council
Andorra la Vella

Angola

Office of the President
Protocolo de Estado
Futungo de Belas
Luanda
Tel.: +244 2 350409
www.angola.org/

Office of the Prime Minister
Palácio do Povo
Luanda

Antigua and Barbuda

Office of the Governor-General
Government House
St John's
Tel.: +1 268 462 0003
Fax: +1 268 462 2566
Email: govg@candw.ag
www.antiguagov.com/office.htm

Office of the Prime Minister
Queen Elizabeth Highway
St John's
Tel.: +1 268 462 4956
Fax: +1 268 462 3225
Email: primeminister@lesterbird.com
www.antiguagov.com/pm.htm

Argentina

Office of the President
Balcarce 50 Piso 1
1064 Buenos Aires
Tel.:   +54 11 4344 3600
Fax: +54 11 4331 1398
Email: scyc@presidencia.gov.ar
www.presidencia.gov.ar/

Armenia

Office of the President
Marshall Baghramian Street 26
375077 Yerevan
Tel.:   +374 10 52 02 04
Fax: +374 10 52 15 51
Email: web@president.am
www.president.am/

Office of the Prime Minister
Government House
1 Republic Square
375010 Yerevan
Tel.:   +374 1 52 03 60
Fax: +374 1 15 10 35
www.gov.am/en/

Australia

Office of the Governor-General
Government House
Dunrossil Drive
Yarralumla ACT 2600
Tel.:   +61 2 6283 3533
Fax: +61 2 6283 3760
Email: governor-general@gg.gov.au
www.gg.gov.au

Office of the Prime Minister
3–5 National Circuit
Barton ACT 2600
Tel.:   +61 2 6271 5111
Fax: +61 2 6271 5414
Email: firstname.surname@dpmc.gov.au
www.dpmc.gov.au/

Austria

Office of the Federal President
Hofburg
Leopoldinischer Trakt
1014 Vienna
Tel.:   +43 1 534 22
Fax: +43 1 535 6512
Email: heinz.fischer@hofburg.at
www.hofburg.at/

Office of the Federal Chancellor
Ballhausplatz 2
1014 Vienna
Tel.:   +43 1 531 150
Fax: +43 1 535 0338
Email: praesidium@bka.gv.at
www.austria.gv.at/

Azerbaijan

Office of the President
Istiklal Street 19
370066 Baku
Tel.:   +994 12 492 79 06
Fax: +994 12 498 08 22
Email: root@lider.baku.az
www.president.az/

Office of the Prime Minister
Lermontov Street 63
370066 Baku
Tel.:   +994 12 495 75 28
Fax: +994 12 498 97 86

Bahamas

Office of the Governor-General
Government House
Government Hill
PO Box N-8301
Nassau
Tel.:   +1 242 322 1875
Fax: +1 242 322 4659
www.bahamas.gov.bs/bahamasweb/home.nsf

Office of the Prime Minister
Sir Cecil Wallace-Whitfield Centre
Cable Beach
PO Box CB-10980
Nassau
Tel.:   +1 242 327 5826
Fax: +1 242 327 5806
Email: info@opm.gov.bs
www.opm.gov.bs/

Bahrain

Office of the King
The Amiri Court
Rifa'a Palace
PO Box 555
Manama
Tel.:　+973 17 666 666
Fax:　+973 17 663 070

Office of the Prime Minister
Government House
Government Road
PO Box 1000
Manama
Tel.:　+973 17 200 000
Fax:　+973 17 532 839

Bangladesh

Office of the President
Bangabhaban
Dhaka 1000
Tel.:　+880 2 831 2066
Fax:　+880 2 956 6242

Office of the Prime Minister
Old Sangshad Bhaban
Tejgaon
Dhaka 1000
Tel.:　+880 2 811 5100
Fax:　+880 2 811 3244
Email:　pm@pmobd.org
www.pmo.gov.bd/

Barbados

Office of the Governor-General
Government House
St Michael
Tel.:　+1 246 429 2646
Fax:　+1 246 436 5910

Office of the Prime Minister
Government Headquarters
Bay Street
St Michael
Tel.:　+1 246 436 6435
Fax:　+1 246 436 9280
Email:　info@primeminister.gov.bb
www.primeminister.gov.bb/

Belarus

Office of the President
Dom Urada
ulitsa K. Marksa 38
220016 Minsk
Tel.:　+375 172 223217
Fax:　+375 172 260610
Email:　contact@president.gov.by
www.president.gov.by/

Office of the Prime Minister
House of Government
Independence Square
220010
Minsk
Tel.:　+375 172 226905
Fax:　+375 172 226665

Belgium

Office of the King
Palais Royal/Koninklijk Paleis
rue de Bréderode
B-1000 Brussels
Tel.:　+32 2 551 20 20

Office of the Prime Minister
16 rue de la Loi
B-1000 Brussels
Tel.:　+32 2 501 02 11
Fax:　+32 2 512 69 53
www.premier.fgov.be/

Belize

Office of the Governor-General
Belize House
Belmopan
Tel.:　+501 8222521
Fax:　+501 8222050

Office of the Prime Minister
New Administrative Building
Belmopan
Tel.:　+501 8222346
Fax:　+501 8223323
Email:　primeminister@belize.gov.bz
www.belize.gov.bz/pm/welcome.shtml

Benin

Office of the President
BP 1288
Place de l'Indépendence
Cotonou
Tel.: +229 30 02 28
Fax: +229 30 06 36
www.gouv.bj/

Bhutan

Office of the King
Royal Palace
Tashichhodzong
Thimpu
Tel.: +975 2 322521
Fax: +975 2 322079

Bolivia

Office of the President
Palacio de Gobierno
Plaza Murillo
La Paz
Tel.: +591 2 2430700
Fax: +591 2 2391216
Email: webmaster@presidencia.gov.bo
www.presidencia.gov.bo/

Bosnia & Herzegovina

Office of the President
Musala 5
71000 Sarajevo
Tel.: +387 3366 4941
Fax: +387 3347 2791
www.predsjednistvohih.ba/

Office of the Prime Minister
Vojvode Putnika 3
71000 Sarajevo
Tel.: +387 3366 4941
Fax: +387 3344 3446
Email: kabprem@fbihvlada.gov.ba
www.fbihvlada.gov.ba/

Botswana

Office of the President
Private Bag 001
Gaborone
Tel.: +267 3950800
Fax: +267 3950888
Email: op.registry@gov.bw
www.gov.bw/

Brazil

Office of the President
Palácio do Planalto
Praça dos Três Poderes
70150-900
Brasília DF
Tel.: +55 61 3211 1221
Fax: +55 61 3226 7566
Email: casacivil@planalto.gov.br
www.presidencia.gov.br/

Brunei

Office of the Sultan
Istana Nurul Iman
BA1000
Bandar Seri Begawan
Tel.: +673 2229988
Fax: +673 2244150
Email: pro@jpm.gov.bn
www.bruneisultan.com/

Bulgaria

Office of the President
2 Dondukov Boulevard
Sofia 1000
Tel.: +359 2 983 3839
Email: president@president.bg
www.president.bg/

Office of the Prime Minister
1 Dondukov Boulevard
Sofia 1000
Tel.: +359 2 940 2770
Fax: +359 2 980 2056
Email: primeminister@government.bg
www.government.bg/

Burkina Faso

Office of the President
BP 7030
Ouagadougou 03
Tel.:   +226 50 30 66 30
Fax: +226 50 31 05 78
www.presidence.bf/presidence/index.php

Office of the Prime Minister
BP 7027
Ouagadougou
Tel.:   +226 50 32 48 89
Fax: +226 50 31 47 61
www.primature.gov.bf/republic/
    fgouvernement.htm

Burundi

Office of the President
Boulevard de l'Uprona
Rohero I
BP 1870
Bujumbura
Tel.:   +257 226063
Fax: +257 227490
Email: sindamuk@cbinf.com
www.burundi.gov.bi/

Cambodia

Office of the King
Royal Palace
Phnom Penh
Tel.:   +855 23 426801
Fax: +855 23 426802
www.phnompenhdaily.com/royalpal.htm

Office of the Prime Minister
Phnom Penh

Cameroon

Office of the President
Palais de l'Unité
Yaoundé
Tel.:   +237 223 40 25
www.camnet.cm/celcom/homepr.htm

Office of the Prime Minister
c/o the Central Post Office
Yaoundé
Tel.:   +237 223 57 50
Fax: +237 223 57 50
Email: spm@spm.gov.cm
www.spm.gov.cm/

Canada

Office of the Governor-General
Rideau Hall
One Sussex Drive
Ottawa ON K1A 0A1
Tel.:   +1 613 993 8200
Fax: +1 613 990 7636
Email: info@gg.ca
www.gg.ca/

Office of the Prime Minister
Room 309-S Centre Block
House of Commons
111 Wellington Street
Ottawa ON K1A 0A6
Tel.:   +1 613 992 4211
Fax: +1 613 995 0101
Email: pm@pm.gc.ca
http://pm.gc.ca/

Cape Verde

Office of the President
Presidência da República
CP100
Plateau
Praia
São Tiago
Tel.:   +238 61 26 69
Fax: +238 61 43 56
www.presidenciarepublica.cv/

Office of the Prime Minister
Palácio do Governo
CP 16
Várzea
Praia
São Tiago
Tel.:   +238 61 05 13
Fax: +238 61 30 99
Email: gab.imprensa@gpm.gov.cv
www.governo.cv/

Central African Republic

Office of the President
Palais de la Renaissance
Bangui
Tel.:   +236 661 03 23
Fax.:   +236 661 75 08
www.socatel.cf/patasse.htm

Office of the Prime Minister
Bangui
www.rca-gouv.net/

Chad

Office of the President
BP 74
N'Djamena
Tel.:   +235 51 44 37
Fax: +235 51 45 01
Email: presidence@tchad.td
http://rapidrecettes.com/sodt/

Office of the Prime Minister
N'Djamena
Tel.:   +235 52 60 64
Fax: +235 52 45 40

Chile

Office of the President
Palacio de La Moneda
Santiago
Tel.:   +56 2 690 4000
Fax: +56 2 698 4656
Email: opinion@presidencia.cl
www.presidencia.cl/

China

Office of the President
State Council Secretariat
Zhong Nan Hai
Beijing
Tel.:   +86 10 6309 8375
Fax: +86 10 6238 1025
Email: gov@govonline.cn
www.gov.cn/

Office of the Premier
Beijing
Tel.:   +86 10 6207 2370
Fax: +86 10 6205 3995
Email: gov@mail.ctca.com.cn
www.gov.cn/

Chinese Communist Party
Beijing
Email: master@ccp.org.cn
www.ccp.org.cn/

Colombia

Office of the President
Palácio de Nariño
Carrera 8a
No 7–26
Santafé de Bogotá
Tel.:   +57 1 562 9300
Fax: +57 1 336 1128
www.presidencia.gov.co/

Comoros

Office of the President
BP 521
Moroni
Tel.:   +269 74 4808
Fax: +269 74 4829
www.presidence-uniondescomores.com/

Democratic Republic of the Congo

Office of the President
Mont Ngaliema
Kinshasa
Tel.:   +243 12 313 12

Republic of the Congo

Office of the President
Palais du Peuple
Brazzaville
Tel.:   +242 810235
Fax: +242 814557
Email: collgros@altanet.fr
www.gouv.cg/

Office of the Prime Minister
Brazzaville
Tel.:   +242 815239
Fax: +242 813348

Costa Rica

Office of the President
Casa Presidencial
Apartado 10.089
San José 1000
Tel.: +506 225 3211
Fax: +506 253 9676
Email: presidente@casapres.go.cr
www.casapres.go.cr/

Côte d'Ivoire

Office of the President
alais de la Présidence
BP V11
Abidjan 01
Tel.: +225 20 21 02 88
Fax: +225 20 21 34 25
Email: lepresident@pr.ci
www.presidence.gov.ci/

Office of the Prime Minister
Boulevard Angoulvand
01 BP 1533
Abidjan 01
Tel.: +225 20 22 00 20

Croatia

Office of the President
Pantovčak 241
Zagreb
Tel.: +385 1 456 51 91
Fax: +385 1 456 52 99
Email: ured@predsjednik.hr
www.predsjednik.hr/

Office of the Prime Minister
Trg svetog Marka 2
10 000 Zagreb
Tel.: +385 1 456 92 01
Fax: +385 1 630 30 19
Email: premijer@vlada.hr
www.vlada.hr/

Cuba

Office of the President
Palacio del Gobierno
Havana
www.cubagob.cu/

Cyprus

Office of the President
Presidential Palace
Demosthenis Severis Avenue
1400 Nicosia
Tel.: +357 22 661333
Fax: +357 22 665016
Email: grafio-proedrou@cytanet.com.cy
www.cyprus.gov.cy/

Turkish Republic of Northern Cyprus

Office of the President
(Lefkoşa)
Mersin 10
Turkey
Tel.: +90 392 22 83 444
Fax: +90 392 22 72 252
Email: info@kktc-cb.org
www.trncpresidency.org

Office of the Prime Minister
(Lefkoşa)
Mersin 10
Turkey
Tel.: +90 392 22 83141
Fax: +90 392 22 75281
Email: pressdpt@brimnet.com
www.cm.gov.nc.tr/

Czech Republic

Office of the President
Prazsky Hrad
119 08 Prague 1
Tel.: +420 2 2437 1111
Fax: +420 2 2437 3300
Email: president@hrad.cz
www.hrad.cz/

Office of the Prime Minister
nábřeží Eduarda Beneše 4
118 01 Prague 1
Tel.: +420 2 2400 2224
Fax: +420 2 2481 0231
Email: posta@vlada.cz
www.vlada.cz/

Denmark

Office of the Queen
The Lord Chamberlain's Office
Det Gule Palæ
Amaliegade 18
1256 Copenhagen K
Tel.:   +45 33 40 10 10
Email: hofmarskallatet@konghuset.dk
www.kongehuset.dk/

Office of the Prime Minister
Christiansborg
Prins Jørgens Gard 11
1218 Copenhagen K
Tel.:   +45 33 92 33 00
Fax: +45 33 11 16 65
Email: stm@stm.dk
www.stm.dk/

Djibouti

Office of the President
BP 6
Djibouti
Tel.:   +253 351145
Fax: 253 358296
Email: sggpr@intnet.dj
www.presidence.dj/

Office of the Prime Minister
BP 2086
Djibouti
Tel.:   +253 351494
Fax: +253 355049

Dominica

Office of the President
Government Headquarters
Morne Bruce
Roseau
Tel.:   +1 767 4482 054
Fax: +1 767 4498 366

Office of the Prime Minister
Government Headquarters
Kennedy Avenue
Roseau
Tel.:   +1 767 4482 401
Fax: +1 767 4488 200
Email: pmoffice@cwdom.dm

Dominican Republic

Office of the President
Palacio Nacional
Calle Moisés García
Santo Domingo DN
Tel.:   +1 829 695 8000
Fax: +1 829 688 2100
Email: prensa@presidencia.gov.do
www.presidencia.gov.do/

East Timor

Office of the President
Palácio das Cinzas
Kaikoli
Dili
Tel.:   +670 333 9011
Email: president-tl@easttimor.minihub.org
www.gov.east-timor.org

Office of the Prime Minister
Dili
Tel.:   +670 331 2210
Email: info@gov.east-timor.org
www.gov.east-timor.org

Ecuador

Office of the President
Palacio Nacional
García Moreno 1043
Quito
Tel.:   +593 2 2216 300

Egypt

Office of the President
al-Etehadia Building
Heliopolis
Cairo
Tel.:   +20 2 245 9816
Email: webmaster@presidency.gov.eg
www.presidency.gov.eg/

Office of the Prime Minister
Sharia Majlis al-Sha'ab
Cairo
Tel.:   +20 2 355 3192
Fax: +20 2 355 8016
Email: primemin@idsc.gov.eg
www.egypt.gov.eg

El Salvador

Office of the President
Alameda Dr Manuel Enrique Araújo
Km. 6
San Salvador
Tel.:   +503 2271 1555
Fax: +503 2271 0850
Email: casapres@casapres.gob.sv
www.casapres.gob.sv/

Equatorial Guinea

Office of the President
Malabo

Office of the Prime Minister
Malabo

Eritrea

Office of the President
PO Box 257
Asmara
Tel.:   +291 1 12 21 32
Fax: +291 1 12 51 23

Estonia

Office of the President
Weizenbergi 39
15050
Tallinn
Tel.:   +372 631 6202
Fax: +372 631 6250
Email: sekretar@vpk.ee
www.president.ee/

Office of the Prime Minister
Stenbock House
Rahukohtu 3
15161
Tallinn
Tel.:   +372 693 5701
Fax: +372 693 5994
Email: peaminister@rk.ee
www.peaminister.ee/

Ethiopia

Office of the President
PO Box 1031
Addis Ababa
Tel.:   +251 1 55 02 24
Fax: +251 1 55 20 41

Office of the Prime Minister
PO Box 1031
Addis Ababa
Tel.:   +251 1 55 20 44
Fax: +251 1 55 20 20
www.ethiospokes.net/

Fiji

Office of the President
Government Buildings
PO Box 2513
Suva
Tel.:   +679 3314 244
Fax: +679 3301 645
Email: info@fiji.gov.fj
www.fiji.gov.fj/president/index.shtml

Office of the Prime Minister
4th Floor
New Government Buildings
PO Box 2353
Suva
Tel.:   +679 3211 201
Fax: +679 3306 034
Email: pmsoffice@connect.com.fj
www.fiji.gov.fj/publish/pm_office.shtml

Finland

Office of the President
Mariankatu 2
FIN-00170
Helsinki
Tel.:   +358 9 661 133
Fax: +358 9 638 247
Email: presidentti@tpk.fi
www.tpk.fi/

Office of the Prime Minister
Snellmaninkatu 1A
PO Box 23
FIN-00023 Government
Helsinki
Tel.:   +358 9 16001
Fax: +358 9 1602 2165
Email: firstname.surname@vnk.fi
www.vn.fi/vnk/

France

Office of the President
Palais de l'Elysée
55–57 rue du Faubourg Saint Honoré
75008 Paris Cédex
Tel.:   +33 1 42 92 81 00
Fax: +33 1 47 42 24 65
www.elysee.fr/

Office of the Prime Minister
Hôtel Matignon
57 rue de Varenne
75700 Paris Cédex
Tel.:   +33 1 42 75 80 00
Fax: +33 1 45 44 15 72
Email: premier-ministre@premier-
    ministre.gouv.fr
www.premier-ministre.gouv.fr/

Gabon

Office of the President
BP 546
Libreville
Tel.:   +241 172 20 30
www.presidence-gabon.com/

Office of the Prime Minister
BP 546
Libreville
Tel.:   +241 177 89 81

Gambia

Office of the President
Private mail bag
State House
Banjul
Tel.:   +220 4223 811
Fax: +220 4227 034
Email: info@statehouse.gm
www.statehouse.gm/

Georgia

Office of the President
Ingorovka 7
380007
Tbilisi
Tel.:   +995 32 99 96 53
Fax: +995 32 99 08 79
Email: office@presidpress.gov.ge
www.presidpress.gov.ge/

Office of the State Minister
Ingorokva 7
380018
Tbilisi
Tel.:   +995 32 93 59 07
Fax: +995 32 98 23 54

Germany

Office of the Federal President
Schloß Bellevue
Spreeweg 1
10557
Berlin
Tel.:   +49 30 2000 0
Fax: +49 30 2000 1999
Email: poststelle@bpra.bund.de
www.bundespraesident.de/

Office of the Federal Chancellor
Willy-Brandt Straße 1
10178
Berlin
Tel.:   +49 30 4000 0
Fax: +49 30 4000 1818
Email: bundeskanzler@bundeskanzler.de
www.bundesregierung.de/

Ghana

Office of the President
The Castle
Osu
PO Box 1627
Accra
Tel.:   +233 21 665 415
www.ghana.gov.gh/

Greece

Office of the President
17 Odos Stissichorou
106 74 Athens
Tel.: +30 210 728 3111
Fax: +30 210 724 8938

Office of the Prime Minister
Maximos' Mansion
19 Hrodou Attikou
106 71 Athens
Tel.: +30 210 671 7732
Fax: +30 210 671 5799
Email: mail@primeminister.gr
www.primeminister.gr/

Grenada

Office of the Governor-General
Government House
St George's
Tel.: +1 473 440 2401
Fax: +1 473 440 6688

Office of the Prime Minister
Ministerial Complex
6th Floor
Botanical Gardens
St George's
Tel.: +1 473 440 2255
Fax: +1 473 440 4116
Email: gndpm@caribsurf.com
www.spiceisle.com/gndpm/

Guatemala

Office of the President
Palacio Nacional
6a Calle y 7a Avenida
Zona 1
Guatemala City
Tel.: +502 2221 4428
www.guatemala.gob.gt

Guinea

Office of the President
State House
Conakry
Tel.: +224 44 11 47
www.guinee.gov.gn/1_bienvenue/
    president.htm

Office of the Prime Minister
Cité des Natíons
BP 5141
Conakry
Tel.: +224 44 51 19
Fax: +224 41 52 82
www.guinee.gov.gn/

Guinea-Bissau

Office of the President
Conselho de Estado
Bissau

Office of the Prime Minister
Avenida Unidade Africana
CP 137
Bissau
Tel.: +245 211308
Fax: +245 201671

Guyana

Office of the President
New Garden Street
Georgetown
Tel.: +592 225 1330
Fax: +592 226 9969

Office of the Prime Minister
Wight's Lane
Kingston
Georgetown
Tel.: +592 226 6955
Fax: +592 225 7573

Haiti

Office of the President
rue Champ-de-Mars
Port-au-Prince
Tel.: +509 228 2128
Fax: +509 228 2320
www.palaishaiti.net/

Office of the Prime Minister
Villa d'Accueil
Musseau
Port-au-Prince
Tel.: +509 245 0025
Fax: +509 298 3900

Honduras

Office of the President
Casa Presidencial
Boulevard Juan Pablo II
Tegucigalpa
Tel.:   +504 239 1515
Fax: +504 231 0097

Hungary

Office of the President
Kossuth Lajos tér 1–3
1055 Budapest
Tel.:   +36 1 441 4000

Office of the Prime Minister
Kossuth Lajos tér 1–3
1055 Budapest
Tel.:   +36 1 441 4000
Fax: +36 1 268 3050
www.kancellaria.gov.hu/

Iceland

Office of the President
Stadastadur
Sóleyjargata 1
150 Reykjavík
Tel.:   +354 540 4400
Fax: +354 562 4802
Email: forseti@forseti.is

Office of the Prime Minister
Stjórnarrádshúsinu v/ Lækjargtorg
150 Reykjavík
Tel.:   +354 545 8400
Fax: +354 562 4014
Email: postur@for.stjr.is
www.stjr.is/for/

India

Office of the President
Rashtrapati Bhavan
New Delhi 110 004
Tel.:   +91 11 2301 5321
Fax: +91 11 2301 7290
Email: poi_gen@rb.nic.in
http://presidentofindia.nic.in/

Office of the Prime Minister
South Block
Kaisina Hill
New Delhi 110 011
Tel.:   +91 11 2301 2312
Fax: +91 11 2301 6857
http://pmindia.nic.in/

Indonesia

Office of the President
Istana Merdeka
Jakarta
Tel.:   +62 21 331 097
www.indonesia.go.id/

Iran

Office of the Spiritual Leader
Tehran

Office of the President
Pasteur Avenue
13168-43311
Tehran
Tel.:   +98 21 614451
Email: info@president.ir
www.president.ir/

Iraq

Office of the President
Baghdad
www.iraqigovernment.org/

Office of the Prime Minister
Baghdad

Ireland

Office of the President
Áras an Uachtaráin
Phoenix Park
Dublin 8
Tel.:   +353 1 6772 815
Fax: +353 1 6710 529
Email: webmaster@aras.irlgov.ie
www.irlgov.ie/aras/

Office of the Prime Minister
Government Buildings
Upper Merrion Street
Dublin 2
Tel.:   +353 1 6624 888
Fax: +353 1 6789 791
Email: webmaster@taoiseach.irlgov.ie
www.taoiseach.gov.ie/

Israel

Office of the President
3 Hanassi Street
Jerusalem 92188
Tel.:   +972 2 670 7211
Fax: +972 2 561 0037
www.president.gov.il/

Office of the Prime Minister
PO Box 187
3 Kaplan Street
Kiryat Ben-Gurion
Jerusalem 91919
Tel.:   +972 2 670 5555
Fax: +972 2 651 2631
Email: pm_eng@pmo.gov.il
www.pmo.gov.il/

Italy

Office of the President
Palazzo del Quirinale
00187 Rome
Tel.:   +39 06 46991
Fax: +39 06 46992384
Email: presidenza.repubblica@quirinale.it
www.quirinale.it/

Office of the Prime Minister
Palazzo Chigi
Piazza Colonna 370
00187 Rome
Tel.:   +39 06 67791
Fax: +39 06 6783998
www.palazzochigi.it/

Jamaica

Office of the Governor-General
King's House
Hope Road
Kingston 10
Tel.:   +1 876 927 6424
Fax: +1 876 927 4561

Office of the Prime Minister
Jamaica House
1 Devon Road
Kingston 10
Tel.:   +1 876 927 9941
Fax: +1 876 929 0005
Email: pmo@opm.gov.jm
www.cabinet.gov.jm/

Japan

Imperial Household Agency
1-1 Chiyoda
Chiyoda-ku
Tokyo 100-8111
Tel.:   +81 3 3213 1111
Fax: +81 3 3282 1407
Email: information@kunaicho.go.jp
www.kunaicho.go.jp/eindex.html

Office of the Prime Minister
1-1-6 Nagata-cho
Chiyoda-ku
Tokyo 100-8968
Tel.:   +81 3 3581 2361
Fax: +81 3 3581 1910
www.sorifu.go.jp/english/index.html

Jordan

Office of the King
Royal Palace
Amman
Tel.:   +962 6 4637 341
Email: info@nic.gov.jo
www.kingabdullah.jo/

Office of the Prime Minister
PO Box 1577
Amman
Tel.:   +962 6 4641 211
Fax: +962 6 4642 520
Email: prime@pm.gov.jo
www.pm.gov.jo/

Kazakhstan

Office of the President
11 Beybitshilik Street
473000 Astana
Tel.:   +7 317 2152000
Fax: +7 317 2326182
www.president.kz/

Office of the Prime Minister
11 Beybitshilik Street
473000 Astana
Tel.:   +7 317 2323104
Fax: +7 317 2323003

Kenya

Office of the President
Harambee House
Harambee Avenue
PO Box 30510
Nairobi
Tel.:   +254 20 2227 411
www.officeofthepresident.go.ke/

Kiribati

Office of the President
PO Box 68
Bairiki
Tarawa
Tel.:   +686 21183
Fax: +686 21145

North Korea

Supreme People's Assembly
Mansoudong Central District
Pyongyang
Tel.:   +850 2 18 111
Fax: +850 2 381 2100

Office of the National Defence Commission
Pyongyang

Office of the Premier
Pyongyang

South Korea

Office of the President
Cheong Wa Dae
1 Sejong-no
Jongno-gu
Seoul
Tel.:   +82 2 770 0011
Fax: +82 2 770 0344
Email: president@cwd.go.kr
www.cwd.go.kr/

Office of the Prime Minister
77-6 Sejong-no
Jongno-gu
110 760 Seoul
Tel.:   +82 2 737 0094
Fax: +82 2 737 0109
Email: m_opm@opm.go.kr
www.opm.go.kr/

Kuwait

Office of the Amir
PO Box 799
13008 Safat
Kuwait City
Tel.:   +965 539 6144
Fax: +965 534 7696

Office of the Prime Minister
PO Box 4
13001 Safat
Kuwait City
Tel.:   +965 539 1111
Fax: +965 539 0430
Email: info@dpm.gov.kw
www.dpm.gov.kw/

Kyrgyzstan

Office of the President
Government House
720000 Bishkek
Tel.:   +996 312 212466
Fax: +996 312 218627
Email: office@mail.gov.kg
www.president.kg/

Office of the Prime Minister
Government House
Dom Pravitelstva
720000 Bishkek
Tel.:   +996 312 225656
Fax: +996 312 218627
www.kyrgyzstan.org/persons/bakiev.htm

Laos

Office of the President
Sethathirath Road
Vientiane
Tel.:   +856 21 214210
Fax: +856 21 214208

Office of the Prime Minister
Lane Xang Avenue
Vientiane
Tel.:   +856 21 213652
Fax: +856 21 213560

Latvia

Office of the President
Pils lauk 3
Riga 1900
Tel.:   +371 7377 548
Fax: +371 7325 800
Email: chancery@president.lv
www.president.lv/index.php

Office of the Prime Minister
Brivibas bulvaris 36
Riga 1520
Tel.:   +371 7082 900
Fax: +371 7280 469
Email: vk@mk.gov.lv
www.mk.gov.lv/

Lebanon

Office of the President
Presidential Palace
Baabda
Beirut
Tel.:   +961 1 387200
Fax: +961 5 922400
Email: president_office@presidency.gov.lb
www.presidency.gov.lb/

Office of the Prime Minister
Grand Sérail
rue des Arts et Métiers
Sanayeh
Beirut
Tel.:   +961 1 862001
Fax: +961 1 865630

Lesotho

Office of the King
The Royal Palace
PO Box 524
Maseru 100
Tel.:   +266 22322170
Fax: +266 22310083
Email: sps@palace.org.ls
www.lesotho.gov.ls/ministers/mnking.htm

Office of the Prime Minister
PO Box 527
Maseru 100
Tel.:   +266 22311000
Fax: +266 22310444
www.lesotho.gov.ls/ministers/
      mndefence.htm

Liberia

Office of the President
Executive Mansion
Capitol Hill
PO Box 9001
Monrovia
Tel.:   +231 224961
Email: emansion@liberia.net
www.executive-mansion.gov.lr/

Libya

Office of the Leader of the Revolution
Secretariat of the General People's
      Committee
Tripoli
Tel.:   +218 21 48210
Email: greenbook2001@yahoo.com
www.qadhafi.org/

Office of the Secretary-General
Secretariat of the General People's
      Committee
Tripoli
Tel.:   +218 21 48210

Liechtenstein

Office of the Prince
Schloß Vaduz
9490 Vaduz
Tel.:   +423 2321212
Fax: +423 2326862
www.fuerstenhaus.li/

Office of the Head of Government
9490 Vaduz
Tel.:   +423 2366111
Fax: +423 2366022
Email: office@liechtenstein.li
www.firstlink.li/regierung/

Lithuania

Office of the President
S. Daukanto apylinke 3
Vilnius 2008
Tel.: +370 526 64154
Fax: +370 521 64145
Email: info@president.lt
www.president.lt/

Office of the Prime Minister
Gedimino prospekt 11
Vilnius 2039
Tel.: +370 521 21088
Fax: +370 521 27452
Email: kanceliarija@lrvk.lt
www.lrvk.lt/

Luxembourg

Office of the Grand Duke
Palais Grand-Ducal
Marché-aux-Herbes
1728 Luxembourg-Ville
Tel.: +352 47 48741

Office of the Prime Minister
Hôtel de Bourgogne
4 rue de la Congrégation
2910 Luxembourg-Ville
Tel.: +352 47 82106
Fax: +352 46 1720
Email: me@me.smtp.etat.lu
www.gouvernement.lu/

Macedonia

Office of the President
11 Oktomvri bb
91000 Skopje
Tel.: +389 2 3113 318
Fax: +389 2 3112 643
www.president.gov.mk/

Office of the Prime Minister
Ilindenska bb
91000 Skopje
Tel.: +389 2 3115 389
Fax: +389 2 3112 561
Email: office@primeminister.gov.mk
www.primeminister.gov.mk/

Madagascar

Office of the President
BP 955/1310
Ambohitsirohitra
101 Antananarivo
Tel.: +261 20 2227474

Office of the Prime Minister
BP 248
Mahazoarivo
101 Antananarivo
Tel.: +261 20 2225258
Fax: +261 20 2235258

Malawi

Office of the President
Government Offices
Private Bag 301
Lilongwe 3
Tel.: +265 1 789311
Fax: +265 1 788456
Email: opc@malawi.gov.mw
www.malawi.gov.mw/

Malaysia

Office of the Head of State
Istana Negara
50500 Kuala Lumpur
Tel.: +60 3 2078 8332
Fax: +60 3 2010 4646

Office of the Prime Minister
Blok Utama, Tingkat 1-5
Pusat Pentadbiran Kerajaan Persekutuan
62502 Putrajaya
Tel.: +60 3 8888 8000
Fax: +60 3 8888 3424
Email: ppm@pmo.gov.my
www.pmo.gov.my/

Maldives

Office of the President
Medhuziyaaraiy Magu
Malé 20113
Tel.: +960 323701
Fax: +960 325500
Email: info@po.gov.mv
www.presidencymaldives.gov.mv

Mali

Office of the President
BP 1463
Koulouba
Bamako
Tel.:   +223 2 22 80 30
Fax: +223 2 22 01 29
Email: presidence@koulouba.pr.ml
http://koulouba.pr.ml/

Office of the Prime Minister
BP 97
Quartier du Fleuve
Bamako
Tel.:   +223 2 22 55 34
Fax: +223 2 22 85 83

Malta

Office of the President
The Palace
Valletta CMR 02
Tel.:   +356 21 221221
Fax: +356 21 241241
Email: president@gov.mt
http://president.gov.mt/

Office of the Prime Minister
Auberge de Castille (Kastilja)
Valletta CMR 02
Tel.:   +356 21 242560
Fax: +356 21 249888
Email: info.msp@magnet.mt
www.opm.gov.mt/

Marshall Islands

Office of the President
PO Box 2
MH 96960 Majuro
Tel.:   +692 625 3213
Fax: +692 625 4021
Email: presoff@ntamar.com

Mauritania

Office of the President
Présidence de la République
BP 184
Nouakchott
Tel.:   +222 5252 317
www.mauritania.mr/

Office of the Prime Minister
Présidence de la République
BP 184
Nouakchott
www.mauritania.mr/

Mauritius

Office of the President
State House
Le Réduit
Port Louis
Tel.:   +230 454 3021
Fax: +230 464 5370
Email: president@mail.gov.mu
http://ncb.intnet.mu/presiden.htm

Office of the Prime Minister
Intendance Street
Port Louis
Tel.:   +230 207 9595
Fax: +230 208 7907
Email: secab@intnet.mu
http://primeminister.gov.mu/

Mexico

Office of the President
Los Pinos
Colonia San Miguel Chapultepec
11850 Mexico DF
Tel.:   +52 55 5277 7455
Fax: +52 55 5510 3717
www.presidencia.gob.mx/

Federated States of Micronesia

Office of the President
PO Box PS-53
Palikir
96941 FM Pohnpei
Tel.:   +691 320 2228
Fax: +691 320 2785
www.fsmgov.org/bio/falcam.html

Moldova

Office of the President
Ştefan cel Mare 154
Chişinau
Tel.:   +373 2 234 793
Fax: +373 2 245 089
http://presedinte.md/

Appendix: Contact Details

Office of the Prime Minister
Piaţa Marii Adunari Naţionale 1
227033 Chişinau
Tel.:   +373 2 233 092
Fax: +373 2 242 696

Monaco

Office of the Prince
Palais de Monaco
Place du Palais
BP 518
98015 Monaco
Tel.:   +377 93 25 18 31
Fax: +377 93 30 26 26
Email: centre-info@gouv.mc
www.gouv.mc/

Office of the Minister of State
Place de la Visitation
BP 522
98015 Monaco
Tel.:   +377 93 15 80 00
Fax: +377 93 15 82 17
Email: centre-info@gouv.mc
www.gouv.mc/

Mongolia

Office of the President
State Palace
Sukhbaatar Square 1
Ulan Bator 12
Tel.:   +976 11 323240
Fax: +976 11 329281
Email: webmaster@presi.pmis.gov.mn
http://gate1.pmis.gov.mn/president/

Office of the Prime Minister
State Palace
Sukhbaatar Square 1
Ulan Bator 12
Tel.:   +976 11 3236731
Fax: +976 11 328329
Email: webmaster@pmis.gov.mn
www.pmis.gov.mn/cabinet

Morocco

Office of the King
Palais Royal
Rabat
Tel.:   +212 37 760122

Office of the Prime Minister
Al Méchouar
Essaid
Rabat
Tel.:   +212 37 761763
Fax: +212 37 769995
www.pm.gov.ma/

Mozambique

Office of the President
Avenida Julius Nyerere 1780
Maputo
Tel.:   +258 1 491121
Fax: +258 1 492065
www.presidencia.gov.mz/

Office of the Prime Minister
Praça da Marinha
Maputo
Tel.:   +258 1 426861
Fax: +258 1 426881
Email: dgpm.gov@teledata.mz
www.mozambique.mz/governo/mocumbi.htm

Myanmar

Office of the Chair of the SPDC
15–16 Windermere Park
Rangoon
Tel.:   +95 1 282445
www.myanmar.com/

Office of the Prime Minister
Ministers' Office
Rangoon
Tel.:   +95 1 283742

Namibia

Office of the President
State House
Private Bag 13339
Windhoek
Tel.:   +264 61 220 010
Fax: +264 61 221 780
Email: angolo@op.gov.na
www.op.gov.na/

Office of the Prime Minister
Private Bag 13338
Windhoek
Tel.:   +264 61 287 9111
Fax: +264 61 226 189
www.opm.gov.na/

Nauru

Office of the President
Government Offices
Yaren
Tel.:   +674 444 3100
Fax: +674 444 3199

Nepal

Office of the King
Narayamhity Royal Palace
Durbar Marg
Kathmandu
Tel.:   +977 1 4413 577
Fax: +977 1 4227 395

Office of the Prime Minister
Central Secretariat
Singha Durbar
Kathmandu
Tel.:   +977 1 4228 555
Fax: +977 1 4227 286
Email: info@pmo.gov.np
www.pmo.gov.np/

Netherlands

Office of the Queen
Paleis Noordeinde
PO Box 30412
2500 GK
The Hague
www.koninklijkhuis.nl/

Office of the Prime Minister
Binnenhof 20
Postbus 20001
2500 EA
The Hague
Tel.:   +31 70 356 4100
Fax: +31 70 356 4683
www.postbus51.nl/

New Zealand

Office of the Governor-General
Government House
Wellington
Tel.:   +64 4 389 8055
Fax: +64 4 389 5536
www.gov-gen.govt.nz/

Office of the Prime Minister
PO Box 18888
Parliament Buildings
Wellington
Tel.:   +64 4 471 9998
Fax: +64 4 473 3579
Email: pm@ministers.govt.nz
www.primeminister.govt.nz/

Nicaragua

Office of the President
Avenida Bolívar y dupla sur
Managua
Tel.:   +505 228 2803
Fax: +505 228 6771
Email: presidente@presidencia.gob.ni
www.presidencia.gob.ni/

Niger

Office of the President
Palais Présidentiel
BP 550
Niamey
Tel.:   +227 722381
www.delgi.ne/presidence/

Office of the Prime Minister
BP 893
Niamey
Tel.:   +227 722699
Fax: +227 723859

Nigeria

Office of the President
Federal Secretariat Phase II
Shehu Shagari Way
Abuja
Tel.:   +234 9 2341 010
Fax: +234 9 2341 733
Email: ssa@nopa.net
www.nopa.net/

Norway

Office of the King
Det Kongelige Slott
0010 Oslo
Tel.:   +47 22 04 87 00
Fax: +47 22 04 87 90
www.kongehuset.no/

Office of the Prime Minister
Akersgaten 42
PO Box 8001 Dep.
0030 Oslo
Tel.: +47 22 24 90 90
Fax: +47 22 24 95 00
Email: postmottak@smk.dep.no
http://odin.dep.no/smk/

Oman

Office of the Sultan
Royal Palace
PO Box 875
Muscat 113
Tel.: +968 736 222
Fax: +968 739 427
www.diwan.gov.om

Pakistan

Office of the President
Aiwan-e-Sadr
Islamabad
Tel.: +92 51 920 2723
Fax: +92 51 921 1018
Email: psecyp@isb.paknet.com.pk

Office of the Prime Minister
F6/5 Cabinet Division
Cabinet Block
Constitution Avenue
Islamabad
Tel.: +92 51 920 6111
www.pak.gov.pk/

Palau

Office of the President
PO Box 100
PW 96940
Koror
Tel.: +680 488 2702
Fax: +680 488 1725
Email: roppressoffice@palaunet.com

Palestine

Office of the President
Abu Khdra Building
Omar al-Mukhtar Street
Gaza
Tel.: +970 8 2824670
Fax: +970 8 2822365
www.gov.ps/

Panama

Office of the President
Palacio Presidencial
San Felipe zona 1
Panamá
Tel.: +507 227 9600
Fax: +507 227 6944
Email: ofasin@presidencia.gob.pa
www.presidencia.gob.pa/

Papua New Guinea

Office of the Governor-General
Government House
PO Box 79
Konedobu
Tel.: +675 321 4466
Fax: +675 321 4543

Office of the Prime Minister
Morauta Haus
PO Box 639
Waigani
Tel.: +675 327 6525
Fax: +675 327 3943
Email: primeminister@pm.gov.pg
www.pm.gov.pg/pmsoffice/PMsoffice.nsf

Paraguay

Office of the President
Palacio de Lopez
Asunción
Tel.: +595 21 441 889
Fax: +595 21 493 154
www.presidencia.gov.py/

Peru

Office of the President
Plaza Mayor 5
Cercado de Lima
Lima 1
Tel.:   +51 1 426 6770
Fax: +51 1 426 6770
www.pres.gob.pe/

Office of the Prime Minister
Avenida 28 de Julio no 878
Miraflores
Lima 18
Tel.:   +51 1 446 9800
Fax: +51 1 444 9168
Email: webmastre@pcm.gob.pe
www.pcm.gob.pe/

Philippines

Office of the President
Malacanang Palace
J.P. Laurel Street
San Miguel 1005
Manila
Tel.:   +63 2 564 1451
Fax: +63 2 929 3968
Email: opnet@ops.gov.ph
www.opnet.ops.gov.ph/

Poland

Office of the President
ulica Wiejska 10
00-902 Warsaw
Tel.:   +48 22 695 2900
Fax: +48 22 695 2257
Email: listy@prezydent.pl
www.prezydent.pl/

Office of the Prime Minister
aleje Ujazdowskie 1/3
00-583 Warsaw
Tel.:   +48 22 694 6000
Fax: +48 22 625 2637
Email: cirinfo@kprm.gov.pl
www.kprm.gov.pl/

Portugal

Office of the President
Presidência da República
Palácio de Belém
1300 Lisbon
Tel.:   +351 213 637 141
Fax: +351 213 636 603
Email: presidente@presidenciarepublica.pt
www.presidenciarepublica.pt/

Office of the Prime Minister
Presidência do Conselho de Ministros
Rua Professor Gomes Teixeira
1399-022 Lisbon
Tel.:   +351 213 927 600
Fax: +351 213 927 615
Email: relacoes.publicas@pcm.gov.pt
www.portugal.gov.pt/

Qatar

Office of the Amir
PO Box 923
Doha
Tel.:   +974 446 2300
Fax: +974 436 1212
Email: adf@diwan.gov.qa
www.diwan.gov.qa/

Office of the Prime Minister
Doha

Romania

Office of the President
Cotroceni Palace
Bulevard Geniului 1
76238 Bucharest
Tel.:   +40 21 410 0581
Fax: +40 21 312 1179
Email: procetatean@presidency.ro
www.presidency.ro/

Office of the Prime Minister
Piaţa Victoriei 1
71201 Bucharest
Tel.:   +40 21 614 3400
Fax: +40 21 222 5814
Email: premier@gov.ro
www.guv.ro/

Russian Federation

Office of the President
Staraya ploshchad 42
103073 Moscow
Tel.:   +7 095 925 3581
Fax: +7 095 206 5173
Email: president@gov.ru
http://president.kremlin.ru/

Office of the Prime Minister
Krasnopresenskaya 2
103274 Moscow
Tel.:   +7 095 2055735
Fax: +7 095 205 4219
www.gov.ru/

Rwanda

Office of the President
BP 15
Urugwiro Village
Kigali
Tel.:   +250 584085
Fax: +250 584390
Email: presirep@rwanda1.com
www.rwanda1.com/government/presindex.html

Office of the Prime Minister
Kigali
Tel.:   +250 585444
Fax: +250 583714

St Kitts and Nevis

Office of the Governor-General
Government House
Basseterre
Tel.:   +1 869 465 2315

Office of the Prime Minister
Government Headquarters
Basseterre
Tel.:   +1 869 465 2521
Fax: +1 869 465 1001
Email: sknpmoffice@caribsurf.com
www.stkittsnevis.net

St Lucia

Office of the Governor-General
Government House
Morne Fortune
Castries
Tel.:   +1 758 452 2481
Fax: +1 758 453 2731
*Email:*privsec@stluciagovernmenthouse.com
www.stluciagovernmenthouse.com/

Office of the Prime Minister
Greaham Louisy Administrative Building
The Waterfront
Castries
Tel.:   +1 758 468 2111
Fax: +1 758 453 7352
Email: pmoffice@candw.lc
www.stlucia.gov.lc/

St Vincent and the Grenadines

Office of the Governor-General
Government House
Old Montrose
Kingstown
Tel.:   +1 784 456 1111
Fax: +1 784 457 9710

Office of the Prime Minister
Administrative Centre
Bay Street
Kingstown
Tel.:   +1 784 456 1111
Fax: +1 784 457 2152
Email: pmosvg@caribsurf.com

Samoa

Office of the Head of State
Government House
Vailima
Apia
Tel.:   +685 20438
www.samoa.ws/govtsamoapress/
    head_of_state.htm

Office of the Prime Minister
PO Box 1864
Apia
Tel.:   +685 24799
Fax: +685 21742
Email: contact@govt.ws
www.govt.ws/

San Marino

Office of the Captains Regent
Palazzo Pubblico
47031 San Marino
Tel.: +378 882259

São Tomé and Príncipe

Office of the President
Palácio do Povo
Avenida da Independência
São Tomé
Tel.: +239 221 143
Fax: +239 221 226

Office of the Prime Minister
Rua do Município
CP 302
São Tomé
Tel.: +239 223 596
Fax: +239 221 670

Saudi Arabia

Office of the King
Royal Diwan
Riyadh
Tel.: +966 1 401 4576
Email: kfb@saudinf.com
www.saudinf.com/

Senegal

Office of the President
avenue Léopold Sédar Senghor
BP 168
Dakar
Tel.: +221 8231 088
Fax: +221 8218 660
www.gouv.sn/institutions/president.html

Office of the Prime Minister
Immeuble Administratif
avenue Léopold Sédar Senghor
BP 4029 Dakar
Tel.: +221 8231 088
Fax: +221 8225 578
www.gouv.sn/

Serbia & Montenegro

Office of the Union Presidency
Bulevar Mihajla Pupina 2
11 070 Belgrade
Tel.: +381 11 311 8063
Fax: +381 11 301 5055
Email: kabinet@predsednikscg.yu
www.gov.yu/

Office of the President of Serbia
Andrićev venac 1
11 000 Belgrade
Tel.: +381 11 323 2915
Fax: +381 11 658 584

Office of the Prime Minister of Serbia
Nemanjina 11
11 000 Belgrade
Tel.: +381 11 361 7719
Fax: +381 11 361 7609
Email: oomr@srbija.sr.gov.yu
www.srbija.sr.gov.yu/

Office of the President of Montenegro
Bulevar Blaža Jovanovića 2
81000 Podgorica
Tel.: +381 81 242382
Fax: +381 81 242329
www.predsjednik.cg.yu/

Office of the Prime Minister of Montenegro
Jovana Tomaševića bb
81000 Podgorica
Tel.: +381 81 242530
Fax: +381 81 242329
Email: kabinet.premijera@mn.yu
www.vlada.cg.yu/

Seychelles

Office of the President
PO Box 55
State House
Victoria
Mahé
Tel.: +248 224155
Fax: +248 225117
Email: state@seychelles.net
www.virtualseychelles.com/gover/po.htm

Sierra Leone

Office of the President
State House
State Avenue
Freetown
Tel.: +232 22 232101
Fax: +232 22 231404
Email: info@statehouse-sl.org
www.statehouse-sl.org/

Singapore

Office of the President
Istana
Orchard Road
238823 Singapore
Tel.: +65 6737 5522
Fax: +65 6735 3135
Email: istana_general_office@istana.gov.sg
www.istana.gov.sg/

Office of the Prime Minister
Istana Annexe
Orchard Road
238823 Singapore
Tel.: +65 6235 8577
Fax: +65 6732 4627
Email: pmo_hq@pmo.gov.sg
www.pmo.gov.sg/

Slovakia

Office of the President
Hod zovo nam 1
PO Box 128
81000 Bratislava
Tel.: +421 2 5720 1121
Fax: +421 2 5441 7010
Email: informacie@prezident.sk
www.prezident.sk/

Office of the Prime Minister
Námestie Slobody 1
81370 Bratislava
Tel.: +421 2 5729 5111
Fax: +421 2 5249 7595
Email: urad@government.gov.sk
www.government.gov.sk/

Slovenia

Office of the President
Erjavčeva 17
1000 Ljubljana
Tel.: +386 1 478 1222
Fax: +386 1 478 1357
Email: gp.uprs@up-rs.s
www.sigov.si/up-rs/

Office of the Prime Minister
Gregorčičeva 20
1000 Ljubljana
Tel.: +386 1 478 1000
Fax: +386 1 478 1721
Email: vlada@gov.si
www.sigov.si/pv/

Solomon Islands

Office of the Governor-General
PO Box 252
Honiara
Tel.: +677 22222
Fax: +677 23335

Office of the Prime Minister
PO Box G1
Honiara
Tel.: +677 21863
Fax: +677 21863

Somalia

Office of the President
People's Palace
Mogadishu
Tel.: +252 1 723

Office of the Prime Minister
Mogadishu

South Africa

Office of the State President
Private Bag X1000
0001 Pretoria
Tel.: +27 12 300 5200
Fax: +27 12 321 8870
Email: president@po.gov.za
www.gov.za/dept/president/

Spain

Office of the King
Palacio de la Zarzuela
28071 Madrid
Tel.:   +34 91 599 2424
Fax: +34 91 599 2525
www.casareal.es/casareal/

Office of the Pime Minister
Complejo de la Moncloa
Edificio Consejo
Avenida de Puerta de hierro s/n
28071 Madrid
Tel.:   +34 91 335 3535
Fax: +34 91 335 3338
Email: portal.presidencia@mp.boe.es
www.la-moncloa.es/

Sri Lanka

Office of the President
Republic Square
Colombo 01
Tel.:   +94 11 2248 010
Email: info@presidentsl.org
www.priu.gov.lk/execpres/presecretariat.html

Office of the Prime Minister
58 Sir Ernest de Silva Mawatha
Colombo 07
Tel.:   +94 11 2575 317
Fax: +94 11 2437 017
Email: prime_minister@sltnet.lk
www.gov.lk/pm/office.htm

Sudan

Office of the President
People's Palace
PO Box 281
Khartoum
Tel.:   +249 1 8377 9426

Office of the Prime Minister
Khartoum
Tel.:   +249 1 8377 0726

Suriname

Office of the President
Onafhankelijkheidsplein
Paramaribo
Tel.:   +597 472 841
Fax: +597 475 266
www.sr.net/users/burpres/

Office of the Vice President
Dr S Redmondstraat
1st floor
Paramaribo
Tel.:   +597 474 805
Fax: +597 472 917

Swaziland

Office of the King
Lozitha Palace
Private Bag 1
Kwaluseni
Tel.:   +268 51 84022
Fax: +268 51 85028
www.swazi.com/king/king.html

Office of the Prime Minister
PO Box 395
Mbabane
Tel.:   +268 40 42251
Fax: +268 40 43943
Email: ppcu@realnet.co.sz
www.gov.sz/

Sweden

Office of the King
Kungliga Slottet
Slottsbacken
Gamla Stan
111 30 Stockholm
Tel.:   +46 8 402 6000
Fax: +46 8 402 6005
Email: webmaster@royalcourt.se
www.royalcourt.se/

Office of the Prime Minister
Rosenbad 4
103 33 Stockholm
Tel.:   +46 8 405 1000
Fax: +46 8 723 1171
Email: webmaster@primeminister.ministry.se
http://statsradsberedningen.regeringen.se/

Switzerland

Office of the President
Bundeshaus West
3003 Bern
Tel.:   +41 31 332 2111
Fax: +41 31 322 3706
www.admin.ch/

Syria

Office of the President
Mouhajreen
Presidential Palace
Abu Rumanch
Al-Rashid Street
Damascus
Tel.:   +963 11 2231 112
www.basharassad.org/

Office of the Prime Minister
Shahbandar Street
behind Central Bank
Damascus
Tel.:   +963 11 2226 001
Fax: +963 11 2233 373

Taiwan

Office of the President
Chiehshou Hall
122 Chungking South Road
Section 1
Taipei
Tel.:   +886 2 2311 3731
Fax: +886 2 2314 0746
Email: public@mail.oop.gov.tw
www.president.gov.tw/index_e.html

Office of the Premier
1 Chunghsiao East Road
Section 1
Taipei
Tel.:   +886 2 2356 1500
Fax: +886 2 2394 8727
Email: eyemail@eyemail.gio.gov.tw
www.ey.gov.tw/

Tajikistan

Office of the President
prospect Rudaki 80
734023 Dushanbe
Tel.:   +992 372 210 418
Fax: +992 372 211 837

Office of the Prime Minister
prospect Rudaki 80
734023 Dushanbe
Tel.:   +992 372 215 110
Fax: +992 372 211 510

Tanzania

Office of the President
The State House
Magogoni Road
PO Box 9120
Dar es Salaam
Tel.:   +255 22 211 6898
Fax: +255 22 211 3425
www.tanzania.go.tz/government/

Office of the Prime Minister
Magogoni Road
PO Box 3021
Dar es Salaam
Tel.:   +255 22 211 2850
Fax: +255 22 211 3439
www.tanzania.go.tz/government/

Thailand

Office of the King
The Grand Palace
Bangkok 10200
Tel.:   +66 2 221 1151
Fax: +66 2 226 4949
www.kanchanapisek.or.th/

Office of the Prime Minister
Government House
Thanon Nakhon Pathom
Bangkok 10300
Tel.:   +66 2 280 3693
Fax: +66 2 280 0858
Email: opm@opm.go.th
www.opm.go.th/

Togo

Office of the President
Palais Présidentiel
ave de la Marina
Lomé
Tel.:　+228 221 2701
Fax:　+228 221 1897
Email:　presidence@republicoftogo.com
www.republicoftogo.com/

Office of the Prime Minister
Lomé
Tel.:　+228 221 1564
Fax:　+228 221 2040
Email:　info@republicoftogo.com

Tonga

Office of the King
PO Box 6
Nuku'alofa
Tel.:　+676 25064
Fax:　+676 24102

Office of the Prime Minister
PO Box 62
Hala Taufa'ahau
Nuku'alofa
Tel.:　+676 24644
Fax:　+676 23888
Email:　pmomail@pmo.gov.to
www.pmo.gov.to/

Trinidad and Tobago

Office of the President
President's House
St Ann's
Port of Spain
Tel.:　+1 868 624 1261
Fax:　+1 868 625 7950
Email:　presoftt@carib-link.net
www.gov.tt/government/president.html

Office of the Prime Minister
Whitehall
Maraval Road
Port of Spain
Tel.:　+1 868 622 1625
Fax:　+1 868 622 0055
Email:　opm@trinidad.net
www.opm.gov.tt/

Tunisia

Office of the President
Palais Présidentiel
Tunis and Carthage
Tel.:　+216 71 260 348

Office of the Prime Minister
place du Gouvernment
La Kasbah
1008 Tunis
Tel.:　+216 71 565 400
Fax:　+216 71 569 205
Email:　prm@ministeres.tn
www.ministeres.tn/

Turkey

Office of the President
Cumhurbaşkanlıgı Köşkü
Cankaya
Ankara
Tel.:　+90 312 468 5030
Fax:　+90 312 427 1330
Email:　cumhurbaskanligi@tccb.gov.tr
www.cankaya.gov.tr/

Office of the Prime Minister
Başbakanlık
Vekaletler Caddesi
06573 Bakanlıklar
Ankara
Tel.:　+90 312 413 7000
Fax:　+90 312 417 0476
Email:　hiliskiler@basbakanlik.gov.tr
www.basbakanlik.gov.tr/

Turkmenistan

Office of the President
Presidential Palace
ulitsa 2001 24
744000 Ashkhabad
Tel.:　+993 12 354534
Fax:　+993 12 354388

Tuvalu

Office of the Governor-General
Vaiaku
Funafuti atoll
Tel.:　+688 20715

Office of the Prime Minister
Vaiaku
Funafuti atoll
Tel.:   +688 20716
Fax: +688 20819

Uganda

Office of the President
Parliament Building
PO Box 7168
Kampala
Tel.:   +256 41 254 881
Fax: +256 41 235 459
Email: info@gouexecutive.net
www.statehouse.go.ug/

Office of the Prime Minister
Post Office Building
St. Clement Hill Road
PO Box 341
Kampala
Tel.:   +256 41 258 721
Fax: +256 41 242 341
www.government.go.ug/

Ukraine

Office of the President
vulitsa Bankova 11
01220 Kiev
Tel.:   +380 44 291 5333
Fax: +380 44 293 1001
Email: viktor@yuschenko.com.ua
www.yuschenko.com.ua/

Office of the Prime Minister
vulitsa M. Hrushevskoho 12/2
01008 Kiev
Tel.:   +380 44 226 2289
Fax: +380 44 293 2093
Email: web@kmu.gov.ua
www.kmu.gov.ua

United Arab Emirates

Office of the President
Manhal Palace
PO Box 280
Abu Dhabi
Tel.:   +971 2 665 2000
Fax: +971 2 665 1962

Office of the Prime Minister
PO Box 12848
Dubai
Tel.:   +971 4 353 4550
Fax: +971 4 353 0111
www.uae.gov.ae/

United Kingdom

Office of the Queen
Buckingham Palace
London
SW1 1AA
Tel.:   +44 20 7930 4832
www.royal.gov.uk/

Office of the Prime Minister
10 Downing Street
London
SW1A 2AA
Tel.:   +44 20 7270 1234
Fax: +44 20 7925 0918
www.pm.gov.uk/

United States of America

Office of the President
The White House
1600 Pennsylvania Ave
NW Washington D.C. 20500-0001
Tel.:   +1 202 456 1414
Fax: +1 202 456 1907
Email: president@whitehouse.gov
www.whitehouse.gov/

Uruguay

Office of the President
Edificio Libertad
Avda Dr Luis Alberto de Herrera 3350
Montevideo
Tel.:   +598 2 487 2110
Fax: +598 2 480 9397
Email: presidente@presidencia.gub.uy
www.presidencia.gub.uy/

Uzbekistan

Office of the President
43 Uzbekistanskaya Avenue
700163 Tashkent
Tel.:   +998 71 139 5040
Fax: +998 71 139 5525
Email: presidents_office@press-service.uz
www.press-service.uz/

Office of the Prime Minister
Government House
700008 Tashkent
Tel.:   +998 71 239 8295
Fax: +998 71 239 8601
www.gov.uz/

Vanuatu

Office of the President
Private Mail Bag 100
Port Vila
Tel.:   +678 230 55
Fax: +678 266 93
www.vanuatugovernment.gov.vu/
    president.html

Office of the Prime Minister
Private Mail Bag 053
Port Vila
Tel.:   +678 224 13
Fax: +678 228 63
www.vanuatugovernment.gov.vu/
    primeminister.html

Vatican City

Office of the Pope
Palazzo Apostolico Vaticano
00120 Vatican City
Email: apsa-ss@apsa.va
www.vatican.va/

Secretariat of State
Palazzo Apostolico Vaticano
00120 Vatican City
Tel.:   +39 066982 83913
Fax: +39 066982 85255
Email: vati026@relstat-segstat.va

Venezuela

Office of the President
Palacio de Miraflores
Caracas 1010
Tel.:   +58 212 860 0811
Fax: +58 212 860 1101
Email: presidencia@venezuela.gov.ve
www.venezuela.gov.ve/

Viet Nam

Office of the President
Hoang Hoa Tham
Hanoi
Tel.:   +84 4 8258 261

Office of the Prime Minister
Hanoi

Communist Party of Viet Nam
1 Hoang Van Thu, Hanoi
Email: cpv@hn.vnn.vn
www.cpv.org.vn

Yemen

Office of the President
Zubairy Street
Sana'a
Tel.:   +967 1 273092

Office of the Prime Minister
Sana'a

Zambia

Office of the President
PO Box 30208
Lusaka
Tel.:   +260 1 260312
Email: state@zamnet.zm
www.statehouse.gov.zm/

Zimbabwe

Office of the President
Munhumutapa Building
Samora Machel Avenue
Causeway
Harare
Tel.:   +263 4 707091
Fax: +263 4 734644
www.gta.gov.zw/

INDEX BY DATE OF TAKING POWER

Index: Dates of Taking Power

INDEX OF PERSONAL NAMES

INDEX BY TYPE OF REGIME

Monarchies

Bahrain, Bhutan, Brunei, Jordan,
Kuwait, Monaco, Nepal, Oman,
Qatar, Saudi Arabia, Swaziland,
United Arab Emirates

One-party states

China, Cuba, North Korea,
Laos, Libya, Syria, Turkmenistan,
Viet Nam

Nonparty systems

Micronesia, Nauru, Palau, Tuvalu

Transitional regimes

Afghanistan, Congo, Dem. Rep.,
Eritrea, Iraq, Liberia, Somalia

Presidential systems

Algeria	Dominican Rep.	Malawi	Sierra Leone
Angola	Ecuador	Maldives	Sudan
Argentina	Egypt	Mali	Taiwan
Armenia	El Salvador	Mauritania	Tajikistan
Azerbaijan	Equatorial Guinea	Mexico	Tanzania
Belarus	Gabon	Mozambique	Togo
Benin	Gambia	Namibia	Tunisia
Bolivia	Georgia	Nicaragua	Uganda
Botswana	Ghana	Niger	Ukraine
Brazil	Guatemala	Nigeria	United States
Burkina Faso	Guinea	Pakistan	of America
Burundi	Guinea-Bissau	Panama	Uruguay
Cameroon	Guyana	Paraguay	Uzbekistan
Chad	Haiti	Peru	Venezuela
Chile	Honduras	Philippines	Yemen
Colombia	Indonesia	Romania	Zambia
Comoros	Kazakhstan	Russia	Zimbabwe
Congo, Rep.	Kenya	Rwanda	
Costa Rica	Kiribati	São Tomé and	
Côte d'Ivoire	South Korea	Príncipe	
Cyprus	Kyrgyzstan	Senegal	
Djibouti	Madagascar	Seychelles	

Parliamentary systems

Albania	Denmark	Latvia	St Lucia
Andorra	Dominica	Lebanon	St Vincent and
Antigua and	East Timor	Lesotho	the Grenadines
Barbuda	Estonia	Lithuania	Samoa
Australia	Ethiopia	Luxembourg	San Marino
Austria	Fiji	Malaysia	Singapore
Bahamas	Finland	Malta	Slovakia
Bangladesh	Germany	Marshall Islands	Slovenia
Barbados	Greece	Mauritius	Solomon Islands
Belgium	Grenada	Moldova	Spain
Belize	Hungary	Mongolia	Sri Lanka
Bosnia and	Iceland	Netherlands	Sweden
Herzegovina	India	New Zealand	Switzerland
Bulgaria	Ireland	Norway	Thailand
Cambodia	Israel	Papua New Guinea	Trinidad and Tobago
Canada	Italy	Poland	Turkey
Croatia	Jamaica	Portugal	United Kingdom
Czech Republic	Japan	St Kitts and Nevis	Vanuatu

Mixed presidential–parliamentary systems

Cape Verde, Central African Republic, France, Macedonia,
Serbia and Montenegro, South Africa, Suriname

Mixed monarchical–parliamentary systems

Liechtenstein, Morocco, Tonga

Others

Iran (Islamic theocracy)
Myanmar (military-based regime)
Mauritania (military-based regime)
Palestine (unrecognized state)
Vatican City (papal state)

The Politics of Series

This new series from Routledge provides a fresh perspective on various political issues world-wide. Subjects including **Terrorism, Oil, Migration, the Environment, Water** and **Religion** are analysed in detail, with statistics and maps providing a thorough examination of the topic.

Each book comprises an A-Z glossary of key terms specific to the subject, as well as relevant organizations, individuals and events.

A selection of 8-10 chapters in essay format, each around 5,000 words in length, written by a group of acknowledged experts from around the world provide in-depth comment on some of the issues most relevant to each title.

Key Features:

- This mixture of analytical and statistical information is a unique aspect of this series, and provides the reader with a comprehensive overview of the subject matter
- Information can now be found on each of these topics in these one-stop resources
- This series provides the only detailed examination of politics relating to specific subjects currently available.

For more information on this series, including a full list of titles, please contact
reference@routledge.co.uk

Routledge
Taylor & Francis Group